# THE ILLUSTRATED DIRECTORY OF

# GUNS

## DAVID MILLER

CHARTWELL
BOOKS, INC.

This edition published in 2014 by CHARTWELL BOOKS, INC.
A division of BOOK SALES, INC.
276 Fifth Avenue Suite 206
New York, New York 10001
USA
Reprinted 2013, 2014

ISBN-13 978-0-7858-2801-3

Printed in China

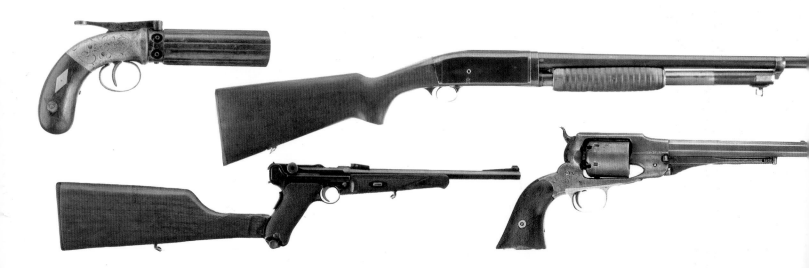

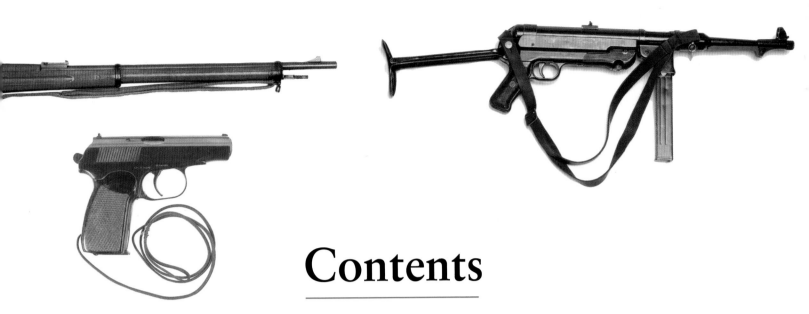

# Contents

# ARGENTINA

## BERSA MODEL 383A

### SPECIFICATIONS

**Type:** double action, semi-automatic
**Origin:** FabricaRamos Mejia, Argentina
**Caliber:** .380 ACP
**Barrel Length:** 3.5in

This small semi-automatic pistol was produced by the Argentinean firm of Ramos Mejia in three versions. The Model 323 was a single-action .32 ACP caliber, while the Models 383 and 383A (shown here) were .380 ACP caliber, single- and double-action, respectively. All had a 3.5in barrel with fixed sights and a seven-round, detachable box magazine.

## HAFDASA ARMY MODEL 1927

### SPECIFICATIONS

**Type:** semi-automatic pistol
**Origin:** HAFDASA, Argentina
**Caliber:** .45 ACP
**Barrel Length:** 5in

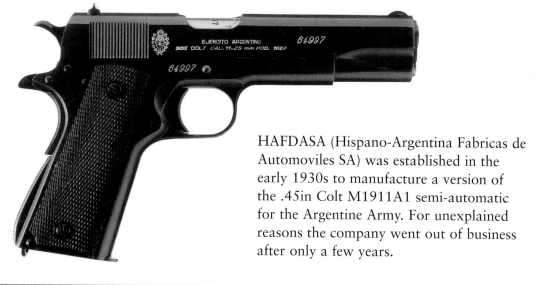

HAFDASA (Hispano-Argentina Fabricas de Automoviles SA) was established in the early 1930s to manufacture a version of the .45in Colt M1911A1 semi-automatic for the Argentine Army. For unexplained reasons the company went out of business after only a few years.

## BALLESTER-MOLINA SEMI-AUTOMATIC

### SPECIFICATIONS

**Type:** Semi-automatic pistol
**Origin:** Ballester-Molina, Argentina
**Caliber:** .45 ACP
**Barrel Length:** 5in

Ballester-Molina took over production of this pistol from HAFDASA (*see previous entry*) and made a few minor changes to the design. These included a marginally longer slide and a butt sized for a slightly smaller hand. The only visual distinction between the HAFDASA and Ballester-Molina weapons is that the former has the standard Colt regular finger grips on the slide, whereas those on the latter are irregularly spaced. A small number of Ballester-Molinas were purchased by the British early in World War two and were issued to various clandestine organisations.

# AUSTRIA

## GLOCK MODEL 21

The Glock company was established in 1963 and for twenty years produced minor items of military hardware such as knives and entrenching tools. In 1983, however, it won a competition for a totally new design of 9mm automatic pistol for the Austrian army with its 9mm Glock 17 pistol and it has enjoyed much success ever since. The pistol gained some notoriety as a 'plastic' pistol, undetectable by security screening devices. This was uninformed rubbish – some 40 percent of the weapon is made from plastic materials, but there remains enough metal in the critical parts, such as the slide and barrel, that any X-Ray or magnetic screening devise will detect it. The Models 20 and 21 are identical in design except that the former is chambered for the 10mm Auto round and the latter for the .45in ACP round. The Model 21 shown here has a 13-round magazine and weighs approximately 25.25oz.

**SPECIFICATIONS**

**Type:** semi-automatic pistol
**Origin:** Glock AG, Deutsch-Wagram, Austria
**Caliber:** .45 ACP
**Barrel Length:** 4.6in

## GLOCK MODEL 22

**SPECIFICATIONS**

**Type:** semi-automatic pistol
**Origin:** Glock AG, Deutsch-Wagram, Austria
**Caliber:** .40 S&W
**Barrel Length:** 4.5in

The original Glock pistol was the Model 17 which was chambered for the 9mm Parabellum round. The Model 17 entered the market in 1985 and in 1990 the company introduced the Model 22, which is virtually identical to the Model 17, but chambered for the 0.40 S&W round. It is very slightly larger and heavier than the Model 17 and has a 15-round magazine.

## GLOCK MODEL 34

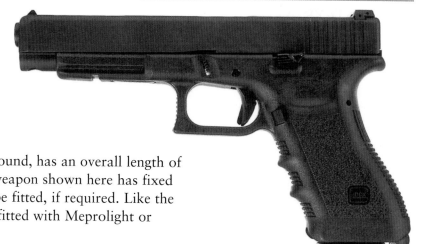

### SPECIFICATIONS

**Type:** semi-automatic pistol
**Origin:** Glock AG, Deutsch-Wagram, Austria
**Caliber:** 9 x 19mm
**Barrel Length:** 5.3in

The Glock 34 is chambered for the 9 x 19mm round, has an overall length of 8.2in and the magazine holds ten rounds. The weapon shown here has fixed front and rear sights, but adjustable sights can be fitted, if required. Like the others in the Glock range, the Glock 34 can be fitted with Meprolight or Trijicon night sights.

## MANNLICHER MODEL 1905

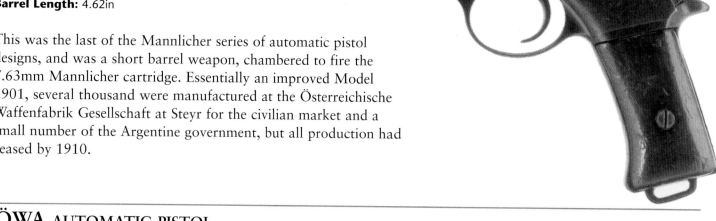

### SPECIFICATIONS

**Type:** semi-automatic pistol
**Origin:** Mannlicher, Austria-Hungary
**Caliber:** 7.63mm Mannlicher
**Barrel Length:** 4.62in

This was the last of the Mannlicher series of automatic pistol designs, and was a short barrel weapon, chambered to fire the 7.63mm Mannlicher cartridge. Essentially an improved Model 1901, several thousand were manufactured at the Österreichische Waffenfabrik Gesellschaft at Steyr for the civilian market and a small number of the Argentine government, but all production had ceased by 1910.

## ÖWA AUTOMATIC PISTOL

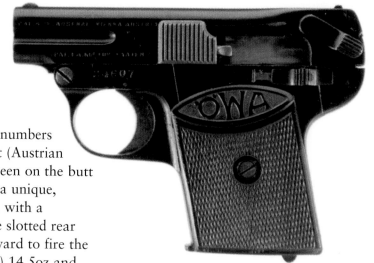

### SPECIFICATIONS

**Type:** semi-automatic pistol
**Origin:** Österreichische Werke Anstalt, Austria
**Caliber:** 6.35mm Auto
**Barrel Length:** 1.97in

This small automatic pistol was manufactured in some numbers in the early 1920s by the Österreichische Werke Anstalt (Austrian Works establishment) always abbreviated to ÖWA, as seen on the butt of the weapon in the picture. The weapon operated on a unique, patented system, with a separate slide and breechblock, with a hammer, mounted in the frame, which rises through the slotted rear portion of the block to hit the firing pin, forcing it forward to fire the round. The weapon was 4.7in long, weighed (unloaded) 14.5oz and had a six-round box magazine.

# ROTH-STEYR M 1907

This pistol entered service with the Austro-Hungarian army in 1907 – the first time a major power had adopted a self-loading pistol. Unusually in a pistol, the Roth-Steyr fires from a locked bolt, and when fired the bolt and barrel recoil together within the hollow receiver. The barrel actually rotates through ninety degrees before unlocking and beginning the extraction/reloading cycle. The 10-shot magazine is fixed, and has to be reloaded through the open breech using a charger clip.

FEGYVERGYÁR BUDAPEST

## SPECIFICATIONS

**Type:** semi-automatic pistol
**Origin:** Österreichische Waffenfabrik, Steyr, Austria
**Caliber:** 8 x 18.5mm Roth
**Barrel Length:** 5in

# STEYR M 1912

## SPECIFICATIONS

**Type:** semi-automatic pistol
**Origin:** Österreichische Waffenfabrik, Steyr, Austria
**Caliber:** 9 x 23mm Steyr
**Barrel Length:** 5in

The M 1907 was issued mainly to the Austrian cavalry, but the rest of the army was given the later M 1912. The barrel still rotated, but the receiver was now a moving slide, closer in concept to today's automatics. The magazine was still an integral fixed box, holding up to 8 of the powerful 9mm cartridge.

## BROWNING MODEL 10/71

### SPECIFICATIONS

**Type:** semi-automatic pistol
**Origin:** Fabrique Nationale, Herstal,
Belgium
**Caliber:** .38
**Barrel Length:** 4.5in

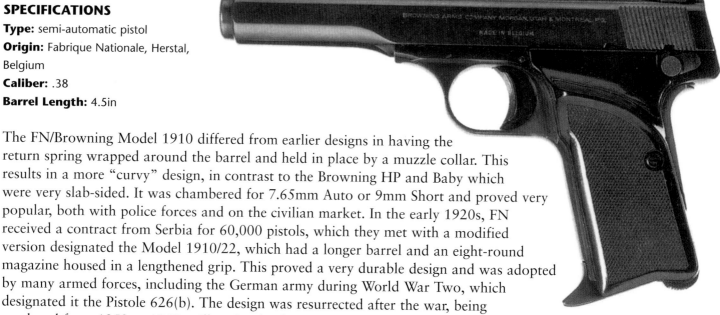

The FN/Browning Model 1910 differed from earlier designs in having the
return spring wrapped around the barrel and held in place by a muzzle collar. This
results in a more "curvy" design, in contrast to the Browning HP and Baby which
were very slab-sided. It was chambered for 7.65mm Auto or 9mm Short and proved very
popular, both with police forces and on the civilian market. In the early 1920s, FN
received a contract from Serbia for 60,000 pistols, which they met with a modified
version designated the Model 1910/22, which had a longer barrel and an eight-round
magazine housed in a lengthened grip. This proved a very durable design and was adopted
by many armed forces, including the German army during World War Two, which
designated it the Pistole 626(b). The design was resurrected after the war, being
produced from 1950 to 1959, still under the designation Model 1910/22. The second time was in the 1970s when
a number were produced as the Model 1910/71, as seen here, with a 4.5in barrel and both fore and backsights,
and firing the .380 round.

## BROWNING HI POWER

### SPECIFICATIONS

**Type:** semi-automatic pistol
**Origin:** Fabrique Nationale,
Herstal, Belgium
**Caliber:** 9mm
**Barrel Length:** 4.75in

John Browning worked on this design from 1914 until his death in 1926, and
it is a logical development of the M1911, which he had designed when working with
Colt. After his death FN, Herstal continued to work on the project and, following a
number of modifications, it entered production in 1935. Since then it has been adopted
by many armed forces, and has also sold well on the civilian market. There were many
versions, including one with a combined holster/stock of the type found on the original
Mausers. When the Germans overran Belgium in 1940 some FN engineers escaped to
Britain with the drawings and in 1942 they were sent onwards to Canada, where the Inglis
factory undertook production for the Allies. Meanwhile, production continued at Herstal for
the German Wehrmacht under the designation Pistole Modell 640(b) and carrying the factory code
"ch." Following the German defeat, manufacture continued at the FN factory and the weapon was also put on the
civil market as the "High Power."

A crucial development was the adoption of the weapon in 1954 by the British army who designated it "Pistol, 9mm, Browning, Mk1*" and it has served with over fifty armies since. Illustrated here are just three of the many dozens of varieties of this great weapon.

The standard civilian model shows the basic shape, the only difference from the military models is that it has walnut, as opposed to plastic, grips.

The Capitan model, introduced in 1993, added tangent rear sights and other minor modifications.

## FN-BROWNING MODEL 49

**SPECIFICATIONS**
**Type:** police/civilian semi-automatic pistol
**Origin:** FN Herstal, Belgium
**Caliber:** 9mm
**Barrel Length:** 4.25in

This weapon, introduced in 2000, is built for police (16 rounds) or civil use (10 rounds) and is available chambered for either .40 S&W or 9mm Parabellum ammunition. The frame is made of polymer and the slide of steel, which can be either black-coated or stainless steel (as seen here). Sights are fixed and marked with white dots.

## ROBAR JIEFFECO (2) SAP

The patent for this design was owned by a Belgian firm named Janssen et Fiels Compagnie, which was abbreviated to J.F. Co, and then expanded, apparently for the U.S. market, to Jieffeco. The original pistol, the Jieffeco (1), was marketed immediately prior to World War One, and was available in 7.65mm and 6.35mm versions. After the war, production was restarted and marketed in the U.S. by the Davis-Warner Arms Corporation of New York City. This new weapon, chambered for the 0.25in round, was known either as the Jieffeco (2) or the New Model Melior. Davis-Warner went out of business in the late 1920s and the pistol was no longer imported.

**SPECIFICATIONS**
**Type:** semi-automatic pistol
**Origin:** Robar et Cie, Liege, Belgium
**Caliber:** .25in
**Barrel Length:** 3.5in

## ROBAR LIEGOISE MELIOR

**SPECIFICATIONS**
**Type:** semi-automatic pistol
**Origin:** Robar et Cie, Liege, Belgium
**Caliber:** .380in
**Barrel Length:** 3.5in

The Melior pistol was essentially a variant of the Jieffeco (2), chambered for the .380in round for the U.S. market.

## NAGANT ROLLING-BLOCK PISTOL

**SPECIFICATIONS**
**Type:** single-round pistol
**Origin:** Fabrique d'Armes E&L Nagant, Liege, Belgium
**Caliber:** 9mm
**Barrel Length:** 5.5in

The Belgian firm of Nagant, founded in 1859, made weapons fitted with the Remington rolling-block under license, the first of which was a somewhat ungainly double-barreled pistol for the Belgian gendarmerie (military police). The company also produced this, equally ungainly, single barrel version.

## PIEPER BAYARD MODEL 1908

### SPECIFICATIONS

**Type:** semi-automatic pistol
**Origin:** Henri Pieper et Cie Nagant, Liege, Belgium
**Caliber:** .380in
**Barrel Length:** 2in

Chevalier de Bayard (1475–1524) was a French knight and national hero who was renowned for his bravery and his personal qualities, and his name was taken as a trademark for a series of pistols produced by the Belgian firm of Henry Pieper, based on the patents of a M. Clarus. The Clarus action involved a unique hammer and sear system, and it was claimed that it was these features that made it possible for such a small pistol (length 4.92in; weight 16.6oz) to fire such a large round. This picture shows the Model 1908, the first in the line.

## PIEPER BAYARD MODEL 1912

### SPECIFICATIONS

**Type:** semi-automatic pistol
**Origin:** Anciennes Établissements Pieper, Herstal-lèz-Liege, Belgium
**Caliber:** 6.35mm Auto
**Barrel Length:** 2.2in

A further model in the Bayard series, the Model 1912 was chambered for 6.35mm and was marginally small (length 4.8in) and lighter (12oz) than its predecessors. It remained in production until 1914, when production ceased due to the German invasion, but restarted in 1919. On all pistols bearing this name there is an engraving of a medieval knight on the left side of the weapon.

## BELGIAN DOUBLE BARREL

### SPECIFICATIONS

**Type:** double-barrel percussion pistol
**Origin:** unknown Belgium gunsmith
**Caliber:** .40
**Barrel Length:** 2.63in

Muzzle-loading pistols were too slow to reload in action so the double-barreled weapon gave the firer a second chance at an adversary. Such "pocket" pistols were produced in large quantities by Belgian gunsmiths in the early 19th century and this is one of the better quality weapons to survive. The pistol is some 6.5in long and weighs 12oz, enabling it to be carried in one of the capacious pockets of coats then in style.

# (PIEPER) BERGMANN BAYARD MODEL 1910

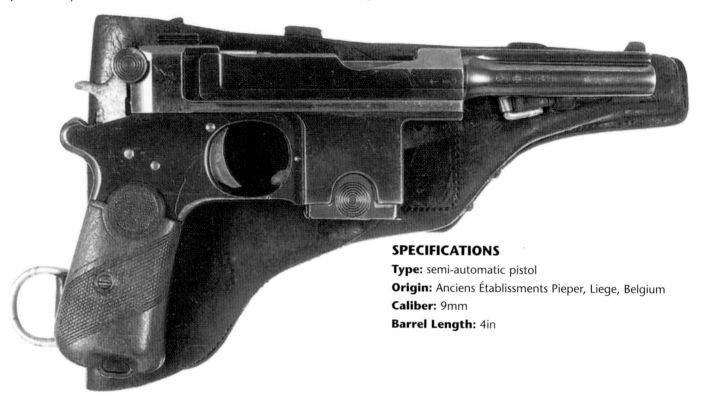

**SPECIFICATIONS**
**Type:** semi-automatic pistol
**Origin:** Anciens Établissments Pieper, Liege, Belgium
**Caliber:** 9mm
**Barrel Length:** 4in

The German company, Bergmann, won an order for their Mars pistol from the Spanish Army, which was to have been manufactured by another German company, Schilling, based at Suhl. When the latter withdrew, Bergmann negotiated a production deal with Pieper of Belgium who then fulfilled the Spanish contract with a slightly modified weapon, now designated the Bergmann-Bayard Model 1908 (Bayard was Pieper's trade name). Shortly afterwards, Pieper won a pistol contract from the Danish Army; these weapons, although virtually identical to the Model 1908, were designated the Model 1910.

# BRAZIL

## TAURUS MODEL PT-99AF

Taurus is a Brazilian arms manufacturer that has been in business since 1889. The PT-99 was based on the earlier PT092 and weighs 34oz with a 15-round magazine. It has a fully adjustable, three-dot rear sight and is chambered for the 9mm round.

### SPECIFICATIONS
**Type:** semi-automatic pistol
**Origin:** Taurus International, Porta Alegre, Brazil
**Caliber:** 9mm
**Barrel Length:** 5in

## TAURUS MODEL PT-111

The neat and business-like PT-111 was introduced in 1997. It operates on a double-action only system and has a 3.3in barrel firing 9mm rounds. It has a polymer frame, with a ten-round magazine housed in the butt. It weighs about 16oz.

### SPECIFICATIONS
**Type:** semi-automatic pistol
**Origin:** Taurus International, Porta Allegre, Brazil
**Caliber:** 9mm
**Barrel Length:** 3.3in

## TAURUS MODEL PT-908

### SPECIFICATIONS
**Type:** semi-automatic pistol
**Origin:** Taurus International, Porta Allegre, Brazil
**Caliber:** 9mm
**Barrel Length:** 3.8in

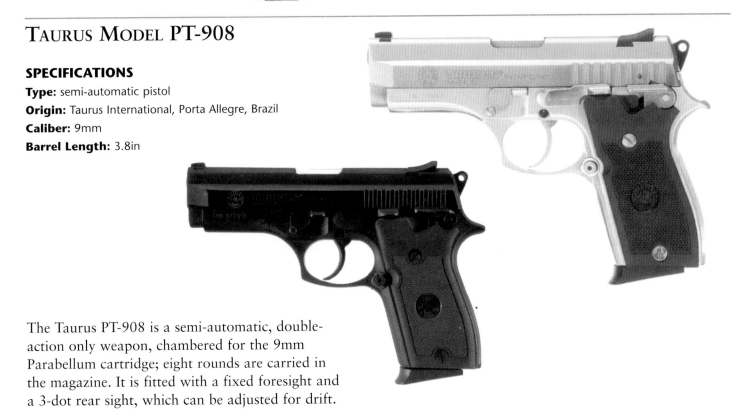

The Taurus PT-908 is a semi-automatic, double-action only weapon, chambered for the 9mm Parabellum cartridge; eight rounds are carried in the magazine. It is fitted with a fixed foresight and a 3-dot rear sight, which can be adjusted for drift.

# CHINA (PRC)

## NORINCO TYPE 51 (TT1933)

The Russian weapon designer, Fedor Tokarev, was working at the Tula Arsenal in the USSR when he designed his famous pistol, which was chambered for the 7.63mm Mauser cartridge. This was adopted by the Red Army under the designation Tula Tokarev Model 1933 (TT1933) and was immediately placed in large volume production (*see below*). The TT1933 was also manufactured in Hungary (Model 1948) and in the People's Republic of China (as seen here) as the Type 51.

**SPECIFICATIONS**
**Type:** semi-automatic pistol
**Origin:** NORINCO, PRC
**Caliber:** 7.62mm
**Barrel Length:** 3.5in

## NORINCO TYPE 54

**SPECIFICATIONS**
**Type:** semi-automatic pistol
**Origin:** NORINCO, PRC
**Caliber:** 7.62mm
**Barrel Length:**
4.5in

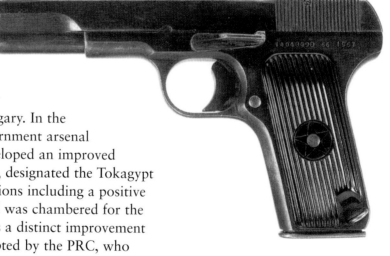

As described in the previous entry, the Tokarev TT1933 was produced in Hungary. In the late 1950s the Hungarian government arsenal at Fegyvergyan, Budapest, developed an improved version for the Egyptian police, designated the Tokagypt 58. This had various modifications including a positive safety, wrap-around stocks and was chambered for the 9mm Luger cartridge. This was a distinct improvement and was immediately also adopted by the PRC, who placed it in production as the Type 54, superseding their earlier Type 51.

## NORINCO TYPE 59

**SPECIFICATIONS**
**Type:** semi-automatic pistol
**Origin:** NORINCO, PRC
**Caliber:** 9mm Makarov
**Barrel Length:** 3.75in

This is a copy of the Soviet Pistolet Makarov (PM), which is chambered for the standard Makarov 9mm cartridge, which is known in the PRC as the Type 59 round. The Type 59 is 6.3in long and has an empty weight of 23oz. The detachable box carries a maximum of eight rounds.

# CZECHOSLOVAKIA

## CESKA ZBROJOVKA CZ 1924

**SPECIFICATIONS**
**Type:** semi-automatic pistol
**Origin:** Ceska Zbrojovka, Strakonitz, Czechoslovakia.
**Caliber:** 9mm
**Barrel Length:** 3.5in

The Ceska Zbrojovka arsenal was established in Pilsen in 1919, almost at the same time as Czechoslovakia became a nation. Moving to Strakonitz in 1921, it began the design and production of a range of military and civilian pistols. This one was based on a design by Josef Nickl, a Mauser engineer at the time helping Czech industry to set up for the licensed production of Mauser rifles. Nickl's CZ Model 1922 was a simple blowback weapon firing 9mm Short cartridges, and the later Model 1924 shown here is a further development of the design. It uses a conventional barrel and slide blowback system, slightly unusual in that the barrel unlocks from the slide by rotating slightly. The hammer is partially shrouded, although just visible.

## CESKA ZBROJOVKA CZ 1927

**SPECIFICATIONS**
**Type:** semi-automatic pistol
**Origin:** Ceska Zbrojovka, Strakonitz, Czechoslovakia.
**Caliber:** 7.65mm
**Barrel Length:** 3.9in

Frantisek Myska developed Nickl's Model 1922/24 design further to create this Model 1927. He remodeled it for the less powerful 7.65 x 17mm cartridge, allowing him to dispense with the barrel/slide locking mechanism. Instead the pistol relied on the inertia of the slide to hold the breech shut until the gas pressure had dropped to a safe level. It was a successful design, and even remained in production for the Wehrmacht after the Germans occupied Czechoslovakia. The last Model 1927 was made in 1951.

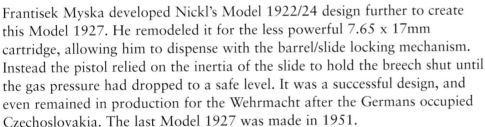

Ceska Zbrojovka CZ 1927

## CESKA ZBROJOVKA CZ 1938/39

### SPECIFICATIONS

**Type:** semi-automatic pistol
**Origin:** Ceska Zbrojovka, Strakonitz, Czechoslovakia.
**Caliber:** 9mm
**Barrel Length:** 4.65in

First entering service in 1938, this pistol was designed to be simple to use and quick to get into action. As such it had no safety device and didn't need any cocking operation. Once a round was chambered, the mechanism was double-action only, the user simply pulling the trigger to fire. Unfortunately it was a clumsy handful with no safety mechanism, while heavy trigger pressure made accurate shooting difficult. Another unusual feature is that access to the mechanism and barrel is by hinging the whole barrel and slide upward around a pivot under the muzzle.

## DUSEK "DUO" PISTOL

### SPECIFICATIONS

**Type:** semi-automatic pistol
**Origin:** F. Dusek, Opocno, Czechoslovakia.
**Caliber:** 6.35mm
**Barrel Length:** 2.25in

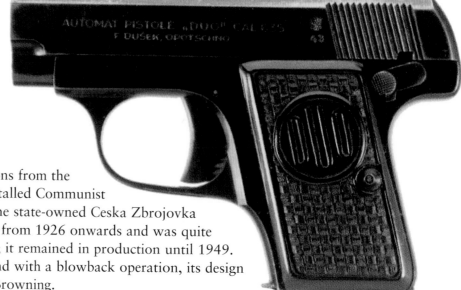

The Dusek factory manufactured weapons from the mid-1920s to 1948, when the newly-installed Communist government transferred its facilities to the state-owned Ceska Zbrojovka (CZ) factory. The "Duo" was marketed from 1926 onwards and was quite successful, being sold all over the world; it remained in production until 1949. Chambered for the 6.35mm cartridge and with a blowback operation, its design was based on that of the 1906-pattern Browning.

# FRANCE

## FLOBERT TIP-UP PISTOL

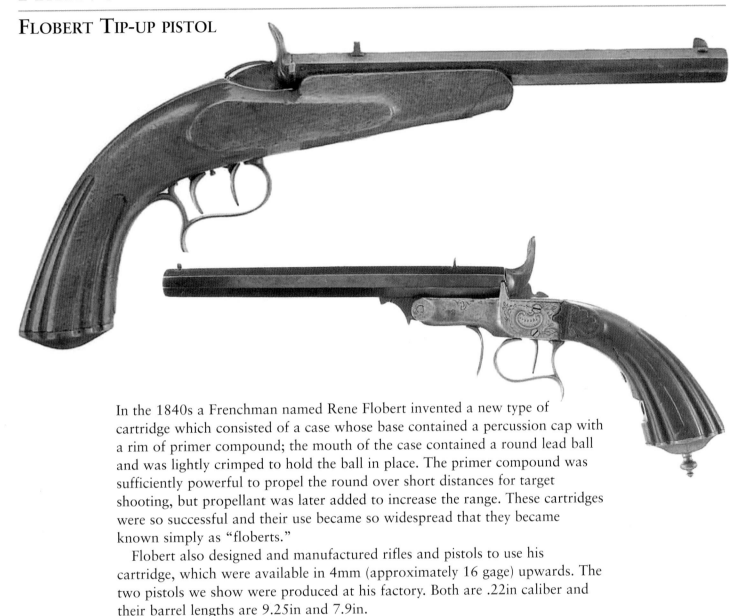

In the 1840s a Frenchman named Rene Flobert invented a new type of cartridge which consisted of a case whose base contained a percussion cap with a rim of primer compound; the mouth of the case contained a round lead ball and was lightly crimped to hold the ball in place. The primer compound was sufficiently powerful to propel the round over short distances for target shooting, but propellant was later added to increase the range. These cartridges were so successful and their use became so widespread that they became known simply as "floberts."

Flobert also designed and manufactured rifles and pistols to use his cartridge, which were available in 4mm (approximately 16 gage) upwards. The two pistols we show were produced at his factory. Both are .22in caliber and their barrel lengths are 9.25in and 7.9in.

## ST ETIENNE MODEL 1822 PERCUSSION CONVERSION

When the percussion mechanism became widely accepted, many older flintlock weapons were converted to this way of firing, either by their original makers or by independent gunsmiths. Shown here is a pistol originally made as a Model 1822 flintlock at the St Etienne arsenal, but subsequently converted by an unknown hand to the percussion method. It's a large military-caliber pistol with a part-octagonal barrel, an unusually, no ram appears to have been fitted.

### SPECIFICATIONS
**Type:** percussion conversion
**Origin:** National Arsenal, St. Etienne, France
**Caliber:** .70
**Barrel Length:** 8in

# MAB Model A

**SPECIFICATIONS**

**Type:** semi-automatic pistol
**Origin:** Manufacture d'Armes de Bayonne, France (MAB)
**Caliber:** .25 ACP
**Barrel Length:** 2in

MAB was established in 1921 and produced a number of successful pistols until it was forced to close in the mid-1980s. The Model A, shown here, was the first to be produced. It was chambered for the 6.35mm cartridge and, like so many automatics of that period, was based on the 1906 Browning. The weapon pictured here has grips bearing the logo of the U.S. importer, WAC, but the logo for models not intended for the U.S. market was the parent company's "MAB."

# MAB Model D 1933

**SPECIFICATIONS**

**Type:** semi-automatic pistol
**Origin:** Manufacture d'Armes de Bayonne, France (MAB)
**Caliber:** 7.65mm
**Barrel Length:** 3.2in

Another MAB pistol based on the Browning, this one was first issued as the Model C, in 1933, and used a simple unlocked blowback operating cycle. The butt and grip were soon redesigned and the pistol renamed Model D. In this form it turned out to be a successful compact pistol, and remained in production until 1988.

# MAPF Mikros

**SPECIFICATIONS**

**Type:** semi-automatic pistol
**Origin:** Manufacture d'Armes de Pyrénées Françaises, Hendaye, France (MAPF)
**Caliber:** .25 ACP
**Barrel Length:** 2in

MAPF was established in 1923 to manufacture rifles and automatic pistols and up to 1939 it concentrated on the French military and police market, although numbers were also sold on the civilian market. The weapons were given model names rather than numbers and the Mikros was manufactured between 1934 and 1939. The design was based closely on that of the Walther Model 9 and most were chambered for the 6.35mm cartridge (*seen here*) although some were chambered for the more powerful 7.35mm round.

# GERMANY

## BORCHARDT PISTOL

### SPECIFICATIONS

**Type:** semi-automatic pistol/carbine
**Origin:** Hugo Borchardt and Loewe & Cie, Berlin
**Caliber:** 7.65mm
**Barrel Length:** 6.5in

Hugo Borchardt designed this complex weapon in 1893 using similar principles to those devised by Maxim in his machine gun. When a round was chambered, the barrel and breech were held together by a straight locking piece (with a pivoting joint in the centre) behind the breech. When fired, the barrel, breech and lock recoiled together until lugs in the receiver pushed a central pivot joint in the locking piece upwards, causing it to bend rather like a knee. The barrel stopped, while the breechblock was now able to continue to the rear, extracting the empty case. A powerful spring forced the barrel and breechblock forward, picking up the next round from the top of the magazine and loading it into the chamber. As they reached the firing position, the locking piece snapped back straight, holding the breech block in place.

The pistol was large and rather clumsy to use, and was normally seen with the combined wooden stock/holster as seen here. It was also expensive and complex to make. However, it was one of the first reasonable successful semi-automatic pistols, and the design concepts were developed further to make the outstanding Luger series (*see below*).

## BSW PROTOTYPE

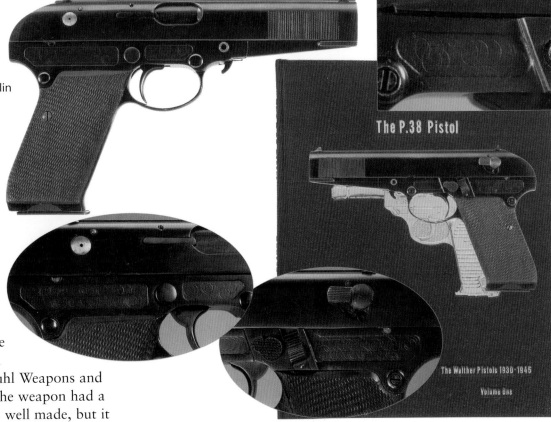

The P.38 Pistol

The Walther Pistols 1930-1945

Volume One

### SPECIFICATIONS

**Type:** semi-automatic pistol
**Origin:** Berlin-Suhler Waffen und Fahrrad Fabrik (BSW), Berlin
**Caliber:** 9mm
**Barrel Length:** 5in

This pistol was one of a number of designs submitted to the German army in the late 1930s as a replacement for the Luger. It was designed and made by the Berlin-Suhler Waffen und Fahrrad Fabrik (Berlin/Suhl Weapons and Bicycle Factory; BSW). The weapon had a neat appearance and was well made, but it was too complicated for service use and never got beyond the prototype stage.

## DREYSE 6.35MM MODEL 1907

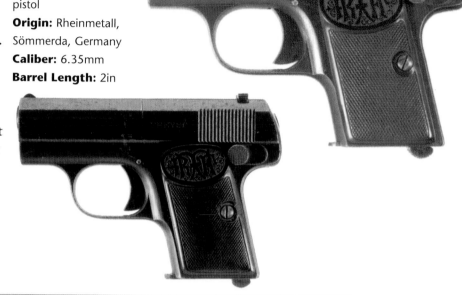

The German company Rheinmetall purchased the assets of the failing gunsmith Dreyse Waffenfabrik in 1901 but continued to produce weapons under the original name for some years. One of these was the 6.35mm Model 1907; there was also an unrelated 7.65mm Model 1907. The overall design of the weapon was similar to that of the 1906 Browning (but without the grip safety) but the famous designer Louis Schmeisser devised a novel method of assembly, for which he took out a patent. Note that the weapon shown here has the word "Dreyse" on the side, with the Rheinmetall logo at the head of the grip.

**SPECIFICATIONS**
**Type:** semi-automatic pistol
**Origin:** Rheinmetall, Sömmerda, Germany
**Caliber:** 6.35mm
**Barrel Length:** 2in

## HECKLER & KOCH USP

**SPECIFICATIONS**
**Type:** semi-automatic pistol
**Origin:** Heckler & Koch, Oberndorf
**Caliber:** .45
**Barrel Length:** 4.4in

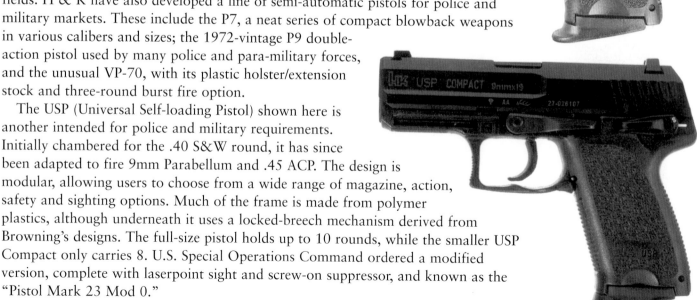

Heckler & Koch established themselves in Oberdorf-Neckar after World War Two, and began producing weapons as soon as they were permitted. The company has created a reputation for high-quality products, and weapons such as the G3 rifle and MP-5 sub-machine gun have been world-beaters in their respective fields. H & K have also developed a line of semi-automatic pistols for police and military markets. These include the P7, a neat series of compact blowback weapons in various calibers and sizes; the 1972-vintage P9 double-action pistol used by many police and para-military forces, and the unusual VP-70, with its plastic holster/extension stock and three-round burst fire option.

The USP (Universal Self-loading Pistol) shown here is another intended for police and military requirements. Initially chambered for the .40 S&W round, it has since been adapted to fire 9mm Parabellum and .45 ACP. The design is modular, allowing users to choose from a wide range of magazine, action, safety and sighting options. Much of the frame is made from polymer plastics, although underneath it uses a locked-breech mechanism derived from Browning's designs. The full-size pistol holds up to 10 rounds, while the smaller USP Compact only carries 8. U.S. Special Operations Command ordered a modified version, complete with laserpoint sight and screw-on suppressor, and known as the "Pistol Mark 23 Mod 0."

# DWM LUGER MODEL 1900 US

## SPECIFICATIONS

**Type:** semi-automatic pistol
**Origin:** Deutsche Waffen und Munitionsfabriken, Erfurt, Germany
**Caliber:** 7.65mm Luger
**Barrel Length:** 4.75in

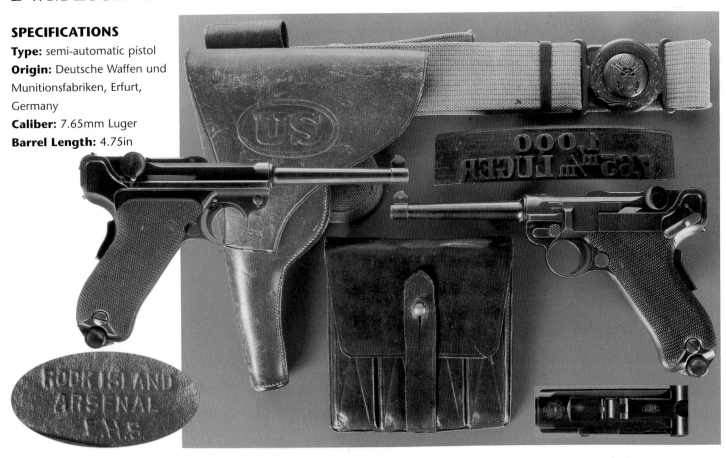

This exceptionally clear picture shows one of the 1,000 Model 1900 Lugers sent for trials by the U.S. army. An American eagle device is stamped above the chamber and a grip safety incorporated. These weapons were issued to the U.S. Cavalry for field trials, but no order was ever placed. This particular weapon obviously remained in service after the trials, as it comes complete with a Model 1910 Officer's Garrison Belt, an unusual left-handed leather, russet-colored leather holster and a pouch for four magazines.

# DWM COMMERCIAL MODEL 1900

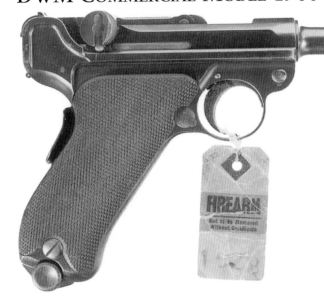

## SPECIFICATIONS

**Type:** semi-automatic pistol
**Origin:** Deutsche Waffen und Munitionsfabriken, Erfurt, Germany
**Caliber:** 7.65mm Luger
**Barrel Length:** 4.75in

The first Lugers were produced in 1899/1900 in a successful bid to win a contract for the Swiss Army and although DWM clearly saw the military market as potentially the most profitable, a number of weapons were produced for the civil market as the Model 1900 Commercial. This beautifully preserved specimen has the serial number 4907 and has the DWM crest on the toggle and the word "Germany" below the serial number. There is no crest above the chamber.

## DWM MODEL 1902 COMMERCIAL "AMERICAN EAGLE"

### SPECIFICATIONS

**Type:** semi-automatic pistol
**Origin:** Deutsche Waffen und
Munitionsfabriken, Erfurt, Germany
**Caliber:** 9mm Parabellum
**Barrel Length:** 4in

As explained in the introduction, Georg Luger designed a new cartridge for his pistol – the 9mmm Parabellum round – which was introduced from about 1902 onwards. This model was intended for the U.S. civil market and had an American eagle engraved above the chamber. The barrel was some 0.75in shorter than on other Lugers, leading to the nickname which is occasionally applied of "the Fat Barrel Luger."

## DWM MODEL 1906 NAVY 1ST ISSUE

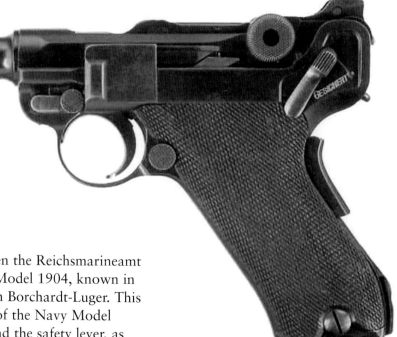

### SPECIFICATIONS

**Type:** semi-automatic pistol
**Origin:** Deutsche Waffen und Munitionsfabriken,
Erfurt, Germany
**Caliber:** 9mm Parabellum
**Barrel Length:** 6in

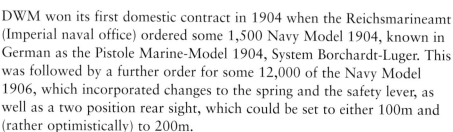

DWM won its first domestic contract in 1904 when the Reichsmarineamt (Imperial naval office) ordered some 1,500 Navy Model 1904, known in German as the Pistole Marine-Model 1904, System Borchardt-Luger. This was followed by a further order for some 12,000 of the Navy Model 1906, which incorporated changes to the spring and the safety lever, as well as a two position rear sight, which could be set to either 100m and (rather optimistically) to 200m.

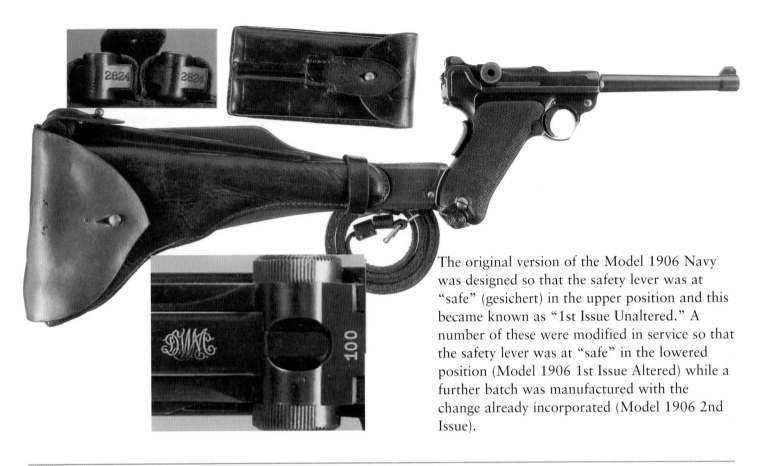

The original version of the Model 1906 Navy was designed so that the safety lever was at "safe" (gesichert) in the upper position and this became known as "1st Issue Unaltered." A number of these were modified in service so that the safety lever was at "safe" in the lowered position (Model 1906 1st Issue Altered) while a further batch was manufactured with the change already incorporated (Model 1906 2nd Issue).

# DWM Parabellum M 1908

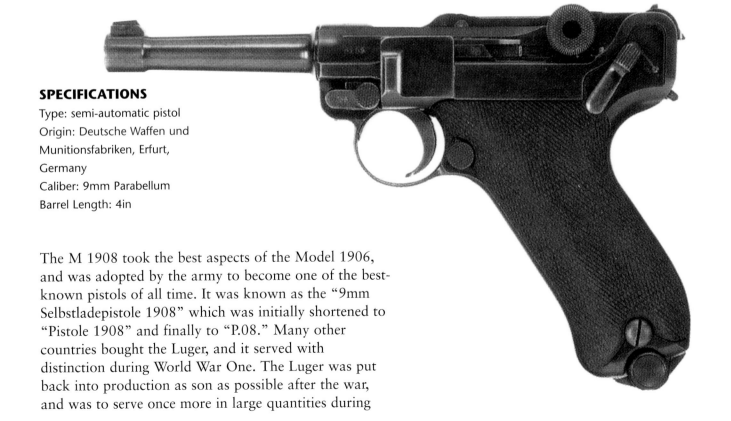

**SPECIFICATIONS**

Type: semi-automatic pistol
Origin: Deutsche Waffen und Munitionsfabriken, Erfurt, Germany
Caliber: 9mm Parabellum
Barrel Length: 4in

The M 1908 took the best aspects of the Model 1906, and was adopted by the army to become one of the best-known pistols of all time. It was known as the "9mm Selbstladepistole 1908" which was initially shortened to "Pistole 1908" and finally to "P.08." Many other countries bought the Luger, and it served with distinction during World War One. The Luger was put back into production as son as possible after the war, and was to serve once more in large quantities during

## DWM Long Model 1918 Reissued to Weimar Navy

### SPECIFICATIONS
**Type:** semi-automatic pistol
**Origin:** Deutsche Waffen und Munitionsfabriken, Erfurt, Germany
**Caliber:** 9mm Parabellum
**Barrel Length:** 8in

This weapon is unusual for three reasons. It is a Langepistole 1908 (artillery model) but with a 1918 date of manufacture stamped atop the chamber and Imperial German proof marks stamped on the right side of the receiver. This year of manufacture is, in itself, unusual, but it is also rare that it should have survived the Allied occupation, since they had taken a major dislike to this weapon and destroyed a great number. Finally, the weapon has stamps to show that it was issued to the Reichsmarine, the name given to the reconstituted navy formed in 1921 under the Weimar Republic, and which served until 1935 when Hitler redesignated it the Kriegsmarine.

## DWM Model 1920 Carbine

### SPECIFICATIONS
**Type:** semi-automatic carbine
**Origin:** Simson & Co, Suhl, Germany
**Caliber:** 9mm Parabellum
**Barrel Length:** 11.75in

The first carbine version of the Luger was produced in 1902, but the version shown here is the Model 1920, produced by Simson & Co of Suhl, Germany, in the immediate aftermath of World War One. These carbines were built on P.08 weapons, but with a much longer barrel, ramped foresight, tangent backsight and other changes. This particular weapon has an American eagle over the chamber indicating that it was made for export. Note the grip safety.

## MAUSER BYF-41 (LUGER P.08)

**SPECIFICATIONS**
**Type:** semi-automatic carbine
**Origin:** Mauser, Oberndorf, Germany
**Caliber:** 9mm Parabellum
**Barrel Length:** 3.9in

DWM had been forbidden to manufacture guns by the Allies in 1919 and the production machinery was moved from Erfurt to the Simson factory at Suhl. In 1923, DWM, now part of a consortium which included Mauser and redesignated the Berlin Karlsruhe Industrie-Werke re-entered production, only to have all its Parabellum staff and machinery move to the Mauser works at Oberndorf in 1930. Mauser continued to manufacture Parabellums until 1942. In about 1939 all weapons factories were allocated production codes, which had to be stamped on their weapons; in Mauser's case this was initially "42" but it then changed to "byf" which was followed by the last two digits of the calendar year. Thus, the "byf 41 Luger was produced by Mauser in 1941.

This particular weapon belonged to the adjutant to General Maximilian Fretter-Pico (1892–1984), who in March/April 1945 was the Commanding-General of Military District IX. Fretter-Pico and his adjutant were captured by troops of the U.S. army's 1st Infantry Division, and both were relieved of their weapons by their American captors.

# MAUSER MODEL 1896 (C/96)

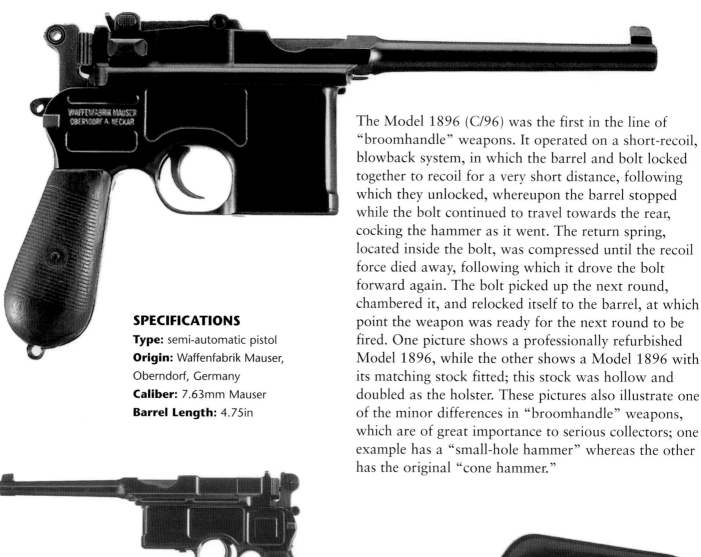

**SPECIFICATIONS**

**Type:** semi-automatic pistol
**Origin:** Waffenfabrik Mauser, Oberndorf, Germany
**Caliber:** 7.63mm Mauser
**Barrel Length:** 4.75in

The Model 1896 (C/96) was the first in the line of "broomhandle" weapons. It operated on a short-recoil, blowback system, in which the barrel and bolt locked together to recoil for a very short distance, following which they unlocked, whereupon the barrel stopped while the bolt continued to travel towards the rear, cocking the hammer as it went. The return spring, located inside the bolt, was compressed until the recoil force died away, following which it drove the bolt forward again. The bolt picked up the next round, chambered it, and relocked itself to the barrel, at which point the weapon was ready for the next round to be fired. One picture shows a professionally refurbished Model 1896, while the other shows a Model 1896 with its matching stock fitted; this stock was hollow and doubled as the holster. These pictures also illustrate one of the minor differences in "broomhandle" weapons, which are of great importance to serious collectors; one example has a "small-hole hammer" whereas the other has the original "cone hammer."

## VARIATIONS ON THE BROOMHANDLE THEME

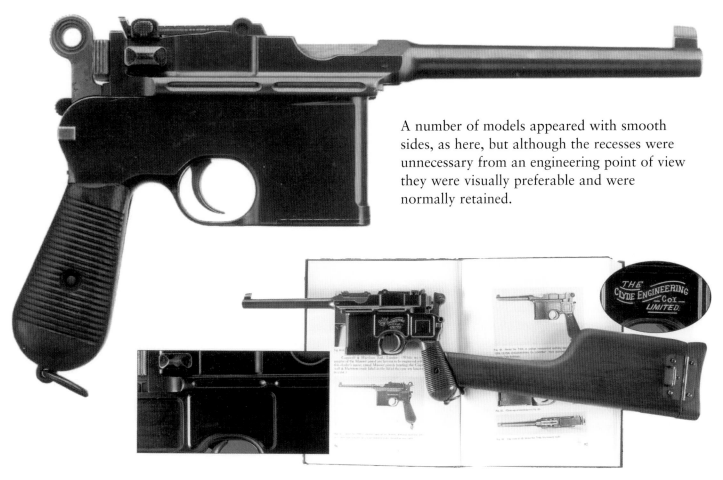

A number of models appeared with smooth sides, as here, but although the recesses were unnecessary from an engineering point of view they were visually preferable and were normally retained.

It was common for arms dealers to "buy-in" foreign products which retained their original identity but were marked with the retailer's name, as in this example which carries the name of "The Clyde Engineering Company."

During World War One some 150,000 Model 1896s were produced chambered for the 9mm Parabellum round. Other than in caliber, these were identical to the 7.63mm version, so a large figure "9" was cut into the butt and painted red. This particular weapon is one of that series, but has been reworked in the early 1920s for police use by having the barrel shortened and the rear sight removed.

## MAUSER MODEL 1914

### SPECIFICATIONS

**Type:** semi-automatic pistol
**Origin:** Waffenfabrik Mauser, Oberndorf, Germany
**Caliber:** 7.65mm Auto
**Barrel Length:** 3.5in

In 1914 Mauser introduced a new version of the Model 1910, slightly enlarged and chambered for the 7.65mm Auto round. The unusual shape of the slide, as shown in the right-hand picture, led to it being referred to as "the hunchback" model. The German army ordered a large number of these pistol in 1915 and production continued well into the 1930s.

# MAUSER MODEL 1910

Mauser introduced a totally new blowback pistol in 1909, chambered for the increasingly popular 9mm Parabellum round, but the weapon was not particularly successful. As a result, in the following year the company introduced a modified version chambered for the 6.35mm Auto (Browning) round, which proved much more popular, with some 60,000 being sold between 1910 and the outbreak of war in 1914. The weapon shown here bears a Portuguese marking.

## SPECIFICATIONS

**Type:** semi-automatic pistol
**Origin:** Waffenfabrik Mauser, Oberndorf, Germany
**Caliber:** 6.35mm Auto
**Barrel Length:** 3in

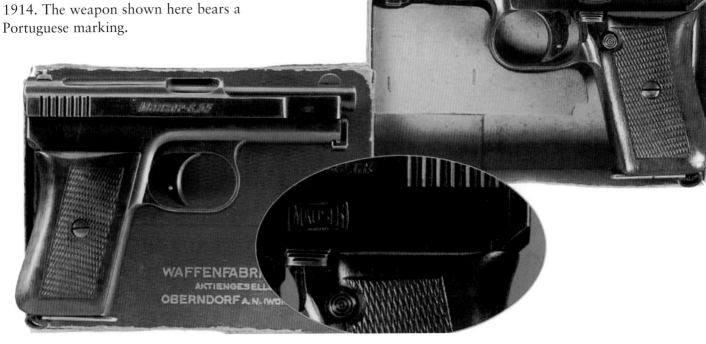

# MAUSER MODEL 1934

## SPECIFICATIONS

**Type:** semi-automatic pistol
**Origin:** Waffenfabrik Mauser, Oberndorf, Germany
**Caliber:** 7.65mm Auto
**Barrel Length:** 3.4in

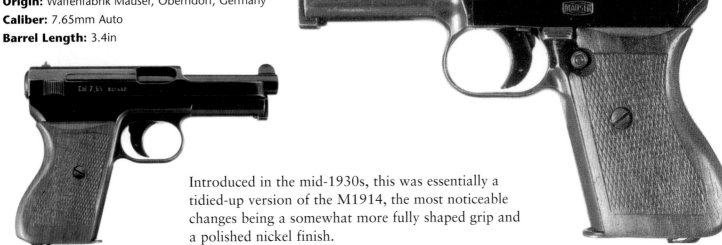

Introduced in the mid-1930s, this was essentially a tidied-up version of the M1914, the most noticeable changes being a somewhat more fully shaped grip and a polished nickel finish.

## MAUSER "BYF 42" (WALTHER P.38)

### SPECIFICATIONS

**Type:** semi-automatic pistol
**Origin:** Waffenfabrik Mauser,
Oberndorf, Germany
**Caliber:** 9mm Parabellum
**Barrel Length:** 5in

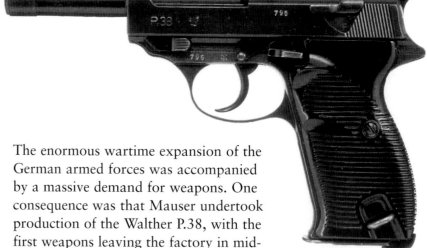

The enormous wartime expansion of the German armed forces was accompanied by a massive demand for weapons. One consequence was that Mauser undertook production of the Walther P.38, with the first weapons leaving the factory in mid-1942. This is one of those, as proved by the marking "byf 42" – the Mauser production code accompanied by the last two digits of the calendar year. The mark can be seen to the right of the "P38" on the body of the weapon.

## MAUSER (BYF 44) (WALTHER P.38)

### SPECIFICATIONS

**Type:** semi-automatic pistol
**Origin:** Waffenfabrik Mauser, Oberndorf, Germany
**Caliber:** 9mm Parabellum
**Barrel Length:** 5in

Produced in 1944 this P.38 can only be distinguished from a Walther-built version by the code "byf 44" stamped on the body. This particular weapon appears to have been initially issued to the police, but it was in military use when captured by Gerard P. Finn of Springfield, Virginia during the Battle of the Bulge in late 1944.

## MAUSER WTP

### SPECIFICATIONS

**Type:** semi-automatic pistol
**Origin:** Waffenfabrik Mauser, Oberndorf, Germany
**Caliber:** 6.35mm Auto
**Barrel Length:** 2.4in

The Westentaschenpistole (waistcoat pocket pistol or WTP) was designed following the end of World War One and entered production in 1921. It was a blowback design, carried six 6.35mm rounds, weighed 10.6oz and was a mere 4.0 in long. A slightly modified version appeared in 1938, but production ended in 1940.

## MAUSER 9MM NICKL EXPERIMENTAL

**SPECIFICATIONS**
**Type:** semi-automatic pistol
**Origin:** Waffenfabrik Mauser,
Oberndorf, Germany
**Caliber:** 9mm Parabellum
**Barrel Length:** 3.44in

Josef Nickl, an Austrian,
worked in the production
department of the Mauser
factory from about 1912
to 1921, when he moved
to Czechoslovakia. Apart
from being a production
engineer he was also
interested in design, and a
small number of pistols to
his design were produced
in 1916–17. This weapon
was designed around the
9mm Kurz (Luger) round
and featured a rotating barrel and a locked-breech mechanism on a Mauser
Model 1912/14 frame. The weapon seems not to have found favour with
Mauser (although the company took copyright of the design) and it was later
licensed for production in Czechoslovakia as the vz.22 and vz.24.

## MAUSER HSC

Faced in the 1930s with increasing
competition in 7.65mm caliber
from the Walther PP and PPK,
Mauser developed a new weapon
designated the Seblstspannerpistole
mit Hahn (self-cocking pistol with
hammer). When however, it
appeared that this might infringe
some Walther patents, the design
was completely recast to
produce the Hahnlos,
Selbsladung Pistole Modelle a (hammerless,
self-loading pistol, model a, or HSa). Initial
trials led to modifications, resulting in the
HSb, but yet further modifications were
found necessary and the HSc finally entered
production in 1940. Some 250,000 had been

**SPECIFICATIONS**
**Type:** semi-automatic pistol
**Origin:** Waffenfabrik Mauser,
Oberndorf, Germany
**Caliber:** 7.65mm Auto
**Barrel Length:** 3.4in

produced by May 1945, the main users being the Luftwaffe (air force), Kriegsmarine (navy) and police, although some were also sold commercially.

After the war, some 20,000 were completed from existing components for the French armed forces. Production restarted in 1970, but ended in Germany in the 1970s, when a production licence was granted to an Italian company.

## MAUSER PROTOTYPE 0.45 SELF-LOADING PISTOL

The completion details of this pistol are beyond doubt, as it is clearly stamped with the company's name "WAFFENFABRIK MAUSER A.G. OBERNDORF a.N" and "KONSTRUKTIONSDATUM 17:2:1915." (date of manufacture February 17, 1915). Other than that, however, its history is somewhat obscure. It is known that Mauser (and also Luger) produced a small number of prototype .45in caliber pistols in the years prior to World War One with the aim of breaking into the American market, at least one of which was tested (and rejected) by the U.S. army.

Work on this caliber would, of course, have been going on prior to the outbreak of war in August 1914 and the declaration of war between Germany and the United States did not take place until 1917, so Mauser may have still been hoping for a breakthrough when this pistol was made and it may even have been delivered there, as it came to light in a U.S. collection.

### SPECIFICATIONS
**Type:** semi-automatic pistol
**Origin:** Waffenfabrik Mauser, Oberndorf, Germany
**Caliber:** .45
**Barrel Length:** 4.5in

## MENZ MODEL II

### SPECIFICATIONS

**Type:** semi-automatic pistol
**Origin:** Waffenfabrik August Menz, Suhl, Germany
**Caliber:** 7.65mm auto
**Barrel Length:** 2in

Menz introduced a new small, blowback pistol in 1920, named, appropriately, the Lilliput. It was chambered for the unusual caliber of 4.25mm and although it proved a popular weapon Menz offered a 6.25mm Auto version in 1925, followed by a few in 7.65mm Auto. This more powerful round may have proved too much for the design, as the company then marketed a new, slightly larger version of the weapon chambered for the 6.35mm Auto, designated the Model II (*seen here*), with the caliber carefully marked in red on the grip.

## ORTGIES SEMI-AUTOMATIC POCKET PISTOL

### SPECIFICATIONS

**Type:** semi-automatic pistol
**Origin:** Heinrich Ortgies & Co, Erfurt, Germany
**Caliber:** 7.65mm auto
**Barrel Length:** 3.4in

Heinrich Ortgies returned to his native Germany in 1918 armed only with a patent for a new design of semi-automatic, blowback operated pistol. Despite the depressed and chaotic conditions in post-war Germany, he managed to put this into production and enjoyed such success that he was bought out by Deutsche Werke in 1921. The Ortgies pistol weighed some 22.6oz and had an eight-round box magazine housed in the butt. As produced by Ortgies, the pistol was available only in 7.65mm caliber, but Deutsche Werke introduced further models in 6.35mm and 9mm Short.

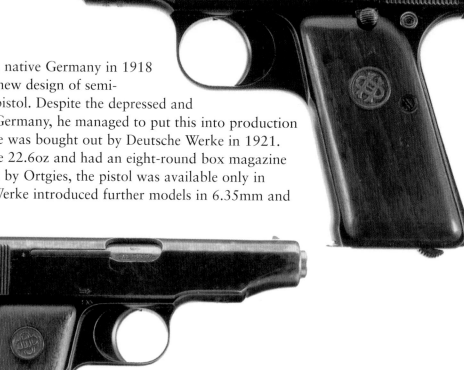

# RHEINMETALL PROTOTYPE 9MM

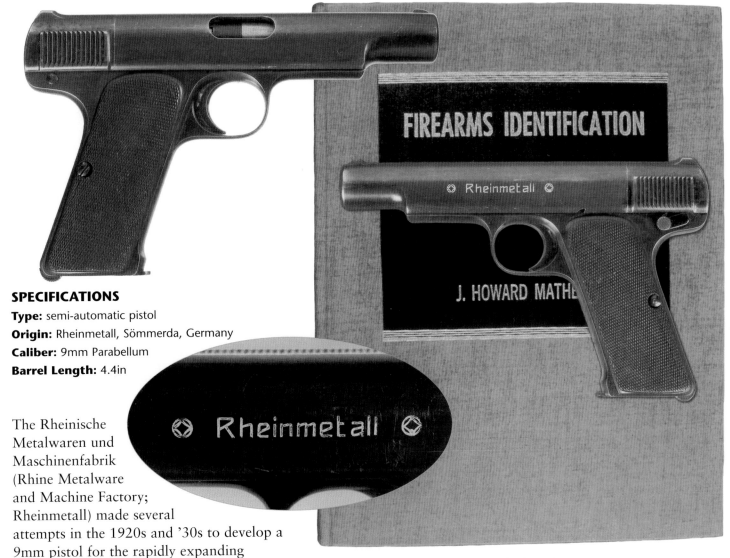

## SPECIFICATIONS

**Type:** semi-automatic pistol
**Origin:** Rheinmetall, Sömmerda, Germany
**Caliber:** 9mm Parabellum
**Barrel Length:** 4.4in

The Rheinische Metalwaren und Maschinenfabrik (Rhine Metalware and Machine Factory; Rheinmetall) made several attempts in the 1920s and '30s to develop a 9mm pistol for the rapidly expanding German armed forces. The first was an adaptation of the Dreyse 7.65mm described in the previous entry, but rechambered for 9mm, while the second was the totally new design shown here. This example is finished to a very high standard but has no serial number or proof marks, suggesting that it was a prototype. No order was ever received.

# SAUER MODEL 1930

The Sauer company produced firearms from 1751, but only became involved in pistols in 1900, producing various models under licensed. This led to their own design, the Sauer Model 1913, a 7.65mm weapon of which some 100,000 were manufactured. The company then developed the Model 1930, which was essentially a product-improved Model 1913, with detailed modifications resulting from some twenty years' service.

This is the Behörden-Modell (official model), developed for the police market. Production of all versions of the Model 1930 ended in 1937.

## SPECIFICATIONS

**Type:** semi-automatic pistol
**Origin:** J.P. Sauer & Sohn, Erfurt and Eckenförde, Germany
**Caliber:** 7.65mm auto
**Barrel Length:** 3in

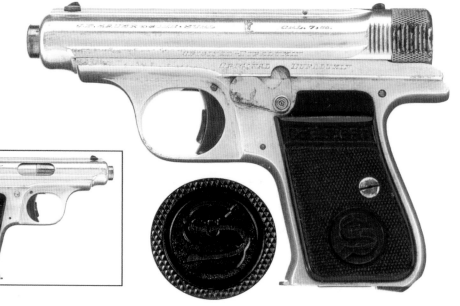

This picture shows a duralumin-framed version of this weapon.

# SAUER MODEL 38-H

## SPECIFICATIONS

**Type:** semi-automatic pistol
**Origin:** J.P. Sauer & Sohn, Erfurt and Eckenförde, Germany
**Caliber:** 7.65mm auto
**Barrel Length:** 3.270in

Sauer produced a small 6.35mm pistol, designated the WTM (Westentasche Modelle (waistcoat-pocket model), from 1925 to 1939, but its major success came with the Model 38 and the later Model 38-H. There is some discussion over the meaning of the suffix "H", which is taken to mean either Hahn, indicating that it was fitted with a hammer rather than a striker, or Heer, meaning that it was an army model. However, both Model 38 and 38-H were excellent handguns, being well made, reliable and accurate. There were five variations in the design, partly resulting from improvements, but also due to the war, as increasing shortages of time and materiel meant that the standard of finish became lower. The pictures show three variations. The first one we show is a standard Model 38-H in blue finish, with black plastic grips.

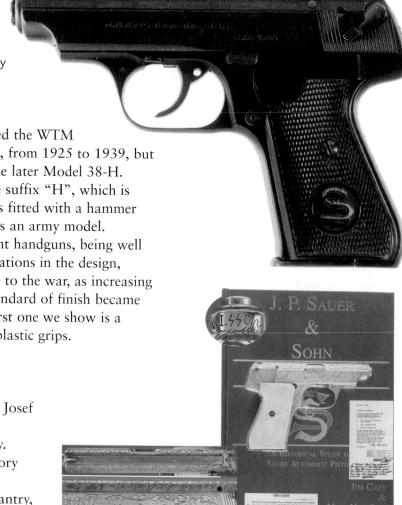

This one was the personal weapon of Oberstgruppenführer und General der Waffen-SS Josef "Sepp" Dietrich, whose Waffen-SS rank was equivalent to colonel-general in the German army. This was in heavily-engraved silver finish with ivory grips and was "liberated" in Munich in 1945 by Sergeant Sever B. Lone of Company B, 179th Infantry, who took it back to the States, where it remained the property of his family for many years.

# WALTHER MODEL 3

## SPECIFICATIONS

**Type:** semi-automatic pistol
**Origin:** Carl Walther, Zella-Mehlis, Germany
**Caliber:** 7.65mm auto
**Barrel Length:** 2.62in

The Model 1 was followed by the Model 2, which was a simplified version of the first design, with a full-length slide and the recoil spring, which was concentric with the barrel, held in place by a prominent muzzle bush. This was followed in 1913 by the Model 3, seen here, which was enlarged to accommodate the 7.65mm cartridge. One surprising – and unwelcome – characteristic was that the ejection port was on the left side of the weapon, which meant that, for a right-handed firer, the empty cartridge case flew across the firer's face. The recoil-spring retaining bush, which had been screwed on in the Model 2, was now retained by a bayonet joint, which engaged in locking-studs inside the frame.

# WALTHER MODEL 4

## SPECIFICATIONS

**Type:** semi-automatic pistol
**Origin:** Carl Walther, Zella-Mehlis, Germany
**Caliber:** 7.65mm auto
**Barrel Length:** 3.35in

Models 1 through 3 had a six-round magazine, but in the Model 4 this was increased to eight, necessitating a slightly longer butt. In addition, the barrel was lengthened as was the slide, although the left-side ejection slot was retained. This model was ordered in large numbers which were delivered between 1915 and 1918, with production continuing, albeit at a slower pace until 1923.

## WALTHER MODEL 5

### SPECIFICATIONS

**Type:** semi-automatic pistol

**Origin:** Carl Walther, Zella-Mehlis, Germany

**Caliber:** 6.35mm auto

**Barrel Length:** 2in

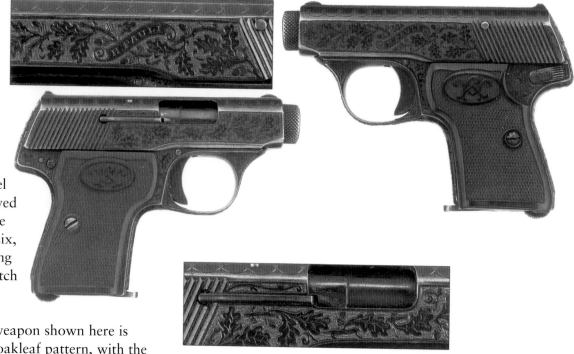

The Model 5 was not a successor to the Model 4, but a product-improved Model 2, firing the same 6.35mm round. It had six, as opposed to two, rifling grooves, and a fixed-notch rear sight, and was manufactured to higher tolerances. The actual weapon shown here is heavily engraved in an oakleaf pattern, with the name "H. PAULI" appearing on the left side.

## WALTHER MODEL 6

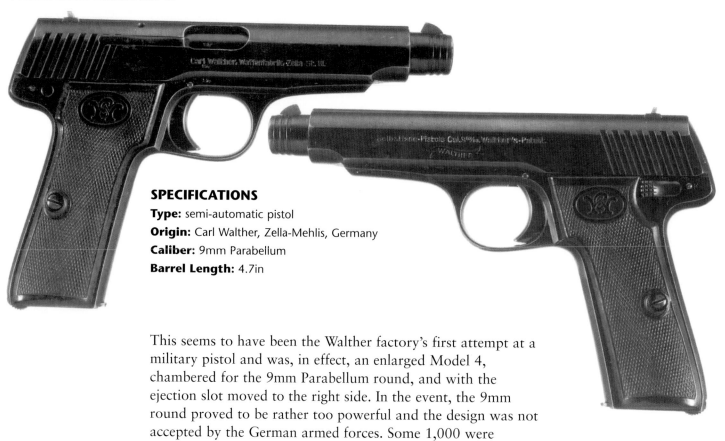

### SPECIFICATIONS

**Type:** semi-automatic pistol

**Origin:** Carl Walther, Zella-Mehlis, Germany

**Caliber:** 9mm Parabellum

**Barrel Length:** 4.7in

This seems to have been the Walther factory's first attempt at a military pistol and was, in effect, an enlarged Model 4, chambered for the 9mm Parabellum round, and with the ejection slot moved to the right side. In the event, the 9mm round proved to be rather too powerful and the design was not accepted by the German armed forces. Some 1,000 were produced in 1916–17

# WALTHER MODEL 7

## SPECIFICATIONS

**Type:** semi-automatic pistol
**Origin:** Carl Walther, Zella-Mehlis, Germany
**Caliber:** 6.35mm auto
**Barrel Length:** 3in

The Model 7 was a 6.35mm version of the Model 4, but with a longer slide, shorter barrel and ejection, much more sensibly, to the right. The Model 7 was not procured by the military, but it became fashionable among staff officers, who had to buy them at their own expense on the commercial market.

# WALTHER MODEL 8

The Model 8 was Walther's first post-war pistol and its popularity can be gauged by the fact that some 250,000 were sold between 1920 and the end of production in 1943. It had a longer butt to house an eight-round magazine and an unusual feature was that the trigger guard served also as the stripping catch. Although the vast majority of those produced were in the conventional dull black finish, there were, as usual, some presentation models, such as the example seen here, with its elaborate engravings and ivory grips.

## SPECIFICATIONS

**Type:** semi-automatic pistol
**Origin:** Carl Walther, Zella-Mehlis, Germany
**Caliber:** 6.35mm auto
**Barrel Length:** 2.8in

# WALTHER MODEL 9

## SPECIFICATIONS

**Type:** semi-automatic pistol
**Origin:** Carl Walther, Zella-Mehlis, Germany
**Caliber:** 6.35mm auto
**Barrel Length:** 2in

The Model 9 Pocket Pistol was smaller than its predecessors, being only 4 inches long and weighing 9.5oz. A simple blowback design, it held 6 rounds in the magazine, and was a useful and neat self-defense pistol easily carried in a bag or pocket.

# WALTHER MODEL 1925 SPORT

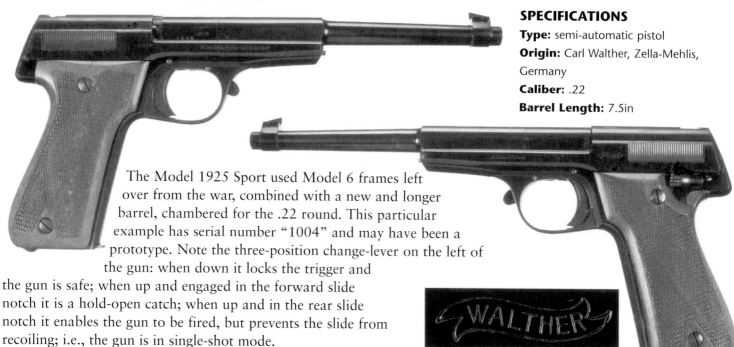

## SPECIFICATIONS
**Type:** semi-automatic pistol
**Origin:** Carl Walther, Zella-Mehlis, Germany
**Caliber:** .22
**Barrel Length:** 7.5in

The Model 1925 Sport used Model 6 frames left over from the war, combined with a new and longer barrel, chambered for the .22 round. This particular example has serial number "1004" and may have been a prototype. Note the three-position change-lever on the left of the gun: when down it locks the trigger and the gun is safe; when up and engaged in the forward slide notch it is a hold-open catch; when up and in the rear slide notch it enables the gun to be fired, but prevents the slide from recoiling; i.e., the gun is in single-shot mode.

# WALTHER MODEL 1936 OLYMPIA

## SPECIFICATIONS
**Type:** semi-automatic pistol
**Origin:** Carl Walther, Zella-Mehlis, Germany
**Caliber:** .22 LR
**Barrel Length:** 7.4in

A German competitor won a silver medal at the 1932 Los Angeles Olympics using the Model 1926 pistol, so the Walther factory produced an improved version for the 1936 Berlin Olympics. There were various barrel lengths and chambering for either .22LR or .22Short depending upon the competition, weights could be added to improve balance, and all had ten round magazines, except for the Modern Pentathlon weapon which carried six. The design was so good that it was reintroduced by the Swedish Hämmerli company in the 1950s.

The main picture shows a beautifully prepared example presented by Fritz Walther to his son Karl Heinz and engraved "Zur Erinnerung am Deiner Sieg im Ausscheidungsschießen am 16.8.1942." (In memory of your success in shooting August 16, 1942).

## WALTHER GRIP SAFETY EXPERIMENTAL

### SPECIFICATIONS

**Type:** semi-automatic pistol
**Origin:** Carl Walther, Zella-Mehlis, Germany
**Caliber:** 7.65mm
**Barrel Length:** 3.5in

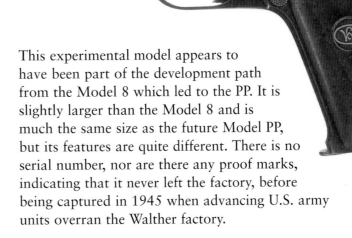

This experimental model appears to have been part of the development path from the Model 8 which led to the PP. It is slightly larger than the Model 8 and is much the same size as the future Model PP, but its features are quite different. There is no serial number, nor are there any proof marks, indicating that it never left the factory, before being captured in 1945 when advancing U.S. army units overran the Walther factory.

# WALTHER PPK

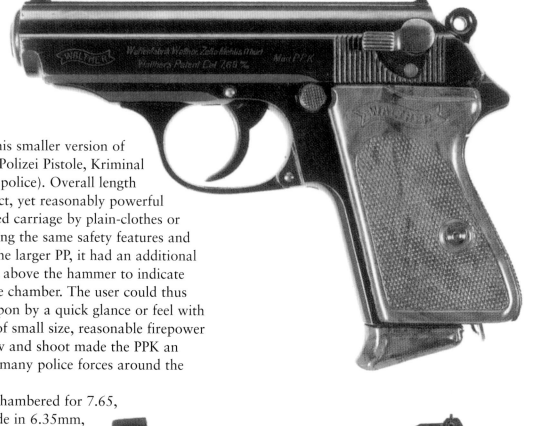

## SPECIFICATIONS

**Type:** semi-automatic pistol
**Origin:** Carl Walther, Zella-Mehlis, Germany
**Caliber:** 7.65mm
**Barrel Length:** 3.1in

In 1931 Walther introduced this smaller version of the PP, known as the PPK, or Polizei Pistole, Kriminal Polizei (police pistol, criminal police). Overall length was 5.8in and it was a compact, yet reasonably powerful weapon, intended for concealed carriage by plain-clothes or undercover police officers. Using the same safety features and double-action mechanism as the larger PP, it had an additional feature where a pin protruded above the hammer to indicate that a round was loaded in the chamber. The user could thus check to load state of his weapon by a quick glance or feel with a fingertip. The combination of small size, reasonable firepower and the ability to quickly draw and shoot made the PPK an instant hit, and it was sold to many police forces around the world.

As with the PP, most were chambered for 7.65, although there were some made in 6.35mm, .22LR and 9mm Short. The grip area is quite short, so many PPKs used a plastic grip extension at the bottom of the 7-shot magazine.

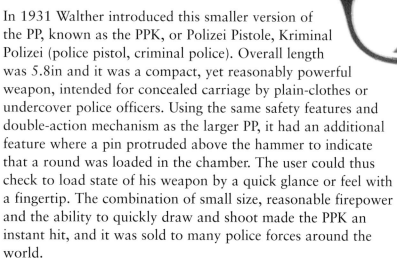

# WALTHER ARMEE-PISTOLE (AP)

## SPECIFICATIONS
**Type:** semi-automatic pistol
**Origin:** Carl Walther, Zella-Mehlis, Germany
**Caliber:** 9mm Parabellum
**Barrel Length:** 5in

As always with automatics, military contracts were the key to real success, and in 1934 Walther produced the MP (Militärische Pistole, military pistol). However, only a few prototypes were ever made and the next design was the totally new Armee-Pistole of 1936–37, of which perhaps 100 were made, that shown here being the 48th in the series. It had a lightweight duralumin frame and the top of the frame was open, enabling the breech end of the barrel to be seen. The weapon had an internal hammer and this was one particular feature that the Germany army singled out for adverse comment. The barrel on the weapon seen here is 5in long, but versions of the AP with longer barrels have also been seen.

# WALTHER MODEL HEERES-PISTOLE (HP)

## SPECIFICATIONS
**Type:** semi-automatic pistol
**Origin:** Carl Walther, Zella-Mehlis, Germany
**Caliber:** 9mm Parabellum
**Barrel Length:** 4.9in

Walther's next effort to win army approval was the Model HP (Heeres-Pistole; army pistol) of 1937, which sought to correct the problems with the Model AP, being fitted with a revised slide and an external hammer. After careful examination the German Army requested certain minor modifications, which resulted in the famous P.38 (*see below*). The Model HP was also offered on the civilian market, with versions being advertised chambered for 7.65mm, 9mm Parabellum, .38 Super Auto and .45 ACP. However, the model shown here is a military version marked with the German army acceptance stamp. One thousand Model HP were also supplied to the Swedish army.

# WALTHER P.38

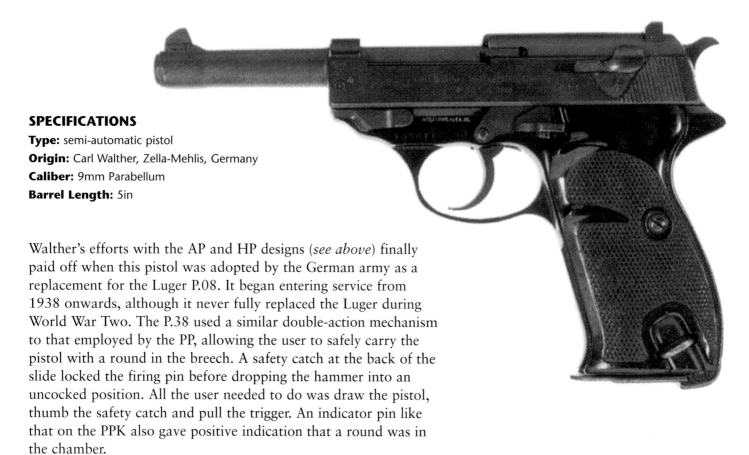

## SPECIFICATIONS

**Type:** semi-automatic pistol
**Origin:** Carl Walther, Zella-Mehlis, Germany
**Caliber:** 9mm Parabellum
**Barrel Length:** 5in

Walther's efforts with the AP and HP designs (*see above*) finally paid off when this pistol was adopted by the German army as a replacement for the Luger P.08. It began entering service from 1938 onwards, although it never fully replaced the Luger during World War Two. The P.38 used a similar double-action mechanism to that employed by the PP, allowing the user to safely carry the pistol with a round in the breech. A safety catch at the back of the slide locked the firing pin before dropping the hammer into an uncocked position. All the user needed to do was draw the pistol, thumb the safety catch and pull the trigger. An indicator pin like that on the PPK also gave positive indication that a round was in the chamber.

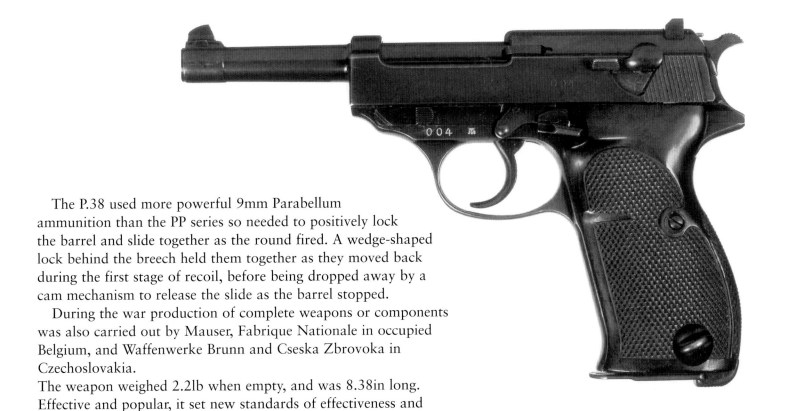

The P.38 used more powerful 9mm Parabellum ammunition than the PP series so needed to positively lock the barrel and slide together as the round fired. A wedge-shaped lock behind the breech held them together as they moved back during the first stage of recoil, before being dropped away by a cam mechanism to release the slide as the barrel stopped.

During the war production of complete weapons or components was also carried out by Mauser, Fabrique Nationale in occupied Belgium, and Waffenwerke Brunn and Cseska Zbrovoka in Czechoslovakia.

The weapon weighed 2.2lb when empty, and was 8.38in long. Effective and popular, it set new standards of effectiveness and safety for military pistols. It was adopted by the Swedish army before World War Two as the Pistole Model 39, and by the German and other armies when production restarted after the war (*see the P1 below*).

## WALTHER 9MM ULTRA

### SPECIFICATIONS

**Type:** semi-automatic pistol
**Origin:** Carl Walther, Zella-Mehlis, Germany
**Caliber:** 9 x 18mm Ultra
**Barrel Length:** 5in

The German World War Two 9mm Ultra project was an attempt to develop the most powerful cartridge that could be used with a simple blowback mechanism, ie in a pistol that needed no barrel locking mechanism. The most powerful round the unlocked PP series could handle was the 9mm Short (also known as .380 ACP), while the Parabellum pistols such as the P.38 all needed some sort of locking arrangement. The Ultra round involved using the projectile from the 9mm Parabellum system, but mounted in a slightly shorter straight-sided case. Some 20,000 of these rounds were manufactured by the Genschow company and Walther designed this pistol to use them, the aim being to satisfy a Luftwaffe requirement for a weapon that was more powerful than the .38 ACP caliber Model PP, but smaller than the P.38 and Model 8. The weapon combined some aspects of the P.38 and PP, but overall it was quite a revolutionary design.

## WALTHER P1

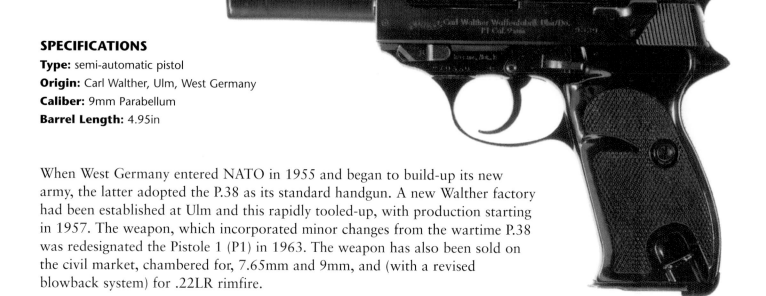

### SPECIFICATIONS

**Type:** semi-automatic pistol
**Origin:** Carl Walther, Ulm, West Germany
**Caliber:** 9mm Parabellum
**Barrel Length:** 4.95in

When West Germany entered NATO in 1955 and began to build-up its new army, the latter adopted the P.38 as its standard handgun. A new Walther factory had been established at Ulm and this rapidly tooled-up, with production starting in 1957. The weapon, which incorporated minor changes from the wartime P.38 was redesignated the Pistole 1 (P1) in 1963. The weapon has also been sold on the civil market, chambered for, 7.65mm and 9mm, and (with a revised blowback system) for .22LR rimfire.

## GERMAN TARGET PISTOL

### SPECIFICATIONS

**Type:** target pistol
**Origin:** unknown German gunsmith
**Caliber:** .22
**Barrel Length:** 11.2in

This .22in caliber German target pistol is marked with the name "J.H. Hampe, Gettingen" on the top of the barrel, but no gunsmith of this name is recorded in any of the authorities on the subject. The weapon is made in the old style of target pistol, with a long (11.2in) barrel and a gracefully curved stock. The frame is decorated with light scroll engraving.

# EAST GERMANY (DDR)

## MAKAROV PISTOL

### SPECIFICATIONS

**Type:** semi-automatic pistol
**Origin:** Ernst Thaelmann VEB, Suhl, East Germany
**Caliber:** 9 x 18mm
**Barrel Length:** 3.75in

The former German Democratic Republic, or GDR (generally known as "East Germany") was totally under the thumb of the former Soviet Union. The GDR took over the former arms factories at Suhl in Thuringia in the late 1940s and designated them a Volkeigener Betrieb (VEB; "people-owned factory"), named after an obscure Communist "hero," Ernst Thaelmann. This factory undertook licensed production of various Soviet-designed weapons, one of which was the Makarov pistol, two examples of which are shown here.

# HUNGARY

## FEGYVERGYAR MODEL 29M

### SPECIFICATIONS

**Type:** semi-automatic pistol
**Origin:** Fémáru Fegyver és Gépgyár,
Budapest, Hungary
**Caliber:** 9mm Short (.380 ACP)
**Barrel Length:** 3.94in

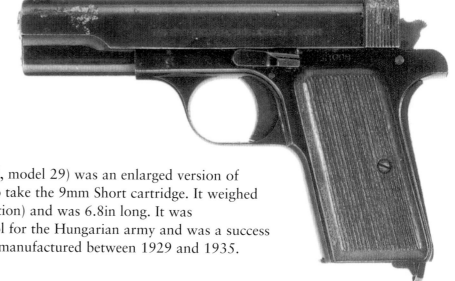

The Model 29M (Pisztoly 29 Minta; pistol, model 29) was an enlarged version of Rudolph Frommer's Lilliput, chambered to take the 9mm Short cartridge. It weighed 26oz (with magazine but without ammunition) and was 6.8in long. It was immediately accepted as the standard pistol for the Hungarian army and was a success for the company, with some 50,000 being manufactured between 1929 and 1935.

## FEGYVERGYAR MODEL 37M

### SPECIFICATIONS

**Type:** semi-automatic pistol
**Origin:** Fémáru Fegyver és Gépgyár, Budapest,
Hungary
**Caliber:** 7.65mm Auto
**Barrel Length:** 4.3in

Frommer died in 1936 and his last design appeared a year later as the Model 37M. This was, essentially, a mechanically simpler version of the Model 29M, intended to be easier and cheaper to produce and maintain. This was produced initially for the Hungarian army, but in 1941 the Germans placed an order for 50,000 (later increased to 90,000) for the Luftwaffe, most of which were issued to aircrew. These weapons were officially designated Pistole M.37 Kaliber 7.65mm, shortened on the weapons themselves to "P. Mod.37, Kal. 7,65" which were also stamped with the German production code "jvh" and the last two digits of the year of manufacture. The only significant change requested by the Luftwaffe was the addition of a mechanical safety catch, which had not been fitted to the original Hungarian version.

## FEGYVERGYAR PJK-9HP

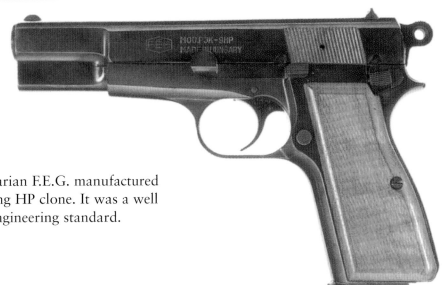

**SPECIFICATIONS**

**Type:** semi-automatic pistol
**Origin:** Fémáru Fegyver és Gépgyár,
Budapest, Hungary
**Caliber:** 9mm
**Barrel Length:** 4.5in

In the post-World War Two era the Hungarian F.E.G. manufactured
the Model PJK-9HP, which was a Browning HP clone. It was a well
regarded weapon, being made to a high engineering standard.

# IRELAND

## JOHN RIGBY DUELLING PISTOL

**SPECIFICATIONS**

**Type:** duelling pistol
**Origin:** John Rigby, Dublin, Ireland
**Caliber:** .60
**Barrel Length:** 10in

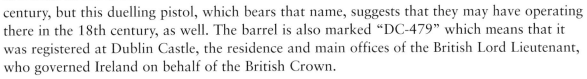

The Rigby family is
known to have been in
the gunmaking business
in Dublin in the 19th
century, but this duelling pistol, which bears that name, suggests that they may have operating
there in the 18th century, as well. The barrel is also marked "DC-479" which means that it
was registered at Dublin Castle, the residence and main offices of the British Lord Lieutenant,
who governed Ireland on behalf of the British Crown.

## IRISH FLINTLOCK PISTOL

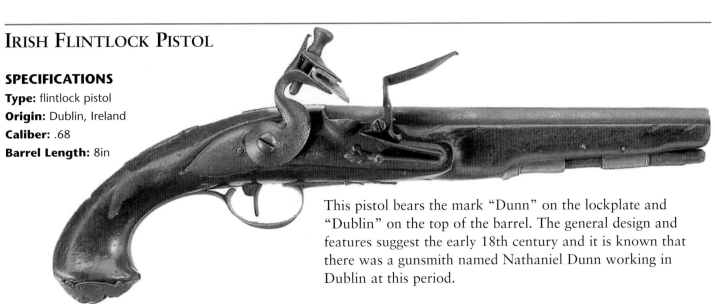

**SPECIFICATIONS**

**Type:** flintlock pistol
**Origin:** Dublin, Ireland
**Caliber:** .68
**Barrel Length:** 8in

This pistol bears the mark "Dunn" on the lockplate and
"Dublin" on the top of the barrel. The general design and
features suggest the early 18th century and it is known that
there was a gunsmith named Nathaniel Dunn working in
Dublin at this period.

## Beretta Model 1935

**SPECIFICATIONS**
**Type:** semi-automatic pistol
**Origin:** Armi Beretta SpA, Brescia, Italy
**Caliber:** 7.65mm
**Barrel Length:** 3.5in

A year after the introduction of the Model 1934, Beretta released a similar pistol but this time chambered for the less powerful 7.65mm round, It was taken up by the Italian navy, air force and police.

## Beretta Model 70

**SPECIFICATIONS**
**Type:** semi-automatic pistol
**Origin:** Armi Beretta SpA, Brescia, Italy
**Caliber:** 9mm Short (.380 ACP)
**Barrel Length:** 3.5in

The Model 70 design could be traced back via the Model 948 to the Model 1934, with minor changes to the safety and holding-open device. The basic model was chambered for the 7.65mm cartridge, but variants included the Model 70S, which had a magazine safety and was produced in .22LR, 7.65mm Auto (*seen here*) and 9mm Short versions.

# BERETTA MODEL 92/92S

After World War Two, Beretta finally designed an automatic pistol for the 9mm Parabellum round. The Model 1951 was the first Beretta pistol to use used a breech locking mechanism to handle such a powerful cartridge. The Model 92 was introduced in 1976, and was a further development of this pistol, with a larger butt to hold a 15-shot magazine. It also used a double-action mechanism, allowing the user to fire without having to cock the hammer first. The Model 92S introduced some further safety features, and had the safety catch moved from the frame to the slide. It also acts as a decocking lever for the hammer and moves the firing pin out of position. Users can safely carry a Model 92S with a round chambered, and only need to thumb the safety catch before pulling the trigger to fire. It was adopted by the Italian and other armies, and by a number of police forces.

**SPECIFICATIONS**
**Type:** semi-automatic pistol
**Origin:** Armi Beretta SpA, Brescia, Italy
**Caliber:** 9mm Parabellum
**Barrel Length:** 4.3in

By 1980 the U.S. army had accepted that the long-serving Colt M1911A1 (*see below*) had reached the end of its service life, and trials were undertaken to find a replacement. Beretta put the slightly modified Model 92SB forward, and it eventually won the trials, seeing off tough competition from a range of homegrown and international products.

## BERETTA MODEL 75

### SPECIFICATIONS

**Type:** semi-automatic pistol
**Origin:** Armi Beretta SpA, Brescia, Italy
**Caliber:** .22LR
**Barrel Length:** 4.2in

The Beretta Jaguar .22 pistol was introduced into the US market in the mid-1950s and was available with two barrel lengths. The parallel versions for the European market were designated the Models 72 thru 75, the actual designation depending on the length of the barrel. The weapon seen here, the Model 75, had a 4.2in barrel.

## BERETTA MODEL 92F

### SPECIFICATIONS

**Type:** semi-automatic pistol
**Origin:** Armi Beretta SpA, Brescia, Italy
**Caliber:** 9mm
**Barrel Length:** 4.3in

Despite its success in the U.S. armed forces' competition, the U.S. authorities required some minor changes to the Model 92SB before it was put into production. Changes were made to the safety system, the shape of the trigger guard, the base of the grip and the finish. This resulted in the Model 92F, which was designated M9 in US service.

Selection of the M9 was not without controversy, as some serving personnel felt that the 9mm Parabellum wasn't sufficiently powerful compared to the well-liked .45 of the Colt. There were also some problems with an early batch where some slides cracked in use.

However, the M9 has now seen hard service in large quantities, and has proven to be an effective military pistol in both American and other hands. Two civil versions of the weapon are seen here: the basic Model 92F (left) and the Model 92F with a built-in laser sight (right) which also has a slightly longer barrel. Both are chambered for the 9mm Parabellum cartridge.

# JAPAN

## NAMBU 4TH YEAR PISTOL 8MM TYPE A

Colonel Kirijo Nambu designed this pistol, the first Japanese semi-automatic to be produced. Known as the Model 04 (and also as the Nambu Type A or Papa Nambu), it bears a visual resemblance to the P.08 Luger, although there is no design commonality whatsoever. It is a locked breech design, the breechblock being held in place by floating block attached to the barrel extension. One unusual feature was the grip safety under the trigger guard. The magazine follower held the slide open after the last shot was fired, giving a clear indicator the 8-shot magazine was empty, if making it cumbersome to change magazines. Adopted by the Japanese navy in 1909 and by the Thai government, in the 1920s, the Model 04 was never adopted in quantity by the Japanese army. Commercial sales were few, as were independent sales to military officers. It was a rather cumbersome, fragile, unreliable piece, and within the context of Japanese industry at the time, expensive to make.

**SPECIFICATIONS**
**Type:** semi-automatic pistol
**Origin:** Koshikawa Arsenal, Japan
**Caliber:** 8mm Nambu
**Barrel Length:** 4.7in

## NAMBU 4TH YEAR PISTOL 7MM TYPE B

**SPECIFICATIONS**
**Type:** semi-automatic pistol
**Origin:** Koshikawa Arsenal, Japan
**Caliber:** 7mm Nambu
**Barrel Length:** 3.25in

In an attempt to overcome customer resistance to the larger Model 04, Nambu redesigned it to produce this smaller pistol chambered for his newly developed 7mm cartridge. Also know as the "Baby Nambu", it remained more expensive than contemporary western types, and was still less reliable than most of them. Only a few thousand were made.

# NAMBU 14TH YEAR PISTOL

## SPECIFICATIONS
**Type:** semi-automatic pistol
**Origin:** Koshikawa Arsenal, Japan
**Caliber:** 8mm Nambu
**Barrel Length:** 4.8in

Introduced in 1925, this was an attempt to improve the Model 04 by simplifying the design to reduce manufacturing costs. The grip safety was removed and replaced by an awkward safety catch. The magazine hold open device was retained, and combined with the strong recoil springs made it very difficult to remove an empty magazine in a hurry. It saw extensive service in Manchuria and in World War Two, and one of the results of combat experience was an early modification to enlarge the trigger guard to enable users to wear winter gloves. It was still a bulky and expensive design, however, and as Japanese army officers had to by their own pistols, it struggled to gain widespread acceptance.

## NAMBU TYPE 94

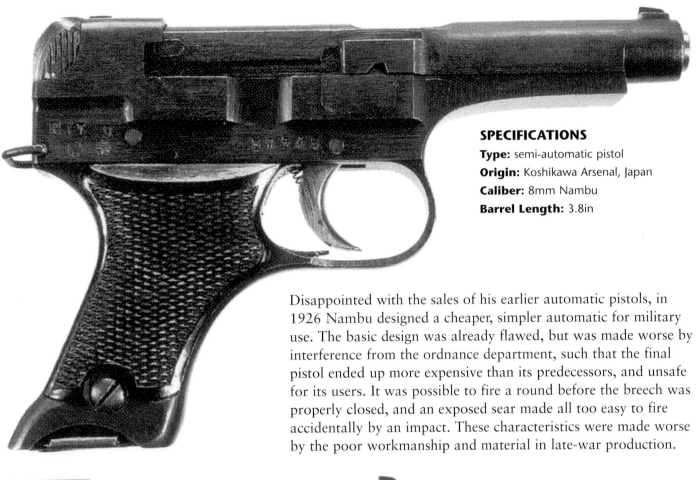

**SPECIFICATIONS**
**Type:** semi-automatic pistol
**Origin:** Koshikawa Arsenal, Japan
**Caliber:** 8mm Nambu
**Barrel Length:** 3.8in

Disappointed with the sales of his earlier automatic pistols, in 1926 Nambu designed a cheaper, simpler automatic for military use. The basic design was already flawed, but was made worse by interference from the ordnance department, such that the final pistol ended up more expensive than its predecessors, and unsafe for its users. It was possible to fire a round before the breech was properly closed, and an exposed sear made all too easy to fire accidentally by an impact. These characteristics were made worse by the poor workmanship and material in late-war production.

# MEXICO

## OBREGON 0.45IN

### SPECIFICATIONS

**Type:** semi-automatic pistol
**Origin:** Fabrica Nacional de Armas
Mexicanos, Mexico City, Mexico.
**Caliber:** .45 ACP
**Barrel Length:** 5.0in

The Mexican Army used the Colt M1911A1 from 1925 onwards, but in the early 1930s the government encourage the development of this weapon, which looks, at first sight, to be yet another M1911A1 clone. It is, however, a different weapon, which was designed by a Mexican, Alejandro Obregon, for use by his country's armed forces. The "Obregon system" involved a rotating bolt which moved through some 17 degrees before unlocking; some weapons also had a safety system in which removing the magazine caused the hammer to be locked. When the weapon was not accepted by the military, the approximately one thousand weapons completed between 1934 and 1938 were then sold on the civil market, making the example shown here very rare, indeed.

# POLAND

## RADOM VIS-35

### SPECIFICATIONS

**Type:** semi-automatic pistol
**Origin:** Fabryka Broni Radom
**Caliber:** 9mm Parabellum
**Barrel Length:** 4.53in

This Polish weapon appeared in 1935, and like many, if not most, other automatic pistols owed a lot to the designs of John M. Browning. One of the differences was the addition of a grip safety, and a decocking lever on the slide, which allowed the user to safely

carry the pistol with a round in the chamber. Manually cocking the hammer was all that was needed to get the pistol ready for action.

A heavy piece (at 2.31 lb empty), the Radom was a well-made, reliable and easy to shoot weapon, popular with its users. During the German occupation of Poland it was made for German forces as the Pistole 35(p), although these ones have much cruder finish and a simplified safety system. Polish pistols can be identified by the Polish eagle engraved on the slide.

# RUSSIA/USSR

## PISTOLET MAKAROV (PM)

**SPECIFICATIONS**

**Type:** semi-automatic pistol
**Origin:** Soviet State Arsenals
**Caliber:** 9mm Makarov
**Barrel Length:** 8.86in

The Makorov bears a close resemblance to the
Walther PP, and entered service as the standard
military pistol for the Soviet Army and client states in
the 1950s. A simple, unpretentious design, it fires a
specially-designed 9mm x 18 round from an 8-shot
magazine, which as about as powerful a cartridge as
can be handled in a simple unlocked blowback pistol.
It has a double-action mechanism and a decocking
lever, allowing the user to carry it safely with a round
chambered. Like almost all Russian weapons, the
Makarov is a no-nonsense cheap, tough, reliable and
easy to use piece.

## TULA-TOKAREV MODEL 1930 (TT-30)/ MODEL 1933 (TT-33)

**SPECIFICATIONS**

**Type:** semi-automatic pistol
**Origin:** Tula Arsenal
**Caliber:** 7.62 x 25mm Russian
**Barrel Length:** 8.86in

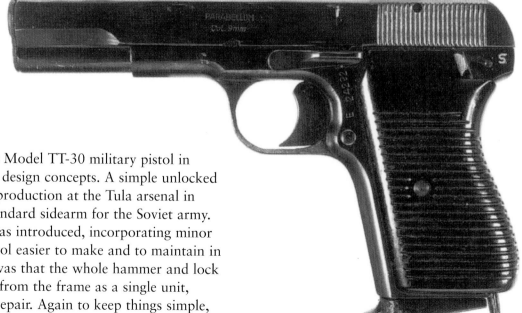

Feodor Tokarev developed the Model TT-30 military pistol in
1930, basing it on Browning's design concepts. A simple unlocked
blowback weapon, it entered production at the Tula arsenal in
1930 and soon became the standard sidearm for the Soviet army.
Three years later, the TT-33 was introduced, incorporating minor
modifications to make the pistol easier to make and to maintain in
field conditions. One feature was that the whole hammer and lock
mechanism could be removed from the frame as a single unit,
giving much easier access for repair. Again to keep things simple,

there was no safety device other than allowing the hammer to be set at half-cock.

The TT-33 quickly replaced the earlier TT-30, and served as the Russian's main military pistol throughout the Russo-Finnish War and World War Two. It also equipped most of the Soviet Union's allies and client states, and has been made in Poland, Yugoslavia, Hungary, China and North Korea. A version was also made in Egypt.

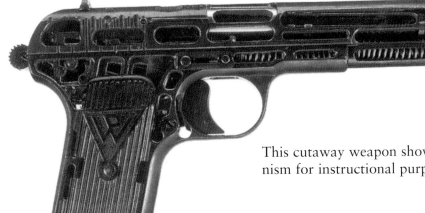

This cutaway weapon shows the internal construction and mechanism for instructional purposes.

## SEMI-AUTOMATIC TARGET PISTOL

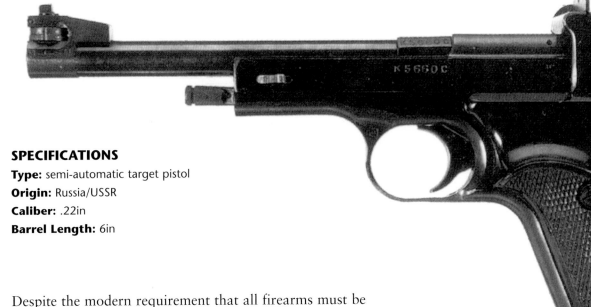

**SPECIFICATIONS**
**Type:** semi-automatic target pistol
**Origin:** Russia/USSR
**Caliber:** .22in
**Barrel Length:** 6in

Despite the modern requirement that all firearms must be fully documented, weapons can still be found without any trace as to their origin. Thus, this well-made and carefully designed .22 caliber target pistol bears no evidence as to its manufacture apart from the serial number "K5660C." Both front and rear sights are adjustable.

# REPUBLIC OF SOUTH AFRICA

## PRETORIA ARMS FACTORY (PAF) JUNIOR

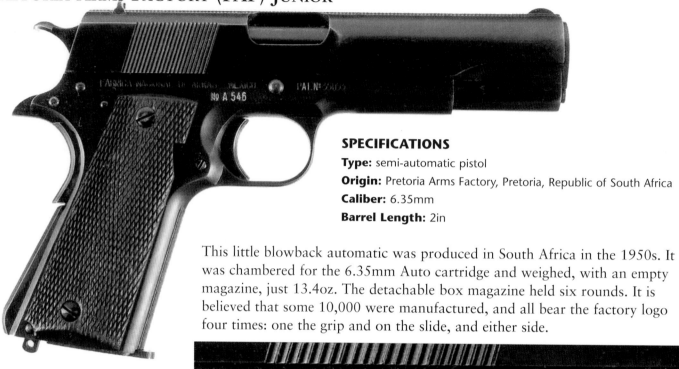

### SPECIFICATIONS

**Type:** semi-automatic pistol
**Origin:** Pretoria Arms Factory, Pretoria, Republic of South Africa
**Caliber:** 6.35mm
**Barrel Length:** 2in

This little blowback automatic was produced in South Africa in the 1950s. It was chambered for the 6.35mm Auto cartridge and weighed, with an empty magazine, just 13.4oz. The detachable box magazine held six rounds. It is believed that some 10,000 were manufactured, and all bear the factory logo four times: one the grip and on the slide, and either side.

# SPAIN

## ARIZMENDI WALMAN

### SPECIFICATIONS

**Type:** semi-automatic pistol
**Origin:** Francisco Arizmendi, Eibar, Spain
**Caliber:** 7.65mm
**Barrel Length:** 3in

This weapon was produced in Spain, primarily for the U.S. market, and early production models were marked "American Automatic Pistol Walman Patent" although the word "American" was later dropped. The pistols were available in either 6.35mm or 7.65mm, the example shown here being of the latter caliber. The Walman was in production throughout most of the 1920s, but the company went out of business in 1936.

## ASTRA-UNCETA MODEL 300

**SPECIFICATIONS**
**Type:** semi-automatic pistol
**Origin:** Astra-Unceta SA, Guernica, Spain
**Caliber:** 7.65mm
**Barrel Length:** 3.5in

Curiously, the Astra 300 seems to have followed the Astra 400 into production. Both were the result of improving the Campo-Giro Model 1913--16 "tubular" design (*see below*), in which an annular recoil spring surrounded the barrel and was retained by a muzzle bush. The Model 300 was manufactured in 7.65mm Browning and 9mm Short calibers, with the latter being procured by both the Spanish prison service and the navy in the 1920s. It remained in production throughout the 1930s and some 85,000 were purchased for use by the German army and navy during World War Two; production ended in 1947.

## ASTRA-UNCETA MODEL 600/43

**SPECIFICATIONS**
**Type:** semi-automatic pistol
**Origin:** Astra-Unceta SA, Guernica Spain
**Caliber:** 9mm Parabellum
**Barrel Length:** 5.5in

The Model 600 was manufactured in 1943-4 for the German armed forces, which took delivery of some 10,500, following which approximately 50,000 more examples were produced for the commercial market. It was descended from the Campo-Giro design and was chambered (as here) for the 9mm Parabellum round, although some may have been chambered for the 7.65mm Parabellum round.

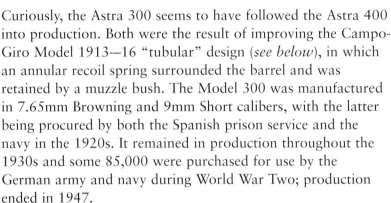

## ASTRA-UNCETA CUB

### SPECIFICATIONS

**Type:** semi-automatic pistol
**Origin:** Astra-Unceta SA, Guernica Spain
**Caliber:** .22
**Barrel Length:** 2in

The Astra 200 had a production run lasting from 1920 to 1966 and was particularly successful in the United States where it was generally known as the "Firecat." This was succeeded by the Astra 2000, chambered for either 6.35mm or .22 (as seen here) and was sold in the United States, first, as the "Colt Junior" and, later, as the "Cub."

## BERNEDO 6.35MM

### SPECIFICATIONS

**Type:** semi-automatic pistol
**Origin:** Vincente Bernedo y Cia, Eibar, Spain
**Caliber:** 6.35mm
**Barrel Length:** 2in

During World War One, the Bernedo company was involved in the manufacture of Ruby pistols, but once the war finished they produced this pocket blowback pistol. Cheap and simple, it carried six rounds in the magazine.

## CAMPO GIRO MODEL 1913-16

### SPECIFICATIONS

**Type:** semi-automatic pistol
**Origin:** Lieutenant Colonel, the Count of Campo Giro, Spain
**Caliber:** 9mm Bergmann
**Barrel Length:** 6.4in

Venancio López de Caballos y Aguirre, Count of Campo Giro, a lieutenant colonel in the Spanish Army, developed an automatic pistol which was entered for army trials in 1904. The design was constantly refined over the following decade. A stamp on this weapon identifies it as the Model 1913–16 which had an amended safety, the magazine release catch moved to the base of the butt and other minor changes. The Spanish army acquired 13,000 between 1916 and 1919, and a further 5–600 were sold on the commercial market. When complaints of frame failures were made the weapon was modified and returned to the market as the "Astra 400" (*see Astra-Unceta above*).

## Echeverria (Star) Model B

**SPECIFICATIONS**
**Type:** semi-automatic pistol
**Origin:** Star Bonnifacio Echeverria, Eibar, Spain
**Caliber:** 9 x 23mm Largo
**Barrel Length:** 5in

"Star" is the brand name used by the firm of Echeverria who have been making military self-loading pistols since 1908. This Star Model B was introduced in 1928 and is based on the Colt M1911A1, although with no grip safety and firing 9mm Parabellum rather than .45 ACP. Robust and simple, it was an effective enough pistol and remained in Spanish military service until the 1980s.

## Llama-Gabilondo Model Omni

**SPECIFICATIONS**
**Type:** semi-automatic pistol
**Origin:** Llama-Gabilondo y Urresti, Vitoria, Spain
**Caliber:** 9mm Parabellum
**Barrel Length:** 4.25in

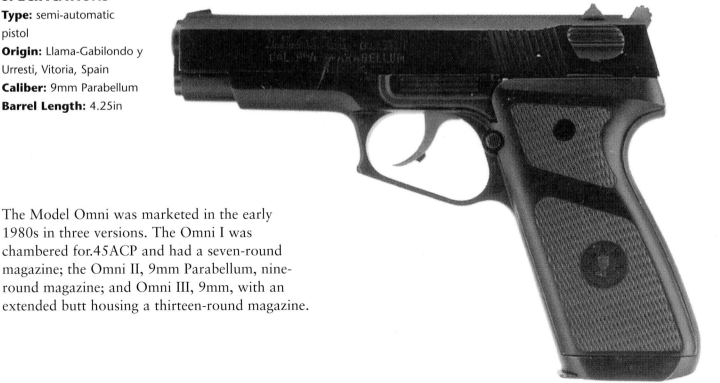

The Model Omni was marketed in the early 1980s in three versions. The Omni I was chambered for.45ACP and had a seven-round magazine; the Omni II, 9mm Parabellum, nine-round magazine; and Omni III, 9mm, with an extended butt housing a thirteen-round magazine.

# SWEDEN

## HUSQVARNA MODEL 1907

### SPECIFICATIONS
**Type:** semi-automatic pistol
**Origin:** Husqvarna Vapensfabrik Aktiebolag,
Sweden
**Caliber:** .38
**Barrel Length:** 5.2in

The Husqvarna Model 1907 was a licensed copy of the FN Browning Model 1903, which was made in Sweden for the Swedish Army. This was identical with the original in every respect except for the markings, which bore the legend "HUSQVARNA VAPENSFABRIK AKTIEBOLAG" and the Swedish royal arms at the top of the black, hard rubber grips. As made for the Swedish army they were 9mm caliber, but when replaced in Swedish service many were converted to .38 and exported to the United States, as was this specimen.

# SWITZERLAND

## SIG/SIG-SAUER P-226

### SPECIFICATIONS
**Type:** semi-automatic pistol
**Origin:** SIG / J.P. Sauer & Sohn, Switzerland and
Germany
**Caliber:** 9mm Parabellum
**Barrel Length:** 4.4in

Schweizerische Industrie Gessellschaft (SIG) of Switzerland design a range of high quality, superbly engineered automatic pistols for police and military customers. Swiss arms export laws are extremely restrictive, so they work in partnership with J.P. Sauer & Sohn in Germany, who make the pistols and sell them to a wider market than would otherwise be available.

Tracing its design back to the successful SIG P-210 of 1949 and the P-220 and P-225 police pistols of the 1970s, the P-226 was developed to enter the 1980 U.S. army competition to replace the Colt M1911A1. In the event the SIG lost out to the Beretta 92 (*see above*), mainly on price. This hasn't stopped the P-226 from going on to sell successfully to police forces and military users around the world, and it is a fine example of modern high-quality weapon engineering. Chambered for the 9mm Parabellum cartridge, it carries 15 rounds in the butt. Using a double-action mechanism with decocking lever and mechanical safety devices it can safely be carried with a round chambered, and the user can simply pull the trigger to fire the first shot. Alternatively, if time allows the hammer can be cocked manually as in a double-action revolver.

There are versions of the P226 with a longer 5in barrel, and others chambered for .357 SIG rounds.

## SIG/SIG-Sauer P-228/P-229

### SPECIFICATIONS

**Type:** semi-automatic pistol
**Origin:** SIG / J.P. Sauer & Sohn, Switzerland and Germany
**Caliber:** 9mm Parabellum, .40 S&W, .357 SIG
**Barrel Length:** 3.9in

The P-228 is based on the earlier P-225 police model, but carries 13 rounds instead of the former's 8. The P-299 is the same weapon chambered for larger .40 S&W or .357 SIG rounds – the only difference being a change of barrel. Both these weapons and the P-226 series have been adopted by a wide range of agencies, including the FBI and United States Drug Enforcement Agency.

## SIG/SIG-Sauer P-239

### SPECIFICATIONS

**Type:** semi-automatic pistol
**Origin:** SIG / J.P. Sauer & Sohn, Switzerland and Germany
**Caliber:** 9mm Parabellum, .40 S&W, .357 SIG
**Barrel Length:** 3.6in

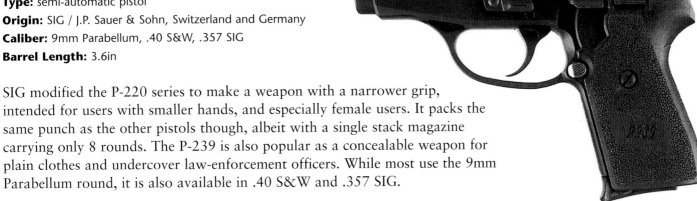

SIG modified the P-220 series to make a weapon with a narrower grip, intended for users with smaller hands, and especially female users. It packs the same punch as the other pistols though, albeit with a single stack magazine carrying only 8 rounds. The P-239 is also popular as a concealable weapon for plain clothes and undercover law-enforcement officers. While most use the 9mm Parabellum round, it is also available in .40 S&W and .357 SIG.

## Knap Percussion

### SPECIFICATIONS

**Type:** percussion-fired target pistol
**Origin:** A. Knap, Rheinfelden, Switzerland
**Caliber:** 0.50in
**Barrel Length:** 9.5in

This very handsome target pistol was made in the middle of the 19th century at Rheinfelden in Switzerland. It is marked with the name "A. KNAP" who is known to have been an active gunsmith in that town at that time.

# UNITED KINGDOM

## BLANCHARD PERCUSSION TARGET PISTOL

**SPECIFICATIONS**

**Type:** percussion target pistol
**Origin:** Blanchard, London, England
**Caliber:** .62
**Barrel Length:** 8in

A target pistol from the 19th Century, this one was made by Blanchard of London. Finely made with microgroove rifling in the 8 inch barrel, it has a finely checkered butt, with a cap box inside, and the ram held in the wooden stock.

## BRUNN DOUBLE-BARRELED PISTOL

**SPECIFICATIONS**

**Type:** double-barreled flintlock pistol
**Origin:** Brunn, London, England
**Caliber:** 28 bore
**Barrel Length:** 6in

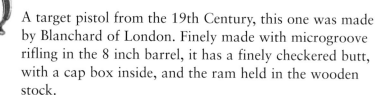

Before the advent of revolvers, one of the only ways to get more than one shot from a pistol without reloading was to have more than one barrel. This fine c.1790 example, from a London gunsmith, has two side-by-side barrels, and two separate triggers operating two complete flintlock mechanisms.

## BUNNEY CANNON-BARRELED PISTOL

**SPECIFICATIONS**

**Type:** double-barreled flintlock pistol
**Origin:** Bunney, London, England
**Caliber:** 24 bore
**Barrel Length:** 5.25in

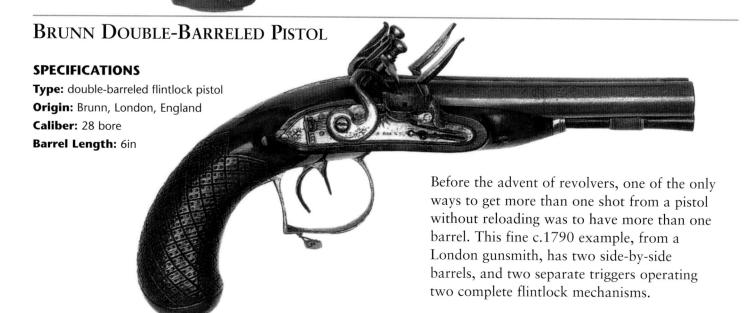

As is obvious from the picture, the shape of this kind of pistol gave rise to the "cannon-barrel" description. This flintlock example dates from around 1770 and is typical of the type. The bronze barrel can be unscrewed, giving access to the breech for reloading, while a sliding trigger guard safety gives the user some protection from accidental discharges.

## COLLUMBELL HOLSTER

### SPECIFICATIONS

**Type:** double-barreled flintlock pistol
**Origin:** Collumbell, London, England
**Caliber:** 20 bore
**Barrel Length:** 8in

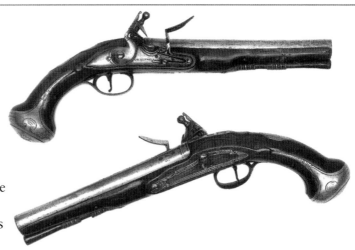

Made in around 1740, by David Collumbell of London, this is a solid example of a holster pistol of the time. The lock has the maker's name engraved on it, and uses a "swan-neck" cock. The stock is from walnut, and comes

## DEANE PERCUSSION BELT PISTOL

### SPECIFICATIONS

**Type:** percussion pistol
**Origin:** G. & J. Deane, London, England
**Caliber:** .60
**Barrel Length:** 4.9in

G & J. DEANE, 30. KING WILLIAM ST LONDON BRIDGE.

This mid-19th century pistol was designed and manufactured by G. & J. Deane at 30 King William Street at London Bridge. Parts are engraved and there is a captive swivelling ramrod. The large caliber of this weapon would have created considerable recoil – and would have considerably damaged the target if the firer hit it.

## EGG FLINTLOCK

### SPECIFICATIONS

**Type:** percussion pistol
**Origin:** D.Egg, London, England
**Caliber:** 24 bore
**Barrel Length:** 7in

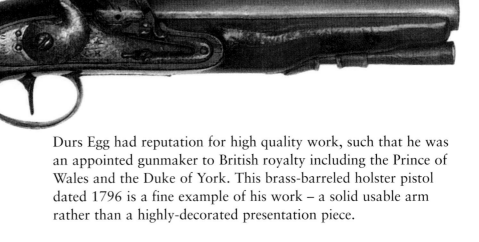

Durs Egg had reputation for high quality work, such that he was an appointed gunmaker to British royalty including the Prince of Wales and the Duke of York. This brass-barreled holster pistol dated 1796 is a fine example of his work – a solid usable arm rather than a highly-decorated presentation piece.

## EIG M1842 CAVALRY PISTOL

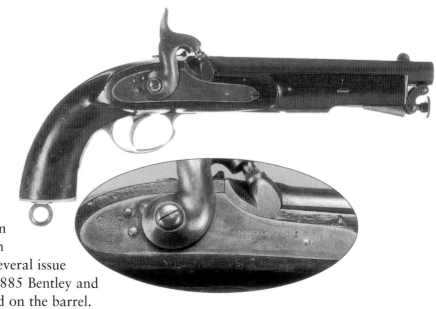

### SPECIFICATIONS

**Type:** service percussion pistol
**Origin:** East India Gun Company
**Caliber:** .65
**Barrel Length:** 8in

The East India Company ran India almost as if the company were an independent state, to the extent that it even formed, trained and equipped its own armed forces. This heavy military pistol was made by the East India Gun Company for such use, and is dated 1871 with Birmingham proof marks on the lock. It has several issue marks stamped on the stock, including one "1885 Bentley and Playfair". Indian issue marks are also engraved on the barrel.

## FISHER FLINTLOCK TRAVELER'S PISTOL

### SPECIFICATIONS

**Type:** flintlock pistol
**Origin:** Fisher, Bristol, England
**Caliber:** .50
**Barrel Length:** 8in

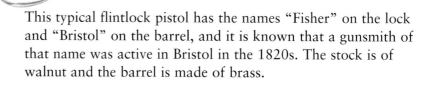

This typical flintlock pistol has the names "Fisher" on the lock and "Bristol" on the barrel, and it is known that a gunsmith of that name was active in Bristol in the 1820s. The stock is of walnut and the barrel is made of brass.

## GALTON FLINTLOCK PISTOLS

### SPECIFICATIONS

**Type:** flintlock pistols
**Origin:** Galton, England
**Caliber:** .64
**Barrel Length:** 7in

This pair of flintlock pistols are housed in a specially-made case, together with the original bullet mold, although the powder flask appears to have come from another weapon. These pistols were made by Galton and there were several gunsmiths of that name active in London and Birmingham between 1750 and 1812.

## HOLLIS & SHEATH PERCUSSION POCKET PISTOL

**SPECIFICATIONS**
**Type:** percussion pistol
**Origin:** Hollis & Sheath, London, England
**Caliber:** .40
**Barrel Length:** 4in

Hollis & Sheath were gunsmiths in Birmingham and London in the middle of the 19th century. This pistol is about 6 inches long and was designed to be hidden about the firer's person and used as a "last ditch" defense.

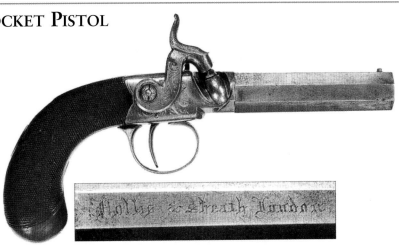

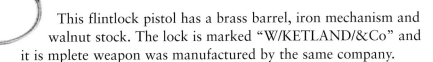

## KETLAND FLINTLOCK PISTOL

**PECIFICATIONS**
**Type:** flintlock pistol
**Origin:** William Ketland & Co, Birmingham, England
**Caliber:** .60
**Barrel Length:** 7.75in

This flintlock pistol has a brass barrel, iron mechanism and walnut stock. The lock is marked "W/KETLAND/&Co" and it is mplete weapon was manufactured by the same company. Several generations of this family were employed in the weapons business from the mid-18th to mid-19th centuries, based in Birmingham and London. The family also had close ties with the United States and two brothers, John and Thomas Ketland, were resident in Philadelphia from 1797 to 1800 and supplied a large number of weapons to the Commonwealth of Pennsylvania.

## KETLAND DRAGOON FLINTLOCK PISTOL

**SPECIFICATIONS**
**Type:** flintlock pistol
**Origin:** William Ketland & Co, Birmingham, England
**Caliber:** .70in
**Barrel Length:** 9.0in

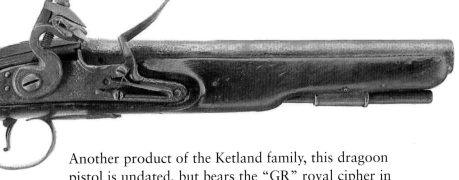

Another product of the Ketland family, this dragoon pistol is undated, but bears the "GR" royal cipher in front of the cock. Various parts of this weapon are replacements, including the cock, hammer and ramrod, but it is still of considerable value as an antique.

## MANTON TRAVELER PISTOLS

Joseph and John Manton were brothers who traded
independently, and were two of England's finest
gunsmiths in the early 19th century. Shown here are a
pair of so-called "Travelers Pistols", handy but effective
weapons for self-protection from robbers and brigands
while on the unpoliced roads of the time. The pistol has
a full-length walnut stock, finely checkered butt and
Birmingham proof marks. The barrel shows the distinctive
markings of the manufacturing process known as "Damascus
twist." Thin rods of metal and steel are twisted together then wrapped around
a barrel mandrel, then hammer-welded into a single solid piece. If done well, it
made for a strong and light barrel, although if not done do carefully
weaknesses and flaws in the weld could end up with the barrel splitting. Twist
barrels were often treated with acid after manufacture to bring out the fine
underlying pattern.

**SPECIFICATIONS**
**Type:** flintlock pistol
**Origin:** Joseph Manton & Son,
London, England
**Caliber:** .55in
**Barrel Length:** 9in

## MEWIS LONDON BLUNDERBUSS PISTOL

**SPECIFICATIONS**
**Type:** flintlock blunderbuss pistol
**Origin:** Mewis & Co, Birmingham,
England
**Caliber:** .50
**Barrel Length:**
7.4in

This pistol is marked "Mewis & Co" and a
gunsmithing company of that name was in
business in Birmingham, England in the late 18th
century. It was proofed in
Birmingham and has London retailer's
marks indicating that it was supplied
to a London trader. The effect of such
a blunderbuss weapon would have
been devastating against a human being or an
animal at short range.

## NOCK FLINTLOCK .45IN PISTOL

**SPECIFICATIONS**
**Type:** flintlock pistol
**Origin:** Nock, England
**Caliber:** .45
**Barrel Length:** 2.4in

The Nock family were active gunsmiths from the
1770s to the 1860s and had numerous
government contracts, particularly with the
Royal Navy. Many of their weapons are also
marked "Gunmakers to His Majesty"
suggesting that they were in the privileged
position of supplying weapons to the Royal
Household. This weapon is marked "London" but has Birmingham proofs suggesting that while Nock's trading
premises were in London, they had either a factory in Birmingham or the weapon was supplied by a sub-
contractor.

## RICHARDS OVER/UNDER

**SPECIFICATIONS**
**Type:** over/under flint-lock pistol
**Origin:** Richards, London, England
**Caliber:** .44in
**Barrel Length:** 1.6in

The over/under pistol was one of the early attempts at obtaining a compact multi-barrel weapon without the breadth involved in the double-barrel design. As with many weapons of this period this pistol was manufactured and proofed in Birmingham but sold in London.

## SAUNDERS QUEEN ANNE

**SPECIFICATIONS**
**Type:** flintlock pistol
**Origin:** T. Saunders, London, England
**Caliber:** 20 bore
**Barrel Length:** 12in

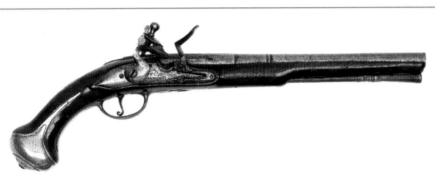

This style of pistol is often referred to as the "Queen Anne" type, although most pistols of this type they were in the main produced after that Queen died in 1714. It has the cannon-barrel shape with a "three stage" barrel. Made by T. Saunders, a London gunsmith of the time, it has a finely engraved lockplate and a serpent engraving in the stock on the opposite side.

## SCOTTISH DRESS PISTOL

**SPECIFICATIONS**
**Type:** flintlock dress pistol
**Origin:** Scottish gunsmith
**Caliber:** 36 bore
**Barrel Length:** 6.25in

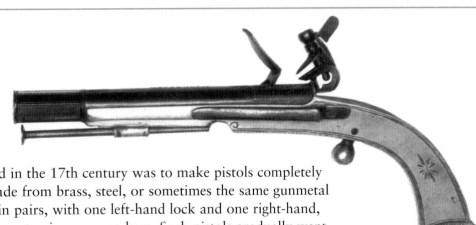

The gunsmithing tradition in Scotland in the 17th century was to make pistols completely out of metal, with the stock being made from brass, steel, or sometimes the same gunmetal as the barrel. They were often made in pairs, with one left-hand lock and one right-hand, and the butts often had "rams-horn" protrusions as seen here. Such pistols gradually went out of favor in the 18th and 19th century as Scottish gunmakers turned to English methods and designs.

In the early Victorian years, however, there was an increase in popularity of a romantic view of Scotland and Highland culture, partly inspired by the novels of Sir Walter Scott. Unlikely versions of so-called "Highland Dress" became popular at society gatherings, and wearers often completed their ensemble with their pastiches of "traditional Highland weapons."

The c.1840 pistol shown here was intended for this market, and is a light, finely engraved item, more a decoration than serious weapon. The metal butt has the rams horn protrusions and starburst engravings, the trigger is the ball-type and the stocks are largely silver-plated. The lockplate is engraved with "MacLeod".

## Smith Boarding Pistol

**SPECIFICATIONS**
**Type:** percussion service pistol
**Origin:** Smith, London
**Caliber:** 18 bore
**Barrel Length:** 4.75in

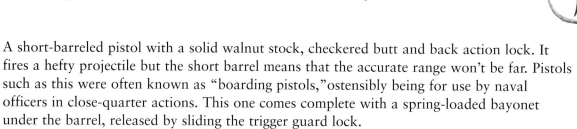

A short-barreled pistol with a solid walnut stock, checkered butt and back action lock. It fires a hefty projectile but the short barrel means that the accurate range won't be far. Pistols such as this were often known as "boarding pistols,"ostensibly being for use by naval officers in close-quarter actions. This one comes complete with a spring-loaded bayonet under the barrel, released by sliding the trigger guard lock.

## Thomas Holster Pistols

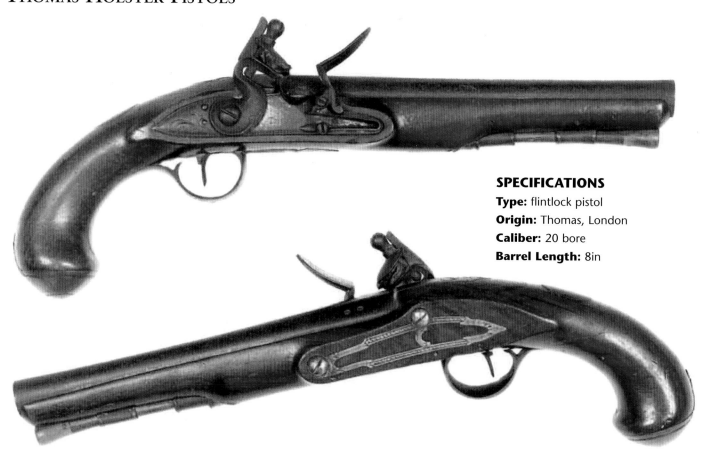

**SPECIFICATIONS**
**Type:** flintlock pistol
**Origin:** Thomas, London
**Caliber:** 20 bore
**Barrel Length:** 8in

A long pistol, typical of those used by cavalrymen and mounted troops. Dated around 1775, if has an early-style rounded lock with silver wire inlay. The pistol also has engraved teardrop panels.

# TIPPING & LAWDEN MODEL 3 FOUR-BARREL PISTOL

## SPECIFICATIONS

**Type:** four-barrel pistol
**Origin:** Tipping & Lawden, London, England
**Caliber:** 9mm
**Barrel Length:** 4.25in

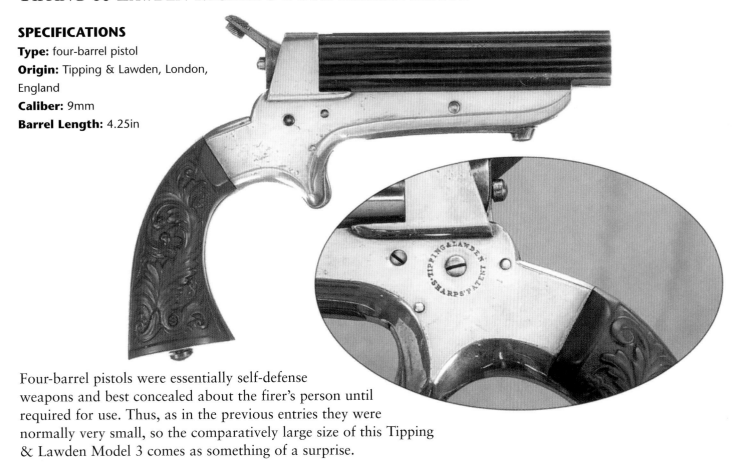

Four-barrel pistols were essentially self-defense weapons and best concealed about the firer's person until required for use. Thus, as in the previous entries they were normally very small, so the comparatively large size of this Tipping & Lawden Model 3 comes as something of a surprise.

# TOWER SEA SERVICE PISTOL

## SPECIFICATIONS

**Type:** flintlock service pistol
**Origin:** Tower Armouries, London, England
**Caliber:** .58
**Barrel Length:** 8in

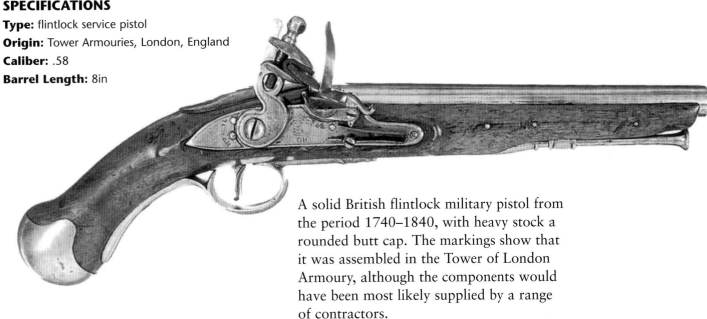

A solid British flintlock military pistol from the period 1740–1840, with heavy stock a rounded butt cap. The markings show that it was assembled in the Tower of London Armoury, although the components would have been most likely supplied by a range of contractors.

## WEBLEY NO1 MK1 .455IN PISTOL

**SPECIFICATIONS**
**Type:** semi-automatic pistol
**Origin:** Webley & Scott, Birmingham, England
**Caliber:** .455
**Barrel Length:** 5in

As the 19th century drew to a close, gunmakers were waking up to the fact that the automatic pistol had a military future. Webley and Scott experimented with a couple of designs, including the Webley-Mars then the Model of 1904. Revolvers were proven, reliable and popular with service users, and Webley faced an uphill struggle to get any new design taken seriously by the services.

Eventually they developed this pistol, chambered for a massively powerful .455 cartridge, similar to but slightly larger than, the one used in service revolvers. A recoil-operated arm, the barrel is locked to the slide at the moment of firing by a lug which engages on a recess on the slide.

The angular butt held 7 rounds, while a grip safety protruded from the back. It was adopted in 1915 by the Royal Navy as the Webley No. 1 Mk I. Later models had provision for a wooden stock, and some were issued to the Royal Flying Corps.

# UNITED STATES OF AMERICA

## ALLEN & THURBER SINGLE-SHOT PISTOL

**SPECIFICATIONS**

**Type:** single-shot, side-hammer pistol

**Origin:** Allen & Thurber, Worcester, Massachusetts.

**Caliber:** .41

**Barrel Length:** 8in

This single-shot pistol is one of a batch of some 300 manufactured by Allen & Thurber, one of the companies in which Ethan Allen (1806–1871) was involved. These pistols were produced in the late 1840s/early 1850s and were intended for competition use, for which they were fitted with an adjustable rear sight. The cast-steel barrel, which is part octagonal/part round is marked "Allen & Thurber, Worcester."

## AMES MODEL 1842 NAVY

**SPECIFICATIONS**

**Type:** service percussion pistol

**Origin:** N.P. Ames, Springfield, Massachusetts

**Caliber:** .54

**Barrel Length:** 6in

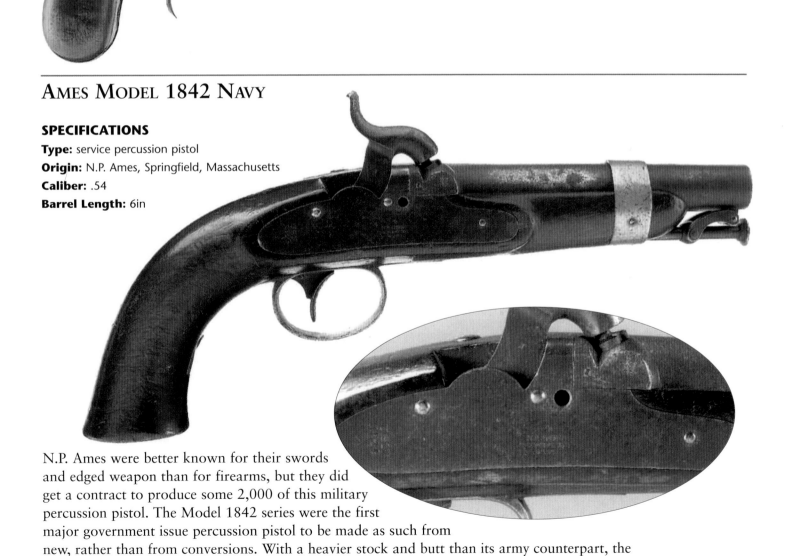

N.P. Ames were better known for their swords and edged weapon than for firearms, but they did get a contract to produce some 2,000 of this military percussion pistol. The Model 1842 series were the first major government issue percussion pistol to be made as such from new, rather than from conversions. With a heavier stock and butt than its army counterpart, the Model 1842 Navy had a brass barrel band and butt cap, while the hammer pivot and spring are actually on the inside of the lockplate.

## AMT MODEL 1911A1 HARDLINER

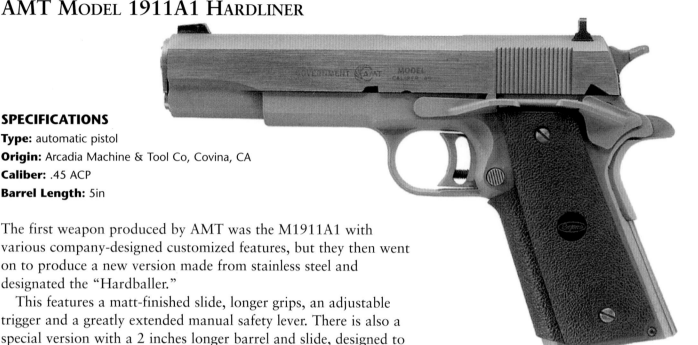

### SPECIFICATIONS

**Type:** automatic pistol
**Origin:** Arcadia Machine & Tool Co, Covina, CA
**Caliber:** .45 ACP
**Barrel Length:** 5in

The first weapon produced by AMT was the M1911A1 with various company-designed customized features, but they then went on to produce a new version made from stainless steel and designated the "Hardballer."

This features a matt-finished slide, longer grips, an adjustable trigger and a greatly extended manual safety lever. There is also a special version with a 2 inches longer barrel and slide, designed to achieve higher muzzle velocity from the same .45 ACP round.

## AMT BACK-UP

### SPECIFICATIONS

**Type:** automatic pistol
**Origin:** Arcadia Machine & Tool Co
Covina, CA
**Caliber:** .38 ACP
**Barrel Length:** 2.52in

The AMT Back-Up, as its name implies, is a very small weapon designed to be used as a last resort when other weapons have failed or are otherwise unavailable. It was originally produced in .22LR caliber, but has since appeared in .38 ACP (as in this example) and, in a slightly modified form, 9mm. It is made mainly from stainless steel and weighs 18 ounces. It is fitted with both grip and manual safeties, and the magazine holds five rounds. The weapon is fitted with recessed sights, although at the ranges it is likely to be used, these would be of only limited value.

## AMT AUTO MAG BABY

### SPECIFICATIONS
**Type:** automatic pistol
**Origin:** Arcadia Machine & Tool Co Covina, CA
**Caliber:** .22 Winchester rimfire
**Barrel Length:** 6in

This weapon has a complicated history. It was originally designed in the 1960s around the .44 Auto Magnum cartridge (hence the name) and marketed by Sanford Arms in the early 1970s. This company became the Auto-Mag Corp in October 1970 but went out of business in 1972, when the rights were purchased by the TDE Corp. Production then restarted, with TDE doing the manufacturing while Hi Standard were responsible for marketing. This arrangement ended in 1977, but production restarted only to end again in 1980. Finally, AMT produced about 100 Model Cs chambered for the .22 Winchester round, of which the first two were presented to Clint Eastwood.

## ASTON MODEL 1842

### SPECIFICATIONS
**Type:** percussion pistol
**Origin:** H. Aston & Co, Middleton, CT
**Caliber:** .56in
**Barrel Length:** 8.5in

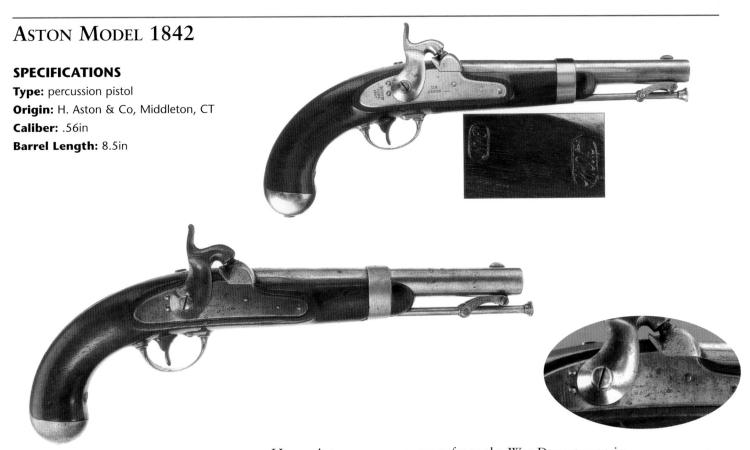

## BROWNING
See Belgium

Henry Aston won a contract from the War Department in 1845 to provide the Army with 30,000 of these Model 1842 pistols. The first percussion pistol generally adopted, it was a solid arm which was still used my many during the Civil War.

# COLT MODEL 1900

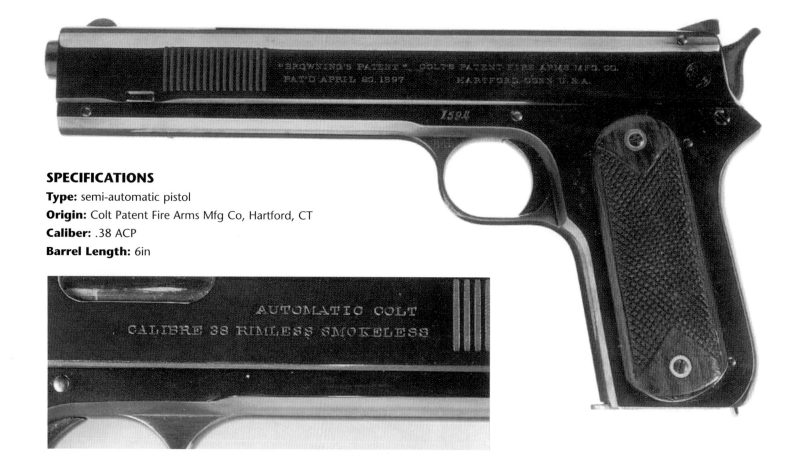

## SPECIFICATIONS

**Type:** semi-automatic pistol
**Origin:** Colt Patent Fire Arms Mfg Co, Hartford, CT
**Caliber:** .38 ACP
**Barrel Length:** 6in

In the latter part of the 19th century the US handgun scene was dominated by the revolver, although Colt was the first among US weapons companies to appreciate the importance of the automatic pistol. As in all aspects of the weapons industry, the crucial factor was to gain a military contract and with this aim in view, Colt set about developing a reliable and effective pistol for the US army and navy. The first fruit of this was the M1898 and this was quickly developed into the M1900, chambered for the .38 ACP cartridge, and which had exceptionally functional lines as shown in this beautifully restored example.

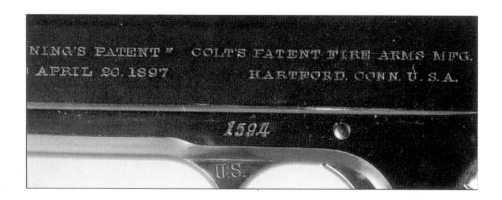

# COLT MODEL 1902 SPORTING PISTOL

The Model 1902 Sporting pistol was essentially a Model 1900 for the civil market, which incorporated a number of minor modifications, including a revised firing pin and hammer, and moulded rubber grips. Curiously, there was a parallel Military Model 1902, which was marginally larger than the Sporting model and incorporated a number of other refinements, including a larger magazine holding eight rounds. The US army bought only 200 for trials, but did not adopt it for service. The Military Model 1902 was then sold on the civil market and remained in production until 1928, whereas the Sporting Model was phased out of production in 1908.

**SPECIFICATIONS**
**Type:** semi-automatic pistol
**Origin:** Colt Patent Fire Arms Mfg Co, Hartford, CT
**Caliber:** .38 ACP
**Barrel Length:** 6in

# COLT MODEL 1903 POCKET PISTOL

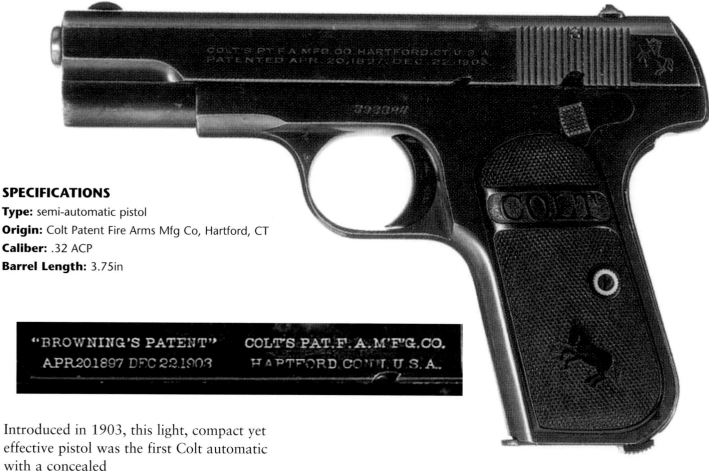

## SPECIFICATIONS

**Type:** semi-automatic pistol
**Origin:** Colt Patent Fire Arms Mfg Co, Hartford, CT
**Caliber:** .32 ACP
**Barrel Length:** 3.75in

Introduced in 1903, this light, compact yet effective pistol was the first Colt automatic with a concealed hammer. Based on Browning's design (although not marked as such) it carried 8 rounds of .32 ammunition in the butt magazine, and operated using a simple unlocked blowback method. A grip safety also sat in the rear of the grip, while post-1926 models had an extra safety disconnect which operated when the magazine was removed.

A neat, well-balanced arm it was one the most popular Colt pistols ever. Many thousands were made for both military and civilian use, and it was sold around the world. Other companies produced their own pistols based on this design, sometimes even as exact copies, and they can still be found in large quantities today.

# COLT MODEL 1911

**SPECIFICATIONS**

**Type:** semi-automatic pistol

**Origin:** Colt Patent Fire Arms Mfg Co, Hartford, CT

**Caliber:** .45 ACP

**Barrel Length:** 5in

One of the classic all-time greats, this superbly effective pistol was another developed from Browning's design but intended from the start to be a service pistol. Built to chamber Colt's new .45 ACP (Automatic Colt Pistol) cartridge, a lethal round with more than enough stopping power, it carried 7 shots in the magazine. Such a powerful rounds demands the barrel and slide be locked when firing, and lugs on the barrel upper surface are designed to do just that. After both have recoiled a sufficient distance, the barrel is cammed downwards to release the slide, which continues to the rear to eject the round, cock the hammer and prepare to feed the next round from the magazine. The pistol also has a grip safety in the rear of the butt. Adopted by the U.S. army in 1911, the pistol served in huge numbers in World War One. The Model 1911 turned out to be easy to handle with the grip at a comfortable angle for accurate shooting. It is also extremely solid and tough, reliable, easy to maintain and has exceptional shooting performance and stopping power.

# COLT MODEL 1911A1

Effective as then Model 1911 was, combat experience indicated that some minor improvements could still be made. The hammer shape was changed slightly, the butt safety enlarged, some internal changes made and two chamfered cutouts added to the frame, just behind the trigger. The ensuing Model 1911A1 entered service in 1926, and ended up even more successful than the earlier version. It gave sterling service through World War Two, then Korea, Vietnam and anywhere else the American fighting man was sent. The M1911A1 was also adopted by other armies, including Norway, Argentina and others, and

**SPECIFICATIONS**
**Type:** semi-automatic pistol
**Origin:** Colt Patent Fire Arms Mfg Co, Hartford, CT
**Caliber:** .45 ACP
**Barrel Length:** 5in

made in several countries (*see below*). During both World Wars, manufacture was taken up by other companies, such as Remington, Ithaca, Singer, and the Springfield Armory. The pistol has also been manufactured overseas (both licensed and unlicensed copies) in Canada, Norway, Argentina, Spain, Brazil and elsewhere.

A large civilian market also exist for this pistol, with variations in sights, materials and calibers all being offered. A model was also made for British use, chambered for the .455 Webley round. But it's the classic, straightforward no-nonsense military pistol that remains at the heart of the M1911 story. It did the job so well that it wasn't until 1985 that the army announced the final replacement of this old war-horse by the Beretta 92 – and many soldiers still regret its passing. Colt still sell a version today, known as the Model 1991.

## COLT LIGHTWEIGHT COMMANDER

### SPECIFICATIONS

**Type:** semi-automatic pistol
**Origin:** Colt Patent Fire Arms
Mfg Co, Hartford, CT
**Caliber:** 9mm Parabellum
**Barrel Length:** 4.25in

In the late 1940s the U.S. armed forces started what was to prove a very long search for a replacement for the Colt Model 1911A1, among the requirements being a maximum weight of 25 ounces and length of 7.0 inches, and they were to fire the .45 ACP round. The Colt submission was the Commander, which had a frame fabricated from Coltalloy, a lightweight aluminum alloy. None of the participants in this competition obtained a military order, but Colt placed the Commander in production for civil use, chambered for .45 ACP, 9mm Parabellum, .38 Super and 7.65mm. In 1970 a new model with a steel frame was introduced as the Combat Commander (*see below*) whereupon the aluminum-framed version was redesignated the Lightweight Commander, one of which is seen here.

## COLT GOVERNMENT MODEL NATIONAL MATCH

### SPECIFICATIONS

**Type:** semi-automatic pistol
**Origin:** Colt Patent Fire Arms Mfg Co, Hartford, CT
**Caliber:** .45 ACP
**Barrel Length:** 5in

This exceptional engraving was done by Master Engraver Alvin A. White on a Colt Government Model M1911A1 National Match pistol, chambered for .45 ACP. Inlaid gold wire outlines all the edges on the gun, including the trigger guard, the back strap and the front strap, and virtually all flat surfaces are engraved. The grips are of ivory, one having a carved buffalo's head, with the eyes being picked out by diamonds.

# COLT COMBAT COMMANDER

## SPECIFICATIONS

**Type:** semi-automatic pistol
**Origin:** Colt Patent Fire Arms Mfg Co, Hartford, CT
**Caliber:** .45 ACP, 9mm Parabellum
**Barrel Length:** 4.25in

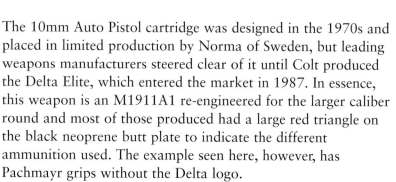

The Combat Commander, introduced in 1971, was the steel-framed version of the aluminum-framed Commander/Lightweight Commander, which resulted in an increase in weight to 33 ounces. We show one chambered for .45 ACP with a 4 inch barrel.

The lower one fires 9mm Parabellum and has a 4.25 inch barrel.

# COLT DELTA ELITE

## SPECIFICATIONS

**Type:** semi-automatic pistol
**Origin:** Colt Patent Fire Arms Mfg Co, Hartford, CT
**Caliber:** 10mm Auto Pistol
**Barrel Length:** 5in

The 10mm Auto Pistol cartridge was designed in the 1970s and placed in limited production by Norma of Sweden, but leading weapons manufacturers steered clear of it until Colt produced the Delta Elite, which entered the market in 1987. In essence, this weapon is an M1911A1 re-engineered for the larger caliber round and most of those produced had a large red triangle on the black neoprene butt plate to indicate the different ammunition used. The example seen here, however, has Pachmayr grips without the Delta logo.

# COLT WOODSMAN SEMI-AUTOMATIC PISTOLS

## SPECIFICATIONS

**Type:** semi-automatic pistol
**Origin:** Colt Patent Fire Arms Mfg Co, Hartford, CT
**Caliber:** .22LR
**Barrel Length:** 6.6in

The "Woodsman" proper was divided into three production runs: First Series 1927–47; Second Series 1947–55; and Third Series 1955–1977. Within each of those series, there were three models: Target, Sport and Match Target, and in the Second and Third Series only, additional economy models, designated Challenger, Huntsman and Targetsman.

Seen here is a variety of Woodsman models, but it should be noted that, in addition, to the variations seem here, there were also differences in barrel length and more minor characteristics.

First we show a Series 1 Woodsman with standard markings and features, including a 6.5in barrel, walnut grips and the magazine catch on the heel of the butt.

Next is a Series 2 Woodsman, made in 1954, which has been further modified by the addition of wrap-around walnut grips.

## COLT HUNTSMAN SEMI-AUTOMATIC PISTOL

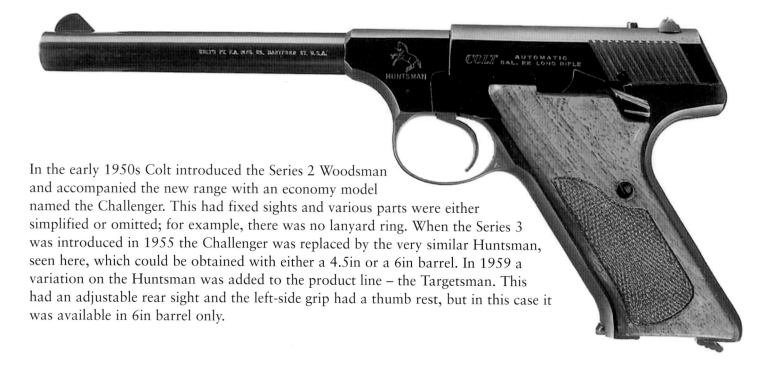

In the early 1950s Colt introduced the Series 2 Woodsman and accompanied the new range with an economy model named the Challenger. This had fixed sights and various parts were either simplified or omitted; for example, there was no lanyard ring. When the Series 3 was introduced in 1955 the Challenger was replaced by the very similar Huntsman, seen here, which could be obtained with either a 4.5in or a 6in barrel. In 1959 a variation on the Huntsman was added to the product line – the Targetsman. This had an adjustable rear sight and the left-side grip had a thumb rest, but in this case it was available in 6in barrel only.

### SPECIFICATIONS

**Type:** semi-automatic pistol
**Origin:** Colt Patent Fire Arms Mfg Co, Hartford, CT
**Caliber:** .22LR
**Barrel Length:** 6in

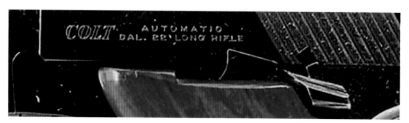

## COLT ALL AMERICAN MODEL 2000

**SPECIFICATIONS**
**Type:** semi-automatic pistol
**Origin:** Colt Patent Fire Arms Mfg Co, Hartford, CT
**Caliber:** 9mm
**Barrel Length:** 4.5in

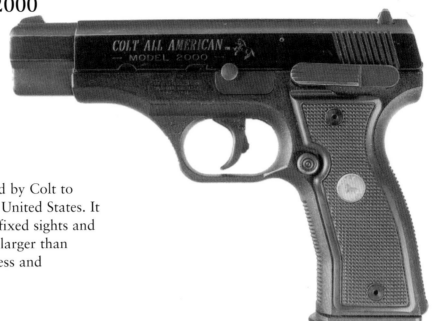

The All American Model 2000 was designed by Colt to achieve a return to the police market in the United States. It was produced only in 9mm, had white-dot fixed sights and the magazine (and, thus, also the butt) was larger than usual, holding 15 rounds. It was not a success and remained in production only until 1993.

## COLT FIRST MODEL DERINGER

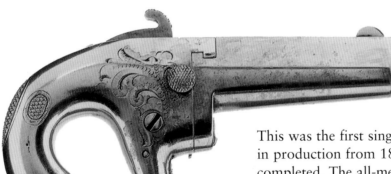

**SPECIFICATIONS**
**Type:** deringer-type pocket pistol
**Origin:** Colt Patent Fire Arms Mfg Co, Hartford, CT
**Caliber:** .44 rimfire
**Barrel Length:** 2.5in

This was the first single-shot pistol to be manufactured by Colt and was in production from 1870 to 1890, during which some 6,500 were completed. The all-metal weapon was loaded by releasing the barrel using the small round catch, which can be seen below the hammer, and swinging it to the left and then down, whereupon the empty cartridge case could be removed and replaced by a full one.

## COLT SECOND MODEL DERINGER

**SPECIFICATIONS**
**Type:** deringer-type pocket pistol
**Origin:** Colt Patent Fire Arms Mfg Co, Hartford, CT
**Caliber:** .44 rimfire
**Barrel Length:** 2.5in

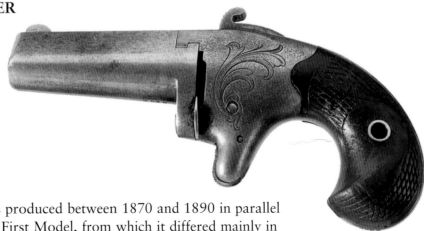

This was produced between 1870 and 1890 in parallel with the First Model, from which it differed mainly in the varnished walnut grips.

## COLT THIRD MODEL DERINGER

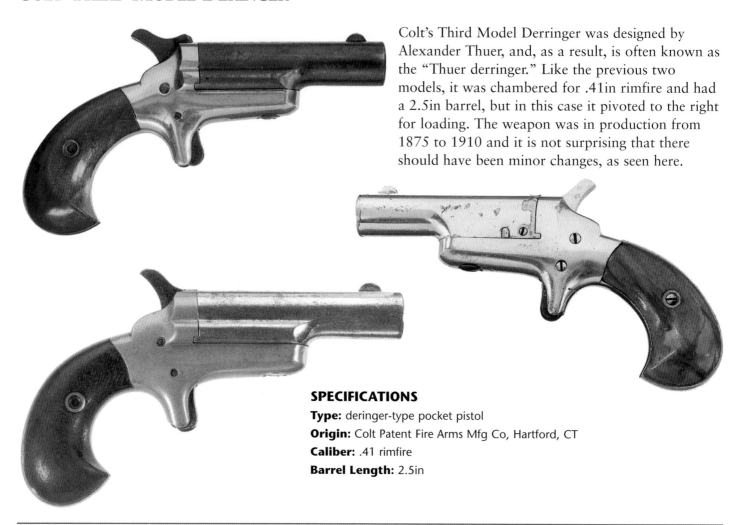

Colt's Third Model Derringer was designed by Alexander Thuer, and, as a result, is often known as the "Thuer derringer." Like the previous two models, it was chambered for .41in rimfire and had a 2.5in barrel, but in this case it pivoted to the right for loading. The weapon was in production from 1875 to 1910 and it is not surprising that there should have been minor changes, as seen here.

**SPECIFICATIONS**
**Type:** deringer-type pocket pistol
**Origin:** Colt Patent Fire Arms Mfg Co, Hartford, CT
**Caliber:** .41 rimfire
**Barrel Length:** 2.5in

## CHARLES DALY MODEL 1911A1

**SPECIFICATIONS**
**Type:** semi-automatic pistol
**Origin:** K.B.I Inc (Charles Daly), Harrisburg, Pa.
**Caliber:** .45 ACP
**Barrel Length:** 3.6in/4in/5in

The M1911A1's continuing popularity is attested by its continuing production, one range being marketed under the Charles Daly label (part of KBI Inc of Harrisburg, Pa). This company produces three basic models, all of which include an extended hi-rise beavertail grip safety, combat trigger, combat hammer, beveled magazine housing, modified ejection port, dovetailed front and dovetailed snag-free low profile rear sights, and hardwood grips! There are three standards of finish – Field, Empire and Target – and three barrel lengths – 5in barrel (eight round magazine); 4in barrel (eight round magazine) and 3.6in barrel (six round magazine).

## ESSEX M1911A1

**SPECIFICATIONS**
**Type:** semi-automatic pistol
**Origin:** Essex Arms Corp,
Island Pond, Vermont
**Caliber:** .45 ACP
**Barrel Length:** 5in

The original patents of the
M1911A1 have long since
expired and it remains in
production in a variety of
forms. The Essex Arms
Corp of Island Pond,
Vermont, markets a
number of versions based
on the company's own
frames. The pictures show
examples of the various
finishes available.

## GRENDEL P10

**SPECIFICATIONS**
**Type:** semi-automatic pistol
**Origin:** Grendel Inc, Rockledge,
Florida
**Caliber:** .38
**Barrel Length:** 3in

The P10 appeared in 1988 and was
intended to be a really compact, semi-
automatic handgun. It made considerable
use of polymers to lighten the design, but its
most unusual feature was that the butt served as
a fixed magazine with the eleven rounds of
ammunition being loaded from a stripper clip
inserted through the top of the receiver. This doers not appear to
have been particularly successful as a new version, the P-12, appeared
in 1991 which featured a conventional detachable box magazine
housing, reducing capacity to ten rounds, but this, too, had problems and
went out of production in 1995.

## GRENDEL P30

**SPECIFICATIONS**
**Type:** .22 semi-automatic
pistol
**Origin:** Grendel Inc,
Rockledge, Florida
**Caliber:** .22 WMR
**Barrel Length:** 5in

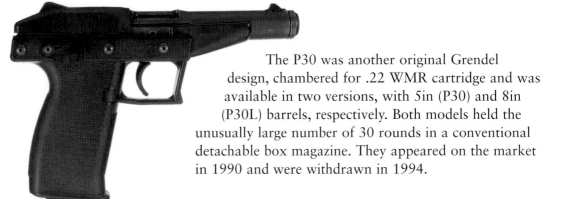

The P30 was another original Grendel
design, chambered for .22 WMR cartridge and was
available in two versions, with 5in (P30) and 8in
(P30L) barrels, respectively. Both models held the
unusually large number of 30 rounds in a conventional
detachable box magazine. They appeared on the market
in 1990 and were withdrawn in 1994.

## L.A.R. GRIZZLY MARK I

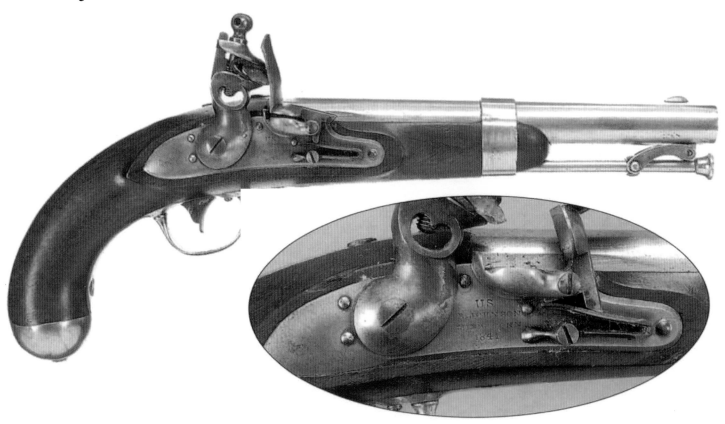

### SPECIFICATIONS
**Type:** semi-automatic pistol
**Origin:** L.A.R. Manufacturing, West Jordan, Utah
**Caliber:** .45 Winchester
**Barrel Length:** 6.5in

L.A.R. Manufacturing produces a series of handguns under the Grizzly name. The Grizzly Mark I is produced in .45 ACP, 10mm or .45 Winchester Magnum, and a variety of barrel lengths: 5.4in, 6.5in, 8in and 10in, resepectively (seen here is the 6.5in, 0.45 Winchester version). Various finishes are also available, as well as mountings for telescopic sights and a compensator, but all have adjustable sights and an ambidextrous safety.

## ROBERT JOHNSON MODEL 1836 PISTOL

### SPECIFICATIONS
**Type:** flintlock pistol
**Origin:** Robert Johnson, Middletown, Connecticut
**Caliber:** .54
**Barrel Length:** 8.5in

This is a Model 1836 pistol manufactured by Robert Johnson to meet a government contract for 3,000 weapons at $9.00 each. It is a conventional design but made to a very high standard; this particular example was made in 1841 and as the close-up of the action shows, it has lasted particularly well.

## HAMMOND BULLDOG

**SPECIFICATIONS**

**Type:** single shot pocket pistol
**Origin:** Connecticut Arms and Manufacturing Company
**Caliber:** .44
**Barrel Length:** 4in

A single shot self-defense weapon in the deringer class, this crudely finished breechloading pistol fired a powerful .44 cartridge and was patented in 1864. It would be effective enough at close range, and pistols of this nature became popular with many soldiers in the Civil War, who bought them to carry as concealed last-ditch back-up weapons.

## HARPER'S FERRY MODEL 1805 FLINTLOCK PISTOL

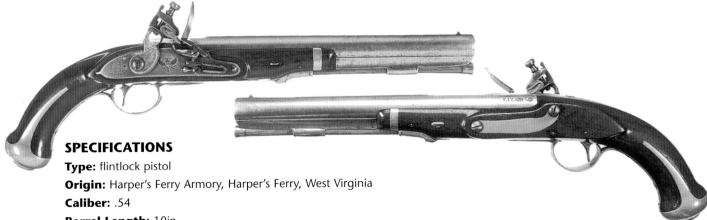

**SPECIFICATIONS**

**Type:** flintlock pistol
**Origin:** Harper's Ferry Armory, Harper's Ferry, West Virginia
**Caliber:** .54
**Barrel Length:** 10in

The United States government established a southern "Armory and Arsenal" at Harpers Ferry in 1799 to take advantage of the water power supplied by the Potomac and Shenandoah rivers, which meet there. Between 1801 and the outbreak of the Civil War over 600,000 muskets, pistols and rifles were manufactured, one of the earliest types being this Model 1805, which was the first military pistol to be manufactured at a United States' government arsenal. A total of 4,086 were produced between 1806 and 1808.

## HENRY SAW-HANDLE FLINTLOCK

**SPECIFICATIONS**

**Type:** flintlock pistol
**Origin:** Joseph Henry, Philadelphia
**Caliber:** .60
**Barrel Length:** 10in

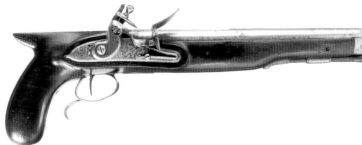

A pistol of this shape, with the stock spur extending horizontally back over the grip is often known as a "Saw Handle" pistol. The spur was intended to help keep the muzzle down, and the straight top edge was supposed to improve instinctive aiming. This one has a Model 1907 lock and may either have been a target pistol or one of a pair of duelling pistols.

# HIGH STANDARD MODEL E

## SPECIFICATIONS

**Type:** semi-automatic pistol
**Origin:** High Standard Mfg Corp, New Haven, Connecticut
**Caliber:** .22LR
**Barrel Length:** 4.5in or 6.75in

The Model E was a development of the Model D, but with an even heavier and more substantial barrel. Like the Model D, the barrel was available in either 4.5in or 6.75in lengths. Some 2,000 Model Es were produced in 1940–41.

# HIGH STANDARD MODEL G-B

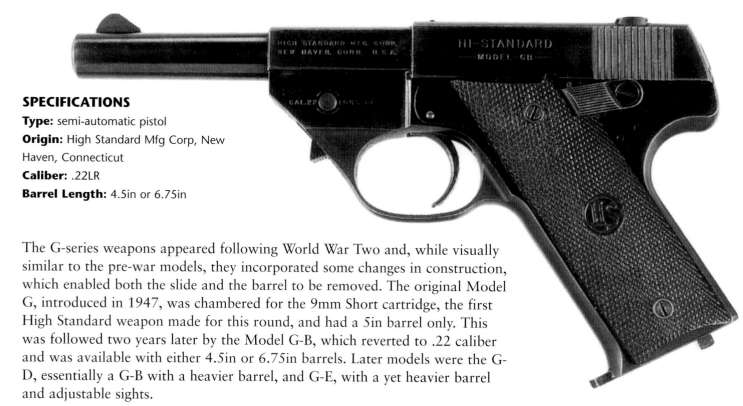

## SPECIFICATIONS

**Type:** semi-automatic pistol
**Origin:** High Standard Mfg Corp, New Haven, Connecticut
**Caliber:** .22LR
**Barrel Length:** 4.5in or 6.75in

The G-series weapons appeared following World War Two and, while visually similar to the pre-war models, they incorporated some changes in construction, which enabled both the slide and the barrel to be removed. The original Model G, introduced in 1947, was chambered for the 9mm Short cartridge, the first High Standard weapon made for this round, and had a 5in barrel only. This was followed two years later by the Model G-B, which reverted to .22 caliber and was available with either 4.5in or 6.75in barrels. Later models were the G-D, essentially a G-B with a heavier barrel, and G-E, with a yet heavier barrel and adjustable sights.

# HIGH STANDARD OLYMPIC

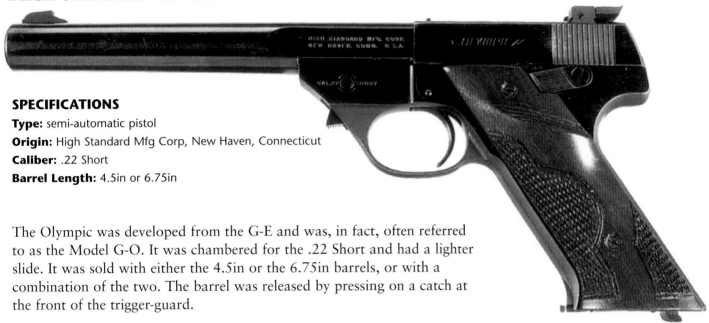

## SPECIFICATIONS

**Type:** semi-automatic pistol
**Origin:** High Standard Mfg Corp, New Haven, Connecticut
**Caliber:** .22 Short
**Barrel Length:** 4.5in or 6.75in

The Olympic was developed from the G-E and was, in fact, often referred to as the Model G-O. It was chambered for the .22 Short and had a lighter slide. It was sold with either the 4.5in or the 6.75in barrels, or with a combination of the two. The barrel was released by pressing on a catch at the front of the trigger-guard.

# HIGH STANDARD SUPERMATIC/SUPERMATIC MILITARY

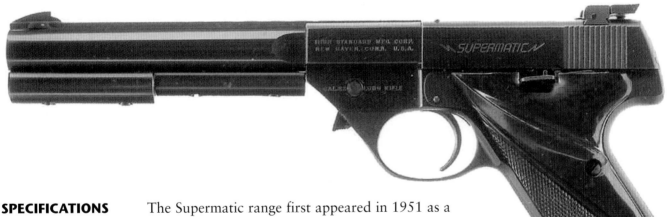

## SPECIFICATIONS

**Type:** semi-automatic pistol
**Origin:** High Standard Mfg Corp, New Haven, Connecticut
**Caliber:** .22
**Barrel Length:** 4.5in or 6.75in

The Supermatic range first appeared in 1951 as a replacement for the G-series and was, in essence, a development of the Olympic (G-O), and eventually numbered five models. The original Supermatic featured aids for target shooting, including balance weights, a slide stop and micrometer sights, but with similar parallel-sided barrels to the G-series. In 1959 the Supermatic Trophy was introduced with a new design of light, tapered barrel, with longitudinal fluted grooves, which, apart from aiding cooling, were also used to secure the barrel weights; 6.75in, 8in and 10in barrels were available. The Supermatic Citation was very similar to the Trophy, but with a more economical finish, while the Olympic was a Citation chambered for the .22 Short cartridge. Supermatic Tournament was the cheapest in the range without either stabilizer or weights, while the sights were simplified and there were only two choices of barrel length. The first pistol we show is an original Supermatic but with removable weights fitted under the barrel.

# HIGH STANDARD SERIES 103 MODEL SPORT KING

## SPECIFICATIONS

**Type:** semi-automatic pistol
**Origin:** High Standard Mfg Corp, New Haven, Connecticut
**Caliber:** .22
**Barrel Length:** 4.5in or 6.75in

High Standard's Series 103 models were in production from 1960 to 1963 and differed very little from the 102 series. The pictures show the pistols with 6.75in and 4.5in barrels.

# HIGH STANDARD SERIES 107 MODEL VICTOR

## SPECIFICATIONS

**Type:** semi-automatic pistol
**Origin:** High Standard Mfg Corp, New Haven, Connecticut
**Caliber:** .22
**Barrel Length:** 4.5in or 5.5in

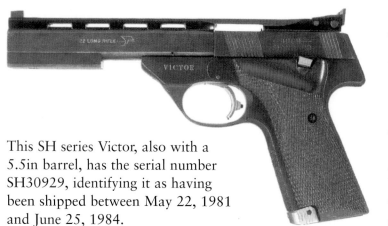

This SH series Victor, also with a 5.5in barrel, has the serial number SH30929, identifying it as having been shipped between May 22, 1981 and June 25, 1984.

The Victor was introduced in 1970 and combined the G-type frame with a new slab-sided barrel, topped by a heavy rib, which was continued to the rear of the weapon to carry the backsight. The barrel came in two lengths, 4.5in and 5.5in, and were either ventilated or solid, while both types carried an under rib upon which the weights could be mounted. Shown here is a 104 series Victor with 5.5in barrel.

# KIMBER M1911A1

## SPECIFICATIONS

**Type:** semi-automatic pistols
**Origin:** Kimber Mfg Inc, Yonkers, New York
**Caliber:** .45ACP
**Barrel Length:** various

Kimber originated in Oregon in 1979 where it manufactured some 60,000 rimfire and centerfire rifles for twelve years until it was forced to close in 1991. It reopened under new management in 1993 and in 1995 added new-build M1911A1s to its product line. In 1997 it moved to New York where it is still located. (It should be noted that the suffix "II" means that the weapon is fitted with the Kimber firing-pin safety system.) Seen on this page are five of the many variations of the M1911A1 produced by Kimber.

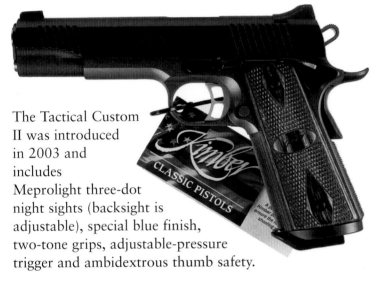

The Tactical Custom II was introduced in 2003 and includes Meprolight three-dot night sights (backsight is adjustable), special blue finish, two-tone grips, adjustable-pressure trigger and ambidextrous thumb safety.

This is a Pro Shadow LE II, from a limited edition of just 500 weapons produced in 2001. It has a 4 inch barrel, anodized aluminum frame, black steel slide, two-tone laminate grips, and stainless steel vented trigger and hammer.

The Team Match II was selected by the U.S. National Rapid Fire event team at the 2004 Olympics and, apart from those used by the team, a number were made available on the open market, with Kimber donating $100 from each sale to the team. The Team Match II .45 ACP has a stainless steel slide and frame, eight-round magazine, Kimber tactical extraction device and red, white and blue U.S. Shooting Team grips. The weapon also has a vented aluminum trigger.

The Heritage is one of many customized series produced for funds or to commemorate special events. The basic weapon is the Kimber Classic version of the M1911A1, but it has been customized to support the Hunting & Shooting Sports Heritage Fund.

Finally, the Kimber Classic Custom Royal 1911 is a top-of-the-range model, chambered for 0.45 and with an eight-round magazine. What makes it special, however, is that, in addition to all the Custom features, it has Kimber's traditional "royal blue" finish, hand checkered, double diamond rosewood grips and lightweight aluminium spoked trigger.

## SIMEON NORTH PISTOLS

Simeon North (1765–1852) is one of America's forgotten heroes. He owned a farm in Berlin, Connecticut, but had a lifelong fascination with engineering and, in particular, with the idea of producing equipment with standardized parts so that spares would be fully interchangeable. He started in the engineering business by producing scythes, but after only four years he obtained his first contract to make pistols for the U.S. government. In 1813 he obtained a further contract to produce 20,000 pistols and, for the first time ever in such a government contract, it was specified that the parts were to be fully standardized. He later visited the arsenal at Harper's Ferry, where he helped introduce the concept of standardization.

The North Model 1811 flintlock shown here had a caliber of .73 and an 8.6 inch barrel, and its origins are clearly shown in the markings on the lock: "S. NORTH, BERLIN, CONN" and "U. STATES" topped by the eagle.

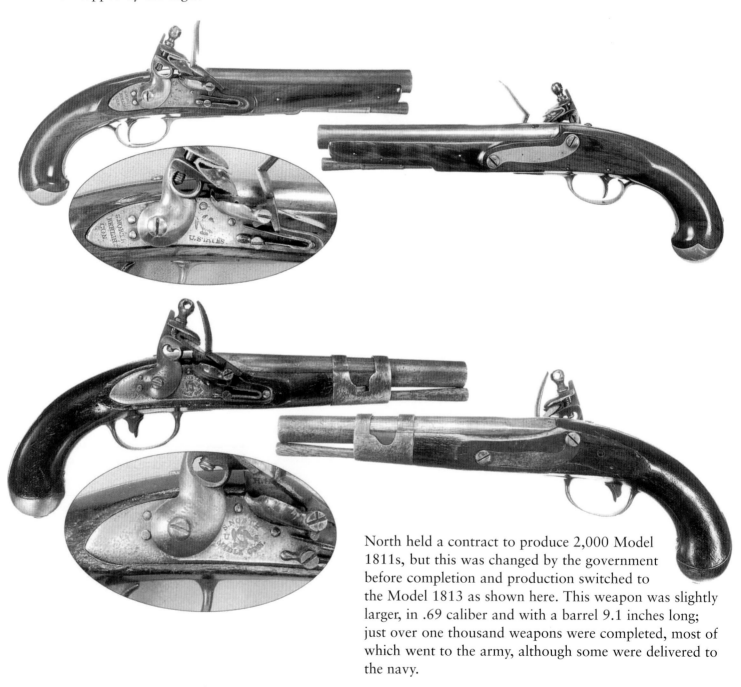

North held a contract to produce 2,000 Model 1811s, but this was changed by the government before completion and production switched to the Model 1813 as shown here. This weapon was slightly larger, in .69 caliber and with a barrel 9.1 inches long; just over one thousand weapons were completed, most of which went to the army, although some were delivered to the navy.

## PARA-ORDNANCE P14.45

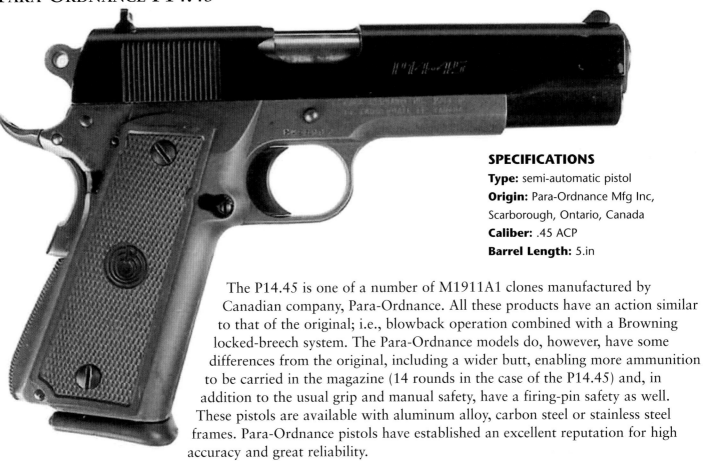

### SPECIFICATIONS

**Type:** semi-automatic pistol
**Origin:** Para-Ordnance Mfg Inc, Scarborough, Ontario, Canada
**Caliber:** .45 ACP
**Barrel Length:** 5.in

The P14.45 is one of a number of M1911A1 clones manufactured by Canadian company, Para-Ordnance. All these products have an action similar to that of the original; i.e., blowback operation combined with a Browning locked-breech system. The Para-Ordnance models do, however, have some differences from the original, including a wider butt, enabling more ammunition to be carried in the magazine (14 rounds in the case of the P14.45) and, in addition to the usual grip and manual safety, have a firing-pin safety as well. These pistols are available with aluminum alloy, carbon steel or stainless steel frames. Para-Ordnance pistols have established an excellent reputation for high accuracy and great reliability.

## PHOENIX PISTOL

### SPECIFICATIONS

**Type:** semi-automatic pistol
**Origin:** Phoenix, Lowell, Massachusetts (but see text)
**Caliber:** .25 ACP
**Barrel Length:** 2.1in

The origins of this rather undistinguished weapon are somewhat obscure. It is marked "PHOENIX. LOWELL. MASS. USA PATENT" but there was no known U.S. gunsmith of that name. It is most probable that this was the name of an importer and that the weapon was manufactured elsewhere, most probably in Belgium by Robar of Liege. Caliber is .25 ACP (6.35mm) and the weapon is quite small, with a barrel length of just 2.1in.

## REMINGTON-RIDER PARLOR PISTOL

### SPECIFICATIONS
**Type:** parlor pistol
**Origin:** Remington Arms Co., Inc., Ilion, New York
**Caliber:** .17
**Barrel Length:** 3in

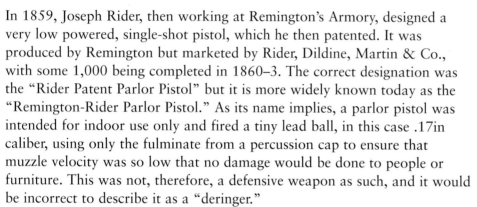

In 1859, Joseph Rider, then working at Remington's Armory, designed a very low powered, single-shot pistol, which he then patented. It was produced by Remington but marketed by Rider, Dildine, Martin & Co., with some 1,000 being completed in 1860–3. The correct designation was the "Rider Patent Parlor Pistol" but it is more widely known today as the "Remington-Rider Parlor Pistol." As its name implies, a parlor pistol was intended for indoor use only and fired a tiny lead ball, in this case .17in caliber, using only the fulminate from a percussion cap to ensure that muzzle velocity was so low that no damage would be done to people or furniture. This was not, therefore, a defensive weapon as such, and it would be incorrect to describe it as a "deringer."

## REMINGTON MAGAZINE PISTOL

### SPECIFICATIONS
**Type:** multi-shot "deringer" pistol
**Origin:** Remington Arms Co., Inc., Ilion, New York
**Caliber:** .32 Extra Short
**Barrel Length:** 3in

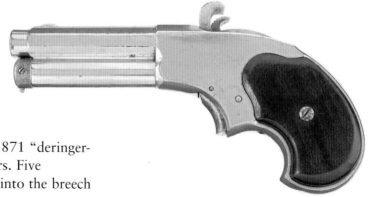

Another Joseph Rider patent design, this neat, 1871 "deringer-style" pistol is more effective than it first appears. Five cartridges are held in the tubular magazine, fed into the breech using the short lever next to the hammer.

## REMINGTON-ELLIOT ZIG-ZAG DERINGER

### SPECIFICATIONS

**Type:** multi-barrel derringer pistol

**Origin:** Remington Arms Co., Inc., Ilion, New York.

**Caliber:** .22

**Barrel Length:** 3.25in

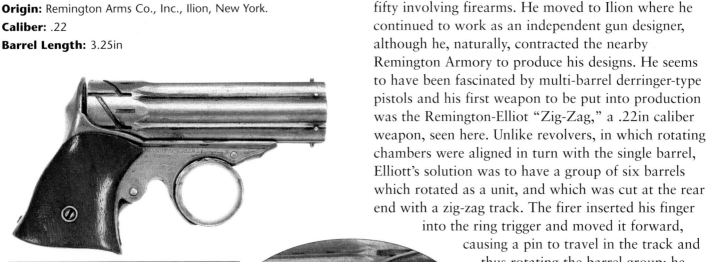

Dr William H. Elliot was a dentist and a prolific inventor, who patented many devices including over fifty involving firearms. He moved to Ilion where he continued to work as an independent gun designer, although he, naturally, contracted the nearby Remington Armory to produce his designs. He seems to have been fascinated by multi-barrel derringer-type pistols and his first weapon to be put into production was the Remington-Elliot "Zig-Zag," a .22in caliber weapon, seen here. Unlike revolvers, in which rotating chambers were aligned in turn with the single barrel, Elliott's solution was to have a group of six barrels which rotated as a unit, and which was cut at the rear end with a zig-zag track. The firer inserted his finger into the ring trigger and moved it forward, causing a pin to travel in the track and thus rotating the barrel group; he then pulled backwards to cock the internal hammer and fire the weapon. This was a clever solution to the problem, but was mechanically complicated and fragile – and the one essential characteristic in such a close-quarter self-defense weapon is absolute dependability!

## REMINGTON-ELLIOT FIVE/FOUR BARREL DERINGER

### SPECIFICATIONS

**Type:** multi-barrel deringer-type pistol

**Origin:** Remington Arms Co., Inc., Ilion, New York.

**Caliber:** .22 and .32

**Barrel Length:** 3in

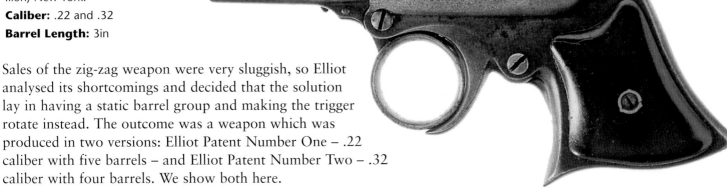

Sales of the zig-zag weapon were very sluggish, so Elliot analysed its shortcomings and decided that the solution lay in having a static barrel group and making the trigger rotate instead. The outcome was a weapon which was produced in two versions: Elliot Patent Number One – .22 caliber with five barrels – and Elliot Patent Number Two – .32 caliber with four barrels. We show both here.

In both weapons the barrels were 3 inches long. A total of some 12,000 of both types was manufactured between 1862 and the late 1870s. It should be noted that in modern collectors' circles, these weapons are known as "Elliot's Ring-Trigger Pistols."

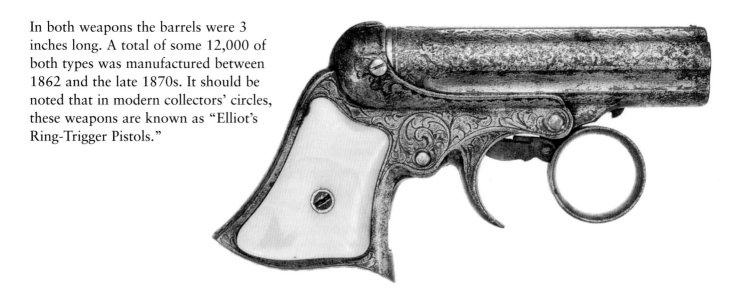

## REMINGTON VEST-POCKET PISTOL

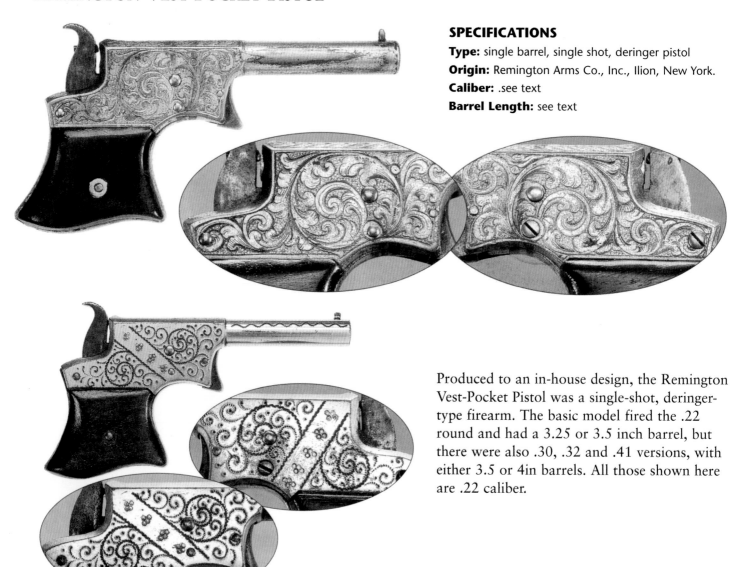

### SPECIFICATIONS
**Type:** single barrel, single shot, deringer pistol
**Origin:** Remington Arms Co., Inc., Ilion, New York.
**Caliber:** .see text
**Barrel Length:** see text

Produced to an in-house design, the Remington Vest-Pocket Pistol was a single-shot, deringer-type firearm. The basic model fired the .22 round and had a 3.25 or 3.5 inch barrel, but there were also .30, .32 and .41 versions, with either 3.5 or 4in barrels. All those shown here are .22 caliber.

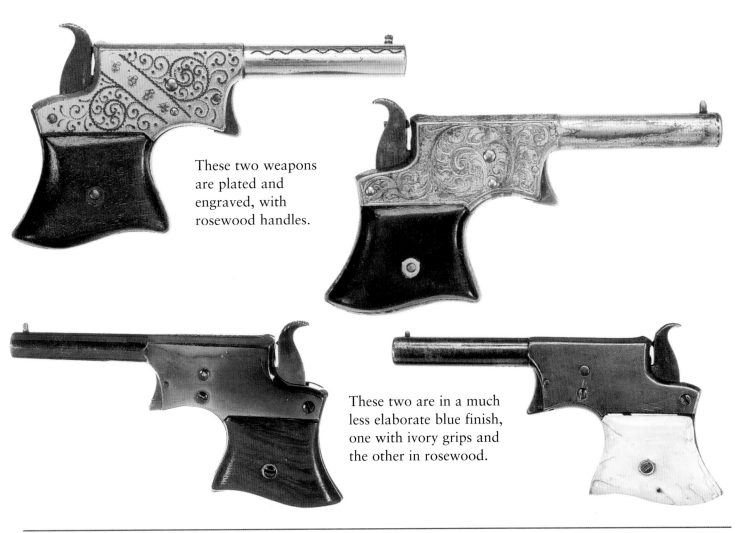

These two weapons are plated and engraved, with rosewood handles.

These two are in a much less elaborate blue finish, one with ivory grips and the other in rosewood.

## REMINGTON NO.2 VEST-POCKET PISTOL

### SPECIFICATIONS

**Type:** single barrel, single shot, split-breech deringer pistol

**Origin:** Remington Arms Co., Inc., Ilion, New York.

**Caliber:** .30, .32

**Barrel Length:** 3.25in

Having seen the parlor pistol into production, Joseph Rider designed a new type of split breech, which led to the No 2 Vest-Pocket pistol seen here. This was available in .30 rimfire and .32 rimfire, and in a variety of finishes.

## REMINGTON DOUBLE DERINGERS (OVER-AND-UNDER)

### SPECIFICATIONS

**Type:** double barrel "over-and-under" deringer-type pistol

**Origin:** Remington Arms Co., Inc., Ilion, New York.

**Caliber:** .41 rimfire

**Barrel Length:** 3in

Anyone in a "last-ditch" situation wanted to be sure that he or she would have as many opportunities as possible to repel an attack. Most multi-barrel deringers were either complicated or large and heavy (or both), but the twin-barrel version seemed to offer a compromise. Thus, these Remington "over-and-under" derringers were popular and were manufactured, with minor variations, from 1866 to as late as 1935, during which time some 150,000 were completed. All known versions were in .41 caliber, but in a variety of finishes.

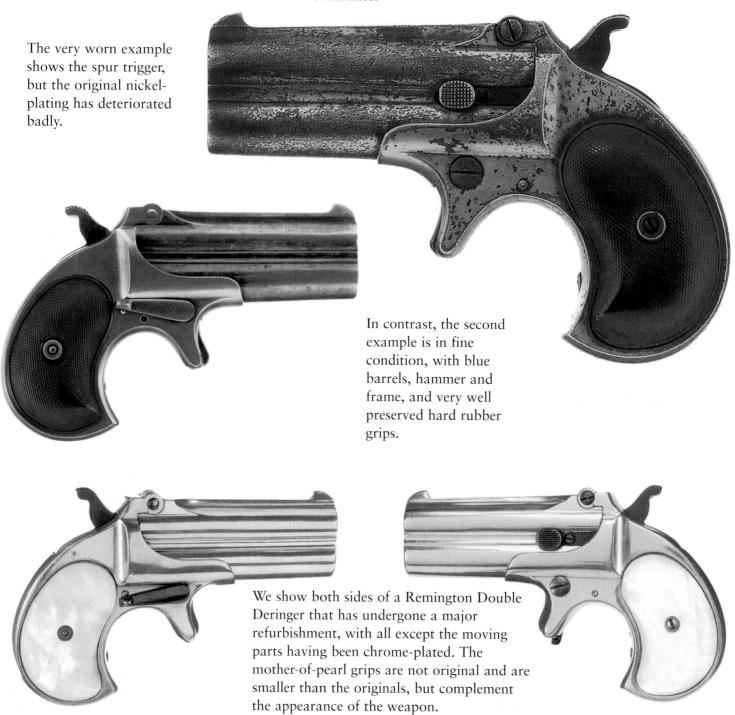

The very worn example shows the spur trigger, but the original nickel-plating has deteriorated badly.

In contrast, the second example is in fine condition, with blue barrels, hammer and frame, and very well preserved hard rubber grips.

We show both sides of a Remington Double Deringer that has undergone a major refurbishment, with all except the moving parts having been chrome-plated. The mother-of-pearl grips are not original and are smaller than the originals, but complement the appearance of the weapon.

# REMINGTON MODEL 1867 NAVY ROLLING BLOCK PISTOL

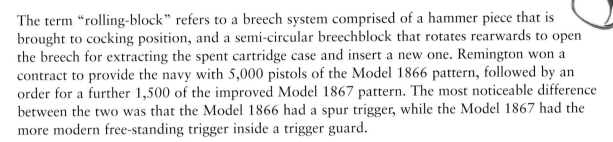

## SPECIFICATIONS

**Type:** single-shot, rolling-block pistol
**Origin:** Remington Arms Co., Inc., Ilion, New York.
**Caliber:** .50 centerfire
**Barrel Length:** 7in

The term "rolling-block" refers to a breech system comprised of a hammer piece that is brought to cocking position, and a semi-circular breechblock that rotates rearwards to open the breech for extracting the spent cartridge case and insert a new one. Remington won a contract to provide the navy with 5,000 pistols of the Model 1866 pattern, followed by an order for a further 1,500 of the improved Model 1867 pattern. The most noticeable difference between the two was that the Model 1866 had a spur trigger, while the Model 1867 had the more modern free-standing trigger inside a trigger guard.

# REMINGTON MODEL 1871 ARMY

## SPECIFICATIONS

**Type:** single-shot, rolling-block pistol
**Origin:** Remington Arms Co., Inc., Ilion, New York.
**Caliber:** .50 centerfire
**Barrel Length:** 8in

Remington won a government contract which led to the supply of the Model 1871 Army pistol; a number were also made for the civilian market. The two examples shown here illustrate the wide difference between a standard model and a custom-built, fully decorated "de luxe" example.

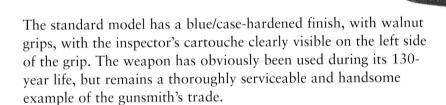

The standard model has a blue/case-hardened finish, with walnut grips, with the inspector's cartouche clearly visible on the left side of the grip. The weapon has obviously been used during its 130-year life, but remains a thoroughly serviceable and handsome example of the gunsmith's trade.

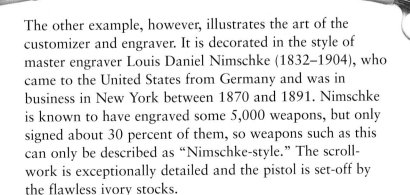

The other example, however, illustrates the art of the customizer and engraver. It is decorated in the style of master engraver Louis Daniel Nimschke (1832–1904), who came to the United States from Germany and was in business in New York between 1870 and 1891. Nimschke is known to have engraved some 5,000 weapons, but only signed about 30 percent of them, so weapons such as this can only be described as "Nimschke-style." The scroll-work is exceptionally detailed and the pistol is set-off by the flawless ivory stocks.

# REMINGTON ROLLING BLOCK "PLINKER" TARGET PISTOLS

## SPECIFICATIONS

**Type:** single-shot, rolling-block pistol

**Origin:** Remington Arms Co., Inc., Ilion, New York.

**Caliber:** .22LR, .32 WCF

**Barrel Length:** 8in

On several occasions Remington took surplus frames lying in the factory stockrooms to produce target pistols, which were also known as "plinkers."

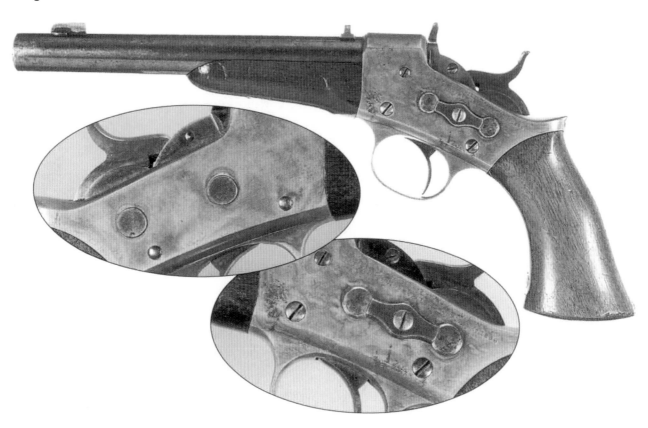

The example shown here is based on a Model 1871 action, sleeved down to .22LR.

This picture shows a Model 1867 action, sleeved down to .32 WCF. Both examples have 8in round barrels.

# REMINGTON MODEL 1901 ROLLING BLOCK TARGET PISTOL

## SPECIFICATIONS
**Type:** single-shot, rolling-block pistol
**Origin:** Remington Arms Co., Inc., Ilion, New York.
**Caliber:** see text
**Barrel Length:** 10in

Remington continued to cater for the target-shooting fraternity with a series of rolling-block models. The Model 1891 was produced in .22LR and .32 S&W calibers (the latter is seen here) with the backsight mounted on the 10in half round/half octagonal barrel. Only about 100 were made, making this a very rare collectors' piece.

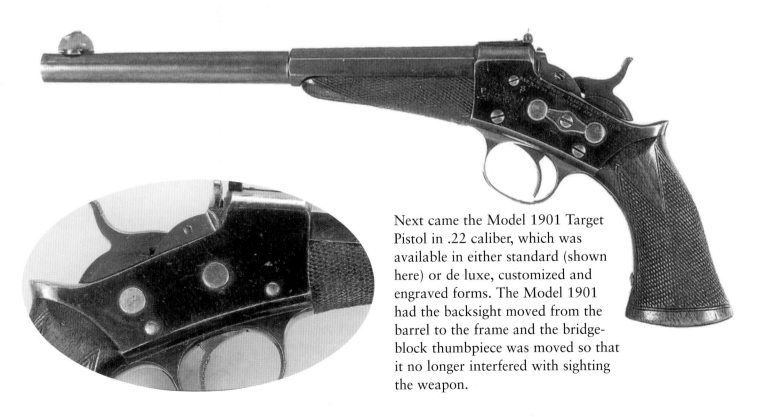

Next came the Model 1901 Target Pistol in .22 caliber, which was available in either standard (shown here) or de luxe, customized and engraved forms. The Model 1901 had the backsight moved from the barrel to the frame and the bridge-block thumbpiece was moved so that it no longer interfered with sighting the weapon.

# REMINGTON MODEL 1911

## SPECIFICATIONS

**Type:** semi-automatic pistol
**Origin:** Remington Arms Co., Inc.,
Ilion, New York.
**Caliber:** .45ACP
**Barrel Length:** 5in

With America's entry into World War One massive orders for weapons were placed, one of the many recipients being Remington, which was awarded a contract for 150,000 Colt Model 1911 autoloading pistols, with first delivery on June 1, 1918. In the event, Remington did not make the first delivery until August 1918, not long before the end of the war on November 11 resulted in suspension of the contract on December 17. A few more were produced but the final total was 21,677.

# REMINGTON MODEL 51

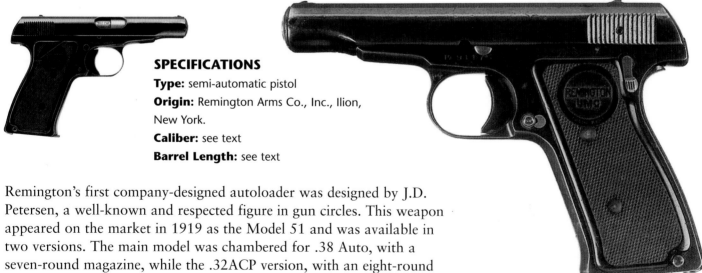

## SPECIFICATIONS

**Type:** semi-automatic pistol
**Origin:** Remington Arms Co., Inc., Ilion, New York.
**Caliber:** see text
**Barrel Length:** see text

Remington's first company-designed autoloader was designed by J.D. Petersen, a well-known and respected figure in gun circles. This weapon appeared on the market in 1919 as the Model 51 and was available in two versions. The main model was chambered for .38 Auto, with a seven-round magazine, while the .32ACP version, with an eight-round magazine, was made in much smaller numbers. The mechanism used a combination delayed blowback/recoil system, in which when the cartridge was fired the slide and breechblock moved back together very briefly, before the block stopped and unlocked, allowing the slide to continue to the rear. The Model 51 was an excellent weapon but was expensive to produce and its relatively high made between 1918 and 1934. A Model 53, similar to the Model 51, but chambered for .45ACP and with a hammer was produced in very small numbers for government trials, but was not proceeded with.

## REMINGTON MODEL XP-100 LONG-RANGE TARGET PISTOL

**SPECIFICATIONS**

**Type:** single-shot, bolt-action pistol
**Origin:** Remington Arms Co., Inc., Ilion, New York.
**Caliber:** .221 Remington
**Barrel Length:** 14.5in

The XP-100 series started with Remington's early 1960s decision to produce a high-powered, bolt-action varmint pistol, chambered for a newly-developed .221 Remington "Fireball" centerfire cartridge. The first model was the singleshot XP-100 (seen here with fitted scope) which, according to company claims "shoots faster, flatter, farther and tighter than any handgun in history." Since then a number of variations have been produced featuring different sights, calibers and stocks.

## RUGER MARK I TARGET MODEL

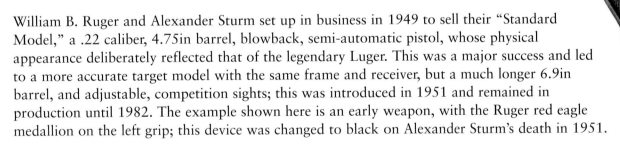

**SPECIFICATIONS**

**Type:** semi-automatic target pistol
**Origin:** Sturm, Ruger & Co, Southport, Connecticut
**Caliber:** .22LR
**Barrel Length:** 6.9in

William B. Ruger and Alexander Sturm set up in business in 1949 to sell their "Standard Model," a .22 caliber, 4.75in barrel, blowback, semi-automatic pistol, whose physical appearance deliberately reflected that of the legendary Luger. This was a major success and led to a more accurate target model with the same frame and receiver, but a much longer 6.9in barrel, and adjustable, competition sights; this was introduced in 1951 and remained in production until 1982. The example shown here is an early weapon, with the Ruger red eagle medallion on the left grip; this device was changed to black on Alexander Sturm's death in 1951.

## RUGER MARK II TARGET MODEL

**SPECIFICATIONS**

**Type:** semi-automatic target pistol
**Origin:** Sturm, Ruger & Co, Southport, Connecticut
**Caliber:** .22LR
**Barrel Length:** 5.5in

The Ruger Mark II was introduced in 1982. It retained the appearance of the original Mark I, but included some significant improvements, including a redesigned safety, magazine capacity increased to ten rounds, bolt-stop thumb-piece, and small grooves to improve the grip on the bolt. As with the Mark I there was a parallel Mark II Target model, with the same mechanical characteristics, but with a variety of target-type barrels and adjustable sights. This example has the 5.5in bull barrel.

## RUGER MODEL P85

**SPECIFICATIONS**

**Type:** semi-automatic pistol
**Origin:** Sturm, Ruger & Co, Southport, Connecticut
**Caliber:** 9mm Parabellum
**Barrel Length:** 4.5in

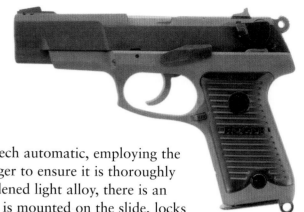

The P85, which appeared in 1985, is a double-action, locked breech automatic, employing the Browning swinging-link lock, but with changes developed by Ruger to ensure it is thoroughly reliable and accurate. The frame is fabricated from specially-hardened light alloy, there is an external hammer and the large ambidextrous safety catch, which is mounted on the slide, locks the firing-pin, blocks the hammer, and disconnects the trigger.

## SAVAGE MODEL 1907

**SPECIFICATIONS**

**Type:** semi-automatic pistol
**Origin:** Savage Arms Corp, Utica, New York
**Caliber:** .32
**Barrel Length:** 3.6in

The design of this weapon originated with Major Elbert H. Searle, whose patent included the use of the bullet's torque to twist the barrel to unlock the breech, and a magazine with staggered rounds, increasing capacity compared to contemporary models. Although the pistol worked well, the supposed use of torque was often disputed, and many experts claimed that it was, in reality, a delayed blowback system. Searle sold his patent to Savage, resulting in the Model 1907. The example shown here is the .32 caliber, 3.75 inch model; there was also a .38 version with a 4.25inch barrel.

## SAVAGE MODEL 1907 TEST

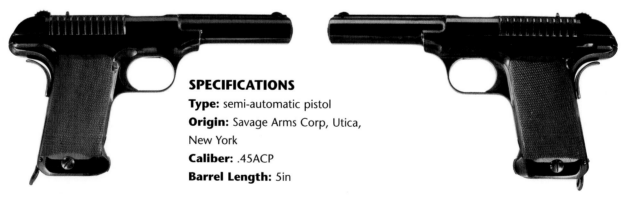

**SPECIFICATIONS**

**Type:** semi-automatic pistol
**Origin:** Savage Arms Corp, Utica, New York
**Caliber:** .45ACP
**Barrel Length:** 5in

Savage developed a special version of the Model 1907, chambered for the .45in ACP cartridge, which was entered in the competition for the U.S. army's standard automatic. The prototypes survived the army's initial trials and some 290 were then produced between 190 and 1911, which were issued to the 3rd, 6th and 11th Cavalry for field trials in competition with the Colt-Browning design. The army selected the latter which was put into production as the M1911 and the trial batch of Savage pistols were returned to the company for disposal. Savage sold them at auction in 1912 and no further development was undertaken.

## SHARPS & HANKINS SINGLE-SHOT PISTOL

**SPECIFICATIONS**

**Type:** breechloading single-shot pistol

**Origin:** Sharps & Hankins, Hartford, Connecticut

**Caliber:** see text

**Barrel Length:** see text

Christian Sharps (1811–74) was an inventor better known for designing his own rifles, although in the early days he licensed them out to others for production. In 1855, however, he established his own factories in Hartford, Connecticut and Philadelphia, Pennsylvania (the latter becoming Sharps & Hankins in 1863). There, apart from rifles, he also produced designs for one pistol and a number of multi-barrel "pepperpots."

His breechloading percussion pistol was produced in various calibers. We show two examples, a .31 pistol with a small frame and a 5 inch barrel, and a .36 pistol with a larger frame and a 6.4 inch barrel.

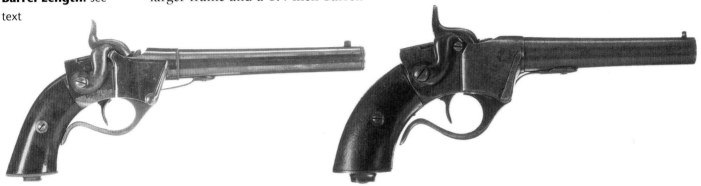

## SHATTUCK UNIQUE PALM PISTOL

**SPECIFICATIONS**

**Type:** vest-pocket, multi-round pistol

**Origin:** C. S. Shattuck, Hatfield, Massachusetts

**Caliber:** .32

**Barrel Length:** 1.4in

This extraordinary weapon was made by C.S. Shattuck in the 1880s. The rectangular portion on the right of the weapon housed four .22 caliber barrels; it was released by the knurled knob at the top and was then moved forwards and down on the pivot screw, whose head can be seen. The rounds were fired by squeezing the trigger at the bottom of the weapon.

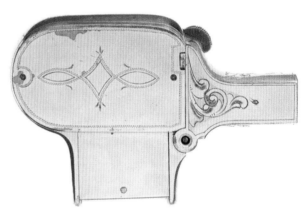

## SHERIDAN TIP-UP SINGLE-SHOT PISTOL

**SPECIFICATIONS**

**Type:** tip-up, single-shot pistol

**Origin:** Sheridan Products Inc, Racine, Wisconsin

**Caliber:** .22LR

**Barrel Length:** 5in

Sheridan Products normally produced air-guns and gas-guns, but made this single essay into conventional pistols in 1953. It was a single-shot weapon designed to look like an automatic and was made of plastic and steel pressings. Since it fired .22 rounds it was clearly not a toy, but it was of little real use other than for not-too-serious target practise. It had the unofficial title of "the Knockabout" and remained in production until 1963.

## SMITH & WESSON VOLCANIC PISTOL

**SPECIFICATIONS**
**Type:** lever-action repeating pistol
**Origin:** Smith & Wesson, Norwich, Connecticut
**Caliber:** .40
**Barrel Length:** 8in

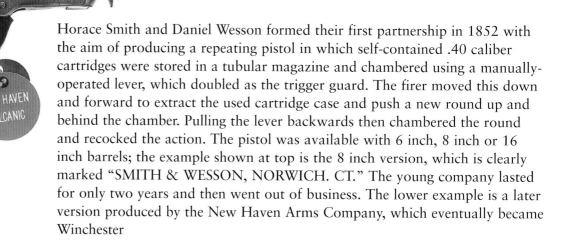

Horace Smith and Daniel Wesson formed their first partnership in 1852 with the aim of producing a repeating pistol in which self-contained .40 caliber cartridges were stored in a tubular magazine and chambered using a manually-operated lever, which doubled as the trigger guard. The firer moved this down and forward to extract the used cartridge case and push a new round up and behind the chamber. Pulling the lever backwards then chambered the round and recocked the action. The pistol was available with 6 inch, 8 inch or 16 inch barrels; the example shown at top is the 8 inch version, which is clearly marked "SMITH & WESSON, NORWICH. CT." The young company lasted for only two years and then went out of business. The lower example is a later version produced by the New Haven Arms Company, which eventually became Winchester

## SMITH & WESSON THIRD MODEL SINGLE-SHOT

**SPECIFICATIONS**
**Type:** single-shot pistol
**Origin:** Smith & Wesson, Springfield, Massachusetts
**Caliber:** .22LR
**Barrel Length:** 8in

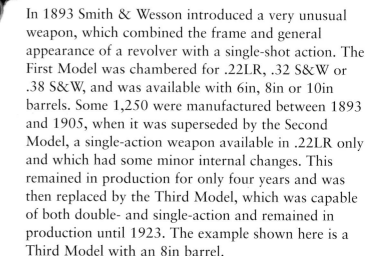

In 1893 Smith & Wesson introduced a very unusual weapon, which combined the frame and general appearance of a revolver with a single-shot action. The First Model was chambered for .22LR, .32 S&W or .38 S&W, and was available with 6in, 8in or 10in barrels. Some 1,250 were manufactured between 1893 and 1905, when it was superseded by the Second Model, a single-action weapon available in .22LR only and which had some minor internal changes. This remained in production for only four years and was then replaced by the Third Model, which was capable of both double- and single-action and remained in production until 1923. The example shown here is a Third Model with an 8in barrel.

# SMITH & WESSON AUTOMATIC MODEL OF 1913

**SPECIFICATIONS**
**Type:** semi-automatic pistol
**Origin:** Smith & Wesson, Springfield, Massachusetts
**Caliber:** .35 S&W automatic
**Barrel Length:** 3.5in

Smith & Wesson had continuing and outstanding success with revolvers and hesitated for many years before attempting to move into the automatic field. The result was this pistol, which appeared in 1913, which was sometimes known (incorrectly) as the Model 35. This was chambered for the specially-developed rimless .35 S&W Automatic cartridge, and based (under license) on patents held by a Belgian, Charles Clément of Liege. The weapon employed a simple, if unusual, blowback system, with the recoil spring above the barrel and a grip safety located immediately below the trigger guard. The magazine held seven rounds. Some 8,300 were produced between 1913 and 1921, but the type was not popular, mainly because not only was the gun expensive to buy, but the ammunition was also expensive and difficult to obtain. We show two standard weapons here.

This one Serial Number 2102, and is interesting in that it is resting on its letter of authenticity, signed by Smith & Wesson's official historian.

# SMITH & WESSON AUTOMATIC MODEL OF 1924

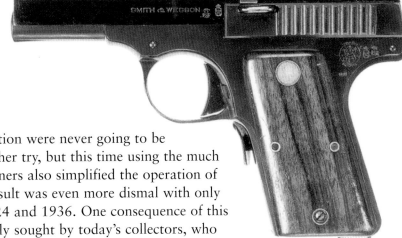

**SPECIFICATIONS**
**Type:** semi-automatic pistol
**Origin:** Smith & Wesson, Springfield, Massachusetts
**Caliber:** .32 ACP
**Barrel Length:** 3.5in

Realising that the .35 Automatic and its ammunition were never going to be a commercial success, Smith & Wesson had another try, but this time using the much more readily available .32 ACP round. The designers also simplified the operation of the gun and smartened its appearance, but the result was even more dismal with only about one thousand being produced between 1924 and 1936. One consequence of this small production run is that this weapon is eagerly sought by today's collectors, who will pay a high price for one in excellent condition.

## SMITH & WESSON MODEL 41

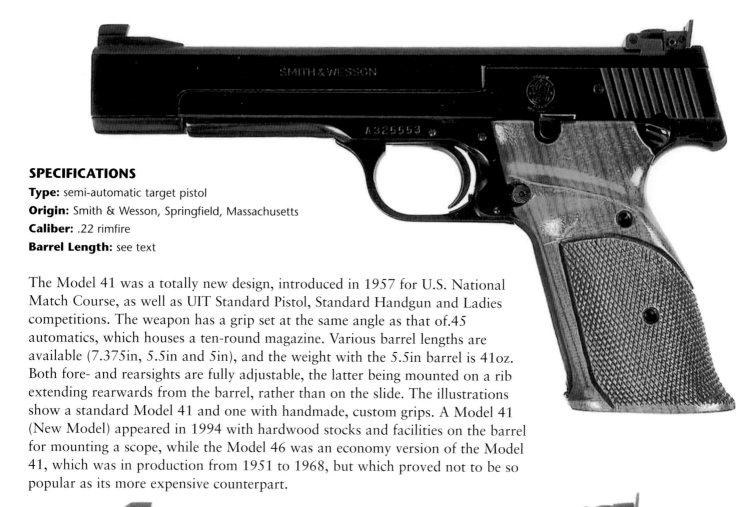

### SPECIFICATIONS

**Type:** semi-automatic target pistol
**Origin:** Smith & Wesson, Springfield, Massachusetts
**Caliber:** .22 rimfire
**Barrel Length:** see text

The Model 41 was a totally new design, introduced in 1957 for U.S. National Match Course, as well as UIT Standard Pistol, Standard Handgun and Ladies competitions. The weapon has a grip set at the same angle as that of.45 automatics, which houses a ten-round magazine. Various barrel lengths are available (7.375in, 5.5in and 5in), and the weight with the 5.5in barrel is 41oz. Both fore- and rearsights are fully adjustable, the latter being mounted on a rib extending rearwards from the barrel, rather than on the slide. The illustrations show a standard Model 41 and one with handmade, custom grips. A Model 41 (New Model) appeared in 1994 with hardwood stocks and facilities on the barrel for mounting a scope, while the Model 46 was an economy version of the Model 41, which was in production from 1951 to 1968, but which proved not to be so popular as its more expensive counterpart.

## SMITH & WESSON MODELS 59 AND 459

**SPECIFICATIONS**

**Type:** semi-automatic pistol
**Origin:** Smith & Wesson, Springfield, Massachusetts
**Caliber:** 9mm Parabellum
**Barrel Length:** 4in

Developments of the Model 59 included the Model 459, which had improved sights, marginally longer barrel (4.1in) and an alloy frame, and the Model 559 (not shown) which had a stainless steel frame, but was otherwise identical to the 459.

The Model 59 was generally similar in design to the Model 39, but had a wider grip which enabled a larger magazine to hold 14 rounds in a double column, compared to seven for the earlier model. It was in production from 1971 to 1982.

## SMITH & WESSON MODEL 61

**SPECIFICATIONS**

**Type:** semi-automatic pocket pistol
**Origin:** Smith & Wesson, Springfield, Massachusetts
**Caliber:** .22LR
**Barrel Length:** 2.1in

The Model 61, also known as "The Escort," is the only pocket automatic ever to be marketed by Smith & Wesson. A very small and handy design, it was chambered for the .22LR cartridge and had a five-round magazine. Barrel length was 2.1in. It was available in two finishes – nickel or blue (*as seen here*). It remained in production for a mere four years.

## SMITH & WESSON MODEL 3914

**SPECIFICATIONS**
**Type:** semi-automatic pistol
**Origin:** Smith & Wesson,
Springfield, Massachusetts
**Caliber:** 9mm Parabellum
**Barrel Length:** 3.5in

Smith & Wesson revamped their existing range of 9mm automatics in 1989 resulting in a more "modern" outward appearance, as well as internal refinements. Lead model was the 3904, which had a 4in barrel, eight-round magazine, squared trigger guard to facilitate two-hand use, and an alloy frame. The Model 3906 was identical except that it was made of stainless steel. Also introduced was the Model 3914, seen here, which was slightly smaller than the Model 3904, with a 3.5in barrel and reduced overall length. It had an alloy frame and blued carbon-steel slide, and an eight round magazine.

## SMITH & WESSON MODEL 1066

**SPECIFICATIONS**
**Type:** semi-automatic pistol
**Origin:** Smith & Wesson,
Springfield, Massachusetts
**Caliber:** 9mm Parabellum
**Barrel Length:** 4in

The Model 1006 is a full-size weapon chambered for the 10mm cartridge and with a nine-round magazine. Both frame and slide were made of stainless steel. This was complemented by the slightly smaller Model 1066, seen here, which had a 4.25in barrel, plastic grips and white-dot sights.

# SMITH & WESSON MODEL 4506

The Smith & Wesson Model 4506 was a new version of the .45 ACP pistol with a 5in barrel and an eight-round magazine. The first example shown here is the original Model 4506.

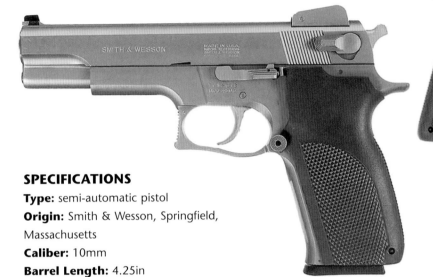

## SPECIFICATIONS
**Type:** semi-automatic pistol
**Origin:** Smith & Wesson, Springfield, Massachusetts
**Caliber:** 10mm
**Barrel Length:** 4.25in

We also show the slightly different Model 4506-1. Both have stainless steel finish, white-dot sights and black Delrin grips.

# SMITH & WESSON MODEL 745

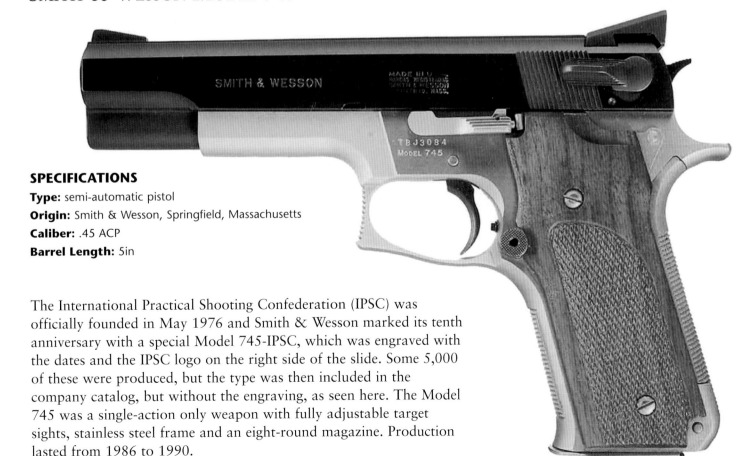

## SPECIFICATIONS
**Type:** semi-automatic pistol
**Origin:** Smith & Wesson, Springfield, Massachusetts
**Caliber:** .45 ACP
**Barrel Length:** 5in

The International Practical Shooting Confederation (IPSC) was officially founded in May 1976 and Smith & Wesson marked its tenth anniversary with a special Model 745-IPSC, which was engraved with the dates and the IPSC logo on the right side of the slide. Some 5,000 of these were produced, but the type was then included in the company catalog, but without the engraving, as seen here. The Model 745 was a single-action only weapon with fully adjustable target sights, stainless steel frame and an eight-round magazine. Production lasted from 1986 to 1990.

## STANDARD ARMS OF NEVADA MODEL SA-9

**SPECIFICATIONS**

**Type:** semi-automatic pistol

**Origin:** Standard Arms of Nevada, Reno, Nevada

**Caliber:** 9mm

**Barrel Length:** 3in

This tiny pistol has an overall length of 6in and weighs 16oz. It is manufactured by Standard Arms of Nevada, which was established in 1999 by James Waldof, the former owner of Lorcin Engineering Inc.

## STEVENS NUMBER 41 TIP-UP PISTOL

**SPECIFICATIONS**

**Type:** single-shot pocket pistol

**Origin:** J Stevens Arms Co., Chicopee Falls, Massachusetts

**Caliber:** .22

**Barrel Length:** 6in

From 1864 onwards, Stevens produced a series of vest-pocket pistols and deringers, leading up to this Number 41, of which some 90,000 were manufactured between 1896 and 1916. There were several models, chambered for either .22 or .30 Short and with either 3.5in or, as seen here, 6in barrels. It was described in the company catalogue as a "pocket pistol" but in this 6in version, at least, that seems to be something of an over-statement.

## STEVENS NO 10 TARGET PISTOL

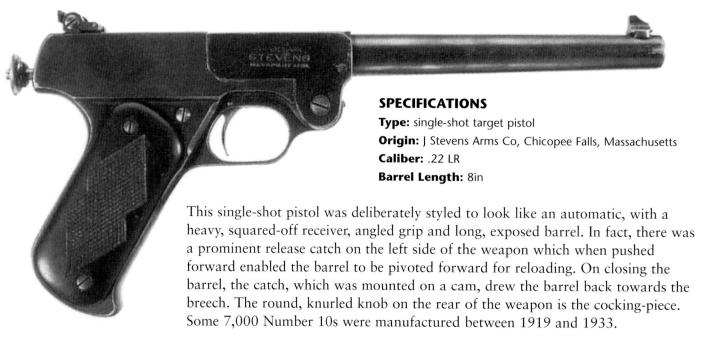

**SPECIFICATIONS**

**Type:** single-shot target pistol

**Origin:** J Stevens Arms Co, Chicopee Falls, Massachusetts

**Caliber:** .22 LR

**Barrel Length:** 8in

This single-shot pistol was deliberately styled to look like an automatic, with a heavy, squared-off receiver, angled grip and long, exposed barrel. In fact, there was a prominent release catch on the left side of the weapon which when pushed forward enabled the barrel to be pivoted forward for reloading. On closing the barrel, the catch, which was mounted on a cam, drew the barrel back towards the breech. The round, knurled knob on the rear of the weapon is the cocking-piece. Some 7,000 Number 10s were manufactured between 1919 and 1933.

## WHEELER DOUBLE DERINGERS

**SPECIFICATIONS**

**Type:** double-barrel deringer-type pistols
**Origin:** American Arms Co, Boston, Massachusetts
**Caliber:** see text
**Barrel Length:** see text

The American Arms Co was established in the early 1870s to produce revolvers, pistols and shotguns and continued until 1901 when its machinery was bought by Marlin Fire Arms and transferred to their plant at New London, Connecticut. Among the weapons it produced were a number of deringers, whose design had been patented by Henry F. Wheeler. This design featured two vertically mounted barrels, and weapons were produced in the following combinations: .22 + .32, 3in barrels; .32 + .32, 3in barrels; .32 + .32, 2.6in barrels; .38 + .38, 2.6in barrels; .41 + .41, 2.6in barrels. The pistols had a nickel-plated brass frame, spur trigger and blued barrels, which were rotated manually. Some 2–3,000 were manufactured between 1866 and 1878. The two examples shown here are: .32 + .32 with 2.6in barrels and .32 +.32 with 3in barrels.

## WILDEY SURVIVOR

**SPECIFICATIONS**

**Type:** double-action automatic pistol
**Origin:** Wildey Inc, Brookfield, Connecticut
**Caliber:** .45 Win Mag
**Barrel Length:** 5in

This range of pistols was developed by W.J. "Wildey" Moore and has an adjustable gas system, which can be easily configured for differing loads. Two rounds – the .45 Winchester Magnum and 9mm Winchester Magnum – were developed specially for these weapons, although only the former is still available. The Wildey pistol is gas-operated and has a three-lug rotating bolt. The patented gas system is adjusted using the ring ahead of the piston and users report that, despite its power, the pistol is comfortable to use. The version shown here is chambered for the .45 Winchester Magnum round, has a 5in barrel, and has a stainless steel finish.

# AUSTRIA

## GASSER MODEL 1870 AUSTRO-HUNGARIAN ARMY SERVICE REVOLVER

Leopold Gasser owned two factories which produced vast numbers of handguns for both the Imperial Austro-Hungarian Army and the civilian market. The company continued in family ownership until the early 20th century when it became Rast & Gasser. Gasser's first major success was the Model 1870, seen here, which was adopted as the standard cavalry weapon of the Imperial Austro-Hungarian Army. This had an "open frame" which meant that there was no bridge across the top of the cylinder and had the barrel attached to the frame by a heavy screw beneath the cylinder arbor, as is shown very clearly in the inset. The inset also shows the company's crest – an apple pierced by an arrow.

**SPECIFICATIONS**
**Type:** six-round, double-action, revolver
**Origin:** Leopold Gasser, Ottakring, Austria
**Caliber:** 11mm
**Barrel Length:** 7.4in

## RAST & GASSER MODEL 1898 SERVICE REVOLVER

In the late 19th century Gasser produced a series of six-shot revolvers, chambered for the 11mm cartridge, which are known collectively as "Montenegrin Gassers." The true situation is, however, clouded by the fact that so-called "Montenegrin Gasser-style" revolvers were also produced in Belgium, as well as by smaller Austrian gunsmiths. There was also an authentic Gasser-Kropatschek Officers' Model in which the caliber was reduced to 9mm, resulting in a slightly smaller and lighter weapon. The final model known to have carried the company's name was the Rast & Gasser Model 1898 Service Revolver, seen here, which was also adopted by the Austro-Hungarian Army. This had eight cylinders for the 8mm cartridge and this time the barrel group was secured to the frame by both a screw at the foot and a strap across the top of the cylinder. This weapon was very well made and proved to be reliable, but as can be seen in the illustration, the grip was at right angles to the barrel making it uncomfortable to aim properly.

**SPECIFICATIONS**
**Type:** eight-round, double-action revolver
**Origin:** Leopold Gasser, Ottakring, Austria
**Caliber:** 8mm
**Barrel Length:** 4.5in

# BELGIUM

## FRANCOTTE PINFIRE REVOLVER

Auguste Francotte established his firm of Liege gunsmiths in 1805, and the company is still in existence today, making a range of superb sporting and hunting weapons. This well made pinfire revolver was made to the Lefacheaux pattern, and actually carries Lefacheaux patent markings as well as the maker's marks.

### SPECIFICATIONS
**Type:** six-round, double-action, revolver
**Origin:** Leopold Gasser, Ottakring, Austria
**Caliber:** 11mm
**Barrel Length:** 7.4in

## FRANCOTTE ADAMS PERCUSSION

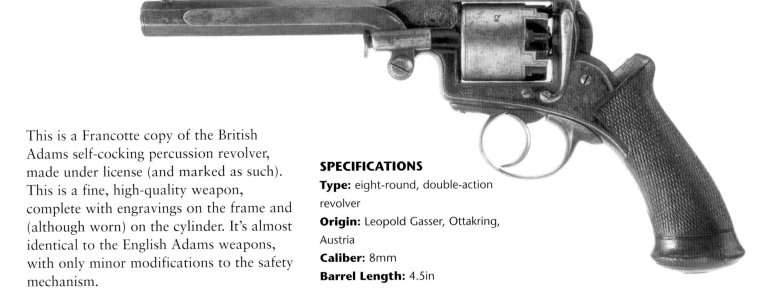

This is a Francotte copy of the British Adams self-cocking percussion revolver, made under license (and marked as such). This is a fine, high-quality weapon, complete with engravings on the frame and (although worn) on the cylinder. It's almost identical to the English Adams weapons, with only minor modifications to the safety mechanism.

### SPECIFICATIONS
**Type:** eight-round, double-action revolver
**Origin:** Leopold Gasser, Ottakring, Austria
**Caliber:** 8mm
**Barrel Length:** 4.5in

## BELGIAN VELO-DOG REVOLVERS

"Velo-Dog" was a generic term for a type of small, cheap pocket revolver, which became fashionable in the late 19th century; they were produced in vast numbers in western Europe, particularly in Belgium and Spain. The name resulted from combining the term "velocipede" (the then current name for a bicycle) and "dog", although this seems to be an odd mixture of French and English terms. Early cyclists seem to have been greatly troubled by fierce dogs and these little revolvers were designed to deter them through the use of rounds filled with salt, pepper or dust, or to wound them using light bullets.

All five models shown here are chambered for the specially-developed 5.5mm Velo-Dog round.

Another clearly identified revolver, this time marked as "Rousseaux."

This Le Page is well made and clearly-marked with the maker's name.

Finally, this one has inferior finish and no name, but is probably of Belgian origin.

The revolver is well-finished and heavily engraved but bears no maker's marks, although it does have Belgian proof marks.

The fourth Velo-Dog revolver has no marks at all other than a maker's serial "15," although from its design it is clearly of Belgian origin.

# FRANCE

## DEVISME PERCUSSION REVOLVER

### SPECIFICATIONS

**Type:** five-round
double-action revolver
**Origin:** F.P. Devisme,
Paris, France
**Caliber:** .30
**Barrel Length:** 4.25in

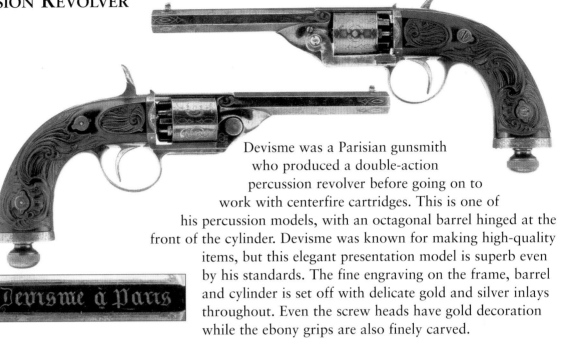

Devisme was a Parisian gunsmith
who produced a double-action
percussion revolver before going on to
work with centerfire cartridges. This is one of
his percussion models, with an octagonal barrel hinged at the
front of the cylinder. Devisme was known for making high-quality
items, but this elegant presentation model is superb even
by his standards. The fine engraving on the frame, barrel
and cylinder is set off with delicate gold and silver inlays
throughout. Even the screw heads have gold decoration
while the ebony grips are also finely carved.

## LEFAUCHEUX POCKET REVOLVER

### SPECIFICATIONS

**Type:** pinfire pocket revolver.
**Origin:** F. Lefaucheux, Paris, France
**Caliber:** .30 pinfire
**Barrel Length:** 3.4in

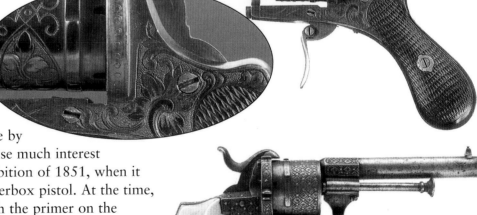

The pinfire cartridge was
invented by a Frenchman, Casimir
Lefaucheux, in 1828 and was in
fairly wide use in Continental Europe by
about 1840, although it did not arouse much interest
in Great Britain until the Great Exhibition of 1851, when it
appeared in conjunction with a pepperbox pistol. At the time,
many felt that centerfire designs, with the primer on the
bottom of the cartridge case, weakened the case and risked it
bursting to the rear when fired. Pinfire cartridges had their
primer embedded within the cartridge, and a metal pin
sticking sideways out of the case. As can be seen from
this model, the hammer comes down on the edge of the
cylinder, striking the pin and driving it into the
cartridge, igniting the primer.

Casimir's son, Eugene, designed a series of revolvers which
made use of the pinfire principle and was soon producing his
designs for many European armies and navies; many were also
exported to the United States and used during the Civil War.
Many other gunsmiths were given licenses to produce weapons
using pinfire ammunition (*see the Francotte pinfire above*).

The second picture shows a superbly-
engraved presentation model with ivory
grips. The pinfire system didn't last long, as
the cartridges themselves were relatively
fragile, they had to be loaded into the
cylinder at exactly the correct angle, and
centerfire cartridges proved themselves to
reliable, effective and easier to use.

## LEFAUCHEUX PINFIRE REVOLVER

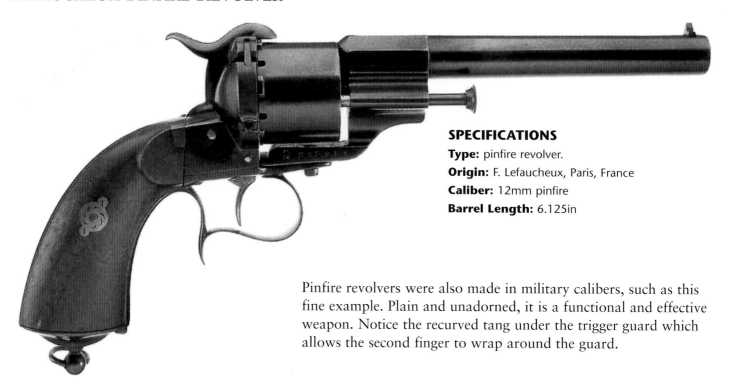

### SPECIFICATIONS

**Type:** pinfire revolver.
**Origin:** F. Lefaucheux, Paris, France
**Caliber:** 12mm pinfire
**Barrel Length:** 6.125in

Pinfire revolvers were also made in military calibers, such as this fine example. Plain and unadorned, it is a functional and effective weapon. Notice the recurved tang under the trigger guard which allows the second finger to wrap around the guard.

## LEFAUCHEUX 20-ROUND PINFIRE REVOLVER

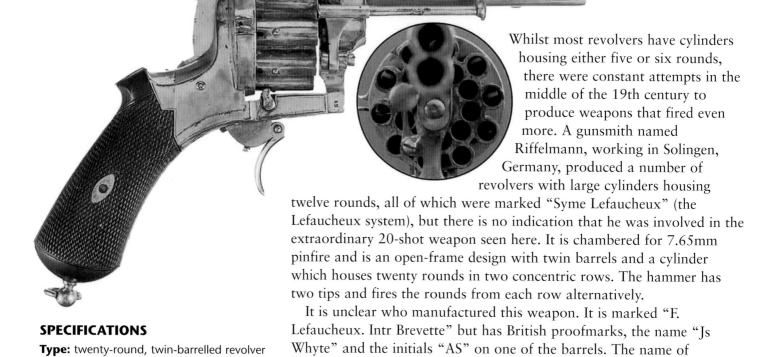

Whilst most revolvers have cylinders housing either five or six rounds, there were constant attempts in the middle of the 19th century to produce weapons that fired even more. A gunsmith named Riffelmann, working in Solingen, Germany, produced a number of revolvers with large cylinders housing twelve rounds, all of which were marked "Syme Lefaucheux" (the Lefaucheux system), but there is no indication that he was involved in the extraordinary 20-shot weapon seen here. It is chambered for 7.65mm pinfire and is an open-frame design with twin barrels and a cylinder which houses twenty rounds in two concentric rows. The hammer has two tips and fires the rounds from each row alternatively.

It is unclear who manufactured this weapon. It is marked "F. Lefaucheux. Intr Brevette" but has British proofmarks, the name "Js Whyte" and the initials "AS" on one of the barrels. The name of Lefaucheux may simply be an acknowledgement of his ownership of the patent for the pinfire round, but the name of Whyte and the initials AS cannot be traced.

### SPECIFICATIONS

**Type:** twenty-round, twin-barrelled revolver
**Origin:** F. Lefaucheux, Paris, France
**Caliber:** 7.65mm pinfire
**Barrel Length:** 4.75in

## MODELE D'ORDONNANCE 1892 (LEBEL)

### SPECIFICATIONS

**Type:** six-round, service revolver.
**Origin:** Manufacture Nationale d'Armes de St Etienne, St Etienne, France
**Caliber:** 8mm
**Barrel Length:** 4.4in

[A number of efforts were made to improve the Model 1873 and Model 1874 revolvers, but although a few prototypes were produced in the 1880s they offered little improvement. Instead, a totally new weapon was designed, chambered for a new 8mm smokeless round, and known variously as the Modele 1892, Modele d'Ordonnance, or the 8mm Lebel. This six-shot weapon had a solid frame and a cylinder which swung sideways for reloading, with collective ejection by means of a hand-operated lever. It should be noted that the lever to the immediate rear of the cylinder is not a loading gate, as on the Models 1873 and 1874, but is actually the cylinder release lever.

## PERRIN CENTERFIRE REVOLVER

### SPECIFICATION

**Type:** six-round, centerfire cartridge revolver.
**Origin:** L. Perrin et cie, Paris, France
**Caliber:** 11mm
**Barrel Length:** 6in

In 1859, Perrin & Delmas patented the first European centerfire revolver and produced a successful range of weapons. The large European-style centre-fire revolver shown here was one of the many foreign weapons that found their way into the hands of American fighting men during the Civil War. Some 550 or so were purchased by the Federal Government, but it is not known if this was one of them, or one bought privately. A heavy and powerful enough weapon, it must have been difficult for an American owner to find a reliable supply of the 11mm centerfire cartridges it used.

# GERMANY

## REICHSREVOLVER MODEL 1879

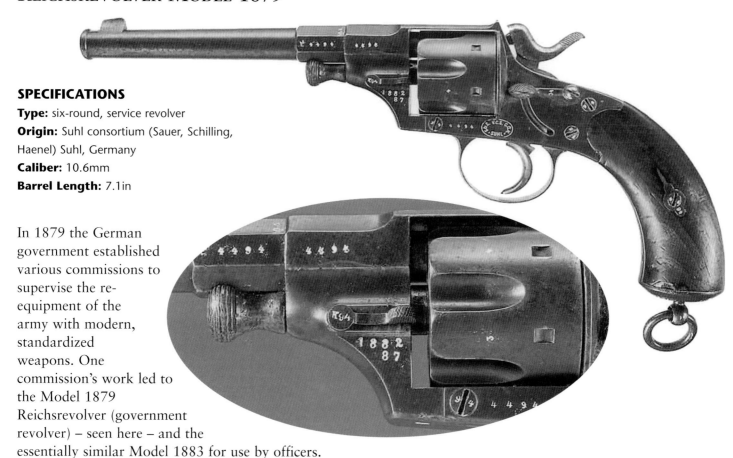

**SPECIFICATIONS**

**Type:** six-round, service revolver
**Origin:** Suhl consortium (Sauer, Schilling, Haenel) Suhl, Germany
**Caliber:** 10.6mm
**Barrel Length:** 7.1in

In 1879 the German government established various commissions to supervise the re-equipment of the army with modern, standardized weapons. One commission's work led to the Model 1879 Reichsrevolver (government revolver) – seen here – and the essentially similar Model 1883 for use by officers.

The Model 1879 was a solid-frame revolver with a six-round, fluted cylinder and was manufactured by various gunsmiths under contract to the government. This particular weapon was produced by a consortium of three firms, C.G. Haenel, J.P. Sauer & Sohn, and V. Chr. Schilling, all based at Suhl, one of the centers of German gunmaking.

## REICHSREVOLVER MODEL 1883 (DREYSE)

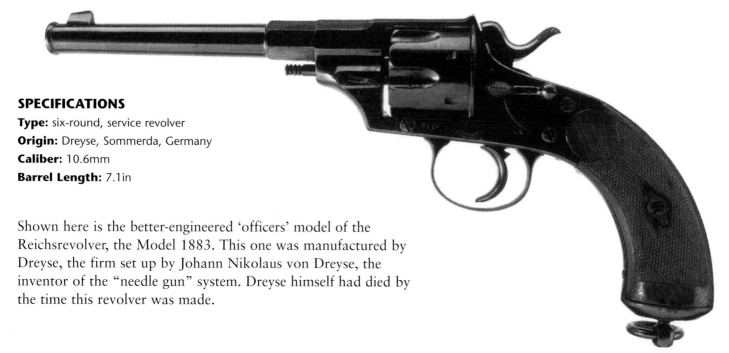

**SPECIFICATIONS**

**Type:** six-round, service revolver
**Origin:** Dreyse, Sommerda, Germany
**Caliber:** 10.6mm
**Barrel Length:** 7.1in

Shown here is the better-engineered 'officers' model of the Reichsrevolver, the Model 1883. This one was manufactured by Dreyse, the firm set up by Johann Nikolaus von Dreyse, the inventor of the "needle gun" system. Dreyse himself had died by the time this revolver was made.

## KORTH REVOLVERS

Korth Vertriebs-GmbH was established in Ratzeburg, in the state of Holstein in northern Germany in 1954 and started to produce revolvers to its own design in the 1970s. There is, in effect, just one design – a conventional solid-frame, double-action weapon with a sideways swinging fluted cylinder and a cylinder-release catch mounted, most unusually, alongside the hammer. All have a double action trigger with three adjustable let-off regulating points. The two models are offered with a variety of calibers, interchangeable barrels and cylinders, and various patterns of grip, but all are made to a very high standard of engineering and finish.

Here is a Combat model chambered for .22LR and with a 3 in raised (but unvented) rib. The frame, barrel and cylinder are finished in matte blue, while the hammer, release catch and trigger are gold-plated. The grips are of walnut.

Four examples of combat and sports are shown here.

Here is a Combat model chambered for .22LR and with a 3 in raised (but unvented) rib. The frame, barrel and cylinder are finished in matte blue, while the hammer, release catch and trigger are gold-plated. The grips are of walnut.

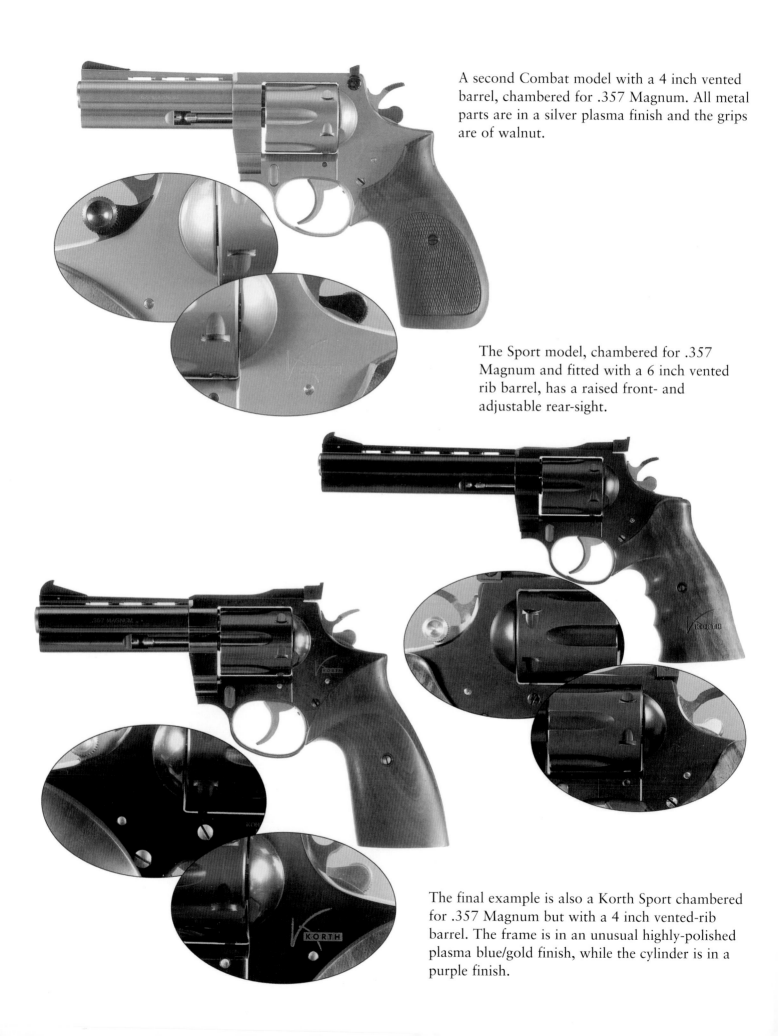

A second Combat model with a 4 inch vented barrel, chambered for .357 Magnum. All metal parts are in a silver plasma finish and the grips are of walnut.

The Sport model, chambered for .357 Magnum and fitted with a 6 inch vented rib barrel, has a raised front- and adjustable rear-sight.

The final example is also a Korth Sport chambered for .357 Magnum but with a 4 inch vented-rib barrel. The frame is in an unusual highly-polished plasma blue/gold finish, while the cylinder is in a purple finish.

# ITALY

## MATEBA MODEL 6 SEMI-AUTOMATIC REVOLVER

It does not matter how well-established some aspects of design may be, there will always be somebody who will challenge them – sometimes even stand them completely on their head, as, quite literally, has been done in this case. Thus, in the Mateba Model 6, the barrel aligns with the bottom, rather than the top, cylinder; it is the front sight that is adjustable, while the rear sight is fixed; and although it has a revolving cylinder, it is, in fact, a semi-automatic weapon.

Mateba's original weapon, the MTR-8, was also a revolver, but with the cylinder in front of, rather than above, the trigger, and was made in a variety of calibers, including .22LR, for which a 20-round cylinder was available. In the Model 6 the cylinder returns to its customary place above the trigger, but, in order to minimize the recoil forces, the barrel is placed at the bottom rather than the top of the cylinder. The operation of the weapon is comparatively simple. The first pressure on the trigger cocks the hammer and then releases it, firing the first round. The upper part of the frame then recoils, recocks the hammer and rotates the cylinder, until it hits the backplate, whereupon it is pushed forward by the return spring. It comes to rest in the forward position and the firer then pulls the trigger again, but this time requiring only a light pressure. The Model 6 is considered to be a very accurate weapon and continues in production.

**SPECIFICATIONS**
**Type:** target revolver
**Origin:** Macchini Termo Ballistiche (Mateba), Pavia, Italy.
**Caliber:** .44 Remington
**Barrel Length:** 5in

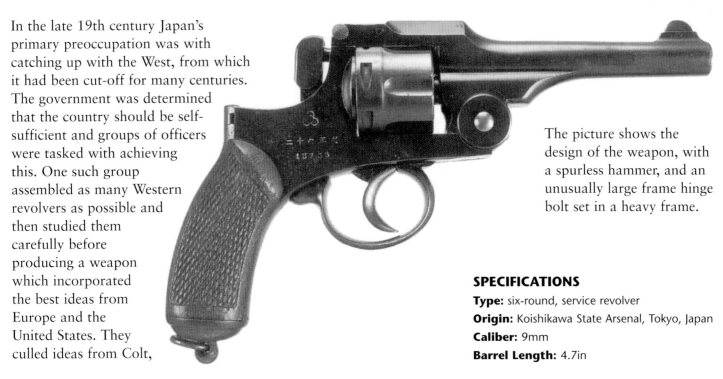

# JAPAN

## NAMBU MEIJI 26TH YEAR SERVICE REVOLVER

In the late 19th century Japan's primary preoccupation was with catching up with the West, from which it had been cut-off for many centuries. The government was determined that the country should be self-sufficient and groups of officers were tasked with achieving this. One such group assembled as many Western revolvers as possible and then studied them carefully before producing a weapon which incorporated the best ideas from Europe and the United States. They culled ideas from Colt,

The picture shows the design of the weapon, with a spurless hammer, and an unusually large frame hinge bolt set in a heavy frame.

**SPECIFICATIONS**
**Type:** six-round, service revolver
**Origin:** Koishikawa State Arsenal, Tokyo, Japan
**Caliber:** 9mm
**Barrel Length:** 4.7in

# RUSSIA/USSR

## NAGANT M1895 GAS-SEAL REVOLVER

The design and production rights to the Nagant patented gas-seal revolver (*see Belgium above*) were purchased by the Imperial Russian government in 1895 and deliveries started from the Tula Arsenal in 1899. Production continued following the Revolution and the establishment of the USSR in 1918, and throughout World War Two, ending only in 1945. The stopping power of the high-velocity 7.62mm bullet was not particularly great, but the cylinder housed seven rounds and the weapon was extremely reliable, making it very popular with its users.

**SPECIFICATIONS**

**Type:** seven-round, service revolver
**Origin:** Tula State Arsenal, Russia/USSR.
**Caliber:** 7.62mm
**Barrel Length:** 4.3in

The pictures illustrate the variety of markings applied during this weapon's long production run. The first is marked as having been produced at Tula in 1915 for the Imperial Russian Army.

This later one is marked "CCCP" (Cyrillic script for USSR) and is dated 1928.

# SWITZERLAND

## ORDNANCE REVOLVER MODEL 1882

In 1880 the Swiss Army was armed with revolvers chambered for the 10.4mm round and which resulted in a heavy weapon. So the director of the Bern weapons factory, Lieutenant-Colonel Rudolf Schmidt, designed a new 7.5 x 23R round and a revolver to fit it. Both were accepted and the weapon was placed in production as the Ordnance Revolver Model 1882.

This was a conventional, double-action weapon with a hexagonal barrel and a six-round, fluted cylinder. The weapon remained in production for many years and was succeeded in 1929 by a slightly refined version, the Model 1888/29, of which some 18,000 were produced. Three examples are shown here, their identity being clarified by their serial numbers.

**SPECIFICATIONS**
**Type:** six-round double-action service revolver
**Origin:** Eidgenossischen Waffenfabrik, Bern, Switzerland
**Caliber:** 7.5mm
**Barrel Length:** 4.5in

Weapon serial number 4396 is an early production Model 1882 with hard rubber grips and is one of those modified to accept a shoulder stock, although, as far as is known, such stocks were never officially acquired by the Swiss Army.

Finally, the third weapon is one of the Model 1882s produced for the civilian market, identified by its serial number "P7121" where the prefix "P" stands for privat.

Weapon serial number 58915 is a Model 1882/29, one of those produced in the second production run.

# UNITED KINGDOM

## BEAUMONT-ADAMS PERCUSSION REVOLVER

Robert Adams was an English gun designer who took out a large number of patents in the middle of the 19th century, while his brother, John was responsible for marketing. Their main business activity seems to have been licensing other companies to produce and market the Adams patents. (*See the Francotte Adams in the Belgium section and the Hollis and Sheath below*). They achieved some success with a series of self-cocking percussion revolvers which could be fired only by bringing quite heavy pressure on the trigger, which made them relatively inaccurate, except at close range. This problem was overcome in 1855 when a Lieutenant Beaumont of the Royal Engineers invented a double-locking system, which allowed preliminary cocking without affecting the rate of fire. The resulting Beaumont-Adams revolvers were manufactured in two calibers, the smaller of the two, in .44in, being seen here.

**SPECIFICATIONS**
**Type:** six-round, percussion revolver
**Origin:** Adams Patent Small-Arms Co., London, England
**Caliber:** .44
**Barrel Length:** 6in

The boxed example demonstrates how percussion pistols were sold, complete with a full set of tools, a number of balls and a tin of percussion caps, all housed in a handsome box. Even though some of the tools are missing, the box has ensured that this weapon is preserved in excellent condition.

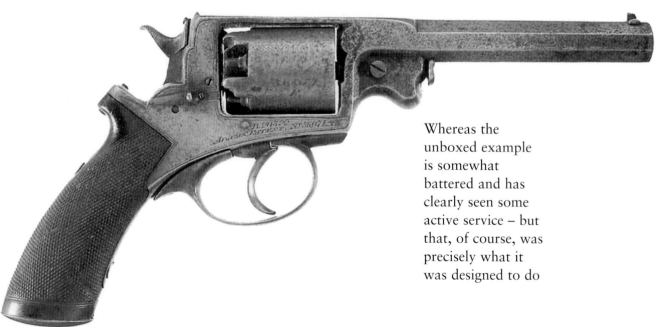

Whereas the unboxed example is somewhat battered and has clearly seen some active service – but that, of course, was precisely what it was designed to do

## ADAMS CONVERSION REVOLVER

### SPECIFICATIONS
**Type:** six-round, cartridge revolver
**Origin:** Unknown, England
**Caliber:** .50
**Barrel Length:** 3in

The basic frame and mechanism of this neat, well-made revolver is Adams, but the barrel and cylinder have been added later, presumably to convert the weapon to cartridge firing. Instead of a top strap, there is an unusual lever system, which, when operated, draws the cylinder forward to help unload the empty cartridge cases.

## BRITISH PERCUSSION REVOLVER

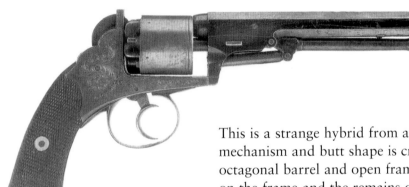

### SPECIFICATIONS
**Type:** six-round, percussion revolver
**Origin:** unknown, England
**Caliber:** .46
**Barrel Length:** 6.87in

This is a strange hybrid from an unknown British gunmaker. The self-cocking mechanism and butt shape is crudely reminiscent of the Adams style, but the octagonal barrel and open frame reflect Colt's early designs. There is engraving on the frame and the remains of engraving on the cylinder.

## ENFIELD NO 2 MARK 1/MARK 1* REVOLVER

### SPECIFICATIONS
**Type:** six-round, service revolver
**Origin:** see text
**Caliber:** .38 S&W
**Barrel Length:** 5in

Throughout most of its colonial campaigns the British Army insisted on powerful revolvers, whose heavy bullets would bring down the heaviest and most determined targets in close-quarter combat. This resulted in the use of large calibers such as .45in or even .476in, but following the experiences of World War One it was decided that a smaller caliber would suffice and .38in was eventually selected. This still had effective stopping power, but could be fired from a weapon which was smaller, lighter and easier to fire.

The revolver developed for this round was the Enfield Number 2 Mark 1 (No 2 Mk 1), in essence, a smaller version of the old Webley & Scott Mk VI, which began to reach troops in 1932 and was produced in very large numbers.

Shown opposite, below, the standard issue revolver had an octagonal barrel with a screwed-in foresight blade, while the rear sight was integrated with the barrel-release catch. The hammer had a prominent spur and the fluted cylinder housed six rounds.

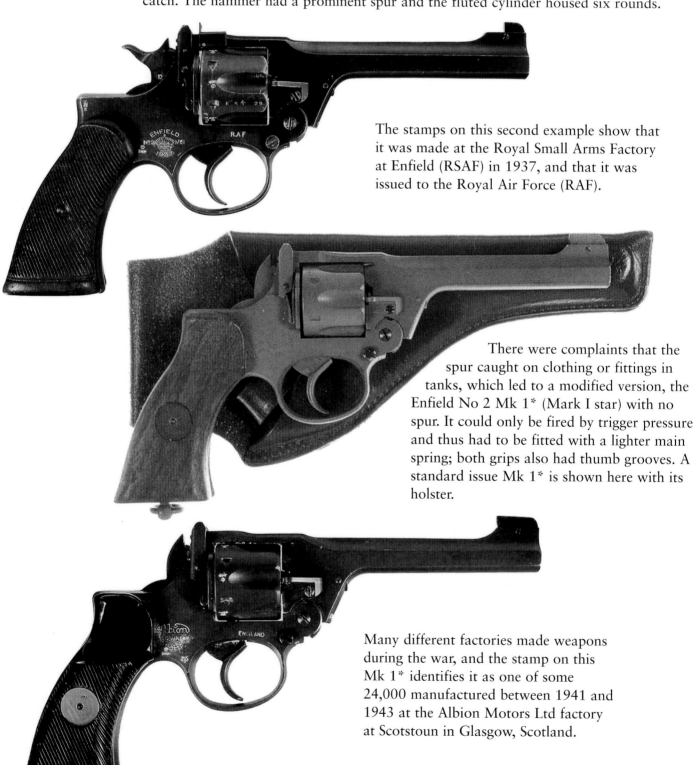

The stamps on this second example show that it was made at the Royal Small Arms Factory at Enfield (RSAF) in 1937, and that it was issued to the Royal Air Force (RAF).

There were complaints that the spur caught on clothing or fittings in tanks, which led to a modified version, the Enfield No 2 Mk 1* (Mark I star) with no spur. It could only be fired by trigger pressure and thus had to be fitted with a lighter main spring; both grips also had thumb grooves. A standard issue Mk 1* is shown here with its holster.

Many different factories made weapons during the war, and the stamp on this Mk 1* identifies it as one of some 24,000 manufactured between 1941 and 1943 at the Albion Motors Ltd factory at Scotstoun in Glasgow, Scotland.

## HOLLIS & SHEATH MODEL 1851 ADAMS DRAGOON

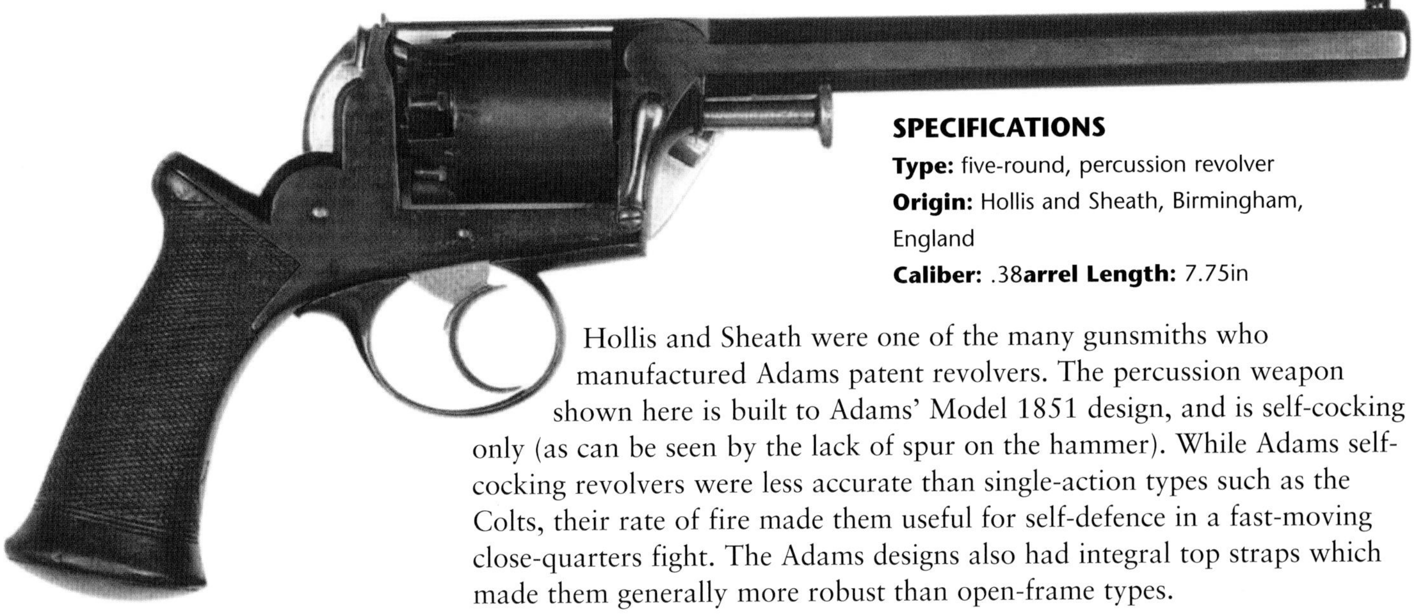

### SPECIFICATIONS

**Type:** five-round, percussion revolver
**Origin:** Hollis and Sheath, Birmingham, England
**Caliber:** .38 **arrel Length:** 7.75in

Hollis and Sheath were one of the many gunsmiths who manufactured Adams patent revolvers. The percussion weapon shown here is built to Adams' Model 1851 design, and is self-cocking only (as can be seen by the lack of spur on the hammer). While Adams self-cocking revolvers were less accurate than single-action types such as the Colts, their rate of fire made them useful for self-defence in a fast-moving close-quarters fight. The Adams designs also had integral top straps which made them generally more robust than open-frame types.

## TRANTER FIRST MODEL

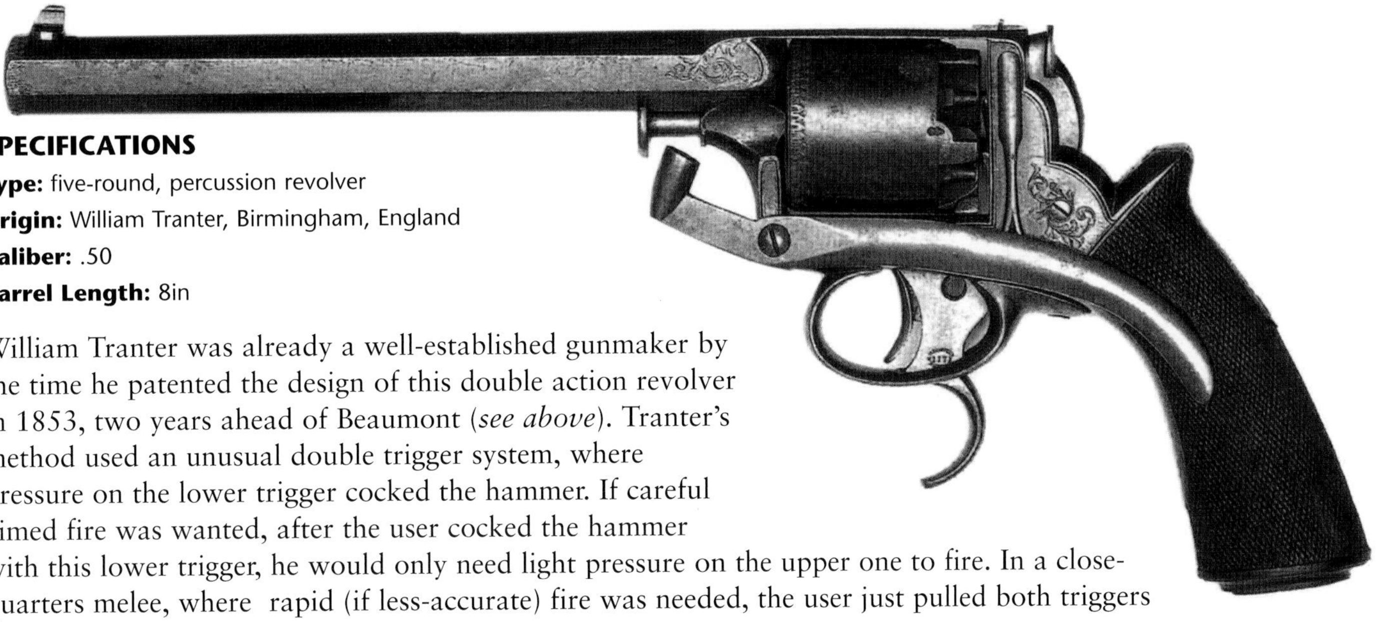

### SPECIFICATIONS

**Type:** five-round, percussion revolver
**Origin:** William Tranter, Birmingham, England
**Caliber:** .50
**Barrel Length:** 8in

William Tranter was already a well-established gunmaker by the time he patented the design of this double action revolver in 1853, two years ahead of Beaumont (*see above*). Tranter's method used an unusual double trigger system, where pressure on the lower trigger cocked the hammer. If careful aimed fire was wanted, after the user cocked the hammer with this lower trigger, he would only need light pressure on the upper one to fire. In a close-quarters melee, where rapid (if less-accurate) fire was needed, the user just pulled both triggers at once.

Tranter also incorporated a unique safety device, where if the hammer was pulled back a little, a spring-loaded blanking piece inserted itself between the hammer and the percussion nipple. When the hammer was cocked using the bottom trigger, the blanking piece was disengaged.

Early Tranter models were based on Adams (*see above*) frames, as Tranter prefered to pay the fee for a well-proven and solid design than go to the trouble of developing his own.

The one shown here has the Adams frame, and as such is marked "Adams Patent No. 20,580Y." It's also marked "W&J Rigby, Dublin", and was one of a batch delivered to that dealer for retail.

Tranter's revolvers were made in a range of sizes and calibers, but can be divided into three main classes. The First Model, pictured here, usually had a separate detachable ram, although the one shown actually has a non-standard permanently screwed ram, fitted by Rigby. The Second Models had a larger ram which normally stayed on the weapon, lying along the barrel, but which could be easily removed. The Third Models had a permanently mounted ram held on by a screw fitting.

## TRANTER FIRST MODEL POCKET REVOLVER

Tranter revolvers were also made in small pocket sizes, using the same Adams frame and double trigger mechanism of their larger military brethren. Shown here is a First Model with the detachable ram missing. It was one made for a London dealer, and carries their markings: "Wm Powell & Son".

### SPECIFICATIONS
**Type:** five-round, percussion revolver
**Origin:** William Tranter, Birmingham, England
**Caliber:** .31
**Barrel Length:** 3in

## WEBLEY LONGSPUR

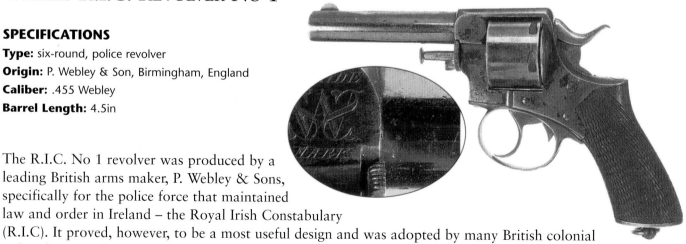

Philip and James Webley had a gunmaking business in Birmingham from the early 19th century, and they eventually became the main manufacturer of service revolvers in the United Kingdom. This early Webley was patented by James in 1853, three years before his death in 1856. Known as the Longspur, it was an open-frame design with the barrel assembly attached to the rest of the frame by the large flat-headed screw visible in front of the cylinder. There were three models of Longspur – the First Model had a detachable ram, the Second had a simple swivel ram, and the Third the more complex ram shown here. The Longspur is genrally known as a single-action revolver, but one shown here is unusual, in that it has a double-action mechanism.

### SPECIFICATIONS
**Type:** five-round, police revolver
**Origin:** P. Webley & Son, Birmingham, England
**Caliber:** .44
**Barrel Length:** 7in

## WEBLEY R.I.C. REVOLVER No 1

### SPECIFICATIONS
**Type:** six-round, police revolver
**Origin:** P. Webley & Son, Birmingham, England
**Caliber:** .455 Webley
**Barrel Length:** 4.5in

The R.I.C. No 1 revolver was produced by a leading British arms maker, P. Webley & Sons, specifically for the police force that maintained law and order in Ireland – the Royal Irish Constabulary (R.I.C). It proved, however, to be a most useful design and was adopted by many British colonial police forces and was also sold commercially, as was the example shown here, which is stamped with the name of the retailer, "S.W. Silver & Co." It is a no-nonsense design, with a short, thick-walled barrel and a smooth-sided cylinder housing six-rounds. The R.I.C. No 1 revolver was made in a number of large calibers, the example shown here being .45. Many illegal copies were also produced, particularly in Belgium and Spain.

## WEBLEY MARK II SERVICE REVOLVER

### SPECIFICATIONS

**Type:** six-round service revolver
**Origin:** P. Webley & Son, Birmingham, England
**Caliber:** .455 Webley
**Barrel Length:** 4in

The Webley Mark I entered service in 1887 and remained in wide-scale use in the British and Imperial forces for many years, being periodically upgraded. For example, as late as 1915, Mark Is were being modified in army workshops by having their 4 inch barrels replaced by 6 inch versions, and a new cylinder fitted. The production successor to the Mark I was the Mark II, first issued in 1894, which differed from the Mark I in having a new hammer with a larger spur, a revised butt and a modified recoil shield. Like the earlier version, the Mark II was chambered for the .455 Webley round and had a six-round fluted cylinder.

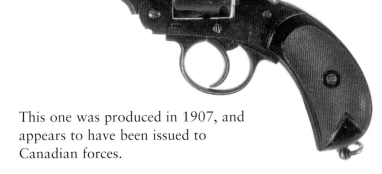

This one was produced in 1907, and appears to have been issued to Canadian forces.

This was produced in 1899. The inset shows the broad arrow stamped above the letters "WD." The broad arrow had been a mark of government property in England since the 13th century, while the initials "WD" indicated that the government body concerned was the War Department; i.e., the Army.

## WEBLEY & SCOTT MARK IV SERVICE REVOLVER

### SPECIFICATIONS

**Type:** service revolv
**Origin:** Webley & Scott, Birmingham, England
**Caliber:** .38
**Barrel Length:** 5in

Webley & Scott was the main supplier of revolvers to the British Army from the introduction of their Mark I in 1887, and the Mark IV, which was approved in 1899, continued that tradition. It was being issued as the British Army deployed to South Africa to take part in the Boer War, which resulted in the popular nickname, the "Boer War model." The Mark IV was, in reality, little different in overall design from the Mark III, but was fabricated from higher grade steel and the hammer spur was made wider for ease of handling. All Mark IVs made for military use were .445 caliber, but when the British Army switched to the Enfield No 2 Mk 1 (*see above*) in 1927, Webley & Scott produced a .38 version of the Mk IV for the civilian market. Both the weapons shown here were produced during World War One in .455 caliber but were later modified to .38.

## WEBLEY & SCOTT MARK VI SERVICE REVOLVER

The Mark VI was the last Webley & Scott revolver to be accepted for service by the British Army and was also the best. It did not differ very greatly from its predecessors except that the butt was of a more "squared-off" shape in contrast to the earlier "bird beak" designs. It was a hinged-frame design with a substantial, stirrup-type barrel catch, which also incorporated the rear sight. It did excellent work in the trenches of World War One, standing up well to the dirty and damp conditions, and was particularly useful in trench raids, with a short bayonet being developed for such close-quarter combat (although it was never officially adopted).

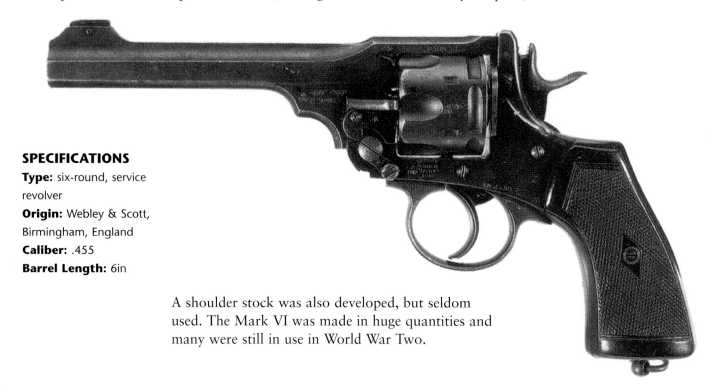

### SPECIFICATIONS

**Type:** six-round, service revolver
**Origin:** Webley & Scott, Birmingham, England
**Caliber:** .455
**Barrel Length:** 6in

A shoulder stock was also developed, but seldom used. The Mark VI was made in huge quantities and many were still in use in World War Two.

## WITTON BROS TRANTER PATENT PERCUSSION

### SPECIFICATIONS

**Type:** five-round, percussion revolver
**Origin:** Witton Bros, London, England
**Caliber:** .54
**Barrel Length:** 6in

William Tranter was an English gunsmith (based in Birmingham) who developed a fast-firing double-action mechanism to rival the Beaumont Adams, recognisable by a unique "double trigger". This is a later revolver to one of Tranter's patents, made by Witton Brothers, without the double trigger and with a spurred hammer. It has the Tranter signature lever ram alongside the barrel. This particular item was sold to the Confederate forces during the Civil War, although it never reached them. The shipment was intercepted by Northern Revenue cutter "Harriet Jane" in February 1862.

# UNITED STATES OF AMERICA

## ALLEN & WHEELOCK 2ND TYPE SIDEHAMMER REVOLVER

**SPECIFICATIONS**

**Type:** five-round, single-action, revolver

**Origin:** Allen & Wheelock, Worcester, Massachusetts

**Caliber:** see text

**Barrel Length:** see text

These revolvers had a barrel screwed into the frame, a spur trigger and a hammer mounted on the right-hand side.

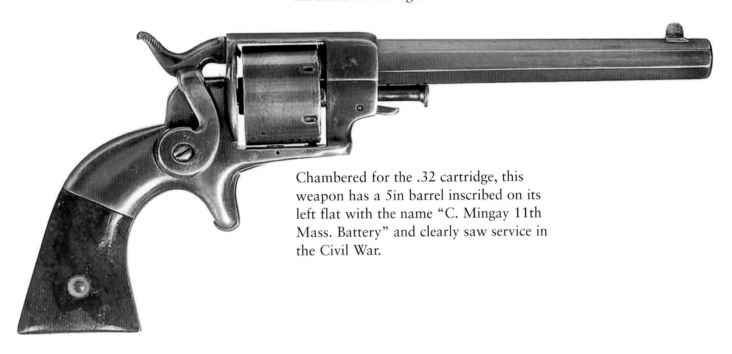

Chambered for the .32 cartridge, this weapon has a 5in barrel inscribed on its left flat with the name "C. Mingay 11th Mass. Battery" and clearly saw service in the Civil War.

This one is in .22 caliber with a 3in octagonal barrel and is fitted with ivory grips.

## ALLEN & WHEELOCK "PROVIDENCE POLICE" REVOLVER

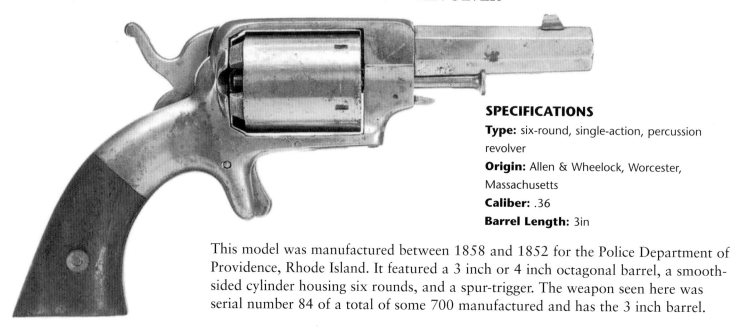

### SPECIFICATIONS

**Type:** six-round, single-action, percussion revolver

**Origin:** Allen & Wheelock, Worcester, Massachusetts

**Caliber:** .36

**Barrel Length:** 3in

This model was manufactured between 1858 and 1852 for the Police Department of Providence, Rhode Island. It featured a 3 inch or 4 inch octagonal barrel, a smooth-sided cylinder housing six rounds, and a spur-trigger. The weapon seen here was serial number 84 of a total of some 700 manufactured and has the 3 inch barrel.

## ALLEN & WHEELOCK CENTER HAMMER ARMY REVOLVER

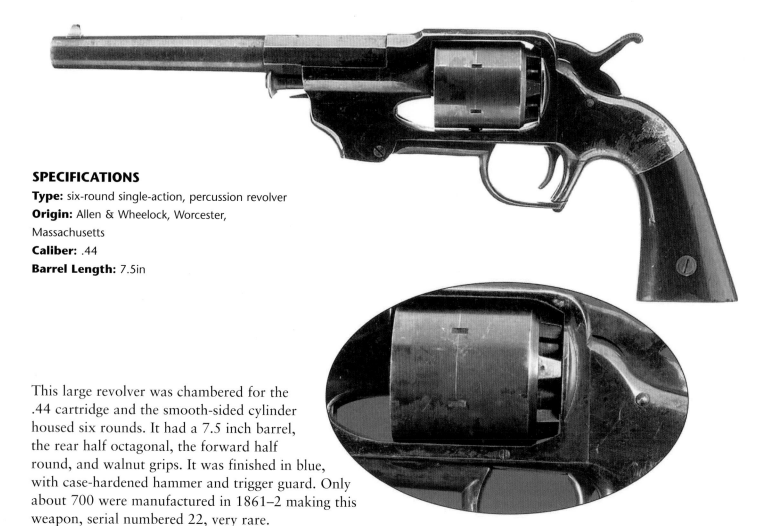

### SPECIFICATIONS

**Type:** six-round single-action, percussion revolver

**Origin:** Allen & Wheelock, Worcester, Massachusetts

**Caliber:** .44

**Barrel Length:** 7.5in

This large revolver was chambered for the .44 cartridge and the smooth-sided cylinder housed six rounds. It had a 7.5 inch barrel, the rear half octagonal, the forward half round, and walnut grips. It was finished in blue, with case-hardened hammer and trigger guard. Only about 700 were manufactured in 1861–2 making this weapon, serial numbered 22, very rare.

## BROOKLYN FIREARMS POCKET REVOLVER

**SPECIFICATIONS**

**Type:** five-round, sleeved, revolver

**Origin:** Brooklyn Fire Arms Co., Brooklyn, New York

**Caliber:** .32 rimfire

**Barrel Length:** 3in

Because Rollin White held the patent on drilled-through revolver cylinders – and sued anyone who tried to infringe it – several inventors sought alternative methods of loading. One of these was Frank Slocum whose revolver's cylinder contained five chambers, each covered by a forward-sliding sleeve. To load, the firer placed his finger-tip on the serrated section of an exposed sleeve and pushed it forward; he then placed the cartridge in the chamber, closed the sleeve and moved the cylinder through one-fifth of a turn. He then repeated the process until all troughs were full. The Slocum revolver was manufactured by the Brooklyn Fire Arms Co. and some 10,000 were completed between 1863 and 1865.

## BROOKLYN BRIDGE COLT COPY

**SPECIFICATIONS**

**Type:** five-round, percussion revolver

**Origin:** unknown

**Caliber:** .38

**Barrel Length:** 4in

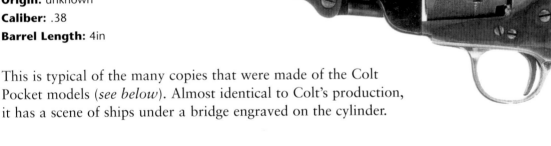

This is typical of the many copies that were made of the Colt Pocket models (*see below*). Almost identical to Colt's production, it has a scene of ships under a bridge engraved on the cylinder.

## BUTTERFIELD ARMY PERCUSSION REVOLVER

**SPECIFICATIONS**

**Type:** five-shot, single-action percussion revolver

**Origin:** Jesse Butterfield, Philadelphia, Pennsylvania

**Caliber:** .41

**Barrel Length:** 7in

Patented in 1855 by Jesse Butterfield, this design is reminiscent of the earlier 'transition' revolvers. It had a unique priming system, where a tubular magazine (accessed from in front of the trigger guard) held paper "pellet-style" percussion primers. When the single-action hammer was cocked, a pellet was slid over the cylinder nipple at the firing position.

The Butterfield was ordered in small numbers by the US Government, but the contract was cancelled after only about 600 were delivered. A few saw service on both sides during the Civil War.

# Colt's Patent Fire Arms Manufacturing Company

The name of Colt is virtually synonymous with revolvers and "six-shooters" and this world-famous company has been in the firearms business since it was founded in 1836 in Paterson, New Jersey. The main factory moved to Hartford, Connecticut in 1850 but the head office remained in New York, while the company's official name has changed several times over the many years it has been in business. As a result, the style in which the name and location have been stamped on its products have become a matter of serious study among collectors and authors. For the purposes of this book, and to avoid confusion, all Colt firearms are shown as being produced by Colt's Patent Fire Arms Manufacturing Company (Colt PFA Mfg Co) of Hartford, Connecticut, although in some cases the actual weapon may be marked differently. It is also the case that Colt has produced vast numbers of models, together with many varieties within those models, and the company's system of naming and dating is frequently bewildering, even to experts.

## Colt Dragoon 1st Model

**SPECIFICATIONS**
**Type:** single-action percussion revolver
**Origin:** Colt PFA Mfg Co., Hartford, Connecticut
**Caliber:** .44
**Barrel Length:** 7.5in

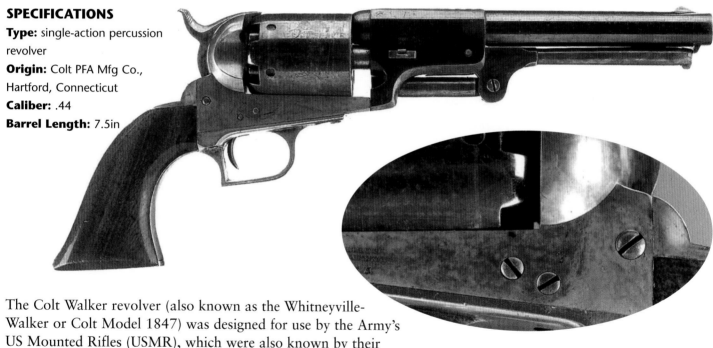

The Colt Walker revolver (also known as the Whitneyville-Walker or Colt Model 1847) was designed for use by the Army's US Mounted Rifles (USMR), which were also known by their European name of "Dragoons." The Walker was a six-shot, .44 caliber weapon with a 9 inch barrel and an overall length of 15.5 inches, which weighed no less than 4 pounds 9 ounces. This, plus problems of unreliability, led to the development of the Colt Dragoon, or Model 1848, of which some 20,000 were produced for government service between 1848 and 1860, with more made for sale on the civilian market.

All Colt Dragoons carried six .44 caliber rounds in an unfluted cylinder, many of which were engraved with battles scenes and marked "U.S. DRAGOONS." It was a single-action revolver, with a 7.5 inch barrel and an overall length of 14 inches; weight was brought down to 4 pounds. It was very robust, with the barrel keyed to the chamber axis pin and supported by a solid lug keyed to the lower frame.

The Dragoon was made in three production runs which differed only in minor details, although these differences are of immense importance to today's historians and collectors. The one shown here is the First Model, the main distinguishing mark being that the notches on the cylinder are oval-shaped. Some 7,000 First Model Dragoon revolvers were made in 1848–50, and the item shown here was one of those made for individual purchase rather than government contract.

## COLT DRAGOON 3RD MODEL

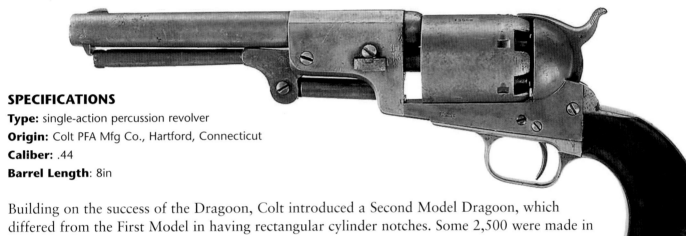

### SPECIFICATIONS

**Type:** single-action percussion revolver
**Origin:** Colt PFA Mfg Co., Hartford, Connecticut
**Caliber:** .44
**Barrel Length:** 8in

Building on the success of the Dragoon, Colt introduced a Second Model Dragoon, which differed from the First Model in having rectangular cylinder notches. Some 2,500 were made in 1850 through 1851. The most successful version of the Dragoon, however, was the Third Model, the main production version. Over 10,000 of these were completed in 1851 through 1860, and they can be identified by the round trigger guard, whereas the guards on the earlier two versions were square-backed. The Third Model also had notches for attaching a shoulder stock, although such stocks were seldom, so far as is known, issued. Some late-production Third Model Dragoons (such as the one shown here) had a slightly longer 8 inch barrel.

## COLT MODEL 1848 BABY DRAGOON

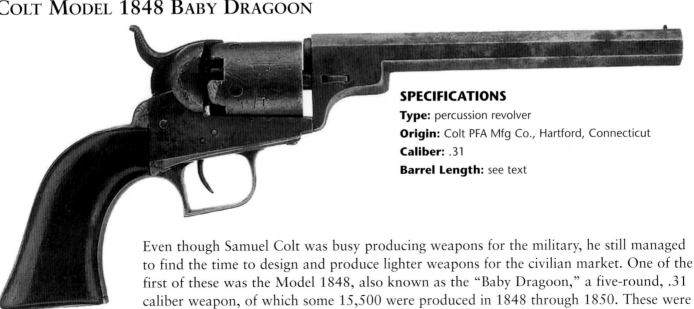

### SPECIFICATIONS

**Type:** percussion revolver
**Origin:** Colt PFA Mfg Co., Hartford, Connecticut
**Caliber:** .31
**Barrel Length:** see text

Even though Samuel Colt was busy producing weapons for the military, he still managed to find the time to design and produce lighter weapons for the civilian market. One of the first of these was the Model 1848, also known as the "Baby Dragoon," a five-round, .31 caliber weapon, of which some 15,500 were produced in 1848 through 1850. These were made with 3 inch, 4 inch, 5 inch or, as seen here, 6 inch barrels.

# COLT MODEL 1849 POCKET REVOLVER

## SPECIFICATIONS

**Type:** percussion revolver
**Origin:** Colt PFA Mfg Co., Hartford, Connecticut
**Caliber:** .31
**Barrel Length:** see text

Successor to the Baby Dragoon, the Model 1849 Pocket Revolver was produced in vast numbers, with some 325,000 being completed from 1850 through to 1873. They were made with either 3 inch, 4 inch, 5 inch or 6 inch barrels and with five-or six-shot cylinders, but there were many more minor variations, as is inevitable over such a long production run.

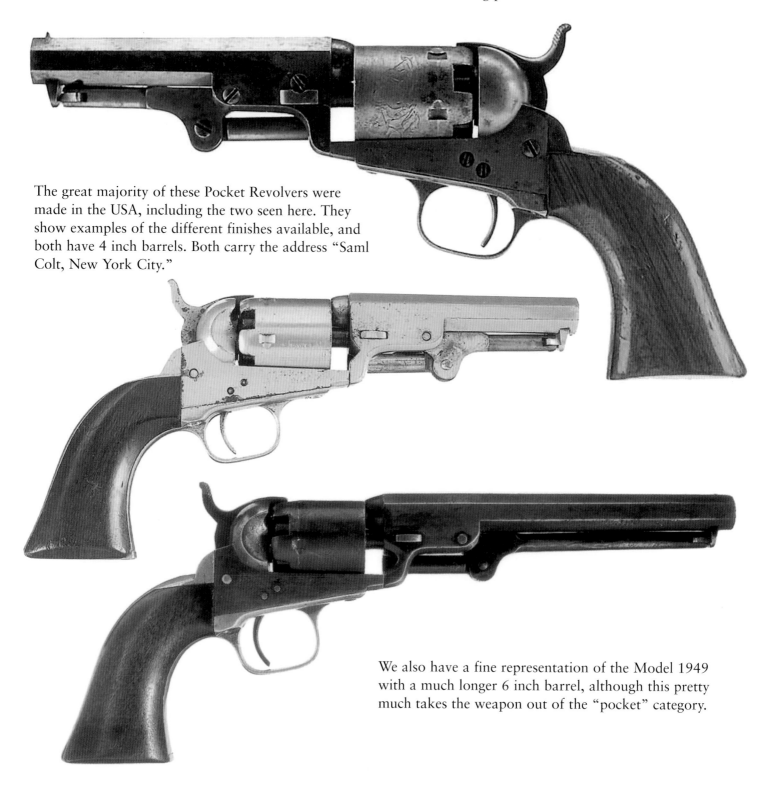

The great majority of these Pocket Revolvers were made in the USA, including the two seen here. They show examples of the different finishes available, and both have 4 inch barrels. Both carry the address "Saml Colt, New York City."

We also have a fine representation of the Model 1949 with a much longer 6 inch barrel, although this pretty much takes the weapon out of the "pocket" category.

# COLT MODEL 1849 WELLS FARGO

Colt made great efforts to sell its products on the civil market and was very happy to meet requests for special versions for companies or even for individuals. Nothing is more evocative of the Wild West than a coach driver, under attack from marauding bandits, pulling out his revolver in a despairing final attempt to protect his coach and passengers, and it is not surprising that Wells Fargo turned to Colt to meet their requirements for a small, easily-handled weapon as a back-up to a rifle or carbine. The two examples shown here are identical in every respect save one – the revolver on the left is serial number 99995 and that on the right serial number 99996 – and having been produced one after the other on the same day some 150 years ago, they turned up together in the same auction in 2004!

## SPECIFICATIONS

**Type:** percussion revolver
**Origin:** Colt PFA Mfg Co., Hartford, Connecticut
**Caliber:** .31
**Barrel Length:** 3in

# COLT NAVY MODEL 1851

The Colt Model 1851 Navy revolver was one of the most popular handguns ever made, with some 215,000 manufactured in various Colt factories in 1850 through 1873. It has a 7.5 inch octagonal barrel and a smooth sided cylinder which houses six .36 caliber rounds. In most cases, the cylinder was decorated with a scene involving a naval battle between United States' and Mexican fleets. It was this decoration that gave the type its "Navy" designation, and the term ended up being used to describe any military percussion revolver in .36 caliber. Revolvers made for .44 rounds were usually called "Army". Many fighting men, whether on land or at sea, preferred the lighter weight and smaller size of the .36, and revolvers of both sizes were used by all branches of the armed forces, whether Federal or Confederate.

A shoulder stock was available for the Model 1851, which could be attached to the butt for more accurate long-range shooting. The company applied three different forms of address on these revolvers, some being marked "Saml. Colt New York City," while others bore "Saml. Colt Hartford, Ct;" and there was a yet further variation of "Saml. Colt New York U.S. America."

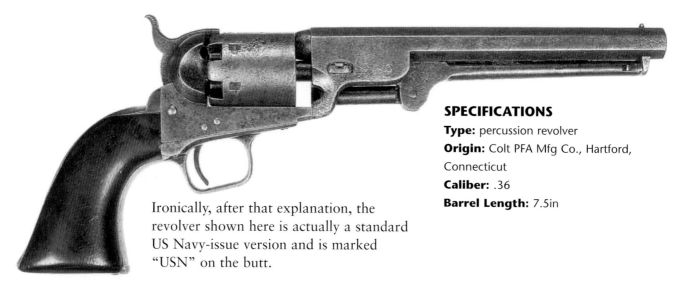

**SPECIFICATIONS**
**Type:** percussion revolver
**Origin:** Colt PFA Mfg Co., Hartford, Connecticut
**Caliber:** .36
**Barrel Length:** 7.5in

Ironically, after that explanation, the revolver shown here is actually a standard US Navy-issue version and is marked "USN" on the butt.

Like most Colt service revolvers, the Model 1851 Navy was also sold on the civilian market, a fine example being this weapon which was manufactured in 1861-2, and which was purchased for presentation to Major Hill, of the 45th Regiment, Ohio Volunteer Infantry. The insets show the higher standard of finish applied to weapons intended for sale on the open market, while the photograph actually shows Major Hill holding his saber and his revolver.

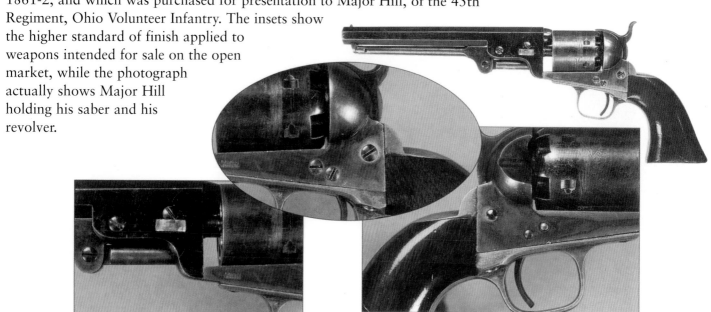

## COLT MODEL 1855 ROOT REVOLVER

This design was developed by a Colt employee, Elijah Root, and was the company's first-ever, solid-frame design, with a top-strap across the cylinder joining the barrel and frame. It was fitted with a side-mounted hammer, a stud-trigger without guard, and a single-action lock. It was produced in .28 and .31 calibers, but all have a 3.5 inch barrel. It is very popular with modern gun-collectors, who know it simply as "the Root," and who have identified no less than twelve minor variations in the actual production weapons.

**SPECIFICATIONS**

**Type:** six-shot, single-action, side-hammer revolver
**Origin:** Colt PFA Mfg Co., Hartford, Connecticut
**Caliber:** .28 or .31
**Barrel Length:** 3.5in

This picture shows a Root Model 2, complete with hand pointing to the Colt address on the barrel.

Another Root, this time a Model 7, complete with screw holding the cylinder pin in place. At some point in its history this one has been modified by one of its owners and incorporates some replacement parts.

# COLT MODEL 1860 ARMY

## SPECIFICATIONS

**Type:** percussion revolver
**Origin:** Colt PFA Mfg Co., Hartford, Connecticut
**Caliber:** .44
**Barrel Length:** 7.5in and 8in

The production figures for the Colt Model 1860 are self-explanatory – the total produced between 1860 and 1873 was 200,500, of which the US Government accepted no less than 127,156. Designed as the successor to the Third Model Dragoon (*see above*) it became one of the most widely used of all handguns during the Civil War and was equally popular in both the Union and Confederate armies. It was a percussion revolver, with rammer loading from the front of the cylinder and any reasonably experienced shooter ensured that he had a stock of paper cartridges close at hand for rapid reloading. The weapon weighed 2.74 pounds and was fitted with either a 7.5in or 8in barrel.

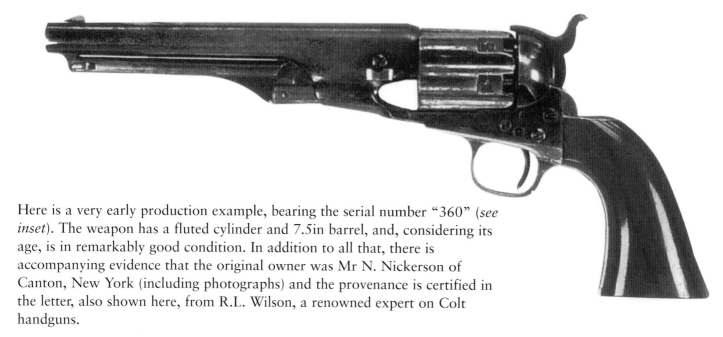

Here is a very early production example, bearing the serial number "360" (*see inset*). The weapon has a fluted cylinder and 7.5in barrel, and, considering its age, is in remarkably good condition. In addition to all that, there is accompanying evidence that the original owner was Mr N. Nickerson of Canton, New York (including photographs) and the provenance is certified in the letter, also shown here, from R.L. Wilson, a renowned expert on Colt handguns.

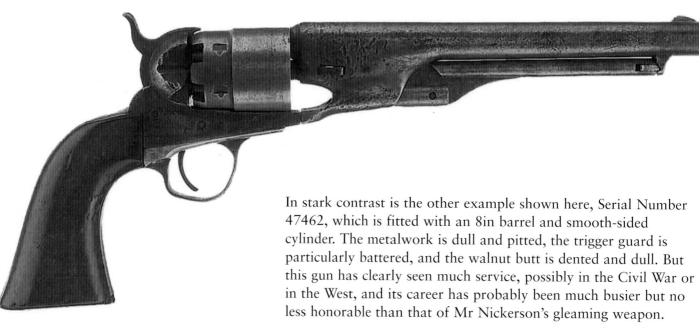

In stark contrast is the other example shown here, Serial Number 47462, which is fitted with an 8in barrel and smooth-sided cylinder. The metalwork is dull and pitted, the trigger guard is particularly battered, and the walnut butt is dented and dull. But this gun has clearly seen much service, possibly in the Civil War or in the West, and its career has probably been much busier but no less honorable than that of Mr Nickerson's gleaming weapon.

# COLT MODEL 1861 NAVY

## SPECIFICATIONS
**Type:** percussion revolver
**Origin:** Colt PFA Mfg Co., Hartford, Connecticut
**Caliber:** .36
**Barrel Length:** 7.5in

Although some 39,000 were made, there were remarkably few variations in the Model 1861 Navy revolver, which had a 7.5 inch barrel and a smooth-sided cylinder housing six shots.

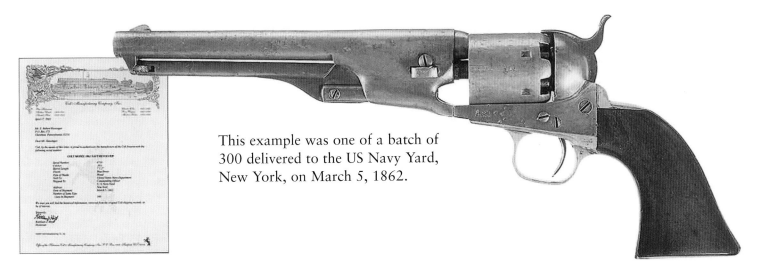

This example was one of a batch of 300 delivered to the US Navy Yard, New York, on March 5, 1862.

This Model 1861 is accompanied by what would appear to be its original black leather holster, although it has not stood the test of time so well as the gun.

## COLT MODEL 1861 NAVY CONVERSION

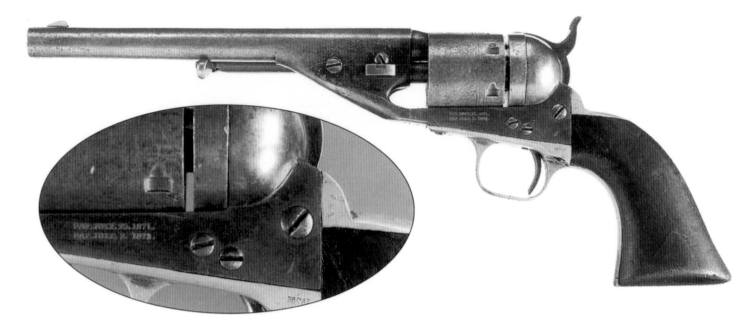

When Rollin White's patent expired, most manufacturers began converting their well-proven designs to fire cartridge ammunition. Colt produced about 2,000 new-build Model 1861s, assembled from existing parts but with a new cylinder and barrel assembly. They also modified a large batch for the US Navy and existing weapons from individual purchases. The weapon shown here has the rammer replaced with an ejection rod for removing empty cases from the cylinder. It is marked as belonging to a Lt Robert I. Netts from Celina, Ohio.

**SPECIFICATIONS**
**Type:** single-action cartridge revolver
**Origin:** Colt PFA Mfg Co., Hartford, Connecticut
**Caliber:** .38 centerfire
**Barrel Length:** 7.5in

## COLT MODEL 1862 POCKET NAVY

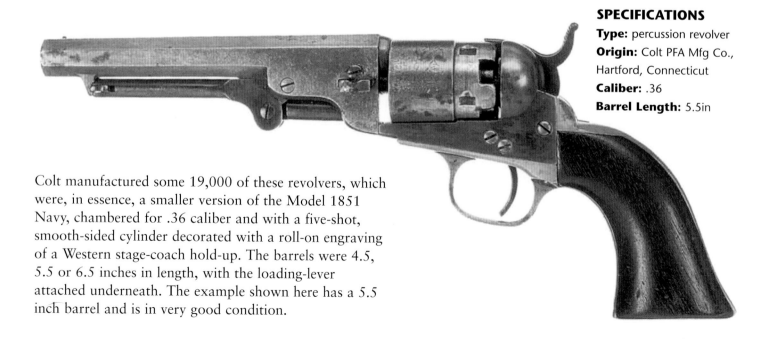

**SPECIFICATIONS**
**Type:** percussion revolver
**Origin:** Colt PFA Mfg Co., Hartford, Connecticut
**Caliber:** .36
**Barrel Length:** 5.5in

Colt manufactured some 19,000 of these revolvers, which were, in essence, a smaller version of the Model 1851 Navy, chambered for .36 caliber and with a five-shot, smooth-sided cylinder decorated with a roll-on engraving of a Western stage-coach hold-up. The barrels were 4.5, 5.5 or 6.5 inches in length, with the loading-lever attached underneath. The example shown here has a 5.5 inch barrel and is in very good condition.

# COLT MODEL 1862 POLICE

## SPECIFICATIONS

**Type:** percussion revolver
**Origin:** Colt PFA Mfg Co., Hartford, Connecticut
**Caliber:** .36
**Barrel Length:** see text

There were some 28,000 of the Model 1862 Police revolver manufactured between 1861 and 1873, but because many of these were later converted to accept the metallic-cased cartridges, unaltered originals have become fairly rare. It had a five-round fluted cylinder and barrel lengths were 3.5, 4.5, 5.5 or 6.5 inches.

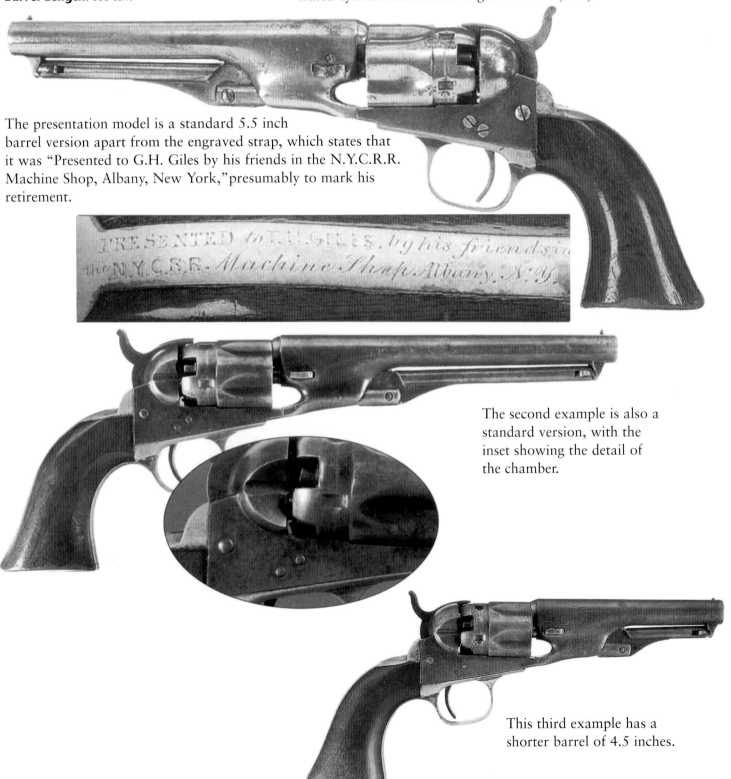

The presentation model is a standard 5.5 inch barrel version apart from the engraved strap, which states that it was "Presented to G.H. Giles by his friends in the N.Y.C.R.R. Machine Shop, Albany, New York," presumably to mark his retirement.

The second example is also a standard version, with the inset showing the detail of the chamber.

This third example has a shorter barrel of 4.5 inches.

## COLT RICHARDS CONVERSION

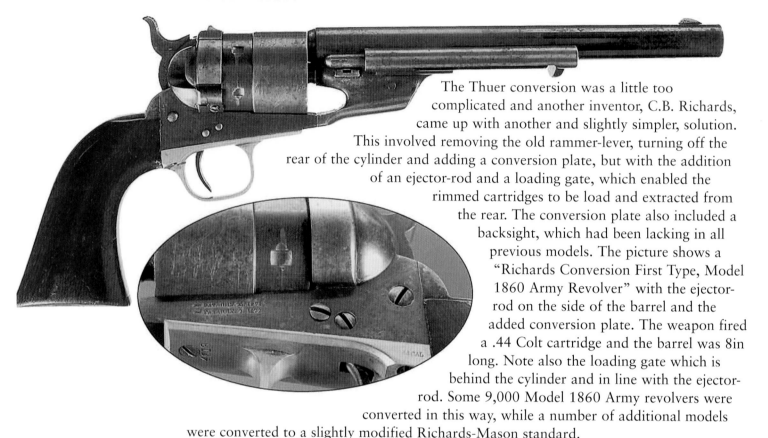

The Thuer conversion was a little too complicated and another inventor, C.B. Richards, came up with another and slightly simpler, solution. This involved removing the old rammer-lever, turning off the rear of the cylinder and adding a conversion plate, but with the addition of an ejector-rod and a loading gate, which enabled the rimmed cartridges to be load and extracted from the rear. The conversion plate also included a backsight, which had been lacking in all previous models. The picture shows a "Richards Conversion First Type, Model 1860 Army Revolver" with the ejector-rod on the side of the barrel and the added conversion plate. The weapon fired a .44 Colt cartridge and the barrel was 8in long. Note also the loading gate which is behind the cylinder and in line with the ejector-rod. Some 9,000 Model 1860 Army revolvers were converted in this way, while a number of additional models were converted to a slightly modified Richards-Mason standard.

## COLT DERINGERS

Like other US gunmakers, Colt made a series of deringers – single-shot, close-quarter weapons. The Colt National No 1 Deringer was of all-metal construction and fired a .41 rimfire round from a 2.5 inch barrel. On pressing the release catch the barrel rotated to the left and downwards, automatically ejecting the used cartridge case, whereupon the firer inserted a new round and closed the weapon, cocked and fired again.

Colt's No 2 Deringer had the same design and mechanics as the No 1, but with wooden grips.

## COLT MODEL 1871/2 OPEN TOP RIMFIRE

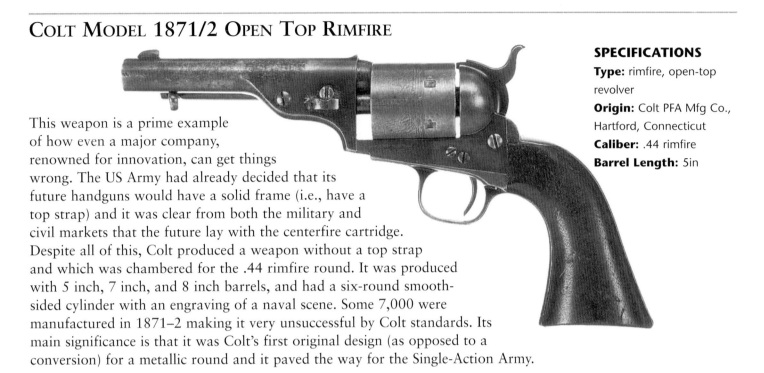

**SPECIFICATIONS**
**Type:** rimfire, open-top revolver
**Origin:** Colt PFA Mfg Co., Hartford, Connecticut
**Caliber:** .44 rimfire
**Barrel Length:** 5in

This weapon is a prime example of how even a major company, renowned for innovation, can get things wrong. The US Army had already decided that its future handguns would have a solid frame (i.e., have a top strap) and it was clear from both the military and civil markets that the future lay with the centerfire cartridge. Despite all of this, Colt produced a weapon without a top strap and which was chambered for the .44 rimfire round. It was produced with 5 inch, 7 inch, and 8 inch barrels, and had a six-round smooth-sided cylinder with an engraving of a naval scene. Some 7,000 were manufactured in 1871–2 making it very unsuccessful by Colt standards. Its main significance is that it was Colt's first original design (as opposed to a conversion) for a metallic round and it paved the way for the Single-Action Army.

## COLT MODEL 1873 SINGLE-ACTION ARMY REVOLVER

The Colt Single-Action Army revolver is one of the greatest handguns in history and was not only purchased in vast numbers for the US Army, but was also widely sold on the civilian market, particularly in the American West where it came to symbolize the cowboy era. Its story began in 1872 when the US Army conducted a rigorous competition for a new revolver; this was won by Colt, whose entry was accepted for service as the Model 1873. It was then continuously in production for 67 years (1873–1940) during which time exactly 357,859 were produced. Later it was reintroduced into production in 1956, and even today the Single-Action Army is still available from Colt, although made in very small numbers and at considerable expense.

There is nothing particularly unusual about the design and construction of the Model 1873, but the inspired combination of simplicity, ruggedness, ease of use and dependability has made for an enduring and unpretentious classic.

**SPECIFICATIONS**
**Type:** centerfire, single-action revolver
**Origin:** Colt PFA Mfg Co., Hartford, Connecticut
**Caliber:** .45 Colt (but see text)
**Barrel Length:** see text

The basic Model 1873 was produced in three barrel lengths. This revolver is an early (Serial Number 19393) .45 caliber weapon with a 7.5 inch barrel, showing the elegance of line, with bare metal finish and plain walnut grips.

# COLT MODEL 1877 DOUBLE-ACTION "LIGHTNING" AND "THUNDERER"

**SPECIFICATIONS**

**Type:** centerfire, double-action revolver

**Origin:** Colt PFA Mfg Co., Hartford, Connecticut

**Caliber:** Lightning .38 Colt; Thunderer .41 Colt

**Barrel Length:** see text

Samuel Colt was not keen on the idea of double-action revolvers, but when effective systems appeared from other manufacturers he had little choice but to follow suit. The first Colt double-action revolver was the Model 1877 which appeared in two forms, .38 caliber, known as the Lightning, and .41 caliber, known as the Thunderer; both were six-shooters, and both came in a variety of barrel lengths.

In appearance, the Model 1877 resembled a slightly scaled down Single-Action Army, except for the butt which was a bird's head shape made of hard rubber or wood. Both types proved over-complicated and were very difficult to repair; even so, some 166,000 were made between 1877 and 1909.

The Lightning was chambered for the .38 Colt and came in three barrel lengths. All are shown here: 4.5 inch (complete with ejector rod); 3.5 inch and 2.5 inch (note the cylinder arbor with a knurled head, which had to be unscrewed and the cylinder removed completely before the cartridge cases could be removed).

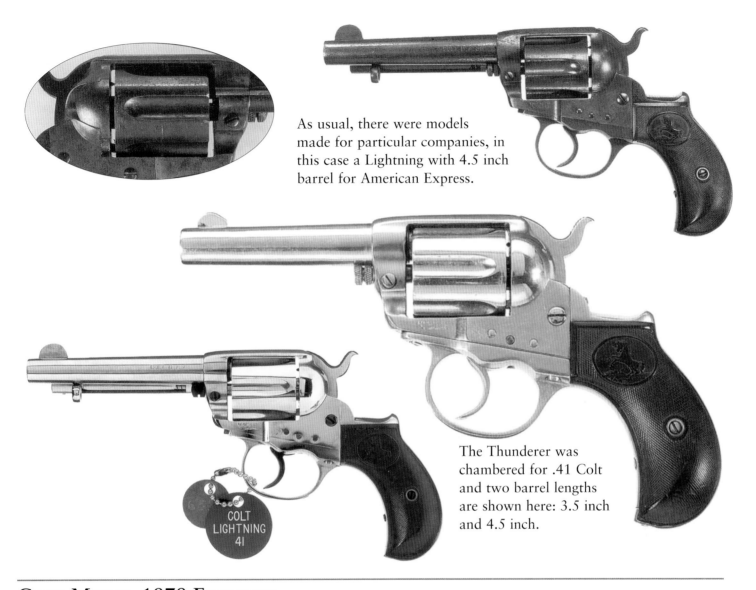

As usual, there were models made for particular companies, in this case a Lightning with 4.5 inch barrel for American Express.

COLT LIGHTNING 41

The Thunderer was chambered for .41 Colt and two barrel lengths are shown here: 3.5 inch and 4.5 inch.

## COLT MODEL 1878 FRONTIER

The Colt Model 1878 appeared shortly after the Model 1877 and was another double-action revolver but larger and more robust, with a strong frame and a removable trigger guard. The fluted cylinder held six cartridges and was not removable, being loaded via narrow gate on the right side of the frame. There were six barrel lengths (3, 3.5, 4, 4.75, 5.5, and 7.5 inches) and a wide variety of chambering from .22 to .476. A total of some 51,000 was produced in 1878 through 1905, which included some 4,000 Model 1878/1902, ordered by the US Army in 1902 for use in Alaska and the Philippines.

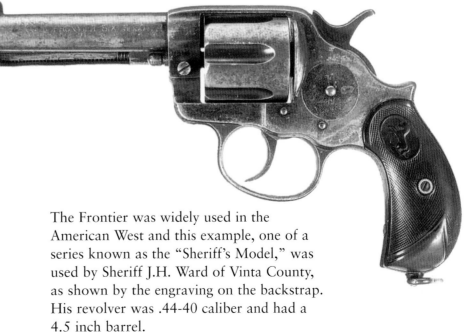

The Frontier was widely used in the American West and this example, one of a series known as the "Sheriff's Model," was used by Sheriff J.H. Ward of Vinta County, as shown by the engraving on the backstrap. His revolver was .44-40 caliber and had a 4.5 inch barrel.

## SPECIFICATIONS

**Type:** centerfire, double-action revolver
**Origin:** Colt PFA Mfg Co., Hartford, Connecticut
**Caliber:** see text
**Barrel Length:** see text

This later model was similar but chambered for .45 Colt and with a 6 inch barrel, while the trigger was longer and trigger guard larger to enable the weapon to be used while the firer was wearing gloves – hence the nickname, the "Alaskan model."

## COLT BISLEY FLAT-TOP REVOLVER

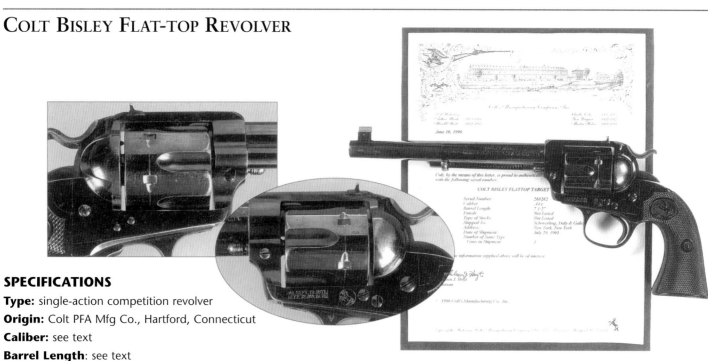

## SPECIFICATIONS

**Type:** single-action competition revolver
**Origin:** Colt PFA Mfg Co., Hartford, Connecticut
**Caliber:** see text
**Barrel Length:** see text

A major range for competitive shooting was established in England in 1860 on Wimbledon Common, but after only a few years the expansion of London southwards forced a move. A new site was found at Bisley in Surrey, which opened with the 1890 competition, and the name quickly became a byword for national and international shooting; indeed, so prestigious was the revolver competition that Colt designed a weapon specially for it. The first Colt Bisley appeared in 1894 and it continued in production until 1915, during which time some 44,350 were manufactured and although many were sold in England the great majority went to US customers.

The Colt Bisley was produced in three barrel lengths

– 4.75 inch, 5.5 inch and 7.5 inch – and in sixteen different calibers. It was a single-action revolver with a fluted, six-round cylinder and a specially-designed grip with a rather "hump-backed" profile. However, a variation was the "Flat-top" whose name derived from the flattening of the top-strap so that a competition backsight could be mounted. Some 976 of these weapons were produced between 1894 and 1913 and the example shown here with its letter of authenticity, is chambered for .44-40 caliber. Barrels in this sub-type were a standard length of 7.5 inches but the usual wide variety of chamberings were available. The insets show the exceptional workmanship and finish on such competition models.

## COLT NEW SERVICE MODEL

**SPECIFICATIONS**

**Type:** six-round, double-action, service revolver

**Origin:** Colt PFA Mfg Co., Hartford, Connecticut

**Caliber:** see text

**Barrel Length:** see text

Colt developed this revolver from the New Army and Navy Models of 1892, but with minor refinements to improve handling, reliability and strength. It was intended specifically for the military market and was first offered to the U.S. Army in 1898. Initial orders were relatively small, but eventually large numbers were produced, particularly during World War One, when the British and Canadian Armies also took many, with a total of some 355,000 manufactured during a production run lasting from 1898 to 1944. The New Service Model was originally designed to chamber .45 ACP, but was eventually produced in no less than eighteen separate calibers, ranging from .38 Special through .44 Russian to .476 Eley, while barrel lengths ranged from 2 to 7.5 inches. The empty weight of the .45 Colt version with a 5.5 inch barrel was 41 ounces. The illustration shows a New Service Model chambered for .455 Eley and with a 6 inch barrel, which was delivered to the Canadian Army during World War One.

## COLT OFFICER'S MODEL

**SPECIFICATIONS**

**Type:** six-shot, double-action revolver

**Origin:** Colt PFA Mfg Co., Hartford, Connecticut

**Caliber:** see text

**Barrel Length:** see text

The Officer's Model entered production in 1904 and was produced in a wide variety of calibers and barrel lengths, although the quality was always very high. It was used on active duty, but it was intended more for competition shooting. There were many different models, but the most numerous were:
• **Officer's Target Model.** In .32 and .38 calibers, with various barrel lengths from 4 to 7.5 inches. In production from 1904 to 1972.
• **Officer's Target Model, Rimfire version.** This was chambered for .22 rimfire and was made only with a 6.0 inch barrel. In production from 1930.
• **Officer's Model, Special.** In .22 and .38 calibers only. In production from 1949 to 1952.
• **Officer's Model Match.** A development of the Special with a change of metal used in the frame. In production from 1953 to 1972.

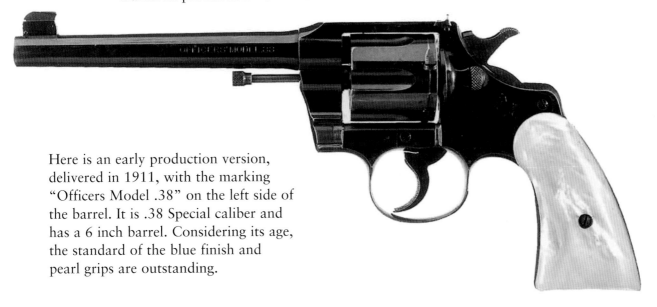

Here is an early production version, delivered in 1911, with the marking "Officers Model .38" on the left side of the barrel. It is .38 Special caliber and has a 6 inch barrel. Considering its age, the standard of the blue finish and pearl grips are outstanding.

## COLT POLICE POSITIVE

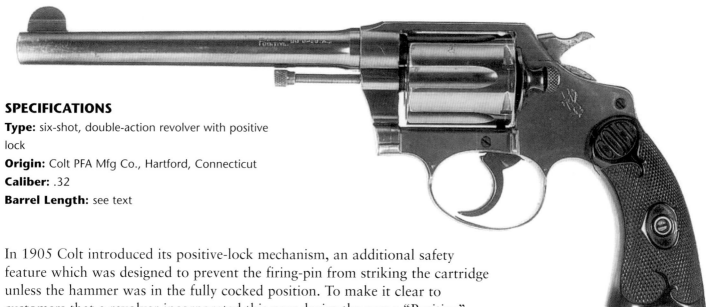

### SPECIFICATIONS

**Type:** six-shot, double-action revolver with positive lock
**Origin:** Colt PFA Mfg Co., Hartford, Connecticut
**Caliber:** .32
**Barrel Length:** see text

In 1905 Colt introduced its positive-lock mechanism, an additional safety feature which was designed to prevent the firing-pin from striking the cartridge unless the hammer was in the fully cocked position. To make it clear to customers that a revolver incorporated this new device the name "Positive" was added to the name, and so when the lock was added to the New Police Model, the latter became the Police Positive. This weapon was then in production from 1907 until 1939, by which time some 200,000 had been sold, mainly to police forces in the United States and elsewhere. It was chambered for .32, and 2.5 inch, 4 inch, 5 inch and 6 inch barrels were available. A target model was also produced chambered for .22 rimfire (although a .32 centerfire was also available) with a 6 inch barrel only. A number of Pequano Police Positive were also made from left-over parts, some of which were bought by the British Purchasing Commission in 1940. There was also a Police Positive .38 Model.

This beautifully preserved Police Positive was chambered for .38 Special and has a 6 inch barrel.

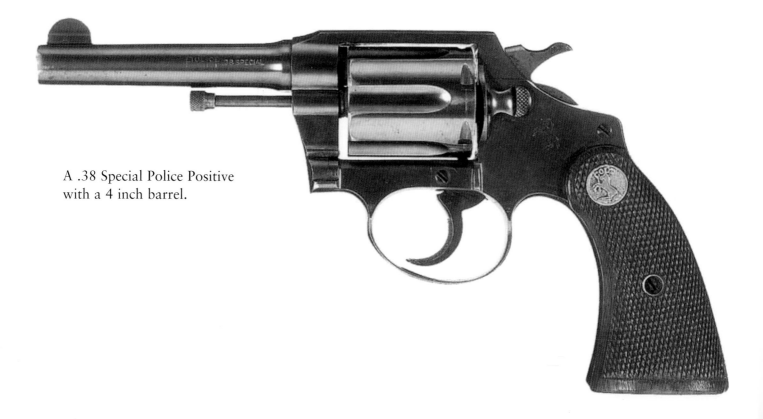

A .38 Special Police Positive with a 4 inch barrel.

# COLT ARMY SPECIAL

## SPECIFICATIONS

**Type:** six-shot, double-action revolver
**Origin:** Colt PFA Mfg Co., Hartford, Connecticut
**Caliber:** see text
**Barrel Length:** see text

The Army Special was an improved version of the New Army Revolver, and was introduced in 1908. It had a heavier frame, the cylinder rotation was changed to clockwise and it was given a more "modern" appearance, for example, by sloping the front face of the frame.

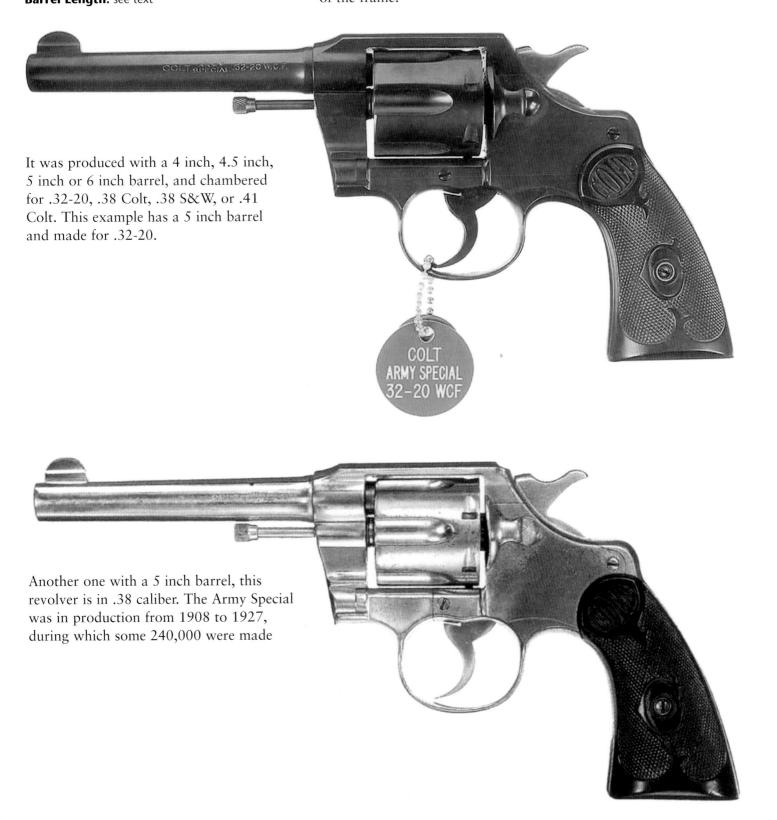

It was produced with a 4 inch, 4.5 inch, 5 inch or 6 inch barrel, and chambered for .32-20, .38 Colt, .38 S&W, or .41 Colt. This example has a 5 inch barrel and made for .32-20.

Another one with a 5 inch barrel, this revolver is in .38 caliber. The Army Special was in production from 1908 to 1927, during which some 240,000 were made

# COLT US ARMY MODEL 1917

### SPECIFICATIONS

**Type:** six-round, service revolver
**Origin:** Colt PFA Mfg Co., Hartford, Connecticut
**Caliber:** .45ACP
**Barrel Length:** 5.5in

This was developed from the New Service model and was produced only in .45 caliber (rimless) and with a 5.5 inch barrel. The main difference to the New Service model was the ammunition loading/ejection system , which involved loading in two clips of three rounds. When the Army contract ended Colt used the spares in the factory to produce some 1,000 for the civilian market. The only difference between the two types is that the Army revolver has its designation stamped on the butt; the civilian version does not.

In excellent condition, this is a military version, and the insets show the U.S. Army's markings on the butt.

This revolver is an early production example – Serial Number 728 – which was originally issued to the military and marked as such, but was later disposed of. The military marks have been ground off, but in such a way that it is clear what has been done.

# COLT OFFICIAL POLICE

## SPECIFICATIONS

**Type:** six-round, double-action revolver
**Origin:** Colt PFA Mfg Co., Hartford, Connecticut
**Caliber:** see text
**Barrel Length:** see text

The Official Police model was introduced by Colt on 1927 and was, in effect, a minor updating of the 1908 Army Special, but with a change in name. The changes included a wider, square-shaped backsight notch, and a darker blue coloring of the metalwork. Concerning calibers, .38 was available throughout its life, while .41 Colt was available until 1932 and .32-20 until 1942, while .22 OR was introduced in 1930. Barrel lengths were 2in, 4in, 5in and 6in. The model remained in production until 1969, during which time some 400,000 were sold.

The first example is a .38 caliber revolver with a 4 inch barrel.

This is a standard model which an owner has modified by installing a powerful scope and changing the grips.

This one has a 5 inch barrel version and is chambered from the .38-20 round and was supplied to the British Purchasing Commission in October 1941.

# COLT COMMANDO (1942)

## SPECIFICATIONS

**Type:** double-action revolver
**Origin:** Colt PFA Mfg Co., Hartford, Connecticut
**Caliber:** .38
**Barrel Length:** 4in

The Colt Commando's dramatic name covers its rather more prosaic purpose, which was to equip security guards and other security men at defense factories. It was, in fact, the 1939 .38 Official Police revolver with a 4 inch barrel (although a few were produced with 6 inch barrels).

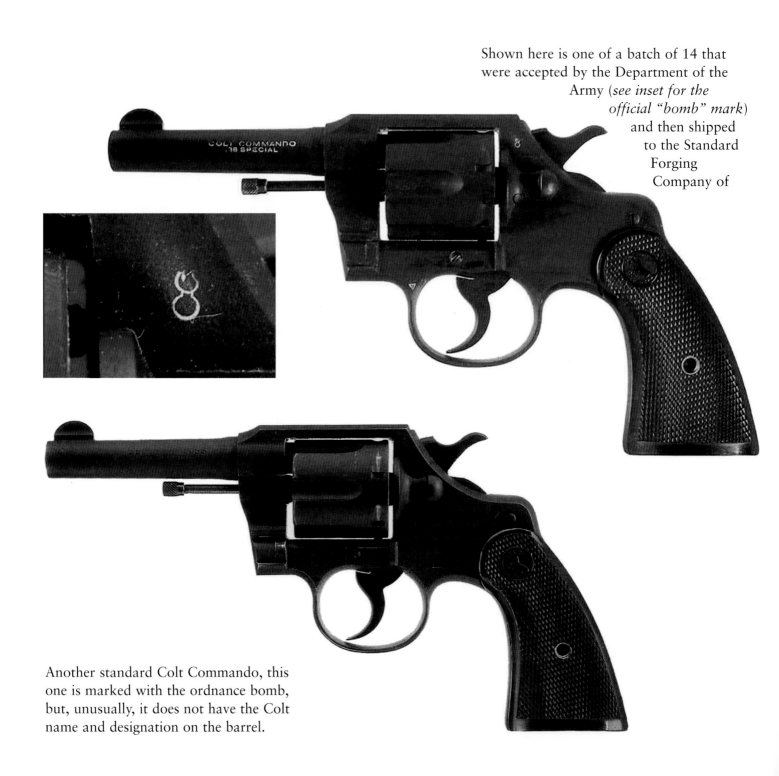

Shown here is one of a batch of 14 that were accepted by the Department of the Army (*see inset for the official "bomb" mark*) and then shipped to the Standard Forging Company of

Another standard Colt Commando, this one is marked with the ordnance bomb, but, unusually, it does not have the Colt name and designation on the barrel.

## COLT PYTHON DOUBLE-ACTION REVOLVER

The Python was introduced as a "top-of the-range" model in 1955 and was Colt's first totally new design since the early 1900s, featuring a heavy barrel with a vented rib (which is stippled to prevent reflections). All models are chambered for .357 Magnum, with 2.5 inch, 4 inch, 6 inch or 8 inch barrels (a 3 inch barrel has been discontinued).

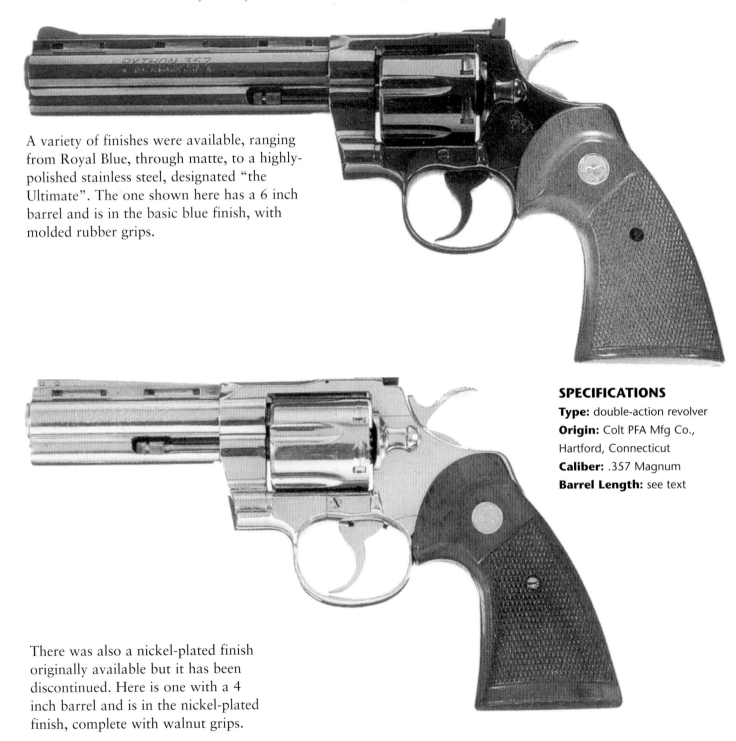

A variety of finishes were available, ranging from Royal Blue, through matte, to a highly-polished stainless steel, designated "the Ultimate". The one shown here has a 6 inch barrel and is in the basic blue finish, with molded rubber grips.

### SPECIFICATIONS
**Type:** double-action revolver
**Origin:** Colt PFA Mfg Co., Hartford, Connecticut
**Caliber:** .357 Magnum
**Barrel Length:** see text

There was also a nickel-plated finish originally available but it has been discontinued. Here is one with a 4 inch barrel and is in the nickel-plated finish, complete with walnut grips.

## COLT COBRA

### SPECIFICATIONS

**Type:** double-action revolver

**Origin:** Colt PFA Mfg Co., Hartford, Connecticut

**Caliber:** see text

**Barrel Length:** see text

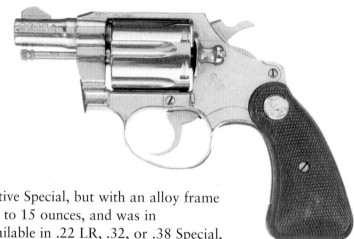

The Cobra was developed from the Detective Special, but with an alloy frame which reduced the weight from 22 ounces to 15 ounces, and was in production from 1950 to 1973. It was available in .22 LR, .32, or .38 Special, and most of those produced had a 2 inch barrel. A variant was the "Aircrewman Special" which weighed a mere 11 ounces, but was never sold commercially. Shown here is an excellent example of the Cobra, chambered for .38 Special, and with a 2 inch barrel, nickel-plated finish and walnut grips.

## COLT DIAMONDBACK

### SPECIFICATIONS

**Type:** double-action revolver

**Origin:** Colt PFA Mfg Co., Hartford, Connecticut

**Caliber:** .22LR and .38 Special

**Barrel Length**: see text

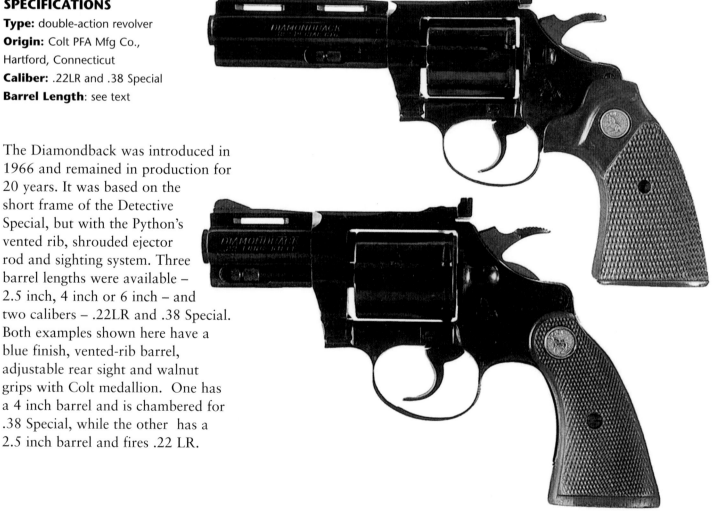

The Diamondback was introduced in 1966 and remained in production for 20 years. It was based on the short frame of the Detective Special, but with the Python's vented rib, shrouded ejector rod and sighting system. Three barrel lengths were available – 2.5 inch, 4 inch or 6 inch – and two calibers – .22LR and .38 Special. Both examples shown here have a blue finish, vented-rib barrel, adjustable rear sight and walnut grips with Colt medallion.  One has a 4 inch barrel and is chambered for .38 Special, while the other  has a 2.5 inch barrel and fires .22 LR.

## COLT ANACONDA

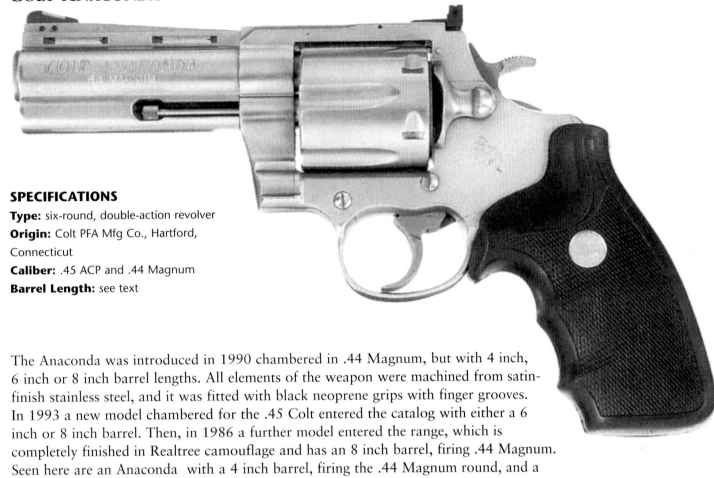

### SPECIFICATIONS

**Type:** six-round, double-action revolver
**Origin:** Colt PFA Mfg Co., Hartford, Connecticut
**Caliber:** .45 ACP and .44 Magnum
**Barrel Length:** see text

The Anaconda was introduced in 1990 chambered in .44 Magnum, but with 4 inch, 6 inch or 8 inch barrel lengths. All elements of the weapon were machined from satin-finish stainless steel, and it was fitted with black neoprene grips with finger grooves. In 1993 a new model chambered for the .45 Colt entered the catalog with either a 6 inch or 8 inch barrel. Then, in 1986 a further model entered the range, which is completely finished in Realtree camouflage and has an 8 inch barrel, firing .44 Magnum. Seen here are an Anaconda with a 4 inch barrel, firing the .44 Magnum round, and a scoped Realtree, also firing the .44 Magnum round, but with an 8 inch barrel.

## COOPER POCKET REVOLVER

### SPECIFICATIONS

**Type:** six-chamber, double-action percussion revolver
**Origin:** Cooper Firearms Manufacturing Co., Philadelphia, Pennsylvania
**Caliber:** .31
**Barrel Length:** see text

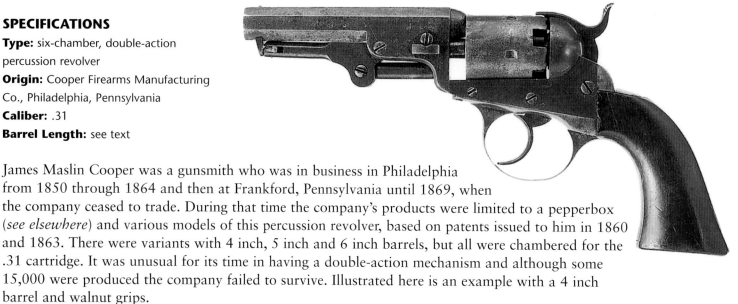

James Maslin Cooper was a gunsmith who was in business in Philadelphia from 1850 through 1864 and then at Frankford, Pennsylvania until 1869, when the company ceased to trade. During that time the company's products were limited to a pepperbox (*see elsewhere*) and various models of this percussion revolver, based on patents issued to him in 1860 and 1863. There were variants with 4 inch, 5 inch and 6 inch barrels, but all were chambered for the .31 cartridge. It was unusual for its time in having a double-action mechanism and although some 15,000 were produced the company failed to survive. Illustrated here is an example with a 4 inch barrel and walnut grips.

## DARDICK MODEL 1500

This was a most unusual weapon, based on patents held by New York inventor, David Dardick, which, in effect, combined the rotating cylinder of a revolver with the magazine feed of an automatic. The rounds were conventional commercial rounds (e.g., .38 Special, 9mm Parabellum, .22LR) which were loaded into trochoidal-shaped carriers known as "trounds." The trounds were then placed in a box magazine, which was loaded into the butt in the normal manner. The cylinder was mounted on a horizontal axis inside a circular housing and had three recesses, each sized to hold one tround. Each pull of the trigger,

rotated the cylinder to pick a new tround, brought a second in line with the barrel and fired it, and ejected the previously-fired tround. The weapon did not fire automatically, but depended on a trigger-stroke to continue the process until the magazine was empty. The Dardick was marketed in two versions; Model 1100 with a small butt and eleven-round magazine, and the Model 1500 (*seen here*) with a larger butt and a fifteen-round magazine. There was also a carbine version. The system worked but was not a commercial success.

### SPECIFICATIONS

**Type:** fifteen-round, automatic revolver
**Origin:** Dardick Corporation, Hamden, Connecticut
**Caliber:** see text
**Barrel Length:** 6in

## DEFENDER (JOHNSON, BYE) SPUR-TRIGGER REVOLVER

**SPECIFICATIONS**
**Type**: spur-trigger revolver
**Origin**: Johnson, Bye & Company, Worcester, Massachusetts
**Caliber**: .32 rimfire
**Barrel Length**: 2.4in

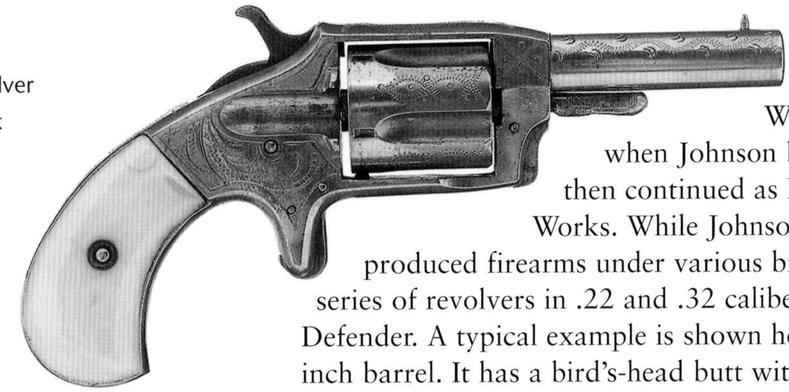

Iver Johnson and Martin Bye ran a joint business in Worcester from 1871 to 1883, when Johnson bought out Bye and the firm then continued as Iver Johnson Arms & Cycle Works. While Johnson and Bye were together they produced firearms under various brand-names, including one series of revolvers in .22 and .32 caliber under the brand-name Defender. A typical example is shown here, in .32 caliber with a 2.4 inch barrel. It has a bird's-head butt with ivory grips and, as the name indicates, a spur trigger.

## EAGLE ARMS CUP-PRIMER REVOLVER

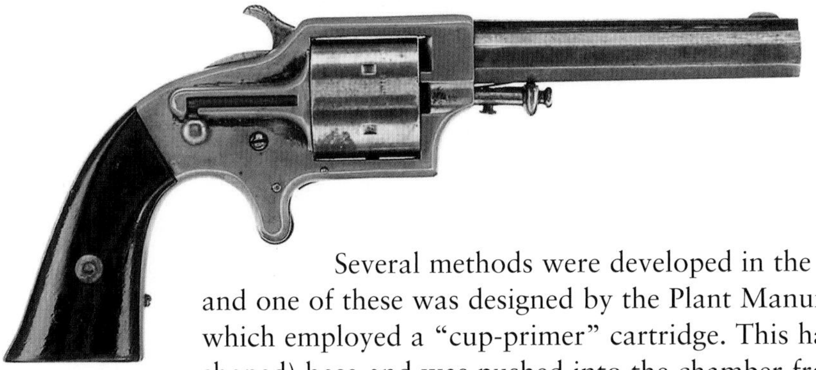

**SPECIFICATIONS**
**Type:** five-round, double-action, cup-primer revolver
**Origin:** Johnson, Bye & Company, Worcester, Massachusetts
**Caliber:** .31
**Barrel Length:** 3.5in

Several methods were developed in the 1860s which sought to evade Rollin White's patent and one of these was designed by the Plant Manufacturing Company based in Norwich, Connecticut, which employed a "cup-primer" cartridge. This had a straight-sided, metal case with a dished (cup-shaped) base and was pushed into the chamber from the front. The base of the cartridge was struck by the nose of the hammer through a small hole in the rear-face of the chamber. The Plant revolver was made in .41 and .36 caliber, but the Eagle Arms Company produced the smaller version, seen here, in .31 caliber (Eagle Arms was another brand-name used by the Johnson & Bye company). This revolver had a 3.5 inch barrel, smooth-sided cylinder and spur trigger. The slot which can be seen behind the cylinder houses the ejector-rod which was pushed forward through the hammer-aperture in rear of each cylinder to eject the empty cartridge case forward.

## FOREHAND & WADSWORTH POCKET REVOLVER

**SPECIFICATIONS**
**Type:** five-shot, double-action pocket revolver
**Origin:** Forehand & Wadsworth, Worcester, Massachusetts
**Caliber:** .32 S&W
**Barrel Length:** 3.25in

When Ethan Allen, the renowned New England gunsmith, died in 1871 his business passed to his two sons-in-law, Sullivan Forehand and Henry Wadsworth, who changed the company's name to reflect the new ownership. Among the first products of the renamed company was a series of pocket revolvers, which featured a solid-frame and a five-round fluted cylinder, such as that seen here. Wadsworth's involvement in the company decreased, presumably due to ill-health, as he sold out to his brother-in-law in 1890 and died in 1892.

## FOREHAND & WADSWORTH BRITISH BULLDOG

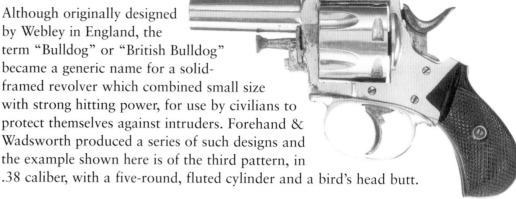

### SPECIFICATIONS

**Type:** double-action pocket revolver

**Origin:** Forehand & Wadsworth, Worcester, Massachusetts

**Caliber:** .38 centerfire

**Barrel Length:** 2in

Although originally designed by Webley in England, the term "Bulldog" or "British Bulldog" became a generic name for a solid-framed revolver which combined small size with strong hitting power, for use by civilians to protect themselves against intruders. Forehand & Wadsworth produced a series of such designs and the example shown here is of the third pattern, in .38 caliber, with a five-round, fluted cylinder and a bird's head butt.

## HARRINGTON & RICHARDSON MODEL 22

### SPECIFICATIONS

**Type:** seven-round, solid-frame, double-action, target revolver

**Origin:** Harrington & Richardson, Worcester, Massachusetts

**Caliber:** .22 LR

**Barrel Length:** 5.75in

Gilbert Harrington & William Richardson started their business in Worcester, Massachusetts in 1874 and produced a large range of designs over the next 113 years, until the company failed in 1987. During this time it produced many revolver designs, but just one is shown here, the .22 Special, a seven shot, tip-up design, with walnut grips and a ribbed (but un-vented) 5.75 inch barrel.

## HOPKINS & ALLEN XL DOUBLE-ACTION

### SPECIFICATIONS

**Type:** double-action revolver

**Origin:** Hopkins & Allen, Norwich, Connecticut

**Caliber:** .32 S&W

**Barrel Length:** 3in

Hopkins & Allen was founded in 1868 and, following a disastrous fire in 1900, was purchased by the Forehand Arms Company. It continued until 1917 when it was absorbed by the Malin-Rockwell Company. In its heyday Hopkins & Allen produced a large number of low-priced revolvers under – as was the style of the time – a host of brand-names, such as Captain Jack, Mountain Eagle, etc. The weapon seen here was one of the XL-series, which were produced for about twelve years from 1871 and were five-shot, solid-frame weapons, in a variety of calibers. The early versions had spur triggers, but later models, as with the one seen here, had the more modern, free-standing trigger.

## HOPKINS & ALLEN "DICTATOR"

**SPECIFICATIONS**

**Type:** single-action revolver
**Origin:** Hopkins & Allen, Norwich, Connecticut
**Caliber:** .30
**Barrel Length:** 2.75in

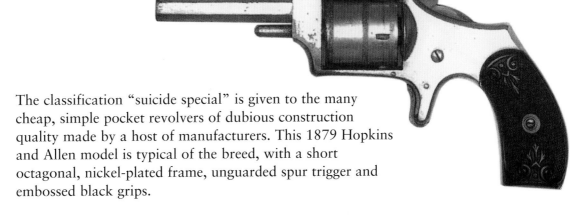

The classification "suicide special" is given to the many cheap, simple pocket revolvers of dubious construction quality made by a host of manufacturers. This 1879 Hopkins and Allen model is typical of the breed, with a short octagonal, nickel-plated frame, unguarded spur trigger and embossed black grips.

## HOPKINS & ALLEN HAMMERLESS TOP-BREAK REVOLVER

**SPECIFICATIONS**

**Type:** five-round, hammer-less revolver
**Origin:** Hopkins & Allen, Norwich, Connecticut
**Caliber:** .32 S&W
**Barrel Length:** 3in

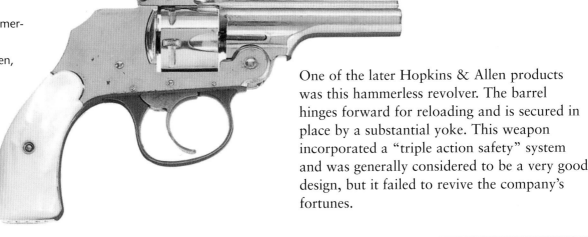

One of the later Hopkins & Allen products was this hammerless revolver. The barrel hinges forward for reloading and is secured in place by a substantial yoke. This weapon incorporated a "triple action safety" system and was generally considered to be a very good design, but it failed to revive the company's fortunes.

## IVER JOHNSON HAMMERLESS REVOLVER

**SPECIFICATIONS**

**Type:** hammerless revolver
**Origin:** Iver Johnson Arms & Cycle Works, Fitchburg, Massachusetts
**Caliber:** .32 S&W
**Barrel Length:** 3in

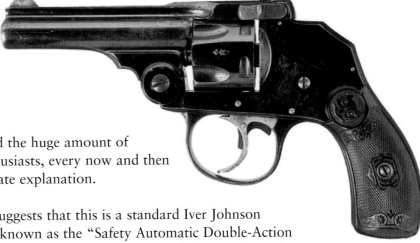

Despite the vast volumes of documentation and the huge amount of research carried out over the years by gun enthusiasts, every now and then weapons turn up for which there is no immediate explanation.

An initial inspection of the weapon seen here suggests that this is a standard Iver Johnson Hammerless revolver, a design which was also known as the "Safety Automatic Double-Action Model." This was produced by the company from 1894 until the 1970s, and the grips bear the company's famous "Owl Head" logo. However, the safety mechanism is operated by a second trigger mounted in a slot in the main trigger, a highly unusual modification of the usual Iver Johnson safety arrangement. In addition, the frame bears a number of German proofmarks; again, this is curious as in those instances where US-made arms of this period do carry foreign proofmarks, these are almost invariably British.

The second weapon is an Iver Johnson cut-away of the type prepared by most manufacturers for use at trade fairs and when instructing customers. But, again, this has a curious feature in that there are no cuts in the barrel or cylinder, which means that it is a functioning firearm under Federal Law.

# MANHATTAN NAVY

## SPECIFICATIONS

**Type:** five-shot percussion revolver
**Origin:** Manhattan Firearms Co., Newark, New Jersey
**Caliber:** .36
**Barrel Length:** 5in

The Manhattan firearms company were one of the many who began manufacturing revolvers when Colt's patent expired. Their main products were copies of the Model 1851 Navy and Model 1949 pocket series, and were so close that Colt took legal action to have production stopped. Even so, over 80,000 Manhattan revolvers were made. This is one of the Manhattan "Navy" models, which has features from both the Colt Navy and pocket revolvers.

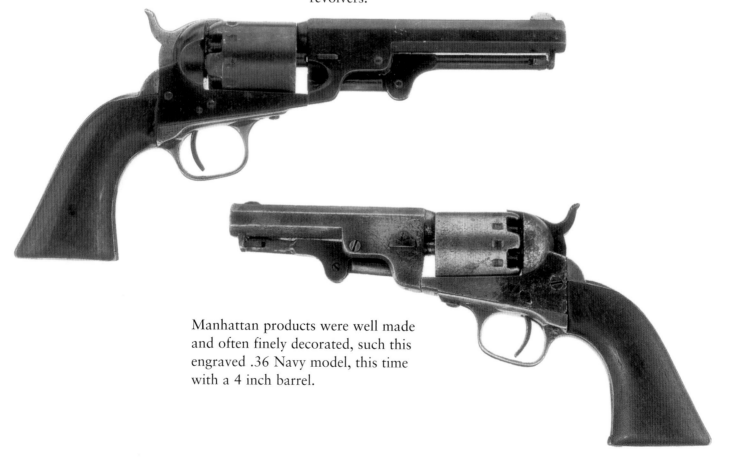

Manhattan products were well made and often finely decorated, such this engraved .36 Navy model, this time with a 4 inch barrel.

## MANHATTAN TIP-UP

**SPECIFICATIONS**

**Type:** seven-shot cartridge revolver
**Origin:** Manhattan Firearms Co., Newark,
New Jersey
**Caliber:** .22
**Barrel Length:** 3.3in

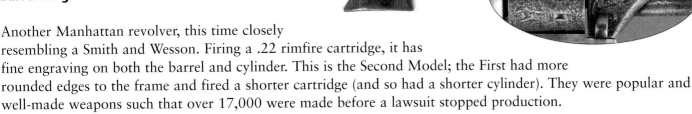

Another Manhattan revolver, this time closely
resembling a Smith and Wesson. Firing a .22 rimfire cartridge, it has
fine engraving on both the barrel and cylinder. This is the Second Model; the First had more
rounded edges to the frame and fired a shorter cartridge (and so had a shorter cylinder). They were popular and
well-made weapons such that over 17,000 were made before a lawsuit stopped production.

## MARLIN XXX 1872 REVOLVER

**SPECIFICATIONS**

**Type:** single-action percussion revolver
**Origin:** Marlin Firearms Co., New Haven, Connecticut
**Caliber:** .30
**Barrel Length:** 3in

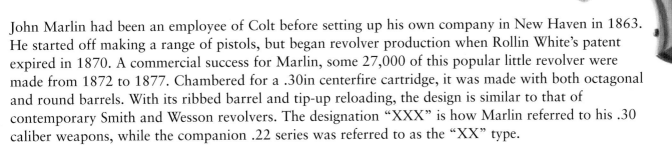

John Marlin had been an employee of Colt before setting up his own company in New Haven in 1863.
He started off making a range of pistols, but began revolver production when Rollin White's patent
expired in 1870. A commercial success for Marlin, some 27,000 of this popular little revolver were
made from 1872 to 1877. Chambered for a .30in centerfire cartridge, it was made with both octagonal
and round barrels. With its ribbed barrel and tip-up reloading, the design is similar to that of
contemporary Smith and Wesson revolvers. The designation "XXX" is how Marlin referred to his .30
caliber weapons, while the companion .22 series was referred to as the "XX" type.

## MASSACHUSETTS ARMS CO. DRAGOON PERCUSSION REVOLVER

**SPECIFICATIONS**

**Type:** percussion revolver
**Origin:** Massachusetts Arms Company,
Chicopee Falls, Massachusetts
**Caliber:** .40
**Barrel Length:** 7.1in

The Massachusetts Army Company operated at Chicopee Falls, Massachusetts from 1849
to 1876, during which time it produced rifles and revolvers under licence from other
patent-holders. One such was Daniel Leavitt of Cabotsville whose design was produced
first by Wesson, Stevens & Miller at Hartford, and subsequently by the Massachusetts
Arms Co., and is now commonly known as the "Wesson and Leavitt." This example,
made in the early 1850s shows the good finish and neat design, and the side hammer is
shown in the inset.

## MERWIN HULBERT AND CO. POCKET ARMY

### SPECIFICATIONS

**Type:** six-shot single-action revolver
**Origin:** Hopkins and Allen, Norwich, Connecticut
**Caliber:** .44-40
**Barrel Length:** 3.25in

Merwin Hulbert and Co. were New York dealers, promoters and marketers of firearms. They made no weapons themselves but instead contracted with other manufacturers to supply them with guns, usually under their own brand. This 1880s range of neat, compact centerfire revolvers was made for them by Hopkins and Allen, and came in a number of styles. All used an unusual loading mechanism, where the barrel and cylinder assembly were twisted sideways them pulled forwards to allow the cartridge cases to drop out and new rounds to be inserted. One of the early Hulbert/Hopkins and Allen pocket models, the single-action weapon shown here has an open frame with no top strap, nickel plating finish, ivory grips and "scallop-style" cylinder flutes. It fires the .44-40 cartridge, although it was also made in .44 "Russian" and .44 Merwin Hulbert calibers. Later models had a top strap and more conventional flutes.

## MERWIN HULBERT AND CO. POCKET DOUBLE ACTION

### SPECIFICATIONS

**Type:** six-shot double-action revolver
**Origin:** Hopkins and Allen, Norwich, Connecticut
**Caliber:** .44
**Barrel Length:** 3.5in

Hopkins and Allen also made a double-action version of their .44 Merwin Hulbert pocket revolvers, which used the same unique unloading method. This one has a top strap and ivory grips.

## METROPOLITAN NAVY PERCUSSION

### SPECIFICATIONS

**Type:** six-shot single-action revolver
**Origin:** Metropolitan Arms Co., New York
**Caliber:** .36
**Barrel Length:** 7.5in

When the Colt factory was damaged by fire in 1864, the Metropolitan Arms C. began to manufacture copies of Colt weapons. This "Navy" model is almost indistinguishable from the Colt original of the time, even down to the faint remnants of the naval battle scene engraved on the cylinder. It also has a brass trigger guard with walnut grips.

# NEPPERHAN REVOLVER

## SPECIFICATIONS

**Type:** five-shot single-action revolver
**Origin:** Nepperhan Fire Arms Co.,
Yonkers, New York
**Caliber:** .31
**Barrel Length:** 4.25in

The Nepperhan Fire Arms Company made about 5,000 of these .31 Colt copies for a while during the Civil War.

# PETTENGILL ARMY MODEL

## SPECIFICATIONS

**Type:** six-shot self-cocking revolver
**Origin:** Rogers, Spencer & Co., Willow Dale, New York
**Caliber:** .44
**Barrel Length:** 6.5in

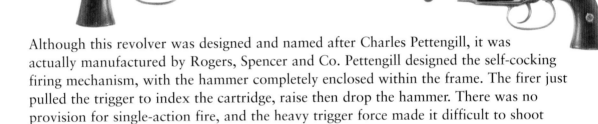

Although this revolver was designed and named after Charles Pettengill, it was actually manufactured by Rogers, Spencer and Co. Pettengill designed the self-cocking firing mechanism, with the hammer completely enclosed within the frame. The firer just pulled the trigger to index the cartridge, raise then drop the hammer. There was no provision for single-action fire, and the heavy trigger force made it difficult to shoot accurately.

The Pettengill was the subject of a 5,000 item order from the US Ordnance Department in 1861, but had to be modified when the first batch was rejected as unsuitable, Eventually only some 2,000 of the modified weapon were delivered.

# PHILLIPS & RODGERS MODEL 47

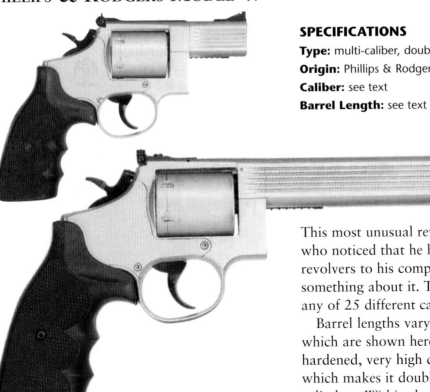

## SPECIFICATIONS

**Type:** multi-caliber, double-action revolver
**Origin:** Phillips & Rodgers, Huntsville, Texas
**Caliber:** see text
**Barrel Length:** see text

This most unusual revolver was designed by Jonathan Rodgers, who noticed that he had to carry a number of different caliber revolvers to his competition shoots and decided to do something about it. The result is this weapon which can handle any of 25 different cartridges in the .38/9mm, .357 range.

Barrel lengths vary between 2.5 inches and 6 inches, both of which are shown here. The cylinder is made from specially hardened, very high quality MilSpec 4330 vanadium steel, which makes it double the strength of normal revolver cylinders. Within the chambers, there are special springs to hold rimless cartridges in place.

# POND SEPARATE CHAMBER REVOLVER

## SPECIFICATIONS

**Type:** separate chamber revolver

**Origin:** Lucius W. Pond, Worcester, Massachusetts

**Caliber:** see text

**Barrel Length:** see text

Lucius Pond designed a pocket revolver which had to be withdrawn because it infringed Rollin White's drilled-through chamber patent. Like a number of others, he then set about designing a system which avoided this, and the result was a single-action, solid-frame revolver with a unique cylinder arrangement. The cylinder had a solid rear wall with six small ports to enable the nose of the hammer to strike the rear of the cartridge. Forward of this wall were six chambers, each accommodating a removable sleeve, into which the cartridge was inserted and then pushed back by the ejector rod. It was a very complicated system and its defects are well-illustrated by the example seen here, which is missing four of the removable sleeves, while the other two are rusted in place.

# REMINGTON-BEALS 1ST MODEL POCKET REVOLVER

## SPECIFICATIONS

**Type:** five-shot single-action revolver

**Origin:** Remington Armory, Ilion, New York.

**Caliber:** .31

**Barrel Length:** 3in

The Remington Armory became a magnet for many skilled engineers and designers, and one such was Fordyce Beal. After an earlier stint at Remington, he went to the Whitneyville Armory in 1854, but was enticed back to Remington after only two years. Back at Remington, he helped the company enter the civilian market with its first ever pistol, this 1st Model Remington Beals, patented in June 1856.

A small, reliable and effective single-action 5-shot percussion arm, the basic weapon was subject to significant design changes through its life (*see below*).

# REMINGTON-BEALS 2ND MODEL POCKET REVOLVER

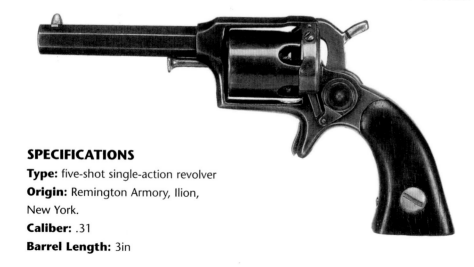

## SPECIFICATIONS

**Type:** five-shot single-action revolver

**Origin:** Remington Armory, Ilion, New York.

**Caliber:** .31

**Barrel Length:** 3in

Beal's second model .31caliber single-action pocket revolver for Remington had some minor improvements over the first. The main difference was that it now had a spur trigger rather than the trigger and guard of the first model. The butt had also been reshaped and squared off, while the grips were now either checkered rubber or, as shown in this case, walnut.

## REMINGTON-BEALS 3RD MODEL POCKET REVOLVER

**SPECIFICATIONS**
**Type:** five-shot single-action revolver
**Origin:** Remington Armory, Ilion, New York.
**Caliber:** .31
**Barrel Length:** 4in

Fordyce Beals continued to develop his pocket revolver line with this third model. Larger than the previous two models, it had a 4 inch barrel while keeping the spur trigger and squared butt of the 2nd Model. The main distinguishing feature is the solid frame extension under the barrel and the attached pivoting rammer.

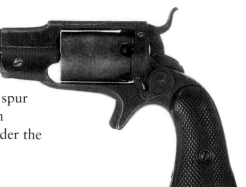

## REMINGTON-RIDER DOUBLE-ACTION REVOLVER

**SPECIFICATIONS**
**Type:** five-shot double-action revolver
**Origin:** Remington Armory, Ilion, New York.
**Caliber:** .31
**Barrel Length:** 3in

Remington formed another design partnership, this time with Joseph Rider of Newark, Ohio. Rider chose Remington to manufacture his double-action design patented in 1859. It had an unusual 'mushroom-style' cylinder with the percussion nipples set in towards the chambers and angled outwards to meet the hammer. The trigger guard was also rather large, with a distinctive straight trigger. Many such weapons were later converted to fire metallic cartridges, and have a claim to be the first American double-action cartridge revolver.

## REMINGTON-BEALS NAVY REVOLVER

**SPECIFICATIONS**
**Type:** six-shot single-action revolver
**Origin:** Remington Armory, Ilion, New York.
**Caliber:** .36
**Barrel Length:** 7in

By the end of the 1850s Remington was producing a range of pocket revolvers, pistols and rifles, but had no weapons suitable for military use. In 1858 Fordyce Beals took the principles of his 3rd Model, and developed an entirely new arm in .36 caliber. It had a large solid frame, complete with integral top strap, octagonal barrel and single-action lock. A large hinged ram sat beneath the barrel. This turned out to be a reliable and effective weapon, and was ordered by the US Government as they rearmed in preparation for the Civil War. The first government deliveries to see service were actually the .44 Army version.

## REMINGTON-BEALS ARMY REVOLVER

When Col. Ripley, the Chief of Ordnance examined the Remington-Beals Navy prototypes, he immediately placed a large order – but for revolvers in .44 Army caliber. This revolver has similar appearance to the original .36 version but is slightly larger and has a longer barrel. The first deliveries were made in August 1862; the first of a long line of Remington large caliber percussion revolvers.

**SPECIFICATIONS**
**Type:** six-shot single-action revolver
**Origin:** Remington Armory, Ilion, New York.
**Caliber:** .44
**Barrel Length:** 8in

## REMINGTON MODEL 1861 ARMY REVOLVER

Soon after the Remington-Beals military revolvers entered production, the company looked to improve the design. The main difference was a modification to the way the cylinder axle pin was retained. A channel was cut in the top of the rammer arm to allow the pin to be removed easily. The system was patented by Dr Elliott, and the weapon is sometimes referred to as the Model 1861 Elliott's Patent Army Revolver. In service conditions this system was found to be too fragile, and many revolvers had a small screw added to block this channel.

The Model 1861 is also known as the "Old Model Army". It had a distinctive outline, with an integral top strap, large gap in front of the lower edge of the cylinder, and a long sloping web on the loading ram under the barrel. This form set the pattern for all subsequent Remington military percussion revolvers.

Solid, reliable and popular, thousands were made and used during the Civil War and after. Many were manufactured at the Remington facility at Utica created to meet the demands of the Civil War, although they bear "Remington, Ilion", markings.

**SPECIFICATIONS**
**Type:** six-shot single-action revolver
**Origin:** Remington Armory, Ilion and Utica, New York.
**Caliber:** .44
**Barrel Length:** 8in

## REMINGTON MODEL 1861 NAVY REVOLVER

**SPECIFICATIONS**
**Type:** six-shot single-action revolver
**Origin:** Remington Armory, Ilion and Utica, New York.
**Caliber:** .36
**Barrel Length:** 7.42in

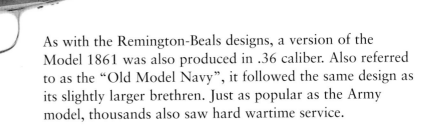

As with the Remington-Beals designs, a version of the Model 1861 was also produced in .36 caliber. Also referred to as the "Old Model Navy", it followed the same design as its slightly larger brethren. Just as popular as the Army model, thousands also saw hard wartime service.

# REMINGTON NEW MODEL ARMY REVOLVER

## SPECIFICATIONS

**Type:** six-shot single-action revolver

**Origin:** Remington Armory, Ilion, New York.

**Caliber:** .44

**Barrel Length:** 8in

Wartime experience showed up some weaknesses in Remington's Model 1861, especially concerning the cylinder fixing system. Remington modified the design by improving the fixing pin and adding safety notches around the rear edge of the cylinder. The end result was one of the finest percussion revolvers ever, and the only one to really challenge Colt's dominance of the military market. Over 120,000 were delivered during the Civil War, and at its peak, production reached over 1,000 a week.

Of course, a version of the New Model was made in .36 Navy caliber, but this didn't sell quite so well – although the 28,000 produced was still a healthy number.

# REMINGTON-RIDER DOUBLE-ACTION BELT REVOLVER

## SPECIFICATIONS

**Type:** six-shot double-action revolver

**Origin:** Remington Armory, Ilion, New York.

**Caliber:** .36

**Barrel Length:** 6.5in

Remington continued to concentrate on their traditional civilian market, and from around 1865 produced a range of "belt" revolvers based on the New Model Navy. They were slightly smaller than their military brethren but were equally effective and reliable. With the Remington-Rider they also returned to a double-action lock, presumably on the basis that a weapon for civilian self-defence needed to be quick-reacting for use in a close-quarters brawl rather than designed for carefully aimed fire. Some of the double-action weapons also had cylinders with external fluting.

# REMINGTON NEW MODEL POLICE REVOLVER

## SPECIFICATIONS

**Type:** five-shot single-action revolver

**Origin:** Remington Armory, Ilion, New York.

**Caliber:** .36

**Barrel Length:** see text

Again taking the New Model design as a basis, this was a much smaller weapon manufactured from around 1865 and intended to compete with the smaller Colt Police and Pocket revolvers. Only single-action, it was made in a range of barrel lengths from 3 to 6 inches. The one shown has a 3 inch barrel, and is a compact concealable, reliable weapon that still packs a hefty punch. It proved to be popular and over 17,000 were sold.

## REMINGTON NEW MODEL POCKET REVOLVER

### SPECIFICATIONS

**Type:** five-shot single-action revolver
**Origin:** Remington Armory, Ilion, New York.
**Caliber:** .31
**Barrel Length:** see text

After the Civil War, Remington brought out this popular series of pocket revolvers to replace the Remington-Beal pocket models. The revolver had a small frame and unguarded spur trigger, but still had the typical Remington outline. Early production was percussion type, but later models were made to fire a rimfire cartridge. Some 26,000 were made in 3 inch, 3.5inch, 4 inch and 4.5 inch barrel lengths.

Many percussion models were also factory-modified to fire cartridges as well.

## REMINGTON-KITTREDGE CONVERSION REVOLVERS

### SPECIFICATIONS

**Type:** five-shot single-action revolver
**Origin:** Remington Armory, Ilion, New York.
**Caliber:** .46
**Barrel Length:** 8in

As the Civil War was coming to an end, it was clear that the metallic cartridge had superseded the percussion mechanism and was the way of the future. As far as revolvers were concerned, Rollin White's 1855 patent prevented manufacturers from legally using a bored-through cylinder in new or converted weapons until 1869. Smith and Wesson had bought the rights to the patent from White, and had an almost exclusive market until 1868.

Remington signed an agreement with Smith and Wesson in 1868 which allowed them to convert some 4,500 New Model Army large-calibre percussion revolvers to fire .46 rimfire cartridges. Complete with a new five shot cylinder they were mainly sold via the Kittredge company of Cincinnati, Ohio. Kitteridge, Smith and Wesson, Rollins White and Remington all had a cut of the sales price.

Note that the under-barrel ram was left in place on this conversion.

# REMINGTON ARMY MODEL 1875 REVOLVER

## SPECIFICATIONS

**Type:** six shot single-action cartridge revolver
**Origin:** Remington Armory, Ilion, New York.
**Caliber:** .44 and .45
**Barrel Length:** 7.5in (plus some 5in)

A heavy Army caliber single-action cartridge revolver, this was launched in 1875 to compete with highly-successful Colt Model 1873. Originally made for Remington's own .44 caliber centerfire cartridge, they were later produced in .44-40 and .45 long Colt calibers. Note how this cartridge revolver kept the Remington "signature" triangular web under the ejector rod.

An effective, reliable weapon, the Model 1875 never managed to seriously challenge the Colt's supremacy. No large military contracts were awarded, although a few hundred were purchased by the Interior department for use in policing the western reservations. A large order was placed by Egypt, but as the Egyptian government were in behind in paying for earlier orders of rifles and carbines, only a few were actually delivered.

# REMINGTON ARMY MODEL 1888 REVOLVER

## SPECIFICATIONS

**Type:** six-shot single-action cartridge revolver
**Origin:** Remington Armory, Ilion, New York.
**Caliber:** .44-40
**Barrel Length:** 5.5in

Scant records of this weapon exists, and there is some dispute that it really was a genuine Remington factory design. However, it appears that these shorter, large caliber revolvers were made in small numbers (less than 1,000) for New York dealers Hartley and Graham, perhaps from parts and sub-assemblies already available at the factory. Notice the absence of the normal Remington triangular web under the barrel.

# ROGERS & SPENCER ARMY REVOLVER

## SPECIFICATIONS

**Type:** six-shot, percussion revolver
**Origin:** Rogers & Spencer, Utica, New York
**Caliber:** .44
**Barrel Length:** 7.5in

The partnership of Rogers and Spencer was established in about 1861 and produced a number of firearms, including this Army contract six-round percussion revolver. The order placed by the ordnance department was for 5,000, but it is believed that only about 2,000 had been delivered by the time the Civil War ended and contracts were terminated.

## RUGER MODEL 117 SECURITY SIX REVOLVER

**SPECIFICATIONS**

**Type:** six-shot, double-action revolver

**Origin:** Sturm, Ruger & Co., Southport, Connecticut

**Caliber:** .357 Magnum

**Barrel Length:** see text

The Ruger line of revolvers started with the Single-Six model in 1953 which, like the rest of the line, was an original Ruger design but with the general visual impact of a Colt Single-Action Army. In 1970 the company turned to double-action revolvers with the weapon shown here, the Model 117, which was chambered for .357 Magnum and produced with 2.75 inch, 4 inch, or 6 inch barrels. The weapon was originally named the "Security Six" but this was later changed to "Service-Six." The model shown here is a 2.75 inch version with blue finish, walnut grips and adjustable rear sight.

## SAVAGE NAVY REVOLVER

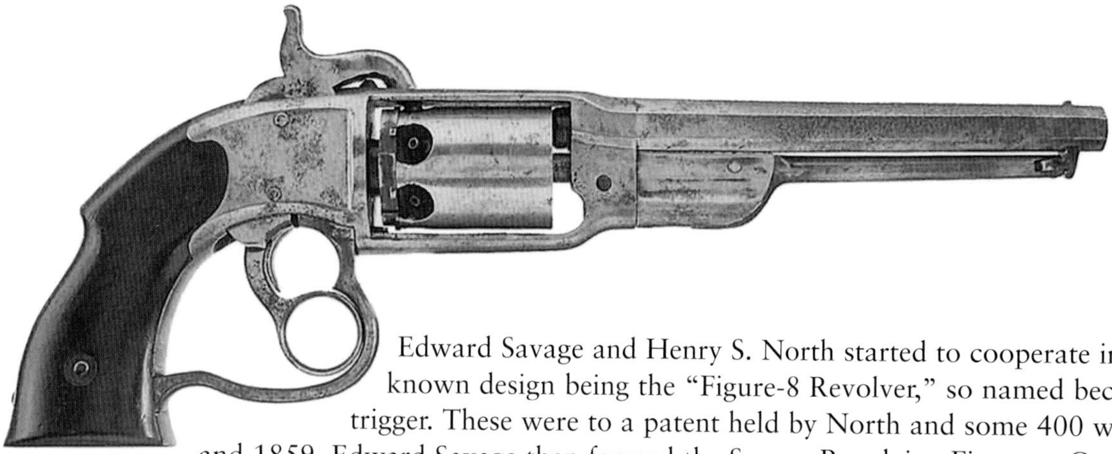

**SPECIFICATIONS**

**Type:**

**Origin:** Savage Revolving Firearms Co., Middletown, Connecticut

**Caliber:** .36

**Barrel Length:** 7.1in

Edward Savage and Henry S. North started to cooperate in the early 1850s, their only known design being the "Figure-8 Revolver," so named because of the shape of the trigger. These were to a patent held by North and some 400 were produced between 1856 and 1859. Edward Savage then formed the Savage Revolving Firearms Company in 1860 and received two known major government contracts, the first of which was for some 25,000 Model 1861 Springfield muskets. The second contract was for the revolver seen here, which was marked as being to North's patents of 1856, 1859 and 1860, and some 20,000 were produced, of which 11,284 went to the Navy. The two examples seen here differ in that one has a fluted cylinder and the other a smooth cylinder, but both have clearly seen a lot of service.

## OTIS SMITH MODEL 1883 SPUR-TRIGGER REVOLVER

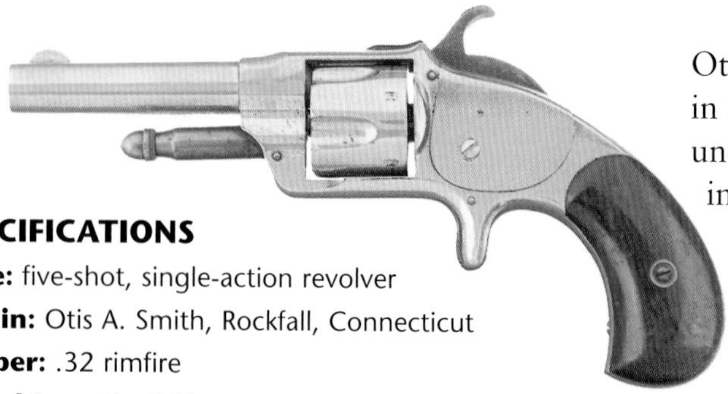

**SPECIFICATIONS**

**Type:** five-shot, single-action revolver

**Origin:** Otis A. Smith, Rockfall, Connecticut

**Caliber:** .32 rimfire

**Barrel Length:** 2.9in

Otis Smith appears to have established his gunmaking business in 1872–3 and his company produced a number of undistinguished revolver designs before going out of business in 1898. The Model 1883, seen here, was chambered for .32 rimfire and has a 2.9 inch barrel. The protruding rod below the barrel is not a cylinder arbor pin but is a patented device for releasing the cylinder for reloading. This was one of the last revolvers to be manufactured with a spur-trigger and without a trigger guard.

## SMITH & WESSON MODEL 1– 2ND ISSUE

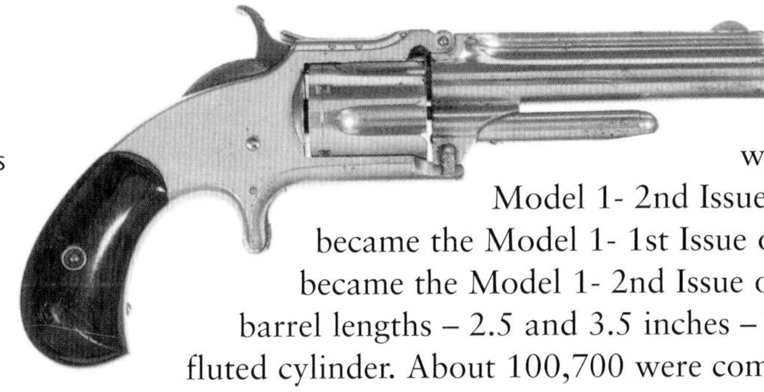

**SPECIFICATIONS**

**Type:** five-round revolver
**Origin:** Smith & Wesson, Springfield, Massachusetts
**Caliber:** .32 rimfire
**Barrel Length:** 3.5in

The S&W Model 1 went through various "types" and "issues" before the Model 1- appeared in 1865, which was followed in 1868 by the Model 1- 2nd Issue (*seen here*) whereupon the 1865 became the Model 1- 1st Issue or "Old Model") and the 1868 weapon became the Model 1- 2nd Issue or "New Model." It was made with two barrel lengths – 2.5 and 3.5 inches – had a bird's head grip and a five-round fluted cylinder. About 100,700 were completed between 1868 and 1875.

## SMITH & WESSON MODEL 2 ARMY REVOLVER (1861)

**SPECIFICATIONS**

**Type:** six-round, service revolver
**Origin:** Smith & Wesson, Springfield, Massachusetts
**Caliber:** .32 rimfire
**Barrel Length:** 3.5in

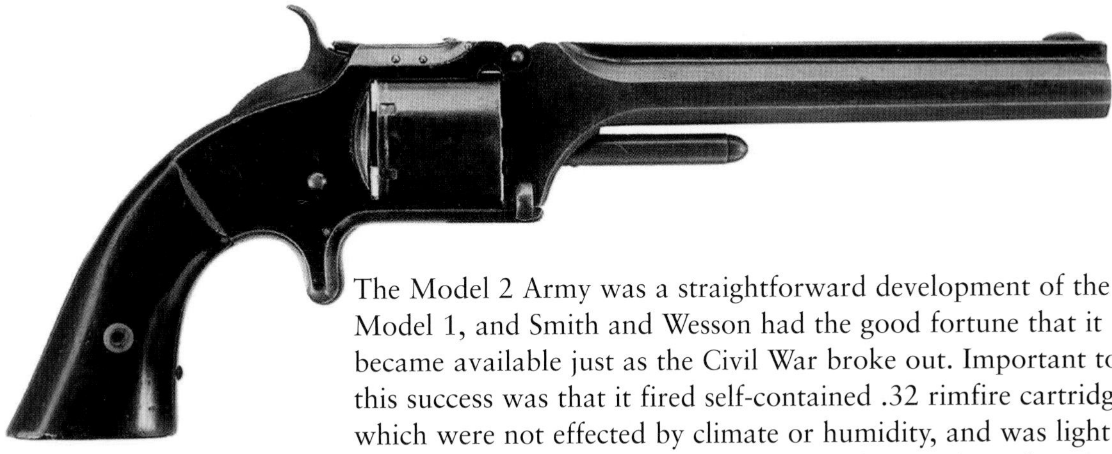

The Model 2 Army was a straightforward development of the Model 1, and Smith and Wesson had the good fortune that it became available just as the Civil War broke out. Important to this success was that it fired self-contained .32 rimfire cartridges which were not effected by climate or humidity, and was light enough to be carried as a back-up to rifle or saber. Thus, it was the very latest design and became an immediate success with Union troops, resulting in a huge backlog of orders for the company. The Model 2 had a six-round, fluted cylinder, was chambered for the .32 rimfire round, and was available with 4, 5, or 6 inch barrels. Over 77,000 were sold between 1861 and the end of production in 1874.

## SMITH & WESSON 0.38 SINGLE-ACTION 2ND MODEL

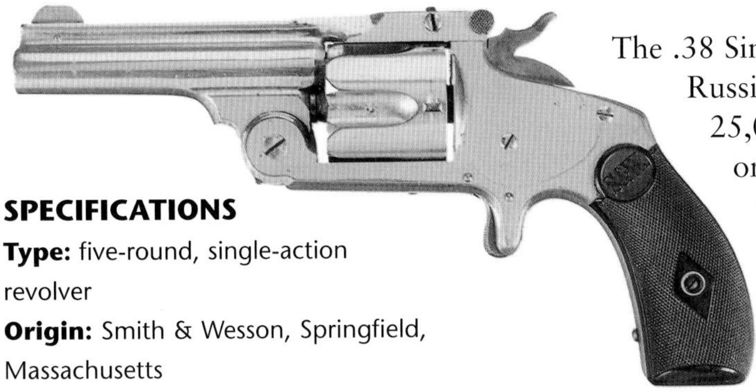

**SPECIFICATIONS**

**Type:** five-round, single-action revolver
**Origin:** Smith & Wesson, Springfield, Massachusetts
**Caliber:** .38
**Barrel Length:** see text

The .38 Single-Action 1st Model, sometimes known as the "Baby Russian" was produced in 1876–7, during which time some 25,000 were completed. The weapon had either a 3.25 inch or 4 inch barrel and a spur-trigger. The 2nd Model, seen here, looked identical to the 1st Model but had a better extractor mechanism and was available in six barrel lengths: 3.25, 4, 5, 6, 8 and 10 inches. The 2nd Model remained in production from 1877 to 1891 and some 108,225 were completed. The example shown here is in typical nickel-plated finish, with a ribbed barrel, five-round fluted cylinder and unguarded spur trigger.

## SMITH & WESSON MODEL 3 SCHOFIELD

The Model 3 was a major success for the company and there were many variations, one of the most interesting being the "Schofield model." Major George Schofield of the US Cavalry liked the Model 3 Smith & Wesson but he patented a number of improvements, designed to make it easier to use on horseback and, in particular, to reload while holding the reins. His proposals were accepted and in 1875 a government order for what was now designated the "Model 3 Schofield" was placed. In essence, Schofield's improvements included a modified barrel catch, improved extraction and a barrel reduced to 7 inches. A new round, the .45 Smith & Wesson (which was not interchangeable with the .45 Colt) was also developed for this weapon.

Major Schofield's heavy revolver proved very popular with users, particularly in the cavalry, but by this time the Colt Single-Action Army was so well-established that it stood no chance of long-term adoption and the Army discarded it after some 9,000 had been made. Army stocks were sold off in 1887, some going to National Guard units, some to Wells Fargo (with barrels shortened to 5 inches) and the balance to civilian arms dealers, many of which then found their way to the Western frontier. According to historians of the period, Schofields were carried by outlaws such as Frank and Jesse James, and Bill Tilghman.

**SPECIFICATIONS**
**Type:** six-round, hinged-frame, single-action revolver
**Origin:** Smith & Wesson, Springfield, Massachusetts
**Caliber:** .45 S&W
**Barrel Length:** 7in

During production there were some minor variations, which have been labeled Schofield First and Second Models, the most visible difference being in the latch. The First Model shown here has a latch with a pointed spur and a washer around the head of the latch retaining screw.

The Second Model shown here has a large circular device at the head of the latch and no washer surrounding the retaining screw.

## SMITH & WESSON MODEL 3 "RUSSIAN"

**SPECIFICATIONS**
**Type:** six-round, hinged-frame, single-action revolver
**Origin:** Smith & Wesson, Springfield, Massachusetts
**Caliber:** .44 Russian
**Barrel Length:** 6in

The Model 3 series was one of the most successful revolvers Smith and Wesson produced, and included a bewildering array of sub-types and variations to the basic design. Some of the most popular Model 3s were known as the "Russians." In 1871 the Russian Government selected the Model 3 to re-equip their army, and once it was modified to take the Russian .44 necked cartridge, some 130,000 revolvers were delivered over the next 8 years.

Smith and Wesson also used the Russian cartridge in commercial weapons, and many thousands were sold, both on the US domestic market and to overseas governments. Smith and Wesson "Russians" were adopted in various quantities by Turkey, Japan, Australia, Argentina, Spain, England and others.

All followed the same basic outline, with the barrel and cylinder tipping forward

around a large hinge pin in front of the cylinder. A star ejection system allowed for quick reloading, while a retaining catch locked the weapon closed just in front of the hammer.

The "Russian" shown here was made for the US civilian market, and is a beautifully prepared piece, with extensive engraving on the frame, barrel and cylinder, all offset by gilt inlay. The finely checkered grips are walnut.

## SMITH & WESSON .38 SAFETY HAMMERLESS REVOLVER ("NEW DEPARTURE")

### SPECIFICATIONS

**Type:** five-round, hinged-frame, double-action revolver
**Origin:** Smith & Wesson, Springfield, Massachusetts
**Caliber:** .38 S&W Special
**Barrel Length:** see text

The .38 Safety Hammerless revolver remained in continuous production from 1886 to 1940 and had the hammer completely enclosed within the frame, and which could only be fired by a long pull on the trigger. Known today as "double-action only," at that time it was introduced as "The New Departure." There is a legend that the design originated when Daniel B. Wesson read a press report that a child had been killed when it cocked and fired a conventional revolver and, as a result, he determined to produce a design in which this was impossible. The resulting weapon also included a grip safety on the rear of the butt, which had to be activated by the shooter's hand in order to disengage an internal hammer block before the trigger could be pulled. Whether the story about Wesson and the child is true or not, the result was an exceptionally safe weapon.

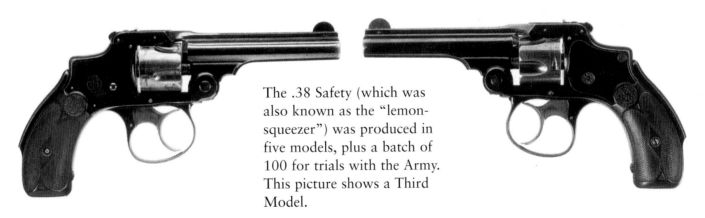

The .38 Safety (which was also known as the "lemon-squeezer") was produced in five models, plus a batch of 100 for trials with the Army. This picture shows a Third Model.

| MODEL | CALIBER | BARREL | PRODUCTION YEAR | NUMBER PRODUCED |
|---|---|---|---|---|
| FIRST | .38S&W | 3.25/4/5in | 1887 | 5,250 |
| SECOND | | 3.25/4/5in | 1887–90 | 37,200 |
| THIRD | | 3.25/4/5in | 1890–98 | 73,500 |
| ARMY TEST | | 6in | 1890 | 100 |
| FOURTH | | 3.25/4/5in | 1898–1907 | 104,000 |
| FIFTH | | 2/3.25/4/5in | 1907–1940 | 41,500 |
| TOTAL | | | | 261,550 |

The changes between Models 1 through 4 mainly concerned the latch which secured the barrel to the frame, and shown here is a Fourth Model. The later Model 5 introduced some changes to ease production. In all models, the barrel was ribbed, with lengths shown in the table.

# SMITH & WESSON .38 HAND-EJECTOR, MILITARY & POLICE MODEL

## SPECIFICATIONS

**Type:** six-round, solid-frame, hand-ejection revolver
**Origin:** Smith & Wesson, Springfield, Massachusetts
**Caliber:** .38 S&W Special (but see text)
**Barrel Length:** see text

The .38 Hand-Ejector, first produced in 1899, has enjoyed a production run of more than one hundred years; well over six million have been produced and it has been estimated that at the peak of its popularity it armed over 80 percent of the police forces in the Continental USA.

For the first sixty years it was known as the Military & Navy Model, but when Smith & Wesson introduced a numbering system in 1958 it was re-designated the Model 10.

The name "hand ejector" derived from the fact that, unlike the top-break revolvers that ejected the empty cases mechanically as the weapon was broken, in the S & W design the cylinder-pin extension was pulled forward allowing the cylinder assembly to swing out sideways for the cases to be removed manually. It was a simple and effective system which proved very popular with users.

The Military & Police Model First Model (also known as the Model of 1899) was produced in two calibers and a variety of barrel lengths: .38 S&W Special with 4, 5, 6, 6.5 or 8 inch barrels, or the .32-20 Winchester cartridge with 4. 5 or 6.5 inch barrels – all had a six-round, fluted cylinder.

A total of 26,286 of all versions was produced between 1899 and 1902, the example shown here being one of 1,000 supplied to the US Navy as the Model 1899.

The .38 Hand-Ejector, Military & Police Second Model appeared in 1902 and had minor changes, including a larger ejector rod; some 12,800 were produced between 1902 and 1911 and, again, the US Navy took 1,000 as the Model 1902.

The Second Model First Change had a minor alteration to the shape of the butt and was in production from 1903 and 1905, some of which (shown here) were delivered to the Canadian Army.

Vast numbers were produced during World War One, including many for the British and Empire Armed Forces, of which the Model 1917 is shown here. Note the "parkerized"(manganese phosphate) finish.

# SMITH & WESSON MODEL 19-5

## SPECIFICATIONS

**Type:** six-round, solid-frame revolver
**Origin:** Smith & Wesson, Springfield, Massachusetts
**Caliber:** .357 Magnum
**Barrel Length:** see text

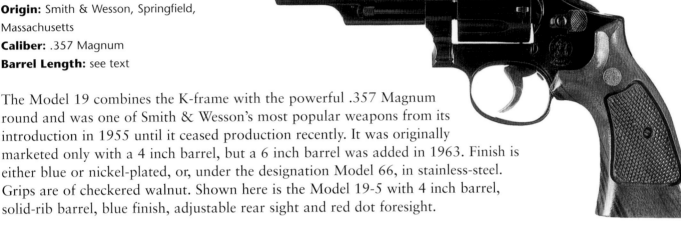

The Model 19 combines the K-frame with the powerful .357 Magnum round and was one of Smith & Wesson's most popular weapons from its introduction in 1955 until it ceased production recently. It was originally marketed only with a 4 inch barrel, but a 6 inch barrel was added in 1963. Finish is either blue or nickel-plated, or, under the designation Model 66, in stainless-steel. Grips are of checkered walnut. Shown here is the Model 19-5 with 4 inch barrel, solid-rib barrel, blue finish, adjustable rear sight and red dot foresight.

# SMITH & WESSON MODEL 29

## SPECIFICATIONS

**Type:** six-round, solid-frame, double-action revolver
**Origin:** Smith & Wesson, Springfield, Massachusetts
**Caliber:** .44 Magnum
**Barrel Length:** see text

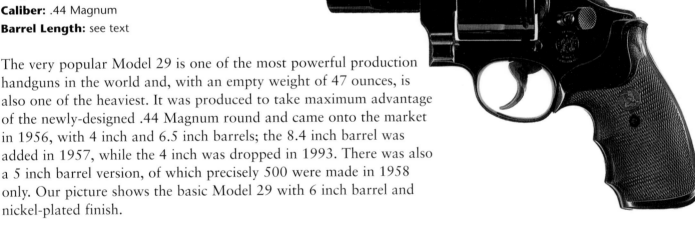

The very popular Model 29 is one of the most powerful production handguns in the world and, with an empty weight of 47 ounces, is also one of the heaviest. It was produced to take maximum advantage of the newly-designed .44 Magnum round and came onto the market in 1956, with 4 inch and 6.5 inch barrels; the 8.4 inch barrel was added in 1957, while the 4 inch was dropped in 1993. There was also a 5 inch barrel version, of which precisely 500 were made in 1958 only. Our picture shows the basic Model 29 with 6 inch barrel and nickel-plated finish.

This Model 29-4 has a 4 inch barrel and unfluted cylinder.

The Model 629 is mechanically identical, but is normally finished in satin-chrome. The one we show here has a 6 inch barrel and is finished in stainless steel.

The Model 29-6 has a blue finish, 5 inch barrel, unfluted cylinder, and rubber grips.

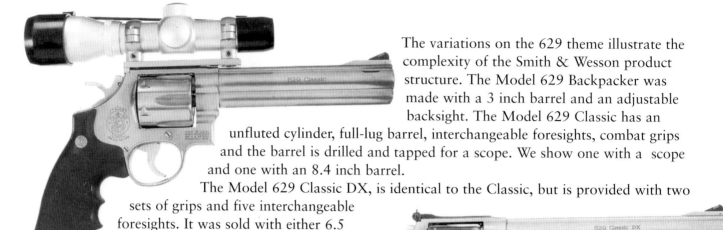

The variations on the 629 theme illustrate the complexity of the Smith & Wesson product structure. The Model 629 Backpacker was made with a 3 inch barrel and an adjustable backsight. The Model 629 Classic has an unfluted cylinder, full-lug barrel, interchangeable foresights, combat grips and the barrel is drilled and tapped for a scope. We show one with a scope and one with an 8.4 inch barrel.

The Model 629 Classic DX, is identical to the Classic, but is provided with two sets of grips and five interchangeable foresights. It was sold with either 6.5 inch or 8.4 inch, or, in 1992–3 only, a 5 inch barrel. The Model 629 Classic Powerport has a 6.5 inch full lug barrel and fully adjustable backsight. The Model 629 Mountain Gun was a limited edition with 4 inch barrel, which was drilled and tapped for a scope, as well as special grips and sights; it was introduced in 1993 and later reintroduced in 1999.

## SMITH & WESSON MODELS 34 AND 43

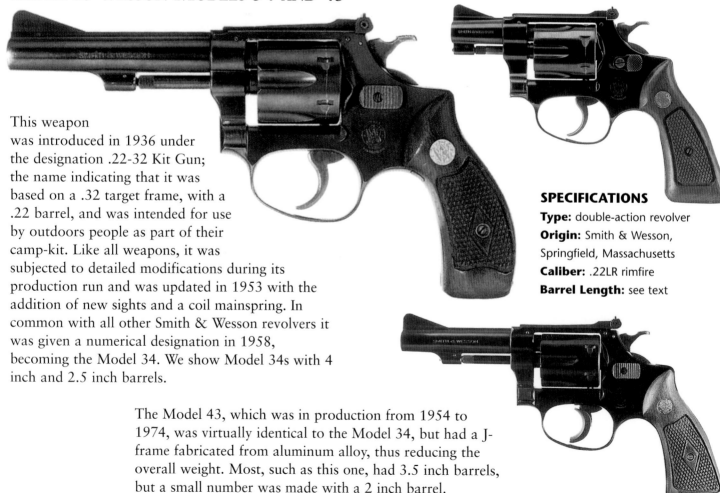

This weapon was introduced in 1936 under the designation .22-32 Kit Gun; the name indicating that it was based on a .32 target frame, with a .22 barrel, and was intended for use by outdoors people as part of their camp-kit. Like all weapons, it was subjected to detailed modifications during its production run and was updated in 1953 with the addition of new sights and a coil mainspring. In common with all other Smith & Wesson revolvers it was given a numerical designation in 1958, becoming the Model 34. We show Model 34s with 4 inch and 2.5 inch barrels.

**SPECIFICATIONS**
**Type:** double-action revolver
**Origin:** Smith & Wesson, Springfield, Massachusetts
**Caliber:** .22LR rimfire
**Barrel Length:** see text

The Model 43, which was in production from 1954 to 1974, was virtually identical to the Model 34, but had a J-frame fabricated from aluminum alloy, thus reducing the overall weight. Most, such as this one, had 3.5 inch barrels, but a small number was made with a 2 inch barrel.

# SMITH & WESSON MODEL 35

## SPECIFICATIONS

**Type:** six-round, solid-frame, double-action revolver
**Origin:** Smith & Wesson, Springfield, Massachusetts
**Caliber:** .22LR
**Barrel Length:** 6in

This model traced its lineage to the .32 Hand Ejector of 1896 and a suggestion by a San Francisco gun dealer named Bekeart that its frame would be a suitable basis for a .22LR target weapon. This eventually found favor with Smith & Wesson who put the new weapon into production in 1912 as the .22/32 Target, thus starting a long series which culminated in the Model 35 which was in production from 1953 to 1973.

The example shown here is a standard Model 35 with blue finish, oversize butt and red-insert foresight blade.

# SMITH & WESSON MODEL 36 CHIEF'S SPECIAL

## SPECIFICATIONS

**Type:** five-round, solid-frame, double-action revolver
**Origin:** Smith & Wesson, Springfield, Massachusetts
**Caliber:** .38 Special
**Barrel Length:** see text

The Chief's Special dates from 1950 and was based on Smith & Wesson's J-frame and chambered for the .38 Special cartridge. It had either a 2 inch or 3 inch barrel and a five-round fluted cylinder. The Model 36LS (LS = Ladysmith) was identical to the original Model 36, except that it came only with a 2 inch barrel and had rosewood grips. The Model 36 Chief's Special Target was marketed between 1955 and 1965, but then continued until 1975 under a new designation – Model 50. It had 2 or 3 inch barrels, adjustable sights and round or square butts. Examples shown here are the Model 36 with 2 inch barrel in blue and nickel-plated finishes, and one with a 3 inch barrel.

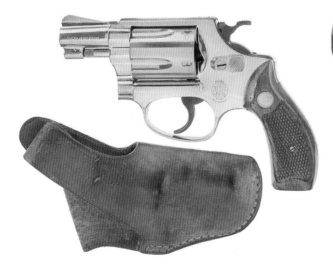

## MODEL 14 (K-38 MASTERPIECE)

### SPECIFICATIONS

**Type:** five-round, solid-frame, double-action and single-action revolver
**Origin:** Smith & Wesson, Springfield, Massachusetts
**Caliber:** .38 Special
**Barrel Length:** see text

Originally designated the K-38 Masterpiece this weapon was introduced in 1946 as a target-shooting version of the Model 10 Military & Police, but with a 6 inch barrel and adjustable sights. Other barrel lengths were added to the range in 1959 and in 1961 a single-action version was introduced. We show two early K-38s with 6 inch barrels.

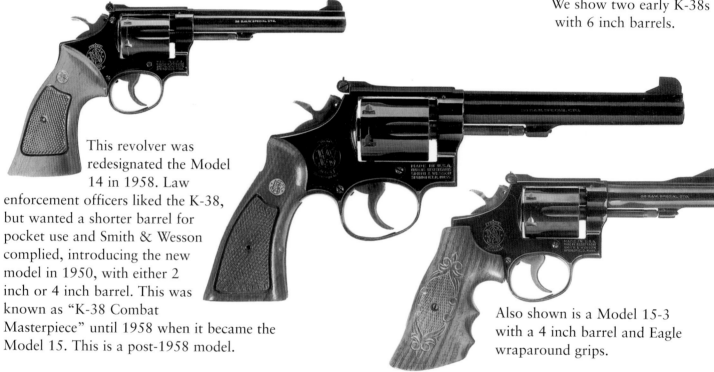

This revolver was redesignated the Model 14 in 1958. Law enforcement officers liked the K-38, but wanted a shorter barrel for pocket use and Smith & Wesson complied, introducing the new model in 1950, with either 2 inch or 4 inch barrel. This was known as "K-38 Combat Masterpiece" until 1958 when it became the Model 15. This is a post-1958 model.

Also shown is a Model 15-3 with a 4 inch barrel and Eagle wraparound grips.

## SPRINGFIELD ARMS REVOLVER

### SPECIFICATIONS

**Type:** six-round, percussion revolver
**Origin:** Springfield Arms Company, Springfield, Massachusetts
**Caliber:** .36
**Barrel Length:** 6in

The Springfield Arms Company (which was not related to the US Government's Springfield Armory) was in business from 1851 to 1869, when it was taken over by the Savage Arms Corporation. The general manager, James Warner, patented a number of designs, but he ran foul of Smith & Wesson who sued him for infringing their patents and won, as a result of which Springfield Arms had to hand over some 1,500 weapons.

The weapons seen here are both Springfield-Warner Navy Models of 1851, with a six-shot, smooth-sided cylinder, six-inch .36 caliber barrel, and walnut grips.

## SPILLER & BURR REVOLVER

**SPECIFICATIONS**

**Type:** six-round, percussion revolver
**Origin:** Spiller & Burr, Atlanta, Georgia
**Caliber:** .36
**Barrel Length:** 7in

On the outbreak of the Civil War, two rich Virginia gentlemen, Edward N. Spiller and David J. Burr, combined with a weapons expert, James H. Burton, to establish a factory to produce a revolver for the Confederate States Army cavalry. The factory was initially sited in Richmond, Virginia, but then moved to Atlanta, Georgia and finally to Macon, also in Georgia, where it set up business in the CSA Armory. The undertaking was always hampered by the pressures of the war, shortage of materials and of skilled labor. The main contract was to deliver 15,000 revolvers in 30 months and had they succeed, Spiller, Burr and Burton would have made a very large profit; in the event, however, only some 1,500 were completed between 1862 and 1865.

Burton's design was based on the Whitney 1858 Navy revolver, and specifically on the Second Model, First Variation, which was in production in the North at the Whitneyville factory, located outside New Haven, Connecticut. Due to shortages of material in the South Burton had to adapt the design in two ways, by using iron instead of steel for the cylinder, and brass instead of iron for the lock-frame.

This example shows the strong resemblance to the Whitney but has a poorer standard of finish, although there is no reason to think it did not work as well. Some of the surviving examples are marked with the name "Spiller & Burr" and others with "C.S." (Confederate States.) This revolver highlights the immense industrial disadvantages facing the Confederacy in its struggle against resourced North.

## STARR MODEL 1858 AND 1863 ARMY REVOLVERS

**SPECIFICATIONS**

**Type:** six-round, single-action, percussion revolver
**Origin:** Starr Arms Company, New York, New York
**Caliber:** .44 rimfire
**Barrel Length:** 6in or 8in

The Starr Arms Company had its offices on Broadway, New York, and factories at Binghampton, Morrisania and Yonkers. The company manufactured weapons designed by Ebenezer (Eben) T. Starr and also those designed by its president, H.H. Wolcott. The company produced a number of deringers and pepperpots designed by Starr and also a very effective revolver, which appeared in three models: Model 1858 Navy, Model 1858 Army Double-Action and the 1863 Single-Action Army.

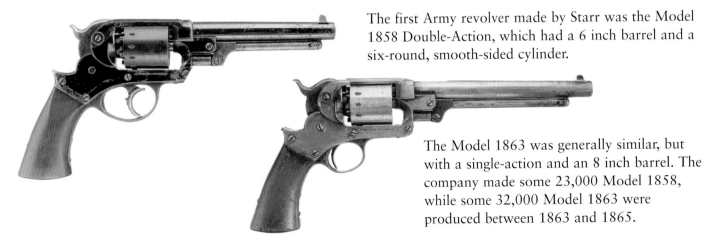

The first Army revolver made by Starr was the Model 1858 Double-Action, which had a 6 inch barrel and a six-round, smooth-sided cylinder.

The Model 1863 was generally similar, but with a single-action and an 8 inch barrel. The company made some 23,000 Model 1858, while some 32,000 Model 1863 were produced between 1863 and 1865.

## WHITNEY NAVY PERCUSSION REVOLVER

### SPECIFICATIONS
**Type:** six shot, single-action percussion revolver.
**Origin:** Whitneyville Armory, New Haven, Connecticut
**Caliber:** .36
**Barrel Length:** 7.5in

Eli Whitney Sr was an engineering genius, but perhaps not as effective in business. His invention of the cotton gin revolutionised the economy of the South, but for various reasons, including competition from other manufacturers, Whitney made very little money from it. He then turned his energies to arms manufacture, and from 1798 onwards, Whitney's company produced a range of longarms and revolvers for both government and civilian markets. Whitney's real strength was in the development of manufacturing techniques, and the company advertised itself as being the first to create standardised parts that could be assembled by workmen with little or no experience.

By the 1860s, the company was in the hands of Whitney's son, Eli Whitney Jr. Financially it was struggling, and most of its efforts were devoted to assembling and selling weapons from surplus parts bought from the government and from other armories.

The Whitney company's first experience of manufacturing handguns was in 1847 when they made over 1,000 .44caliber revolvers for Samuel Colt. At that time Colt had no facilities of his own and needed to sub-contract the manufacture of a government contract he had been awarded.

Whitney went on to develop weapons to their own design, and by the late 1850s were making this series of military caliber weapons to compete with the Colt Navy types. Unlike the Colts, the Whitney revolvers had a solid frame with integral top strap above the cylinder, making for a stronger and more robust design. The one shown is known as the Second Model, and has an octagonal barrel, brass trigger guard and loading ram under the barrel. The Whitney Navy types proved popular in the Civil War, and over 33,000 were made.

## WHITNEY NAVY CONVERSION

### SPECIFICATIONS
**Type:** six shot, single-action cartridge revolver.
**Origin:** Whitneyville Armory, New Haven, Connecticut
**Caliber:** .38 centerfire
**Barrel Length:** 7.75in

This Second Model Whitney has been converted to fire .38 centerfire cartridges, and was renickeled at the same time. It's unlikely that this conversion was carried out in the Whitney factory, but instead was probably the work of another gunsmith. Such cartridge conversions to many makes of percussion revolver were popular once the Rollins White patent had expired, giving a new lease of life to well-proven and reliable weapons.

# AUSTRIA-HUNGARY

## LEGLER TRAPDOOR SCHÜTZEN RIFLE

**SPECIFICATIONS**
**Type:** target rifle
**Origin:** A. Legler, Neustadt
**Caliber:** 9.5mm
**Barrel Length:** 29.5in

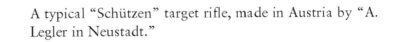

A typical "Schützen" target rifle, made in Austria by "A. Legler in Neustadt."

## LORENZ MODEL 1854 RIFLE MUSKET

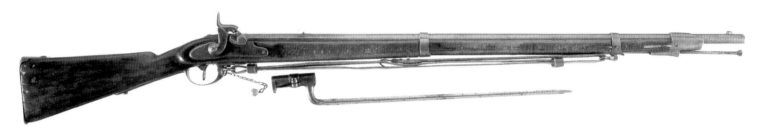

**SPECIFICATIONS**
**Type:** rifled percussion musket
**Origin:** Austro-Hungarian state arsenals
**Caliber:** .54 or .58
**Barrel Length:** n/k

This weapon was designed by Lieutenant Joseph Lorenz of the Imperial Austro-Hungarian Army and entered service with the army in 1854. When the Civil War broke out purchasers from both the Union and the Confederacy scoured Europe looking for firearms of any sort, and as the Lorenz was being replaced by the Model 1862 rifle in Austro-Hungarian service, many thousands were readily available. As a result, the Model 1854 Lorenz rifled musket was widely used by both sides; the Union bought some 225,000 and the Confederacy approximately 100,000.

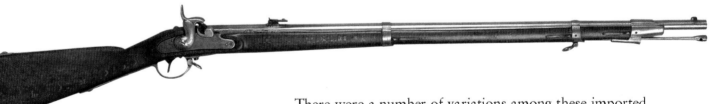

There were a number of variations among these imported weapons. Some were .54 caliber, others .58, and there were also different types of sight. The weapon was well-liked and was considered as accurate as the more widely used Enfield, although it tended to suffer from fouling. The first weapon seen here is .54 caliber with walnut stock and is in generally good condition. The second is in .58 caliber.

## STEYR MANNLICHER MODEL 1893-03 CARBINE

### SPECIFICATIONS
**Type:** bolt-action carbine
**Origin:** Mannlicher, Steyr, Austria
**Caliber:** 6.5mm
**Barrel Length:** 18in

The Mannlicher designs quickly won international acceptance, winning orders from Romania (1892), Switzerland (1893) and the Netherlands (1895), all of which were produced in the factory at Steyr. The initial Romanian order was for the Model 1892 Rifle, which was a typical Mannlicher design but chambered for the Romanian 6.5 x 54R cartridge. This was followed by the Model 1893 Rifle which incorporated some safety improvements, but was otherwise identical to the Model 1892, and by a carbine version, the Model 1893-03 seen here. Compared to the rifle, the carbine's barrel was 10 inches shorter, the bolt-handle was turned down and there were no bayonet fittings. It weighed 7.25 pounds and, like the rifle, had a five-round box magazine.

## STEYR (MAUSER) MODELO 1912

### SPECIFICATIONS
**Type:** bolt-action rifle
**Origin:** Steyr-Mannlicher, Steyr, Austria
**Caliber:** 7mm
**Barrel Length:** 29.5in

The Steyr Modelo 1912 originated with Mexico, which had a long-standing relationship with Mauser, but found that the German company did not have the capacity to meet its needs sufficiently quickly. Mexico then tried to establish its own arms production, setting up a factory to manufacture the FMM 1910 (FMM = Fusil Mauser Mexicano), which was based on the earlier Mauser-produced FMM 1902. When domestic production also proved too slow, an order was placed with Steyr for what was known as the Modelo 1912, based on the FMM Model 1907 but slightly heavier, mainly due to the use of walnut in the stock.

The Modelo 1912 was also ordered by Colombia and Chile, and some of the latter weapons had a curious history. Two battleships were ordered from the

UK by Chile and were nearing completion when World War One broke out in August 1914. They were immediately requisitioned by the Royal Navy and pressed into service as HMS Canada (ex-Almirante Lattore) and HMS Eagle (ex-Almirante Cochrane). Their contents included some 820 Modelo 1912s, which had been ordered by the Chilean Navy, and these were duly put into service by the Royal Navy, being used to arm sailors on second-line vessels such as minesweepers and armed merchant cruisers. On the other side, many Modelo 1912s were awaiting delivery from Steyr and these were seized by the Austro-Hungarian Government before they could be shipped and issued to the Imperial Austro-Hungarian Army. The weapon seen here is a Chilean Modelo 1912, with a fine rendering of the national crest (inset).

# WANZL MODEL 1867

During their short but disastrous 1866 campaign against Prussia, Austrian riflemen with their muzzleloaders were significantly outgunned by the Prussian needle guns. As a result, this conversion was developed to turn existing rifles into cartridge-firing breechloaders. The new Wanzl mechanism had a breechblock which hinged upwards to allow a cartridge to be slotted into the chamber. The block was snapped shut, and locked in place as the hammer descended onto the firing pin. The empty brass case was ejected when the breech was reopened.

This intermediary solution was similar in concept to the British Snider conversion and the American 'Trapdoor' Springfields, and like these was soon superseded by the advent of properly designed breechloaders.

**SPECIFICATIONS**
**Type:** breechloading cartridge conversion
**Origin:** Vienna, Austria
**Caliber:** .55
**Barrel Length:** 32.5in

# WERNDL MODEL 1877 RIFLE AND CARBINE

Josef Werndl (1831–89) joined the army in 1849 and was sent to work in an Imperial arsenal in Vienna, but was then bought out by his father so that he could rejoin the family gunmaking business. Unable to get on with his father, Josef went first to Germany and then to the United States to study gunmaking, returning home in 1853. He took over his father's business in 1855 and turned it into a very successful company – see Steyr Mannlicher Model 1886/90 (above).

Werndl designed a series of firearms under his own name, starting with the Model 1867 and continuing through the Model 1873 to the Model 1877, with a rifle and carbine in each version.

**SPECIFICATIONS**
**Type:** single shot rifle/carbine
**Origin:** Österreichische Waffenfabrik, Steyr, Austria
**Caliber:** 11 x 42mm Werndl
**Barrel Length:** 31.5in (rifle); 23in (carbine)

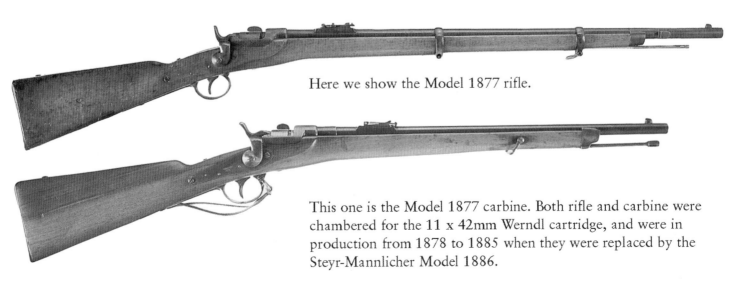

Here we show the Model 1877 rifle.

This one is the Model 1877 carbine. Both rifle and carbine were chambered for the 11 x 42mm Werndl cartridge, and were in production from 1878 to 1885 when they were replaced by the Steyr-Mannlicher Model 1886.

# AUSTRIA

## STEYR-DAIMLER-PUCH MODEL 29/40

### SPECIFICATIONS
**Type:** bolt-action rifle
**Origin:** Steyr-Daimler-Puch, Steyr, Austria
**Caliber:** 7.92mm Mauser
**Barrel Length:** 23in

Following the end of World War One and the dissolution of the Austro-Hungarian Empire, Steyr-Mannlicher became Steyr-Werke AG. In the late 1920s it became involved in the German machinations to circumvent the Versailles Treaty and was absorbed by Steyr-Solothurn, a "shell company," nominally based in Switzerland, in which the German company, Rheinmetall, was a clandestine partner. Following the German Anschluss (military takeover of Austria) in 1938, Steyr-Solothurn became part of the Hermann-Göring-Werke organisation and thus an integral part of the German arms industry.

One of the weapons produced by Steyr during World War Two was this Gewehr 29/40, which was based on the Karabiner 1898k (M1898 Carbine) which had been put into production for the German armed forces in 1935. The Steyr version was produced from parts assembled for export production canceled on the outbreak of war, and was issued to the Kriegsmarine (navy) and Luftwaffe (air force), this example bearing the stamp "M" for Marine. See Germany (*below*) for more information on the Model 1898 series.

## STEYR-MANNLICHER SPORTER MODEL SL

### SPECIFICATIONS
**Type:** bolt-action sporting rifle
**Origin:** Steyr-Mannlicher, Steyr, Austria
**Caliber:** .223 Remington
**Barrel Length:** 23in

One of the first designs of sporting rifles produced by Steyr-Mannlicher after World War Two was the Sporter series. All have a five-round rotary magazine and are available in a wide variety of calibers. They are also produced in four different action lengths (S – Magnum;

M – medium; L – light; and SL – super light) and with either single- or double-set triggers. The model shown here is a Sporter SL, made in 1973, with 23 inch barrel and chambered for the .223 Remington cartridge. It weighs 6.3 pounds.

## STEYR-MANNLICHER LUXUS

### SPECIFICATIONS
**Type:** bolt-action sporting rifle
**Origin:** Steyr-Mannlicher, Steyr, Austria
**Caliber:** 6 x 62 Freres
**Barrel Length:** 26in

The Steyr Luxus range of sporting rifles covers a very wide range of calibers, but this weapon is one of a limited production run chambered for the 6 x 62mm Freres cartridge. This recently-introduced round is manufactured by M.E.N. of Germany and is considered to be equivalent in performance to the North American 6mm-06 Wildcat, combining flat trajectory, good killing power and moderate recoil, and making it very effective against deer, sheep, goats, and antelopes.

## STEYR MODEL 96 SBS

### SPECIFICATIONS
**Type:** bolt-action sporting rifle
**Origin:** Steyr-Mannlicher, Steyr, Austria
**Caliber:** see text
**Barrel Length:** 24in

The Steyr factory was taken over by the Soviet Army in 1945, who stripped out most of the machinery and sent it home to Russia, before handing the site over to the Americans, who converted it to manufacture motor-cycles and tractors. In 1950 Steyr was allowed to restart the production of sporting rifles and since then has produced a succession of well-regarded designs. Seen here is the Model 96 SBS (Safe Bolt System), introduced in 1997, which incorporates considerable enhancements to the safety of the weapon. The bolt is of a modified design, with a forward lug which prevents the trigger being moved while the bolt is unlocked. In addition, powerful rounds can be fired because the bolt and chamber have been designed to take greater stresses.

The Steyr SBS is produced in a wide variety of calibers: .243 Win, 25-06, .270 Win, 6.5x55, 7x64, 7mm/08, .308 Win, .30-06, 7mm Remington Magnum, .300 Winchester Magnum, 8x57JS and 9.3x62. The example shown here is in .25-06 caliber, finished in blue matte and without the scope which would normally be fitted. There is a four-round detachable magazine.

## STEYR AUG

### SPECIFICATIONS
**Type:** automatic assault rifle
**Origin:** Steyr-Mannlicher, Steyr, Austria
**Caliber:** 5.56mm
**Barrel Length:** 20in

Designed in response to an Austrian army requirement, this assault rifle entered service in 1977. The AUG (Armee Universal Gewehr, or army universal rifle) is actually a family of weapons built around the same bullpup frame and plastic stock. Variants can be quickly assembled by replacing components, and the family includes a 5.56mm light machine gun, a 9mm sub-machine gun and a 9mm semi-automatic carbine.

Even more than 25 years after its introduction, the AUG still appears futuristic, and its many design innovations include the bullpup configuration, the smooth one-piece plastic stock (to avoid snagging on uniforms and equipment), integral optical sight and carrying handle, and translucent polymer magazine to enable a quick visual check on the contents. In service the rifle has turned out to be extremely tough and reliable, and has been purchased by many countries, including Australia, Ireland, Morocco, New Zealand and Oman. Carbine variants have also been procured by various police forces.

# AUSTRALIA

## LITHGOW SHORT MAGAZINE LEE-ENFIELD

**SPECIFICATIONS**
**Type:** bolt-action, service rifle
**Origin:** Australian Government Arms Factory, Lithgow, NSW, Australia
**Caliber:** .303 British
**Barrel Length:** 25in

The Australian government established a State armaments factory at Lithgow in New South Wales, which commenced production in 1912. It manufactured exclusively British designs until 1956, including the Short Magazine Lee-Enfield and No. 4 Rifle, as well as Vickers and Bren machineguns. It later produced the FN-FAL under licence (1958–86) and now produces the Austrian Steyr AUG as the F88 assault rifle.

Seen here are three British-designed Short Magazine Lee-Enfield (SMLE) rifles, all built by Lithgow. The first, a Mark 3, was made in 1922 and shows the general characteristics, with the bayonet boss beneath the muzzle, foresight protector, forward sling swivel ramped rear sight, ten-round box magazine and bolt-action (the bolt in the picture is in the cocked position, a breach of normal safety rules).

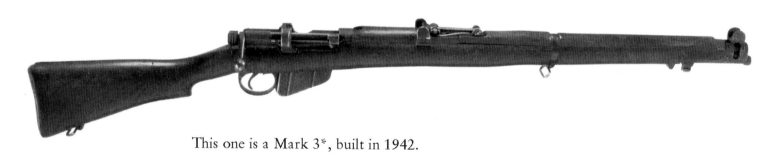

This one is a Mark 3*, built in 1942.

Shown here is a one built in 1944 and then exported to South Africa, which also used British-designed equipment at this time.

# BELGIUM

## PINFIRE REVOLVER RIFLE

**SPECIFICATIONS**
**Type:** pinfire revolving rifle
**Origin:** Liege, Belgium
**Caliber:** 11mm
**Barrel Length:** 23.75in

The pinfire cartridge became popular in Europe in the mid-19th Century and was used extensively in revolvers, although it never caught on in the same way elsewhere or for other applications. However, this unusual piece does shows that some gunsmiths did try to widen the scope of the pinfire system. Made by an unidentified Belgian gunsmith, this rifle takes the cylinder and mechanism of a typical open-frame European pinfire revolver and marries it to a wooden butt and long barrel. Note the ornate scrolled trigger guard.

## COUNA FLINTLOCK FOWLING PIECE

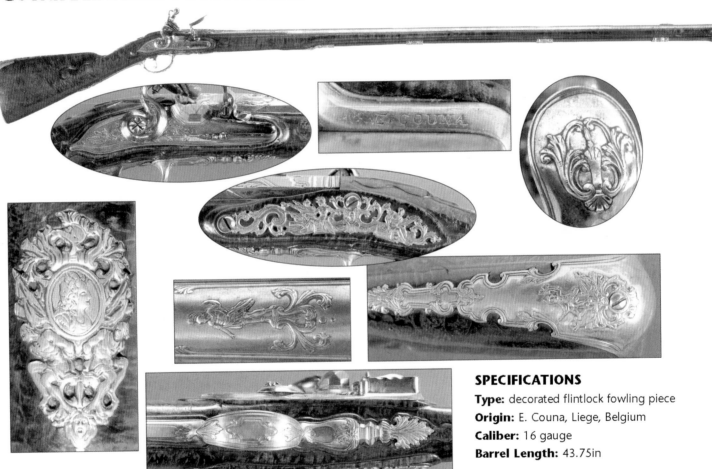

**SPECIFICATIONS**
**Type:** decorated flintlock fowling piece
**Origin:** E. Couna, Liege, Belgium
**Caliber:** 16 gauge
**Barrel Length:** 43.75in

This extraordinary weapon displays the gunsmith's creativity and artistry at its very best. A flintlock fowling piece, it was made at Liege, Belgium, probably in the early 1770s. The woodwork is all carefully selected burl walnut, carefully worked and highly polished. The barrel is almost 44 inches long and is made of high quality steel and engraved along its whole length, apart from the rear 3 inches which are covered with gold and engraved with a picture of a bird sitting on a perch. The lockplate, thumb piece, slide plate,

trigger guard, butt plate and tail pipe are gilded and engraved, while the cock and frizzen are sculpted in matching patterns. This is signed "E. Couna" meaning that it is the work of the Belgian gunsmith, Elizabeth Couna, whose father and husband were both gunmakers in Liege. Elizabeth inherited her father's business on his death in 1767 and she and her husband later moved to Charleville. It is not clear for whom this was made, but he must have been either royalty or extremely wealthy.

## BROWNING BAR RIFLE TYPE I

### SPECIFICATIONS
**Type:** semi-automatic sporting rifle
**Origin:** Browning Arms Co., Morgan, Utah
**Caliber:** see text
**Barrel Length:** 22in, 24in

The Browning BAR Type I was a gas-operated, semi-automatic sporting rifle, introduced in 1967 in various calibers from .243 up to .338 Magnum, and either a 22 or 24 inch barrel. The early models were manufactured by FN in Belgium but later the parts were produced in Belgium but assembled in Portugal.

The BAR Type I was produced in nine standards of finish, from Grade I, the basic, up to Grade V Magnum, the most luxurious, with two sub-grades within grades II, III and V. Four are shown here. This is a Grade II with blued finish and simple scroll engraving on the action with big-game heads.

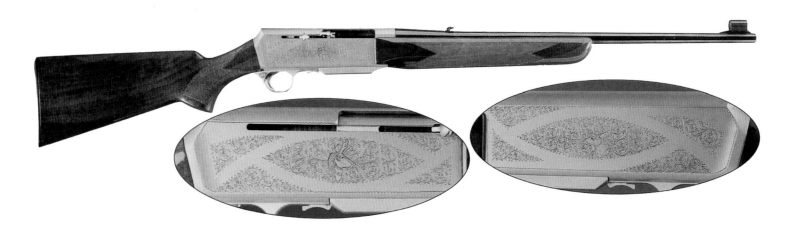

Shown above is a Grade III, also in .243 with 22 inch barrel, with the action plate engraved with English scroll-work and an antelope head on the right, deer head on the left. The trigger is in gold and the stock is more elaborate than on the Grade II.

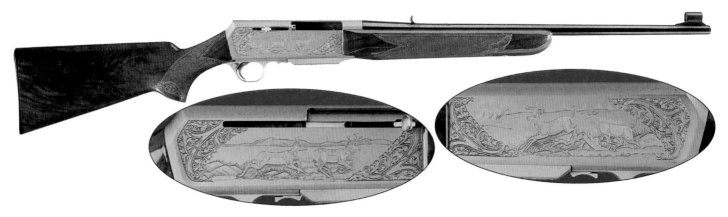

The Grade IV is more elaborate still with big game scenes on either side of the action, antelope on the right side and whitetail deer on the left.

# FN Model 1949

A team led by Dieudonné Saive began work at the FN factory on a semi-automatic rifle in the 1930s, but escaped to England when Belgium was overrun by the Germans in 1940, to continue their work at the Royal Small Arms Factory at Enfield. As soon as their country had been freed in late 1944 the team returned to

Herstal and their work lead, in the first instance, to this weapon, the Model 1949, also known as the SAFN (Saive Automatique Fabrique Nationale). It was a conventionally-shaped rifle, with a full length handguard which totally enclosed the gas cylinder, and a box magazine for ten 7.92mm rounds.

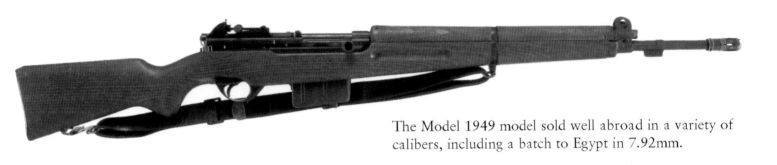

The Model 1949 model sold well abroad in a variety of calibers, including a batch to Egypt in 7.92mm.

# FN FAL 7.62mm

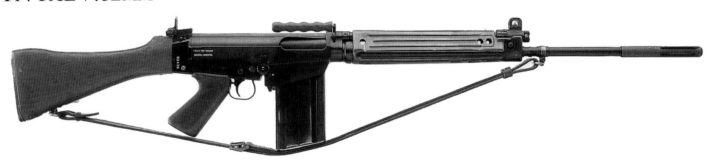

**Type:** semi-automatic service rifle
**Origin:** Fabrique Nationale (FN), Herstal, Belgium
**Caliber:** 7.62 x 51mm NATO
**Barrel Length:** 21in

FN's second post-war rifle, the Model 50, was developed by Saive's team from the Model 1949 and quickly achieved world-wide success. More commonly known as the FAL (Fusil Automatique Leger, or rifle, automatic, light), it was reliable, relatively simple to operate and maintain, and accurate at up to 600 yards. The weapon was originally designed for the 7.92mm cartridge and then adapted for the British .280, but

when it became clear that NATO were going to adopt the 7.62 x 51mm round, the FAL was redesigned yet again and, chambered for this new round, began to enter service in 1953. The original design was capable of fully automatic fire but, following a lead by the British, this was deleted by most buyers, as the powerful cartridge made the weapon unmanageable when firing bursts.

Despite its well-deserved fame, it was not without drawbacks, as it weighed a hefty 9.4 pounds and had an overall length of 43 inches. One particular problem was that when a short butt was fitted for a firer with short arms, the rear sight became too close to his face and could cause injury. In addition, the long, straight magazine made a very low firing position impossible.

Various versions of the FAL were developed including a paratroopers' weapon with folding tubular-steel stock and a heavy barrel version with a folding bipod for service as a light machine gun. In its basic form it was adopted by some 78 armies. Our first example was one that served with Argentina.

The second weapon is the light machinegun/squad automatic weapon version , fitted with a heavy barrel, folding bipod, shortened handguard, and 30-round magazine. This particular example was manufactured by an Israeli company, SBL Industries.

## FN CAL

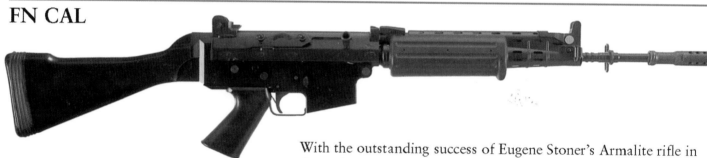

### SPECIFICATIONS
**Type:** experimental semi-automatic rifle
**Origin:** Fabrique Nationale (FN), Herstal, Belgium
**Caliber:** 5.56 x 45mm M193
**Barrel Length:** 18in

With the outstanding success of Eugene Stoner's Armalite rifle in the early 1960s FN decided to develop a new weapon intended for the same .223 round. The result was the CAL, seen here, which was, in effect, a scaled-down version of the FAL. However, the CAL would have been expensive to produce and at the time it was by no means clear that the .223in/5.56mm round was likely to be universally adopted. As a result, this FN weapon found no takers. (Note that the 20-round box magazine is missing from the example shown here).

# BRAZIL

## MAUSER MODEL 1908/34 RIFLE

One of many Mauser-based designs, the Brazilian Model 08/34 had its origins in the German Army's Gewehr 98 (Infantry Rifle Model 1898 – see below). The M1898 then became the basis of the Brazilian M1904, which was, essentially, an M1898 rechambered for the Brazilian Army's standard round, the 7 x 57mm, also known as the "Spanish Mauser." The Brazilian M1908 was virtually identical to the M1904, apart from a new type of nose-cap for a new design of bayonet. The M1908/34 was a new production batch of the M1908, produced at the Brazilian state arsenal at Itajuba.

**SPECIFICATIONS**
**Type:** bolt-action service rifle
**Origin:** Fabrica de Itajuba, Brazil
**Caliber:** 7 x 57mm
**Barrel Length:** 24in

# CANADA

## ROSS RIFLE

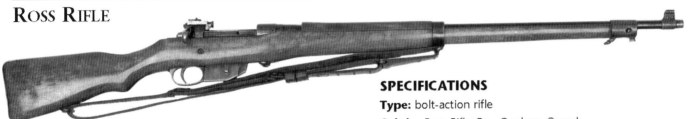

**SPECIFICATIONS**
**Type:** bolt-action rifle
**Origin:** Ross Rifle Co., Quebec, Canada
**Caliber:** .303in
**Barrel Length:** 30in

Sir Charles Ross patented this bolt-action design in 1896, and it was soon adopted for Canadian military service. At the time, British gunmakers, the traditional source of supply for Canada, were fully occupied in making weapons for the British Army in their southern Africa campaigns.

The Ross used an unusual straight-pull bolt design, and at first glance was an extremely accurate weapon. Military service soon showed up its shortcomings however. The Ross was unable to cope with dirt, mud and the rigors of combat, and the mechanism continually jammed in use. In some circumstances the bolt could close without properly locking, causing it to be blown back into the face of the firer.

The rifle went through many changes as Ross continually tried to improve his design, but it never became a reliable or trusted weapon.

There are stories of Canadian soldiers in World War One having to kick the bolts of their rifles to operate the mechanism, and after the first few months of the war, infantrymen tried instead to scavenge Lee-Enfields from British corpses. The Ross was replaced in front line service by the Lee Enfield in 1916, although it did go on to have a worthwhile career as a sniper rifle. We show a Model 1910 Type III.

# REPUBLIC OF CHINA (Nationalist)

## CHINESE TYPE 99 CONVERSION

**SPECIFICATIONS**
**Type:** bolt-action rifle
**Origin:** Chinese Nationalist state arsenal
**Caliber:** 7.92mm Mauser
**Barrel Length:** 26.75in

There is no documentation to attest to the history of this weapon, but it is possible to reconstruct its travels with a reasonable degree of confidence.

It started as a Japanese Arisaka Type 99 infantry rifle, chambered for the 7.7 x 58mm Arisaka cartridge, and produced in Japan from 1939 onwards for the Imperial Japanese Army. It is stamped with the insignia of the Chinese Nationalist North China Army, which indicates that it must have been captured during the fighting in Manchuria during the Sino-Japanese War at

some time between 1939 and 1945, and that its new owners modified it to chamber the 7.92mm cartridge used by Generalissimo Chiang Kai-Shek's army. It appears that it was captured by Mao Tse-tung's Red Army during the Chinese Civil War from whom it was captured by U.S. forces during the Korean war, as a result of which it ended up in its present home, the United States.

## CHINESE MAUSER

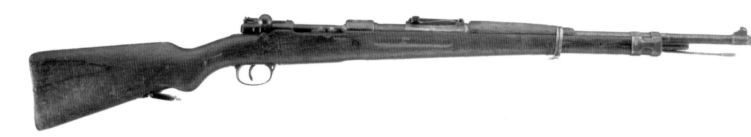

**SPECIFICATIONS**

**Type:** bolt-action rifle
**Origin:** Chinese Nationalist state arsenal
**Caliber:** 7.9 x 57mm Mauser
**Barrel Length:** 24in

The Chinese Army purchased small numbers of Mauser rifles at various times, starting with an unknown quantity of Model 1895s in about 1896–7. The Kwangtung state arsenal then manufactured the Model 21 Short Rifle in the 1930s, which was a crude copy of the FN Modelle 30. The weapon seen here, however, was manufactured in vast numbers, perhaps as many as two million, and was a direct copy of the standard model Mauser, but known in China as the "Chiang Kai-Shek rifle." Production went on from 1936 until 1949. The original workmanship was poor, and as weapons such as this saw many years of hard service in the Sino-Chinese and the Chinese civil wars, it is not surprising that the one shown here is in such a shabby condition.

# CHINA, PEOPLE'S REPUBLIC

## CHINESE TYPE 56 RIFLE

**SPECIFICATIONS**

**Type:** semi-automatic rifle
**Origin:** Chinese (PRC) state arsenals
**Caliber:** 7.62 x 39mm
**Barrel Length:** 21in

The Soviet SKS, entered production in the mid-1940s, and was produced in considerable numbers in Russia, China, East Germany and North Korea (*see Russia section below*). The Chinese version was designated Type 56 and was virtually an identical copy of the Soviet original. It had a folding bayonet, ramped rearsight and an integral, charger-loaded ten-round box magazine.

We also show a paratrooper's version, which differs rather more from the Soviet original, with plastic bodywork and pistol grip, and a composite stock which folds to the right. It has a more elaborate flash eliminator than the original carbine and does not have a bayonet attachment.

## NORINCO TYPE 79 SNIPER RIFLE

### SPECIFICATIONS
**Type:** semi-automatic sniper rifle
**Origin:** NORINCO, China
**Caliber:** 7.62 x 54mm R
**Barrel Length:** 24in

The SVD sniper rifle entered service with the Soviet Army in 1965 (*see Russia section below*). Its use then spread rapidly throughout Soviet client armies and it was put into production in China as the Type 79. As with the Soviet original, it has a 4x PSO sniper scope, which is calibrated for ranges out to 1,300m. The Soviet Army developed sniping to a very high level against the Germans during World War Two and this fine weapon incorporated all the lessons of that conflict. The Type 79 weighs 9.9 pounds with its sight and empty magazine, which is somewhat less than equivalent Western weapons; for example, the British Accuracy International weighs 14.3 pounds in a similar condition.

## NORINCO MODEL 305

### SPECIFICATIONS
**Type:** semi-automatic rifle
**Origin:** NORINCO, China
**Caliber:** 7.62 x 51mm NATO
**Barrel Length:** 24in

The US Garand Rifle M14 was a development of the famous M1, converted to the newly-standardized 7.62mm NATO round and with a box magazine. It was produced in very large numbers, so why NORINCO should have chosen to produce a carbon copy (apart from omitting the bayonet lug) is not at all clear. Nor is there any question of pretense, as the weapon is clearly marked "Made in Rep. of China."

# NORINCO TYPE 86 BULLPUP

**SPECIFICATIONS**
**Type:** bullpup semi-automatic rifle
**Origin:** NORINCO, China
**Caliber:** 7.62 x 39mm
**Barrel Length:** 16.5in

The Type 86 was an attempt by NORINCO designers to adapt the Kalshnikov AK-47 action to a bullpup design. It is of all-metal construction, with an AK-47 bayonet, vertically-mounted, forward-folding handgrip, sight in the fixed carrying handle, and a 30-round magazine. Two examples are shown here, one with a fixed bayonet, but no magazine, while the other has the magazine but no bayonet, enabling the gas cylinder to be seen. Only a few hundred of this weapon were produced, and when it was not adopted by the Peoples Liberation Army (PLA) they were exported to the United States for sale on the civil market.

# NORINCO MAK-90

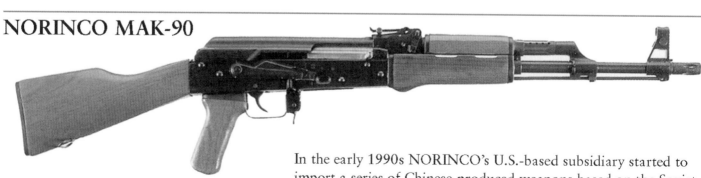

In the early 1990s NORINCO's U.S.-based subsidiary started to import a series of Chinese-produced weapons based on the Soviet AK-47, under the generic title "MAK-90." All are chambered for the Russian 7.62 x 39mm round. Shown here is a standard model, which is virtually identical with the Soviet original.

## M1867 DANISH REMINGTON ROLLING BLOCK

**SPECIFICATION**
**Type:** rolling block,
single-shot rifle
**Origin:** Kjøbenhavns
Tolhuus, Copenhagen,
Denmark
**Caliber:** 11.7 x 27R
Danish
**Barrel Length:** 35.5in

In the early 1860s the Royal Danish Army selected the Remington rolling block rifle (*see below*) for production under licence at the Kjøbenhavns Tolhuus (Copenhagen Arsenal). The rifle was chambered for the Danish 11.7mm rimfire cartridge and used the Remington-Rider rolling block, a very successful design, in which the breech-block pivoted to the rear. Considerable quantities were manufactured in three sub-types: a rifle with bayonet for infantry; a carbine with bayonet for artillery; and a carbine without bayonet for cavalry and engineers. One feature of these weapons which attracts comment is the extraordinary length of the rear-sight leaf – some 3.5 inches – graduated to 2,100 yards. The Model 1867 was replaced in front-line service by the Krag-Jorgensen Model 1889 and withdrawn from service in 1896, converted to 8mm centerfire and then reissued as the Model 1867/86 for use by the artillery. Some were still held in reserve in 1946 and were then sold onto the U.S. civil market. This Model 1867 was made in 1881.

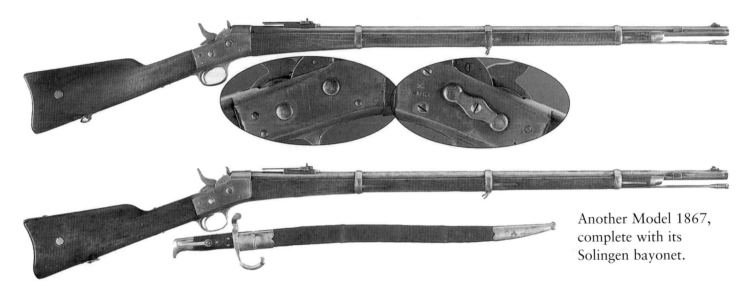

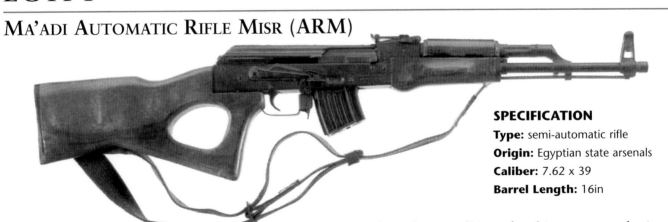

Another Model 1867, complete with its Solingen bayonet.

# EGYPT

## MA'ADI AUTOMATIC RIFLE MISR (ARM)

**SPECIFICATION**
**Type:** semi-automatic rifle
**Origin:** Egyptian state arsenals
**Caliber:** 7.62 x 39
**Barrel Length:** 16in

Egypt has a long tradition of making weapons for its armed forces under license from foreign designers. For many years Swedish rifles were produced, but when the country came under strong Soviet influence in the 1950s and '60s, production switched to the AK-47, then the standard rifle of virtually all Warsaw Pact and Soviet-client state armies. The Ma'adi Company For Engineering Industries is responsible for production of Kalashnikov-based weapons at their factory in Cairo. The weapon seen here has the large butt with thumbhole seen on Chinese versions of the AK-47, and a ten-round magazine.

# FINLAND

## SAKO MODELS M/28-30 AND M/1939

Finland obtained its independence from Russia in 1917, but this was followed by a short and bloody civil war, which ended in 1918. The new government then set about building up the armed forces and a defense industry, one outcome of which was the arms company, Sako. Vast stocks of Mosin-Nagant rifles had been captured from the Russians and this weapon formed the basis of Finnish Army weapons until after World War Two. The Mosin-Nagant was further developed to meet Finnish needs and conditions, but a complicating factor was the existence of two bodies – the regular Army and the Civil Guard (Sk.Y) – whose procurement policies did not always agree.

**SPECIFICATIONS**
**Type:** bolt-action rifle
**Origin:** Suojeluskuntain Ase-ja Konepaja Osakeyhtio (Sako), Riihimaki, Finland
**Caliber:** 7.62 x 54R
**Barrel Length:** 29in (M/28-30); 28in (M/1939)

The M/28-30 was developed from the M/28, but had a better sight and other minor improvements. By the mid-1930s the Army and the Sk.Y had three different versions of the Mosin-Nagant in service and undertook a joint study to agree on one new model. Each organisation put forward a design proposal and this was won by the Sk.Y proposal which was just entering production as the M/1939.

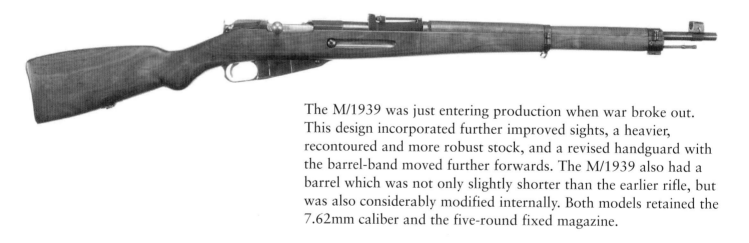

The M/1939 was just entering production when war broke out. This design incorporated further improved sights, a heavier, recontoured and more robust stock, and a revised handguard with the barrel-band moved further forwards. The M/1939 also had a barrel which was not only slightly shorter than the earlier rifle, but was also considerably modified internally. Both models retained the 7.62mm caliber and the five-round fixed magazine.

## VALMET M1962 ASSAULT RIFLE

## SPECIFICATIONS

**Type:** semi-automatic rifle
**Origin:** Valmet, Uusikaupunki, Finland
**Caliber:** 7.62 x 39mm Soviet
**Barrel Length:** 16.5in

The first version of the Kalashnikov AK-47 to be produced in Finland was the Rk 60 (Rynnäkkökivääri 60 or M-60), which underwent user trials, and then, following modifications proposed by the Finnish Army, entered service as the Rk-62 (M 1962). One of the most significant changes to the original Kalashnikov design was that the back sight was moved from the forward end of the receiver cover to the rear end, thus considerably extending the sight-base and improving accuracy. The Finnish Rk-62 also had a folding butt. The workmanship on these Valmet weapons is of a very high standard, and this combined with the rearrangement of the sights makes this one of the most accurate versions of the AK-47.

## VALMET M1978 ASSAULT RIFLE

## SPECIFICATIONS

**Type:** semi-automatic rifle
**Origin:** Valmet, Uusikaupunki, Finland
**Caliber:** 5.56mm (usually 7.62 x 39mm)
**Barrel Length:** 23in

Among the Kalashnikov developments produced by Valmet was the M1978, which was chambered for the Soviet 7.62 x 39mm round, but had a 23 inch barrel (compared to 16 inch in the standard version) with a bipod, to enable it to be used as a squad automatic weapon (SAW). The weapon seen here differs from the usual M1978 made by Valmet in that it is chambered for 5.56mm, lacks a carrying handle and the rear sight is on the distal end of the receiver.

## VALMET M1982 BULLPUP ASSAULT RIFLE

The Valmet M1982 was one of many assault rifles to appear in the late 20th century which employed the "bullpup configuration" in which the magazine is placed behind the trigger/pistol grip. The

## SPECIFICATIONS

**Type:** semi-automatic rifle, bullpup configuration
**Origin:** Valmet, Uusikaupunki, Finland
**Caliber:** 5.56 x 45mm NATO
**Barrel Length:** 16.5in

basic action was the same as in the Kalashnikov, but rearranged to suit the new configuration, and contained in a shockproof plastic polymer housing. Overall length was 28 inches and the box magazine carried 30 rounds. The M1982 was not accepted by the Finnish Army and some of the trials batch were then sold on the U.S. civil market.

## SAKO SPORTER

## SPECIFICATIONS

**Type:** bolt-action sporting rifle
**Origin:** Suojeluskuntain Ase-ja Konepaja
Osakeyhtio (Sako), Riihimaki, Finland
**Caliber:** see text
**Barrel Length:** see text

Sako has produced a large range of sporting rifles, one of the earliest post-war ranges being the "Sporter" which appeared in numerous variations, many of the names being prefixed "Finn..." Among these was the Finnbear seen here in .270 caliber and with a 25 inch barrel, and with a Weaver K series scope on Weaver mounts.

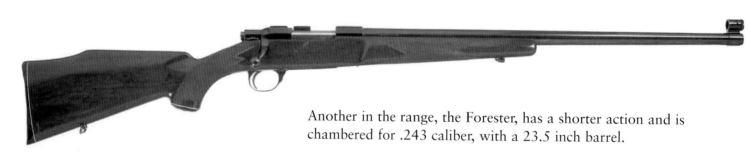

Another in the range, the Forester, has a shorter action and is chambered for .243 caliber, with a 23.5 inch barrel.

# FRANCE

## CHARLEVILLE MUSKET

## SPECIFICATIONS

**Type:** flintlock musket
**Origin:** Manufacture de Charleville, Charleville, France
**Caliber:** .36
**Barrel Length:** 44.5in

The first French standardised model musket appeared in 1717 and this was followed by a series of major and minor modifications over the ensuing century. The weapon seen here was made in France at the government-owned Manufacture de Charleville, with a lock supplied by another of the state arsenals at Maubeuge. The three barrel bands suggest that it is either a Model 1728, but it is not a Model 1777 as the priming-pan is made from iron rather than brass. Of much greater significance, however, is that there is very clear evidence from various marks that this was among the weapons supplied to the United States' Continental Army in 1778, during the Revolutionary War. Such French flintlock muskets served as the pattern for the very similar Springfield M1795.

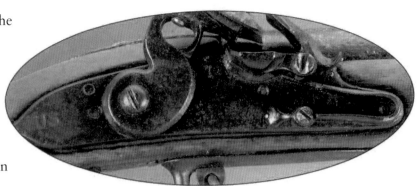

## DAUDETEAU RIFLE

### SPECIFICATIONS
**Type:** bolt-action rifle
**Origin:** Manufacture de St Denis, France
**Caliber:** 6.5 x 53.5SSR Daudeteau No 12
**Barrel Length:** 31.25in

The Daudeteau rifle was developed to fire a special long, round-nosed, parallel-sided round, which required a special design of chamber and barrel. Ammunition was loaded into the action by means of a curved, five-round stripper clip. The design appears to have been around for some years as the weapon seen here is dated 1879, but the only known official consideration was given in 1896 when the Daudeteau was offered to the French Navy. It appears that a small number was accepted, but they were phased out in about 1905.

## MODELLE 66 CHASSEPOT/ MODELLE 1874 GRAS

The French Fusil Modelle 1866 will always be known by the name of its inventor, Antoine Alphonse Chassepot (1833–1905). This Frenchman began his experiments on breechloading systems in 1857 and sufficiently impressed the French Army for his rifle to be adopted as the standard infantry weapon only nine years later. The ammunition was held in a paper cartridge and loaded through the breech, which was then closed by pushing the bolt forwards and turning it down to lock. It was first used at the Battle of Mentana (November 3, 1867) where it inflicted heavy losses on the enemy, but in the Franco-Prussian War (1870) it proved greatly superior to the Prussian Army's much-vaunted Dreyse needle-gun.

## SPECIFICATIONS

**Type:** bolt-action rifle
**Origin:** Manufacture d'Armes Ste Etienne (MAS), France
**Caliber:** 11mm
**Barrel Length:** 31.5in

The weapon seen here is a Modelle 1866 with bright metal parts and a walnut stock, which was made in 1873. The maker's name – Manufacture d'Armes Ste Etienne – is very elegantly engraved.

Chassepot's original concept became outdated very quickly because the metal centerfire cartridge case quickly demonstrated its superiority to paper cartridges. As a result all Chassepots were modified to fire the 11 x 59mm Gras metal cartridge, and the rifle's designation was changed to Gras Modelle 1874. The weapon shown here is a Modelle 1874 with some minor modifications incorporated in 1880.

## FUSIL MAS 36

### SPECIFICATIONS

**Type:** bolt-action service rifle
**Origin:** Manufacture d'Armes Ste Etienne (MAS), France
**Caliber:** 11mm
**Barrel Length:** 31.5in

The French Army fought World War One armed with rifles that dated back to the 1880s, and in the 1920s it became clear that a totally new weapon was required, designed around the 7.5 x 54mm rimless round. Progress was slow and it was not until 1929 that the final two designs were selected, and it was a further eight years before the winner began to reach the troops.

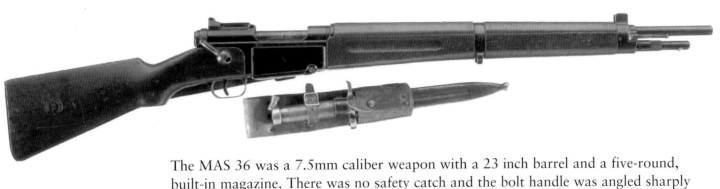

The MAS 36 was a 7.5mm caliber weapon with a 23 inch barrel and a five-round, built-in magazine. There was no safety catch and the bolt handle was angled sharply forward so that the ball lay directly above the trigger. Even though it entered service in 1937 only a relatively small number had reached units by the outbreak of war in 1939. Production restarted after the war and the MAS 36 was in wide-scale use until replaced by the FA MAS in the 1970s.

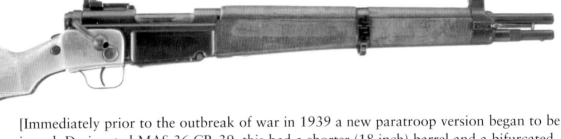

[Immediately prior to the outbreak of war in 1939 a new paratroop version began to be issued. Designated MAS 36 CR-39, this had a shorter (18 inch) barrel and a bifurcated aluminum folding stock, which split into two and swiveled forward to lie either side of the barrel. Curiously, it was left unpainted, exactly as shown in this picture.

Another version appeared in 1951, equipped with a permanently-attached grenade launcher. Designated MAS 36 PG-511, this had a sight for the grenade launcher, which folded back along the top of the handguard when not in use (it can be seen in this picture, just to the left of the foresight guard).

## FUSIL D'ASSAUT MAS 5.56MM ASSAULT RIFLE

The Fusil d'Assaut, Manufacture d'Armes de St Etienne (FA MAS) was introduced into service with the French Army in 1980 and has proven to be an effective and well-specified weapon for both general service and for use by special forces. It uses a delayed blowback mechanism, derived from the French AA-52 general-purpose machinegun, to fire the 5.56 x 45mm French round from a closed bolt position. A black plastic lower handguard, pinned to the barrel and receiver, extends to the magazine well and cannot be removed. Because it has a "bullpup" configuration, the trigger mechanism and pistol grip have been mounted to the lower hand guard,

## SPECIFICATIONS

**Type:** automatic
assault rifle
**Origin:** Manufacture
d'Armes de St Etienne,
St Etienne, France
**Caliber:** 5.56 x 45mm
**Barrel Length:** 19.2in

forward of the magazine housing. Among the features of the FA MAS are the prominent carrying handle (which also houses and protects the sight), left or right-side ejection, a three-round burst option, and a built-in bipod, whose legs fold individually against the receiver when not in use. A slightly modified version, FA MAS G-2, is offered for export, with a revised trigger guard and capable of firing the standard 5.56 x 45mm NATO round. The weapon seen here is a commercial copy of the French Army FA MAS made by MAS, and differs only in being chambered for the .223 Remington round.

# GERMANY

## AYDT SCHUETZEN RIFLE[

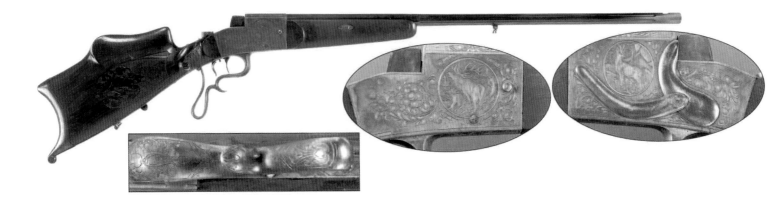

## SPECIFICATIONS

**Type:** Aydt-system, single-shot schuetzen rifle
**Origin:** unknown German gunsmith
**Caliber:** 8.15 x 46R
**Barrel Length:** 32.25in

The "Aydt system" was a type of action which was popular in Continental Europe for target shooting rifles (generally known as "Schuetzen rifles"), particularly in Finland and Germany. It involved a falling-block with the hammer concealed within it. Schuetzen rifles were designed for competitive shooting from the standing position, although they were occasionally used in the kneeling position. They were, however, never used for prone shooting, such "ungentlemanly" conduct being left to the military. The 8.15 x 46R cartridge was designed by a company named Frohn in Suhl, Germany in the 1890s, which suggests that this unsigned and undated weapon may be have been produced at about the turn of the 19th/20th centuries.

# DWM Model 1909 (Argentina)

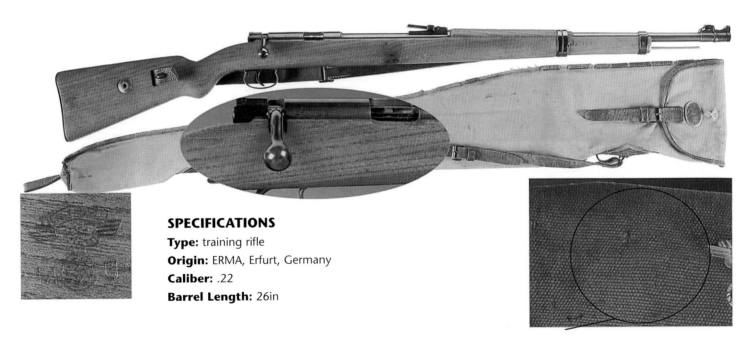

## SPECIFICATIONS
**Type:** bolt-action service rifle
**Origin:** Deutsche Waffen und
Munitionsfabrik, Karlsruhe, Germany
**Caliber:** 7.65 x 53mm Mauser
**Barrel Length:** 30in

The Deutsche Waffen und Munitionsfabrik (DWM, German Weapons and Ammunition Company) was established in Karlsruhe in the Ruhr in 1872 as Henri Ehrmann & Co., but underwent a series of reorganizations, amalgamations and buy-outs until it emerged as DWM in 1896. Apart from its own businesses, DWM also owned substantial shareholdings in FN and Mauser. DWM's weapons business was primarily involved in making other company's designs under licence and in 1909 it started to manufacture the Mauser M1909 for the Argentine Army, as seen here. This weapon was based on the Mauser G98, but was slightly shorter and lighter. Initial production took place in Germany, but from 1942 onwards it was made by FMAP in Argentina. Like the German original, it had a five-round, built-in magazine.

# Erma DSM 34 Training Rifle

## SPECIFICATIONS
**Type:** training rifle
**Origin:** ERMA, Erfurt, Germany
**Caliber:** .22
**Barrel Length:** 26in

ERMA was the acronym for the Erfurter Maschinewerke Gmbh, usually known as Erma-Werke. The company started business in about 1919 as a general engineering undertaking, but expanded into weapons manufacture in 1931. It then specialised in submachine guns, including the famous MP38 and MP40, but also produced .22 caliber training weapons and conversion kits. The weapon seen here is the Deutsche Sport Modell 34 (DSM 34) Training Rifle, one of several such designs produced by various armament firms to meet the Nazis' need for military training for organizations such as the Hitler Youth. This example was produced for the N.S.K.K., the Nationalsozialistisches Kraftfahrkorps (National Socialist Transport Corps), which not only embraced all German (and from 1938, Austrian) motor clubs, but was also responsible for training drivers for the Army and, during the war, providing transport in support of military projects, traffic control in civilian areas, and other support services.

## FRIEDLEIN SCHUETZEN RIFLE

Another of the very large German Schuetzen rifles for competitive shooting, this example was made by gunsmith Friedrich Friedlein of Stockheim. It has a fully adjustable rear sight mounted on the butt and uses a Martini action. It has the holders for a cleaning rod beneath the barrel, but the rod itself is missing.

### SPECIFICATIONS
**Type:** Martini-action, competition rifle
**Origin:** Friedrich Friedlein, Stockheim
**Caliber:** 9mm
**Barrel Length:** 29.6in

## GUSTLOFF KKW TRAINING RIFLE

The Gustloff-Werke was a small weapons production facility located at Suhl in Germany. Its best known product was the VG 1-5 (Volksgerät or People's Weapon), a simple automatic rifle, intended for mass production in 1944/45. However, it also took part in the pre-war KKW program, producing this weapon which was intended to present the user with the same look and feel as the K98 service rifle, but with the minimal recoil of .22 caliber.

### SPECIFICATIONS
**Type:** small caliber, single shot, training and competition rifle
**Origin:** Gustloff Werke, Suhl, Germany
**Caliber:** .22
**Barrel Length:** 24in

## GUSTLOFF-WERKE G43

### SPECIFICATIONS
**Type:** G43 service rifle
**Origin:** Gustloff Werke, Suhl, Germany
**Caliber:** 8mm
**Barrel Length:** 24in

This is a Gustloff-produced version of the Walther G43 (Gewehr 43) and was, in fact, among the first to be produced. It is stamped with the "bcd" production code, which identifies the Gustloff-Werke, but there is reason to believe that this was one of a batch that was assembled at the SS-controlled Buchenwald Concentration Camp.

## HAENEL MASCHINENPISTOLE MP44

**SPECIFICATIONS**

**Type:** automatic assault rifle
**Origin:** Haenel Waffen und Fahrradfabrik, Germany
**Caliber:** 7.92mm Kurz (Short)
**Barrel Length:** 16.5in

Work on this project started before World War Two, after German analysis of earlier combat experience indicated that most targets were engaged at ranges below 300 yards. This meant that infantrymen were carrying rifles and ammunition that fired much further than they needed, and that were larger and heavier than necessary. By 1942 a shorter ("Kurz") version of the standard German 7.92mm rifle cartridge had been developed, one lighter and developing less recoil than the full-sized round. This reduced recoil opened up the possibility of a hand-held infantry weapon firing rifle ammunition that would be controllable during automatic fire.

Trial batches of two new weapons were built around this round, one designed by Walther and the other by Haenel. The intention was to create a universal rifle that would carry out the roles of rifle, sub-machine gun and light machine gun. It didn't – but it did give the infantryman a handy, light weapon that was dramatically effective in real combat conditions.

After early combat experience, the Walther rifle was dropped and the Haenel design modified by Louis Schmeisser to enter service as the Maschinenpistole (machine pistol) MP43.

The MP 43 was gas-operated, where gasses are tapped off from the barrel into a cylinder to operate a piston which drives back, unlocking the bolt and pushing it back to begin the extraction-reloading cycle. Ammunition was fed from a 30-round detachable box magazine under the receiver. The rifle was also designed to be easy to manufacture by the use of stampings and spot welding wherever possible.

The designation was changed to MP 44 in 1944, then later to Sturmgewehr (StG) 44, or "Assault Rifle", supposedly at the instruction of Adolf Hitler himself. Luckily for the Allies, the rifle entered service too late to greatly affect the outcome of the war, and never replaced the bolt-action Kar 98 series. It did set the standard for future military rifles, however, and concepts from it can be seen in almost every automatic weapon since, from the AK 47 to the M16 and beyond.

## HECKLER & KOCH G3

**SPECIFICATIONS**

**Type:** semi-automatic rifle
**Origin:** Heckler & Koch, Oberndorf, Germany
**Caliber:** 7.62 x 51mm NATO
**Barrel Length:** 20in

[Following World War Two, some German weapon designers moved to Spain, where they worked on a new rifle for the Spanish Army. This rifle, known as the CETME, used a roller-operated delayed-blowback system and later became the basis for the standard rifle for the (then) newly established West German Army. This weapon, designated Gewehr 3 (G3), became the start-point for

every new German rifle design until the mid-1990s. The G3A1 had a folding butt, while the G3A2 had a free-floating barrel, and the majority of the original G3s were modified to this standard. The G3A3, fielded in 1964, had a new flash suppressor, drum rear sight, and plastic (as opposed to wood) butt, while the G3A4 was a G3A3 with a retracting butt. Several countries undertook licensed production of the G3A3, including Turkey (G3A7) Iran (G3A6) and Portugal.

This picture shows a G3 carbine with a short barrel and retracting butt.

Like many other assault rifles, the G3 can have a grenade launcher clipped under the barrel.

## HECKLER & KOCH MODEL 91

### SPECIFICATIONS

**Type:** semi-automatic sporting rifle
**Origin:** Heckler & Koch, Oberndorf, Germany
**Caliber:** .308 Winchester
**Barrel Length:** 17.7in

The Heckler & Koch Model 91A2, seen here, was developed from the military G3 specifically for the US civil market, with the first examples going on sale in 1974. Externally, the Model 91 is almost identical to the G3, except that it does not have the grenade-launcher ring on the muzzle. Internally, it is chambered for the .308

Winchester cartridge and the magazine carries 20 rounds. It was sold in the USA as a hunting weapon but a number of states have made ownership illegal. The other version is the Model 91A3, which is identical to the Model 91A2 apart from a retracting stock. The Model 93 is similar to the Model 91 but chambered for the .223 round, while the Model 94 is a slightly smaller weapon chambered for 9mm Parabellum. Both the Model 93 and 94 have 16.4 inch barrels, and in each model there are two versions available: A2 with fixed butt and A3 with retractable butt.

## HECKLER & KOCH MODEL SR9 SPORTING RIFLE

### SPECIFICATIONS
**Type:** semi-automatic sporting rifle
**Origin:** Heckler & Koch, Oberndorf, Germany
**Caliber:** 7.62 x 51
**Barrel Length:** 19.7in

The SR9 was designed to get round the federal ban on the importation of various models of semi-automatic weapons, and it has succeeded in obtaining a certificate from the U.S. Bureau of Alcohol, Tobacco, and Firearms that the SR9 Sporting Rifle and SR9(T) target rifle may legally be imported and owned by civilians. The SR9 is a linear successor to the HK91 but has several important modifications. One is that it has the company's new MSG90 buffer system, which ensures that the SR9 rifle has one of the lowest recoils of any semi-automatic. It is also equipped with a specially-designed thumbhole stock constructed of Kevlar-reinforced fiberglass. The SR9 has either five- or twenty round magazines and weighs 10.9 pounds (with empty magazine). The target version of the SR9 – the SR9(T) – has a special adjustable buttstock, trigger group, and contoured handgrip to make it more suitable for competition shooting.

## MAUSER GEWEHR 1871/84

### SPECIFICATIONS

**Type:** bolt-action rifle
**Origin:** Mauser, Oberndorf, Germany
**Caliber:** 11.15 x 60R Mauser
**Barrel Length:** 32in

The Mauser Gewehr Model 1871 introduced some excellent ideas, including automatic cam cocking which considerable enhanced the safety of the weapon, and was a major advance on the famous needle-gun. It was, however, a single-shot weapon and in 1884 a modified version appeared, fitted with a Mannlicher-pattern tubular magazine under the barrel and a lifting mechanism beneath the bolt, which transformed it into an eight-round repeater and considerably enhanced its tactical value. The barrel was also shortened by some 2 inches. It was produced at five German factories and widely exported. Both the weapons shown here were manufactured in the Imperial Prussian arsenal at Spandau in Berlin.

## MAUSER GEWEHR M 1898

### SPECIFICATIONS

**Type:** bolt-action, single-shot rifle
**Origin:** Mauser, Oberndorf, Germany
**Caliber:** 8mm
**Barrel Length:** 29in

The Gewehr 98 (G98) was the most successful bolt-action rifle ever made, having been produced in vast numbers and used, in one form or another, by most armies around the world. Also known as the Kar 98 or K98, it was a strong and reliable weapon employing Mauser's forward-locking lugs and a five-round magazine whose bottom was level with the stock. As originally produced, the bolt handle stuck out at right angles from the weapon, which was clumsy and liable to catch on clothing, but this was eventually changed to a turned-down design. The example here is an early model with the sticking-out bolt, the type used by German forces throughout World War One.

This is a later carbine model with a cut-down barrel.

## MAUSER K98: EXPORT MODELS

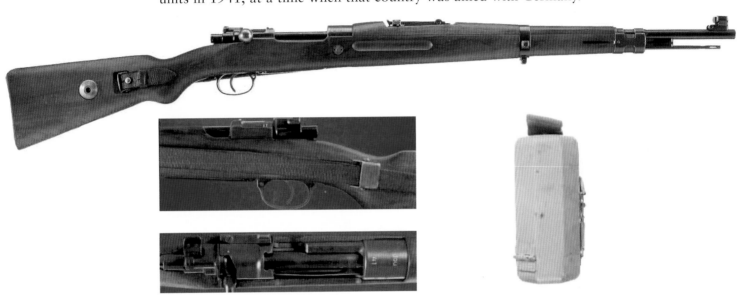

Mauser rifles were supplied to many other European armies, during times of both peace and war, and a small selection is shown here. The first example was supplied to Croatian units in 1941, at a time when that country was allied with Germany.

The history of the second is more complex. When Czechoslovakia was established after World War One, the army was supplied with Mauser G98s made at the former Austro-Hungarian arsenal at Brno; this rifle was then developed into the Model 1923 and 1924 Short Rifles, which were similar to the Kar 98 but with Czech improvements. The Model 1924 remained in production until the German seizure of the country in 1939, but the invaders then ordered production to continue under the factory's new Germanic name, Waffenwerke Brunn AG. The rifle was then supplied to the German Army under the designation G24(t) ("t" was the initial letter of the German name for the country, "Tschechoslovakei").

This one was produced in Hungary during World War Two as the G98/40.

## MAUSER K98: NAZI PRODUCTION IN GERMANY

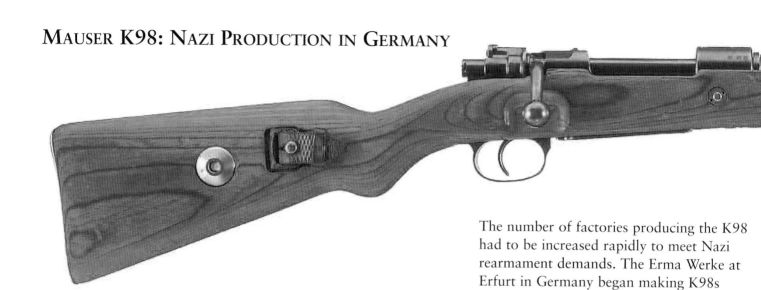

The number of factories producing the K98 had to be increased rapidly to meet Nazi rearmament demands. The Erma Werke at Erfurt in Germany began making K98s such as this one in 1936.

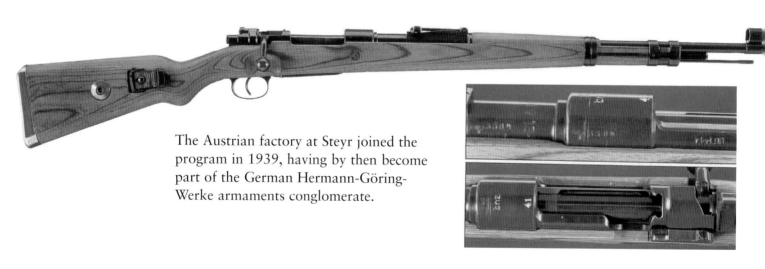

The Austrian factory at Steyr joined the program in 1939, having by then become part of the German Hermann-Göring-Werke armaments conglomerate.

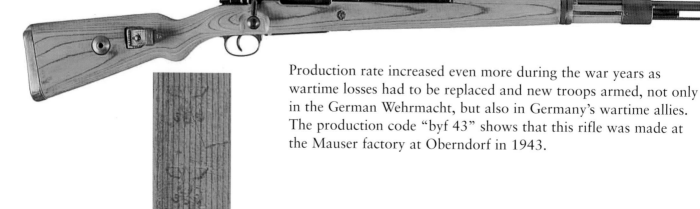

Production rate increased even more during the war years as wartime losses had to be replaced and new troops armed, not only in the German Wehrmacht, but also in Germany's wartime allies. The production code "byf 43" shows that this rifle was made at the Mauser factory at Oberndorf in 1943.

Marked "byf 44", this one was also made at Oberndorf but in the following year. By this time in the war, shortages of labor and materials were starting to have a major influence on the quality of workmanship.

This rifle is marked with the production code "bnz 43" accompanied by a single SS rune and was probably assembled at a concentration camp from parts supplied by the factory at Steyr.

## MAUSER K98 SNIPER VERSIONS

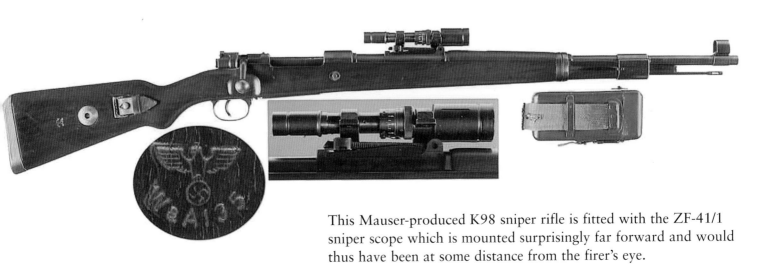

This Mauser-produced K98 sniper rifle is fitted with the ZF-41/1 sniper scope which is mounted surprisingly far forward and would thus have been at some distance from the firer's eye.

## MAUSER G33/40 ALPINE CARBINE

### SPECIFICATIONS

**Type:** bolt-action, service carbine.
**Origin:** Waffen-werke Brünn (German-occupied Czechoslovakia)
**Caliber:** 8mm
**Barrel Length:** 18.0in

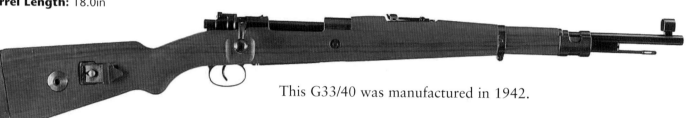

These are two examples of the G33/40, a version of the G33 which had been produced as a carbine for the Czech gendarmerie. It was produced at Brünn (Brno) between 1940 and 1942 to arm the German Army's Alpine (mountain) troops and the Luftwaffe's paratroops. The first one we show was produced in 1940.

This G33/40 was manufactured in 1942.

## MAUSER TRAINING/TARGET RIFLES

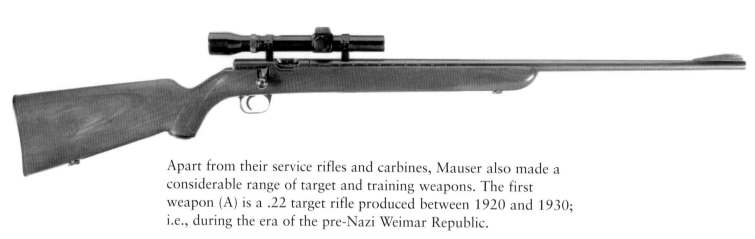

Apart from their service rifles and carbines, Mauser also made a considerable range of target and training weapons. The first weapon (A) is a .22 target rifle produced between 1920 and 1930; i.e., during the era of the pre-Nazi Weimar Republic.

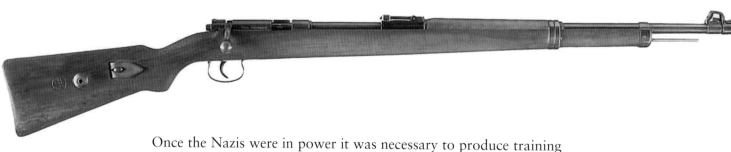

Once the Nazis were in power it was necessary to produce training rifles in large numbers, and lower quality, as with this Mauser-produced .22 rifle, marked "Deutsches Sport Model", which was made to represent the shape, size and weight of the G98.

# RHEINMETALL FALLSCHIRMGEWEHR FG42

**SPECIFICATIONS**

**Type:** automatic paratroop rifle
**Origin:** Rheinmetall-Borsig AG, Germany
**Caliber:** 7.92 x 57mm
**Barrel Length:** 20in

Important from a design point of view rather than for what it achieved in combat, the World War Two FG 42 was another predecessor of the modern assault rifle. The design was intended to be able to fire both fully-automatic and single shot fire, in a light, easy to use package. This was achieved, but it never turned out to be as effective as planned. The main problem was that the rifle used the standard German 7.92 x 57mm cartridge, which was really too powerful for automatic fire from a light hand-held weapon. Ammunition supply was also an issue, in that the 20-shot detachable box magazine wasn't really enough for automatic fire. And as this magazine stuck out to the right of the receiver it also affected the balance and handling.

What really hindered adoption of the rifle, though, was that it was expensive and time-consuming to make. The army wasn't interested, and in the end, under pressure from Herman Goering, it was only adopted by paratroop units. Only some 7,000 were made, although in well-trained hands (which the paratroopers certainly had) it was an effective enough weapon. Notice the folding bayonet under the barrel and the magazine housing on the side of the receiver in this picture.

# SAUER MODEL 98

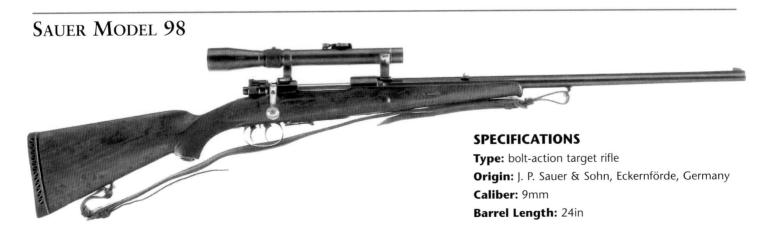

**SPECIFICATIONS**

**Type:** bolt-action target rifle
**Origin:** J. P. Sauer & Sohn, Eckernförde, Germany
**Caliber:** 9mm
**Barrel Length:** 24in

The Sauer company was established in Suhl in 1751 where it remained until 1945. It was re-established at Eckernförde on the Baltic coast near the Danish border in 1948, where it is still in business – the oldest surviving firearms manufacturer in Germany. The company has a long record of manufacturing high quality sporting weapons, although from 1913 onwards it has also been involved with handguns. This Model 98 is a fine example of the company's post-war products. It is chambered for the 9 x 57mm round and is fitted with a Voigtländer scope.

## SAUER MODEL 200 SUPREME

### SPECIFICATIONS

**Type:** high-quality, engraved, bolt-action sporting rifle
**Origin:** J. P. Sauer & Sohn, Eckernförde, Germany
**Caliber:** .30-06
**Barrel Length:** 23.7in

This very high quality sporting rifle was produced in a variety of calibers and barrel lengths; this weapon is chambered for .30-06 and has a 23.7 inch barrel. It is fitted with a five-round magazine, and has iron sights (ramped foresight; adjustable leaf rear sight) and a spoon-shaped bolt handle. The metal work is engraved in unobtrusive, but intricately worked scrolls.

## SPANDAU 1915 SNIPER RIFLE

### SPECIFICATIONS

**Type:** bolt-action, sniper rifle
**Origin:** Spandau Arsenal, Berlin, Germany
**Caliber:** 8mm
**Barrel Length:** 29in

This weapon was produced by the Imperial German Arsenal at Spandau in Berlin. It was originally a standard Gewehr 1898, but was converted during production by fitting a much longer barrel (29 inches against 24 inches) and mountings for a scope (not fitted in this picture). The more elaborate back sight is also clearly shown.

## WALTHER GEWEHR 41 (W)

### SPECIFICATIONS

**Type:** semi-automatic assault rifle
**Origin:** Carl Walther Waffenfabrik, Zella-Mehlis, Thuringia, Germany
**Caliber:** 7.92 x 57mm Mauser
**Barrel Length:** 22in

The Walther brothers, Fritz and Erich, began work on a new semi-automatic rifle in the 1930s but their first product, the Gewehr 41(W), was not a great success. It underwent trials in competition with the Mauser Gewehr 41(M) which the Walther weapon won and was then, with a few modifications, placed in production. Unfortunately, experience in the Russian campaign showed that the muzzle cup became eroded very quickly and the production order was quickly terminated in early 1943.

The Gewehr 41(W) is shown here, with its vertically-mounted cocking handle and the muzzle cap which deflected some of the gasses back on to an annular piston which drove the working parts to the rear. With the gas-flow being reversed by the muzzle cap it is not surprising that there was so much fouling. This one was produced by at the Walther factory (production code "ac").

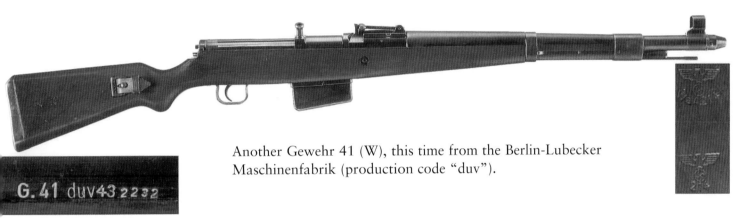

Another Gewehr 41 (W), this time from the Berlin-Lubecker Maschinenfabrik (production code "duv").

This rifle is the Mauser competitor, the equally unsuccessful Gewehr 41(M), which used a similar "Bang" type muzzle cap.

## WALTHER GEWEHR G43

### SPECIFICATIONS

**Type:** semi-automatic assault rifle
**Origin:** Carl Walther Waffenfabrik, Zella-Mehlis, Thuringia, Germany
**Caliber:** 7.92 x 57mm Mauser
**Barrel Length:** 23in

After the failure of the Gewehr 41(W) the Walther brothers worked on a second design, the Gewehr 42(W) which competed with a design by Haenel, but both of these were also failures and had to be abandoned. The next weapon was, however, a major success and the Gewehr 43 was quickly placed into production. The disastrous muzzle cup and annular piston were replaced by a more conventional port-and-piston layout, which was a modified version of that used on the Soviet Tokarev rifle.

This new weapon was produced in two versions, Gewehr 43 (Rifle 1943) and its successor, Karabiner 43 (Carbine 43), which actually differed in only very minor details. The design proved to be a very considerable improvement on the Gewehr 41(W) and would have been an even greater success had it not been for the poor production standards in German industry in the last months of the war, which meant that parts broke easily.

## WALTHER K-43 SNIPER RIFLE

### SPECIFICATIONS
**Type:** semi-automatic sniper rifle
**Origin:** Carl Walther Waffenfabrik, Zella-Mehlis, Thuringia, Germany
**Caliber:** 8mm
**Barrel Length:** see text

These are three examples of the sniper version of the K-43, which was essentially unchanged except for rails on the receiver and a sniper-scope. All shown here are fitted with the Voigtländer ZF-4 scope, which is shown in detail.

This rifle is included to show what can happen to a military weapon when it passes onto the civil market. In this case a Walther-produced G43 sniper has had the one-piece stock and handgrip replaced and all wood- and metalwork refinished. The scope, marked with production code "duw" is, however, original.

## WALTHER KKW TRAINING RIFLE

### SPECIFICATIONS

**Type:** small caliber, single shot, training and competition rifle
**Origin:** Heckler & Koch, Oberndorf, Germany
**Caliber:** .22
**Barrel Length:** 26in

The Walther factory produced a number of weapons for the Nazi Party training programs. Such weapons, all in .22 caliber, were produced by various weapons manufacturers, under the generic title "Kleinkaliber Wehrsportsgewehr" (small caliber, weapons sports rifle) and there were regular competitions sponsored by the KKW organisation. This weapon, which is in excellent condition, was manufactured pre-war but was still in use in target competitions as late as 1944.

# HUNGARY

## FEG Model AK47

**SPECIFICATIONS**

**Type:** AK-47 clone

**Origin:** Fémáru és Gépygár Reszvenutarsasag, Burapest, Hungary.

**Caliber:** 7.62 x 39mm

**Barrel Length:** 17.5in

Fémáru és Gépygár, usually known as FEG, was established in Budapest in the 1880s, at a time when Hungary was part of the Austro-Hungarian Empire. It manufactured Mannlicher rifles and a number of original pistol designs known by the name of the designer, Rudolph Frommer, who was the company's managing director from 1906 to 1935. Following World War Two the company was forced to operate under control from Moscow and, like other Communist satellite states, produced a series of Soviet designs, particularly Kalashnikov rifles. The AK-47 clone seen here is a typical product, but has been given a superior finish and a more elaborate stock with an inbuilt recoil pad to make it attractive to the United States' sporter market.

# ISRAEL

## Galil ARM

**SPECIFICATIONS**

**Type:** semi-automatic assault rifle

**Origin:** Israeli Metal Industries (IMI), Israel

**Caliber:** see text

**Barrel Length:** see text

Designed by an Israeli Army officer, Uziel Gal, the Galil 7.62mm assault rifle was the outcome of some twenty years of constant conflict in the Arab-Israeli Wars. Gal based his design on the gas and rotating-bolt system of the Russian AK-47, of which Israel had captured many thousands of examples, and combined these with the firing mechanism of the US M1 Garand. With the exception of the breech cover which is stamped, all metal components are fully machined, while the foregrip is wood, lined with Dural, with plenty of free space around the barrel for heat dissipation. The tubular butt folds to the right, but when extended is positively latched to prevent any wobble. There is an ambidextrous safety and a carrying handle, while the bipod folds into a slot on the underside of the foregrip.

The Galil ARM entered service in 1973, chambered for the NATO standard 7.62mm round, and was produced in three versions: assault rifle/light machinegun; assault rifle (as the LMG but minus the bipod); and the SAR (Short Assault Rifle) with a shorter 15.8in barrel.

# ITALY

## MANNLICHER-CARCANO M1891

**SPECIFICATIONS**

**Type:** bolt-action, rifle

**Origin:** Fabbrica Nazionale d'Armi, Terni and Brescia, Italy

**Caliber:** see text

**Barrel Length:** see text

The name of this weapon has achieved an infamy attached to few other individual designs in history, because it was a Carcano M91/38 bolt-action rifle, serial number C2766, and chambered for 6.5 x 52mm, which Lee Harvey Oswald used to shoot President John F. Kennedy on November 22, 1963. The rifle design dated back 1887, when the Italian Government set up a committee, chaired by General Parravicino, to design a new rifle and cartridge to replace the Vetterli-Vitali (*see above*). The winning weapon was the result of work by a team headed by Salvatore Carcano and, while the design incorporated ideas from various sources, including Mannlicher, Mauser and a number of others, it was designated the Mannlicher-Carcano Model 1891 and manufactured at the State arsenals at Terni and Brescia. The design was periodically updated, the most significant being in 1938 when fears that the 6.5 x 52mm bullet was insufficiently powerful led to the development of the Model 1891/38 chambered for a new 7.35 x 52mm cartridge. Modifications to existing rifles had only just started when World War Two broke out and it was quickly decided that it would be too complicated to change to a new rifle and a new round, so the few 7.35mm rifles already converted were withdrawn and issued to the militia. We show here two carbines (moschetto) chambered for 6.5mm and with an 18 inch barrel. Notice the permanently attached folding bayonet.

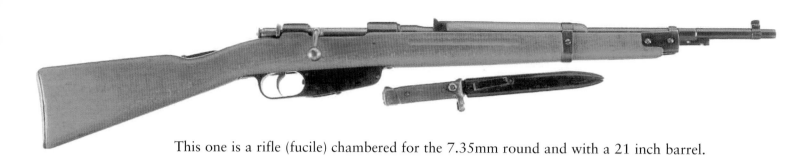

This one is a rifle (fucile) chambered for the 7.35mm round and with a 21 inch barrel.

# BERETTA BM-59

## SPECIFICATIONS

**Type:** semi-automatic rifle
**Origin:** Aram Pietro Beretta SpA, Rome, Italy
**Caliber:** 7.62mm NATO
**Barrel Length:** see text

When Italy joined NATO, the United States supplied a large quantity of M1 Garand rifles from surplus stocks, while Beretta tooled up to supply new-build M1s, whose delivery started in 1952. Beretta engineers then realised that the M1 design was falling behind contemporary standards and redesigned it, the new weapon being accepted by the Italian Army as the BM-59. This picture shows a BM-59 Mark I with a 20 inch barrel (3 inches shorter than the M1 Garand), 20-round detachable box magazine, improved trigger group, integral bipod and a so-called "triple compensator." This latter device fitted on the muzzle and served as a combined muzzle-brake, flash suppressor and grenade launcher; it was also fitted with a bayonet lug.

The second version is a BM-59 Ital Tipo Parachutisti, with an 18.5 inch barrel and a detachable compensator (not fitted in this picture).

# JAPAN

## MEIJI 30TH YEAR RIFLE

### SPECIFICATIONS

**Type:** bolt-action, magazine-fed rifle

**Origin:** Koishikawa arsenal.

**Caliber:** 6.5 x 50mm

**Barrel Length:** 31in

Modern Japan's first overseas campaign was against China in 1894, where the Chinese infantry were armed with the Mannlicher Gewehr 88, which had box magazines and proved to be clearly superior to the tube-magazines on the Murata-designed 22nd Year type. Colonel Arisaka Nariake headed a committee to find a solution and the outcome was the Meiji 29th Year (1896) type with a Mauser action, firing a 6.5 x 50mm round. The trials batch showed shortcomings and these were rectified in the definitive Meiji 30th Year rifle, which remained the basis of all Japanese service rifles until 1945.

It is not generally known that during World War One the United Kingdom, then closely allied to Japan, bought some 150,000 Japanese rifles, a mixture of Meiji 30th and 38th year types, which entered service with the British Army in 1915 as the "Rifle, Magazine, .256 inch, Pattern 1900." Further batches of Japanese rifles entered service with the Royal Navy and with the Royal Flying Corps (later Royal Air Force).

Shown here are two standard Meiji 30th year rifles. Note the massive bayonet on one, and the Arisaka action on both, which proved exceptionally robust and reliable under combat conditions.

This rifle is unusual in that it is a training item used at an Imperial Japanese Navy school and was only ever intended to be used with blank ammunition.

## ARISAKA MEIJI 35TH YEAR

### SPECIFICATIONS

**Type:** bolt-action, magazine-fed rifle

**Origin:** Koishikawa arsenal

**Caliber:** 6.5 x 50mm

**Barrel Length:** 31.5in

Despite all the effort devoted to its development, once the Meiji 30th Year rifle was in full service some shortcomings became apparent and yet further work was required, leading to the Meiji 35th Year rifle, seen here. This had an improved bolt incorporating a new gas-vent, a new tangent back sight, a longer handguard and a spring-loaded, sliding bolt cover. Like the 30th Year rifle it was still chambered for the 6.5mm round and had an integral five-round magazine. A trials batch was being produced when the Russo-Japanese War broke out and, as a result, only a relatively small number (about 30,000) were completed, most of which were issued to the navy. The example shown here is missing the bolt and bolt-cover but is included because of its rarity.

## ARISAKA MEIJI 38TH YEAR

### SPECIFICATIONS

**Type:** bolt-action, magazine-fed rifle
**Origin:** various arsenals, see text
**Caliber:** 6.5 x 50mm
**Barrel Length:** 31.5in

Some shortcomings in the Meiji 30th Year rifle were thought to have been rectified in the 35th Year type, but a trials batch fielded during the Russo-Japanese war revealed yet further problems. These mainly concerned extraction and susceptibility to mud and dust, and were solved by a new and simpler bolt combined with a bolt-cover. The new design was designated the Meiji 38th Year type (1905) and entered service in 1906. This rifle was in continuous production from 1907 to 1944 and a total of well over three million were produced at the Imperial arsenals at Mishawaka, Kokura, Malden and Nagoya, as well as army depots in China at Nanking and Tientsin. There was also a cavalry carbine version. Shown here is a late production 38th Year rifle with its associated bayonet and the Imperial chrysanthemum and "38th Year" markings.

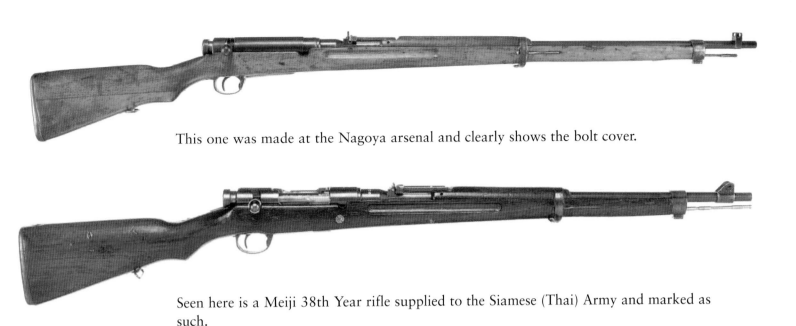

This one was made at the Nagoya arsenal and clearly shows the bolt cover.

Seen here is a Meiji 38th Year rifle supplied to the Siamese (Thai) Army and marked as such.

## ARISAKA MEIJI 44TH YEAR CARBINE

### SPECIFICATIONS

**Type:** bolt-action, magazine-fed carbine
**Origin:** Koishigawa/Nagoya/Mukden arsenals
**Caliber:** 6.5 x 50mm
**Barrel Length:** 20in
SPEC BOX

The Meiji 44th Year type carbine (1911) combined the usual Arisaka action with a much shorter, 20 inch barrel and a permanently fixed bayonet which was attached to a hinge on the nose-cap and swiveled back under the barrel when not in use. This weapon was in production from 1912 to 1942. The two examples shown here are standard production versions, showing the very neat bayonet installation.

## ARISAKA MEIJI 97TH YEAR SNIPER RIFLE

### SPECIFICATIONS

**Type:** bolt-action, magazine-fed sniper rifle
**Origin:** Kokura/Nagoya arsenals
**Caliber:** 6.5 x 50mm
**Barrel Length:** 30in

The Meiji 99th Year sniper rifle (1937) was the outcome of a development program that lasted well over ten years. It was based closely on the Meiji 38th Year rifle but the bolt handle was both longer and angled sharply downwards. A Toka 2.5x telescopic sight was mounted on the left side of the weapon; this position was intended to make recharging the magazine easier, but did, in fact, make holding and aiming (vital characteristics in a sniper rifle) more difficult. Some 19,500 weapons were produced between 1938 and 1941, but it is difficult to see why it took so long to produce such a mediocre weapon.

## ARISAKA TYPE 99 RIFLE

### SPECIFICATIONS

**Type:** bolt-action, magazine-fed rifle
**Origin:** various arsenals
**Caliber:** 7.7 x 58mm
**Barrel Length:** 26in

The Meiji 38th Year rifle entered production in 1907 and remained the unquestioned standard service rifle of the Japanese forces for the following 30 years. Battle experience in the Sino-Japanese war in the late 1930s, however, showed that, once again, Japanese weapons had failed to keep up with modern trends and the 6.5mm round was no real competitor for the 7.9mm round used by the Chinese, especially at longer ranges. As a result, a new 7.7mm round was rushed through development and successfully tested on converted 38th Year rifles. After some teething troubles some Type 99 long rifles were produced, but proved difficult for troops to use and a shorter version was then developed which went into production in 1942. A sniper version of the Type 99 was also developed. By 1944 the war was not going well for the Japanese and raw materials were becoming increasingly difficult to obtain so the Type 99 Model 2 was developed, making use of low-grade steel and inferior quality wood. Manufacturing process were also simplified as much as possible. By the end of the war, production rifles were of abysmal quality, a situation which closely paralleled that in Germany. Shown here is the standard short-barreled (25.5 inches) version.

# PHILIPPINES

## SQUIRES BINGHAM (ARMSCOR) M1600R

**SPECIFICATIONS**
**Type:** semi-automatic carbine
**Origin:** Armscor, Parang, Marikina, Philippines
**Caliber:** .22 LR
**Barrel Length:** 19in

This weapon was produced in the Philippines, the original company being Squires Bingham of Rizal, but the parent company is now Armscor of the Philippines, located at Parang, Marikina, Philippines. The M1600R is a semi-automatic carbine, chambered for the .22 LR round, with a 19 inch barrel. It has either ten or fifteen round magazines and is fitted with a post foresight, peep rearsight, hooded barrel, flash suppressor, and a retractable butt. The grip is made of grey plastic.

# POLAND

## RADOM WZ.29 RIFLE

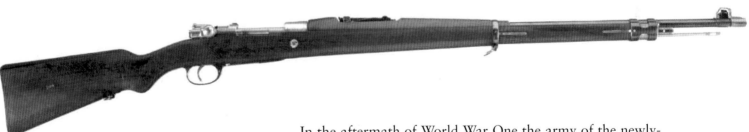

**SPECIFICATIONS**
**Type:** bolt-action magazine rifle
**Origin:** Warsaw, Poland
**Caliber:** 8mm
**Barrel Length:** 24in

In the aftermath of World War One the army of the newly-independent Poland was armed mainly with Mauser rifles of various models. A munitions factory was established in Warsaw, probably using equipment moved there from the former Imperial Prussian arsenal in Gdansk (formerly Danzig), where manufacture of the Mauser Gewehr 98 and Karabiner 98 was undertaken. In the mid-1920s production moved again, this time to the newly-established factor at Radom.

The long Gewehr 98 was not particularly popular and having examined the Mauser-style short rifles produced by the Czechs – the VZ.24 – and FN – the Modelle 24 – the Poles designed their own equivalent, which was then adopted as the wz.29, seen here with its associated bayonet. This was the weapon equipping all Polish units in 1939, but production ceased when the Germans arrived and never re-started during the occupation. The rifle is marked with the Polish shield and Radom stamps.

# PORTUGAL

## GUEDES MODEL 1885 RIFLE

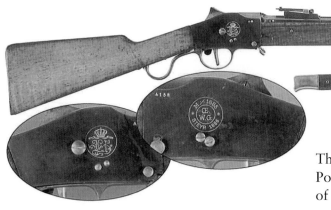

### SPECIFICATIONS

**Type:** block-action, single-shot rifle
**Origin:** Lieutenant Luis Guedes Diaz and ÖWG, Steyr, Austria-Hungary.
**Caliber:** 8 x 60mm
**Barrel Length:** 32.25in

This block-breech action was designed by Lieutenant Guedes of the Portuguese Army and operated by a lever which was an extension of the trigger-guard. It was originally chambered for an 11mm round, and in this form was adopted by the Portuguese Army. Only a very few had been completed, however, when it became obvious that the army would have to adopt the newly-invented smokeless powder and a smaller cartridge. All this, coupled with production difficulties, resulted in the order being switched to the Österreichische Waffenfabrik Gesellshcaft (ÖWG) at Steyr, who also converted the design to take a new 8 x 60mm smokeless cartridge.

The story of the Guedes rifle, was, however, to have an unhappy ending. The Portuguese realized that the day of the single-shot infantry rifle was over, canceled the order with ÖWG forthwith and adopted the Austrian-designed Kropatschek rifle in its place. It would appear that ÖWG was landed with over 10,000 unsold Guedes rifles, but it managed to offload most of these during the Boer war, with some 8,000 going to the Transvaal and a few thousand more to the Orange Free State, where they were used against the British Imperial forces.

The picture shows a Guedes Model 1885 with the maker's seal and Portuguese royal coat-of-arms. Also shown is the bayonet, also made at Steyr, which was no less than 18.5 inches long.

# ROMANIA

## CUGIR AIM SNIPER RIFLE

### SPECIFICATIONS

**Type:** sniper rifle
**Origin:** Cugir armaments factory, Romania
**Caliber:** 5.45 x 39mm
**Barrel Length:** 16in

Kalashnikov clones were produced in Romania at the government arsenal at Cugir, starting with the AK-47 in 1960. Production then switched to the more advanced AKM, which had a few, very minor Romanian modifications. This sniper version, dated 1997, has an unusual butt and a Romanian-made scope.

# RUSSIA (including USSR)

## BERDAN MODEL 1870

### SPECIFICATIONS

**Type:** bolt-action, single-shot rifle
**Origin:** General Hiram Berdan; Russian Imperial arsenals, Tula and Izhevsk
**Caliber:** 10.67 x 58mm
**Barrel Length:** 32.75in

This design was the work of General Hiram Berdan, US Army, who became famous through the sharpshooter (sniper) regiments he formed during the Civil War. He worked on the design in the late 1860s and took out a U.S. patent in 1870, but only two armies ever adopted the design – Imperial Russia and Bulgaria. The Russians designated it *"pekhotniya vintovka Berdana, obr. 1870g"* (infantry rifle, Berdan-pattern, model 1870) although actual production did not start until 1874 at Tula and 1878 at Izhevsk. Several million of these rifles were produced in Russia in a variety of versions, including: infantry model (32.75in barrel); cavalry/artillery carbine (18.7in barrel); dragoon and Cossack rifles (28in barrel).

## DRAGUNOV SVD SNIPER RIFLE

### SPECIFICATIONS

**Type:** semi-automatic sniper rifle
**Origin:** State arsenal Izhevsk
**Caliber:** 7.62 x 54mm rimmed
**Barrel Length:** 22in

Yevgeniy Dragunov began development of the SVD in the 1950s and the weapon entered service with the Soviet Army in 1967. It then became the standard sniper rifle of all Warsaw Pact armies, as well as of many of the USSR's allies; it was also built under license in Bulgaria, China, Egypt, Hungary, Iraq and Romania. Warsaw Pact armies normally had one specially trained SVD-armed sniper per infantry platoon, a far greater scale than in NATO armies.

The Snayperskaya Vintovka Dragunova (SVD) appears long and bulky, but, at 9.9 pounds (with scope and empty magazine), it is actually lighter than previous sniper rifles used by the Soviet Army. At a time when virtually all Western snipers insisted on retaining

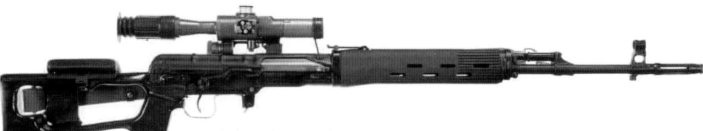

a bolt mechanism, the gas-operated SVD, which fired only in the semi-automatic mode, used a system similar to the AKM assault rifle, but with a much shorter piston stroke to minimize the shift of balance which would upset a sniper's point-of-aim. The SVD had a combined flash suppressor/ compensator and a cheek-pad atop the instantly-recognizable open butt-stock. The example shown here was one of 1,000 imported into the United States in the 1990s, but is typical of those built for the Soviet and other armies. The SVD was widely – and correctly – considered to be among the very best sniper rifles of its era.

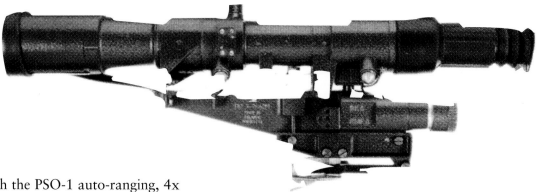

The SVD was fitted with the PSO-1 auto-ranging, 4x telescopic sight, with an extension tube to afford eye relief, and these pictures show both sides of the device. The reticule was calibrated on the height of a man (5.7 feet) and the sight enabled the sniper to take account of the drop of the bullet over ranges up to 1,100 yards, as well as wind strength and direction. It is powered by a 2.4 volt lithium battery.

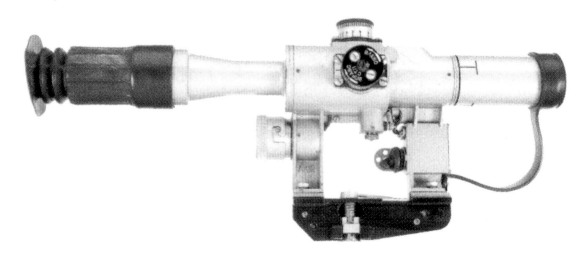

# Kalashnikov AK-47/AK-74 Assault Rifle

## SPECIFICATIONS

**Type:** semi-automatic assault rifles

**Origin:** Soviet state arsenals

**Caliber:** AK-47 – 7.62 x 39mm; AK-74 – 5.45 x 39.5mm

**Barrel Length:** AK-47 – 16.3in; AK-74 – 15.75in

As soon as World War Two was finished the Soviet Red Army set out to develop a weapon that was at least as good as the German MP 44, and preferably better. In this, as in other technological fields, they almost certainly availed themselves of the involuntary help of captured German scientists and engineers. The Soviet designer with final responsibility for the project was Mikhail Kalashnikov and the weapon which bears his name was adopted for use in 1951. Designated the AK-47 (Avtomatiy sistemy Kalashnikova Model 1947), it was, in every respect, an exceptionally fine assault rifle, being well-designed, reliable, light, simple to use and to maintain – and cheap. It is also easy to fire with reasonable accuracy out to the ranges necessary in modern warfare, about 300 yards. All known variants carry a 30-round box magazine.

The AKS was developed with a folding stock, and was intended for paratroopers, vehicle crews and such like. We show it with the butt open and folded.

The AK-47 was produced in a variety of models and was manufactured in factories in Bulgaria, China (PRC); Egypt; East Germany; Hungary; Iraq, North Korea, Poland, Romania and Yugoslavia.See the table below. In addition, a number of other designs were based very closely on the Kalashnikov action, including the Israeli Galil, the Finnish Valmet and South African Vektor.

# SWEDEN

## LJUNGMAN AG-42B RIFLE

**SPECIFICATIONS**
**Type:** semi-automatic rifle
**Origin:** Husqvarna
**Caliber:** 6.5 x 55mm
**Barrel Length:** 24in

Designed by Erik Eklund, the Ljungman semi-automatic rifle was accepted for service by the Swedish Army in 1942 and served until replaced by the German Heckler & Koch G3 in the mid-1960s. The Ljungman employed a gas system which was most unusual at the time, in which the gas was tapped at a point about two-thirds of the way down the barrel and then directed back down through a cylinder to an extension of the bolt carrier, thus delivering its thrust direct to the bolt and avoiding the use of a piston. Similar systems were later used in the French M1949 and the AR-10 and AR-15 developed by Eugene Stoner.

The Ljungman served in the Swedish Army as the AG-42B, but was not a universal rifle, being issued instead on the basis of several per infantry squad, the remaining riflemen carrying Mauser-type weapons. The AG-42B was also manufactured in Egypt, chambered for the 7.92mm round, but prototypes made in Denmark by Madsen did not lead to a production order from the Danish Army.

## SWEDISH MAUSER CARBINES/RIFLES

**SPECIFICATIONS**
**Type:** bolt-action rifle
**Origin:** Mauser, Oberndorf, Germany and Swedish state arsenals
**Caliber:** 6.5 x 55mm
**Barrel Length:** see text

Sweden's first orders for Mauser weapons were for carbines for the cavalry and horse artillery. Designated Karabin M/1894, two batches were ordered from Mauser (5,000 in 1894 and 7,185 in 1895), but in 1900 production of a slightly modified version started at the Carl Gustav Stads Gevärsfactori at Eskilstuna, Sweden. The design was changed slightly in 1917 with the addition of a bayonet boss beneath the muzzle (Carbine M/1894/17). One is shown here with an 18 inch barrel and the bayonet boss on the muzzle plate.

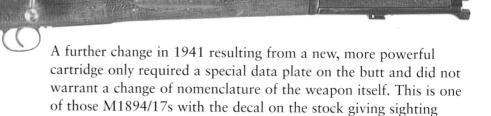

A further change in 1941 resulting from a new, more powerful cartridge only required a special data plate on the butt and did not warrant a change of nomenclature of the weapon itself. This is one of those M1894/17s with the decal on the stock giving sighting data for the new cartridge.

# UNITED KINGDOM

## ACCURACY INTERNATIONAL PM

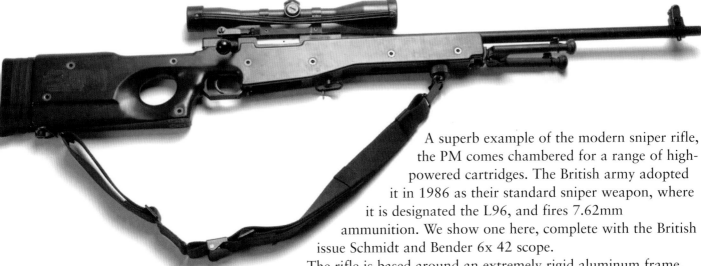

A superb example of the modern sniper rifle, the PM comes chambered for a range of high-powered cartridges. The British army adopted it in 1986 as their standard sniper weapon, where it is designated the L96, and fires 7.62mm ammunition. We show one here, complete with the British issue Schmidt and Bender 6x 42 scope.

The rifle is based around an extremely rigid aluminum frame, with an attached plastic stock with thumbhole grip and a spring-loaded bipod support. A stainless steel barrel is free-floating above the frame, and the action is a short-throw bolt, which can be operated without the firer having to change their head position. All components can be easily removed, and the trigger, stock and bipod are all adjustable.

### SPECIFICATIONS

**Type:** bolt-action sniper rifle
**Origin:** Accuracy International, England
**Caliber:** 7.62mm
**Barrel Length:** 25.8in

## BAKER RIFLE

### SPECIFICATIONS

**Type:** muzzle-loading flintlock rifle
**Origin:** Tower Armouries, England
**Caliber:** .62
**Barrel Length:** 30.25in

Designed by Ezekiel Baker and first selected for service in 1800, the Baker was the first general issue rifled weapon to enter British service. A muzzle-loading flintlock piece, it fired a tight-fitting ball which had to be firmly rammed into the barrel. The first soldiers to be issued with the Baker were also given a wooden mallet to help with reloading, although this was soon superseded by the use of a cloth wadding or "patch" to help the ball slide down the barrel. The Baker was used successfully by British riflemen throughout the Peninsular War and the Waterloo campaign. At this time, riflemen were specialist skirmisher troops, intended to operate in loose, open formations and pick off their targets with aimed fire at longer ranges than possible with smoothbore muskets. The rifle shown here was a volunteer model made by Broomhead in London, and had the earlier full-length stock for use with the sword bayonet.

The sword bayonet proved to be cumbersome in use, so was replaced by a lighter triangular-section socket-mounted item. This rifle has a shorter stock, with the muzzle left clear and fitted with a mounting lug for the new bayonet.

## BROWN BESS SHORT LAND PATTERN MUSKET

**SPECIFICATIONS**

**Type:** muzzle-loading flintlock musket

**Origin:** Tower Armouries, England

**Caliber:** .75

**Barrel Length:** 42in

From about the 1730 onwards, the British Army was equipped with a series of simple, effective flintlock muskets, known by the soldiers' nickname of "Brown Bess." This was never a formal title, and the term covered a multitude of variations in caliber, muzzle length and lock detail.

The Short Land Pattern entered service from about 1763 onwards and became the standard, although other versions remained in use. The "Brown Bess" remained an effective and popular weapon for some 100 years or so, until the flintlock was superseded by the percussion system.

## BROWN BESS MORTIMER 3RD MODEL

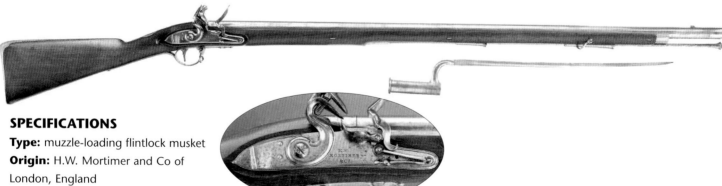

**SPECIFICATIONS**

**Type:** muzzle-loading flintlock musket

**Origin:** H.W. Mortimer and Co of London, England

**Caliber:** .75

**Barrel Length:** 39in

Brown Bess muskets were also manufactured by various contractors, and this one has the markings of H.W. Mortimer and Co. of London.

## BROWN BESS INDIA PATTERN MUSKET

**SPECIFICATIONS**
**Type:** muzzle-loading flintlock smoothbore
**Origin:** Tower Armouries, England
**Caliber:** .75
**Barrel Length:** 39in

The British East India Company had its own armed forces and armories producing weapons to equip them. When Britain became embroiled in the French Revolutionary Wars the government appealed to the company for weapons. The muskets they supplied became known as the India Pattern, and were a simplification of the current "Brown Bess" design. The Indian Pattern proved to be so effective that British contractors were also encouraged to manufacture this model and it became a standard issue from then on.

The one shown here has "9B. ANNAPOLIS.M" stamped in the wooden butt, and was used by the Annapolis Militia during the War of Independence.

## DE LISLE SILENCED CARBINE

**SPECIFICATIONS**
**Type:** single-shot silenced carbine
**Origin:** Sterling Armament Co., Dagenham, England
**Caliber:** .45 ACP
**Barrel Length:** 8.25in

Notwithstanding Hollywood depictions, there is more to silencing a weapon than simply screwing a tube on to the end of a standard pistol. To create such a weapon requires careful engineering, and the effective ones are designed to be so from the start.

This is one such specialized design, intended for use by British Commandos and special forces in World War Two. Silencers and baffles can reduce the muzzle report to a suitably low level, but they can't deal with the crack of a supersonic rifle bullet. To avoid this problem, the De Lisle used pistol ammunition: the .45 ACP round as fired by the Colt M1911 pistol and Thompson sub-machine gun. The stock and bolt mechanism are modified from a standard SMLE, with a new short barrel and integral silencer attached. A 10-shot box magazine fitted under the receiver. The De Lisle was apparently quite effective in its specialized role.

## ENFIELD PATTERN 1853 RIFLE MUSKET (3-BAND)

**SPECIFICATIONS**
**Type:** muzzle-loading percussion rifle
**Origin:** Enfield, England and Tower Armouries, England
**Caliber:** .577
**Barrel Length:** 39in

By 1850, The British Government eventually faced up to the need for a rifled arm as general issue for infantrymen, a decision forced on them by reports of the effectiveness of French Minie rifles. The problem for any muzzle-loader was that for accuracy you needed a bullet that fitted tightly into the barrel rifling. But such a tight fit made it difficult to ram the bullet down the barrel when loading,

and almost impossible to do so once the barrel was fouled with the residue of a few shots. Captain Claude Minie had developed an elongated bullet which was left narrow enough to fit easily into the barrel. When the gun was fired, the gasses drove a plug at the rear of the bullet into the projectile, spreading out the thin lead rim, which engaged in the rifling and formed a tight gas seal as the bullet traveled up the barrel. By 1852 the British were developing an improved Minie, where the elongated bullet had no plug, but instead a hollow base, into which the expanding gasses blew, flaring out the edge of the bullet until it engaged with the rifling. They also created a rifle to fire it, and by 1854 this new 1853 Pattern rifle was reaching the hands of British infantrymen in the Crimea, and rapidly proving to be a success.

Relatively light, well made, popular and effective, it was the first British weapon to use metal bands to fix the barrel to the stock. The standard infantry rifle with the 39in barrel used three such bands, hence the "3-Band" designation. This one was made by Barnett.

Many were made at the Royal Ordnance Factory in Enfield, London, while others were made by various contractors, usually under the markings of the Tower Armouries. We show here another contract rifle; this one was made by Parker Field.

Britain's Volunteer movement was largely a home-defense organisation run by a wealthy middle-class. The only weapons they were offered from government sources were worn out guns from the Crimea, so many units opted to purchase their own. A range of gunmakers met this need, and this London-made rifle is typical of those supplied.

# ENFIELD PATTERN 1856 RIFLE MUSKET (2-BAND)

## SPECIFICATIONS

**Type:** muzzle-loading percussion rifle
**Origin:** Enfield, England and Tower Armouries, England
**Caliber:** .577
**Barrel Length:** 33in

The Enfield rifle, while effective, was also a long piece, and could be cumbersome to aim quickly. A shorter version was produced, with the barrel reduced by 6 inches, and can be identified by the fact it has only two metal bands securing the barrel to the stock. From 1856 it was issued to rifleman skirmishers and to sergeants in line regiments. This 2-Band rifle is a volunteer purchase, although the only markings on it are the Tower armouries crest.

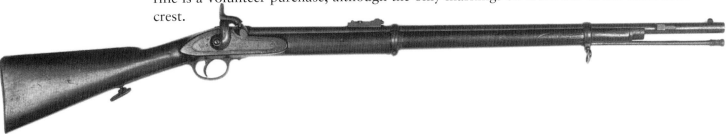

## ENFIELD RIFLES IN AMERICAN SERVICE

**SPECIFICATIONS**
**Type:** muzzle-loading percussion rifle
**Origin:** Various
**Caliber:** .577
**Barrel Length:** 39in

When the Civil War started both sided looked to overseas to make up the shortfall in their infantry weapons. While a range of longarms was procured, the most popular foreign arm quickly became the Enfield Pattern 1853. Along with the Springfield Model 1861 (*see below*) the Enfield became the most popular arm of the line in the war, and in fact, while nominally .577 caliber, it could also fire the .58 Springfield ammunition.

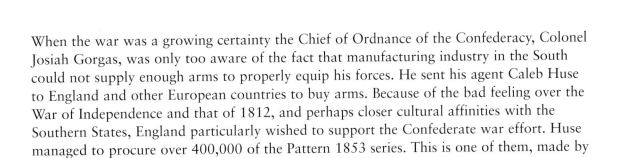

When the war was a growing certainty the Chief of Ordnance of the Confederacy, Colonel Josiah Gorgas, was only too aware of the fact that manufacturing industry in the South could not supply enough arms to properly equip his forces. He sent his agent Caleb Huse to England and other European countries to buy arms. Because of the bad feeling over the War of Independence and that of 1812, and perhaps closer cultural affinities with the Southern States, England particularly wished to support the Confederate war effort. Huse managed to procure over 400,000 of the Pattern 1853 series. This is one of them, made by Potts and Hunt.

A 2-band Enfield Pattern 1856 (with shorter 36in barrel), this also saw Confederate service.

The detail shows a close-up of the lock and Tower marks, while the underside shows the CSA inventory marks "693" stamped into the wood.

Another CSA weapon, this one has inventory mark "729" engraved into the brass buttplate.

The Union used the Enfield too, and this close-up shows New Jersey surcharge markings on the barrel and stock.

As with other weapons, many firms manufactured local copies of the Enfield. This one was made by J.P. Moore's Sons of New York, and US markings can be seen at the rear of the lockplate. The brass muzzle cap has the serial "N232", although the "N" is inverted.

# ENFIELD PATTERN 1853 CAVALRY CARBINE

Carbine versions of the Enfield were also made for cavalry and artillery issue. Using the same lock and mechanism of their larger brethren, they are distinguished by their short 21 inch barrels and swivel ramrod. Many were also ordered by the Confederate States, although fewer than 5,000 of these carbines actually got through the blockade.

**SPECIFICATIONS**
**Type:** muzzle-loading percussion carbine
**Origin:** Enfield, England and Tower Armouries, England
**Caliber:** .577
**Barrel Length:** 21in

## ENFIELD EM-2

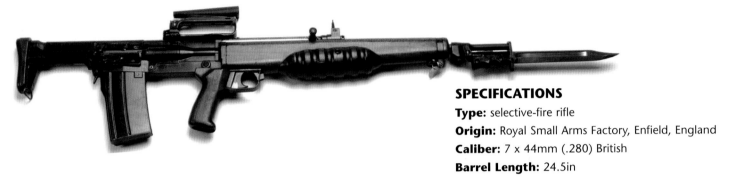

**SPECIFICATIONS**
**Type:** selective-fire rifle
**Origin:** Royal Small Arms Factory, Enfield, England
**Caliber:** 7 x 44mm (.280) British
**Barrel Length:** 24.5in

After World War Two, the British had also come to the conclusion that the .303 round was unnecessarily powerful for combat conditions, and as the SMLE series would soon be due for replacement, now was the time to look anew at the infantry soldier's requirements.

By the late 1940s a new 7 x 44mm (.280) intermediate-powered round was developed, as was this startling new rifle to fire it. Known as the "Rifle, Automatic, No. 9 Mark 1," or EM-2, it was a neat, gas-operated selective-fire weapon firing from a 20-shot detachable box magazine under the receiver. It also pioneered the so-called "bullpup" configuration, where the chamber, bolt and magazine feed are all behind the trigger group and form part of the butt. The advantage of this form is that it makes for a short, handy rifle while still keeping a reasonably long barrel. Other modern features included an optical tube sight integrated with the carrying handle.

In trials, the EM-2 turned out to be reliable and easy to use, and it shot well. It gained service acceptance and all seemed set for production until it ran foul of international politics. At that time the newly formed NATO was attempting to agree standardized ammunition types, and the concept of a small-calibre intermediate-powered cartridge turned out to be too unusual and unproven for most of the other countries, and especially the United States, to accept. After much argument, the 7.62 x 51mm cartridge was chosen by NATO, and as the EM-2 couldn't easily be redesigned to accept this round, it was abandoned. Instead, the British went with a version of the FN FAL (*see below*).

## ENFIELD L1A1 SELF-LOADING RIFLE

**SPECIFICATIONS**
**Type:** semi-automatic rifle
**Origin:** Royal Small arms Factory, Enfield, England
**Caliber:** 7.62 x 51mm NATO
**Barrel Length:** 21in

The British version of the FN FAL, this entered service in 1954, and served until it began to be replaced by the L85 in the mid-1980s. It is only slightly modified from the FAL, the main changes being the removal of the fully-automatic fire option and the addition of a flash hider at the muzzle. The rifle shown here is an early one with wooden stock, pistol grip and foregrip. Later production had these in plastic.

## ENFIELD L85 INDIVIDUAL WEAPON

**SPECIFICATIONS**
**Type:** selective-fire rifle
**Origin:** Royal Small Arms
Factory, Enfield, England
**Caliber:** 5.56 x 45mm NATO
**Barrel Length:** 20.4in

This British design was intended to replace the L1A1, and began to enter service in 1985. While at first glance it resembles the earlier EM-2 prototype, apart from in its basic outline it has no commonality with the earlier design. The bullpup configuration makes for a short rifle, easy to handle while getting in and out of a vehicle, although the downside is the inability to fire from the left shoulder (the ejection port would be in the firer's face) and a certain awkwardness while changing the magazine.

The rifle is gas-operated, and was originally designed for a specially designed British 4.85mm round. When NATO standardized on 5.56mm ammunition it seemed as if another EM-2 debacle might be in the offing, but this time the rifle was quickly redesigned to take the new ammunition.

The L85 is made from stampings and pressings, with a plastic butt-plate, butt cover, pistol grip and fore grip. Ammunition is fed from a 30-shot box magazine. It is unusual in that as standard the L85 is fitted with an optical sight, the Sight Unit, Small Arms, Trilux (SUSAT). A variant for rear-echelon forces doesn't have the SUSAT sight, but instead just simple open sights in an integral carrying handle. There are two variants in use, firstly the L86 Light Support Weapon (*see the Machine Gun section*) and the single-shot, bolt-action Cadet Rifle L98A1. A 40mm grenade launcher is also available to clip under the barrel.

The L85 was designed to a price, and it shows.

## RIFLE, SHORT, MAGAZINE, LEE-ENFIELD (SMLE)

Shortly after the Lee-Metford entered service, it was found that cordite propellant, which burnt at a much higher temperature, caused excessive fouling and wear on the Metford barrel. This meant that the barrel and rifling had to be redesigned, which was done at the Royal Small Arms Factory (RSAF) at Enfield, and when the new rifle was put into production, it was named the "Lee-Enfield." It was next decided to end the existing distinction between infantry rifles and the much shorter cavalry carbines in order to produce a single weapon satisfying all requirements. The result was a new weapon, officially designated the "Rifle, Short, Magazine, Lee-Enfield." It should be noted that this weapon is commonly referred to as the "Short Magazine Lee-Enfield" (SMLE) which suggests that it was the magazine that was short. In fact, as the full title makes clear, it was the rifle that was short, not the magazine.

The SMLE was in service for many years and, not surprisingly, there were many modifications and improvements. The British Army indicated major changes by a new mark number (Mark I, Mark II, etc) and minor changes by a "star" (Mark I*, Mark I**, etc). There were also sniper versions, training versions, grenade launchers and "drill

| DESIGNATION | IN SERVICE (YEAR) | BARREL (INCHES) | WEIGHT (POUNDS) | SIGHTED (YARDS) | MAJOR CHANGES |
|---|---|---|---|---|---|
| MARK I | 1903 | 25.2 | 8.2 | 2,000 | |
| MARK I* | 1906 | 25.2 | 8.2 | | GUNMETAL BUTT-PLATE, DEEPER MAGAZINE |
| MARK I** | 1909 | 25.2 | 8.2 | | RN ONLY. MARK I WITH ALTERED SIGHTS |
| MARK I*** | 1914 | | | | SMLE MARK I* WITH NEW SIGHTS |
| MARK II | 1906 | 25.2 | 8.4LB | | LEE-ENFIELD MARK I/I* AND LEE-METFORD CONVERTED TO SMLE |
| MARK II** | 1909 | 25.2 | 8.2 | | RN ONLY. SAME AS MARK I** BUT ON MARK 2 RIFLE |
| MARK III | 1907 | 25.2 | 8.7 | | CHANGES TO SIGHTS; NEW BRIDGE CHARGER GUIDE. |
| MARK III* | 1916 | 25.2 | 8.7 | | MARK III WITH CHANGES TO EASE PRODUCTION |
| MARK V | TRIALS 1922 | 25.2 | 8.7 | 1,400 | NEW SIGHTS, REINFORCING BAND |
| MARK VI | TRIALS 1924 | 25.2 | 8.7 | | HEAVY BARREL, NEW BACK SIGHT |

purpose rifles" which were old weapons which had been deactivated so that they could be used safely for drill and weapon training by recruits and cadets.

The typical SMLE Mark III had a 25.2 inch barrel and an overall length of 44.6 inches. It weighed 8.7 pounds without ammunition and was fitted with a removable ten-round magazine. It was reloaded either by removing the magazine and loading rounds individually, or, with the magazine in place, using a five-round charger, which was fitted into a guide and the rounds then pushed into the magazine with the right thumb. The Mark III, like most versions, was fitted with a "cut-off" plate which could be slid across the top of the magazine so that the firer had to load and fire round one at a time. In the open position, the bolt lever stuck out at right angles and it was pushed forward and then down, which loaded a new round and cocked the action; once fired, the bolt was raised and then pulled back to extract the empty cartridge case. British regular infantry were so skilled in rapid fire that in August 1914 attacking Germans thought they were under fire from machine guns. The British infantry had great faith in the bayonet and the SMLE's bayonet lug below the muzzle gave the weapon an appearance which could be mistaken for no other weapon.

The only real failure was the SMLE Mark 5 (not to be confused with the Number 5 jungle rifle, described below), which was trialed in the early 1920s. The Mark 5 had a new sighting arrangement and a heavy barrel, but proved very unpopular and never entered production.

British soldiers always complain about their equipment and the SMLE was no exception. It was said to be heavy and so-called experts claimed that the locking lugs could have been better positioned. However, it was lighter and shorter than its contemporaries, very accurate, simple to maintain, and the soldiers who used it trusted it. The SMLE remained in front-line service throughout two world wars and many colonial campaigns, and is one of the greatest of all rifle designs.

## SMLE - RIFLES

This Mark III, shows the major characteristics of all SMLEs. It is stocked to the muzzle, with the foresight at the very end and the bayonet lug below. The rear sight is ramped and protected by two "ears." The bolt lever lies conveniently placed for the firer's right hand and is seen here turned down. Forward of the trigger is the ten-round magazine, which was usually "charged" using a separate metal guide. There are three swivels for the sling which was made of canvas "webbing" with brass ends.

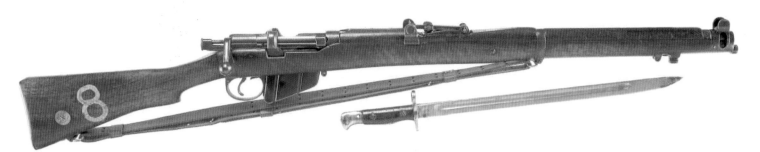

Here we see the action in the cocked position and the very substantial bayonet. This rifle is fitted with a leather sling as an alternative to the more common webbing version.

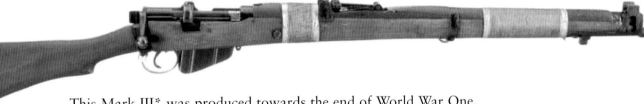

This Mark III* was produced towards the end of World War One, when quality and workmanship were being sacrificed in order to raise production rates. This led to the bindings of copper and brass wire seen here, which were intended to reduce splintering if the barrel should burst.

The only unsuccessful SMLE, the Mark 5 had the rear sight moved back to a position immediately above the trigger and an additional reinforcing band around the bodywork behind the muzzle.

The barrel and action of a combat rifle can be used to produce high quality customized target rifles for civilian use. We show two. One is a very striking weapon, still chambered for the .303 round, but with a totally new stock and butt, coupled with a Weaver telescopic sight and an integral magazine. The barrel has been cut back to 22 inches and is fitted with a new foresight. The other has a 25.4 inch barrel, has a cut-back handgrip, but retains the sights and magazine of the original. Both, however, are at heart, the tried-and-trusted SMLE.

Reworked SMLEs appeared as late as the 1960s when the Rifle Factory at Ishapore, India rebuilt a number of Mark III* chambered for the new NATO 7.62 x 51mm round. The major visual identification for this weapon was the squared-off magazine, replacing the more curved version for the .303 cartridge. Not so obvious was that the barrel and action were made of higher grade steel to withstand the higher stresses and pressures from the more powerful round.

## LEE-ENFIELD RIFLE, NO. 4

The Rifle No. 4 (always known, simply, as "the number 4") was developed from the SMLE Mark VI, which had a heavier barrel and better sights than earlier versions of the SMLE. Testing of small numbers began in the 1920s and development continued at a slow pace throughout the 1930s, but, although approved in late 1939, the first of the new Rifle No. 4 Mark 1s did not reach troops until early 1942.

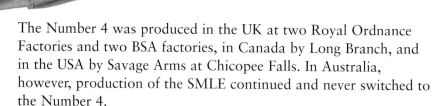

The Number 4 was generally similar to the SMLE, but the nose-cap was removed, the stock cut back to expose about three inches of the muzzle, and the rear sight moved to the rear of the body, all of which combined to make it look like a very different weapon. Inside the rifle, the bolt was improved, and all screw threads were changed from a unique Enfield pattern to national standards.

The Number 4 was produced in the UK at two Royal Ordnance Factories and two BSA factories, in Canada by Long Branch, and in the USA by Savage Arms at Chicopee Falls. In Australia, however, production of the SMLE continued and never switched to the Number 4.

The Number 4 Mark 1* appeared in 1941 with a simplified method of removing the bolt, and shown here is a Number 4 Mark 1* manufactured in the United States for the US Army by Savage.

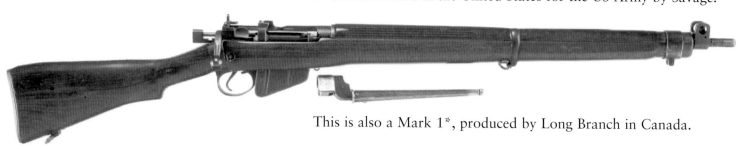

This is also a Mark 1*, produced by Long Branch in Canada.

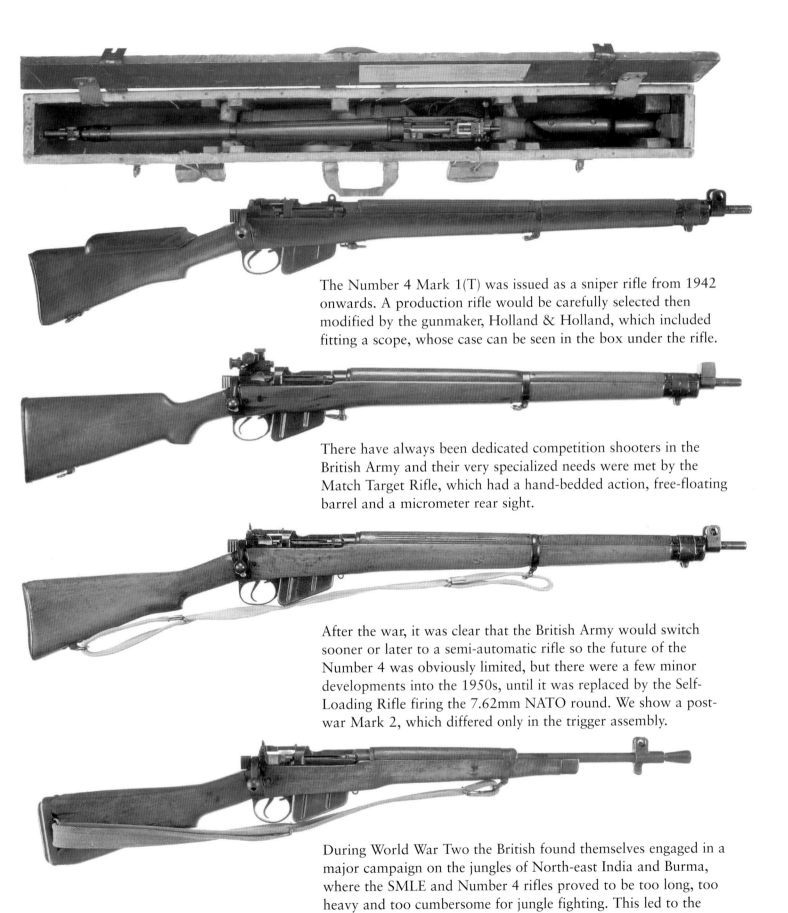

The Number 4 Mark 1(T) was issued as a sniper rifle from 1942 onwards. A production rifle would be carefully selected then modified by the gunmaker, Holland & Holland, which included fitting a scope, whose case can be seen in the box under the rifle.

There have always been dedicated competition shooters in the British Army and their very specialized needs were met by the Match Target Rifle, which had a hand-bedded action, free-floating barrel and a micrometer rear sight.

After the war, it was clear that the British Army would switch sooner or later to a semi-automatic rifle so the future of the Number 4 was obviously limited, but there were a few minor developments into the 1950s, until it was replaced by the Self-Loading Rifle firing the 7.62mm NATO round. We show a post-war Mark 2, which differed only in the trigger assembly.

During World War Two the British found themselves engaged in a major campaign on the jungles of North-east India and Burma, where the SMLE and Number 4 rifles proved to be too long, too heavy and too cumbersome for jungle fighting. This led to the development of the Number 5, usually known as the "jungle carbine." This had the Number 4 action, but with a shorter barrel, a new bayonet, a rubber shoulder-pad on the butt, and a flash-hider fitted to the muzzle. As always, the troops complained, but it was used with great success in the Burma campaign and later in the Malayan Emergency, where it was given up with great reluctance when the Self-Loading Rifle was issued in the later 1950s.

## LORD "SNIDER ACTION" RIFLE

### SPECIFICATIONS

**Type:** Snider-action, breech-loading percussion rifle

**Origin:** J.C. & A. Lord, London and Birmingham, England

**Caliber:** .577 rimmed

**Barrel Length:** 21.5in

The Snider action was not only employed for military purposes, but also saw usage on sporting and hunting arms, such as this short rifle

## MARTINI-HENRY RIFLE

### SPECIFICATIONS

**Type:** Martini-action, breech-loading service rifle

**Origin:** Royal Small Arms Factory, Enfield, England

**Caliber:** .577 rimmed

**Barrel Length:** 36.5in

Despite winning a British War Office competition for a new breech-loading rifle in 1867, the British Martini-Henry Infantry Rifle underwent a lengthy development process and the first model to enter service was the Mark II in 1877. The action had been designed by a Swiss engineer named Friedrich Martini in the 1860s and involved the firer in pushing a lever smartly downwards, causing the front of the breech-block to descend, extract the used cartridge case from the chamber and throw it clear of the weapon. The firer then manually inserted a fresh round and raised the lever, thus closing the breech and cocking the action. This was slow, but considerably faster than what had gone before, although the rate of fire was slowed if the extractor failed to remove the case properly and the firer had to do so by hand. The Martini-Henry Mark II shown was chambered for the .450 cartridge, had a 33 inch barrel and weighed some 8.66 pounds. The type was in service with the British Army from 1877–1881, but remained in production until 1889. Large numbers were sent to India for use by the British Indian Army and as the example seen here has both British and Indian issue marks, it was presumably one of these.

# United States

## ALLEN AND WHEELOCK DROP BLOCK RIFLE

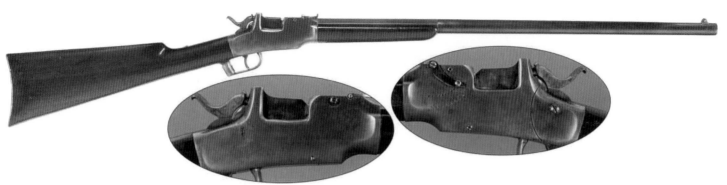

### SPECIFICATIONS

**Type:** single-shot breechloading rimfire rifle
**Origin:** Allen & Wheelock, Worcester, Massachusetts
**Caliber:** .42 A&W rimfire
**Barrel Length:** 26in

A neat single shot breechloader produced from around 1860 to 1871, some saw military service in the Civil War as privately procured weapons. The breech block drops down when the trigger guard is lowered, ejecting the case and allowing a fresh round to be inserted.

## ARMALITE AR-18 RIFLE

### SPECIFICATIONS

**Type:** semi-automatic rifle
**Origin:** Armalite Inc, Costa Mesa, California (now at Geneseo, Illinois)
**Caliber:** .223
**Barrel Length:** 20in

Following the sale of the AR-15 design and the departure of Eugene Stoner to Cadillac Gage in 1963 (*see Colt M16 below*), Arthur Miller and the team at Armalite produced the AR-18 design, intended to be a cheaper alternative to the AR-15. In particular, the AR-18 was meant to be suitable for production in Third World countries which might lack the sophisticated tooling necessary to manufacture the forged aluminum receiver of the AR-15. Thus, the AR-18 employed a rotating bolt with seven-lugs, which locking into the breech end of the barrel, with a short-stroke piston driving the bolt-carrier rearwards. Twin recoil springs ran on guides through the upper part of the carrier to give a well-supported, straight-line recoil, which meant that a rigid, folding butt-stock could be fitted. The AR-18 was of all-steel construction, extensive use being made of pressings for the upper and lower receivers bodies, and for a number of external and internal parts; all furniture was glass-reinforced plastic. The military AR-18 (known as the AR-180 for the civilian market) was manufactured in small numbers by Armalite Inc of California, USA at their Costa Mesa factory, by Howa Machinery of Japan; and by Sterling Armament of Dagenham, England.

We show an early production AR-180, manufactured at the Costa Mesa facility between 1969 and 1972. It looks generally similar to the AR-15, but has pressed steel components and the butt swings forward on the left side by the prominent hinge.

## BRIDESBURG MUSKETS

### SPECIFICATIONS

**Type:** percussion rifle muskets
**Origin:** Bridesburg Machine Works, Pennsylvania
**Caliber:** see text
**Barrel Length:** see text

Two of the Bridesburg muskets are seen here. The first is a Model 1861 musket, with a 40 inch barrel and .64 caliber – the US Government eagle and the maker's name are just visible on the lock plate.

The second is a Model 1863 .58 caliber musket with a 40 inch barrel.

## J.F. BROWN TARGET/SNIPER RIFLE

### SPECIFICATIONS

**Type:** percussion rifle
**Origin:** J. F. Brown, Haverhill, Massachusetts
**Caliber:** .45
**Barrel Length:** 32.5in

This very interesting weapon would certainly have been used for target shooting and may also have been used as a sniper rifle during the Civil War, when it represented the very latest technology. The weapon was made by J.F. Brown, who was based in Poplin from 1840 to 1856 and Fremont from 1856 to 1859, both in New Hampshire, and in Haverhill, Massachusetts from 1859 until his death in 1904. The telescopic sight was manufactured by L.M. Amadon of Bellows Falls, Vermont, who was one of the pioneers of such devices. Both Amadon and Brown were famous in their time for the very high quality of their products.

During the Civil War the Union forces formed Sharpshooter units in which most of the men were armed with Sharp's rifles, but for long-range sniping a few were armed with the much heavier Brown rifle, of the type seen here. The massive cast-steel, octagonal barrel is 32.5 inches long and contributes the most to the overall weight of 30 pounds. The round section a the end of the barrel is a "false muzzle" which was designed to help load the conical-shaped "picket" bullets correctly without damaging the all-important rifling at the true muzzle; it was removed prior to firing. The paper patches used in loading were stored in the elaborately engraved patchbox. The sight could be adjusted by vertical and horizontal screws at the rear end, making it clear this rifle was intended for the highest degree of accuracy. The weight of the Brown rifle was such that the firer would have had to use a rest, but no fitting can be seen on this rifle.

# BROWNING SEMI-AUTOMATIC RIFLE

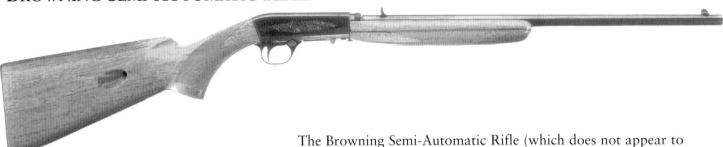

## SPECIFICATIONS

**Type:** semi-automatic rifle
**Origin:** John Browning and FN, Herstal, Belgium or B.C. Hiroku, Kochi, Japan
**Caliber:** .22LR
**Barrel Length:** 19.25in

The Browning Semi-Automatic Rifle (which does not appear to have had an abbreviated designation) was manufactured by FN in Belgium from 1956 to 1974 and from 1976 onwards by B.C. Miroku in Japan. It has a blowback, semi-automatic action, with an eleven-round, tubular magazine inside the butt-stock which is loaded through a hole in the center of the butt. We show one with Grade I finish, with the receiver lightly engraved and parts of the woodwork checkered.

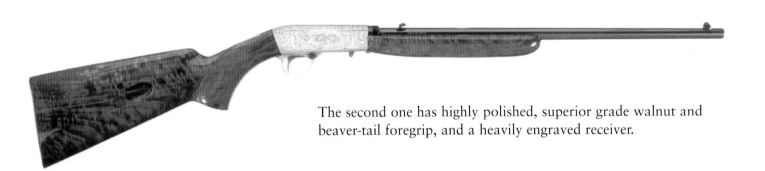

The second one has highly polished, superior grade walnut and beaver-tail foregrip, and a heavily engraved receiver.

# BROWNING HIGH-POWER OLYMPIAN GRADE

## SPECIFICATIONS

**Type:** bolt-action, sporting rifle
**Origin:** John Browning and FN, Herstal, Belgium or Sako, Finland
**Caliber:** see text
**Barrel Length:** see text

The High-Power Bolt-Action Rifle was manufactured from 1959 to 1975, with production taking place at FN, Herstal, Belgium (1959-75) and Sako, Rihimali, Finland (1961–75). It was chambered for a variety of calibers from .22 Remington up to .458 Winchester and featured either a Mauser or a Sako action, with three grades of finish.

Made with the highest "Olympian" finish, this is a .22 caliber weapon fitted with a Leupold Vari XIIc 4 x 12 telescopic sight. The wood is of exceptional quality, namely satin finish walnut with rosewood ends and a finely carved pistol grip, while the action and Leupold scope mounts are finely engraved with hunting scenes.

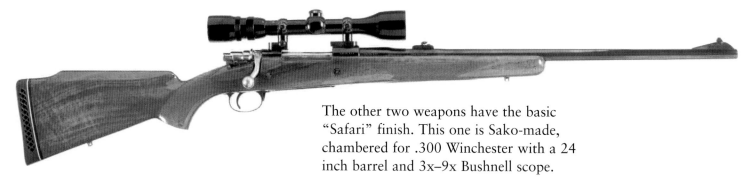

The other two weapons have the basic "Safari" finish. This one is Sako-made, chambered for .300 Winchester with a 24 inch barrel and 3x–9x Bushnell scope.

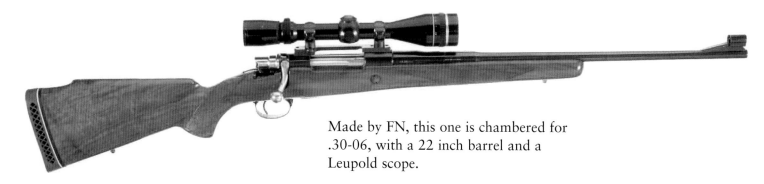

Made by FN, this one is chambered for .30-06, with a 22 inch barrel and a Leupold scope.

## BROWNING BAR HIGH-POWER RIFLE

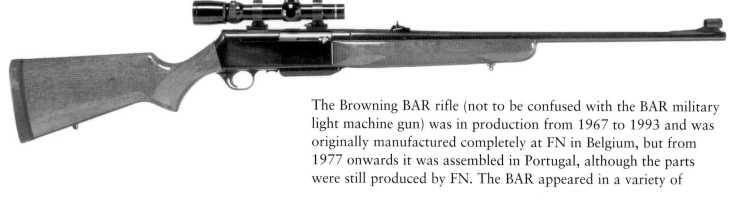

The Browning BAR rifle (not to be confused with the BAR military light machine gun) was in production from 1967 to 1993 and was originally manufactured completely at FN in Belgium, but from 1977 onwards it was assembled in Portugal, although the parts were still produced by FN. The BAR appeared in a variety of

## SPECIFICATIONS

**Type:** gas-operated, semi-automatic rifle
**Origin:** John Browning and FN, Herstal, Belgium
**Caliber:** .338 Winchester Magnum
**Barrel Length:** 24in

chamberings, ranging from .243 to .338 Magnum, with either 22 inch or 24 inch barrels, and, as usual, there were different grades of finish. The weapon seen here is a basic grade I finish, chambered for .338 Magnum with a 24 inch barrel.

# BROWNING GOLD MEDALLION A-BOLT

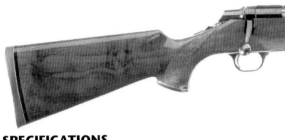

## SPECIFICATIONS

**Type:** target and sporting rifle
**Origin:** John Browning and B. C. Miroku, Kochi, Japan
**Caliber:** .22 LR
**Barrel Length:** 22in

In the 1970s the Browning Arms Co. licensed B.C. Miroku, of Kochi, Japan, to manufacture Browning-designed sporting rifles. This company has a high reputation for good quality weapons, which is borne out by the example seen here. The series is based on the A-Bolt Hunter, for which a deluxe version, the A-Bolt Medallion was introduced in 1985; this had a highly-polish blue finished barrel and action, and a walnut stock with rosewood ends. The Gold Medallion, introduced in 1988, was an even higher quality weapon, which featured the very top grade of walnut, together with light engraving and gold-inlaid lettering. The example seen here has no sights, which would be added by the owner.

# BROWNING BLR

## SPECIFICATIONS

**Type:** lever-action rifle
**Origin:** John Browning and B.C. Miroku, Kochi, Japan
**Caliber:** see text
**Barrel Length:** see text

BLR stands for "Browning Lever-action Rifle." Introduced in 1971, this family of weapons was manufactured for one year at FN, Belgium, but production was then switched to B.C. Miroku in Japan, where it has remained ever since. The Model 81 BLR had a 20 inch barrel, a four-round detachable box magazine and a rotary locking bolt. It was made in a variety of calibers, that seen here being .308. It has adjustable iron sights, but also has mounts for a telescopic sight.

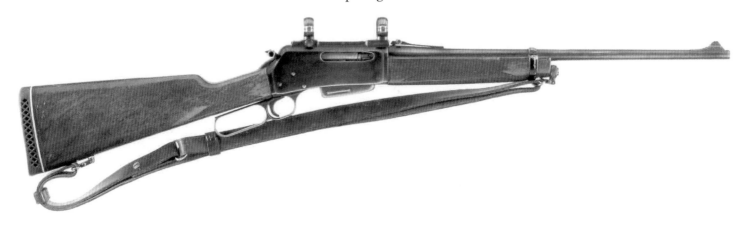

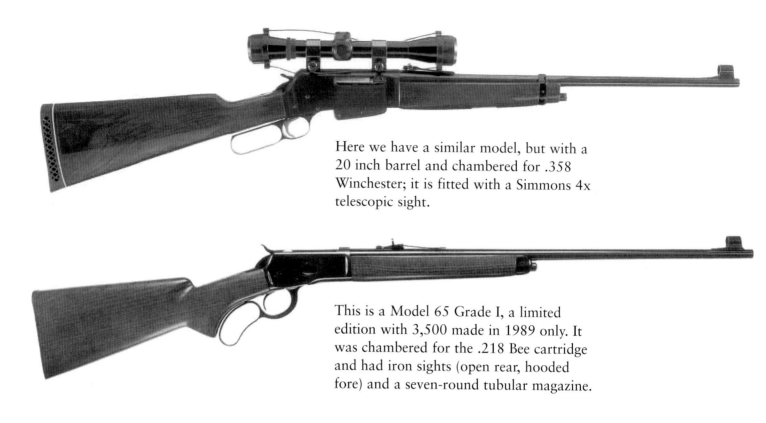

Here we have a similar model, but with a 20 inch barrel and chambered for .358 Winchester; it is fitted with a Simmons 4x telescopic sight.

This is a Model 65 Grade I, a limited edition with 3,500 made in 1989 only. It was chambered for the .218 Bee cartridge and had iron sights (open rear, hooded fore) and a seven-round tubular magazine.

# BURNSIDE CARBINE

A prolific series of Civil War carbines, the Burnside remained in production from 1857 to 1865. Designed by Ambrose E. Burnside, who at that time had formed the Bristol Firearms Co. in Rhode Island, it was later improved by one of his gunsmiths, George P. Foster. The company was also renamed the Burnside Rifle Co and moved to Providence, Rhode Island. After a faltering start, the carbine went on to great success, although most of that was after Burnside had sold his interests in the company. Burnside, of course, went on to greater things himself as the commander of the Army of the Potomac.

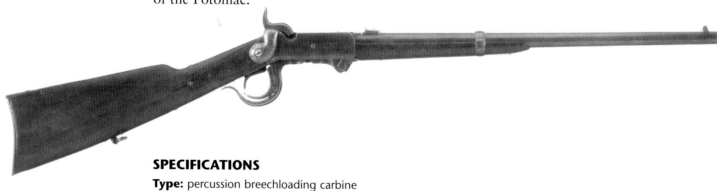

## SPECIFICATIONS
**Type:** percussion breechloading carbine
**Origin:** Bristol Firearms Co., Bristol, and Burnside Rifle Co., Providence, both Rhode Island
**Caliber:** .54
**Barrel Length:** 21in

## BUSHMASTER M17S BULLPUP

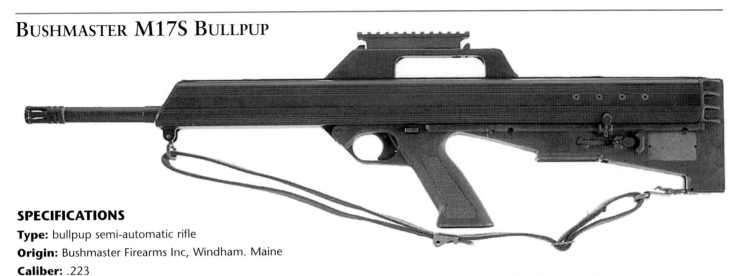

**SPECIFICATIONS**

**Type:** bullpup semi-automatic rifle
**Origin:** Bushmaster Firearms Inc, Windham. Maine
**Caliber:** .223
**Barrel Length:** 21.5in

The M17S Bullpup is a lightweight, short-stroke piston, gas-operated, air-cooled, semi-automatic rifle, chambered for the .223 Remington round. It has a 20 inch, hard chrome lined barrel and a ten-round magazine. Overall length is 30 inches and the weapon (without magazine) weighs 8.2 pounds. In this picture the magazine is not fitted, but the housing can be seen – it is the horizontal portion midway along the angled underside of the stock.

## BUSHMASTER XM15-E2S RIFLE

**SPECIFICATIONS**

**Type:** semi-automatic rifle
**Origin:** Bushmaster Firearms Inc, Windham, Maine
**Caliber:** 5.56mm
**Barrel Length:** 24in

The Bushmaster XM15-ES is based on the M16A2 design, and is marketed in a variety of forms for particular purposes, e.g., shooting varmints. There is also a target shooting version with a long barrel and no carrying handle.

This one is a Bushmaster Assault Rifle, based on the company's XM15, but with all unnecessary items deleted and with a tubular, skeleton folding butt replacing the normal fixed type. Like the XM15 it is chambered for 5.56mm but with a 20 inch barrel.

## CALICO RIFLE

### SPECIFICATIONS

**Type:** semi-automatic rifle
**Origin:** Calico, Bakersfield, California
**Caliber:** see text
**Barrel Length:** see text

The Calico company produces a series of futuristic-looking semi-automatic weapons, first marketed in 1986. Indeed, they are relatively straightforward blow-back weapons, but the exterior is dominated by the large magazine which sits on top of the receiver and holds up to 100 rounds. The Model 100 and Model 100S are both chambered for .22LR and have 17.25in barrels, and differ only in that the first has a folding butt and is intended for tactical military use, while the second is for sporting use.

The Model 900 is chambered for 9mm and has a 16 inch barrel.

## CENTRAL ARMS CO. "KING NITRO" RIFLE

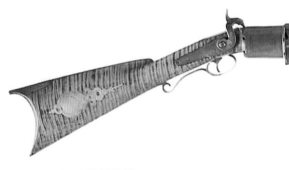

### SPECIFICATIONS
**Type:** slide-action rifle
**Origin:** Davenport Firearms Co, Providence, Rhode Island (see text)
**Caliber:** .22
**Barrel Length:** 24in

The provenance of this weapon is somewhat complicated, but illustrates the tangled web that can sometimes be found in the firearms business. According to the legend engraved on the weapon itself, it was made by "King Nitro, Central Arms Co., St Louis, Mo, United States." But, Central Arms Co was another name for the Central Hardware Co, which, in its turn was part of the Shapleigh Hardware Co, all of St Louis. But all three were wholesalers, not gunsmiths, and they bought in their weapons from whatever source offered the best bargain. In this case, "King Nitro" was one of the many trade names used by the Davenport Firearms Co., which was bought by Hopkins & Allen in 1901. Many companies at the time used such trade names; Hopkins & Allen, for example, used Acme, Blue Jacket, Captain Jack, Chichester, Defender, Dictator, Imperial Arms Co, Monarch, Mountain Eagle, Ranger, Tower, Universal and XL – occasionally they even used their own name of Hopkins & Allen! The design of this weapon bears a remarkable similarity to that of the Savage Model 29.

## CHERRINGTON PILL-LOCK CYLINDER RIFLE

### SPECIFICATIONS
**Type:** seven-shot, revolving chamber, rifle
**Origin:** Thomas P. Cherrington, Jr, Cattawissa, Pennsylvania
**Caliber:** .41
**Barrel Length:** 30in

The search for an efficient multi-shot rifle took many forms, one of the more popular being the revolver rifle, and most arms firms such as Colt produced at least one model. The weapon seen here was made by Thomas P. Cherrington, Junior, who had previously helped to make such rifles when he worked for William Billinghurst at Rochester, New York in the late 1850s and early 1860s. The patent for this particular design belonged to a man named Miller and Cherrington must have obtained a license to make more when he returned to his home town of Cattawissa, Pennsylvania, at some time in the mid-1860s. In this particular design, the seven-round cylinder was rotated by hand and the frame was open; i.e., there was no top strap over the cylinder.

# COLT LIGHTNING

## SPECIFICATIONS

**Type:** tubular magazine, slide-action rifle
**Origin:** Colt Armaments Manufacturing Co, Hartford, Connecticut

The Colt Lightning was the first slide-action rifle to be manufactured by Colt and was produced in three frame-sizes. The small-frame version was available only in .22 caliber, while the medium- and large-frame version were produced in rifle (long barrel) and carbine (short barrel). In addition, a special version of the medium-framed version was produced for the San Francisco Police department. The largest round for the large-frame rifle was the .50-95 Express and earned the nickname "Express model" for all caliber versions.

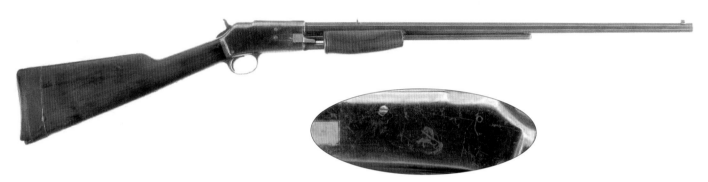

This was the small-frame version, available in .22 Short or Long caliber only, with a 24 inch barrel; this example has seen considerable service and even includes some repair tape.

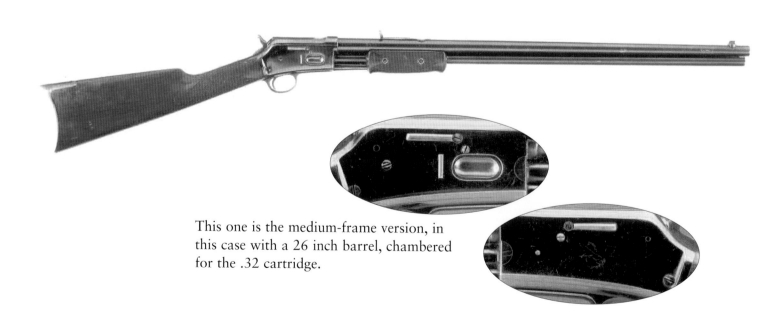

This one is the medium-frame version, in this case with a 26 inch barrel, chambered for the .32 cartridge.

# COLT COLTEER

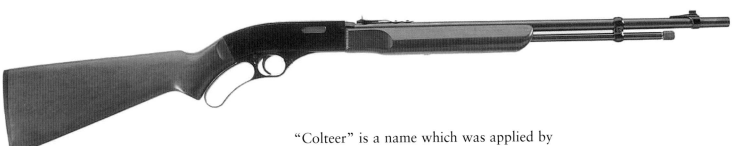

## SPECIFICATIONS

**Type:** tubular magazine, lever-action rifle
**Origin:** Colt Armaments Manufacturing Co, Hartford, Connecticut
**Caliber:** .22LR
**Barrel Length:** 21.5in

"Colteer" is a name which was applied by Colt between 1950 and 1980 to a number of .22 caliber designs, but with different actions. Between 1957 and 1965, for example, the name was given to a bolt-action weapon, then in 1965–75 it was a semi-automatic weapon, and both were manufactured in some numbers. In this case, however, the name Colteer was given to an experimental lever-action weapon, the company's first to use such an action since the Colt-Burgess of 1883 (*see above*). The lever-action and the associated rifle seen here were designed in 1962–3, and produced in an experimental batch, but the action proved much too complicated and the whole design was dropped.

# COLT-SAUER RIFLE

This is a top-of-the-range sporting rifle made in Germany by J.P. Sauer & Son for Colt, who marketed it in the United States. It features an unusual action, with a non-rotating bolt, and a 24 inch barrel. Its undoubted elegance stems from its simplicity, the only decoration on the plain walnut stock being a discreet rosewood fore-end and pistol-grip cap, and a White Line recoil pad. It was marketed in five configurations, depending on the caliber:

| CONFIGURATION | CALIBERS |
|---|---|
| Standard Action | .25-06; .270 Winchester; .30-06 |
| Short Action | .22-250; .243 Winchester; .308 Winchester |
| Magnum Action | 7mm Remington Magnum; .300 Winchester Magnum; .300 Weatherby Magnum |
| Grand Alaskan | .375 Holland & Holland |
| Grand African | .458 Winchester |

## SPECIFICATIONS

**Type:** bolt-action rifle
**Origin:** Colt Armaments Manufacturing Co, Hartford, Connecticut and J.P. Sauer & Son, Eckernförde, Germany
**Caliber:** .458 Winchester Magnum
**Barrel Length:** 24in

The example shown here is the largest and heaviest of them all, the "Grand African."

# COLT M16 ASSAULT RIFLE

In the early 1950s the Fairchild Aircraft Corporation formed the new "Armalite" division, headed by Eugene Stoner, to pursue recent advances in aluminum alloy and glass-reinforced plastic (GRP) technology. One of the division's first tasks was to look at small arms design, and Stoner, who was an aviation rather than a weapons engineer, started with a clean sheet. After some failed attempts at military caliber rifles, Stoner designed a new rifle (the AR-15) around the lighter .223 cartridge, which was intended for use against the shorter range targets now specified by the US Army. Making extensive use of light alloys and glass reinforced plastics, the rifle was light, handy and had minimal recoil. The ammunition was also lighter, and an infantryman could carry 280 rounds of .223 compared to 100 rounds of .30. But the army resisted these new concepts, and in February 1959 Fairchild gave up and sold its design rights to Colt.

At much the same time, the commander-in-chief of the U.S. Air Force, General Curtis Le May, chanced to see a live-firing demonstration of the AR-15, which resulted in small numbers being taken into USAF service under the designation, soon to become famous, of M16. The lack of army interest continued until the first combat troops to deploy to Vietnam noticed the novel rifle being used by USAF airfield guards and demanded that they be issued with them, particularly for jungle fighting.

After many trials and tribulation, the rifle was standardized for all four US forces as the M16, and Colt was soon producing 40,000 per month, with some 400,000 fielded in South Vietnam by early 1966.

The M16 has been sold to many foreign armies, to both U.S. and foreign police forces, and also to civilians. It has also been manufactured under licence in Canada, South Korea, Philippines, Singapore and Taiwan, and a few "sporters" are also known to have been produced by Norinco in China. In addition, the Department of Defense was reluctant to depend upon Colt as the single-source supplier and in 1968 contracts were placed with General Motors (Hydramatic Division) and Harrington & Richardson.

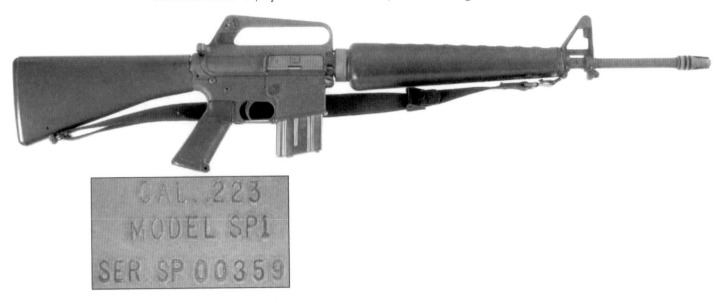

This is an early production Colt M16, chambered for the .223 M193 round and with a 21 inch barrel and 20-round magazine. The M16 has, of course, been modified and adapted over the years, the original 20-round magazine was replaced by a 30-round version, and various add-ons, such as the M203 grenade-launcher were devised.

The M16A2 introduced a new heavier barrel with revised rifling enabling it to take the new NATO SS109 5.46mm round. The fully-automatic capability was also changed to a three-round burst setting.

## M16 SPORT VARIANTS

Colt has sold a large number of "sporter" models on the civilian market. This one is the AR-15A2 Sporter II (Model 711), based on the original M16, with a 21 inch barrel chambered for the .223 round, and normally sold with a five-round magazine (missing in this picture).

The Sporter Match HBAR (Heavy BARrel) has a 20 inch barrel and a TASCO 20x telescopic sight, which is fitted with an extended sunshade.

A Sporter Target Model, with numerous additions for serious target use, including a raised cheek-piece, pistol grip rest and TASCO 3 x 9 telescopic sight, which is protected by a special rubber coating.

A Colt AR15A2 Sporter II carbine with a 16 inch barrel and telescopic, and fiberglass stock.

## COOK AND BROTHER CARBINE

A short carbine typical of the early Civil War period, where muzzleloading weapons were still very much in evidence. And as they had less industrial resources at their disposal, the Confederacy retained more muzzleloaders than did the federal army. America was seen as a great opportunity for foreign gunmakers, and two such were Ferdinand and Francis Cook, a pair of Englishmen who set up shop in New Orleans in 1860. They were in an ideal place to capitalize on the rapid demands of wartime production, and manufactured quantities of this cavalry carbine based on the Enfield pattern.

With the approach of Northern forces around 1862 they decamped to the relative safety of Athens, Georgia where production resumed from 1863–64. Over 1,500 guns of this type were produced. Stocks were either walnut or maple but some pecan wood is believed to have been used, being a close cousin to walnut and more readily available in the South. Furniture was brass with a cast iron ramrod with flat button tip operated by a swivel joint.

It is generally reckoned that the Athens production models were better engineered than the earlier New Orleans models, but collectors will pay far more for earlier, more scarce, guns from the original factory.

**SPECIFICATIONS**
**Type:** percussion carbine
**Origin:** Cook & Brother, New Orleans, later Athens, Georgia
**Caliber:** .58
**Barrel Length:** 21in

## COSMOPOLITAN CARBINE

**SPECIFICATIONS**
**Type:** percussion carbine
**Origin:** Cosmopolitan Arms Co., Hamilton, Ohio
**Caliber:** .52
**Barrel Length:** 19in

This forerunner to the Gwyn & Campbell Carbine was made in the same factory at Hamilton, Ohio. An order for 1,140 units for the State of Illinois was placed through the U.S Ordnance Dept. in December 1861 and delivered the following July. Virtually the whole batch was issued to the 5th and 6th Illinois Cavalry. The 6th Illinois Cavalry, commanded by Benjamin Grierson, took part in the spectacular "Grierson's Raid" in April–May 1863 when they roamed through the whole state of Mississippi, covering 600 miles in 16 days, which is a tribute to both the men and their equipment. The 5th Cavalry, who were issued with some 400 carbines, also saw much action in Arkansas and Mississippi. The first 50 guns produced are recognizable by an enclosed lever extension of the trigger guard which activates the falling block action, whereas all subsequent production examples, known as the contract type, had a serpentine lever like the model shown. This one bears the marking "Hamilton O.,U.S. /Gross Patent".

## DAKOTA ARMS MODEL 76

Dakota Arms was formed by Don Allen in 1987, originally to produce an improved version of the Winchester Model 70, incorporating the Grisel-patented combined bolt-stop/gas-shield/bolt guide, under the designation, Dakota 76. The weapon was produced in two grades, Classic and Safari, and a wide variety of calibers were available ranging from .257 Roberts to .458 Winchester Magnum.

The weapon seen here is the Dakota 76 Classic, chambered for .338 Winchester and with a 23 inch barrel. It has a ported muzzle and an ebony fore-end cap, and is fitted with scope mounts.

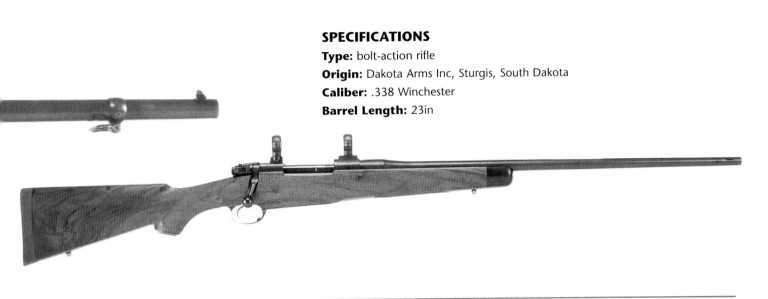

**SPECIFICATIONS**
**Type:** bolt-action rifle
**Origin:** Dakota Arms Inc, Sturgis, South Dakota
**Caliber:** .338 Winchester
**Barrel Length:** 23in

## DAKOTA ARMS MODEL 97 LONG-RANGE HUNTER

**SPECIFICATIONS**
**Type:** bolt-action rifle
**Origin:** Dakota Arms Inc, Sturgis, South Dakota
**Caliber:** .300 Winchester
**Barrel Length:** 26in

The simplicity of line in this design makes it one of the most elegant rifles every made. It was introduced in 1997 and is available in no less than 13 calibers from .250-6 to the company's own .357 Dakota Magnum, with a 24 or 26 inch barrel, depending upon the caliber. The black composition stock is in one piece, complete with a recoil pad. The Model 97 weighs 7.7 pounds and was followed in 1998 by a lightweight version, weighing 6.2–6.5 pounds depending on caliber.
The weapon seen here is the Model 97 in .300 caliber with a 26 inch barrel.

## DAKOTA ARMS MODEL T-76 LONG BOW

**SPECIFICATIONS**
**Type:** bolt-action rifle
**Origin:** Dakota Arms Inc, Sturgis, South Dakota
**Caliber:** .338 Lapua
**Barrel Length:** 28in

If the Dakota 97's lines are simple, then those of the Long Bow are the opposite, but for a good reason. This rifle is designed for long-range sniping or target shooting at a very high level, and consists of a Dakota long-action receiver combined with a heavy, precision-engineered, stainless steel, barrel with an integral muzzle brake. It has a Kevlar/fiberglass stock with an adjustable cheekpiece and is fitted with a Picatinny rail, which, in this example, carries a very powerful telescopic sight graduated from 50 to 2,000 metres. There is also a full-adjustable bipod. The Long Bow is available in three calibers – .338 Lapua (as seen here), .300 Dakota Magnum and .330 Dakota Magnum – all of which have a 28 inch barrel. Total weight is about 13.7 pounds.

## DEMRO XF-7 WASP/T.A.C. MODEL 1

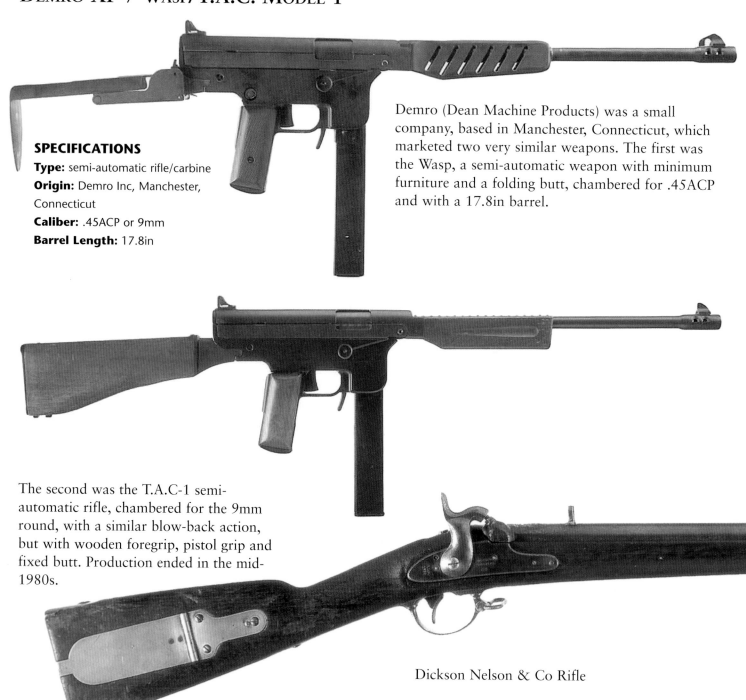

### SPECIFICATIONS

**Type:** semi-automatic rifle/carbine
**Origin:** Demro Inc, Manchester, Connecticut
**Caliber:** .45ACP or 9mm
**Barrel Length:** 17.8in

Demro (Dean Machine Products) was a small company, based in Manchester, Connecticut, which marketed two very similar weapons. The first was the Wasp, a semi-automatic weapon with minimum furniture and a folding butt, chambered for .45ACP and with a 17.8in barrel.

The second was the T.A.C-1 semi-automatic rifle, chambered for the 9mm round, with a similar blow-back action, but with wooden foregrip, pistol grip and fixed butt. Production ended in the mid-1980s.

Dickson Nelson & Co Rifle

## DERINGER MODEL 1814 RIFLE

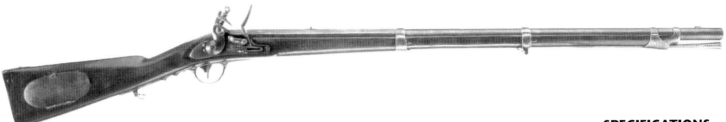

Henry Deringer Sr set up business in Philadelphia in the 1760s and the last government contract he signed before handing over to his son was for 2,000 Model 1814 rifles of the type seen here. The .54 caliber weapon has a 33.5 inch barrel marked "H. Deringer, Philadelphia" and the lock is similarly marked. An unusual feature is the finger ridges on the trigger guard strap.

**SPECIFICATIONS**
**Type:** flintlock rifle
**Origin:** Henry Deringer, Philadelphia, Pennsylvania
**Caliber:** .54
**Barrel Length:** 33.5in

## DERINGER MODEL 1817 PERCUSSION CONVERSION

Deringer was one of the companies who won contracts to manufacture the Model 1817 Rifle musket, often known as the "Common Rifle." Many were later converted to percussion firing, and the one shown was done using the "Belgian" method, where a piece of brass was inserted into the lock plate where the priming pan and frizzen used to be, and a percussion nipple threaded into the barrel vent hole.

**SPECIFICATIONS**
**Type:** percussion modified rifle
**Origin:** Henry Deringer, Philadelphia, Pennsylvania
**Caliber:** .54
**Barrel Length:** 36in

## DICKSON NELSON & CO RIFLE

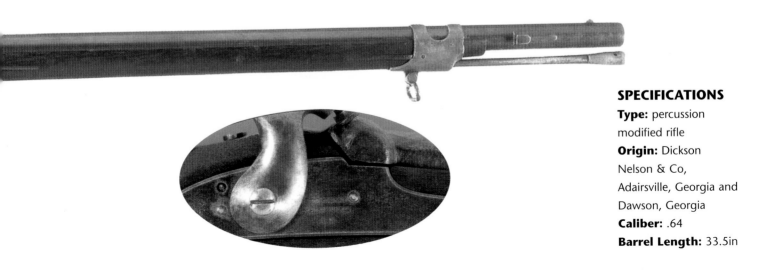

**SPECIFICATIONS**
**Type:** percussion modified rifle
**Origin:** Dickson Nelson & Co, Adairsville, Georgia and Dawson, Georgia
**Caliber:** .64
**Barrel Length:** 33.5in

## DORMANDY PERCUSSION TARGET RIFLE

**SPECIFICATIONS**

**Type:** percussion target rifle
**Origin:** T. Dormandy
**Caliber:** .48
**Barrel Length:** 33in

T. Dormandy is known to have worked at one time for Morgan James, a Utica, New York, gunsmith, who was noted for his very accurate percussion target rifles. The action is marked with Morgan James's name and it is probable that Dormandy made this exceptional weapon whilst still under the tutelage of the master. The 33 inch barrel is octagonal throughout its length and above the muzzle is a globe front sight with an extra broad dovetail base for windage adjustment. The rear sight is also adjustable. The rifle is still kept in its original case with a full range of tools and accessories.

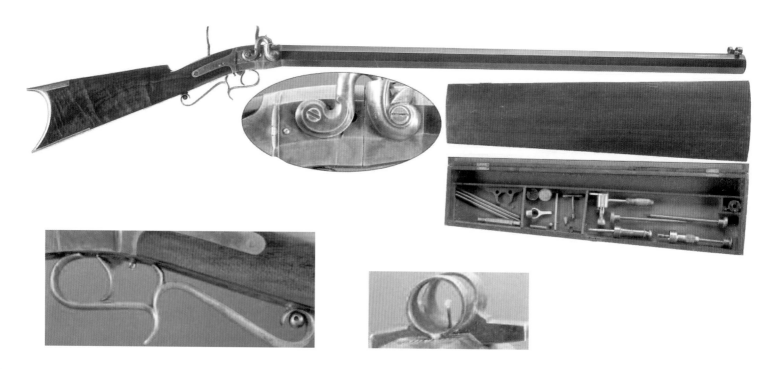

## EAGLE ARMS AR-15 COPY

**SPECIFICATIONS**

**Type:** semi-automatic target rifle
**Origin:** Eagle Arms, Geneseo, Illinois
**Caliber:** 5.56 x 45mm
**Barrel Length:** 20in

Eagle Arms is a division of the Armalite Corporation of Geneseo, Illinois and produces a range of AR-15/M16 clones. This weapon is an exact copy of the M16A2 with a heavy stainless steel barrel for competitive shooting and an 800 meter adjustable rear sight; weight is about 9.4 pounds.

# GARAND M1 SEMI-AUTOMATIC RIFLE

## SPECIFICATIONS

**Type:** magazine-loaded, gas-operated, semi-automatic rifle

**Origin:** National Armory, Springfield

**Caliber:** .30-06

**Barrel Length:** 24in

This outstanding rifle was designed by John C. Garand of the National Armory, Springfield, who worked on various designs throughout the 1920s, eventually taking out a patent for the successful system in April 1930. In the Garand system gas was tapped through a port under the barrel into the gas cylinder where it drove the operating rod to the rear, causing the bolt to rotate slightly, thus releasing it so that they then traveled back together, ejecting the spent round and cocking the action as they went. On hitting the buffer, the rod and bolt were driven forward by a spring, picked up a round from the magazine, chambered it and relocked the bolt. The rifle had a 24 inch barrel and was chambered for the .30-06 round. An eight-round magazine was contained entirely within the stock and was loaded using a special charger; when the last round had been fired, the empty clip was automatically ejected and the bolt left open, serving as a double reminder to the firer that reloading was now necessary.

Commonly known as "the Garand," it was standardized as the M1 on January 9, 1936 but a variety of problems meant that the first production weapons did not reach units until early in 1937. Even then there were further problems, particularly with the gas system, but once these were solved, production built up rapidly. Total U.S. production, which continued well into the 1950s, was just over 6 million: National Armory, Springfield – 4,617,000 (1935–57); Winchester Repeating Arms Co – 513,580 (1940–5); Harrington & Richardson – 445,600 (1951–4); International Harvester – 457,750 (1951–4). The Garand was the standard rifle of the U.S. Army throughout World War Two, and was the only self-loader in general use, giving U.S. forces a great advantage over their enemies who, apart from some German units in 1944–5 continued to use bolt-action weapons to the very end. The Garand remained in front-line use throughout the Korean War, but was eventually replaced by a developed Garand, the M14, then the famous M16.

We show here a very early, Springfield-made, Garand M1 rifle (Serial number 5827; November 1938) with the original 23.75in barrel and Type 1 gas-cylinder, which had to be redesigned. (It should be noted that some parts of the weapon shown here are restorations and some, for example, the gas-trap muzzle-plug, are modern reproductions.)

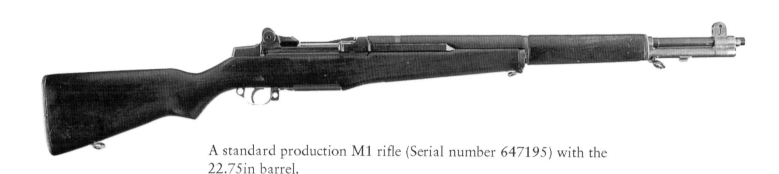

A standard production M1 rifle (Serial number 647195) with the 22.75in barrel.

The M1 was also produced in a carbine version for use by officers and senior NCOs, which had a shorter, 18 inch barrel, as seen in this one, which was made by Winchester.

Another carbine, this time from Rock-Ola. Also produced in World War Two was the M1A1 airborne carbine for use by paratroopers, which had a folding, skeleton butt, with a leather cheek-pad and wooden pistol grip.

After World War Two Garands were supplied to many countries around the world, but licensed production was relatively small. Beretta of Italy produced a straight copy, but then developed version of their own, firing the NATO 7.62mm round, which was designated the BM-59 (*see earlier*).

This one is a post-war Springfield M1A, with a 22 inch barrel which is chambered for 7.62mm NATO. Of the two, the M1A has undergone more modifications, including the fitting of a Hart stainless steel barrel, while every part has been carefully matched and polished to ensure the maximum accuracy and reliability.

## GARAND M14

**SPECIFICATIONS**
**Type:** selective-fire rifle
**Origin:** National Armory, Springfield
**Caliber:** 7.62 x 51mm NATO
**Barrel Length:** 22in

When NATO selected the 7.62 x 51mm round in 1953, everyone then needed a new rifle to fire it. European countries mainly settled on the FAL, but as the Unites States Army already had a superb semi-automatic weapon in the shape of the M1, they looked to this design as a basis of their new M14 rifle.

The M14 takes the Garand as its basis, although there are quite a few improvements and changes. The most obvious is the addition of a 20-shot detachable box magazine and much shorter gas tube and fore-end grip, leaving more exposed barrel at the muzzle. Originally made to fire both semi-automatic single shots and fully-automatic burst fire, it was found that the full-powered cartridge made it too much of a handful in automatic fire. As with the FN FAL, most M14s eventually had the selector switch blocked off or removed, leaving the rifle only capable of single shots. As well as the standard rifle, there was one with a folding stock, the superbly effective M21 sniper rifle, and light machine variant which was proposed but not adopted.

Almost 1,500,000 were made, although the service life of this tough, reliable, effective weapon wasn't as long as might be expected, as it was replaced by the small caliber M16 from the mid 1960s onwards.

## GIBBS CARBINE

**SPECIFICATIONS**
**Type:** breechloading percussion carbine
**Origin:** William F. Brooks, New York, New York
**Caliber:** .52
**Barrel Length:** 22in

Shown here are two of the rarest Civil War carbines to have survived. An order for 10,000 was placed by the federal government with the New York, Phoenix arms factory, owned by W.F Brooks and W.W. Marsden. The factory was destroyed in the New York Draft Riots of 1863, at which time only 1,052 guns had been completed. The action is similar in operation to that of the Gallager with the barrel sliding forward to access the breech.

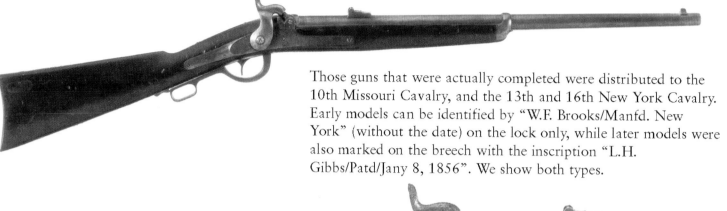

Those guns that were actually completed were distributed to the 10th Missouri Cavalry, and the 13th and 16th New York Cavalry. Early models can be identified by "W.F. Brooks/Manfd. New York" (without the date) on the lock only, while later models were also marked on the breech with the inscription "L.H. Gibbs/Patd/Jany 8, 1856". We show both types.

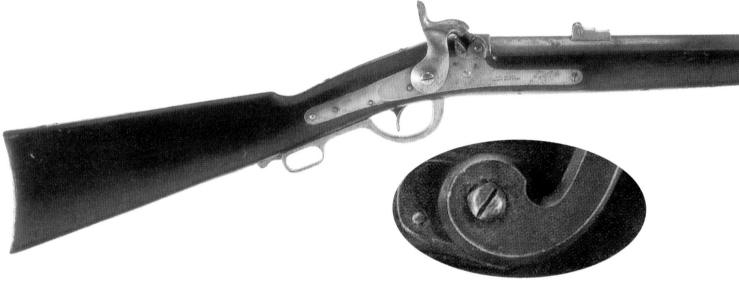

# GREENE CARBINE

The original carbine was produced in limited quantities at the Chicopee Falls factory of the Massachusetts Arms Co. The gun is a .54 caliber single shot breechloader using the Maynard tape primer ignition system. The 22 inch barrel swung down and to the right to allow access to the breech, and the sling was mounted on the rear part of the trigger guard. Some 300 were made in this pattern and some are known to have been issued to the 6th Ohio Cavalry at the outbreak of the Civil War.

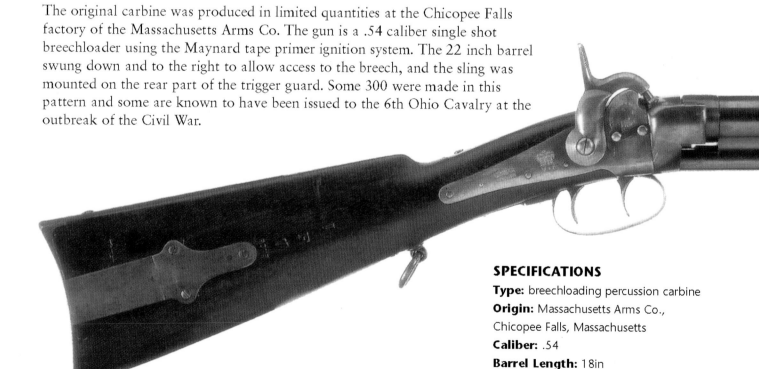

## SPECIFICATIONS
**Type:** breechloading percussion carbine
**Origin:** Massachusetts Arms Co., Chicopee Falls, Massachusetts
**Caliber:** .54
**Barrel Length:** 18in

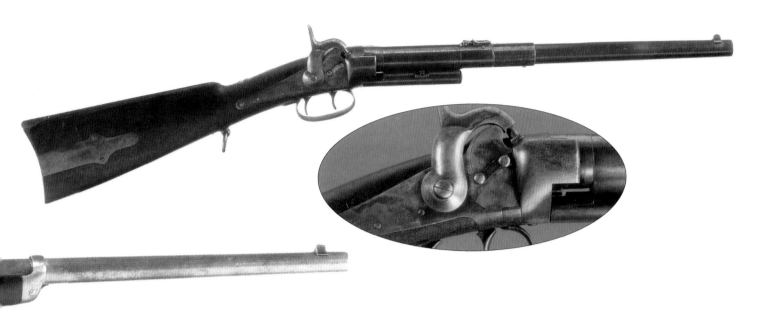

The other Greene variant was
the British Type, easily distinguished by its 18 inch barrel and
with the sling mounting half way down the underside of the
stock. Two thousand of these were made for the British
Government for use in the Crimean War but reputedly some of
the surplus weapons were re-imported to the U.S. for use in the
Civil War. One of the examples shown has "U.S." stamped on
the stock near the buttplate, which would suggest military issue.

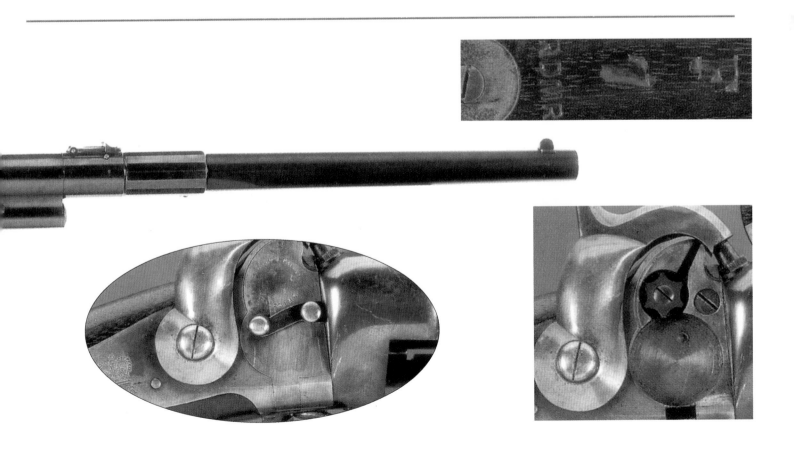

## GREENE BOLT-ACTION RIFLE

### SPECIFICATIONS

**Type:** single shot, bolt-action percussion rifle
**Origin:** A. H. Waters Armory, Millbury, Massachusetts
**Caliber:** .53
**Barrel Length:** 35in

The first bolt-action rifle purchased by the U.S. government, some 900 were delivered during the Civil War in March 1863. Patented by Lt. Col. J. Durrell Greene, it used a twisted oval section bore similar to that developed by Charles Lancaster in England. The bullet fitted into the oval section, and the twist imparted a spin in the same way as rifling. The Greene was also unusual in that the hammer was underneath, in front of the trigger guard. After locking the bolt, the firer still had to insert a percussion priming cap on the nipple beneath the stock.

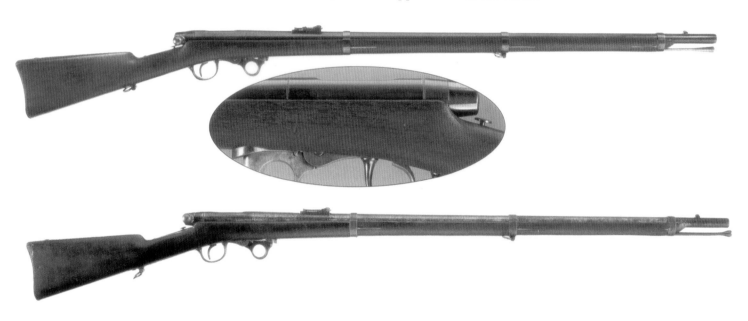

## GRENDEL R-31 CARBINE

### SPECIFICATIONS

**Type:** semi-automatic carbine
**Origin:** Grendel Inc, Rockledge, Florida
**Caliber:** .22 WMR
**Barrel Length:** 16.25in

The Grendel R-31 semi-automatic carbine was in production for just three years – from 1991 to 1994. The R-31 was chambered for the .22 WMR round, it had a 16.75 inch barrel fitted with a muzzle brake, and the 30-round magazine was housed in the pistol grip. The skeleton butt could be extended on two tubes which were housed either side of the receiver. It weighed about 4 pounds and is shown here fitted with a Bushnell Banner scope on a Weaver mount.

# GWINN BUSHMASTER

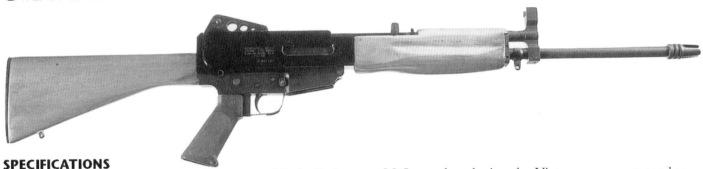

## SPECIFICATIONS

**Type:** semi-automatic rifle
**Origin:** Gwinn Firearms, Bangor, Maine
**Caliber:** .22
**Barrel Length:** 20in

Mack Gwinn, an SOG member during the Vietnam war, returned to the United States with many ideas on how to improve the AR-15/M16. He set up business in 1972 as Gwinn Firearms, of Bangor, Maine, but after only two years the company became part of Quality Products but is now Bushmaster Firearms Inc. of Windham, Maine (*see Bushmaster above*). Gwinn has introduced a number of significant improvements to the M16, including the D-ring which, designed in cooperation with Jim Sullivan, resolves problems associated with the extraction process. The Gwinn Bushmaster, seen here, was produced in the early 1970s and was based on the M16, but with hardwood stock and butt.

# HALL MODEL 1819 RIFLE

## SPECIFICATIONS

**Type:** breechloading, flintlock rifle
**Origin:** Harper's Ferry Armory, Harper's Ferry, Virginia,
**Caliber:** .52
**Barrel Length:** 32.6in

John Hancock Hall (1778–1841) was a gun designer who hailed from North Yarmouth, Maine. In 1811 he was a joint patentee, with William Thornton of Washington, DC, of a novel breech-loading flintlock rifle with a tip-up breech chamber, in which the breech-lock and chamber were incorporated into a single unit. This was manufactured and sold at Portland, Maine from 1811 to 1816, but Hall then moved to Harper's Ferry, Virginia and his weapon was adopted as an official U.S. Army rifle in 1819, the first breech-loader to be so standardized. Hall designed the machinery for his weapon's production, which was housed in a separate building (known for many years as "the rifle works," and remained there until 1840, supervising the manufacture of weapons to his patent.

This Model 1819 was made in 1824 and is very unusual in that it is accompanied by documentary proof that it has passed down through five generations of the same South Carolina family.

# HARPER'S FERRY MODEL 1841 "MISSISSIPPI RIFLE"

## SPECIFICATIONS

**Type:** muzzleloading, percussion rifle
**Origin:** Harper's Ferry Armory, Harper's Ferry, Virginia,
**Caliber:** .54
**Barrel Length:** 33in

When production of the Hall breechloading rifle ended in 1841, the Harper's Ferry "rifle works" was converted to manufacture the newly-adopted U.S. Model 1841 rifle. Some 25,000 were produced at Harper's Ferry between 1846 and 1855. The Model 1841 will always be known as the "Mississippi rifle" in memory of the troops who used it during the Mexican-American War, particularly at the Battle of Buena Vista against General Santa Anna's Mexican army in February 1847. In that battle, Colonel Jefferson Davis's 1st Mississippi Rifles, armed with the new muzzle-loading "U.S. Model 1841 Percussion Rifle," turned the tide for the heavily outnumbered US troops, and this weapon has been known ever since been known as the "Mississippi rifle" in their honor.

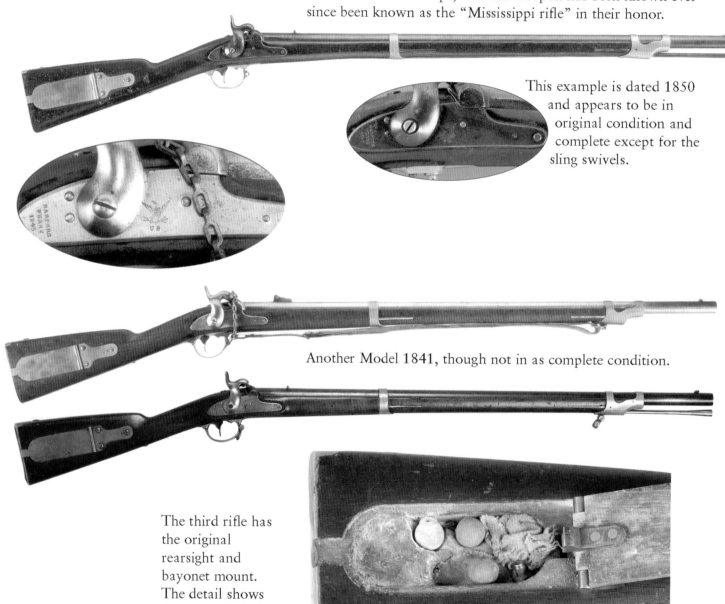

This example is dated 1850 and appears to be in original condition and complete except for the sling swivels.

Another Model 1841, though not in as complete condition.

The third rifle has the original rearsight and bayonet mount. The detail shows the opened patch box, complete with spare nipple, balls and patch material.

## HARPER'S FERRY MODEL 1842 MUSKET

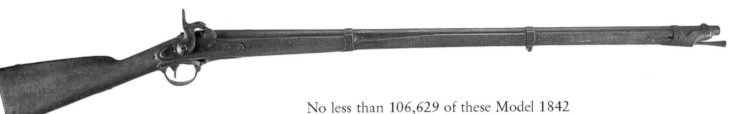

### SPECIFICATIONS

**Type:** muzzleloading, percussion musket
**Origin:** Harper's Ferry Armory, Harper's Ferry, Virginia,
**Caliber:** .69
**Barrel Length:** 42in

No less than 106,629 of these Model 1842 smoothbore muskets were made between 1844 and 1855, the example seen here having left the factory in 1851. Its battered appearance shows that it has seen much hard service, but not so immediately obvious is that, for some reason, two-and-a-half inches have been cut off the muzzle.

Many Model 1842s were rifled after leaving Harper's Ferry, particularly during the Civil War. The second image shows one, which has also been fitted with a long range rearsight.

## HARPER'S FERRY MODEL 1855 PERCUSSION RIFLE MUSKET

### SPECIFICATIONS

**Type:** muzzleloading, percussion musket
**Origin:** Harper's Ferry Armory, Harper's Ferry, Virginia,
**Caliber:** .58
**Barrel Length:** 40in

Over 59,000 of these rifle muskets were made at the Harpers Ferry and Springfield Armories, and most saw extensive service during the Civil War. It was the first issue firearm to fire the .58 expanding Minie bullet, and also used the Maynard Tape Priming system instead of individual percussion primer caps.

## HENDRICKS OVER-AND-UNDER PERCUSSION RIFLE

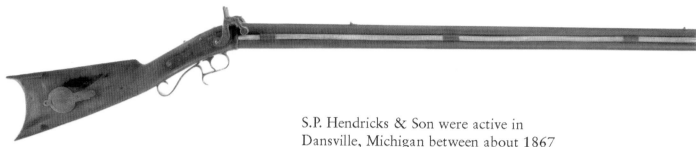

### SPECIFICATIONS

**Type:** superposed (over-and-under) muzzle-loaded, percussion rifle
**Origin:** S.P. Hendrick & Son, Dansville, Michigan
**Caliber:** .44
**Barrel Length:** 30.25in

S.P. Hendricks & Son were active in Dansville, Michigan between about 1867 and 1883, where this weapon was produced. The superposed arrangement was a common alternative to the double-barreled (side-by-side) arrangement and also, as shown here, provided a neat home for the ramrod.

## J.J. HENRY PERCUSSION RIFLE

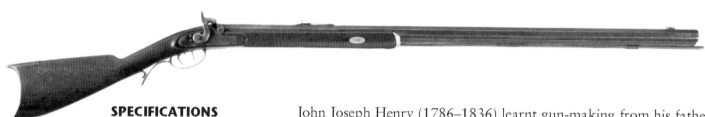

### SPECIFICATIONS

**Type:** half-stock, percussion rifle
**Origin:** J.J. Henry & Son, Philadelphia, Pennsylvania
**Caliber:** .34
**Barrel Length:** 36.7in

John Joseph Henry (1786–1836) learnt gun-making from his father and established his own business in Philadelphia in 1808. He received regular government and state contracts for muskets, rifles and pistols, making his own barrels and locks, as well as assembling the final products. This is a rifle was made for the civil market, and, considering its age, is in an excellent state of preservation.

## HENRY RIFLE

Invented and patented by B. Tyler Henry (1821–1898), the Henry rifle was chambered for the .44 Henry cartridge, with a fifteen-round, tubular magazine in the butt. It had an octagonal 24 inch barrel with no foregrip, but with a walnut buttstock and a brass butt-plate. Some 14,000 of these rifles were made between 1861 and 1866, of which the early examples had iron frames and the remainder, as seen here, brass frame.

## SPECIFICATIONS

**Type:** tubular-magazine, lever-action rifle
**Origin:** New Haven Arms Co, New Haven Connecticut.
**Caliber:** .44 Henry
**Barrel Length:** 24.25in

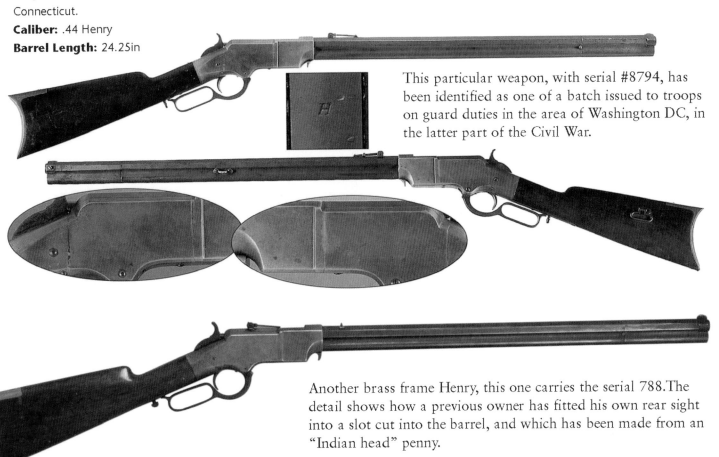

This particular weapon, with serial #8794, has been identified as one of a batch issued to troops on guard duties in the area of Washington DC, in the latter part of the Civil War.

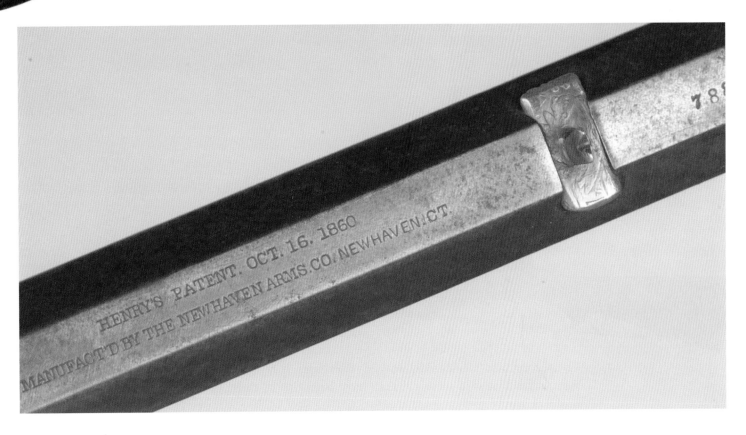

Another brass frame Henry, this one carries the serial 788. The detail shows how a previous owner has fitted his own rear sight into a slot cut into the barrel, and which has been made from an "Indian head" penny.

# JOHNSON M1941 AUTOMATIC RIFLE

**SPECIFICATIONS**

**Type:** automatic rifle

**Origin:** Melvin Johnson, Province, Rhode Island

**Caliber:** .30-06

**Barrel Length:** 22in

This rifle was the brainchild of Melvin Johnson, an inventor as well as an officer in the U.S. Marine Corps Reserve. The action of the weapon was unique and patented in 1937; it involved a combination of short recoil and a bolt with eight lugs, which rotated through 20 degrees to lock/unlock (a concept which reappeared in the 1950s in the Armalite AR-10). There was an integral ten-round rotary magazine, which could be loaded while the bolt was closed. The design included a half-length wooden stock combined with a perforated metal cooling sleeve and a long length of exposed barrel.

Initially, military and civil versions were developed in parallel, but the latter was dropped after half-a dozen prototypes had been completed, and attention then centred on the military version. Prototypes of the military version underwent trials in 1938 and 1939, but in early 1940 an order was issued that attention was to be devoted to solving the problems of the Garand M1 and that work on the Johnson was to cease. At this point (August 1940) Johnson secured an order from the Netherlands East Indies Army, but deliveries were just starting in early 1942 when the Dutch East Indies collapsed under attack from Japan and the undelivered weapons were diverted to the Marine Corps, who allocated them to Raider Battalions in the Far East and to some marine units in the European theater. Production ended in 1944 after some 70,000 had been produced. A small number of Johnson rifles, chambered for the 7 x 57mm rimless cartridge were delivered to Chile.

This one comes complete with its bayonet (also designed by Melvin Johnson); it was manufactured by the Cranston Arms Company.

The second also has its sling and bayonet, and as barrel is dated June 1941 and the rear sight is graduated in meters it may have been one of those intended for the Dutch East Indies Army.

# JOSLYN MODEL 1862 AND 1864 CARBINES

## SPECIFICATIONS

**Type:** single-shot cartridge carbine (see text)
**Origin:** Joslyn Firearms Co., Stonington, Connecticut
**Caliber:** .52 rimfire
**Barrel Length:** 22 in

The Joslyn turned out to be one of the most prolific of Civil War arms, being produced from early in the War through to spring 1865. It evolved during that time from percussion cap ignition to .52 rimfire ammunition in the early 1862 model, with the nipple giving way to the firing pin.

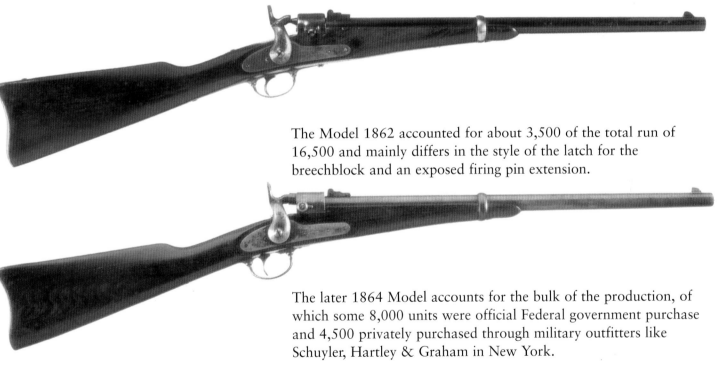

The Model 1862 accounted for about 3,500 of the total run of 16,500 and mainly differs in the style of the latch for the breechblock and an exposed firing pin extension.

The later 1864 Model accounts for the bulk of the production, of which some 8,000 units were official Federal government purchase and 4,500 privately purchased through military outfitters like Schuyler, Hartley & Graham in New York.

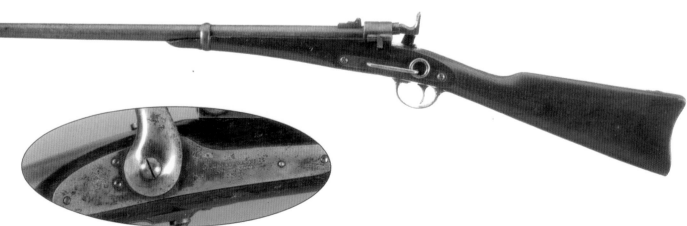

## Justice Rifle Musket

### SPECIFICATIONS

**Type:** percussion rifle musket
**Origin:** P.S. Justice, Philadelphia
**Caliber:** .69
**Barrel Length:** 39in

P.S. Justice began manufacturing rifles and rifle muskets as the Civil War broke out in 1861, one of many new manufacturers trying to meet the rapid demand for weapons from Union forces. Justice rifles were not of particularly high quality, but they were effective enough and were some of the first wartime production to get into the hands of the fighting men. Most were assembled from a mixture of existing components, and this 1861 rifle has some parts dated 1829. It also has the ramrod and one barrel restraining band missing.

## Kel-Tec Sub-9 Rifle

### SPECIFICATIONS

**Type:** semi-automatic rifle
**Origin:** Kel-Tec CNC Industries, Cocoa, Florida
**Caliber:** 9mm Luger
**Barrel Length:** 16.1in

This is one of several semi-automatic rifle designs produced by Florida-based Kel-Tec. This weapon is chambered for 9mm Luger and has a 16.1 inch barrel and operates on the blowback principle. The magazine is in the pistol grip and the weapon folds for storage, the hinge being at the front of the receiver, folded length being 16 inches. It weighs 4.6 pounds.

# LEMAN PERCUSSION RIFLES

## SPECIFICATIONS
**Type:** percussion rifle
**Origin:** H. E. Leman, Conestoga Rifle Works, Lancaster, Pennsylvania
**Caliber:** see text
**Barrel Length:** see text

Henry E. Leman (1812–1887) was the son and grandson of gunsmiths who worked in Lancaster, Pennsylvania. Henry served as an apprentice to two other gunsmiths for three years each before returning to his hometown in 1834 to establish the "Conestoga Rifle Works." His rifles were popular with trappers and explorers, and then in 1837 he received a government contract to supply 1,000 rifles per year, which was then renewed every year until 1860, giving him a very substantial business base. In 1840, he received another government contract, this time from the Department of Indian Affairs, to supply 500 guns, which was the first of many orders for weapons for the "Indian trade" which were handed over either as part of an annual allotment or in implementation of a treaty.

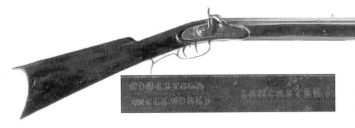

Shown here is a full-stock rifle, with a .45 caliber, 39.25 inch octagonal barrel, walnut stock and brass furniture.

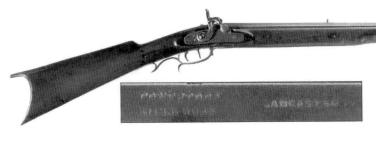

A half-stock rifle, this time in .38 caliber, and with a 38.25 inch octagonal barrel.

This one is altogether more fancy and carries Leman's name, whereas the others are simply marked "Conestoga Iron Works."

The metal can is for gunpowder and bears the picture of an Indian standing with a rifle; it was probably handed over at the same time as the treaty rifles.

## LEONARD PERCUSSION TARGET RIFLE

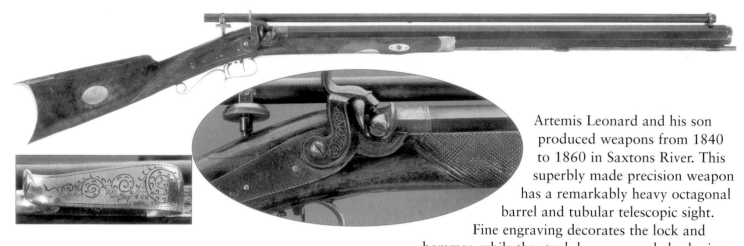

### SPECIFICATIONS

**Type:** percussion rifle target rifle with telescopic sight

**Origin:** Leonard & Son, Saxtons River, Vermont

**Caliber:** .48

**Barrel Length:** 31in

Artemis Leonard and his son produced weapons from 1840 to 1860 in Saxtons River. This superbly made precision weapon has a remarkably heavy octagonal barrel and tubular telescopic sight. Fine engraving decorates the lock and hammer, while the stock has engraved checkering. The lock is the rear action type, with the springs and lockplate behind the hammer. An accurate weapon such as this is typical of the private purchases that found use as sniper rifles during the Civil War.

## NELSON LEWIS BENCH-REST RIFLE

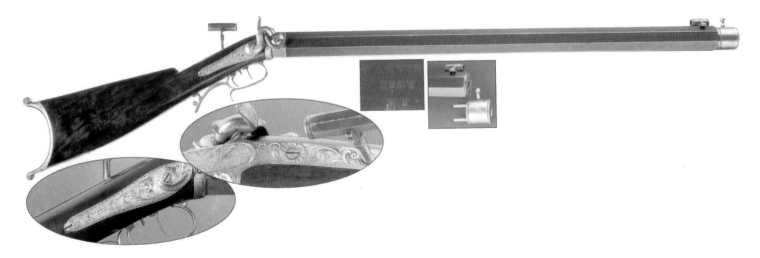

### SPECIFICATIONS

**Type:** bench-rest, muzzle-loading, percussion rifle

**Origin:** Nelson Lewis, Troy, New York

**Caliber:** .52

**Barrel Length:** 28.5in

Nelson Lewis was in the gunmaking business in Troy, New York from 1843 to 1882 and had a good reputation for high quality percussion target rifles, shotguns, and combination rifle/shotguns. Lewis was famed for his barrels and this example shows why, with its monolithic, extra heavy, 28.5 inch octagonal barrel fitted with a false muzzle for loading and a globe-protected foresight. The rearsight is a 2 inch tube mounted on the tang.

## MARLIN-BALLARD/STEVENS-POPE TARGET RIFLE

This weapon has been assembled from the finest components, including a Stevens-Pope barrel, a Marlin-Ballard action, a Sidle telescopic sight and a Stevens stock. It is designed for off-hand (i.e., standing) shooting, using the palm rest and the elaborately curved schuetzen-style butt.

The Stevens-Pope octagonal 30 inch barrel, chambered for .28-30, was designed and engineered by Harry M. Pope (1861–1950), a graduate engineer from MIT who devoted his life to making fine rifles. Pope also supplied the false muzzle and hickory bullet-seating rod, tool-kit and the palm-rest, which is made of walnut and with a leather cover. The scope, which is dated 1918, was made by J.W. Sidle of Philadelphia.

This is a splendid example of the gun-maker's art, but it is of additional interest because of its completeness, with every original component and accessory present.

## MARLIN MODEL 1881 LEVER-ACTION RIFLE

**SPECIFICATIONS**

**Type:** lever-action, repeater rifle
**Origin:** Marlin Firearms Company, New Haven, Connecticut
**Caliber:** .40-60
**Barrel Length:** 24in

The Model 1881 was Marlin's first lever-action rifle, with some 20,000 produced between its introduction in 1881 and its withdrawal in 1892. It featured a smoothly-operating lever action fed from a tubular magazine under the barrel. Five chamberings were offered (.32-40, .38-55, .40-60, .45-70 and .45-85) and three lengths of barrel (24, 28 and 30 inches); the example seen here is .40-60 caliber with a 24 inch barrel. The standard barrel was octagonal, but a round one was available on special request.

## MARLIN MODEL 1889 LEVER-ACTION RIFLE

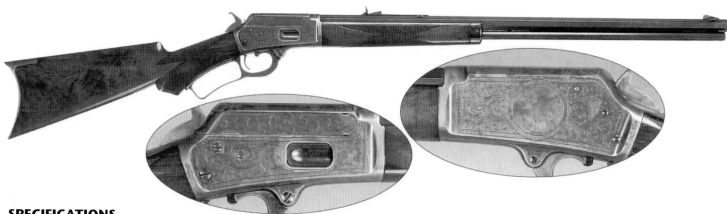

### SPECIFICATIONS

**Type:** lever-action, repeater rifle
**Origin:** Marlin Firearms Company, New Haven, Connecticut
**Caliber:** .32
**Barrel Length:** 24in

This was the first of Marlin's lever-action rifles to be fitted with side-ejection and proved very popular with some 55,000 sold between 1889 and 1899. As usual it was offered in a variety of calibers and barrel lengths; the example seen here is chambered for the .32 cartridge and has the shortest, 24 inch, barrel. There were also a variety of finishes and this is the deluxe version with checkered and highly-polished walnut furniture, blued barrel and engraved receiver with a stag on the left side and scroll work on both sides.

## MARLIN MODELS 1891, 1892, 1897, 39

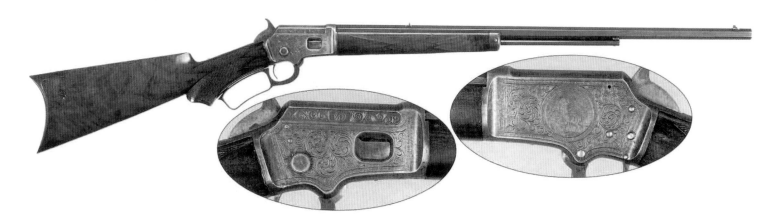

### SPECIFICATIONS

**Type:** lever-action, repeater rifle
**Origin:** Marlin Firearms Company, New Haven, Connecticut
**Caliber:** .22 (see text)
**Barrel Length:** 24in

The Marlin Model 1891, designed by L.L. Hepburn, was the company's first rifle to fire the .22 round and its direct descendants are still in production today, some 115 years later. The Model 1891 was unusual from the start in that it was capable of accepting any of the .22 Short, .22 Long or .22 LR without adjustment. The barrel was a standard 24 inches long and octagonal in profile, and was fitted with rather basic iron sights. Shown is a deluxe version of the Model 1891 with fully engraved receiver and polished, checkered walnut furniture. The weapon seen here is a side-loading "first variation" model, stamped with patent dates of 1878, 1889 and 1890; the "second variation" bore those dates, plus that of 1892, as well.

## MARLIN MODEL 1895

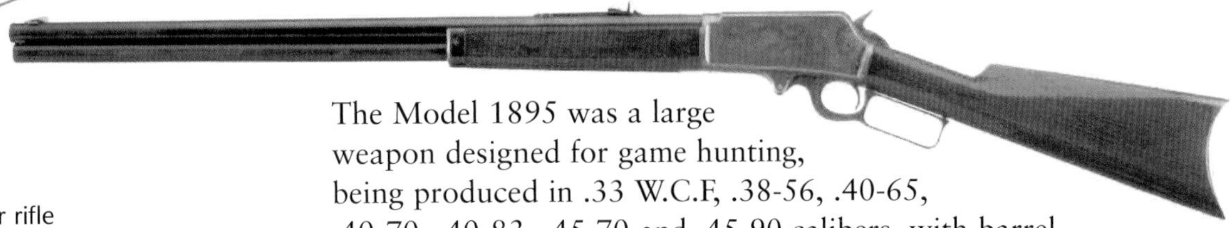

**SPECIFICATIONS**

**Type:** lever-action, repeater rifle

**Origin:** Marlin Firearms Company, New Haven, Connecticut

**Caliber:** see text

**Barrel Length:** see text

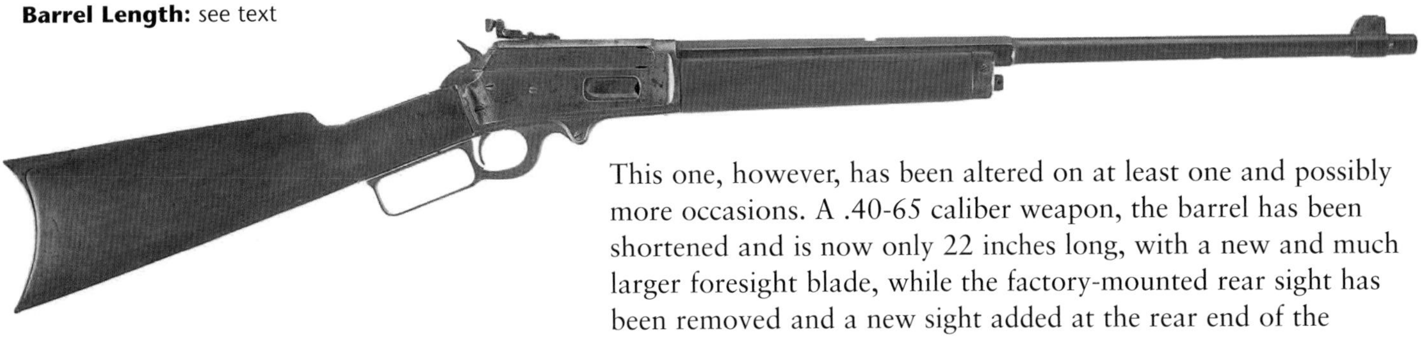

The Model 1895 was a large weapon designed for game hunting, being produced in .33 W.C.F., .38-56, .40-65, .40-70, .40-83, .45-70 and .45-90 calibers, with barrel lengths from 26 to 32 inches. This rifle is in .45-70 caliber with a 26 inch barrel, and, age apart is in "as sold" condition.

This one, however, has been altered on at least one and possibly more occasions. A .40-65 caliber weapon, the barrel has been shortened and is now only 22 inches long, with a new and much larger foresight blade, while the factory-mounted rear sight has been removed and a new sight added at the rear end of the receiver.

## MARLIN MODEL 1936 AND 336

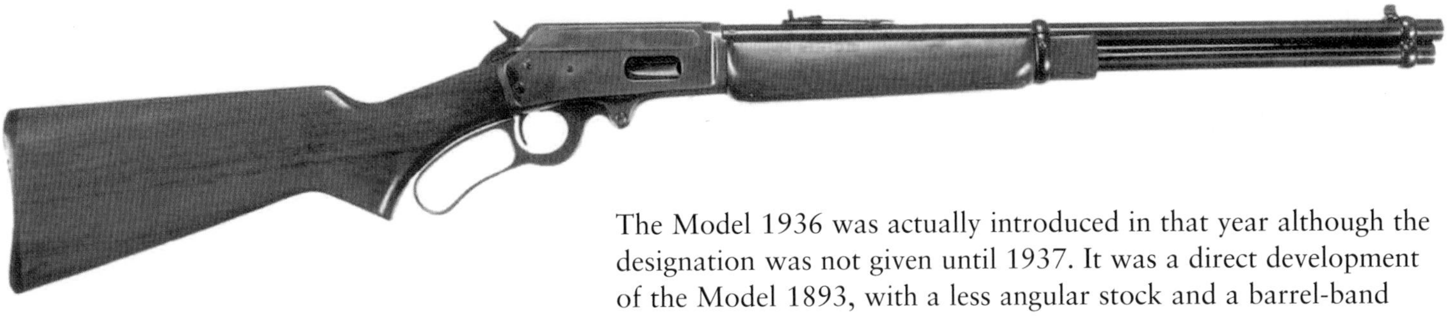

**SPECIFICATIONS**

**Type:** lever-action, repeater rifle

**Origin:** Marlin Firearms Company, New Haven, Connecticut

**Caliber:** .30-30

**Barrel Length:** 20in

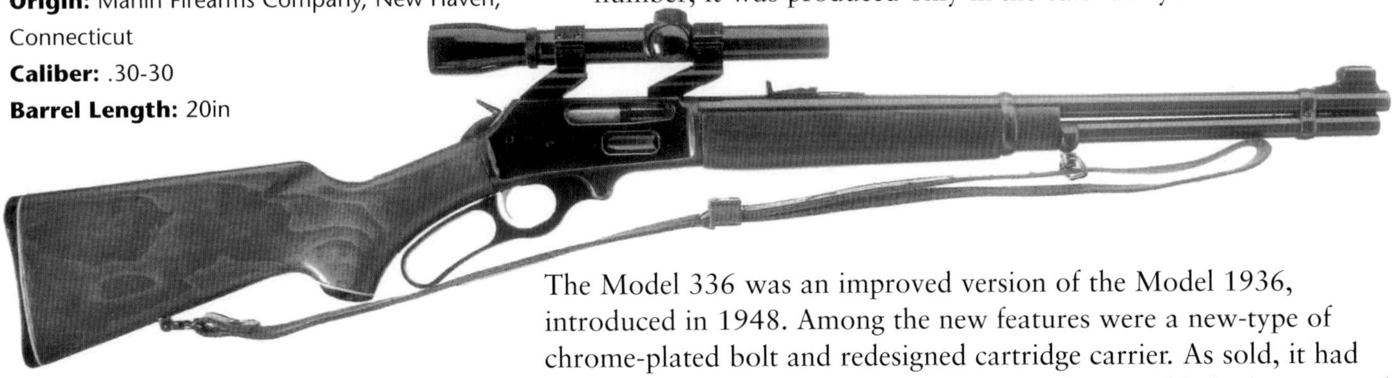

The Model 1936 was actually introduced in that year although the designation was not given until 1937. It was a direct development of the Model 1893, with a less angular stock and a barrel-band fitted on the semi-beavertail forearm. The second variation, seen here, had a thicker forearm, short tang and a B-prefixed serial number; it was produced only in the calendar year 1941.

The Model 336 was an improved version of the Model 1936, introduced in 1948. Among the new features were a new-type of chrome-plated bolt and redesigned cartridge carrier. As sold, it had Rocky Mountain sights, but this example has an added telescopic sight.

## MARLIN MODEL 1894 COWBOY

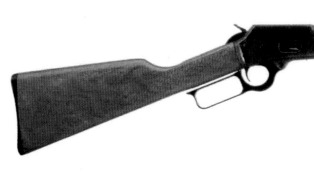

**SPECIFICATIONS**

**Type:** lever-action, repeater rifle
**Origin:** Marlin Firearms Company, New Haven, Connecticut
**Caliber:** .45 Colt
**Barrel Length:** 24in

The Model 336 (*see above*) had some limitations when handling the .44 Magnum round, so the company went back to the Model 1894, which returned to production in 1969, chambered for the .44 Magnum. Since then a wide variety of Model 1894s has appeared, chambered for rounds varying in caliber from .22 through .38 Special to this Model 1894 Cowboy which is chambered for the .45 Long Colt round. This version was first marketed in 1996 and is intended to meet the requirements of the Cowboy Action Shooting sport. The weapon weighs 7.5 pounds and the tubular magazine holds ten rounds.

## MARLIN CAMP 9 MUZZELITE CONVERSION

**SPECIFICATIONS**

**Type:** semi-automatic rifle
**Origin:** Marlin Firearms Company, New Haven, Connecticut
**Caliber:** 9mm
**Barrel Length:** 16.5in

A company named Muzzelite has marketed a series of stocks which can be used to convert an existing, conventionally designed weapon into a bullpup type. This results in a much more compact weapon with a strikingly "modern" appearance. In this case, a Marlin Camp 9 Carbine, chambered for the 9mm Parabellum round, has been changed from its normal appearance with a long barrel and a conventional butt into this very dramatic weapon with built-in carrying handle and the pistol grip and trigger group ahead of the magazine.

# MAYNARD CARBINE

## SPECIFICATIONS

**Type:** percussion, breechloading carbine
**Origin:** Massachusetts Arms Company, Chicopee
Falls, Massachusetts
**Caliber:** .50
**Barrel Length:** 20in

Manufactured by the Massachusetts Arms Co. of Chicopee Falls, the gun was designed by Dr Edward Maynard, inventor of the tape primer ignition system which the weapon (and others) utilized. The Massachusetts Arms Company is worthy of mention in that many famous names are featured in the original board of directors of 1851, including Horace Smith and Daniel B. Wesson (later to form Smith and Wesson), Joshua Stevens (later J. Stevens Arms Co.) and J.T. Ames (Ames Mfg. Co.). The company was originally established in buildings that were part of the Ames plant and was intended to produce revolvers as a rival to Colt. However, the company entered the longarms market in 1855 with the manufacture of the Greene breechloading carbine, followed by the first Maynard Carbines in 1858–59.

The company was dissolved in 1866 when wartime production shriveled away but was bought by T.W. Carter, the factory superintendent. It was taken over again in 1876 but its strong name and heritage was retained on each occasion.

The design of the Maynard Carbine led to the first Maynard sporting model rifles, which became the mainstay of the company's

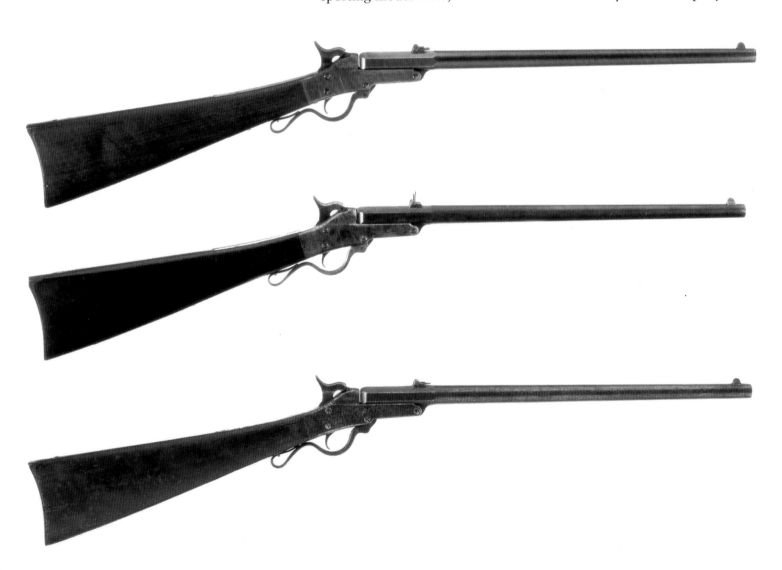

## MERRILL CARBINES

### SPECIFICATIONS

**Type:** percussion breechloading carbine
**Origin:** H. Merrill, Baltimore, Maryland
**Caliber:** .54
**Barrel Length:** 22.25 inches

A simple and effective breechloader, a total quantity of 14,495 carbines were made by H. Merrill of Baltimore, Maryland. The majority of the production was accounted for by federal government purchase. Our first image shows the First Type, which had the patchbox in the butt.

Second Model production was inspired by the need to reduce manufacturing time and cost, which accounts for the patchbox not being present. There were other less apparent changes too, like the copper-faced breech plunger that sealed the percussion cartridge in the breech allowing less gas to escape. The Second Model also had modifications to the breech lever latch, making it a rounded button as opposed to a flat knurled type. There were variations in the sights and lockplates too.

## MERRIMACK ARMS BALLARD RIFLE

### SPECIFICATIONS

**Type:** Ballard-action rifle
**Origin:** Merrimack Arms Company, Newburyport, Massachusetts
**Caliber:** .44
**Barrel Length:** 26in

Merrimack Arms manufactured Ballard-patent weapons between 1867 and 1869 and this rifle was produced early in that period. It has an octagonal, 26 inch long barrel, with the forearm and stock made from extra fancy American walnut. The forearm is tipped with a case-steel cap, and the crescent-shaped butt-plate is also made of case steel. The foresight is a "Martin's Magic Globe" with a long cylindrical hood to expose a glass tube with a gold pinhead post, which proves remarkably effective in low light conditions. The rear sight on the barrel is a folding two-leaf ladder, but there is also a tang-mounted, vernier peep-sight. This is a remarkable weapon in an excellent state of preservation.

## QUACKENBUSH SAFETY RIFLE

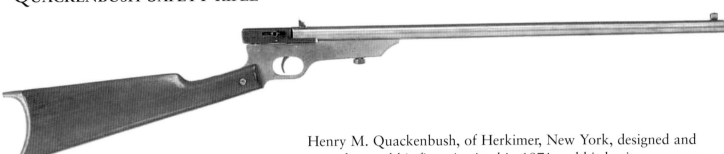

**SPECIFICATIONS**
**Type:** bolt-operated, single shot rifle
**Origin:** H.M. Quackenbush, Herkimer, New York
**Caliber:** .22
**Barrel Length:** 22in

Henry M. Quackenbush, of Herkimer, New York, designed and manufactured his first air pistol in 1871 and his business grew so rapidly that several moves to ever-larger premises were required. He produced a line of air pistols and air rifles, and in 1886 he produced his first .22 rifle design, which, again, proved so successful that a further move became necessary. By 1939 the company employed some one hundred workers, but when war broke out it ceased making air weapons and took up manufacturing steel cores for .50 machinegun bullets. When the war ended the company continued to operate but was no longer in the firearms business. The .22 rifle seen here is elegant in its simplicity, having reduced the individual components to the essential minimum.

## REMINGTON MODEL 1841 MISSISSIPPI RIFLE

**SPECIFICATIONS**
**Type:** percussion rifle musket
**Origin:** E. Remington and Sons, Ilion, New York
**Caliber:** .69
**Barrel Length:** 42in

Eliphalet Remington had a small forge business in Ilion, New York, and from around 1820 his son, Eliphalet Remington II, began making gun barrels there. Young Eli also tried to interest the U.S. government to make use of Remington barrels, made using their 'cast steel' process. By 1828 he was running the company, but at that point had no capacity for mass-producing complete weapons.

This was to change in 1845, when Eli II pulled off a couple of far-sighted business deals to give the family firm a jump-start into the gunmaking business.

N.P. Ames of Chicopee Falls, Massachusetts were renowned sword makers and producers of superior gunmaking equipment and tools. They had contracts to produce the "Mule Ear" carbine for William Jenks (*see above*), but in 1845 Remington offered to buy from Ames one of their contracts for 1,000 rifles. The deal also included the tooling and equipment which was shipped to Remington.

At around the same time, Remington also negotiated the purchase of a contract for 5,000 Model 1841 Mississippi Rifles held by John Griffiths of Cincinnati. This deal also included machinery, although it's not clear if this was actually supplied. Remington delivered the first batch of Model 1841s in 1850, and used this success to gain subsequent government contracts for these and other military weapons. One of the giants of American gunmaking was now in business.

## REMINGTON M1816 MAYNARD CONVERSION

### SPECIFICATIONS

**Type:** muzzleloading, flintlock musket
**Origin:** see text
**Caliber:** .69
**Barrel Length:** 42in

The Maynard Tape Priming system was fitted to many percussion muskets, including the Model 1816. This is one of a batch of about 20,000 that had new Maynard-type locks supplied by Remington, who bid for the contract in an attempt to keep their skilled gunmakers in work. The actual conversions were carried out from 1856–58 by the Frankford Arsenal, Philadelphia, who also rifled the smoothbore barrels.

## REMINGTON MODEL 1863 "ZOUAVE" RIFLE

### SPECIFICATIONS

**Type:** muzzleloading, percussion rifle
**Origin:** E. Remington and Sons, Ilion, New York
**Caliber:** .58
**Barrel Length:** 33in

Remington were awarded the contract to produce some 12,000 of this well made percussion rifle. Similar to the standard Model 1863, it was slightly shorter and had only two barrel bands. It's not known with any certainty why the name "Zouave" was given to this weapon, as there are no records to suggest it was issued particularly to these regiments with their unusual colorful clothing. As can be seen from the examples we show, many surviving Zouave rifles are in excellent condition, and it appears that many didn't see hard active service.

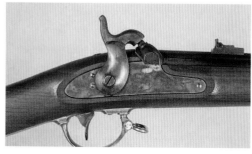

## REMINGTON SPRINGFIELD M1870 ROLLING BLOCK

### SPECIFICATIONS

**Type:** Breechloading rifle
**Origin:** see text
**Caliber:** .50-70
**Barrel Length:** 33in

Remington continually acquired inventions and patents developed by others, and this one was to prove one of their most successful. The original concept for this style of breechloader was devised by Leonard Geiger and developed by Joseph Rider, who took out joint patents with Remington in 1865.

Known as the split breech or "rolling block" system, it was simple to use, reasonably quick to operate, and extremely rugged and reliable. The firer simply had to pull back the hammer to cock it, then rotate the breech block downwards to open it and eject the spent case. A new round was loaded then the block simply thumbed back upwards to lock the breech.

Rolling block arms quickly became popular and Remington eventually developed a bewildering array of service rifles, carbines, sporting guns and even pistols using the system. Many governments procured such weapons (*see Denmark above*), although, surprisingly, the U.S. military never adopted it in a big way.

The rifle shown here was chambered for the government .50-70 cartridge, and was actually manufactured by the Springfield Armory under license for the U.S. Navy. Many of these rifles were subsequently purchased for the French Army to use in the 1870–71 Franco-Prussian War.

## REMINGTON NO 1 SPORTING ARMS

A huge range of sporting, target and hunting arms were also manufactured using the rolling block mechanism, and we show some examples here. These all use the first variant of the rolling block action, subsequently known as the No. 1 action.

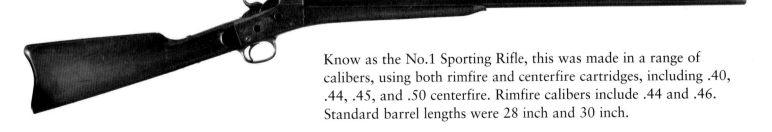

Know as the No.1 Sporting Rifle, this was made in a range of calibers, using both rimfire and centerfire cartridges, including .40, .44, .45, and .50 centerfire. Rimfire calibers include .44 and .46. Standard barrel lengths were 28 inch and 30 inch.

This Sporting Rifle has been made with a much thicker, heavier, barrel than standard.

Creedmoor was the home of American precision long-range target shooting, and many rifle manufacturers used the name to denote specialized long-range target versions of their products. This one was known as the Long Range Creedmoor No.1, and was chambered for .44-90, .44-100 and .44-105 necked and straight cartridges. It had a 34in barrel, a folding long-range sight on the 'tang' (just above the wrist of the stock), a pistol grip shape to the stock, and a globe front sight.

## REMINGTON MODEL 1-1/2 ROLLING BLOCK

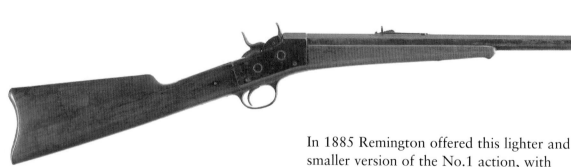

### SPECIFICATIONS
**Type:** breech-loading rolling block rifle
**Origin:** E. Remington & Sons, Ilion, New York
**Caliber:** see text
**Barrel Length:** 24 to 28in

In 1885 Remington offered this lighter and smaller version of the No.1 action, with thinner receiver and less overall weight than the earlier design. It was intended for lower-powered ammunition, and was available in a range of calibers, including .22, 25, .32 and .38 rimfire, together with .32, .38 and .44 centerfire. The later No. 2 Remington was even lighter, with a smaller frame.

# REMINGTON MODEL 12 SLIDE ACTION RIFLE

## SPECIFICATIONS

**Type:** slide action repeating rifle
**Origin:** Remington Arms Co., Ilion, New York
**Caliber:** .22S, .22L, .22LR, .22 Remington
**Barrel Length:** 22in

Another designer who worked with Remington was John D. Pedersen, who in 1907 designed this slide action .22 rifle, which eventually become known as the Remington Model 12. Closely resembling a slide action shotgun, the Model 12 used a similar under-barrel tubular magazine to hold the cartridges. It became one of the best selling sporting rifles ever, with over 831,000 made in a 27-year period from 1909 to 1936. While all Model 12s fired .22 rounds, they came chambered for a range of cartridges, with the magazine capacity varying from 10 to 15 with the size of the cartridge. The first rifle shown is a Model 12 with grooved underbarrel slide.

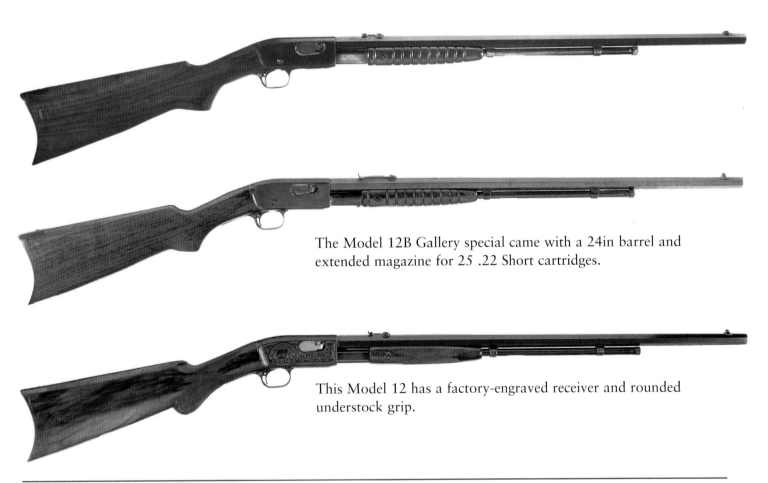

The Model 12B Gallery special came with a 24in barrel and extended magazine for 25 .22 Short cartridges.

This Model 12 has a factory-engraved receiver and rounded understock grip.

# REMINGTON MODEL 14 SLIDE ACTION RIFLE

## SPECIFICATIONS

**Type:** slide action repeating rifle and carbine
**Origin:** Remington Arms Co., Ilion, New York
**Caliber:** Remington .25, .30, .32 and .35
**Barrel Length:** 18in and 22in

The Model 14 was introduced by Pedersen in 1912. In essence it was a Model 12 modified to fire more powerful ammunition, and over 125,000 were sold by the time it was withdrawn in 1935. There were both standard versions with the 22in barrel and "carbine" models with a shorter 18in one.

## REMINGTON PATTERN 1914 (BRITISH) MARK 1

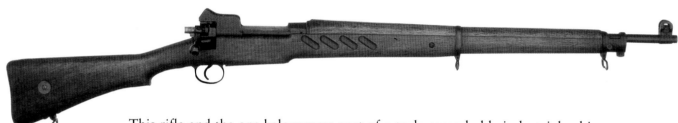

## SPECIFICATIONS

**Type:** bolt-action, magazine-fed rifle
**Origin:** Remington Arms Co., Ilion, New York, and Eddystone, Philadelphia.
**Caliber:** .303 British
**Barrel:** 26in

This rifle and the one below were part of a truly remarkable industrial achievement. The British government placed an order on April 30, 1915 for 1,500,000 rifles to be manufactured by the Remington Arms Co., who then built a huge new plant covering some 14 acres at Eddystone to meet this requirement. Incredibly, the factory was built, workers trained and production started by December 31, 1915, although, mainly due to a shortage of skilled workers, it was some months before it was operating at full capacity.

The contract was for Enfield Pattern 1914 Rifles in .303 caliber. The P14 had been developed in 1913 because of British concerns about the effectiveness of their new SMLE rifle (*see below*), but hadn't entered production when war broke out. Rather than make changes to British factories at this stage, orders for the P14 were placed in the United States with Remington and Winchester (*see below*). As it turned out, fears about the SMLE proved groundless, and that rifle proved to be one of the best military service rifles of all time. The P14 was less effective, being more susceptible to dirt and rough and handling although extremely accurate, and by the time World War One finished, Remington had delivered over 600,000 of them from Ilion and Eddystone.

## REMINGTON U.S. RIFLE MODEL OF 1917

## SPECIFICATIONS

**Type:** bolt-action, magazine-fed rifle
**Origin:** Remington Arms Co., Ilion, New York, and Eddystone, Philadelphia.
**Caliber:** .30-06
**Barrel:** 26in

When the United States entered the war on April 6, 1917, the British contracts were terminated by mutual agreement between the two governments, after some 600,000 rifles had been completed. Remington was at that time tooled up for the Enfield Pattern 1914, so rather than switch production to the standard U.S. M1903 rifle, it was decided the easiest solution was to modify the British P14 to take the standard .30-06 U.S. government cartridge.

When the United States entered the war on April 6, 1917, the British contracts were terminated by mutual agreement between the two governments, after some 600,000 rifles had been completed. Remington was at that time tooled up for the Enfield Pattern 1914, so rather than switch production to the standard U.S. M1903 rifle, it was decided the easiest solution was to modify the British P14 to take the standard .30-06 U.S. government cartridge.

Designated the Model of 1917, the first U.S. government contract for these rifles was signed on July 12, 1917, and between September 1917 and September 1918 one million rifles were completed, a truly astonishing achievement. The Eddystone factory ended production in January 1919 and the buildings were then

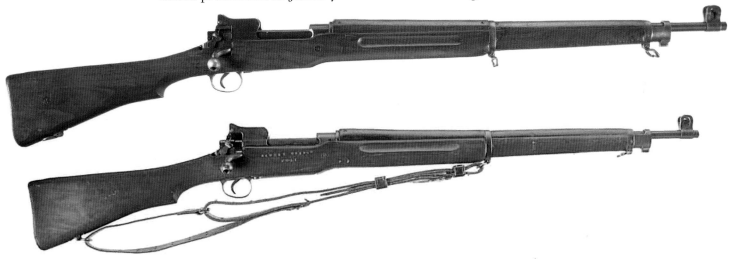

The rifle we shown here is serial number 69,676, was an early production item.

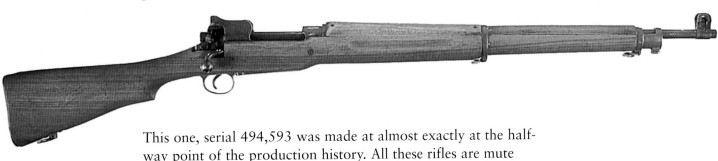

This one, serial 494,593 was made at almost exactly at the half-way point of the production history. All these rifles are mute remainders of a very great story of American production and determination.

## REMINGTON MODEL 30 EXPRESS

### SPECIFICATIONS
**Type:** bolt-action, magazine-fed rifle
**Origin:** Remington Arms Co., Ilion, New York
**Caliber:** see text
**Barrel:** 22in

Once World War One had ended, Remington had many parts left over from the Model 1917 Enfield rifles they had been making in such huge quantities. So in 1922 they announced the Model 30, a civilianized hunting version firing the same .30-06 cartridge. It turned out to be too heavy and expensive to be really popular, so by 1926 Remington switched to this lighter, shorter, improved version, the Model 30 Express. Besides the .30-06, the Express was chambered for the same cartridges as the Model 8 Autoloader, namely .25 Remington, .30 Remington, .32 Remington and .35 Remington centerfire. Later it was also offered in 7mm and .257.

## REMINGTON MODEL 24 AUTOLOADER

**[SPECIFICATIONS**
**Type:** semi-automatic, magazine-fed rifle
**Origin:** Remington Arms Co., Ilion, New York
**Caliber:** .22 Short, .22 Long Rifle
**Barrel:** 19in and 21in

Another self-loading rifle based on the work of John Browning, Remington began selling it in April 1922. The loading slot can be seen in the stock, just behind the semi pistol grip, which fed into a magazine holding up to 15 cartridges. The first model had a 19 inch barrel and only fired .22 S, but later variants were chambered for .22 LR and had 21 inch barrels. The Model 24 remained on sale until 1935.

## REMINGTON MODEL 34

**SPECIFICATIONS**
**Type:** bolt-action, tubular magazine-fed rifle
**Origin:** Remington Arms Co., Ilion, New York
**Caliber:** .22 Long, .22 Long Rifle
**Barrel:** 24in

First delivered in 1932, this neat bolt-action target rifle held between 15 and 17 rounds in its under-barrel tubular magazine. Later variants had higher-quality adjustable rearsights, and the whole series sold a respectable 169,922 through until 1936.

# REMINGTON M 121 "FIELDMASTER"

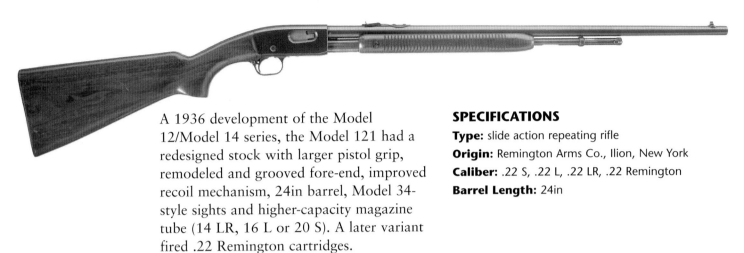

A 1936 development of the Model 12/Model 14 series, the Model 121 had a redesigned stock with larger pistol grip, remodeled and grooved fore-end, improved recoil mechanism, 24in barrel, Model 34-style sights and higher-capacity magazine tube (14 LR, 16 L or 20 S). A later variant fired .22 Remington cartridges.

**SPECIFICATIONS**
**Type:** slide action repeating rifle
**Origin:** Remington Arms Co., Ilion, New York
**Caliber:** .22 S, .22 L, .22 LR, .22 Remington
**Barrel Length:** 24in

# REMINGTON 500 SERIES

In the late 1930s Remington began the development of a series of sporting rifles that would use common components, allowing mass-production, cheaper parts and lower development costs. All were based around a low-cost tubular receiver. The first 500 series rifle was the Model 510 "Targetmaster," delivered from March 1939 as a single shot, bolt-action .22 rifle firing .22S, .22L and .22LR. Later models were also bored for .22 Remington and some had 26in smoothbore barrels. Various designs of sight were used, and a scoped example is shown here. At almost the same time, Remington also introduced the Model 511, another 500-series bolt-action rifle, but this time with a detachable box magazine.

**SPECIFICATIONS**
**Type:** bolt action rifle
**Origin:** Remington Arms Co., Ilion, New York
**Caliber:** .22 S, .22 L, .22 LR, .22 Remington
**Barrel Length:** 24in

# REMINGTON 513T "MATCHMASTER"

The 500 series was further developed to produce this target rifle. Bolt-action, as were most of the 500s, it featured a heavy 27-inch semi-floating barrel, revised stock, adjustable sling swivels, 6-shot detachable box magazine and a Retfield micrometer sight. From 1939 to 1968, over 123,000 of this successful target shooter were produced.

**SPECIFICATIONS**
**Type:** bolt-action target rifle
**Origin:** Remington Arms Co., Ilion, New York
**Caliber:** .22S, .22L, .22LR, .22 Remington
**Barrel Length:** 24in

# REMINGTON M 550 AUTOLOADER

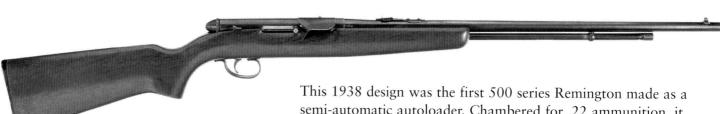

**SPECIFICATIONS**
**Type:** semi-automatic sporting rifle
**Origin:** Remington Arms Co., Ilion, New York
**Caliber:** .22S, .22L, .22LR
**Barrel Length:** 24in

This 1938 design was the first 500 series Remington made as a semi-automatic autoloader. Chambered for .22 ammunition, it used the blowback method, where the recoil force of the cartridge was sufficient to simply move the unlocked breechblock to the rear, eject the case and reload the next round. The various types of .22 cartridge can be used interchangeably without adjustment, and the tubular magazine could hold up to 22 Short, 17 Long or 15 Long Rifle rounds. Over 764,000 of the various models of 550 were sold up until December 1971.

# REMINGTON M720 NAVY TROPHY

A modernized replacement for the Model 30 Express, production was scheduled to begin in 1941. However, only a few thousand components were made before war intervened, causing Remington's attention to switch to military production. Most of the initial production was acquired by the U.S. Navy, mainly with 22in barrels. The navy never put the rifles out on general issue and most remained in storage during the war. They found a use for the stored rifles from 1964 onwards though, when the navy began awarding these pristine, still boxed weapons as marksmanship prizes to navy and marines competition winners. They became known as "Secretary of the Navy Trophies" or "Secretary of Defense Trophies."

**SPECIFICATIONS**
**Type:** bolt action hunting rifle
**Origin:** Remington Arms Co., Ilion, New York
**Caliber:** .30-06
**Barrel Length:** 22in and 24in

# REMINGTON M1903 RIFLE

**SPECIFICATIONS**
**Type:** bolt-action, magazine-fed rifle
**Origin:** Remington Arms Co., Ilion, New York
**Caliber:** .30-06
**Barrel Length:** 24in

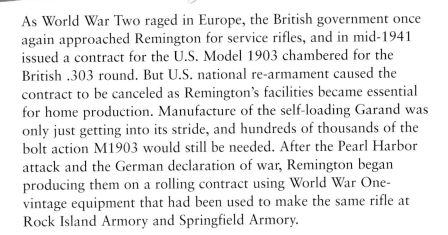

As World War Two raged in Europe, the British government once again approached Remington for service rifles, and in mid-1941 issued a contract for the U.S. Model 1903 chambered for the British .303 round. But U.S. national re-armament caused the contract to be canceled as Remington's facilities became essential for home production. Manufacture of the self-loading Garand was only just getting into its stride, and hundreds of thousands of the bolt action M1903 would still be needed. After the Pearl Harbor attack and the German declaration of war, Remington began producing them on a rolling contract using World War One-vintage equipment that had been used to make the same rifle at Rock Island Armory and Springfield Armory.

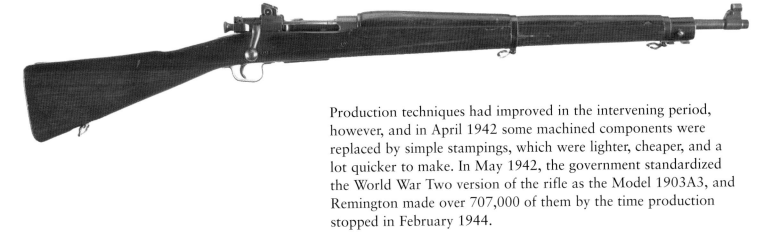

Production techniques had improved in the intervening period, however, and in April 1942 some machined components were replaced by simple stampings, which were lighter, cheaper, and a lot quicker to make. In May 1942, the government standardized the World War Two version of the rifle as the Model 1903A3, and Remington made over 707,000 of them by the time production stopped in February 1944.

## REMINGTON M572 "FIELDMASTER"

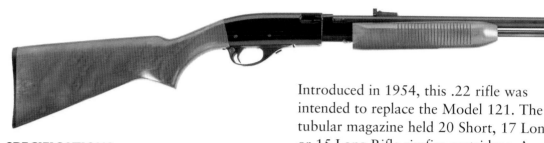

### SPECIFICATIONS

**Type:** slide-action, magazine rifle
**Origin:** Remington Arms Co., Ilion, New York
**Caliber:** .22 S, .22L, .22LR
**Barrel Length:** 24in

Introduced in 1954, this .22 rifle was intended to replace the Model 121. The tubular magazine held 20 Short, 17 Long or 15 Long Rifle rimfire cartridges. A smoothbore variant was introduced in 1962 and a lightweight variant in 1957. The Standard version is still made at the time of writing.

## REMINGTON M40 X "RANGEMASTER"

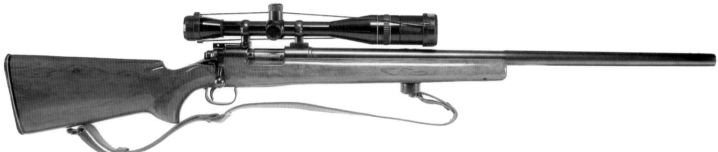

### SPECIFICATIONS

**Type:** bolt-action, single shot target rifle
**Origin:** Remington Arms Co., Ilion, New York
**Caliber:** see text
**Barrel Length:** 24in

The bolt and action of the Remington Model 721 formed the basis of this highly-accurate precision target rifle. The receiver was made to be extremely rigid, the trigger was adjustable, while the barrel rested in large cylindrical bedding surface. The user could even adjust the directional force exerted by the stock. Target rifles were available with standard and heavy barrels and a range of sighting systems. Later, more powerful, models were chambered for .308 Win, .222 Remington, .222 Remington Magnum, .30-06 and .300 H & H Magnum.

The rifle became the Model 40XB in 1965, with modified action and the option of stainless steel barrels. Other variants included a box magazine, while the range of ammunition types available increased to cover pretty much all standard target cartridges. The Model 40XB is still in production at the time of writing, available with walnut, laminate or Kevlar stocks.

## REMINGTON M725

**SPECIFICATIONS**
**Type:** bolt-action, magazine hunting rifle
**Origin:** Remington Arms Co., Ilion, New York
**Caliber:** see text
**Barrel Length:** 22in and 24 in

Introduced in 1958, the Model 725 hunting rifle was based on an improved Model 721, modified by Wayne Leek, Manager of Remington's Research and Design department, and Charlie Campbell, one of his engineers. Intended to compete with Winchester's Model 70, the new rifle had an internal magazine holding four shots, and was designed with adjustable foresights and rearsights, or could be fitted with a range of scopes. It was initially offered in .270 Win, .280 Remington and .30-06, then later in .222 Remington, .244 Remington and .243 Win. The custom-made Model 725 Kodiak was a more powerful weapon in .317 H & H Magnum or .458 Win Magnum, both with 26 inch barrels.

## REMINGTON NYLON 66

**SPECIFICATIONS**
**Type:** self-loading magazine rifle
**Origin:** Remington Arms Co., Ilion, New York
**Caliber:** .22 LR
**Barrel Length:** 19in

Gun users are often thought of as a conservative group, and new technological developments can take time to gain general acceptance. So in December 1959 this .22 caliber autoloader built on a DuPont Zytel nylon frame was seen as a startling departure. A one-piece nylon stock and receiver mounted a 19 inch barrel, steel bolt and a tubular butt magazine holding up to 14 Long Rifle cartridges. The receiver also had metal cover plates, and the whole package was remarkably light, at just over 4 pounds. Variants included green, black and brown stocks, scoped rifles, and presentation weapons with engraved receivers and chrome plating. Almost 989,000 were sold until production stopped in 1985.

## REMINGTON M742 "WOODSMASTER"

### SPECIFICATIONS

**Type:** self-loading magazine rifle
**Origin:** Remington Arms Co., Ilion, New York
**Caliber:** see text
**Barrel Length:** 22in

This 1960 autoloader is unusual in that it used gas operation, a method more commonly seen on military rifles. Based on the Model 760, it used a rotary breech block and working parts coated with Teflon. Ammunition was held in a 4-shot detachable box magazine, and the initial offerings were chambered for .280 Remington, .30-06 and .308 Win. In 1963 Remington introduced a 6mm cartridge, then .243 Win in 1968. A lighter "carbine" version with an 18 inch barrel was also introduced in 1961. This high-powered autoloader was popular in the market, with over 1,433,000 being made before sales ceased in 1981.

## REMINGTON M700 SERIES

### SPECIFICATIONS

**Type:** bolt-action, magazine rifle
**Origin:** Remington Arms Co., Ilion, New York
**Caliber:** many
**Barrel Length:** 22in, 24in and 26in

With this inspired combination of simplicity, strength, reliability and ease of shooting, the Remington design team created a classic – the most popular high-powered commercial bolt action rifle in the world. Based on an improved Model 721/722, it was introduced in 1962 with a fixed magazine and 24in barrel. A significant redesign was launched in 1969, where the rear bolt shroud was extended. From then on a bewildering range of models has been produced, chambered for every important high-powered cartridge and with differing finishes, stock designs, sights and barrel lengths. Magazines were either fixed or detachable boxes. Police variants were made with Kevlar stocks, while the Model 700 also formed the basis of the Marine Corps M40 sniper rifle, some 1,000 of which saw service in Vietnam.

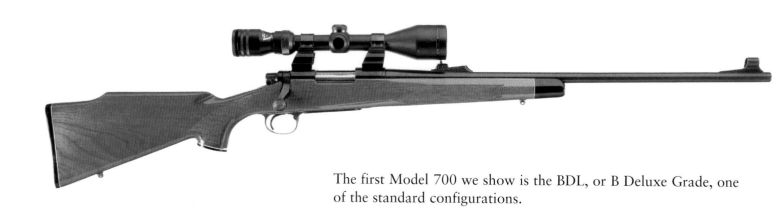

The first Model 700 we show is the BDL, or B Deluxe Grade, one of the standard configurations.

# RICHMOND MUSKETS

## SPECIFICATIONS

**Type:** percussion rifle
**Origin:** Richmond Armory, Richmond, Virginia
**Caliber:** .58
**Barrel Length:** 40in

During the Confederate raid on the Harper's Ferry Armory in April 1861, captured parts and gunmaking equipment were moved to Richmond and Fayetteville (*see above*) to begin production of rifles and muskets. The Richmond Armory produced thousands of weapons from 1861 to 1865, in larger numbers than any other Confederate longarm. Most were based on the Model 1855 and 1863 rifles.

Confederate production didn't use the Maynard system, but as the captured lockplate dies were set for the Model 1855 and its Maynard Tape primer lock, early Richmond lock plates followed the same shape. This gave an unusually high hump where the primer system would have been. Rifles to this design are usually referred to as Type I and Type II, and many minor variations exist. The one shown is a Type II.

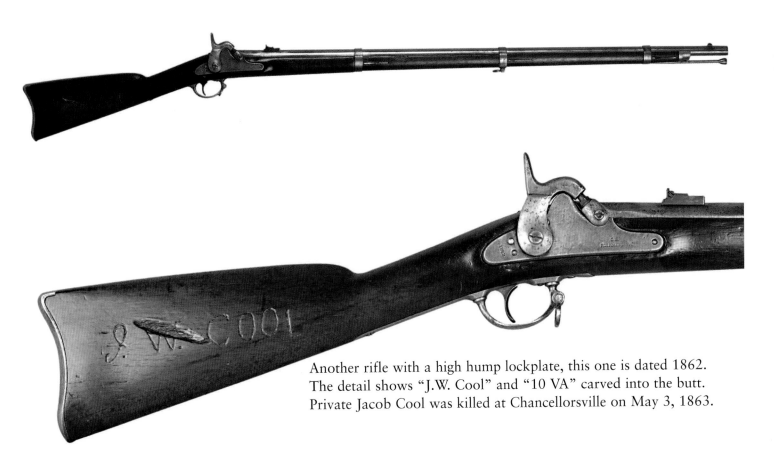

Another rifle with a high hump lockplate, this one is dated 1862. The detail shows "J.W. Cool" and "10 VA" carved into the butt. Private Jacob Cool was killed at Chancellorsville on May 3, 1863.

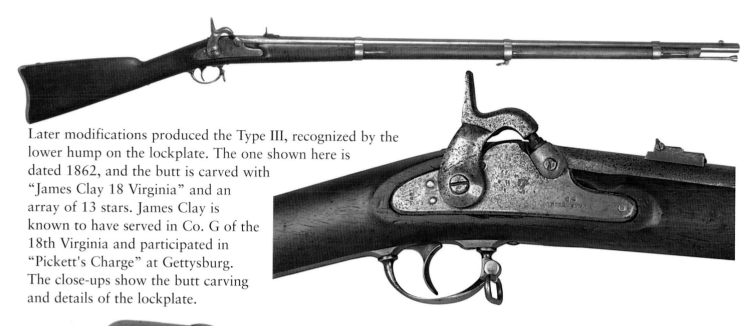

Later modifications produced the Type III, recognized by the lower hump on the lockplate. The one shown here is dated 1862, and the butt is carved with "James Clay 18 Virginia" and an array of 13 stars. James Clay is known to have served in Co. G of the 18th Virginia and participated in "Pickett's Charge" at Gettysburg. The close-ups show the butt carving and details of the lockplate.

## Robinson Sharps Carbine

### SPECIFICATIONS

**Type:** percussion breechloading carbine
**Origin:** Richmond, Virginia
**Caliber:** .52
**Barrel Length:** 21in

Made in Richmond, Virginia between 1862 and 1864 and based on the Hartford-made Model 1859 Sharps, this weapon generally lacked the refinement and quality workmanship of the original. Approximately 1,900 First Type guns were produced by Robinsons between 1862–63. The Confederate Government took over the Robinson factory in March 1863 and introduced the Second Type, which was identical to the First except for the markings on the breech ("Richmond, VA.").

## ROPER REVOLVING RIFLE

**SPECIFICATIONS**

**Type:** revolving chamber rifle

**Origin:** Roper Repeating Rifle Company, Amherst, Massachusetts

**Caliber:** .40

**Barrel Length:** 28in

One of the steps on the road to the multi-shot rifle was the revolving rifle, in which a rotating cylinder presented each cartridge in turn as was done in a revolver-type pistol. One man who tried his hand at such a design was Sylvester Howard Roper, a prolific American inventor, whose other inventions included a steam-carriage and the first-ever steam-powered, motorized-bicycle. In the Roper revolving rifle the cylinder was totally contained and it was, in fact, one of the most compact of all such designs.

## RUGER NO 1 RIFLE

**SPECIFICATIONS**

**Type:** single-shot rifle

**Origin:** Sturm, Ruger & Co, Southport, Connecticut

**Caliber:** see text

**Barrel Length:** see text

The Ruger No. 1 single-shot rifle has been available for many years in a various forms (Sporter, Standard, Tropical, Varminter, etc) and in some thirty discrete calibers; barrel lengths also vary according to the caliber from 20 thru' 22 and 24 to a maximum of 26 inches. Some are offered with open iron sights, others have no sights but are fitted with mounts for scopes.

The weapons shown here are all Number 1-Bs with 26 inch barrels, but are chambered for different calibers and have varying sighting arrangements.

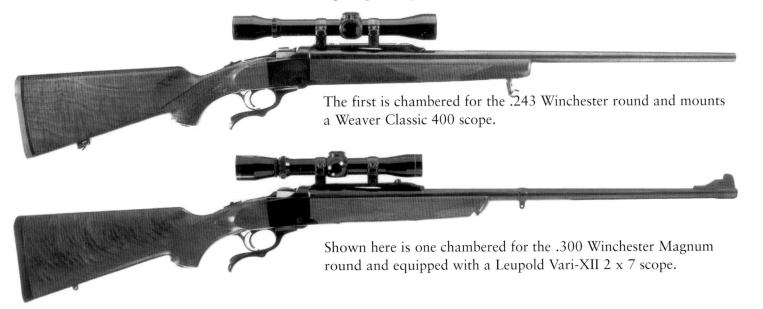

The first is chambered for the .243 Winchester round and mounts a Weaver Classic 400 scope.

Shown here is one chambered for the .300 Winchester Magnum round and equipped with a Leupold Vari-XII 2 x 7 scope.

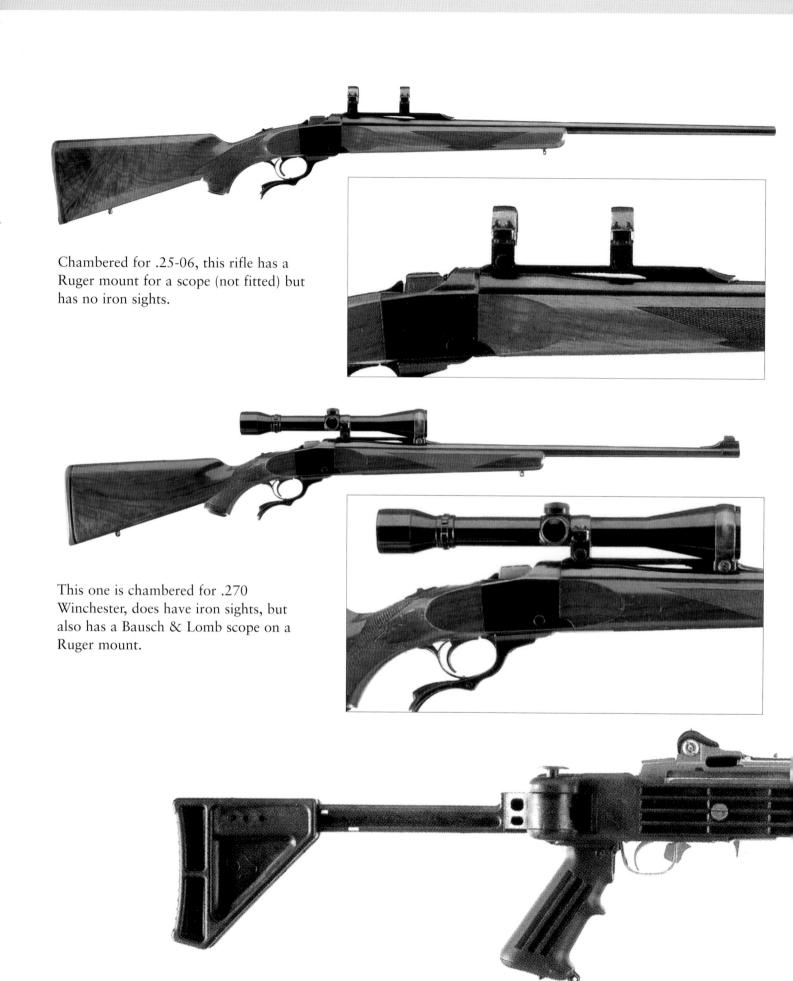

Chambered for .25-06, this rifle has a Ruger mount for a scope (not fitted) but has no iron sights.

This one is chambered for .270 Winchester, does have iron sights, but also has a Bausch & Lomb scope on a Ruger mount.

# RUGER MINI 14 CARBINE

## SPECIFICATIONS

**Type:** semi-automatic carbine
**Origin:** Sturm, Ruger & Co, Southport, Connecticut
**Caliber:** see text
**Barrel Length:** see text

The Mini 14 was introduced in 1975 as a paramilitary-style semi-automatic carbine. It had an 18.5 inch barrel and was chambered for the .223 Remington round, and used a gas-operated action. It was originally sold with either five, ten or twenty round magazines, but the two larger magazines are now available to law-enforcement agencies only.

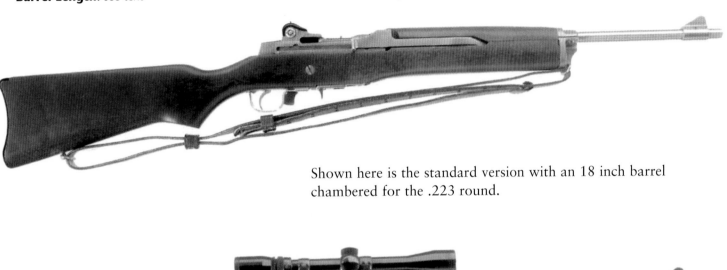

Shown here is the standard version with an 18 inch barrel chambered for the .223 round.

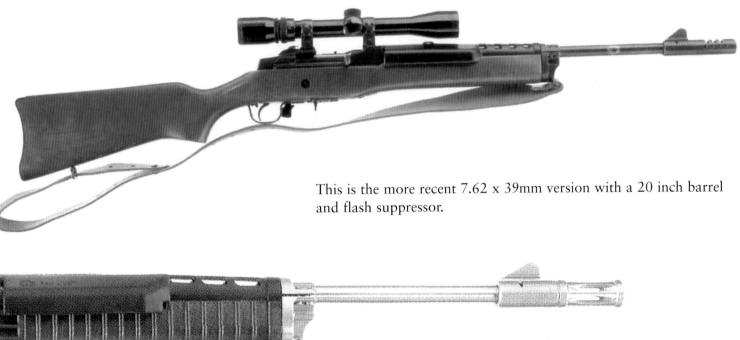

This is the more recent 7.62 x 39mm version with a 20 inch barrel and flash suppressor.

# RUGER MODEL 77 RIFLE

The Model 77 bolt-action rifle has been marketed since 1968 as a hunting rifle combining good quality with a reasonable price, and was in production in many versions until 1991 when it was replaced by the Model 77 Mark II. A five-round magazine was standard on all Model 77s.

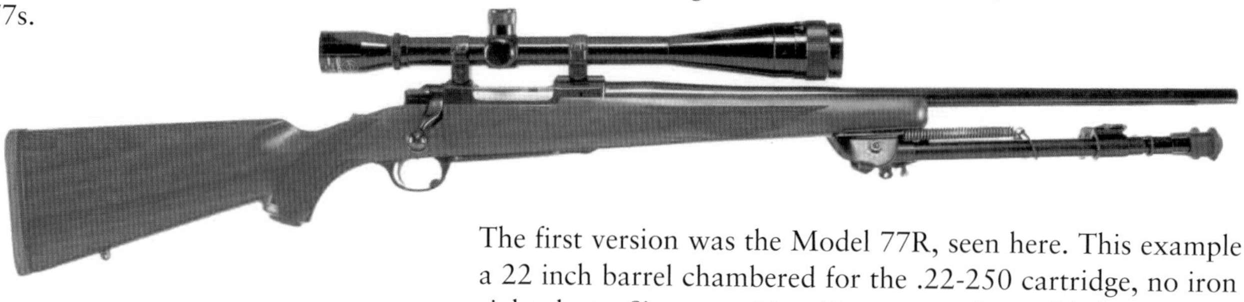

The first version was the Model 77R, seen here. This example has a 22 inch barrel chambered for the .22-250 cartridge, no iron sights but a Simmons 24 x 40 scope, and an added spring-loaded bipod.

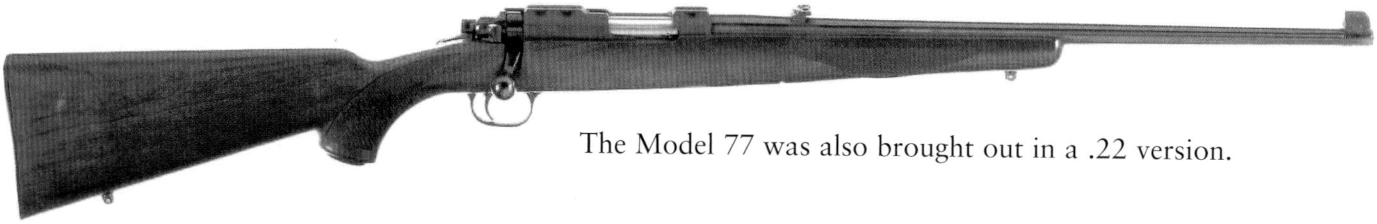

The Model 77 was also brought out in a .22 version.

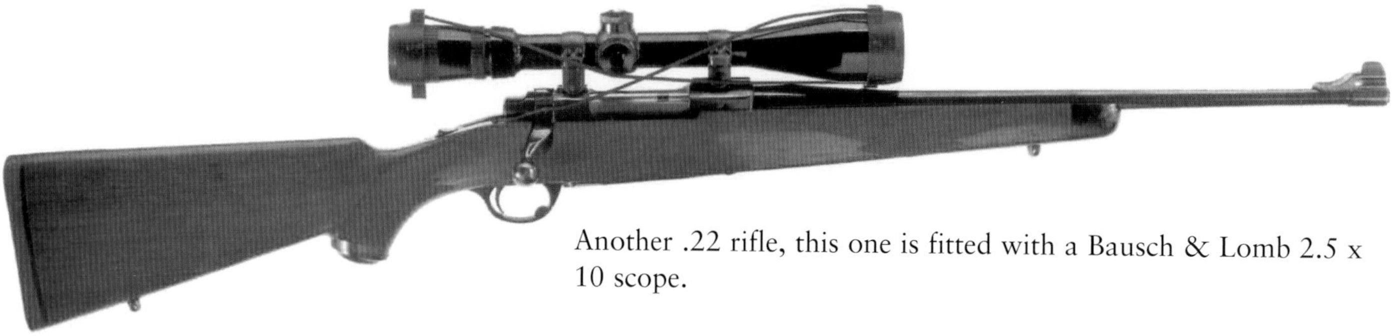

Another .22 rifle, this one is fitted with a Bausch & Lomb 2.5 x 10 scope.

The Model 77 Mark II introduced a number of important changes to the action, safety, bolt, ejector and trigger, while the magazine holds four, rather than five, rounds. The Mark II shown here is intended for bench rest shooting, with a heavy stainless-steel, free-floating barrel and a Redfield 4x – 12x scope. In bench rest competitions rifles are fired, as the name indicates, from a sturdy shooting bench, with the rifle supported by a front and rear rest. For centerfire rifles, the target ranges are 100, 200 and 300 yards, each course of fire consisting of either five rounds in seven minutes or ten rounds in twelve minutes at a single target in order to produce a measurable group.

## RUGER MODEL 10/22 RIFLE

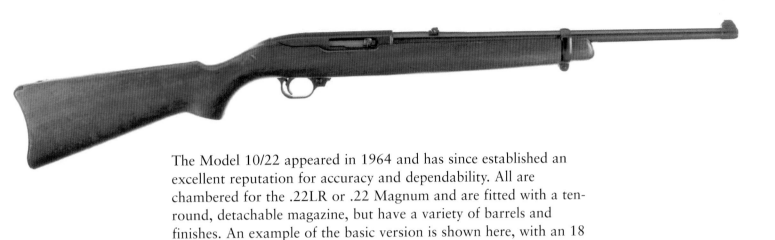

The Model 10/22 appeared in 1964 and has since established an excellent reputation for accuracy and dependability. All are chambered for the .22LR or .22 Magnum and are fitted with a ten-round, detachable magazine, but have a variety of barrels and finishes. An example of the basic version is shown here, with an 18 inch blued barrel, walnut stock and iron sights.

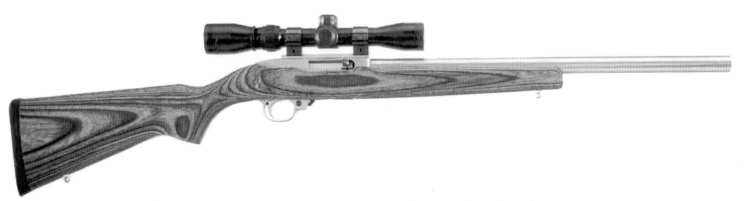

This example is more elaborate with a laminated stock and a hammer-forged steel barrel.

Most elaborate of all is the 10/22 Laminated Stock Sporter here, which has a free-floating, 20.5 inch Volquartsen barrel, Bushnell 4x – 12x scope and a large thumb-hole stock.

## SAVAGE MODEL 1895

### SPECIFICATIONS
**Type:** lever-action sporting rifle
**Origin:** Savage Arms Corporation, Utica, New York
**Caliber:** .303 Savage
**Barrel Length:** see text

The Model 1895 was chambered for the .303 Savage smokeless cartridge, which was so different from the better known British .303 that the latter British army designated the Savage round the ".301 Savage" so that their troops would not get mixed up between the two. This rifle was made by the Marlin Firearms company and about 5,000 were completed between 1895 and 1899. It had an eight-round magazine and weighed about 8.7 pounds. There was a cocking indicator, which was viewed through a .25 inch hole in the top of the breechblock; it showed "C" when the action was cocked and "S" when the striker was down (i.e., safe). We show two standard models with 26 inch barrels, and a third with a shorter 23 inch barrel.

# Savage Model 1899

In the late 1800s European arms manufacturers switched to bolt actions, but lever actions retained their popularity in the United States, mainly because a skilled shooter could fire up to fifteen well-aimed shots within one minute. Such qualities were especially important in the where large areas, particularly in what was then still the "Wild West," were lawless and citizens needed a weapon for self-defense as well as for hunting.

The Savage lever-action was introduced in 1895 (*see previous entry*) but the Model 1899 was much improved model and turned out to be one of those fortunate designs with a combination of features which got things just right and, as a result, over one-and-a-half million have been produced since. In the early years the Model 1899 was chambered for the usual run of low-pressure cartridges, such as 0.30-30, 0.25-35 and 0.32-40, but in 1912 Charles Newton's .22 HP high-velocity round was introduced followed three years later by the 0.250-300, which proved a major breakthrough and placed this rifle in a class of its own. It came about because ballistics expert Charles Newton decided to produce a deer-hunting cartridge by combining a .280 bullet with a cut-down 0.30-40 Krag case, but then Harvey Donaldson, another ballistic expert, suggested using the .30-06 case instead, while Arthur Savage reduced the bullet weight from 100 to 87 grains. The happy outcome of all this was the .250-300, the first commercially loaded American cartridge with a muzzle velocity in excess of 3,000ft/sec.

The original version, the Model 1899A, appeared in two versions: one with a 26 inch barrel, which was manufactured from 1899 to 1927, and the other with a 22 inch barrel (known as the Model 1899A Short) from 1899 to 1922. This is a .30-30, 26 inch version manufactured in 1903, with plain metalwork, furniture and iron sights.

Shown here is also a Model 1899A manufactured in 1903, but is the deluxe version with checkered patterning on the fore-end and pistol grip, and with a tang sight in addition to the barrel-mounted iron sights. It has a 26 inch barrel chambered for .303 Savage.

This Model 1899A Short has a 22 inch barrel, in this case chambered for the .303 Savage, although it was also made in other calibers.

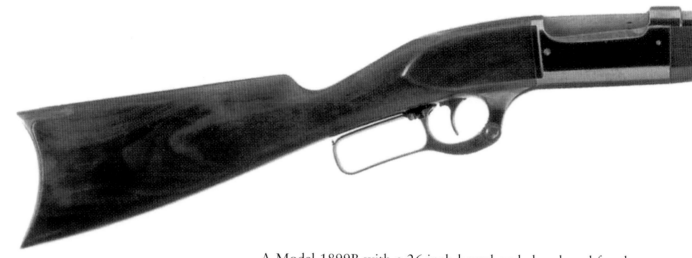

A Model 1899B with a 26 inch barrel and chambered for the unusual .25-35 round; it was shipped in 1905.

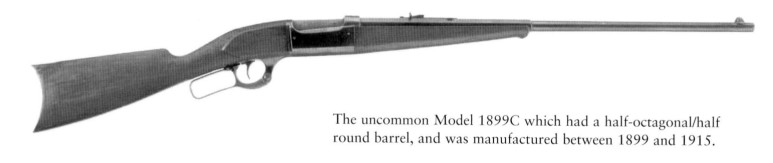

The uncommon Model 1899C which had a half-octagonal/half round barrel, and was manufactured between 1899 and 1915.

Both these rifles are Model 1899Ds, and were among several hundred purchased by a group of Montreal, Canada businessmen in 1914–15 to arm their local militia, in order to free Ross rifles to arm the expeditionary units setting off for France. Most had full-length, military style stocks and 26 inch barrels with a bayonet lug, but all were chambered for the .303 Savage round only.

The Model 1899F Saddle Ring Carbine was made only with a 20 inch barrel, but was available in .25-35, .30-30, .303 Savage, .32-40 (*seen here*) and .38-55 calibers. There is a variation on this model with a single barrel band.

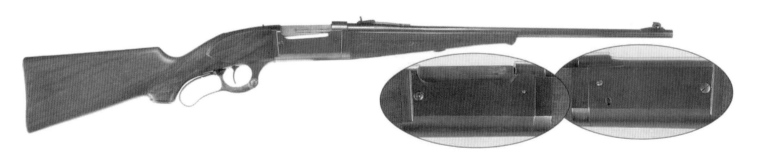

A Model 1899G takedown rifle with checkered fore-end and pistol grip on a special grade walnut. This example also has a tang sight, but this was fitted after purchase.

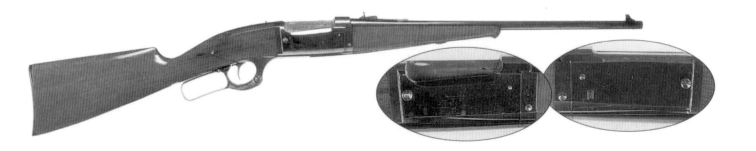

The Model 1899H Featherweight Takedown rifle with a 22 inch barrel and chambered for the revolutionary .22 HP Savage round, which was introduced in 1912.

# SAVAGE MODEL 99

Production of the Savage Model 1899 was suspended in 1917 due to war work, but once the conflict was over production restarted with the Model 99A, which was essentially a minor variant of the pre-1917 weapon and remained in production until 1936. A whole variety of sub-models were produced until 1942 when commercial production was again suspended so that the factory could concentrate on war work. Production recommenced in 1946 and in 1960 the one millionth production Model 1899/99 was presented to the National Rifle Association.

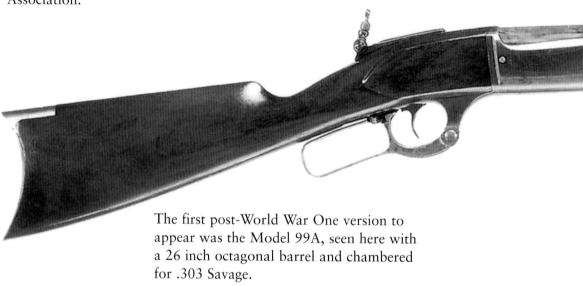

The first post-World War One version to appear was the Model 99A, seen here with a 26 inch octagonal barrel and chambered for .303 Savage.

This is a post-World War Two Model 99E chambered for the .243 Winchester round.

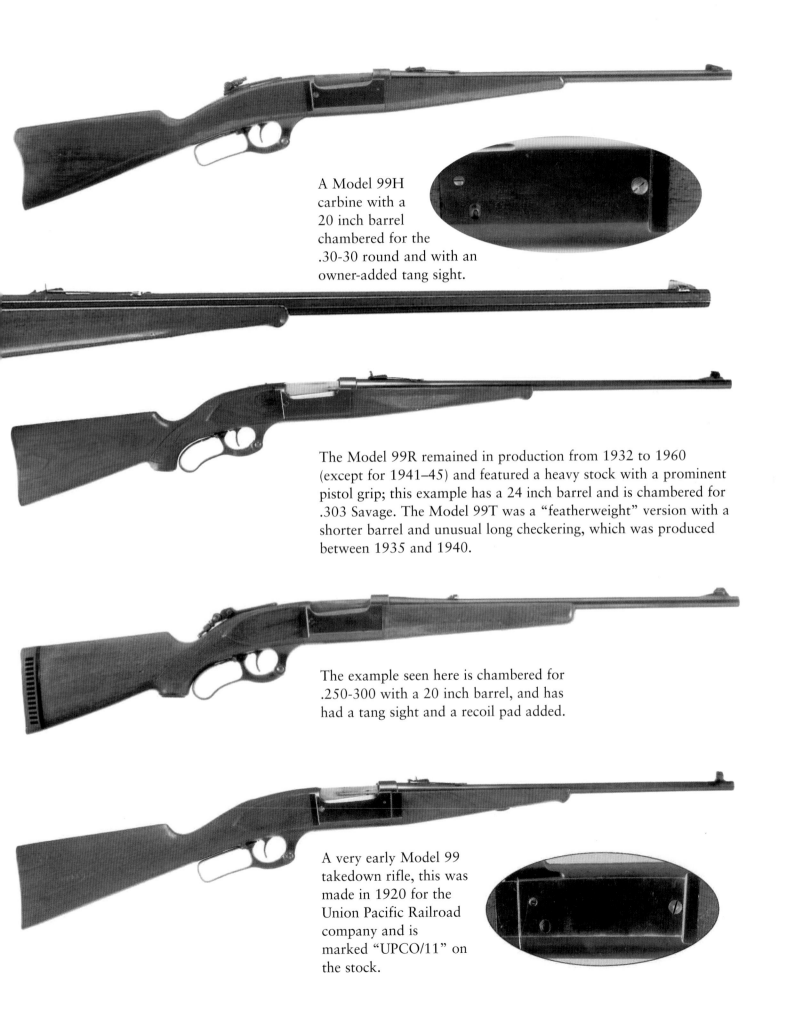

A Model 99H carbine with a 20 inch barrel chambered for the .30-30 round and with an owner-added tang sight.

The Model 99R remained in production from 1932 to 1960 (except for 1941–45) and featured a heavy stock with a prominent pistol grip; this example has a 24 inch barrel and is chambered for .303 Savage. The Model 99T was a "featherweight" version with a shorter barrel and unusual long checkering, which was produced between 1935 and 1940.

The example seen here is chambered for .250-300 with a 20 inch barrel, and has had a tang sight and a recoil pad added.

A very early Model 99 takedown rifle, this was made in 1920 for the Union Pacific Railroad company and is marked "UPCO/11" on the stock.

## SAVAGE MODEL 1903

### SPECIFICATIONS

**Type:** slide-action sporting rifle
**Origin:** Savage Arms Corporation, Utica, New York
**Caliber:** .22 LR
**Barrel Length:** 24in

The Model 1903 was introduced in 1903 and remained in production until 1922. It was a .22 slide-action weapon with a 24 inch octagonal barrel, open, iron sights and a seven-round magazine. The examples shown here are virtually identical standard models, but there were also gallery and some very rare factory-engraved models

## SAVAGE MODEL 1914

### SPECIFICATIONS

**Type:** slide-action sporting rifle
**Origin:** Savage Arms Corporation, Utica, New York
**Caliber:** .22
**Barrel Length:** 24in

Development of the Savage .22 rifle continued from the Model 1903 (previous entry) through the Model 1911 bolt-action and 1912 semi-automatic. Next came this Model 1914, which returned to the slide-action, albeit with an altered slide mechanism and a much longer slide handle. It had a 24 inch octagonal barrel. A factory-engraved Model 1914 with gold inlays, special checkering and a pearl pistol-grip cap, and in mint, unfired condition, was sold at auction in 2002 for $33,600.

## SAVAGE MODEL 29

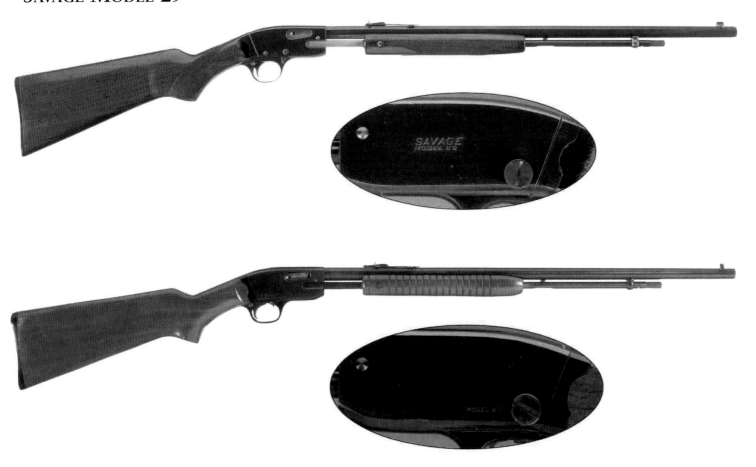

### SPECIFICATIONS

**Type:** slide-action sporting rifle

**Origin:** Savage Arms Corporation, Utica, New York

**Caliber:** .22S, .22L, .22LR

**Barrel Length:** 24in

The Model 29 was introduced in 1929 and remained in production until 1967. Pre-war models had an octagonal barrel and a checkered stock, but these were changed after the war to a round barrel and an undecorated stock. One of those shown is a pre-war model with octagonal barrel, smooth slide handle and checkered pistol grip, while the other is a post-war model with round barrel, serrated slide and no checkering.

## SAVAGE MODEL 10FCM SCOUT

### SPECIFICATIONS

**Type:** bolt-action sporting rifle
**Origin:** Savage Arms Corporation, Utica, New York
**Caliber:** .308 Winchester
**Barrel Length:** 20in

The Model 10 series was introduced in the mid-1990s with the usual variety of sub-models to meet the needs of individual shooters, including a number intended solely for the law enforcement community. The example seen here is a Model 10FCM "Scout," which was introduced in 1999, and is typical of those on offer on the commercial market. It is chambered for the .308 Winchester round and has a 20 inch round barrel. It is fitted with a ramp foresight and a Williams adjustable peep sight on the back of the action, but also has a B-Square one-piece rail for a telescopic sight, which is mounted on the receiver and barrel. It is fitted with a four-round detachable magazine and weighs approximately 6.5 pounds. This particular example is also fitted with an unusually large ball on the bolt lever.

## SAVAGE ANSCHUTZ MODEL 164

### SPECIFICATIONS

**Type:** bolt-action sporting rifle
**Origin:** Savage Arms Corporation, Utica, New York
**Caliber:** .22 LR
**Barrel Length:** 24in

In the 1960s and '70s Savage imported and re-badged the Anschütz Model 164 from Germany. This fired .22 LR ammunition from a five-round removable magazine. This weapon, while not expensive, had a good reputation for accuracy, even with cheap ammunition. The example seen here mounts a Bushnell 4x telescopic sight, but also has a folding-leaf rearsight and a hooded ramp foresight.

## SCHOFIELD PERCUSSION RIFLE

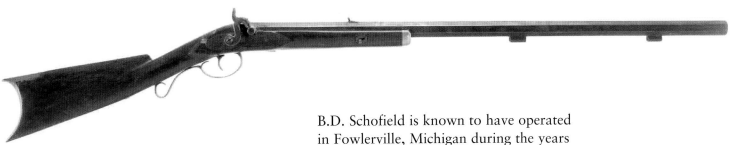

### SPECIFICATIONS
**Type:** half-stock, muzzle-loading, percussion rifle
**Origin:** B.D. Schofield, Fowlerville, Michigan
**Caliber:** .41
**Barrel Length:** 31in

B.D. Schofield is known to have operated in Fowlerville, Michigan during the years 1875 to 1878, but must have been in business for many more years than that. Many gunsmiths were producing half-stock percussion rifles to this general design during this period.

## SCHOYEN BALLARD SCHUTZEN RIFLE

### SPECIFICATIONS
**Type:** Ballard-action rifle
**Origin:** G.C. Schoyen, Denver, Colorado
**Caliber:** .32-40
**Barrel Length:** 30in

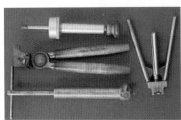

George C. Schoyen (1845–1916) was born in Norway and in about 1869 he emigrated to the United States, settling first in Chicago, but moving to Denver, Colorado in 1873, where he found work with Carlos Gove. On Gove's retirement, Schoyen set up his own gunshop, remaining in Denver until his death. Schoyen was one of the leading gunsmiths during the Schützen era, famous for his outstanding barrels and excellent workmanship, and this .32-40 caliber rifle was one of his finest products.

The 30 inch octagonal barrel was made by Schoyen himself and is fitted with a false muzzle and a Winchester wind gauge Spirit level foresight. There are no mountings or drillings on the barrel for a rear sight or scope; instead there is a Schützen-style short-range vernier sight mounted on the tang. The action is a Marlin-Ballard #6 pistol-grip frame, which is heavily engraved. The large butt ends in a deeply-curved Schützen butt-plate, and there is also a Schoyen-made shotgun buttstock for use in bench-rest shooting. This is an outstanding weapon from a master of his craft.

## SAVAGE MODEL 10FCM SCOUT

### SPECIFICATIONS

**Type:** bolt-action sporting rifle
**Origin:** Savage Arms Corporation, Utica, New York
**Caliber:** .308 Winchester
**Barrel Length:** 20in

The Model 10 series was introduced in the mid-1990s with the usual variety of sub-models to meet the needs of individual shooters, including a number intended solely for the law enforcement community. The example seen here is a Model 10FCM "Scout," which was introduced in 1999, and is typical of those on offer on the commercial market. It is chambered for the .308 Winchester round and has a 20 inch round barrel. It is fitted with a ramp foresight and a Williams adjustable peep sight on the back of the action, but also has a B-Square one-piece rail for a telescopic sight, which is mounted on the receiver and barrel. It is fitted with a four-round detachable magazine and weighs approximately 6.5 pounds. This particular example is also fitted with an unusually large ball on the bolt lever.

## SAVAGE ANSCHUTZ MODEL 164

### SPECIFICATIONS

**Type:** bolt-action sporting rifle
**Origin:** Savage Arms Corporation, Utica, New York
**Caliber:** .22 LR
**Barrel Length:** 24in

In the 1960s and '70s Savage imported and re-badged the Anschütz Model 164 from Germany. This fired .22 LR ammunition from a five-round removable magazine. This weapon, while not expensive, had a good reputation for accuracy, even with cheap ammunition. The example seen here mounts a Bushnell 4x telescopic sight, but also has a folding-leaf rearsight and a hooded ramp foresight.

## SCHOFIELD PERCUSSION RIFLE

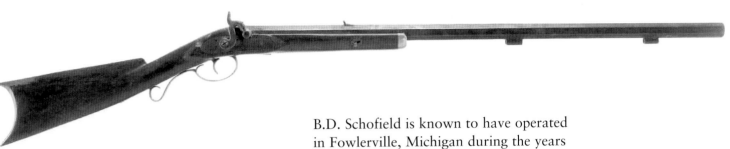

### SPECIFICATIONS

**Type:** half-stock, muzzle-loading, percussion rifle
**Origin:** B.D. Schofield, Fowlerville, Michigan
**Caliber:** .41
**Barrel Length:** 31in

B.D. Schofield is known to have operated in Fowlerville, Michigan during the years 1875 to 1878, but must have been in business for many more years than that. Many gunsmiths were producing half-stock percussion rifles to this general design during this period.

## SCHOYEN BALLARD SCHUTZEN RIFLE

### SPECIFICATIONS

**Type:** Ballard-action rifle
**Origin:** G.C. Schoyen, Denver, Colorado
**Caliber:** .32-40
**Barrel Length:** 30in

George C. Schoyen (1845–1916) was born in Norway and in about 1869 he emigrated to the United States, settling first in Chicago, but moving to Denver, Colorado in 1873, where he found work with Carlos Gove. On Gove's retirement, Schoyen set up his own gunshop, remaining in Denver until his death. Schoyen was one of the leading gunsmiths during the Schützen era, famous for his outstanding barrels and excellent workmanship, and this .32-40 caliber rifle was one of his finest products.

The 30 inch octagonal barrel was made by Schoyen himself and is fitted with a false muzzle and a Winchester wind gauge Spirit level foresight. There are no mountings or drillings on the barrel for a rear sight or scope; instead there is a Schützen-style short-range vernier sight mounted on the tang. The action is a Marlin-Ballard #6 pistol-grip frame, which is heavily engraved. The large butt ends in a deeply-curved Schützen butt-plate, and there is also a Schoyen-made shotgun buttstock for use in bench-rest shooting. This is an outstanding weapon from a master of his craft.

## SEDGELY SPRINGFIELD M1903 SPORTER

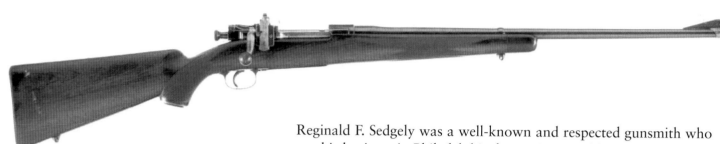

### SPECIFICATIONS

**Type:** Springfield action, sporter rifle
**Origin:** R.F. Sedgely, Philadelphia, Pennsylvania
**Caliber:** .30-06
**Barrel Length:** 24in

Reginald F. Sedgely was a well-known and respected gunsmith who ran his business in Philadelphia from 1910 until his death in 1938. His company made .22 hammerless revolvers and tear-gas guns for the police, but also produced customized sporters based on a variety of actions, including the Mauser and the M1903 Springfield. The one shown here is a typical example and shows a good quality of workmanship, with a blued barrel and a walnut stock, with checkering on the fore-end and pistol grip.

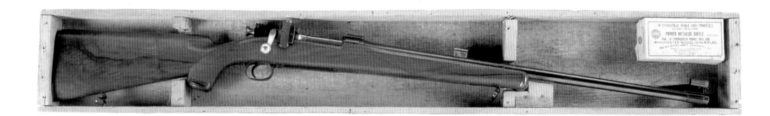

This one is, if anything, even better and is shown here in its original packing case.

## SEDGLEY M 1903 RIFLE

### SPECIFICATIONS

**Type:** Springfield M1903 rifle
**Origin:** R.F. Sedgely, Philadelphia, Pennsylvania
**Caliber:** .30-06
**Barrel Length:** 24in

This is a real curiosity. During the inter-war years Sedgely had bought up many surplus M1903 actions and turned them into good quality sporters (*see previous entry*). However, it appears that at the start of World War Two the company (Sedgely had died in 1938) used some of the actions lying in their stores and assembled them, with other spares and some new production items, to produce an M1903 look-alike for sale to organizations that required a military-looking rifle. Sedgely was well-known for the quality of its output, so it must be assumed that the performance of this odd weapon was, at the very least, satisfactory and safe.

## SEARS & ROEBUCK RANGER

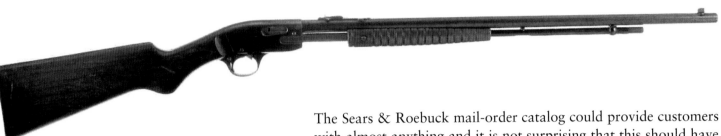

### SPECIFICATIONS

**Type:** sporter rifle
**Origin:** Sears & Roebuck & Co.
**Caliber:** .22S, .22L, .22LR
**Barrel Length:** 24in

The Sears & Roebuck mail-order catalog could provide customers with almost anything and it is not surprising that this should have included firearms. The catalog company bought in models from well-known firearms manufacturers such as Winchester and Savage and sold them under their own label at bargain prices. This weapon, # 102.35 in the relevant Sears catalog, was in reality the Savage Model 29.

## SHARPS 1852 SADDLE RING CARBINE

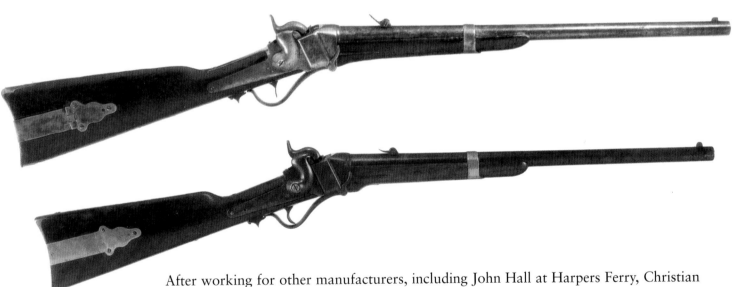

### SPECIFICATIONS

**Type:** single shot, breechloading percussion carbine
**Origin:** see text
**Caliber:** .52
**Barrel Length:** 21.5in

After working for other manufacturers, including John Hall at Harpers Ferry, Christian Sharps eventually set up his own company in 1851, in co-operation with Robbins and Lawrence, in Windsor, Vermont. Robbins and Lawrence made the weapons, while Sharps provided technical advice and marketed them from the Sharps Rifle Manufacturing Company, in Hartford, Connecticut. Sharps developed a range of single-shot breechloading rifles and carbines that were to be heavily used by soldiers in the Civil War and after, and by sportsmen and hunters.

This is one of Sharps' earlier designs, and is a neat .52 caliber cavalry carbine which used the Sharps patent pellet primer mounted on the lockplate. It is recognizable from later models by the "slanting breech" on the side of the frame. The sling ring bar is unusual it that it extends from the breech to the barrel band. This often seems to have been repaired on surviving examples and perhaps the extra length subjected the part to stress. Some 5,000 units were manufactured in serial numbers 2050–7500. Our two examples are early guns, being numbered in the 2600–3950 range.

# SHARPS NEW MODEL CARBINES

## SPECIFICATIONS

**Type:** single shot, breechloading percussion carbine
**Origin:** Sharps Rifle Manufacturing Company, Hartford, Connecticut.
**Caliber:** .52
**Barrel Length:** 21.5in

As a result of experience with the Model 1852, the Sharps Company updated the design to what is known as the straight breech, or New Model rifles and carbines. As far as the carbine series goes, some 98,000 were made of Models 1859, 1863, and 1865, although they can be regarded as a single type. The Model 1863, which we are illustrating, was produced both with and without a patchbox (twice as many without). Both our examples are without. The Sharps pellet priming system is now integral with the lockplate, the furniture is now iron including the cast barrel band, and the sling ring bar on the left side of the receiver is shorter, extending rearwards to the middle of the wrist. Most of the output was put in the hands of federal troops, but the State of Georgia managed to acquire 2,000 for its cavalry and infantry from the first production of the 1859 model, the only batch to retain brass furniture. Ironically, by the time these successful weapons had been developed, Christian Sharps had severed all association with the company, and by 1854 had formed a new partnership with William Hankins (*see below*).

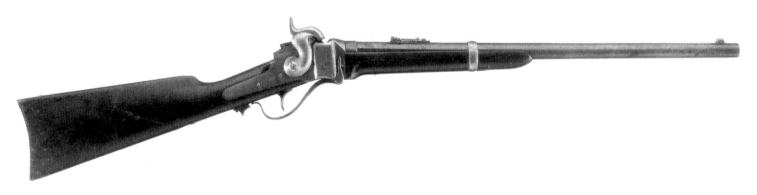

# SHARPS NEW MODEL RIFLES

## SPECIFICATIONS

**Type:** single shot, breechloading percussion rifle
**Origin:** Sharps Rifle Manufacturing Company, Hartford, Connecticut.
**Caliber:** .52
**Barrel Length:** 30in

Sharps rifles were just as successful as their shorter carbine brethren. This model 1859 has the new model breech and is of a similar type to those used by Col. Hiram Berdan's 1st and 2nd regiments of U.S. Sharpshooters.

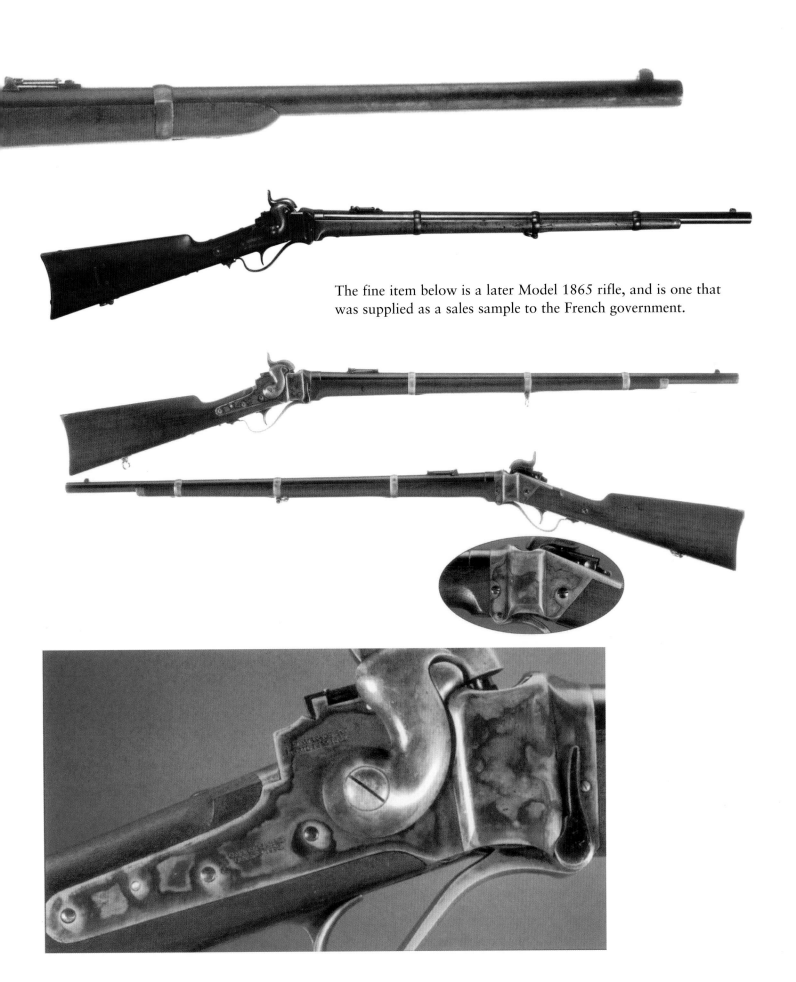

The fine item below is a later Model 1865 rifle, and is one that was supplied as a sales sample to the French government.

## SHARPS CONVERSION CARBINES

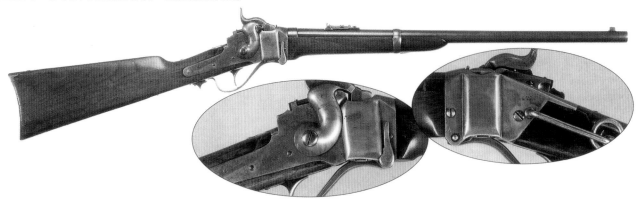

### SPECIFICATIONS

**Type:** single shot, breechloading cartridge carbine
**Origin:** Sharps Rifle Manufacturing Company, Hartford, Connecticut.
**Caliber:** .50-70 centerfire
**Barrel Length:** 21.5in

After the Civil War, many Sharps carbines and rifles were converted to fire metallic cartridges. These three fine examples have all been modified to take .50-70 centerfire, although there were some that were made for .52-70 rimfire.

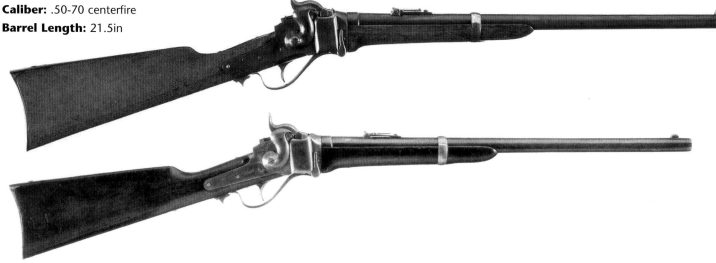

## SHARPS MODEL 1853 SPORTING RIFLE

### SPECIFICATIONS

**Type:** sporting rifle
**Origin:** Sharps Rifle Manufacturing Company, Hartford, Connecticut
**Caliber:** .44
**Barrel Length:** 25.5in

Sharps produced three new weapons in 1853: a military carbine, a military rifle with a longer barrel, and the sporting rifle, seen here. A total of 13,500 of all types were made between 1854 and 1858. The sporting rifle has a 25.5 inch barrel

# SHARPS MODEL 1874 MILITARY RIFLE

## SPECIFICATIONS

**Type:** breech-loading, metallic cartridge, military rifle

**Origin:** Sharps Rifle Manufacturing Company, Hartford, Connecticut

**Caliber:** .45-70

**Barrel Length:** 30in

Although known as the Model 1874, this series of weapons began production in 1871. They come in a bewildering array of calibers and sub-types for both military, sporting and target shooting use. The main difference between this model and the earlier Sharps is that the lock is no longer a modification of the earlier Sharps primer design, but is made as new for cartridge use. The one shown here is a military rifle, and is a hybrid, with lock parts salvaged from older models.

# SHARPS MODEL 1874 MILITARY CARBINE

## SPECIFICATIONS

**Type:** breech-loading, metallic cartridge, military carbine

**Origin:** Sharps Rifle Manufacturing Company, Hartford, Connecticut

**Caliber:** .44

**Barrel Length:** 21in

Sharps regularly produced military carbine versions of their weapons; the British Army, for example, took a number of the Model 1855 carbine. Thus, the company also made a carbine version of the Model 1874, seen here, with a 21 inch barrel. It is not known whether any military sales were made, but, if not, they would certainly have found ready buyers on the civil market.

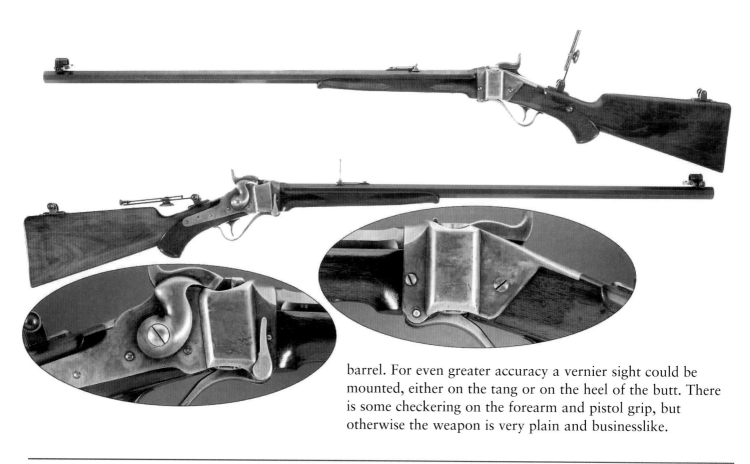

barrel. For even greater accuracy a vernier sight could be mounted, either on the tang or on the heel of the butt. There is some checkering on the forearm and pistol grip, but otherwise the weapon is very plain and businesslike.

## SHARPS BORCHARDT RIFLES

**SPECIFICATIONS**
**Type:** military/sporting rifle
**Origin:** Sharps Rifle Manufacturing Company, Hartford, Connecticut
**Caliber:** .45-70
**Barrel Length:** see text

Hugo Borchardt took out a patent in 1876 on a hammerless, dropping block mechanism, which offered significant improvements to the original Sharps' dropping block mechanism of 1848, being more efficient as well as stronger and quicker acting. This resulted in a series of Sharps-Borchardt rifles which enjoyed a brief vogue in the late 1870s, with some 10,000 military and 12,500 sporting rifles being made. Production ceased when Sharps went out of business in 1881.

The Sharps-Borchardt military rifle was chambered for the US government .45-70 round with a 32 inch barrel, full-length fore-end and two barrel bands. Approximately 12,000 were made; there were sales to National Guard units in the states of North Carolina and Michigan, but the identity of other recipients is not known.

The sporting rifle is also chambered for the .45-70 round, but has a 30 inch barrel with a modern globe foresight. The original barrel-mounted rear sight has been removed and replaced by a vernier sight on the tang.

## SHARPS & HANKINS MODEL 1862 CARBINE

**SPECIFICATIONS**

**Type:** breech-loading, metallic cartridge, military carbine

**Origin:** Sharps and Hankins, Philadelphia, Pennsylvania

**Caliber:** .52 rimfire

**Barrel Length:** 24 in and 19 in.

In 1853 Christian Sharps severed all connections with the Sharps Rifle Manufacturing Company in Hartford, Connecticut. He returned to Philadelphia and set up as C. Sharps & Company and set about manufacturing a breechloading, single shot pistol. In 1862 he formed a partnership with William Hankins to produce weapons for the Civil War, and began manufacture of this sliding barrel action carbine. A total of 8,000 were made between 1862–65.

Production was mainly centered on the navy type, which had the unusual feature of a leather-covered barrel to prevent corrosion. This has not stood the test of time particularly well and many surviving examples have the leather in poor condition. An army type was made in small numbers (around 500) and which lacked the fixings for the leather barrel sleeve.

There was also a cavalry carbine, with a shortened 19 inch barrel and saddle ring. This weapon was used by the 11th New York Volunteer Cavalry and is often known by that name. Confusingly many surviving examples still bear the Navy inspector's markings "P/HKH" despite being issued to the cavalry.

## SIEBERT PLAINS RIFLE

Charles Siebert (1839–1915) started to work for his brother, Christian, at the age of twelve in his gunshop in Columbus, Ohio. He then moved to Circleville, also in Ohio and about 30 miles south of Columbus, where he established his own business. This rifle is unusual in having a round barrel, since most small-town gunsmiths of the period did not have the necessary tools for turning a round barrel.

**SPECIFICATIONS**

**Type:** muzzle-loading hunting rifle

**Origin:** Charles M. Siebert, Circleville, Pickaway County, Ohio

**Caliber:** .58

**Barrel Length:** 39in

# Smith Carbine

## SPECIFICATIONS

**Type:** percussion breechloading carbine
**Origin:** see text
**Caliber:** .50
**Barrel Length:** 21.6 inches

Originally patented by Gilbert Smith of Buttermilk Falls, New York, around 30,000 Smith carbines were made between 1861–65 in Massachusetts. Manufacture took place at the American Machine Works plant in Springfield, at the American Arms Co., and the Massachusetts Arms Co., both located in Chicopee Falls. The gun is loaded by releasing the catch in front of the trigger, allowing the barrel to pivot downward to give access to the breech.

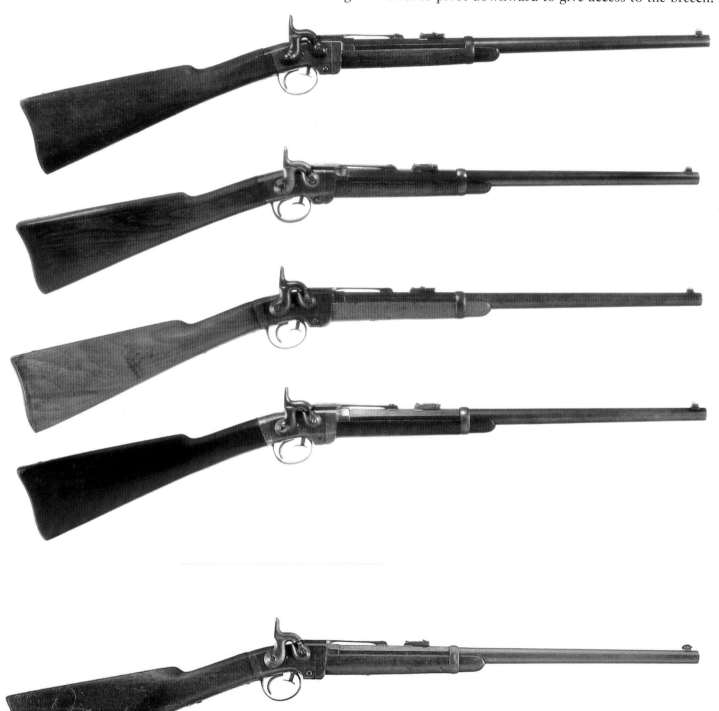

## SMITH-JENNINGS MAGAZINE RIFLE

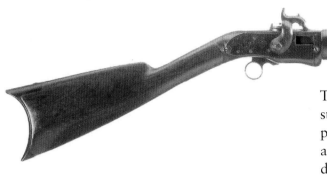

### SPECIFICATIONS

**Type:** magazine-fed rifle
**Origin:** Horace Smith, Daniel Wesson, Norwich, Connecticut.
**Caliber:** .54
**Barrel Length:** 24.5in

This rifle represents a significant stage in the Smith & Wesson story. In 1849 an inventor, Lewis Jennings of Windsor, Vermont, patented a lever-action rifle with a tubular magazine, together with a hollow-base bullet containing the propellant charge; the latter device was known as "Jennings' racket ball." The rifle was initially manufactured by Robbins & Lawrence, but Horace Smith, who was working for that company, introduced some improvements, resulting in the rifle seen here. This particular rifle has been modified at some time since leaving the factory, since the manufacture of Jennings' bullets eventually ceased and there was nothing else with which to replace them, so this weapon has been converted to a muzzleloader by sealing off the magazine and removing the repeater mechanism.

## SMITH & WESSON LIGHT RIFLE

### SPECIFICATIONS

**Type:** semi-automatic military carbine.
**Origin:** Smith & Wesson, Springfield, Massachusetts.
**Caliber:** 9mm
**Barrel Length:** 10in

Even the best companies make mistakes, most managing to prevent them leaving the factory gates, but Smith & Wesson failed in this particular case. The "Light Rifle" was designed to compete with the M1 carbine, and was only made in a small batch for trials purposes. The basic idea was that the empty cartridge cases were ejected downwards through a slot between the magazine and the trigger group; this may have seemed like a good idea in the drawing office, but was extremely dangerous for any unfortunate who tried to fire the weapon. The whole concept was quickly shelved and a red plate has been affixed to the left side of the stock of this example, stating "Extremely hazardous; do not load or fire."

## SPENCER MODEL 1860 RIFLE

**SPECIFICATIONS**

**Type:** magazine-fed repeating rifle
**Origin:** Spencer Repeating Rifle Co., Boston, Massachusetts
**Caliber:** .56-56
**Barrel Length:** 31in

Christopher M. Spencer was born in 1841 and initially made his weapons at South Manchester, Connecticut, until moving to Boston in about 1862. His Model 1860 rifle was similar to the Model 1860 carbine, but with a longer, 30 inch, barrel and a full-length stock extending almost to the muzzle, with an iron tip and secured by three barrel bands. There were two almost identical variants, one for the navy (1,000 produced in 1862–4) the other for the army (11,450 produced in 1863–4).

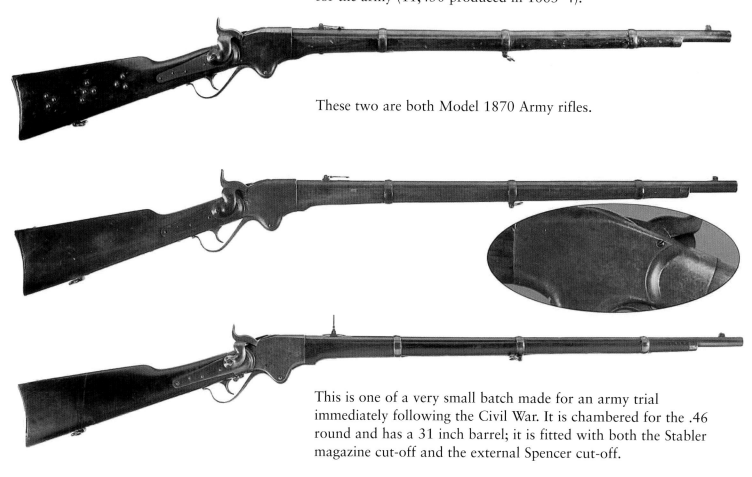

These two are both Model 1870 Army rifles.

This is one of a very small batch made for an army trial immediately following the Civil War. It is chambered for the .46 round and has a 31 inch barrel; it is fitted with both the Stabler magazine cut-off and the external Spencer cut-off.

## SPENCER REPEATING CARBINE

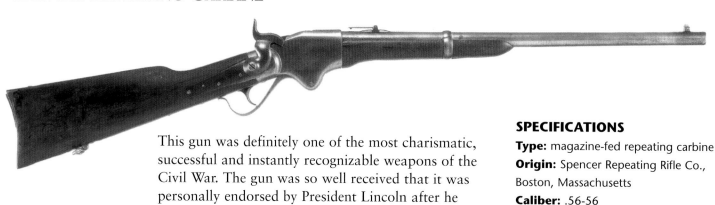

This gun was definitely one of the most charismatic, successful and instantly recognizable weapons of the Civil War. The gun was so well received that it was personally endorsed by President Lincoln after he witnessed a field trial.

**SPECIFICATIONS**

**Type:** magazine-fed repeating carbine
**Origin:** Spencer Repeating Rifle Co., Boston, Massachusetts
**Caliber:** .56-56
**Barrel Length:** 22in

# SPENCER MODEL 1865 CARBINE

## SPECIFICATIONS

**Type:** magazine-fed repeating carbine
**Origin:** Spencer Repeating Rifle Co., Boston, Massachusetts
**Caliber:** .50
**Barrel Length:** 20in

Spencer also produced a later Model 1865, chambered for a .50 cartridge and with a slightly shorter 20in barrel. Many were also fitted with the Stabler cut-off, a device which blocked the magazine. If careful, aimed, fire was needed, the user could block the magazine and feed single cartridges in to the breech, one at a time. The magazine could thus be kept full until rapid fire was needed, whereupon the firer simply slid the cut-off aside and let loose.

## SPENCER 1867 RIFLE

### SPECIFICATIONS

**Type:** magazine-fed repeating rifle
**Origin:** Spencer Repeating Rifle Co., Boston, Massachusetts
**Caliber:** .45
**Barrel Length:** 31in

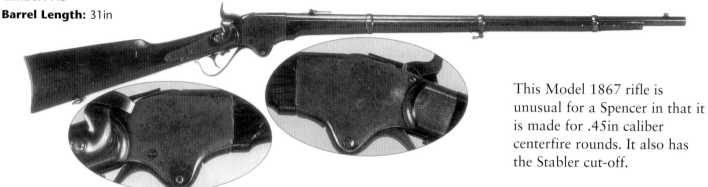

This Model 1867 rifle is unusual for a Spencer in that it is made for .45in caliber centerfire rounds. It also has the Stabler cut-off.

## SPENCER SPORTING RIFLE

### SPECIFICATIONS

**Type:** magazine-fed repeating sporting rifle
**Origin:** Spencer Repeating Rifle Co., Boston, Massachusetts
**Caliber:** .44
**Barrel Length:** 26in

After the Civil War, Spencer attempted to produce weapons for the civilian market, but with limited commercial success. This hunting rifle is chambered for .44 and has a 26 in barrel.

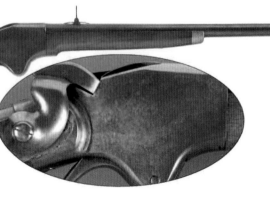

## SPRINGFIELD MODEL 1795 FLINTLOCK MUSKET

### SPECIFICATIONS

**Type:** flintlock musket
**Origin:** National Armory, Springfield, Massachusetts
**Caliber:** .62
**Barrel Length:** 44.4in

This was the first nationally-produced military musket and the first to be made at the newly-established national armory. Unsurprisingly, it was a conventional design with a 44.4 inch barrel and a stock extending almost to the muzzle, which was secured by three barrel bands. There was a metal ramrod housed beneath the barrel.

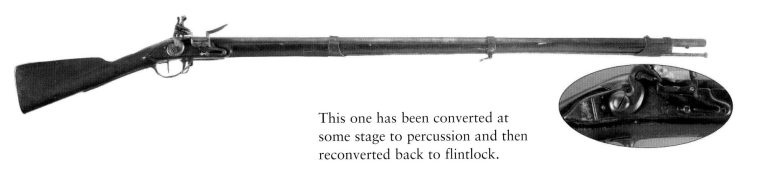

This one has been converted at some stage to percussion and then reconverted back to flintlock.

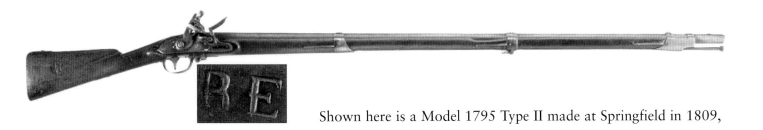

Shown here is a Model 1795 Type II made at Springfield in 1809,

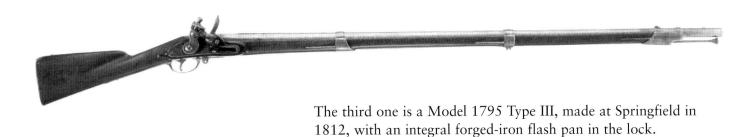

The third one is a Model 1795 Type III, made at Springfield in 1812, with an integral forged-iron flash pan in the lock.

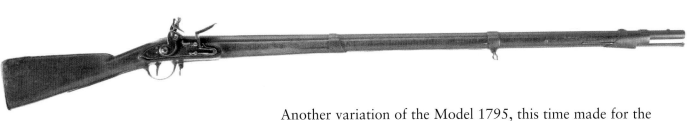

Another variation of the Model 1795, this time made for the U.S. Navy as the Model 1797 Ship's Musket, and which was used on board warships until 1819.

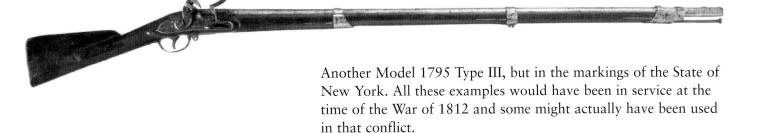

Another Model 1795 Type III, but in the markings of the State of New York. All these examples would have been in service at the time of the War of 1812 and some might actually have been used in that conflict.

# SPRINGFIELD MODEL 1861 RIFLE

## SPECIFICATIONS

**Type:** percussion rifle musket
**Origin:** National Armory, Springfield, Massachusetts
**Caliber:** .58
**Barrel Length:** 40in

Over one million of this percussion rifle were produced during the Civil War years, and together with its British Enfield counterpart they armed over 40 per cent of the fighting men in that conflict. This "Springfield Rifle" was well-balanced, reasonably light, reliable and deadly effective in the right hands. Unlike the Model 1855 it no longer made use of the Maynard system, but instead relied on more conventional separate brass primer caps. Thousands of Model 1861s were also made by individual contractors, and a selection are of shown here.

One manufactured by Jenks.

A Parker's Snow rifle.

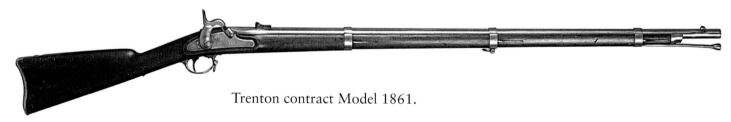

Trenton contract Model 1861.

Trenton close-up.

Bridesburg contract rifle.

## SPRINGFIELD JOSLYN RIFLE

**SPECIFICATIONS**
**Type:** breechloading rifle
**Origin:** National Armory, Springfield, Massachusetts
**Caliber:** .56-50 Spencer
**Barrel Length:** 35.5in

Benjamin F. Joslyn was one of the seemingly inexhaustible supply of inventors with which American was blessed in the 19th century. He had many firearms patents to his credit, one of which led to this rifle, the first true breechloading weapon to be manufactured at the Springfield Armory and issued to the army. The device consisted of a cylindrical section, about two inches long, which fitted on to the end of the barrel. It was hinged on the left and was lifted by a knob to enable a cartridge to be inserted into the chamber, and then closed again. It was a simple and reliable system and 30,007 actions were bought in late 1864 and used in these rifles, which in other respects resembled the Springfield Model 1863 muzzleloading rifle. Because the barrel was some 3 inches shorter than that for the Model 1863, the Joslyn rifle had a new bayonet, two inches longer, to maintain the infantryman's "reach." Approximately 50 percent of these rifles were converted to .50-70 centerfire and sold to the French army in 1870.

## SPRINGFIELD ALLIN "TRAPDOOR" RIFLES

By the end of the Civil War, the US Army had realized that the infantry urgently needed a breech-loading rifle, but funds were urgently needed to rebuild the country after the devastation of war and government funds were short. In addition, there was a huge surplus of muzzle-loaders left over from the war. This problem was overcome by Edwin S. Allin, the Master Armorer at the Springfield Armory who devised and patented the "trapdoor" mechanism where the weapon was opened by means of a front-hinged lifting block on the top of the breech, which was raised to enable a new round to be loaded. Some 30,000 existing rifles and carbines were modified in what was known as the "Allin conversion," but once that program had been completed new rifles and carbines were designed from scratch incorporating the Allin "trapdoor." The first of these was the US Model 1868 which was followed by the Models 1873, 1879, 1880, 1884 and 1889, each of which incorporated only minor changes over its predecessor.

We show one of the earliest Springfield Model 1866 Allin Conversions, which had started life as a muzzle loader.

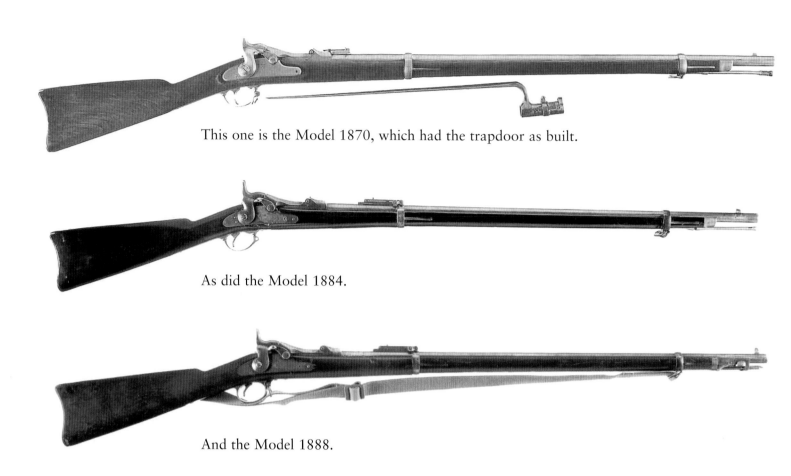

This one is the Model 1870, which had the trapdoor as built.

As did the Model 1884.

And the Model 1888.

# SPRINGFIELD "OFFICER'S MODEL" 1875 RIFLE

**SPECIFICATIONS**

**Type:** breechloading single shot cartridge rifle

**Origin:** National Armory, Springfield, Massachusetts

**Caliber:** .45-70

**Barrel Length:** 26in

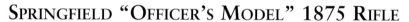

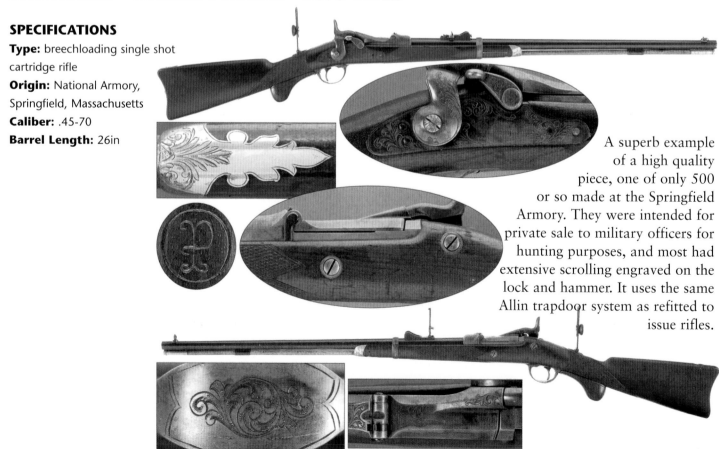

A superb example of a high quality piece, one of only 500 or so made at the Springfield Armory. They were intended for private sale to military officers for hunting purposes, and most had extensive scrolling engraved on the lock and hammer. It uses the same Allin trapdoor system as refitted to issue rifles.

## SPRINGFIELD INDIAN CARBINE

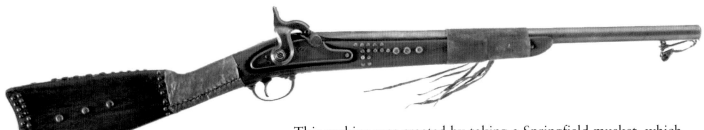

**SPECIFICATIONS**

**Type:** breech-loading carbine
**Origin:** National Armory, Springfield
**Caliber:** .63
**Barrel Length:** 21.75in

This carbine was created by taking a Springfield musket, which would have had a barrel some 44 inches long, and cutting off the front portion to produce a barrel 21.75 inches long. The forearm was suitably shortened and held in place by a single barrel band, covered by a length of cloth, sewn with sinew. There are no sights, as the foresight was discarded with the muzzle, while the holes for the rear sight having been filled in. In common with most Indian weapons of this period, the woodwork has been decorated with patterns of brass tacks.

## SPRINGFIELD MODEL 1879 CARBINE

**SPECIFICATIONS**

**Type:** trapdoor carbine
**Origin:** National Armory, Springfield
**Caliber:** .45-70
**Barrel Length:** 22in

The Model 1873 Cavalry Carbine and its successor the Model 1879 were both made as original Allin trapdoor models. They were also the standard weapons of the US Cavalry in the Indian Wars of the 1870s and 1880s.

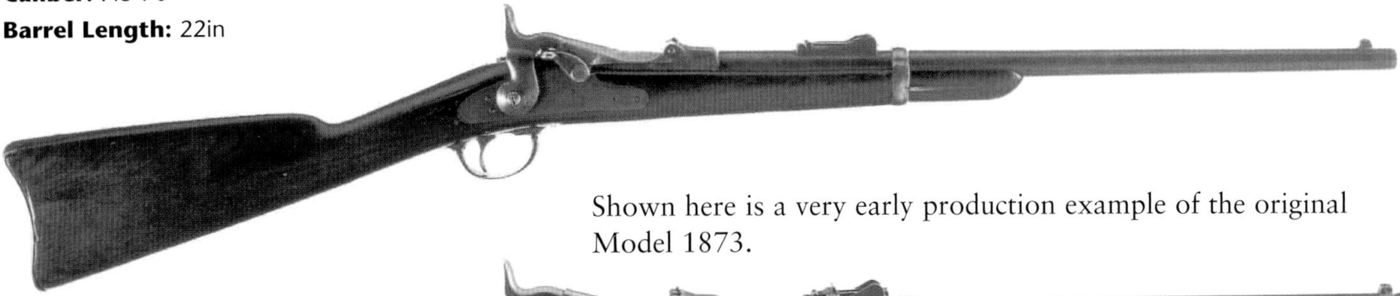

Shown here is a very early production example of the original Model 1873.

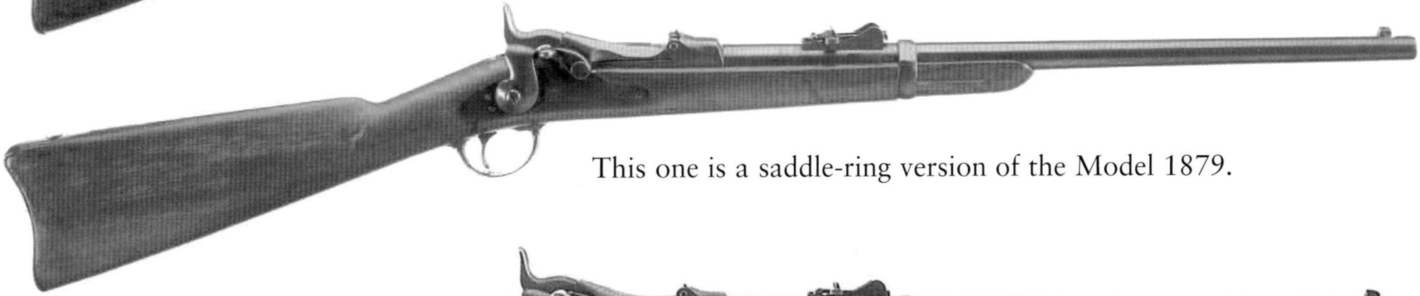

This one is a saddle-ring version of the Model 1879.

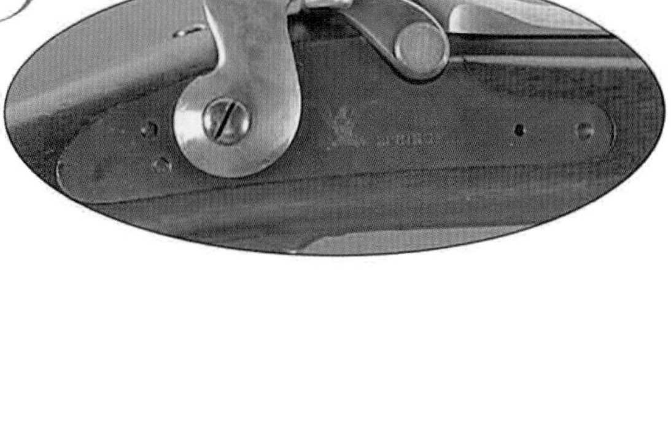

Here we have a particularly fine Model 1879, completed in 1880, which appears to have been neither issued nor fired.

## SPRINGFIELD MODEL 1892 KRAG RIFLE

**SPECIFICATIONS**
**Type:** bolt-action, magazine-fed rifle
**Origin:** Krag and Jørgensen, Norway and Springfield Armory, Massachusetts
**Caliber:** .30-40
**Barrel Length:** 30in

The birth of the Krag-Jørgensen rifle in Norway has already been covered, but this section describes its career in the United States in more detail. The U.S. Army held a competition, which started in 1890, to find a bolt-action, magazine rifle, which would be suitable for service as the basic infantry weapon. More than fifty weapons, many of them minor variations from the same maker, were assembled and subjected to trials, which eventually narrowed down to a choice of three: Krag No.5, Lee No. 3; and Mauser No. 5 which were virtually equal in all respects. Because a choice had to be made, the army finally settled on the Krag on the grounds that its magazine could be recharged while the bolt was closed.

The weapon was put into production, with further minor modifications, as the "U.S. Magazine Rifle, Caliber .30, Model of 1892," with assembly beginning at the National Armory, Springfield on January 1, 1894, although deliveries did not start until October that year.

Seen here is an original Model 1892 with some of the many modifications made in army workshops during its military service.

## SPRINGFIELD M1896 KRAG CAVALRY CARBINE

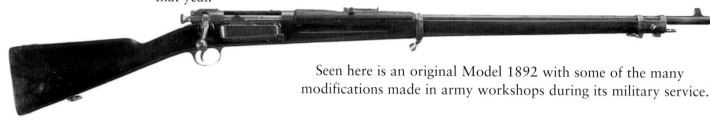

The first experimental Krag carbines were made in 1893 by shortening the M1892 rifle barrel by some eight inches and fixing a saddle ring on the left side of the rifle's wrist. In addition, the carbine's nose-cap did not have a bayonet-ring and the cleaning rod, which was too long to fit under the barrel, was housed in the stock. Development continued until 1895 when the design was finalized and then accepted into service as the Model 1896 Cavalry Carbine, seen here. These had the same action and sights as the infantry rifle, but the barrel was only 22 inches long and the forearm was much shorter; a bar-mounted saddle-ring was on the left side, as usual. Issued in 1896/7, the Model 1896 carbine had a rather short service life, being withdrawn from regular units in 1901 and passed on to militia units.

**SPECIFICATIONS**
**Type:** bolt-action, magazine-fed carbine
**Origin:** Springfield Armory, USA.
**Caliber:** .30-40
**Barrel Length:** 22in

## SPRINGFIELD M1899 KRAG CARBINE

The Model 1898 cavalry carbine, like the Model 1898 rifle, was intended to fire the new high velocity bullet, but when this proved too powerful for the bolt it was withdrawn and only about 5,000 carbines were completed. Attention then turned to the Model 1899

**SPECIFICATIONS**

**Type:** bolt-action, magazine-fed carbine
**Origin:** National Armory, Springfield, Massachusetts
**Caliber:** .30-40
**Barrel Length:** 22in

cavalry carbine, which was derived from the Model 1898 carbine, but with the fore-end lengthened by about three inches and fitted with the M1896 rear sight. This was later replaced, as with the rifle, by the M1902 sight.

## SPRINGFIELD M1898 KRAG RIFLE

The M1898 was the result of a major review of the earlier models; the new pattern was approved in March 1989 and deliveries began in July, although they did not actually reach the troops until October 1899. The most significant aspect of this was the simultaneous introduction of a new high velocity cartridge, which gave the weapon a theoretical range of 2,000 yards, but the new round lasted only a few months when it was discovered that it caused breakages in the bolt locking-lugs. New sights were also fitted on the M1898 as issued, but these were replaced in 1901, by yet another type. Shown here is a standard M1898, but with an M1902 rear sight.

**SPECIFICATIONS**

**Type:** bolt-action, magazine-fed rifle
**Origin:** National Armory, Springfield, Massachusetts
**Caliber:** .30-40
**Barrel Length:** 30in

This one has the original factory-fitted M1898 rear sight

## SPRINGFIELD MODEL 1896 KRAG RIFLE

This was the rifle that equipped most of the U.S. Infantry and Marine Corps units during the Spanish-American war. There were eventually some forty official modifications to the Model 1892 and these were all incorporated into a new production version, the Model 1896. This new version also introduced a completely new backsight with a continuously curved base, which was graduated from 250 yards up to a maximum of 600 yards. In addition, the cleaning rod, which had been a single-piece carried under the barrel in the M1892, could now be disassembled into three sections and carried in a butt-trap.

This one is in excellent condition and has the original M1896 sights. The triangular-shaped object was a used to open the loading-gate, which turned down through 90 degrees, enabling the shooter to load up to five rounds which then lay in a row beneath the bolt and were fed into the gun from the left. The hinged loading-gate door also served to prevent rounds being dropped whilst loading.

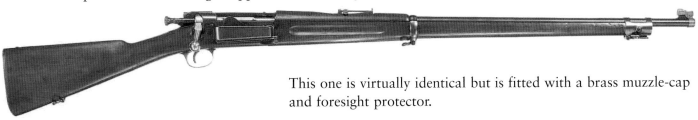

This one is virtually identical but is fitted with a brass muzzle-cap and foresight protector.

## SPRINGFIELD M1903 MARK 1

One of the most important tactical requirements revealed by the U.S. Army's experience in World War One was the need to increase the infantry's firepower, particularly when advancing across "no-man's land". One method of achieving this was the "Pedersen device" which could be inserted, when required, into a modified M1903 to transform the rifle into a semi-automatic, and trials and demonstrations were greeted with great enthusiasm. As a result, the M1903 Mark 1 was developed, which had minor modifications including an ejection port cut into the left side of the receiver, and small changes to the trigger mechanism and to the cut-off. Use in this role required a special round which was fed into the rifle from a 40-round box magazine which stuck out of the top of the rifle, offset slightly to the right.

Orders for 500,000 converted rifles and the associated "Pedersen devices" were immediately placed, but no deliveries had been made by the time the war ended in November 1918. The "Pedersen devices" were kept in store, never used and were scrapped in the early 1930s. Some 100,000 rifles had been converted when the order was canceled and these were issued and used as normal rifles until they wore out. The two examples seen here are both Mark 1 conversions, the clearest evidence of which would be the ejection port on the left side.

## SPRINGFIELD MODEL 1903 SNIPER RIFLES

In 1907 experiments began with a telescopic sight developed by the Warner & Swasey company of Cleveland, Ohio, which led to an order for 1,000 sights under the designation "Telescopic Musket Sights, Model of 1908." These 6x prismatic sights were issued on a trials basis in 1910 but soon proved to be unpopular, being clumsy and uncomfortable, and, even worse, their optical performance was poor. An improved version was then designed which was accepted as the "Model of 1913," with 5.2x magnification, which is seen mounted on an M1903 sniper rifle in this example. Some of the Model 1908 and Model 1913 sights were issued to units in France in 1917–18, but the troops did not like them and they were little used. Thus, the U.S. Army came to accept that the prismatic telescopic sight was greatly inferior to straight tube versions, but the war was over before a satisfactory sight could be produced. This saga represents one of the few failures in the M1903 story.

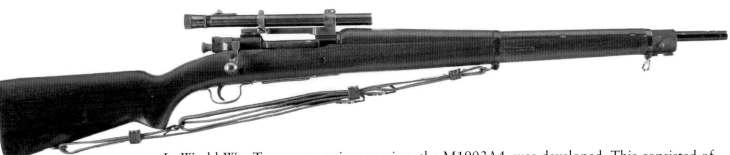

In World War Two a new sniper version, the M1903A4, was developed. This consisted of the M1903A3 action, with a specially selected barrel with two-groove rifling, and a stock with a special pistol grip. The scope was a 2.5x militarized version of the Weaver 330C, designated the M73B1, on a Redfield mount. About 26,000 were produced in 1943–44.

---

# SPRINGFIELD MODEL 1903A3

## SPECIFICATIONS

**Type:** bolt-action, magazine-fed rifle
**Origin:** National Armory, Springfield, Massachusetts
**Caliber:** .30-06
**Barrel Length:** 24in

With the outbreak of World War Two there was a requirement for infantry rifles in vast numbers and the M1903 was re-engineered to make it more suitable for mass production in the quantities now required. Sheet-metal stampings were substituted for machined parts wherever feasible, but the most obvious external changes were the deletion of the leaf backsight on top of the barrel and its replacement by an aperture sight atop the receiver bridge, and the deletion of the grasping groove for the fingers on the forestock. The new sight, which was adjustable for windage, was graduated up to 800yd. About 950,000 of these weapons were produced between 1942 and 1944, when production switched to the semi-automatic M1 Garand rifle. Two examples are shown here.

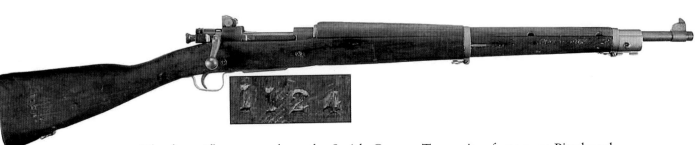

The first rifle was made at the Smith-Corona Typewriter factory at Pittsburgh, Pennsylvania, and delivered in July 1944.

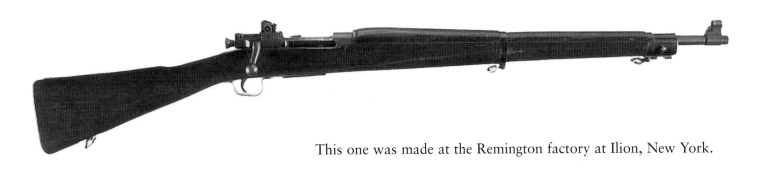

This one was made at the Remington factory at Ilion, New York.

## STEVENS MODEL 416

### SPECIFICATIONS

**Type:** single-shot, bolt action target rifle
**Origin:** J. Stevens Arms Co., Chicopee Falls, Massachusetts
**Caliber:** .22 LR
**Barrel Length:** 26in

The Stevens Model 416–2 was a medium-weight, target-quality rifle, which was introduced in 1938 for civilian target shooting. The armed forces also used .22 caliber for basic marksmanship training and a total of 10,338 were purchased from Stevens between 1941 and 1943, at a cost of $17.98 per weapon. The government also bought similar models from Mossberg, Remington, and Winchester. The two weapons seen here are both Model 416s fitted with Lyman sights on the receiver.

## STEVENS MODEL 414

### SPECIFICATIONS

**Type:** single-shot, bolt action target rifle
**Origin:** J. Stevens Arms Co., Chicopee Falls, Massachusetts
**Caliber:** .22 Short
**Barrel Length:** 26in

The Model 414, also known as the "Armory Model," was produced between 1912 and 1932 in .22 caliber only. It had the same action as the Stevens Model 44, with a Rocky Mountain foresight. It was usually fitted with a Lyman receiver sight, but this example has a Malcolm scope on saddle mounts. The forearm and short, large diameter handgrip is unusual.

## STEVENS MODEL 425

From 1910 until stopped by the switch to war production in 1917, Stevens produced some 26,000 high-powered hunting rifles in the 400-series: Models 425, 430, 435 and 440. These were lever-action weapons, all with a 22 inch barrel, but chambering either .25, .30-30, .32 or the .35 cartridge. The significance of the numbers was that the higher the number, the better the standard of finish and quality of components. The example shown here is a Model 425, chambered for .35 Remington and with simple iron sights.

Specifications
**Type:** single-shot, lever action hunting rifle
**Origin:** J. Stevens Arms Co., Chicopee Falls, Massachusetts
**Caliber:** .35 Remington
**Barrel Length:** 22in

## STEVENS POCKET RIFLE

No matter what system is used to classify weapons there are always a few which do not fit neatly into any particular category and this is certainly true of the so-called "pocket rifles." They look like pistols, but have a metal-framed butt which, when attached, means that they look like and are fired from the shoulder as rifles. Stevens made a variety of such weapons from 1869 onwards, with a single-shot, tip-up action, in calibers ranging from .22 to .45, and with barrel lengths up to 18 inches in length. The example seen here, the Model 40, was one of the most popular, with some 15,000 sold between 1896 and 1916. It is chambered for the .22 round, has a 10 inch, part octagonal barrel. The Model 40_ was identical to the Model 40 except for the addition of a vernier rear sight mounted on the back strap.

**SPECIFICATIONS**
**Type:** single-shot pistol/rifle
**Origin:** J. Stevens Arms Co., Chicopee Falls, Massachusetts
**Caliber:** .22
**Barrel Length:** 10in

## STEVENS LADIES MODEL 14 RIFLE

This was one of the most popular of Stevens' series of ladies rifles and was generally considered to be the best looking. It has a 24 inch, lightweight barrel and is chambered for the .25-20 cartridge. The barrel is fitted with iron sights, but there is also a vernier sight mounted on the tang. All parts of the action are high-quality nickel-plated, as are the forearm knuckle, trigger guard and butt-plate.

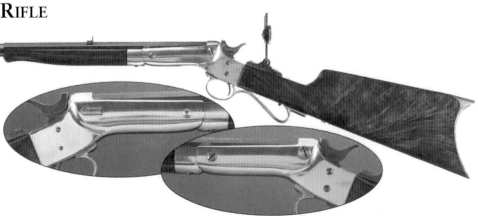

**SPECIFICATIONS**
**Type:** single-shot, tip-up rifle
**Origin:** J. Stevens Arms Co., Chicopee Falls, Massachusetts
**Caliber:** .25-20 Single-shot
**Barrel Length:** 24in

## STEVENS-POPE MODEL 54

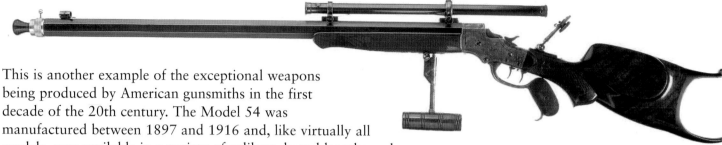

This is another example of the exceptional weapons being produced by American gunsmiths in the first decade of the 20th century. The Model 54 was manufactured between 1897 and 1916 and, like virtually all models, was available in a variety of calibers, barrel lengths and finishes. This example has the Stevens Model 44 action/frame, which is covered in elaborate scroll-work. The heavyweight, fully octagonal, Stevens-Pope barrel is 30 inches long and is fitted with a false muzzle. Sights comprise a globe front sight, Stevens windage adjustable, vernier backsight, and a Stevens Number 487 telescopic sight. The heavy butt has a Swiss-style Schützen butt-plate and a T-handled palm-rest is suspended from the forearm. The weapon is accompanied by a full set of tools which include a buller starter, hickory loading rod, re/de-capper, bullet mold, bullet lubricator, powder measure, and brass drop tube extension.

**SPECIFICATIONS**
**Type:** single-shot, target rifle
**Origin:** J. Stevens Arms Co., Chicopee Falls, Massachusetts
**Caliber:** .32-40
**Barrel Length:** 30in

## TRIPLETT & SCOTT RIFLE AND CARBINE

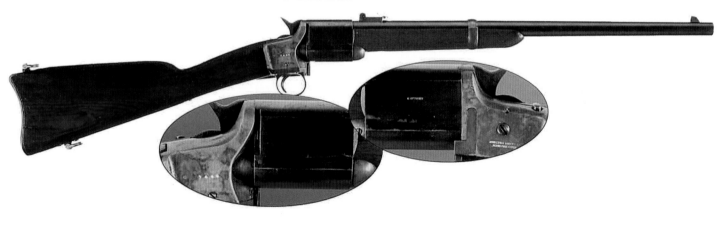

**SPECIFICATIONS**
**Type:** magazine-fed, repeating rifle and carbine
**Origin:** Meriden Manufacturing, Meriden, Connecticut
**Caliber:** .50 Spencer
**Barrel Length:** 20/30in

Louis Triplett of Columbia, Kentucky, and a co-worker named Scott were awarded a patent in December 1864 for a "magazine or self-loading fire-arm." As a result, their home state of Kentucky placed an order for 5,000 of these rifles which were made by the Meriden Company. The two examples shown here are both chambered for the .50 Spencer round, but one has a 22 inch barrel and the other a 30 inch barrel. The Triplett & Scott system was unique and consisted of a barrel assembly which rotated to the right to load from a tubular magazine in the butt-stock. As far as is known no other orders were placed and this somewhat complicated solution to the repeater rifle requirement was not pursued further.

# UNIVERSAL FIREARMS MODEL 3000 ENFORCER CARBINE

## SPECIFICATIONS
**Type:** M1-based carbine
**Origin:** Universal Firearms, Sacksonville, Arkansas
**Caliber:** .30
**Barrel Length:** 11in

Arkansas-based Universal Firearms has made a series of weapons based on the US M1 carbine. The first, the Model 1000 was a direct copy with an 18 inch barrel, and was followed by further full-size copies but with differing barrel lengths and finishes, ranging from blued, through nickel- and gold-plated to the Model 1020 with a Teflon finish. The Model 3000 Enforcer, however, is a redesign, which uses the M1 action, but with an 11 inch barrel, a vented barrel cover, extended forearm and pistol grip, and without a stock-butt. It is difficult to classify being rather large for a pistol and lacking the full automatic capability usually associated with a sub-machine gun. Whatever the correct term, it packs a lot of firepower in a very small envelope.

# VIRGINIA MANUFACTORY FIRST MODEL RIFLE

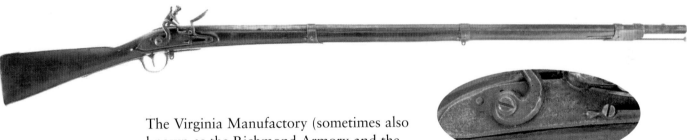

The Virginia Manufactory (sometimes also known as the Richmond Armory and the Virginia State Armory) was established in 1797 to produce weapons for the Virginia State Militia. Production took place between 1802 and 1820, when the building was turned over to a school. The weapon seen here was the first design to be manufactured there and some 14,000 were completed between 1802 and 1809, and is typical of designs of the time. Many of these were still around at the time of the Civil War and were pressed into service by the Confederacy, usually with troops on secondary duties. The former Virginia Manufactory was also returned to its arms-making business in 1860 using machinery assembled from various sources to produce "Richmond rifles."

## SPECIFICATIONS
**Type:** flintlock musket
**Origin:** Virginia Manufactory, Richmond, Virginia
**Caliber:** .69
**Barrel Length:** 44in

## WEATHERBY MARK V RIFLES

Roy Weatherby founded his company in Atascadero, California in 1945 to produce top quality, high velocity rifles, mainly firing cartridges also made to his own design, although other calibers are also catered for. His rifles were originally produced in the former West Germany and a few in Italy, but all production recently moved to Japan, although without any loss in quality or craftsmanship. The Mark V is a bolt-action rifle with a Mauser action that has been produced in a large number of versions, covering many calibers and barrel lengths. This entry is designed to illustrate the wide variety of custom finishes available for one design from a leading gunmaker such Weatherby.

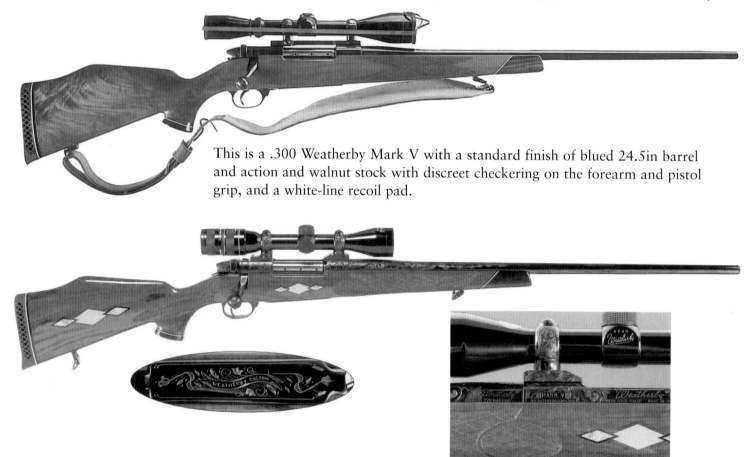

This is a .300 Weatherby Mark V with a standard finish of blued 24.5in barrel and action and walnut stock with discreet checkering on the forearm and pistol grip, and a white-line recoil pad.

A custom .378 Weatherby model with 26in barrel and much more elaborate checkering, jeweled bolts, patterned inlays on forearm and butt, as well as rosewood forearm and pistol-grip caps.

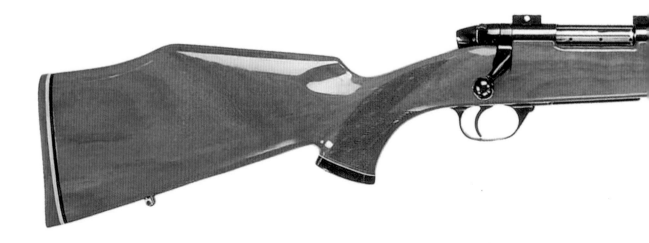

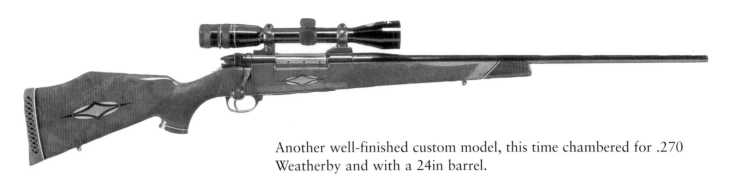

Another well-finished custom model, this time chambered for .270 Weatherby and with a 24in barrel.

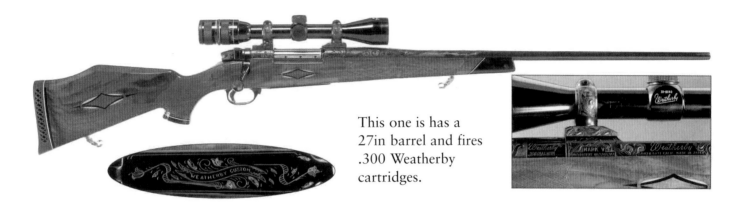

This one is has a 27in barrel and fires .300 Weatherby cartridges.

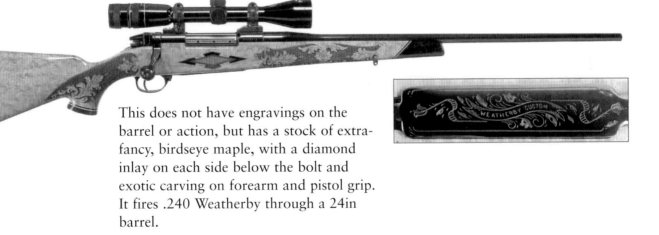

This does not have engravings on the barrel or action, but has a stock of extra-fancy, birdseye maple, with a diamond inlay on each side below the bolt and exotic carving on forearm and pistol grip. It fires .240 Weatherby through a 24in barrel.

A Mark V Varmintmaster, with 24in barrel and chambered for .224 Weatherby, another example of straightforward, but extremely well executed, finish, with minimal checkering, no engraving, but all to the highest possible standard.

## WEATHERBY CROWN CUSTOM

As with the Weatherby Mark V entry, these two rifles show what modern engravers and carvers are capable of when customising gunmakers' products. Both are Crown Custom models with identical bolt-actions and both are fitted with a Weatherby Premier 3x–9x telescopic sight. They both also have damascened bolts, rosewood caps to the pistol grip and to the forearm tip. The differences lie in the engraving on the barrel, receiver and floor plate, on the intricacy of the carving on the forearm and butt, and the contrasting wood inlays on one of them. They are weapons of which any owner would be proud.

## WEATHERBY MARK XXII

The Type XXII was a semi-automatic .22 caliber weapon with a 24 inch barrel, which was originally produced in an Italian factory, and later in Japan. It was available in two versions: one, seen here, had a detachable box magazine, the other a tubular magazine. Although functional in appearance, it had good quality walnut furniture and blued barrel and action, with discreet checkering on the forearm and pistol grip, and a rosewood cap on the pistol grip. Production ended some years ago.

**SPECIFICATIONS**
**Type:** semi-automatic rifle
**Origin:** Roy Weatherby, Atascadero, California
**Caliber:** .22 LR
**Barrel Length:** 24in

## WEAVER NIGHTHAWK CARBINE

**SPECIFICATIONS**
**Type:** semi-automatic carbine
**Origin:** Roy Weaver Arms, Escondido, California
**Caliber:** 9mm Parabellum
**Barrel Length:** 16.5in

The Nighthawk semi-automatic carbine was designed in 1983 and made use of a telescoping wire stock together with a contoured wooden foregrip to assist in accurate shooting. It employed a simple blowback system,

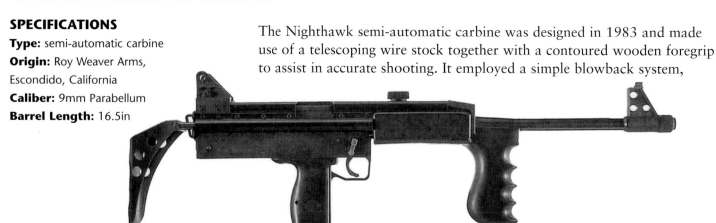

fired 9mm Parabellum ammunition and had a 25-round box magazine, which fitted into the pistol-grip. It enjoyed some success in the 1980s, but sales fell away in the early 1990s. Encouraged by the Nighthawk's initial success, Weaver experimented in the mid-1980s with a selective-fire version, designated PKS-9 Ultralite, which was intended for the law enforcement community, but it only achieved a few sales. The company went bankrupt in the early 1990s.

## WEISS RIFLE

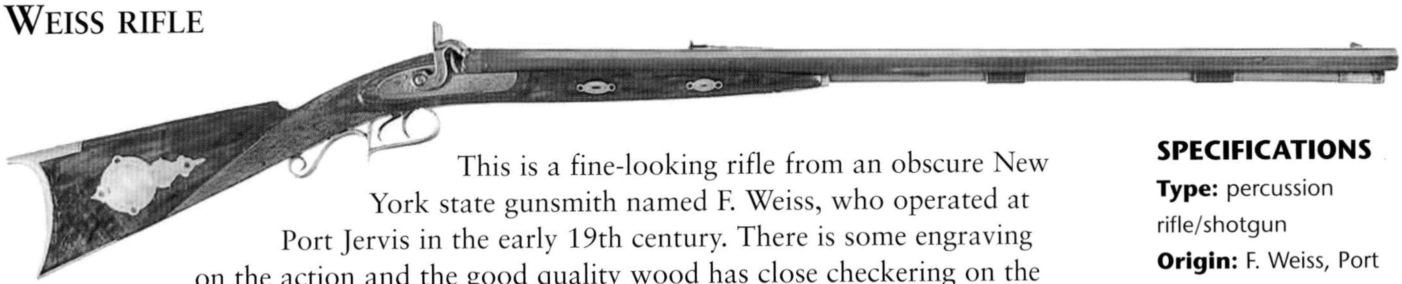

This is a fine-looking rifle from an obscure New York state gunsmith named F. Weiss, who operated at Port Jervis in the early 19th century. There is some engraving on the action and the good quality wood has close checkering on the wrist. There are small brass plates on the forearm and a large brass patch box on the butt (which still contains some chamois patches).

**SPECIFICATIONS**
**Type:** percussion rifle/shotgun
**Origin:** F. Weiss, Port Jervis, New York
**Caliber:** .46/12 gauge
**Barrel Length:** 33.75in

## FRANK WESSON MILITARY CARBINE

**SPECIFICATIONS**
**Type:** tip-up, breechloading carbine
**Origin:** Frank Wesson, Worcester, Massachusetts
**Caliber:** .44RF
**Barrel Length:** 24in

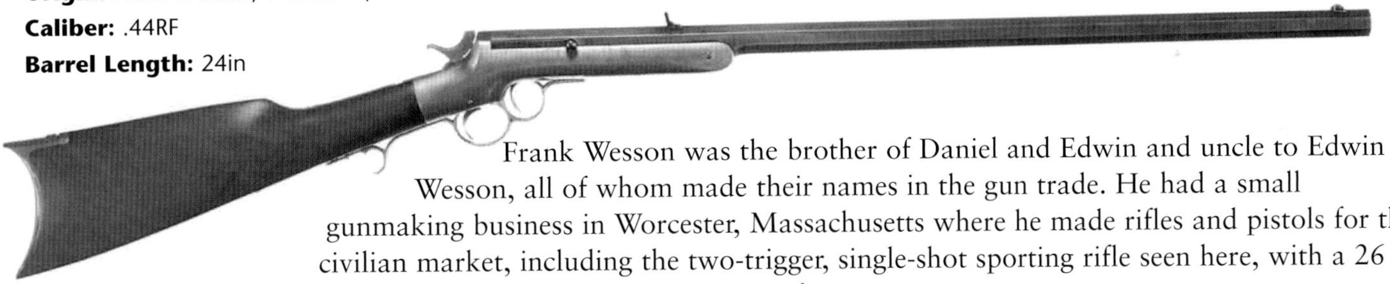

Frank Wesson was the brother of Daniel and Edwin and uncle to Edwin Wesson, all of whom made their names in the gun trade. He had a small gunmaking business in Worcester, Massachusetts where he made rifles and pistols for the civilian market, including the two-trigger, single-shot sporting rifle seen here, with a 26 inch barrel and chambered for .38 rimfire.

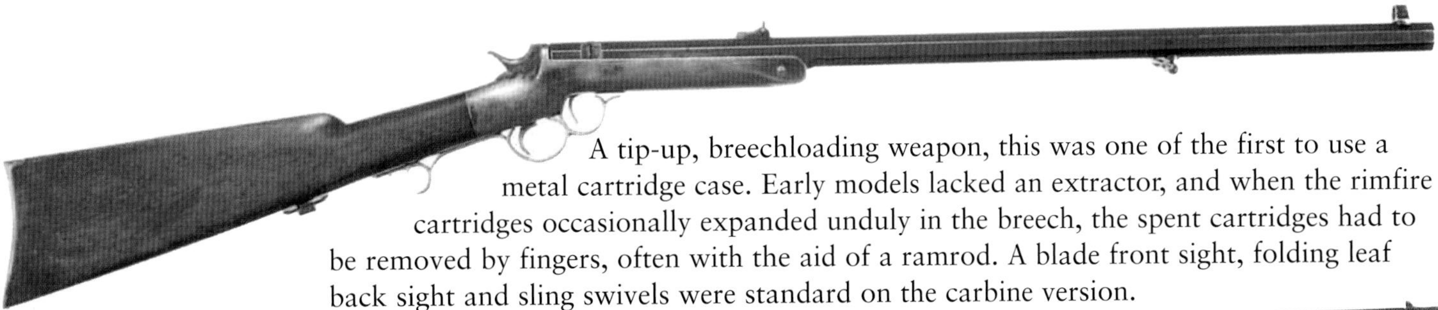

A tip-up, breechloading weapon, this was one of the first to use a metal cartridge case. Early models lacked an extractor, and when the rimfire cartridges occasionally expanded unduly in the breech, the spent cartridges had to be removed by fingers, often with the aid of a ramrod. A blade front sight, folding leaf back sight and sling swivels were standard on the carbine version.

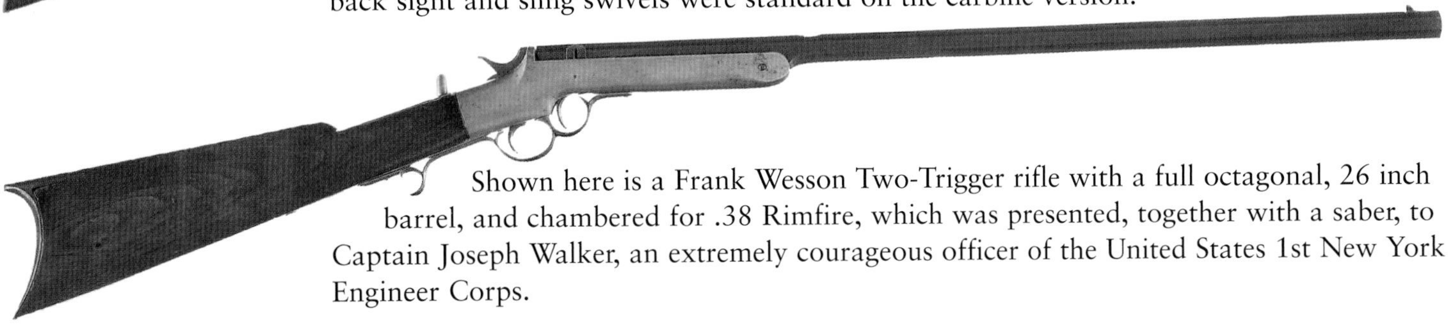

Shown here is a Frank Wesson Two-Trigger rifle with a full octagonal, 26 inch barrel, and chambered for .38 Rimfire, which was presented, together with a saber, to Captain Joseph Walker, an extremely courageous officer of the United States 1st New York Engineer Corps.

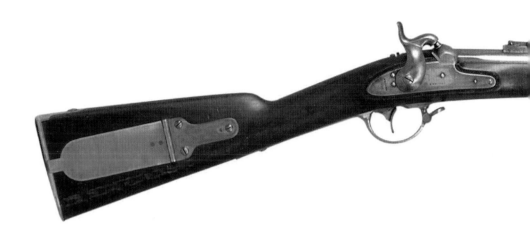

## FRANK WESSON, POCKET RIFLE

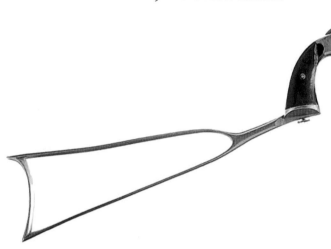

Like the Stevens pocket rifle (*see above*), the Wesson Pocket Rifle was a hybrid – part pistol, part rifle. Wesson produced eight discrete models between 1865 and about 1880, with calibers varying from .22 to .44, and barrel lengths of up to 24 inches, but mostly they were classified according to whether they had small, medium or large frames. The weapon seen here has an 18 inch octagonal barrel and is chambered for the .32 rimfire cartridge.

## WHITNEY MODEL 1822 PERCUSSION CONVERSION

### SPECIFICATIONS
**Type:** single shot percussion musket
**Origin:** Whitneyville Armory, New Haven, Connecticut
**Caliber:** .69
**Barrel Length:** 42in

The Whitney company produced some 39,000 of these flintlock muskets from 1822 to 1841, based on the Model 1816 with minor modifications. Eli Whitney Sr. died in 1824, before the first muskets were delivered, and the company was run for most of this time by Philos and Eli Whitney Blake, his nephews. The musket shown here has been converted to percussion firing using the "Belgian" method.

## WHITNEY MODEL 1841 MISSISSIPPI

### SPECIFICATIONS

**Type:** single shot percussion rifle
**Origin:** Whitneyville Armory, New Haven, Connecticut
**Caliber:** .54
**Barrel Length:** 33in

This rifle was made by Whitney from 1843–55 and was the first contract taken up by Eli Whitney Jr. after he took over the company from the Blakes. It may have only had a 33 inch barrel, but as it was developed to fire the Minie expanding bullet it was effective and accurate at long ranges. Over 26,500 were delivered.

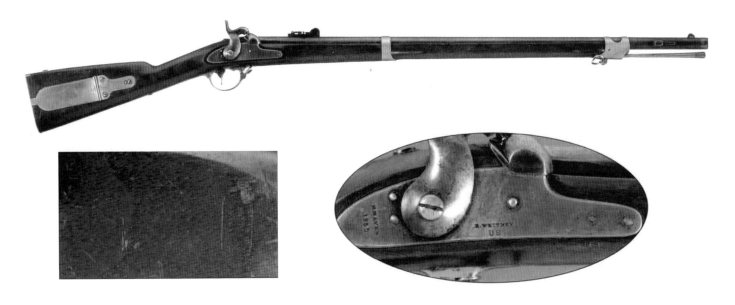

## WHITNEY 1861 NAVY PERCUSSION (PLYMOUTH RIFLE)

### SPECIFICATIONS

**Type:** single shot percussion musket
**Origin:** Whitneyville Armory, New Haven, Connecticut
**Caliber:** .69
**Barrel Length:** 34in

This rifle was developed at the instigation of Captain John Dahlgren, an Ordnance officer for the US. Navy. Much of the development was undertaken on board the ordnance trials ship USS Plymouth, hence the name given to the rifle. Whitney delivered 10,000 of these rifles from 1861–64 and they proved to be accurate and effective. Note the large folding rearsight on this example.

# WINCHESTER MODEL 1866

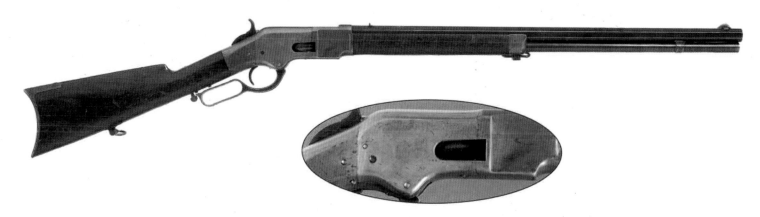

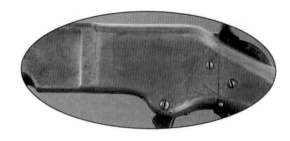

## SPECIFICATIONS

**Type:** tubular magazine, lever-action
rifle/musket/carbine
**Origin:** Winchester Repeating Arms Company,
New Haven, Connecticut
**Caliber:** .44 Henry
**Barrel:** see text

The Model 1860 Henry rifle represented some significant advances, the most important being that the sixteen-round magazine gave the shooter a major increase in firepower. It also, however, suffered from some drawbacks, several of which had tactical implications. The first was the shooter's forehand held the barrel, which became very hot in a prolonged engagement. The second, and more important, was that the tubular magazine had to be disengaged and reloaded from the front, which meant that the weapon had to be taken out of action and engage the shooter's attention until the task had been completed. Thirdly, the magazine had slots, which allowed dirt to enter.

The company changed its name from the New Haven Arms Company to the Henry Repeating Rifle Company in 1865 and to the Winchester Repeating Arms Company in 1866. This meant that when these problems were overcome in a new model which was introduced that year, it carried the now legendary name of the "Winchester Model 1866."

The heating problem was overcome very simply – the weapon was fitted with a forearm so that the shooter's hand never came into contact with the barrel. The ammunition solution was simple from the shooter's point-of-view, but more complicated for the engineers, because the works foreman at the Winchester factory redesigned the gun so that the magazine tube was fixed and rounds were pushed in through a spring-loaded loading-gate at the rear. The result was that the shooter could keep his eye on the battle and hold his weapon in the aiming position with his left hand, while reloading with his right. This also meant that the slots were deleted.

The Model 1866 was in production from 1866 to 1898, during which time some 170,000 were completed. These were split into three main types: carbine, with round barrel (127,000); sporting rifle (28,000) with either round or octagonal barrel; and musket, with round barrel (14,000). All were chambered for the .44 round, either flat or pointed rimfire. There were also some differences in the frames and in the shape of the receiver, which are of interest mainly to the specialist collector.

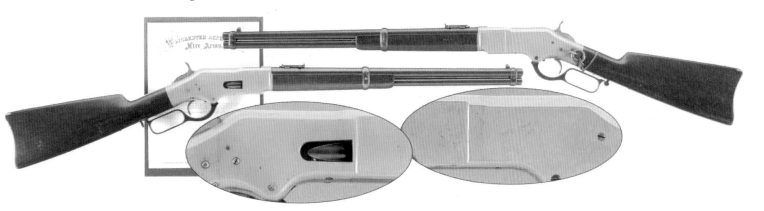

These two are sporting models, made in 1870 and 1878, respectively. Both have 24.4 inch barrels and are chambered for the .44 Henry round. Note the forearm, which solved the hand problem, the color of the brass which earned the weapon its nickname of "the yellow boy" and the loading gate, which solved the reloading problem. There are a few minor differences between the two: they have slightly different rear sights, and one has sling swivels.

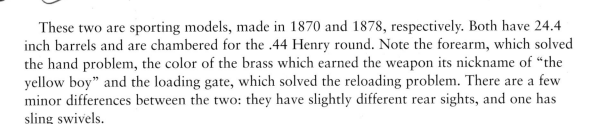

This is the saddle-ring carbine, made in 1883, with a 20 inch barrel, which resulted in a shorter magazine, reducing the capacity from seventeen rounds to thirteen. Note the saddle-ring on the left side of the weapon and the company's latter of authenticity, certifying the details of this particular weapon.

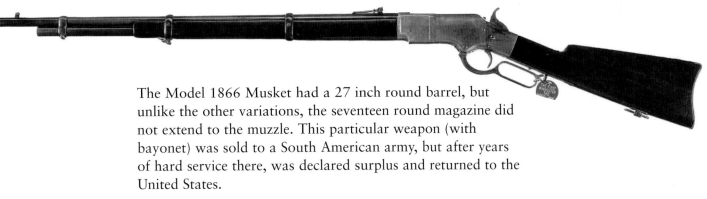

The Model 1866 Musket had a 27 inch round barrel, but unlike the other variations, the seventeen round magazine did not extend to the muzzle. This particular weapon (with bayonet) was sold to a South American army, but after years of hard service there, was declared surplus and returned to the United States.

This oddity is a precise half-scale replica of a saddle-ring carbine, made by Tom P. Weston. It is chambered for the .22 round, and loads, fires and reloads exactly as in the original.

# WINCHESTER MODEL 1873

## SPECIFICATIONS

**Type:** tubular magazine, lever-action rifle/musket/carbine

**Origin:** Winchester Repeating Arms Company, New Haven, Connecticut

**Caliber:** .44 Henry

**Barrel:** see text

The Model 1873 offered three advances over the Model 1866. First, it had a stronger frame, which was originally made of iron, but from 1884 of steel. Secondly, it had a dust-cover over the action. Thirdly, and perhaps most important of all, however, was that although other calibers were available, most were chambered for the .44-40 round, which was the same as that used in the Colt single-action revolver, thus greatly easing the user's logistical problems, particularly in the rigorous environment of the frontier. Indeed, the Model 1873 had a thoroughly well-deserved title of "The Gun That Won The West." As with the Model 1866, the Model 1873 was sold in three versions: musket with 30 inch round barrel; sporting rifle with 24 inch round, octagonal, or round/octagonal barrel; and carbine with 20 inch round barrel. There are also the usual minor changes over the production run, mainly concerning the dust-cover. In 1884, Winchester introduced a new version of the Model 1873 chambered for .22 rimfire, but it did not prove particularly popular, with some 19,000 sold over a twenty-year production run. Overall some 720,000 Model 1873s of all versions had been sold when production ended in 1919.

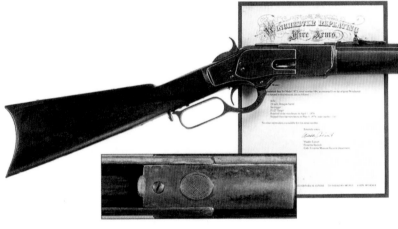

A very early production Model 1873 sporting rifle, this was shipped in 1874 and has serial number #684. It has the 24 inch octagonal barrel. The forearm has an iron cap, and the cover is shown (although this actual cover may be a replacement).

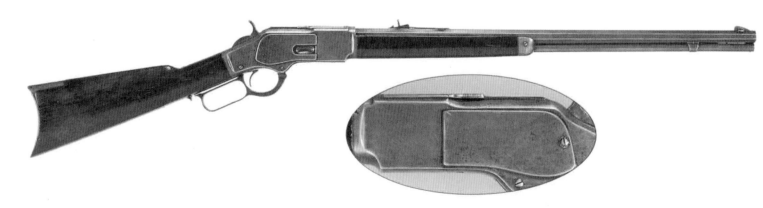

This one is also a sporting rifle with an octagonal barrel, but is what collectors call the "Third Model" with an integral central guide for the dust cover.

## WINCHESTER MODEL 1873 CARBINE AND MUSKET

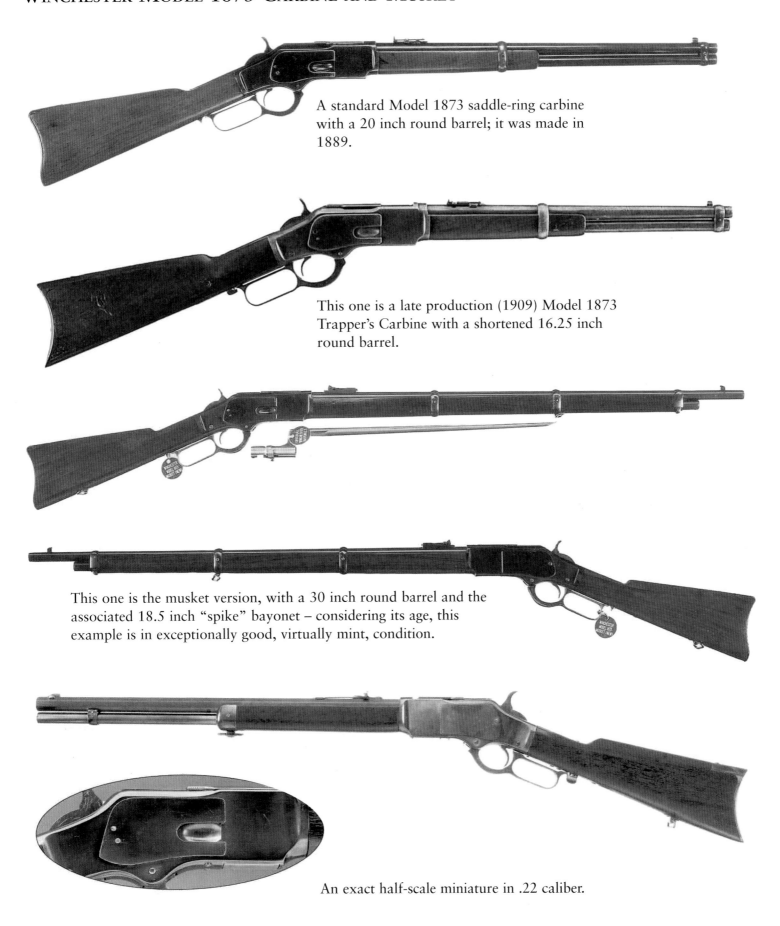

A standard Model 1873 saddle-ring carbine with a 20 inch round barrel; it was made in 1889.

This one is a late production (1909) Model 1873 Trapper's Carbine with a shortened 16.25 inch round barrel.

This one is the musket version, with a 30 inch round barrel and the associated 18.5 inch "spike" bayonet – considering its age, this example is in exceptionally good, virtually mint, condition.

An exact half-scale miniature in .22 caliber.

# WINCHESTER MODEL 1885

**SPECIFICATIONS**
**Type:** single-shot rifle
**Origin:** Winchester
Repeating Arms
Company, New Haven,
Connecticut
**Caliber:** see text
**Barrel:** see text

There were two types of frame – High Wall in which the frame covered the breech and hammer, leaving only the spur visible, and Low Wall in which the breech and hammer were visible, which was done in order to enable shorter length cartridges to be used. Both of these were available in two frame profiles – Thickside with sides that did not widen to meet the stock, and Thinside which did.

A standard Winchester Model 1885 High Wall sporting rifle, with a 30 inch. .38-55 caliber barrel and walnut stock. It has a wind gauge foresight and Lyman tang-mounted elevating peep sight; both are by Lyman. It will be observed that the frame angles upwards rather sharply to leave only the hammer spur visible – this is the "High Wall."

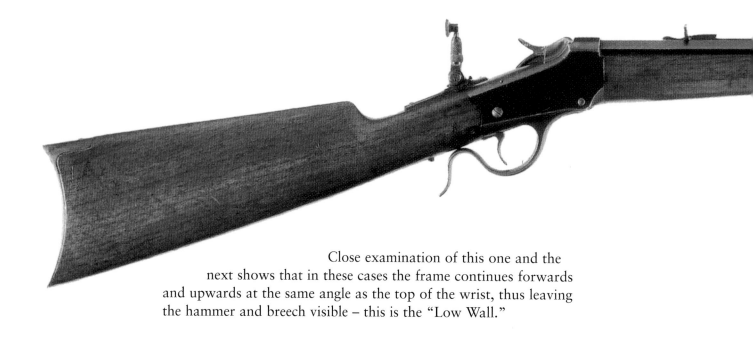

Close examination of this one and the next shows that in these cases the frame continues forwards and upwards at the same angle as the top of the wrist, thus leaving the hammer and breech visible – this is the "Low Wall."

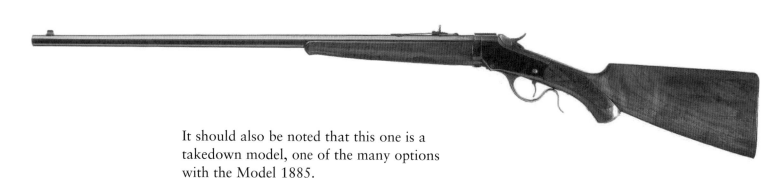

It should also be noted that this one is a takedown model, one of the many options with the Model 1885.

## WINCHESTER MODEL 1885 EXPRESS RIFLES

Express rounds and the associated rifles were designed for a very high muzzle velocity and use at comparatively short ranges – 200 yards or less – so that the round followed a more-or-less flat trajectory and also killed game as cleanly and quickly as possible. Note that all three rifles are of the High Wall variety and all are simple weapons with shotgun butts and iron sights – there was no time for telescopic sights in the game shooting these weapons were intended for.

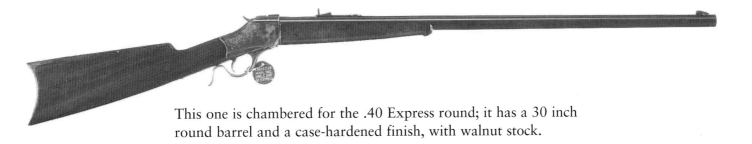

This one is chambered for the .40 Express round; it has a 30 inch round barrel and a case-hardened finish, with walnut stock.

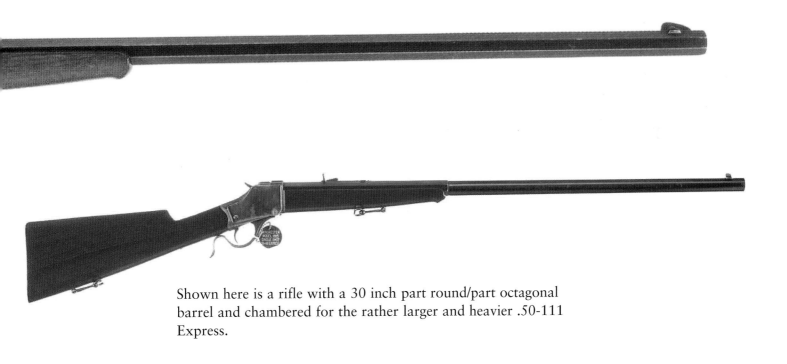

Shown here is a rifle with a 30 inch part round/part octagonal barrel and chambered for the rather larger and heavier .50-111 Express.

Another one fitted with a 30 inch round barrel, it is the only known example to be chambered for the British-made .50 Eley Express.

# WINCHESTER MODEL 1886

## SPECIFICATIONS

**Type:** lever-action rifle

**Origin:** Winchester Repeating Arms Company, New Haven, Connecticut

**Caliber:** see text

**Barrel:** see text

The Model 1886 was introduced to use the more powerful centerfire cartridges then becoming available, the design being based on a John Browning patent. As always, there was an immense range of options for the potential purchaser to choose from. To start with, there were the three basic configurations – Rifle, Musket and Carbine – with the Rifle being sub-divided into Sporting, Fancy Sporting, Takedown, Extra Lightweight and Extra Lightweight Takedown. There were also ten different calibers, ranging from .33 WCF to .50-110 Express, with the government .45-70 being the most popular. Then there were choices to be made on barrel lengths and finishes. However, buyers did make their choices and the Model 1886 quickly established an excellent reputation as a strong and reliable weapon, and it remained in production for no less than 49 years (1886–1935), during which time some 160,000 were made.

By far the most numerous was the Sporting version and this is from the first year of production (serial #569), with a half-round/half-octagonal 26 inch barrel, chambered for .45-90.

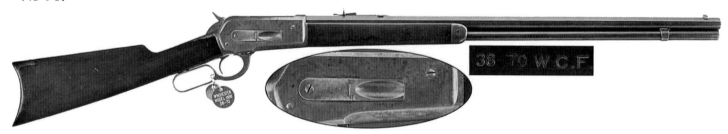

Although also a Sporting version, this one is quite rare, as it is chambered for the .38-70 WCF round, which went out of production soon after the rifle was introduced, being replaced by the smokeless .38-56. This rifle has a 28 inch octagonal barrel, fitted with basic iron sights and was shipped in 1901.

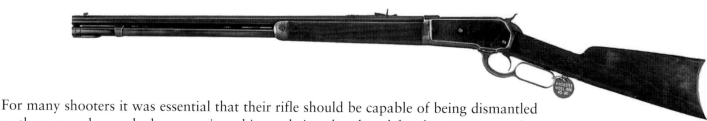

For many shooters it was essential that their rifle should be capable of being dismantled so there was also a takedown version, this one being chambered for the .45-90 round.

# WINCHESTER MODEL 1890

**SPECIFICATIONS**

**Type:** slide-action rifle

**Origin:** Winchester Repeating Arms Company,
New Haven, Connecticut

**Caliber:** .22 (see text)

**Barrel:** 24in

The Model 1890, designed by the brothers John and Matthew Browning, was Winchester's first-ever slide-action rifle and achieved world-wide popularity, with a total of 775,000 produced between 1890 and 1932. All Model 1890s had 24 inch barrels and were available in either .22 Short, .22 Long, or .22 WRF chamberings, with .22 LR being added in 1919 (the .22 WRF was developed specially for the Model 1890).

There were a number of variants. The First Model was the only solid frame version and had a very short production run, with some 15,500 being manufactured between 1809 and 1892. We show a First Model made in 1891 (serial #2482) with solid frame and chambered for .22 Short.

All subsequent Model 1890s had takedown frames; the Second Model being divided into case-hardened and blued frame versions. The picture is of the Second Model case-hardened version, also chambered for the .22 Short.

This later version Second Model has blue finish on the action; it is chambered for .22 WRF. The Third Model also had a blued frame and very minor differences in the breech locking system.

# WINCHESTER MODEL 1892

## SPECIFICATIONS

**Type:** lever-action rifle

**Origin:** Winchester Repeating Arms Company, New Haven, Connecticut

**Caliber:** see text

**Barrel:** see text

The Model 1892 was, in essence, an updated Model 1873 employing a slightly smaller version of Browning's Model 1886 action. It was available in five calibers – .218 Bee, .25-20, .32-20, .38-40 and .44-40 – and various barrel lengths appropriate to the caliber; there was also a choice of magazine sizes in some models. There were five variants: Sporting Rifle, Fancy Sporting Rifle, Carbine, Trapper's Carbine and Musket. More than one million Model 1892s were sold, with the production run extending from 1892 to 1932 for most models, and to 1941 for carbines.

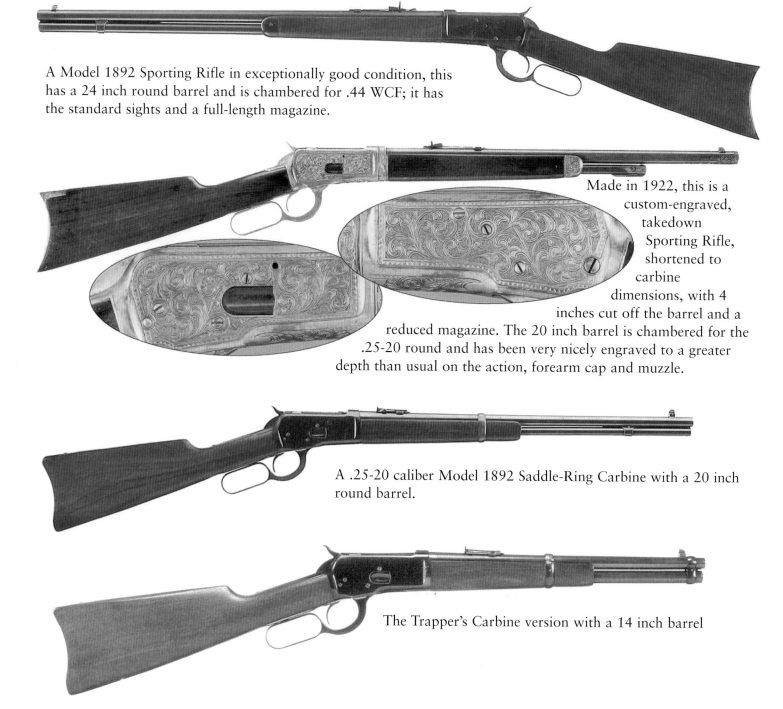

A Model 1892 Sporting Rifle in exceptionally good condition, this has a 24 inch round barrel and is chambered for .44 WCF; it has the standard sights and a full-length magazine.

Made in 1922, this is a custom-engraved, takedown Sporting Rifle, shortened to carbine dimensions, with 4 inches cut off the barrel and a reduced magazine. The 20 inch barrel is chambered for the .25-20 round and has been very nicely engraved to a greater depth than usual on the action, forearm cap and muzzle.

A .25-20 caliber Model 1892 Saddle-Ring Carbine with a 20 inch round barrel.

The Trapper's Carbine version with a 14 inch barrel

# WINCHESTER MODEL 1894

## SPECIFICATIONS

**Type:** lever-action rifle
**Origin:** Winchester Repeating Arms Company, New Haven, Connecticut
**Caliber:** see text
**Barrel:** see text

The Model 1894 was the first Winchester to be designed from the outset to use smokeless powder cartridges and has proved immensely popular; it was the first sporting rifle to exceed one million sales, the total by 1963 was some 2_ million and today the figure stands at about 7 million. With a production run already in excess of 110 years it is not surprising that there have been a bewildering number of variations, with the company's catalog listing fourteen on offer in 2005. In general, however, there have been the usual five basic variants: Sporting, Fancy Sporting, Extra Lightweight, Carbine and Trapper's Carbine.

An early production (serial #102,053; 1897) Model 1894 Sporting Rifle with a 26 inch barrel, chambered for Winchester's smokeless .30-30 cartridge, and a solid frame; it has all the standard features of the time.

An almost identical Sporting Rifle but with a takedown frame.

Made in 1910, with a 26 inch .30-30 octagonal barrel, this rifle was used in the 1970s as the base for a remarkable exercise in the art of engraving by Angelo Bee. There is heavy scroll engraving on virtually all surfaces, with a vignette of two dogs and a bear on the left side and of a moose on the right, all inlaid with gold. All outlines, borders and most lettering are also inlaid with gold. Of equal merit are the forearm and stock, both in Turkish Circassian walnut, which were checkered and carved in oak-leaf style by Angelo's wife, Maria.

A number of carbines were supplied to Canada, as was this example, chambered for .30-30. The carbine is still accompanied by the brassard of the 124th Company of the Pacific Coast Militia Regiment, which patrolled Canada's West coast against Japanese incursions in World War Two.

# WINCHESTER MODEL 1895 LEVER-ACTION RIFLE

**SPECIFICATIONS**
**Type:** lever-action, box magazine-fed rifle
**Origin:** Winchester Repeating Arms Company, New Haven, Connecticut
**Caliber:** see text
**Barrel:** see text

John Browning's Model 1895 was the first Winchester lever-action to feature a box magazine, in this case a non-detachable type with a five-round capacity. It was designed to meet the requirements of the new high-power smokeless cartridge then becoming available and was made in nine calibers. It received the highest possible endorsement when it was adopted by Theodore Roosevelt as his favorite hunting rifle. Some 426,000 were produced between 1895 and 1931.

As with previous models, it was produced in Sporting Rifle, Fancy Sporting Rifle, Carbine and Musket variants, with some interesting examples in the latter category. The U.S. Army purchased a number chambered for the .30-40 Krag round for use in the Spanish-American war, while the Imperial Russian Army bought some 290,000 in 1915–16. Other versions of the Model 1895 Musket were produced for use in NRA competition shooting.

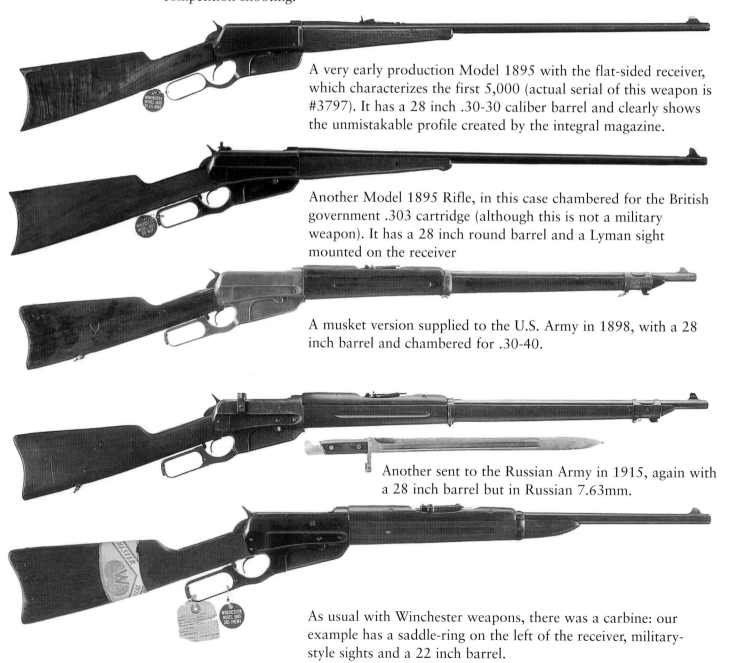

A very early production Model 1895 with the flat-sided receiver, which characterizes the first 5,000 (actual serial of this weapon is #3797). It has a 28 inch .30-30 caliber barrel and clearly shows the unmistakable profile created by the integral magazine.

Another Model 1895 Rifle, in this case chambered for the British government .303 cartridge (although this is not a military weapon). It has a 28 inch round barrel and a Lyman sight mounted on the receiver

A musket version supplied to the U.S. Army in 1898, with a 28 inch barrel and chambered for .30-40.

Another sent to the Russian Army in 1915, again with a 28 inch barrel but in Russian 7.63mm.

As usual with Winchester weapons, there was a carbine: our example has a saddle-ring on the left of the receiver, military-style sights and a 22 inch barrel.

# WINCHESTER MODELS 1900/1902/1904/MODEL 99

## SPECIFICATIONS
**Type:** bolt-action, single-shot rifle
**Origin:** Winchester Repeating Arms Company, New Haven, Connecticut
**Caliber:** .22 Short/Long
**Barrel:** 18in

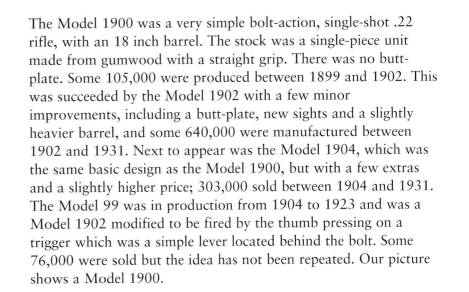

The Model 1900 was a very simple bolt-action, single-shot .22 rifle, with an 18 inch barrel. The stock was a single-piece unit made from gumwood with a straight grip. There was no butt-plate. Some 105,000 were produced between 1899 and 1902. This was succeeded by the Model 1902 with a few minor improvements, including a butt-plate, new sights and a slightly heavier barrel, and some 640,000 were manufactured between 1902 and 1931. Next to appear was the Model 1904, which was the same basic design as the Model 1900, but with a few extras and a slightly higher price; 303,000 sold between 1904 and 1931. The Model 99 was in production from 1904 to 1923 and was a Model 1902 modified to be fired by the thumb pressing on a trigger which was a simple lever located behind the bolt. Some 76,000 were sold but the idea has not been repeated. Our picture shows a Model 1900.

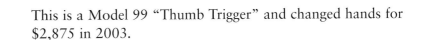

This is a Model 99 "Thumb Trigger" and changed hands for $2,875 in 2003.

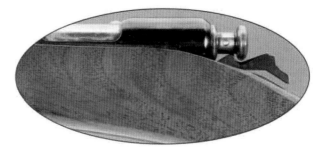

# WINCHESTER MODELS 1903/63

## SPECIFICATIONS (MODEL 1903)

**Type:** semi-automatic, tubular magazine, rifle
**Origin:** Winchester Repeating Arms Company, New Haven, Connecticut
**Caliber:** .22 Win
**Barrel:** 20in

The Model 1903 was the first semi-automatic rifle to be produced by Winchester and had a 20 inch barrel chambered for the .22 Winchester Automatic Rimfire (.22 Win). This round was more powerful than conventional .22 in order to operate the blow-back system and has long since been out of production. The tubular magazine was located in the buttstock. There were two variants: Standard with plain furniture and steel crescent butt, and De Luxe, with high quality furniture. Some 126,000 were sold between 1903 and 1932.

The Model 63 was introduced in 1933 and was designed to use the much more readily-available .22 LR. It had a 20 inch barrel until 1937 when the standard length was increased to 23 inches. Production lasted from 1933 to 1958 and approximately 175,000 were made. Our picture shows a Model 1903 Standard Rifle.

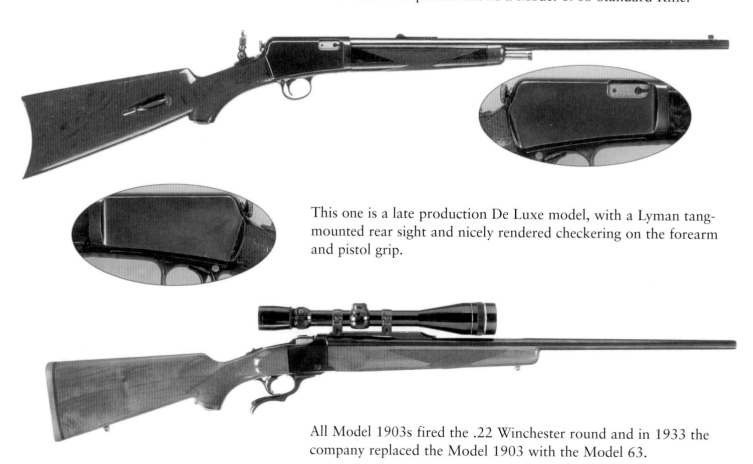

This one is a late production De Luxe model, with a Lyman tang-mounted rear sight and nicely rendered checkering on the forearm and pistol grip.

All Model 1903s fired the .22 Winchester round and in 1933 the company replaced the Model 1903 with the Model 63.

# WINCHESTER MODELS 1905/1907

## SPECIFICATIONS

**Type:** semi-automatic, box magazine, rifle
**Origin:** Winchester Repeating Arms Company, New Haven, Connecticut
**Caliber:** see text
**Barrel:** see text

The Model 1905 was based on the Model 1903 (*see above*) but enlarged slightly to enable it to handle centerfire cartridges, such as the .32 Winchester and .35 Self-Loading rounds. It also had a detachable box magazine and a 22 inch barrel. There were two variants: Sporting Rifle and Fancy Sporting Rifle. About 30,000 were made between 1905 and 1920. The Model 1907 was an improved Model 1903, but with a 20 inch barrel chambered for the new .351 Winchester Self-Loading Cartridge. In addition to the usual Sporting and Fancy Sporting, there was also a Police version. The Model 1910 was a Model 1907 strengthened to handle the .401 Winchester Self-Loading cartridge, then newly-introduced.

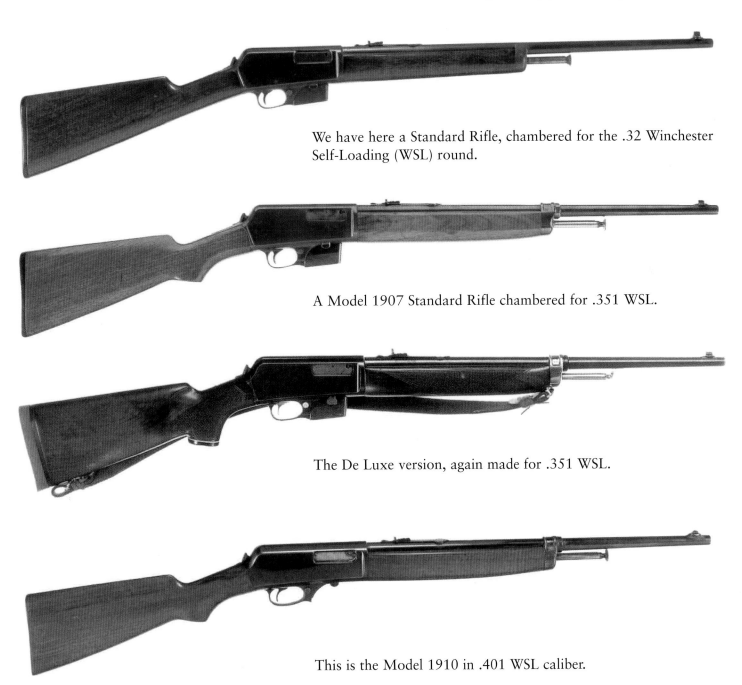

We have here a Standard Rifle, chambered for the .32 Winchester Self-Loading (WSL) round.

A Model 1907 Standard Rifle chambered for .351 WSL.

The De Luxe version, again made for .351 WSL.

This is the Model 1910 in .401 WSL caliber.

## WINCHESTER MODEL 1906

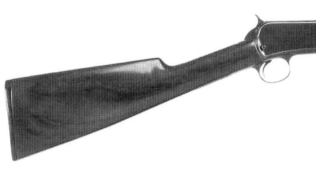

### SPECIFICATIONS

**Type:** slide-action, repeater rifle
**Origin:** Winchester Repeating Arms Company, New Haven, Connecticut
**Caliber:** .22
**Barrel:** 20 in

The Model 1906 was a less-expensive (33 per cent cheaper) development of the Model 1890, with the same receiver but a standard 20 inch barrel and a plain gumwood stock. As introduced, it fired only .22 Short but two years later, and after some 113,000 had been sold, it was altered to accept any of the .22 Short, Long or LR and sales took-off. Production continued until 1932, by which time a total of some 800,000 had been sold. There were three variants: .22 Short only (1906–08); Standard .22S. .22L or .22LR (1908–32) and the Expert with some refinements, including nickel-plating (1918–24). We show a very late production Standard Model 1906 and an Expert which has clearly seen better days.

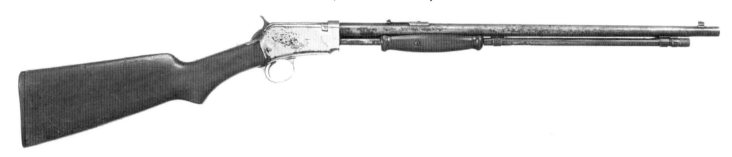

## WINCHESTER PATTERN 1914 (BRITISH) MARK 1

### SPECIFICATIONS

**Type:** bolt-action, magazine-fed rifle
**Origin:** Winchester Repeating Arms Company, New Haven, Connecticut
**Caliber:** .303 British
**Barrel:** 26in

In 1913 and early 1914 the British Army tested a new bolt-action rifle which fired a new rimless .276 round; these trials were a success and it was approved for production as the Pattern 1913. But, when World War One broke out in August 1914, all British domestic production was concentrated on the Short Magazine Lee-Enfield (*see above*) in order to arm the rapidly expanding army. So, an order was placed with Winchester for 200,000 of a rifle based on the Pattern 1913, but modified to take the standard British .303 round. Winchester's design was accepted as the Pattern 1914 and placed in immediate mass-production with Eddystone, Remington-UMC and Winchester. In late 1916, the British reduced their orders and Winchester ended production in December of that year.

The rifle seen here is a Pattern 1914 which was found in the Winchester factory in the 1960s and it would appear that it had been completed after the order had been canceled and never delivered to the British.

## WINCHESTER MODEL 70 (PRE-1964)

The Winchester Model 70, manufactured between 1936 and 1963, is widely and justifiably known as "the Rifleman's Rifle." It started life as a replacement for the Model 54, incorporating a host of minor improvements, and there were a variations in at least eighteen calibers ranging from .22 Hornet to .458 Winchester Magnum during its 27 year production run. The major variants are listed in the table, but it should be noted that there were many minor variations and purchasers could always add "extras" or make changes to suit their personal needs.

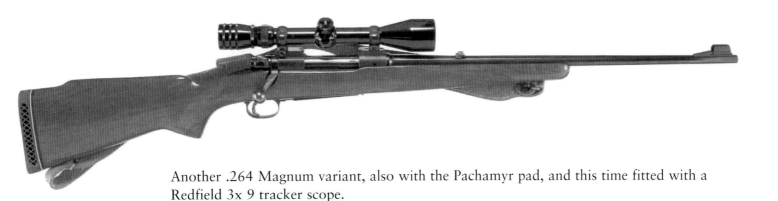

Another .264 Magnum variant, also with the Pachamyr pad, and this time fitted with a Redfield 3x 9 tracker scope.

This one is in .358 Winchester caliber, and although a very rare chambering, it is otherwise typical, with hooded foresight, single folding leaf rear sight, and aluminum floor-plate, trigger guard and butt-plate.

Chambered for the .243 Winchester round, this one is fitted with the Bausch & Lomb Balart 8x scope and has the Winchester aluminum butt-plate.

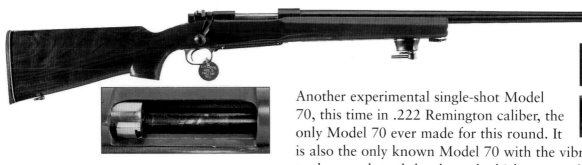

Another experimental single-shot Model 70, this time in .222 Remington caliber, the only Model 70 ever made for this round. It is also the only known Model 70 with the vibration damper fitted to the muzzle and the channel which runs under almost the full length of the forearm to enable swivels and stops to be added/removed and moved to different positions.

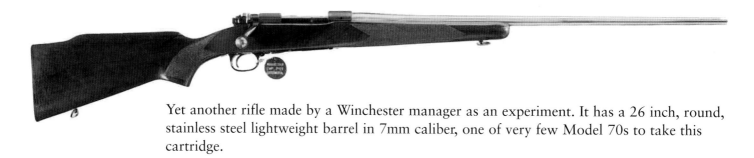

Yet another rifle made by a Winchester manager as an experiment. It has a 26 inch, round, stainless steel lightweight barrel in 7mm caliber, one of very few Model 70s to take this cartridge.

# WINCHESTER MODEL 71

## SPECIFICATIONS

**Type:** lever-action, repeater rifle
**Origin:** Winchester Repeating Arms Company, New Haven, Connecticut
**Caliber:** .348
**Barrel:** 24in and 20in

The Model 71 replaced the Model 1886 in 1935 and was, in effect, the Model 1886 updated and strengthened to take the more powerful .348 cartridge. There were two variants, Rifle (24 inch barrel) and Carbine (20 inch barrel), each with two grades, Standard and De Luxe. A total of about 47,000 were manufactured between 1935 and 1957.

Shown here is a Model 71 Standard Rifle with a 24 inch barrel, made in 1937.

A De Luxe Rifle, also with a 24 inch barrel, but with checkering on the forearm and pistol grip and a Lyman receiver sight.

This is the carbine in De Luxe finish, with 20 inch barrel.

A customized version of the Rifle with 24 inch barrel. It has deep relief scrollwork on all metal parts, including the barrel, action, bolt lever, forearm cap and the rear end of the barrel. There are also gold inlaid vignettes on the action of a buck (left), stag (right) and bear (underside). The forearm and butt stock, made of high-grade American walnut, are also elaborately carved

## WINCHESTER MODEL 72

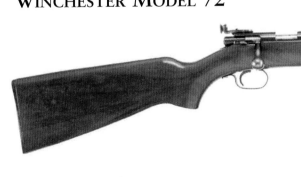

**SPECIFICATIONS**

**Type:** bolt-action rifle
**Origin:** Winchester Repeating Arms Company, New Haven, Connecticut
**Caliber:** .22
**Barrel:** 25in

The Model 72 was another entry in the huge .22 market, being introduced in 1938 and remaining in production until 1959, during which time some 161,000 rifles were manufactured. It was a bolt-action, single-shot rifle, with a tubular, under-barrel magazine. Most were sold with open or peep sights, although some of the earlier sales had simple telescopic sights. We show two Model 72s, one with a simple telescope, while the other has a Lyman receiver-mounted rear sight.

There was also a Gallery Special, chambered for .22 Short, and with a chain for attachment to the booth.

## WINCHESTER MODEL 74

### SPECIFICATIONS

**Type:** semi-automatic, tubular magazine rifle
**Origin:** Winchester Repeating Arms Company, New Haven, Connecticut
**Caliber:** .22 Short/LR
**Barrel:** 24in

This semi-automatic rifle had a 24 inch barrel and was chambered for the .22 Short and .22 LR, the rounds being held in a tubular magazine in the buttstock. There were two variants, one a Sporting Model, the second a Gallery Special, which was chambered for .22 Short only. We show both a standard model and one with an additional snap-on empty case deflector.

## WINCHESTER MODEL 75

### SPECIFICATIONS

**Type:** bolt-action rifle
**Origin:** Winchester Repeating Arms Company, New Haven, Connecticut
**Caliber:** .22
**Barrel:** see text

The Model 75 was a .22 bolt-action rifle which was available in two rather different forms. The Sporting Rifle had a 24 inch round barrel and walnut stock with a checkered pistol grip and forearm. It was supplied with either a Lyman receiver sight or a telescopic sight. The Target Rifle had a 28 inch barrel, lacked any checkering on its furniture and was usually sold with a receiver-mounted rear sight. Apart from civilian users, the Model 75 Target Rifle was bought by the US military in some numbers during World War Two. The Model 75 was taken out of production in 1958 after approximately 89,000 had been sold.

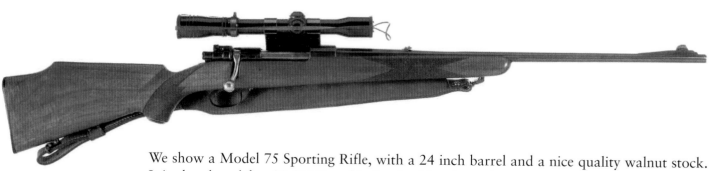

We show a Model 75 Sporting Rifle, with a 24 inch barrel and a nice quality walnut stock. It is chambered for .22 SLLR and is fitted with a Sears 4x scope.

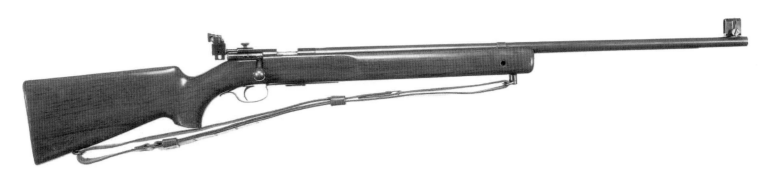

This is the Target version, with the 28 inch barrel, Lyman rear sight and hooded foresight.

## WINCHESTER MODEL 77

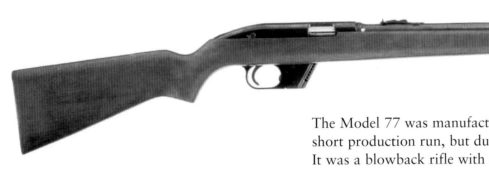

The Model 77 was manufactured from 1955 to 1963, a relatively short production run, but during which some 217,000 were sold. It was a blowback rifle with a 22 inch barrel, and was chambered for the .22LR only, the rounds being fed from either a detachable box magazine or from an under-barrel tubular magazine. There were no variants so we show two standard production models to illustrate the neat, flowing lines of this particular design.

**SPECIFICATIONS**

**Type:** semi-automatic rifle

**Origin:** Winchester Repeating Arms Company, New Haven, Connecticut

**Caliber:** .22

**Barrel:** 22in

## WINCHESTER MODEL 88

**SPECIFICATIONS**

**Type:** lever-action rifle

**Origin:** Winchester Repeating Arms Company, New Haven, Connecticut

**Caliber:** see text

**Barrel:** 25in

The Model 88 was introduced in 1955 to mark the Winchester company's one-hundredth anniversary and is often known as the "Centennial Model." There were two variants, the Rifle, with a 22 inch barrel, introduced in 1955 and the Carbine, with a 19 inch barrel, in 1968, production of both ending in 1968 after some 283,000 had been produced. Both Rifle and Carbine had a short-stroke lever action and were available in three chamberings: .243; .284 and .308, while the Rifle only was also available in .358.

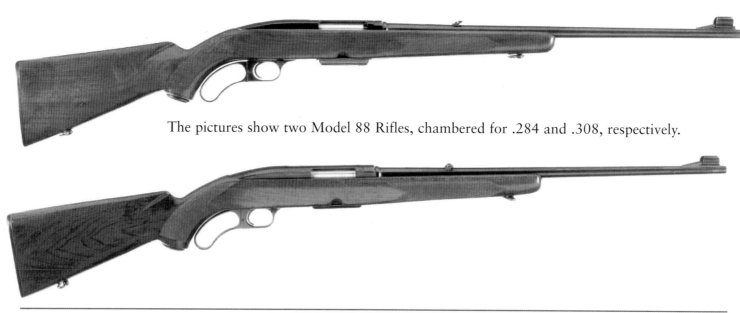

The pictures show two Model 88 Rifles, chambered for .284 and .308, respectively.

# WINCHESTER MODEL 94 (POST-1964)

**SPECIFICATIONS**
**Type:** lever-action rifle
**Origin:** Winchester Repeating Arms Company, New Haven, Connecticut
**Caliber:** see text
**Barrel:** 20 or 24in

The new Model 94 entered production in 1964 as an updated Model 1894, part of the company's drive to introduce updated as well as easier (and cheaper to manufacture) versions of some of the best of the traditional models. Many aspects of the new design were heavily criticized, but production has continued and a large number of variants have been produced. The design features a short-stroke lever action with 20 or 24 inch barrels, chambered for .30-30, 7-30 or .44 Magnum cartridges, and a tubular magazine accommodating six or seven rounds, depending on the barrel length. There have been minor changes over the years; for example, .480 Ruger caliber was added in 2003. There have been the usual variants and the Model 94 has also been used as the basis of a large number of commemorative issues.

It has also been sold under various labels and in a number of different models by other outlets, including K-Mart, Montgomery Wards (Western Field), Western Auto (Revelation) and Sears (Ted Williams).

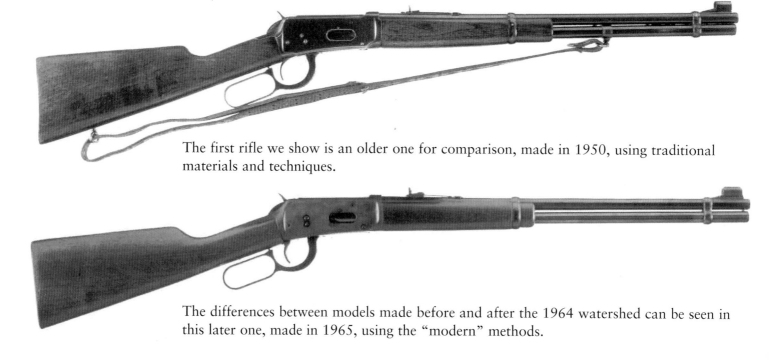

The first rifle we show is an older one for comparison, made in 1950, using traditional materials and techniques.

The differences between models made before and after the 1964 watershed can be seen in this later one, made in 1965, using the "modern" methods.

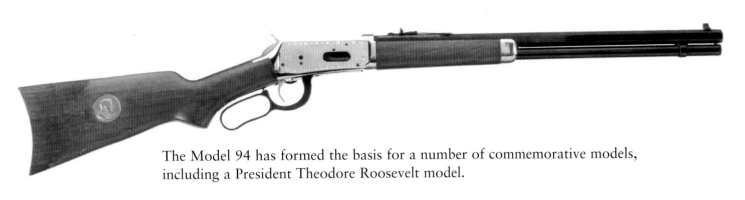

The Model 94 has formed the basis for a number of commemorative models, including a President Theodore Roosevelt model.

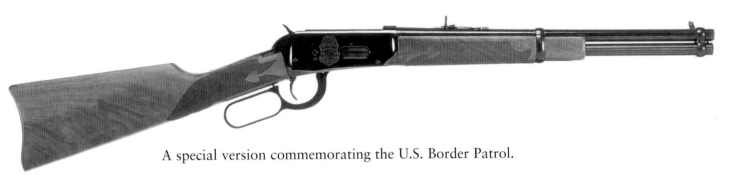

A special version commemorating the U.S. Border Patrol.

The Buffalo Bill commemorative edition.

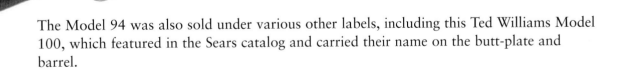

The Model 94 was also sold under various other labels, including this Ted Williams Model 100, which featured in the Sears catalog and carried their name on the butt-plate and barrel.

There were two spectacular special issues by the Custom Shop in support of the Hunting and Shooting Sports Heritage Fund, both with 26 inch part octagonal barrels chambered for .38-55. In the "One-of-a-Thousand" issue the action was engraved with gold wire borders and gold inlaid vignettes on either side, with the stock in very high quality walnut stock with checkered pistol grip and forearm.

The "One-of-a-Hundred" issue was more elaborate, with even finer quality wood and more extensive fleur-de-lis checkering. Both issues had standard iron sights, but the "One-of-a-Hundred" also had a Lyman sight on the tang.

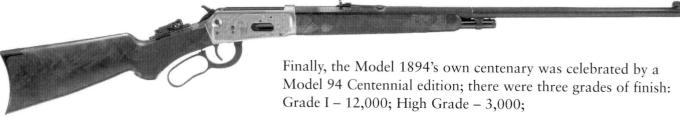

Finally, the Model 1894's own centenary was celebrated by a Model 94 Centennial edition; there were three grades of finish: Grade I – 12,000; High Grade – 3,000;

---

# WINCHESTER MODEL 9422

**SPECIFICATIONS**
**Type:** lever-action rifle
**Origin:** Winchester Repeating Arms Company, New Haven, Connecticut
**Caliber:** .22
**Barrel:** 20.5in

The Model 9422, introduced in 1971, has the appearance of a Model 94 but in the ever-popular .22 caliber, with a 20.5 inch barrel chambered for .22 and .22 Magnum rimfire. It is fitted with a tubular, under-barrel magazine, which houses various numbers of rounds depending on the caliber: .22 Short (21); .22 Long (17); .22 LR (15); and .22 Magnum (11).

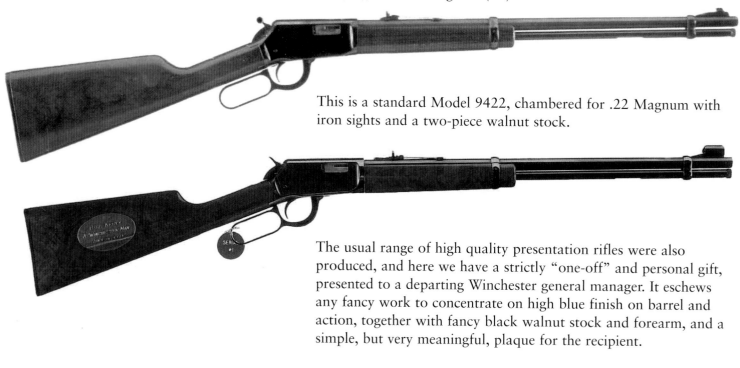

This is a standard Model 9422, chambered for .22 Magnum with iron sights and a two-piece walnut stock.

The usual range of high quality presentation rifles were also produced, and here we have a strictly "one-off" and personal gift, presented to a departing Winchester general manager. It eschews any fancy work to concentrate on high blue finish on barrel and action, together with fancy black walnut stock and forearm, and a simple, but very meaningful, plaque for the recipient.

This is a commercially available High Grade model with engraved action and checkered pistol grip and forearm.

## YOUNG PERCUSSION TARGET RIFLE

John Young was a gunmaker who worked in Michigan City, Indiana, from 1847 to 1871 when he moved to Kingsbury, also in Indiana, where he continued working until his death in 1885. This rifle has a very substantial fully octagonal 32.4 inch barrel, with a hooded foresight. There is a half-length forearm and a ramrod under the barrel. The tang-mounted rear sight is a brass peep-tube (not original and bent as shown). The buttstock is a fine piece of hardwood and has cheekpieces on both sides.

**SPECIFICATIONS**

**Type:** percussion breechloading target rifle
**Origin:** John Young, Michigan City, Indiana
**Caliber:** .45
**Barrel Length:** 32.4in

## ZIEGLER PERCUSSION RIFLE

**SPECIFICATIONS**

**Type:** percussion breechloading rifle
**Origin:** H.D. Ziegler, Portsmouth, Ohio
**Caliber:** .36
**Barrel Length:** 39.6in

Z.D. Ziegler was a gunsmith who is known to have worked in Portsmouth, Ohio from 1858 to 1870. This rifle has a 39.6 inch fully octagonal barrel, chambered for .36 caliber. It mounts two very crude iron sights, whose effectiveness must have been very limited.

## ZETTLER SCHUTZEN RIFLE

The Zettler family had been in the gunmaking business in New York City since at least 1851 and this splendid piece was produced by John Zettler at the turn of the century. The heavy barrel is 30 inches long and is fully octagonal; it is fitted for a false muzzle, which is missing. The sights comprise a hooded globe foresight and a Ballard-improved mid-range, vernier backsight mounted on the tang. The walnut forearm has a Schnabel tip and a built-in hand-rest, which also appears on other Zettler rifles. The buttstock is of the usual Schützen style, with the dramatically curved butt-plate and a recessed cheekpiece.

**SPECIFICATIONS**

**Type:** Ballard action, Schützen rifle
**Origin:** J. Zettler, New York, New York
**Caliber:** .32-40
**Barrel Length:** 30in

# AUSTRIA

## FRANZ SODIA OVER-AND-UNDER

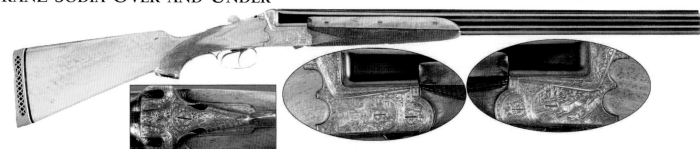

### SPECIFICATIONS

**Type:** over-and-under shotgun
**Origin:** Franz Sodia Jagdgewehrfabrik,
Ferlach, Austria
**Caliber:** 16 gauge
**Barrel Length:** two 28 inch

Franz Sodia was a noted Austrian gunmaker, who made shotguns from 1934 onwards. Following World War Two, he re-established his business in 1947 and this is an excellent example of his work. It is a twin barrel shotgun in an over-and-under configuration, with a three-piece forearm and a very blond walnut butt stock with a white line recoil pad. The action is covered with deep-relief engraving, with a rabbit scene on the left side and a capercaillie on the right, and a woodcock on the bottom. It has a 15 inch pull and the barrels have 2.5 inch chambers.

## FRANZ SODIA SINGLE-BARREL TRAP SHOTGUN

This beautifully finished singe-barrel shotgun has a vent-ribbed 34 inch barrel and highly polished walnut stock and forearm. The box lock action is engraved with games scenes – dog and pheasants on the left and ducks on the right. The stock has a high comb and is fitted with a Pachmayr white-line recoil pad.

### SPECIFICATIONS

**Type:** single-barrel trap shotgun
**Origin:** Franz Sodia Jagdgewehrfabrik,
Ferlach, Austria
**Caliber:** 12 gauge
**Barrel Length:** 34in

## FRANZ SODIA COMBINATION RIFLE/SHOTGUN

### SPECIFICATIONS

**Type: combination** rifle/shotgun
**Origin:** Franz Sodia
Jagdgewehrfabrik, Ferlach, Austria
**Caliber:** 6.5mm/12 gauge
**Barrel Length:** 27in

This combination rifle/shotgun would often be known as a "cape gun," but perhaps that term was not used in Germany. The weapon was made in Austria before World War Two and was confiscated by a U.S. officer in 1945 and brought back to the United States, where it has remained ever since. It consists of a 6.5mm caliber rifle and a 16 caliber shotgun, with cocking indicators on top of the action. There is a bead sight on the muzzle and a two-leaf rearsight – one standing, one folding. There is deep-relief engraving with much scrollwork; there are game scenes on the side plates, a roe-buck on the right and flying woodcock on the left. Unusually, the owners of the gun have managed to retain its original leather muzzle cover.

# BELGIUM

## BROWNING/FN.

The Fabrique Nationale works at Herstal manufactured large numbers of shotguns which were then imported into the United States and sold under the Browning label. These will be found in the United States section.

## DEFOURNEY TRIPLE-BARREL SHOTGUN

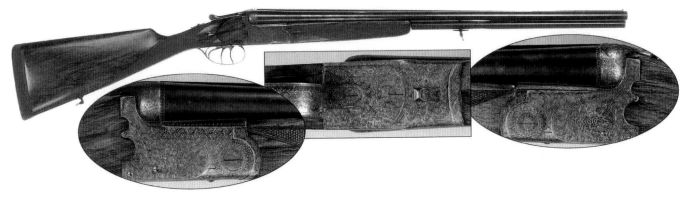

**SPECIFICATIONS**

**Type:** drilling (triple) barrel shotgun
**Origin:** A.J. Defourney, Herstal, Belgium
**Caliber:** 20 gauge
**Barrel Length:** three 26.5in

This is a type of shotgun known as a "drilling" (from the German word dreilling meaning triplets) which usually consists of two shotgun barrels and one rifle barrel, but in this case has three identical 20 gauge shotgun barrels. The intention in such a design is to allow the shooter to fire three cartridges in quicker succession than would be possible on either a slide-action or a semi-automatic gun. The barrels are in a triangular configuration with automatic ejection on the top two, but not the lower barrel, and there are three triggers. A.J. Defourney was a Belgian gunsmith, operating in Herstal, with a small, predominantly bespoke, output.

## FRANCOTTE DOUBLE-BARREL SHOTGUN

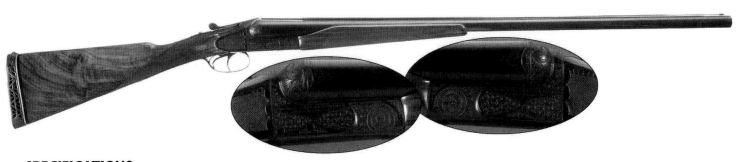

**SPECIFICATIONS**

**Type:** double-barrel trap shotgun
**Origin:** A. Francotte & Cie SA, Liege, Belgium
**Caliber:** 12 gauge
**Barrel Length:** 30in

The Auguste Francotte company has been in business in Liege since 1844, its main products being sporting shotguns and rifles. The example seen here is a double-barrel trap-shooting gun with 30 inch, 12 gauge barrels. It appears from markings on the gun that it was imported into the United States by Francotte's New York agents named von Lengerke & Detmold.

# GERMANY

## AKAH DRILLING

**SPECIFICATIONS**

**Type:** shotgun/rifle

**Origin:** Akah, Germany

**Caliber:** 16 gauge/8mm

**Barrel Length:** 25.5in

Akah is a large (and existing) German sports goods chain, the name being the German phonetic abbreviation for Albrecht Kind (AK = Albrecht and child). Like United States hardware chains and mail order houses, Akah buys in goods such as shotguns from established manufacturers and then sells them under its own name. This drilling has two 16 gauge shotgun barrels and one 8mm rifle barrel.

## COLLATH SIDE-BY-SIDE SHOTGUN/RIFLE

**SPECIFICATIONS**

**Type:** shotgun/rifle

**Origin:** W. Collath & Söhne, Frankfurt a. O, Germany

**Caliber:** 18 gauge/9mm

**Barrel Length:** 27.5in

Collath und Söhne (Collath and sons) were gunsmiths at Frankfurt-an-der-Oder (Frankfurt a.O), a small city some 30 miles to the east of Berlin, which should not be confused with the much larger city of Frankfurt-am-Main in western Germany, north-west of Munich. This weapon has two barrels, a 9mm rifle and 18 gauge shotgun, a combination normally known as a "cape gun." It has underlever action, which is covered in deep-relief engravings depicting fox and duck on the left, rabbit and partridge on the right, with a stag's head, roebuck and capercaillie on the tang. There is also a prominent butterfly-wing safety on the tang.

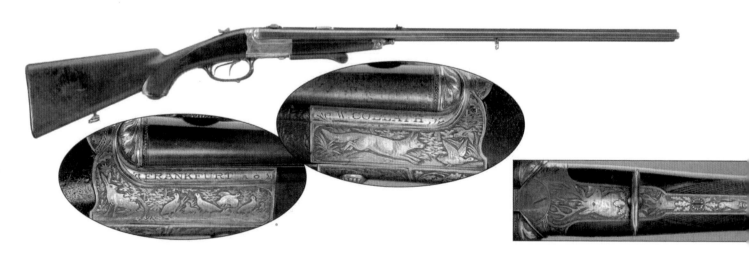

## FUCHS DRILLING

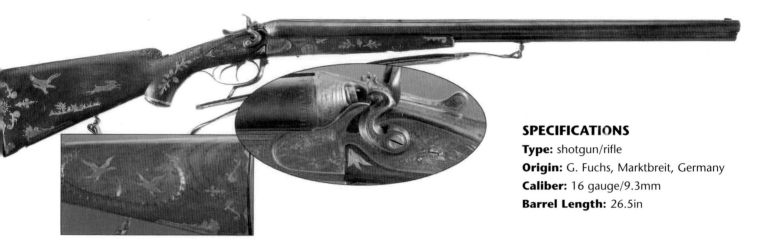

**SPECIFICATIONS**
**Type:** shotgun/rifle
**Origin:** G. Fuchs, Marktbreit, Germany
**Caliber:** 16 gauge/9.3mm
**Barrel Length:** 26.5in

Georg Fuchs was a gunsmith at Marktbreit, a small town on the river Main, some 20 miles south-east of Wurzburg, an area not normally associated with the German gunmaking trade. This highly decorated drilling has two 16 gauge shotgun barrels and a single 9.3mm rifle barrel, all three in Krupp cast steel. The top lever has a dual function, where it positions the firing pin to fire the lower (rifle) barrel while simultaneously raising the tang-mounted rear sight. The lock plates carry game-shooting motifs, but the striking point about this gun is the decoration on the furniture, which consists mostly of inlaid engraved sheet silver in the form of animals, oak leaves and other designs. Altogether a striking and original piece of work.

## S. HEIM SHOTGUNS

There are numerous gunmakers of earlier times whose names live on only in their weapons, but with little known about who they were or when they were in business. Thus, these two shotguns both bear the name "Simon Heim, Nürnberg" and are of very good quality, but little else is known about him.

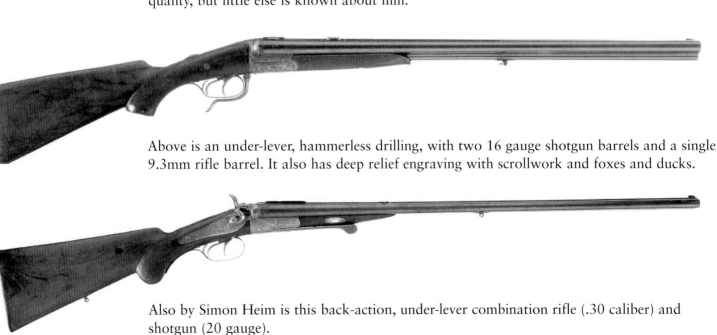

Above is an under-lever, hammerless drilling, with two 16 gauge shotgun barrels and a single 9.3mm rifle barrel. It also has deep relief engraving with scrollwork and foxes and ducks.

Also by Simon Heim is this back-action, under-lever combination rifle (.30 caliber) and shotgun (20 gauge).

## JUNG DRILLING

**SPECIFICATIONS**

**Type:** shotgun/rifle
**Origin:** Aug. Jung, Viernau, Thuringia, Germany
**Caliber:** 16 gauge/5.6mm
**Barrel Length:** 23.5in

This drilling was made by a small German gunsmithing company, named Auguste Jung at Viernau, a small town only a few miles from the great German arms-making centers of Suhl and Zella-Mehlis in Thuringia. This is typical of such products, being well made and with good quality engraving on the action.

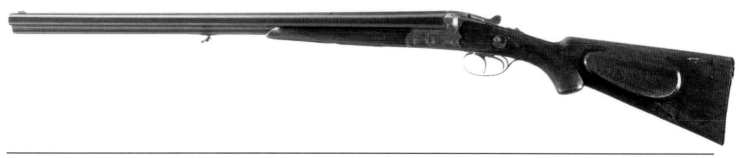

## W. KARL DOUBLE-BARREL SHOTGUN

**SPECIFICATIONS**

**Type:** double-barrel shotgun
**Origin:** Willi Karl, Lüneberg, Germany
**Caliber:** 16 gauge
**Barrel Length:** 25.25in

This elegant and well-balanced double-barrel shotgun was made by a minor German gunsmith, Willi Karl of Lüneberg, a small city about 30 miles south-east of Hamburg. It was then retailed by Stahl & Berger of Hamburg. The engraving is very intricate and covers both the action and the ends of the barrels. The butt has been fitted with a Mershon recoil pad.

## KETTNER DRILLING

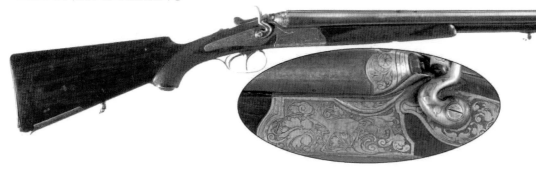

**SPECIFICATIONS**

**Type:** drilling (three-barrel) shotgun
**Origin:** Edward Kettner, Suhl, Thuringia, Germany
**Caliber:** 16 gauge, 9mm
**Barrel Length:** 26.75in

Edward Kettner was a noted gunsmith who worked in Suhl, Germany between the two world wars and this is an excellent example of his work. The drilling has two 16 gauge shotgun barrels and a single rifle barrel in 9mm caliber. There is a bead foresight and two rear sights – one pop-up and one manually raised. The action is totally engraved with a duck on the left lock, a rabbit on the right lock and a deer on either side of the action. There is also a great deal of scrollwork but not of the same standard as many others in this book.

# LINDER (CHARLES DALY) DOUBLE-BARREL SHOTGUN

Shoverling & Daly were well-known New York gunmakers in the latter part of the 19th century but the company then changed to become Charles Daly. This company had a subsidiary factory in Suhl, Thuringia, Germany named the H. A. Linder works, which had no other work than to produce high quality weapons for import into North America under the Charles Daly label. The weapon shown here has double barrels made under the "Damascus" process in which the barrel is made by twisting, forming and welding thin strips of steel around a mandrel. The barrels are marked with the initials "H.A.L" (H.A. Linder) above crossed pistols, while the action is marked "Prussian." The barrels have ejectors, improved and modified full chokes, 2.5 inch chambers and a silver front bead. The engraving is exceptionally detailed, and the triple-X fancy English walnut has very fine checkering on the pistol grip.

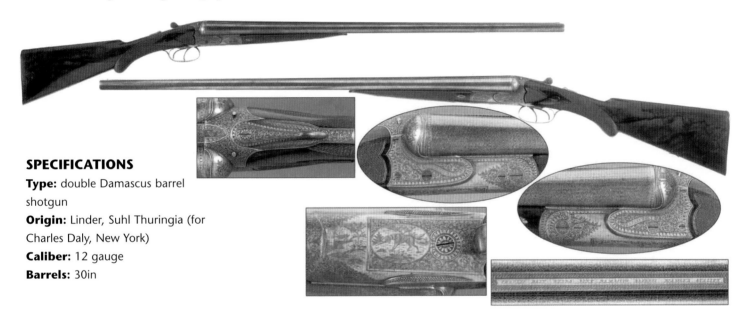

## SPECIFICATIONS
**Type:** double Damascus barrel shotgun
**Origin:** Linder, Suhl Thuringia (for Charles Daly, New York)
**Caliber:** 12 gauge
**Barrels:** 30in

# LINDER (CHARLES DALY) SEXTUPLE MODEL SINGLE-BARREL TRAP SHOTGUN

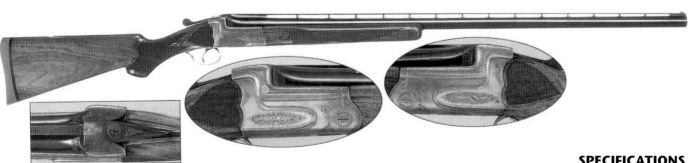

This 12 gauge box-lock, also made in Germany by Linder for Charles Daly (see above) was produced at some time between 1933 and 1939. It is a single-barrel shotgun, which got its name of "sextuple" from the fact that it had six locking lugs. It was fitted with full-choke barrels, a full-length ventilated rib, and automatic ejectors. The action is scroll-engraved in various styles.

## SPECIFICATIONS
**Type:** single barrel shotgun
**Origin:** Linder, Suhl, Thuringia (for Charles Daly, New York)
**Caliber:** 12 gauge
**Barrel Length:** 34in

## GEBRUDER MERKEL MODEL 147SL DOUBLE-BARREL SHOTGUN

**SPECIFICATION**
**Type:** double-barrel
shotgun
**Origin:** Gebrüder
Merkel, Suhl, Thuringia,
Germany
**Caliber:** 20 gauge
**Barrel Length:** 27in

Gebrüder Merkel (Merkel brothers) opened for business in about 1900 in the great German gunmaking center at Suhl in Thuringia. The company quickly earned a high reputation for the quality of its output, which covered most types of firearm, but, in particular, it was famed for its over-and-under shotguns. The company was one of the few to remain in Suhl after World War Two and continued there throughout the Cold War, only to go bankrupt in 1993. After several changes of ownership, it is now part of the Heckler & Koch group.

The Model 147SL is a 20 gauge, side-by-side, double-barrel shotgun with 27 inch barrels, Holland & Holland sidelocks and cocking indicators. The sidelocks are engraved with deep relief scrollwork and hunting scenes – ducks and a dog on the left, fox and birds on the right. The stock and forearm are made of extra fancy walnut, which is checkered.

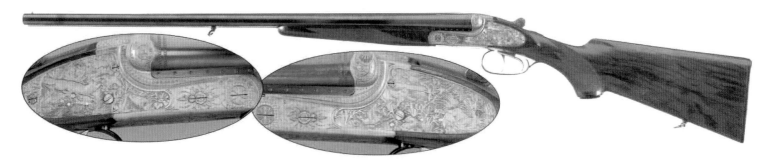

## GEBRUDER MERKEL MODEL 202E OVER-AND-UNDER SHOTGUN

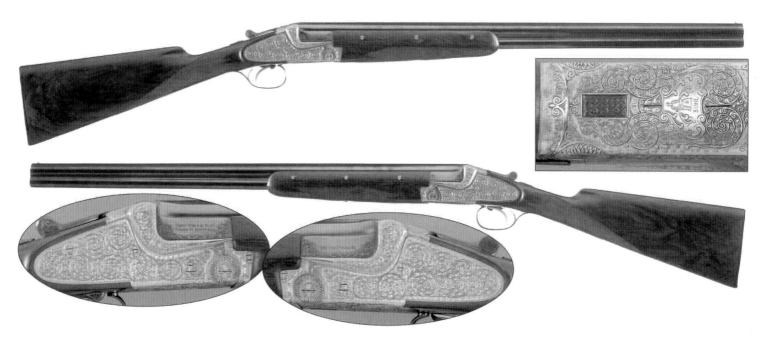

The Model 202E is an over-and-under shotgun with two 27 inch barrels and is fitted with false sideplates with cocking indicators. Those sideplates are covered in Arabesque scrollwork (there are no hunting scenes) and the fine walnut stock and forearm are fine-line Checkered.

**SPECIFICATION**
**Type:** over-and-under shotgun
**Origin:** Gebrüder Merkel, Suhl, Thuringia,
Germany
**Caliber:** 20 gauge
**Barrel Length:** 27in

# J.P. SAUER HAMMERLESS DOUBLE-BARREL SHOTGUN

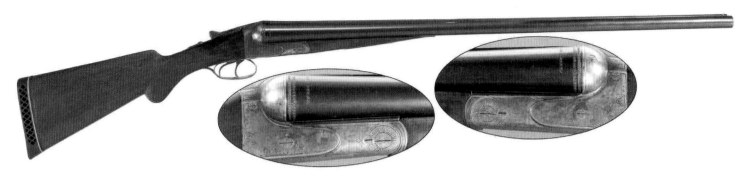

## SPECIFICATIONS

**Type:** hammerless, double-barrel (side-by-side) shotgun
**Origin:** J.P. Sauer & Sohn, Suhl, Germany
**Caliber:** 12 gauge
**Barrel Length:** 30in

J.P. Sauer & Son were located at one of the traditional German gunmaking centers at Suhl in the Thuringian forest until the end of World War Two and subsequently reopened at Eckernförde near the Danish border in what was then West Germany. This double-barrel shotgun has two 12 gauge, 30 inch barrels marked "Fluss Stahl, Krupp Essen" (Flowing steel from Krupp of Essen). There is a limited amount of scrollwork and the walnut stock is fitted with a Pachmayr white line recoil pad.

# J.P. SAUER DRILLING SHOTGUN/RIFLE

## SPECIFICATIONS

**Type:** drilling (side-by-side shotgun, with rifle below)
**Origin:** J.P. Sauer & Sohn, Suhl, Germany
**Caliber:** two 16 gauge, one 9mm
**Barrel Length:** three 26in

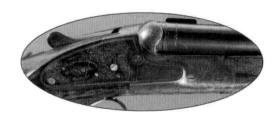

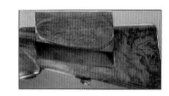

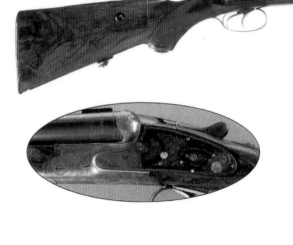

This drilling (shotgun/rifle combination) was made in 1923, at a time when J.P. Sauer & Son were still at their original location at Suhl in Thuringia, Germany. It consists of two 16 gauge barrels with a 9mm rifle barrel below, which has a sub-caliber liner to reduce it to 4mm. The cheekpiece is adjustable and there are cocking indicators for the shotgun barrels on the detachable lockplates and on the upper tang for the rifle. There are scope blocks, which are original factory fits as they are engraved like the rest of the gun, but no scope is installed here.

## W. KUNNA BACK-ACTION DRILLING SHOTGUN/RIFLE

### SPECIFICATIONS
**Type:** three barrel (drilling) shotgun/rifle
**Origin:** W. Kunna, Koblenz, Germany
**Caliber:** two 16 gauge; one 8mm
**Barrel Length:** three 25in

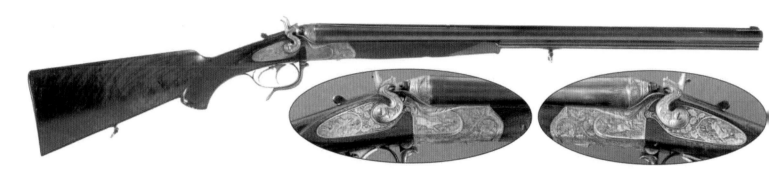

Wilhelm Kunna was a small gunsmithing establishment located in Koblenz, Germany. This drilling has two 16 gauge shotgun barrels and a single 8mm caliber rifle barrel below, with a barrel selector lever between the hammers. There is a flip-up single leaf back sight on the barrels, and a bead front sight. The back-action hammers are heavily engraved, as are the rear ends of the barrels, while the action and locks have both scrollwork and animals, a rabbit on the left and two does on the right.

## GERMAN DOUBLE-BARREL SHOTGUN

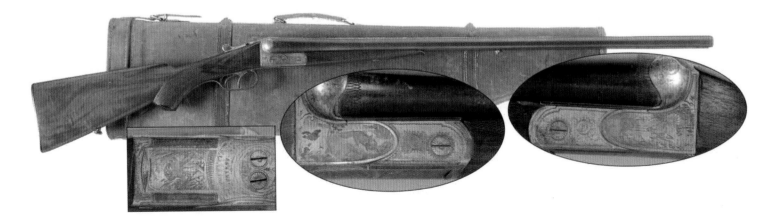

### SPECIFICATION
**Type:** double-barrel shotgun
**Origin:** unknown maker, Germany
**Caliber:** 12 gauge
**Barrel Length:** 30in

The only marking on this splendid shotgun is "Fluss Stahl Krupp Essen" on the barrel, which indicates that it was made from "flowing steel" from Krupp of Essen, but gives no clue as to might have made either the barrels or the gun. Even more intriguing is that there is a very unusual action, which works well. The action is nicely decorated, with auerhuhn (capercaillies) on the left side, fox and game bird on the right and dog and pheasant on the bottom, and there is also a smart carrying case. We shall probably never know why the maker decided not to put his name on such an elegant piece of work.

# ITALY

## BENELLI SHOTGUNS

This successful company was founded in 1967 by Giovanni Benelli as an offshoot of his motorcycle production company. The Benelli "Inertia Drivenbolt" mechanism allows the semi-automatic Super Black Eagle II to shoot 2¾", 3" and even 3½" magnum ammunition without modification. The latest range of Black Eagle semi-autos are extremely light comparatively and come in a variety of finishes, including "Black Synthetic", "Realtree" and "Satin Walnut". The company also offers a range of more basic pump action Nova shotguns and tactical weapons such as the M4 which is a gas operated weapon shown at the bottom of the page.

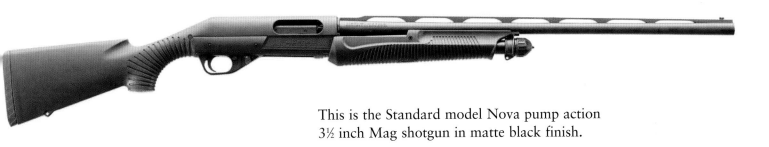

This is the Standard model Nova pump action 3½ inch Mag shotgun in matte black finish.

This is the Super Black Eagle II in camo finish with a "Comfortec" stock.

This is the gas operated M4 Tactical shotgun as used by the U.S. Marine Corps.

### SPECIFICATIONS
**Type:** semi-automatic/pump action shotguns
**Origin:** Giovanni Benelli, Urbino, Italy
**Caliber:** 12 gauge
**Barrel Length:** 24-28 inches
**Weight:** 7.1-7.3 lbs

# ITALY

## BERETTA MODEL AL 390 SILVER MALLARD

**SPECIFICATION**
**Type:** semi-automatic shotgun
**Origin:** Pietro Beretta, Brescia, Italy
**Caliber:** 20 gauge
**Barrel Length:** 28in

Beretta's AL 390 series of semi-automatic shotguns are produced in a variety of models including the Silver Mallard, shown here. This is a 12 gauge gun with a 28 inch vent-rib barrel and a three-round tubular magazine. It has a 2.75 and 3 inch chamber and a screw-in choke system.

## BERETTA BL-SERIES SHOTGUNS

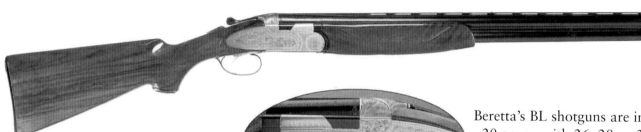

**SPECIFICATION**
**Type:** over-and-under shotgun
**Origin:** Pietro Beretta, Brescia, Italy
**Caliber:** 12 gauge
**Barrel Length:** 28in

Beretta's BL shotguns are in either 12 or 20 gauge with 26, 28 or 30 inch vent-ribbed barrels, or, in the case of the BL-2 only, in 18 inch unribbed. They have boxlock actions (sidelock in BL-6), either manual extraction or automatic ejection, and are fitted with either single or double triggers. The series was in production from 1968 to 1973 and some eleven variants were offered. Our first image shows a BL-6 in 12 gauge with a 28 inch barrel.

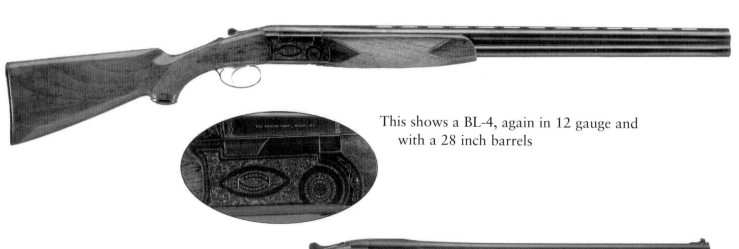

This shows a BL-4, again in 12 gauge and with a 28 inch barrels

Here we show a BL-2 "Stakeout," also in 12 gauge, but with much shorter 18 inch barrels.

## BERETTA MODEL S682X

**SPECIFICATION**

**Type:** over-and-under shotgun
**Origin:** Pietro Beretta, Brescia, Italy
**Caliber:** 12 gauge
**Barrel Length:** 32in

The Beretta 682 series high-quality over-and-under shotguns are made in Italy in four calibers and various barrel lengths. All are fitted with a single trigger and automatic ejectors, and the barrels have a vented-rib. As part of the quality image the stock and forearm are made from high-grade walnut with checkering, and the frame is engraved. The model shown here is the S682X, which has a very prominent vented-rib barrel, 32 inches in length with Briley-type chokes. The Monte Carlo stock has an adjustable butt and a leather-covered adjustable butt.

## BERNARDELLI GAMECOCK DOUBLE-BARREL SHOTGUN

**SPECIFICATION**

**Type:** double-barrel shotgun
**Origin:** Vincenzo Bernardelli, Brescia, Italy
**Caliber:** 20 gauge
**Barrel Length:** 28in

The Bernardelli Gamecock double-barrel shotgun is produced with 25.75 or 27.5 inch barrels in 12, 16, 20, or 28 gauge, with a variety of chokes. Extractors were standard but ejectors could be installed, if requested. The example seen here has 28 inch barrels with modified and improved chokes and 3 inch chambers. It has a walnut stock with a straight grip in what is known as "the English style," and a plastic butt-plate.

## COSMI STANDARD

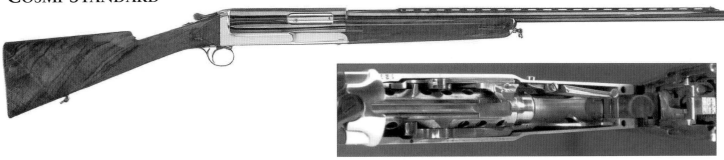

**SPECIFICATION**

**Type:** semi-automatic shotgun
**Origin:** A & F Cosmi, Torrette, Italy
**Caliber:** 20 gauge
**Barrel Length:** 25in

Cosmi is a small Italian gunmaker, whose weapons are imported into the United States by Autumn Sales, Inc, of Fort Worth, Texas. Cosmi's main current product is the Standard Model semi-automatic shotgun, which is available in either 12 or 20 gauge (as seen here). It is of very unusual design, in that it is a top-break weapon, but up to eight cartridges are then loaded through the open action back into the buttstock receiver (see inset). A deluxe model is also made, which differs only in having a higher standard of finish and embellishment.

## FRANCHI MODEL 2004 SINGLE-BARREL TRAP

**SPECIFICATION**
**Type:** single-barrel trap
**Origin:** L. Franchi, Brescia, Italy
**Caliber:** 12 gauge
**Barrel Length:** 34in

Italian weapons manufacturer, Franchi of Brescia, exports a vast range of sporting guns to the United States. One of these was the Model 2004 (the model number has nothing to do with the calendar year), single-barrel trap gun, with a prominent ventilated rib, seen here.

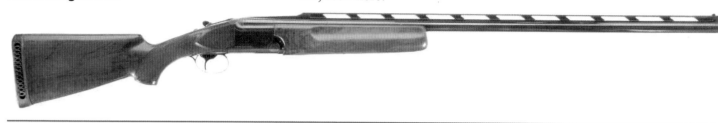

## FRANCHI MODEL 2005 COMBINATION TRAP

**SPECIFICATION**
**Type:** combination trap
**Origin:** L. Franchi, Brescia, Italy
**Caliber:** 12 gauge
**Barrel Length:** 32/34in

Another Franchi shotgun is the Model 2005 (again, the model number is unrelated to the calendar year), seen here with a set of three barrels, all in 12 gauge. One is an over-and-under unit, 32 inches long, which is shown fitted to the gun in this picture. The second is a 32 inch single barrel and the third a 34 inch single barrel, both of which have the under barrel shortened and plugged. The action has a single selective trigger, tang safety and trap-style stock with recoil pad. The whole set is housed in a stylish, trunk-style, hard case.

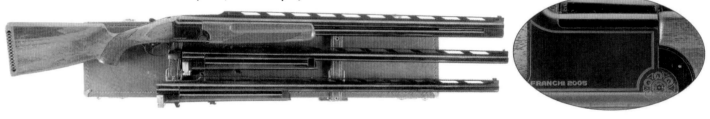

## FRANCHI SPAS 12

Italian company, Luigi Franchi Development, is noted for its line of good quality sporting shotguns, but it also developed the SPAS (Special Purpose Automatic Shotgun) specifically for military or anti-riot duties. The first of a series of models was introduced in 1979 and the SPAS-12 is shown here. The SPAS is capable of operating either in the gas-operated, self-loading mode or in a manually-operated, slide-action mode, which are selected by a small two-position button. The reason for this is to enable the weapon to be used as a manual repeater with special low-pressure ammunition, such as gas munitions, plastic baton rounds, high explosives and flares, which would not be sufficiently powerful to cycle it as a self-loader. In addition, a grenade launcher can be attached to the muzzle. A variety of butts can be fitted, including solid and skeleton, and the weapon can be fired single-handed.

**SPECIFICATION**
**Type:** anti-riot shotgun
**Origin:** Luigi Franchi Development, Brescia, Italy
**Caliber:** 12 gauge
**Barrel Length:** 21.5in

## FRANCHI SEMI-AUTOMATIC SHOTGUN

### SPECIFICATION

**Type:** semi-automatic shotgun
**Origin:** L. Franchi, Brescia, Italy
**Caliber:** 12 gauge
**Barrel Length:** 28in

Franchi has produced a series of semi-automatic shotguns and this one has been given the custom engraving treatment. It has a 28 inch vent-ribbed barrel which is fitted with an adjustable poly choke. The receiver has been engraved with silver lined scenes depicting pheasants on the left and ducks on the right.

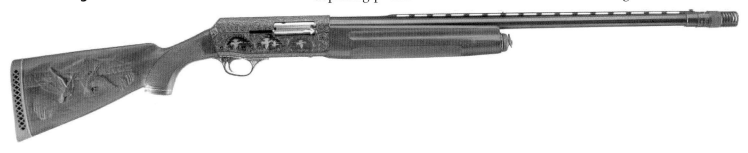

## FRANCHI AL-48 SEMI-AUTOMATIC SHOTGUN

### SPECIFICATION

**Type:** semi-automatic shotgun
**Origin:** L. Franchi, Brescia, Italy
**Caliber:** 12 gauge
**Barrel Length:** 28in

The Franchi AL-48 is a semi-automatic, long-recoil shotgun in 12 or 20 gauge, with 24 or 28 inch barrels, or in 28 gauge with a 26 inch barrel only. All are fitted with a five-round magazine. The example shown here has a 28 inch vent-ribbed barrel and is in the very stylish "Black Magic" finish.

## GAMBA LONDON DOUBLE-BARREL SHOTGUN

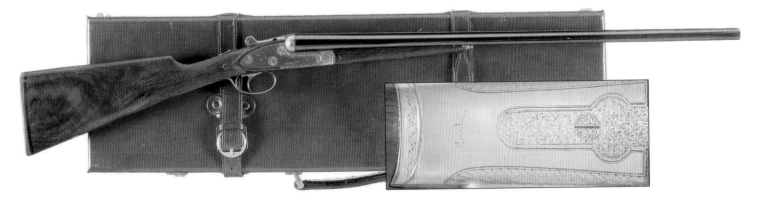

### SPECIFICATION

**Type:** double-barrel shotgun
**Origin:** Armi-Renato Gamba, Gardone V.T., Italy
**Caliber:** 12 gauge
**Barrel Length:** 31.5in

The Gamba London is a 12 or 20 gauge double-barrel shotgun with Holland & Holland type of sidelocks. There are a variety of barrel lengths and a selection of chokes. This particular weapon has a high grade finish with the action being engraved with tight English scrollwork and a good quality walnut stock in the straight "English" style. It is complete with its original leather takedown case with brass hardware.

## GAMBA EDINBURGH TRAP GUN

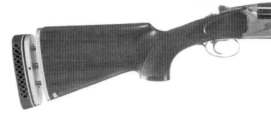

### SPECIFICATION

**Type:** monoblock trap gun
**Origin:** Armi-Renato Gamba, Gardone V.T., Italy
**Caliber:** 20 gauge
**Barrel Length:** 26.75in

Armi-Renato Gamba has given a number of its weapons the names of British cities and, in the case of this weapon, it is Edinburgh. This is a double-barrel, side-by-side shotgun which has two 31.5 inch barrels with 2.75 inch chambers. The action is Holland & Holland-type sidelock, with cocking indicators, single trigger and tang safety. There is very tight scrollwork in the English arabesque style. The shotgun has its own leather takedown case, with brass hardware and a leather sling.

## PERAZZI MX-7 TRAP GUN

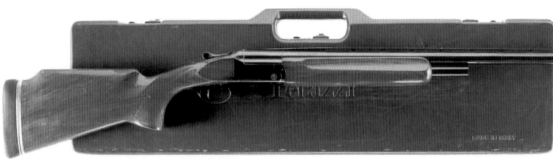

Perazzi started its business in Brescia, Italy in 1965 and by the early 1970s its shotguns were being imported into the United States by Ithaca and Winchester. Later, however, the company established its own business, Perazzi USA, located in Monrovia, California, and handles its own imports. The MX-7 was introduced in 1993 and is available only in 12 gauge, but with either two 29.5 or 31.5 inch barrels in an over-and-under arrangement, or a single barrel which is either 32 or 34 inches in length. The version seen here has a single 34 inch vent-ribbed barrel, a custom stock with terminator-adjustable recoil pad and a 1 inch drop comb 7 inches at the heel.

### SPECIFICATION

**Type:** over-and-under/single-barrel trap gun
**Origin:** Perazzi, Brescia, Italy
**Caliber:** see text
**Barrel Length:** see text

## ANGELO ZOLI OVER-AND-UNDER SHOTGUN

### SPECIFICATION

**Type:** over-and-under shotgun
**Origin:** Angelo Zoli, Brescia, Italy
**Caliber:** 12 gauge
**Barrel Length:** 30in

This over-and-under shotgun was made by Italian gunsmith Angelo Zoli (not to be confused with Antonio Zoli, also of Brescia, Italy). This shotgun has an extra full ventilated rib above the top barrel and vents in the spine between the upper and lower barrels. The gun is very well finished with engraved side plates and a Monte Carlo stock with a white line butt recoil pad.

## ANTONIO ZOLI RITMO SINGLE-BARREL TRAP SHOTGUN

Antonio Zoli of Brescia (not to be confused with Angelo Zoli, see above) makes a range of shotguns, amongst which is this Ritmo trap gun, with an unusually configured vented rib, designed to maximize the heat dissipation from the barrel.

**SPECIFICATION**
**Type:** single-barrel trap shotgun
**Origin:** Antonio Zoli, Brescia, Italy
**Caliber:** 12 gauge
**Barrel Length:** 34in

## ANTONIO ZOLI COMBINATO SAFARI DE LUXE SHOTGUN/RIFLE

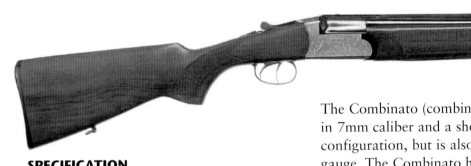

**SPECIFICATION**
**Type:** combined shotgun/rifle
**Origin:** Antonio Zoli, Brescia, Italy
**Caliber:** 12 gauge/ 7 x 57mm
**Barrel Length:** 24in

The Combinato (combination), shown here combines a rifle barrel in 7mm caliber and a shotgun in 12 gauge in an over-and-under configuration, but is also made with barrels in .222 caliber and 20 gauge. The Combinato has box-lock action, double triggers, a folding-leaf rear sight and a 2.75 inch chamber with screw-in choke system. The example shown here is in the Safari deluxe finish with engraved action, but a standard version is also available.

# JAPAN

## CLASSIC DOUBLE MODEL 201 DOUBLE-BARREL SHOTGUN

**SPECIFICATION**
**Type:** double-barrel shotgun
**Origin:** Classic Double, Togichi City, Japan
**Caliber:** 12 gauge
**Barrel Length:** 26in

Classic Double is a Japanese company, several of whose shotgun models were imported into the United States until 1987 by Winchester. The example seen here is the Classic Model 201, which prior to 1987 was imported as the Winchester Model 101 (see below). The Model 201 is a double-barrel, side-by-side boxlock shotgun in either 12 or 20 gauge, but with a barrel length of 26 inches only. The barrels have vented ribs and screw-in chokes, and there is a single selective trigger. The example seen here has a 26 inch barrel.

## MIROKU MODEL 90 SHOTGUN

### SPECIFICATION

**Type:** single barrel, trap shotgun
**Origin:** B. C. Miroku Firearms Company, Kochi, Japan
**Caliber:** 12 gauge
**Barrel Length:** 32in

This weapon is just one representative of the considerable output of B.C. Miroku, which is based in Kochi, Japan, with a workforce some 1,000 strong. The company started making hunting guns in 1893 and has always set great store on combining the centuries old art of Japanese steel-making with the most modern techniques and technology. Following its re-establishment after World War Two, the company's products were aimed for some years at the domestic Japanese market, but it also started to make weapons on behalf of foreign firms for sale on the U.S. market. Their first known customer was Charles Daly and weapons bearing the latter label made between 1963 and 1976 were actually products of the Miroku factory in Japan. In 1976 FN of Belgium and Miroku combined to buy the U.S. Browning company, whereupon Miroku stopped making Charles Daly guns and started producing Brownings, with production of several models being transferred from Belgium to Japan.

Firearms collectors in the United States tend to rate Miroku guns below U.S. or Belgian-made guns for collectability, although experts are virtually unanimous that the quality is, at the very least, the same. Miroku also exports a small, but increasing, number of weapons under their own name, such as this Model 90 shotgun. This Model 90 12 gauge weapon has a 32 inch fully vent-ribbed barrel, with blue finish, walnut stock and white line recoil pad.

# SPAIN

## LAURONA SHOTGUNS

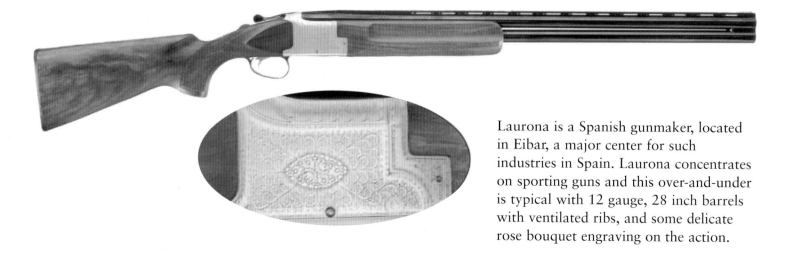

Laurona is a Spanish gunmaker, located in Eibar, a major center for such industries in Spain. Laurona concentrates on sporting guns and this over-and-under is typical with 12 gauge, 28 inch barrels with ventilated ribs, and some delicate rose bouquet engraving on the action.

This second weapon, also by Laurona, is a side-by-side, .410 gauge shotgun with 28 inch barrels, three inch chambers, double triggers, and a recoil pad (somewhat deteriorated due to age). There is light scrollwork on the action.

# TURKEY

## HUGLU OVER-AND-UNDER WITH CUSTOM UPGRADE

### SPECIFICATION

**Type:** over-and-under shotgun
**Origin:** Hu-lu Shotguns, Inc., Huglu-Beysehir-Konya, Turkey
**Caliber:** 12 gauge
**Barrel Length:** 30in

Huglu Shotguns started in 1914 and quickly not only expanded its own business but also attracted other gunsmiths to the area. After some years a cooperative was formed and today there more than 100 separate workshops, employing some 600 craftsmen, with an annual output of approximately 65,000 shotguns (15,000 over-and-unders, 10,000 side-by-sides, 15,000 slide-action, and 25,000 semi-automatics). The weapon seen here is an over-and-under with a customized upgrade with engraved scenes showing pairs of golden geese on either side of the action and a profusely carved stock depicting hunting scenes.

# UNITED KINGDOM

## ADAMS DOUBLE-BARREL SHOTGUN

### SPECIFICATION

**Type:** double-barrel shotgun
**Origin:** Robert Adams, London, England
**Caliber:** 12 gauge
**Barrel Length:** 30in

Robert Adams was another of the prolific inventors who plied the gunmaker's trade in the 19th century, one of his inventions being the Adams revolver, which was technically more advanced than Samuel Colt's design, but failed to achieve sufficient market penetration in the United States. The shotgun shown here is marked "Robert Adams maker to the Royal Family, King William Street, London" and is still housed in its original black leather case. The double barrels are made of Damascus steel, and the gun has underlever action, with back-action locks.

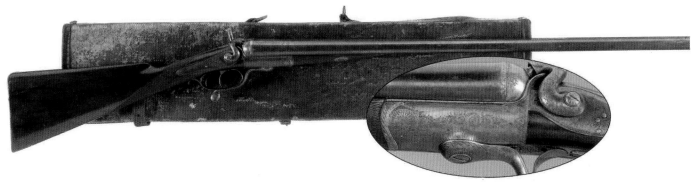

## BLANCH 12 BORE PERCUSSION SHOTGUN

**SPECIFICATION**
**Type:** single-barrel shotgun
**Origin:** J. Blanch, London, England
**Caliber:** 12 gauge
**Barrel Length:** 32in

A fine single barrel weapon with an octagonal breech and a fine "twist" barrel. The lock is engraved with scenes of game birds, dogs, and also holds the makers name. The half-stock is made from walnut halfstock and has a fine checkered pattern on the wrist.

## BLISSETT DOUBLE-BARREL SHOTGUN

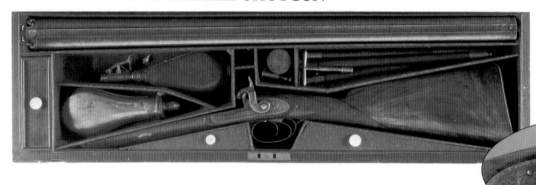

**SPECIFICATION**
**Type:** double-barrel, percussion shotgun
**Origin:** Thomas Blissett, Liverpool, England
**Caliber:** 12 gauge
**Barrel Length:** 30in

The Blissetts were a 19th century English gunmaking family. John Blissett is known to have opened a shop at 321–322 High Holborn, London in 1850, and in 1867 his son, Thomas, joined the firm which then changed its name to John Blissett and Son; in 1878 the name changed yet again, this time to John Blissett, Son & Tomes. The shotgun shown here bears the legend "Thomas Blissett, Liverpool" on both the barrels and the locks, and has Birmingham proofmarks, indicating that the Blissetts had a factory in north-west England.

This weapon is a typical high-quality Blissett product, with twin, solid-ribbed 30 inch barrels, Blissett locks, and a walnut stock. It is housed in its original mahogany case, which has brass corners and straps, and a brass carrying-handle in the lid. The contents include a cleaning rod with steel brush and screw, nipple wrench, box for percussion caps, oil bottle, and an iron powder flask.

## W.W. GREENER DOUBLE-BARREL SHOTGUN

William Greener, the elder, served his apprenticeship in Newcastle-upon-Tyne, England and with the famous gunsmith, John Manton, in London, before setting up his own business in Birmingham, England. His son, W.W. Greener took over the business on his father's death in 1869, and established a reputation for sound workmanship and reasonable prices. The gun shown here is of interest, but is mid-way through restoration work and not looking its best.

**SPECIFICATION**
**Type:** double-barrel shotgun
**Origin:** W.W. Greener, Birmingham and London, England
**Caliber:** 12 gauge
**Barrel Length:** 30in

## CHURCHILL DOUBLE-BARREL SHOTGUN

**SPECIFICATION**
**Type:** double-barrel shotgun
**Origin:** E.J. Churchill, London, England
**Caliber:** 12 gauge
**Barrel Length:** 28in

E.J. Churchill was an English gunmaker situated in the very center of London at 32, Orange Street, Leicester Square, where he was appointed gunmaker to the Prince of Wales (the future King Edward VII). This sidelock, hammerless shotgun is typical of the weapons which would be taken by aristocrats on shooting expeditions and house parties in late Victorian England. It has two 28 inch barrels with 2.75 inch chambers, and the action is decorated and the furniture checkered to a very high standard.

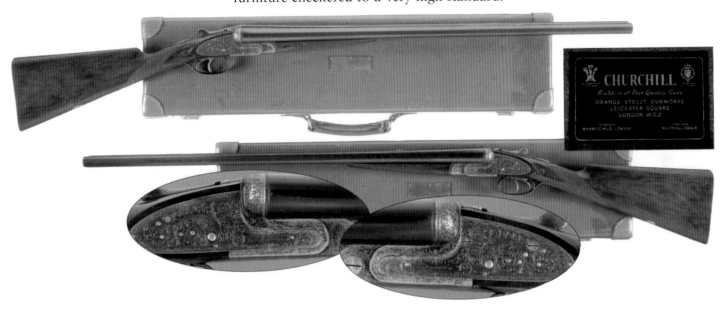

## CHURCHILL DOUBLE-BARREL SHOTGUN

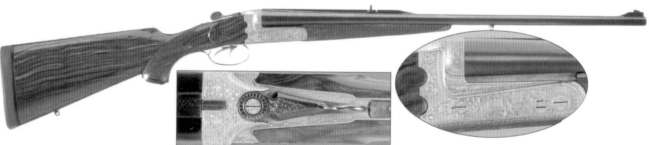

**SPECIFICATION**
**Type:** double-barrel shotgun
**Origin:** E.J. Churchill, London, England
**Caliber:** 12 gauge
**Barrel Length:** 25in

A second example of Churchill's traditional English workmanship is this fine double-barrel shotgun with 25 inch barrels marked with a gold-inlaid "XXV" which was a trademark for such barrels introduced by the company in 1920s. There is also a gold-inlaid St Edward's crown on the bottom plate (see also above).

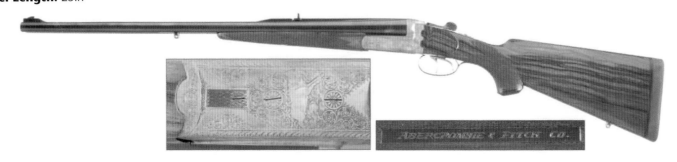

## COGSWELL & HARRISON DOUBLE-BARREL SHOTGUN

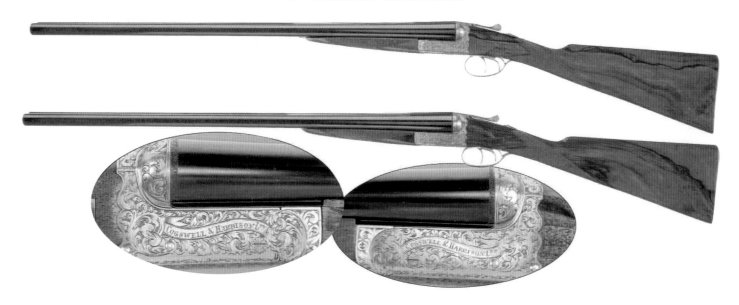

### SPECIFICATION

**Type:** double-barrel shotgun
**Origin:** Cogswell & Harrison, London, England
**Caliber:** 12 gauge
**Barrel Length:** 28in

This pair of shotguns are rather more recent than they may appear to be at first sight. The maker, Cogswell & Harrison, was established in London in 1770 at 168, Piccadilly and is still in business there in 2005 and these guns were part of a bicentenary issue in 1970. The insets show the outstanding quality of the engraving and the guns are marked #1 and #2 in gold to identify them.

## COGSWELL & HARRISON DOUBLE-BARREL SHOTGUN

### SPECIFICATION

**Type:** double-barrel shotgun
**Origin:** Cogswell & Harrison, London, England
**Caliber:** 12 gauge
**Barrel Length:** 28in

This shotgun has two 12 gauge, 28 inch barrels with cylinder chokes, 3 inch chambers and auto ejectors. The frame is heavily engraved and the stock has a round knob pistol grip stock and a rubber recoil pad. This gun was made before 1940 as it is accompanied by a letter from the makers stating that the original paperwork was destroyed when the factory was bombed during the London blitz.

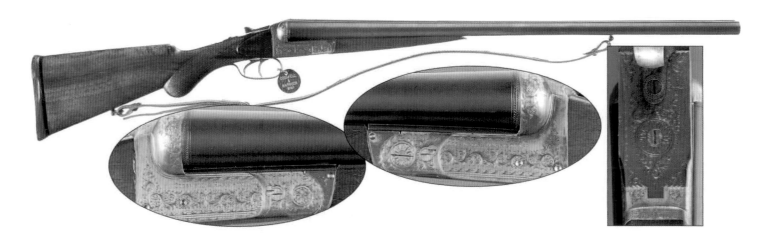

## GREENER MK III POLICE RIOT SHOTGUN

### SPECIFICATION
**Type:** single-barrel Martini-action shotgun
**Origin:** W.W. Greener, Birmingham and London, England
**Caliber:** 12 gauge
**Barrel Length:** 26

This unusual weapon has been converted from a Martini-Henry rifle, and keeps most of the stock and the dropping block mechanism. A 12 gauge, 26in replacement smoothbore barrel has been fitted, and the stock trimmed to fit. It is marked "GREENER/POLICE GUN/MARK III" on the receiver. These conversions were made mainly for riot control and police use in Egypt.

## HOLLAND & HOLLAND ROYAL DOUBLE-BARREL SHOTGUN

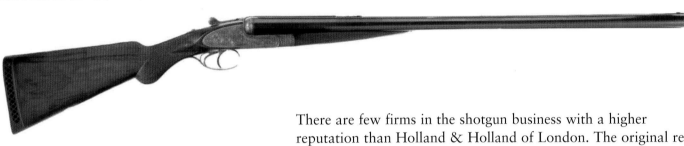

### SPECIFICATION
**Type:** double-barrel, hammerless, paradox, shotgun
**Origin:** Holland & Holland, London, England
**Caliber:** 12 gauge
**Barrel Length:** 28in

There are few firms in the shotgun business with a higher reputation than Holland & Holland of London. The original retail business was established in London in 1835 by Harris Holland (1806–96), a tobacco wholesaler and accomplished shot, and in the 1850s he started to manufacture his own weapons at a factory in nearby Paddington. Harris had no children of his own and took his nephew into apprenticeship in 1861 and as a partner in 1867, changing the company's name to Holland & Holland in 1876. The company has always specialized in sporting guns and rifles, apart from 1914–18 and 1940–45, when it undertook war work.

The gun seen here is a "Royal", a Holland & Holland trade-marked name since 1885, which, according to the company, combines "..all the essentials of a perfect weapon viz: Absolute Safety, Simplicity and Strength of Mechanism with Perfection of Form and Balance." Royal guns may be of any caliber from 4 bore

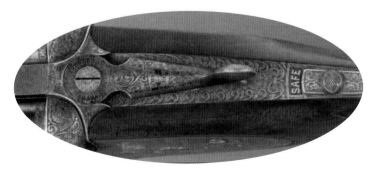

to .410, including all modern Magnums, and each is made to a customer's specific order and involves some 850 hours of highly-skilled precision work.

The gun is 12 gauge with twin 28 inch barrels, with a 2.75 in chamber in the left barrel and 2.88 inches on the right. The barrels incorporate a "Paradox" device, consisting of a short rifled section in the choke, which was devised by Colonel Fosbery (who also designed a famous revolver) and introduced by Holland & Holland in 1886. This imparts spin to a special projectile. There are three folding-leaf sights for ranges of 50, 100 and 150 yards, respectively.

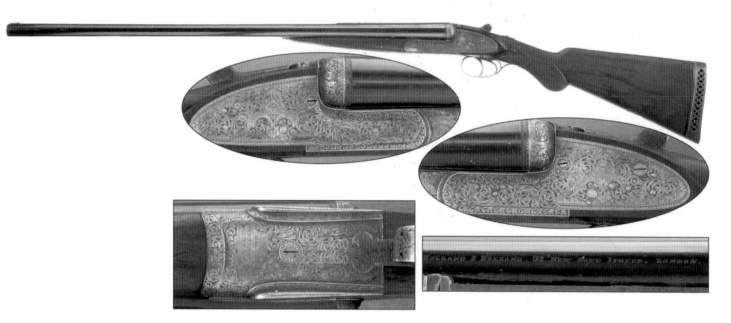

## T.E. MORTIMER DOUBLE-BARREL SHOTGUN

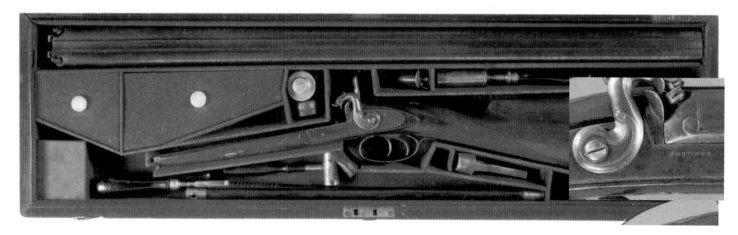

### SPECIFICATION

**Type:** double-barrel percussion shotgun

**Origin:** T.E. Mortimer, London, England

**Caliber:** 12 gauge

**Barrel Length:** 30.5in

Thomas Elsworth Mortimer had shops in George Street, Edinburgh, Scotland, and St James's Street, London, England, in the mid-19th century. This double-barrel shotgun is housed in a mahogany box, lined with green baize, together with its powder flask, wad cutter, five tins, seven tools and a cleaning-rod. The weapon itself has twin 12 gauge, 30.5 inches long barrels, with percussion action and twin triggers.

## HOLLIS & SONS DOUBLE-BARREL SHOTGUN

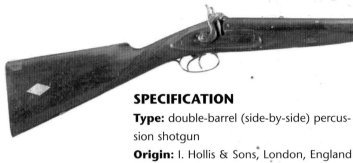

### SPECIFICATION

**Type:** double-barrel (side-by-side) percussion shotgun
**Origin:** I. Hollis & Sons, London, England
**Caliber:** 10 gauge
**Barrel Length:** 35in

Isaac Hollis & Sons was a London, England gunsmithing family firm, which was in business on its own account from 1862 to 1900 when it merged with Bentley & Playfair, the joint company then being known as Hollis, Bentley & Playfair. This large family firm shotgun has side-by-side 10 gauge, 35 inch barrels, which are marked "London Steel Twist" while the locks are marked "I. Hollis & Sons."

## PARKES SPORTING PERCUSSION

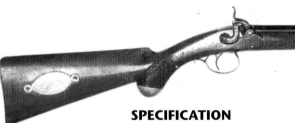

### SPECIFICATION

**Type:** single-barrel percussion shotgun
**Origin:** Isaiah Parkes, Birmingham, England
**Caliber:** .36in
**Barrel Length:** 38.75in

Isaiah Parkes operated from 22 Weamn Street, Birmingham from 1853–1900. This neat single-barreled weapon was made for export to South America and was light enough to be sold as a "Lady's gun". It has the maker's marks "I.Parkes, Birm" engraved on the lock, and a checkered fore-end and grip.

## PROBIN FLINTLOCK SPORTING GUN

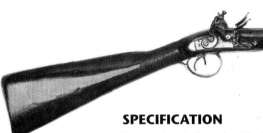

### SPECIFICATION

**Type:** double-barreled flintlock shotgun
**Origin:** John Probin, London, England
**Caliber:** 28 gauge
**Barrel Length:** 33in

A fine example of a flintlock sporting gun, dating from around 1800. It has two slender barrels made in the "Damascus twist" style, and two separate triggers operating two swan-neck cocks. The trigger guard is unusually large.

## WESTLEY RICHARDS DOUBLE-BARREL SHOTGUN

### SPECIFICATION

**Type:** double-barrel percussion shotgun
**Origin:** Westley Richards, London, England
**Caliber:** 12 gauge
**Barrel Length:** 30in

The Richards family established its gun-making business in London in 1812 and made its name manufacturing both military and sporting weapons, and, in particular, combination weapons. It has held "by appointment" status with many members of the British Royal family, starting with Prince Albert in

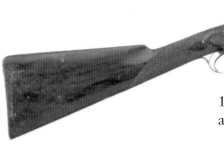

1840, and later with President Theodore Roosevelt and many Indian maharajas and sultans.

This double-barrel shotgun has twin 35 inch barrels, each 35 inches long, with the rib marked "Westley Richards" and there is a brass-tipped wooden ramrod. There is scroll engraving on the locks, hammer and trigger guard and checkering on the wrist. There is a straight grip stock and the steel buttplate bears the company's initials.

## WESTLEY RICHARDS SINGLE-BARREL TRAP GUN

This beautifully finished trap gun has a high-gloss finish on its extra-fancy English walnut stock and forearm, with fine-cut checkering and a "Kickeez" butt pad. The receiver is covered with fine scrollwork engraving on both sides and bottom, as is the tang. The blue/nickel finish, vent-ribbed, 12-bore barrel is 32 inches long.

**SPECIFICATION**
**Type:** single-barrel trap-shooting shotgun
**Origin:** Westley Richards, London, England
**Caliber:** 12 gauge
**Barrel Length:** 32in

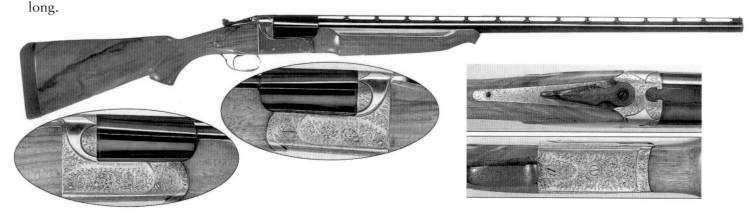

## "WESTLEY RICHARDS" CAPE GUN

This weapon, a combination shotgun and rifle, is something of a curiosity, as it was clearly made in Belgium. It would, therefore, appear to be spurious, and, if so, would be by no means the first Belgian-made gun to masquerade under a foreign maker's logo.

**SPECIFICATION**
**Type:** Cape, combination rifle/shotgun
**Origin:** "W. Richards, London, England"
**Caliber:** .45-70/12 gauge
**Barrel Length:** 30.35in

## W.S. RILEY DOUBLE-BARREL SHOTGUN

### SPECIFICATION
**Type:** double-barrel shotgun
**Origin:** W.S. Riley, Birmingham, England
**Caliber:** 12 gauge
**Barrel Length:** 30in

William S. Riley was an English gunsmith, who is known to have been active in Birmingham over the period 1874–87. This gun is clearly marked "W.S. Riley, Eagle Gun Works, Birmingham" on the rib and has some scrollwork on the action and back-action locks, and triggers. The barrels have a "Damascus" patterning.

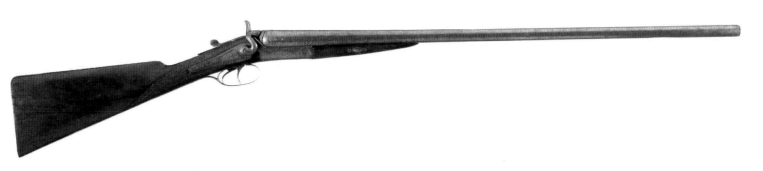

## ROOKE PERCUSSION SPORTING GUN

### SPECIFICATION
**Type:** double-barrel shotgun
**Origin:** G. Rooke, London, England
**Caliber:** 12 gauge
**Barrel Length:** 30in

Another percussion arm with double barrels made using the "Damascus twist" method. The half-stock is walnut and has a checkered wrist and fore-end.

## W & C SCOTT SIDELOCK DOUBLE-BARREL SHOTGUN

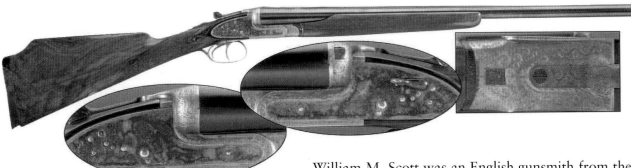

William M. Scott was an English gunsmith from the Bury St Edmunds area of East Anglia, who set up his own business in Birmingham in about 1849, later also establishing a shop in London. The firm later became W. & C. Scott and then in 1898 it amalgamated with P. Webley & Son to form Webley & Scott. This sidelock double-barrel, 12 gauge shotgun has 2.75 inch chambers with automatic ejectors. The sidelock action is detachable, has double triggers and is decorated with fine English scrollwork. The stock is made from extra fancy English walnut.

### SPECIFICATION
**Type:** double-barrel shotgun
**Origin:** W. & C. Scott, London, England
**Caliber:** see text
**Barrel Length:** see text

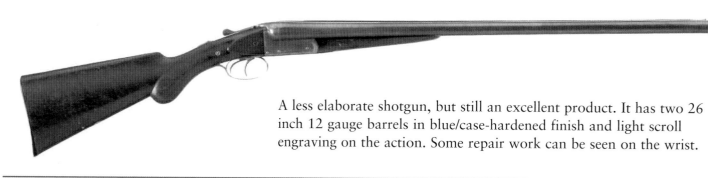

A less elaborate shotgun, but still an excellent product. It has two 26 inch 12 gauge barrels in blue/case-hardened finish and light scroll engraving on the action. Some repair work can be seen on the wrist.

## BRITISH DOUBLE-BARREL SHOTGUN

**SPECIFICATION**
**Type:** double-barrel shotgun
**Origin:** unknown (see text)
**Caliber:** 16 gauge
**Barrel Length:** 27.25in

Among the most basic factors concerning a gun and its value are the name and address of the gunsmith who made it, and this gun exemplifies some of the problems which may be encountered. The gun is a very nice piece of workmanship, with well-made barrels and frame, allied to some very high quality furniture and bears the names "Thompson-Skelton." The barrels bear Birmingham proofmarks, which indicate an English source. The name "Thompson" appears on the locks and breechplugs, but without any initials. There were a number of gunsmiths of that name who operated in the Birmingham area at various times between 1800 and about 1915, but none of them can be identified with this weapon. The wood used is a single piece of maple, with a combination of bird and quills-eye patterns, which is native to North America and not to England.

There has been no recorded English gunsmith named Thompson-Skelton. One possibility is that the barrels and locks were made in England by a man named Thompson and then exported to the United States to be stocked by someone named Skelton, but, if that is so, nobody of that name has been found and the mystery remains.

## BRITISH DOUBLE-BARREL SHOTGUN

**SPECIFICATION**
**Type:** double-barrel shotgun
**Origin:** unknown (see text)
**Caliber:** 10 gauge
**Barrel Length:** 38in

This shotgun is even more anonymous than the previous entry, since the only clue to its origin is a London post-1904 proof mark, suggesting that it was made in England. However, it is of undoubtedly good quality, and is of interest for its huge size, its 38 inch barrels suggesting an overall length of 56 inches. It must have needed a very strong man to control such a weapon, which may well have been intended for shooting "big-game."

# UNITED STATES

## AMERICAN ARMS BRITTANY DOUBLE-BARREL SHOTGUN

### SPECIFICATION
**Type:** double-barrel shotgun
**Origin:** American Arms, Inc., North Kansas City, Missouri
**Caliber:** 12 /20 gauge
**Barrel Length:** 25/27in?

The Brittany model entered production in 1989 and was a double-barrel, boxlock shotgun in either 12 gauge with a 27 inch barrel or 20 gauge with a 25 inch barrel. It had automatic ejectors and a single selective trigger. The action was engraved and the walnut stock was checkered.

## AMERICAN ARMS MODEL SILVER II OVER-AND-UNDER SHOTGUN

### SPECIFICATION
**Type:** over-and-under shotgun
**Origin:** American Arms, Inc., North Kansas City, Missouri
**Caliber:** 28 gauge
**Barrel Length:** 26in

The American Arms company has some manufacturing capability in the United States but the majority of their products are imported from Europe, including shotguns from Spain. This over-and-under shotgun, the Silver II, has two 26 inch vent-ribbed barrels.

## AMERICAN GUN COMPANY DOUBLE-BARREL SHOTGUN

### SPECIFICATION
**Type:** double-barrel shotgun
**Origin:** Crescent Fire Arms Company, Norwich, Connecticut
**Caliber:** .410 gauge
**Barrel Length:** 26in

H & D Folsom of New York City bought the Crescent Fire Arms Company in 1899, following which the latter produced a vast number of shotguns under a wide variety of trade names. One such trade name was regarded by Folsom as their own – "American Gun Company of New York" – until 1922 when guns produced for Folsom were relabeled with Crescent's own name. The first example seen here carries the American Gun Company name and is a double-barrel, hammer shotgun, with two .410 gauge, 26 inch barrels.

The second example, also marketed by Folsom, bears the "Triumph" label but without any maker's name; it has twin 16 gauge, 30 inch barrels.

## AUBREY DOUBLE-BARREL SHOTGUN

Albert J. Aubrey had a gunmaking business at Meriden, Connecticut and much of his output was sold through Sears, Roebuck of Chicago, Illinois. This double-barrel, side-by-side shotgun is a typical product, with 32 inch barrels, sidelock action, extractors, double triggers and tang safety.

**SPECIFICATION**

**Type:** double-barrel shotgun
**Origin:** A.J. Aubrey, Meriden, Connecticut
**Caliber:** 12 gauge
**Barrel Length:** 32in

## BAKER TRAP-GUN ELITE GRADE

**SPECIFICATION**

**Type:** single-barrel trap shotgun
**Origin:** Baker Gun & Forging Co., Batavia, New York
**Caliber:** 12 gauge
**Barrel Length:** 32in

The Baker Gun and Forging company was founded in 1890 to manufacture and market a series of single- and double-barreled shotguns, which soon gained a good reputation for reliability and strength. The company was taken over in December 1919 by the Folsom Arms Company, which then merged with the Crescent Arms company in 1930 and was then absorbed by Stevens Arms in 1933. Baker guns ceased to be produced in about 1923. The Baker Trap Gun was produced in two finishes, of which the one shown here was the higher, Elite Grade. It has a vent-ribbed 32 inch barrel, with two ivory beads and full choke, and a floral engraved action, with bird dog and duck scenes. The extra fancy pistol grip has extensive fleur-de-lis checkering.

## BELKNAP SHOTGUNS

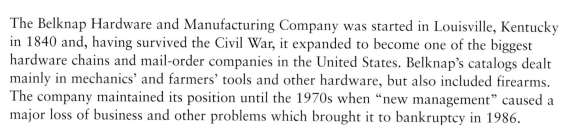

The Belknap Hardware and Manufacturing Company was started in Louisville, Kentucky in 1840 and, having survived the Civil War, it expanded to become one of the biggest hardware chains and mail-order companies in the United States. Belknap's catalogs dealt mainly in mechanics' and farmers' tools and other hardware, but also included firearms. The company maintained its position until the 1970s when "new management" caused a major loss of business and other problems which brought it to bankruptcy in 1986.

Like other mail-order companies (for example, Western Auto, Sears, Roebuck, and Montgomery Ward) Belknap bought their firearms from professional manufacturers such as Savage, Stevens and the Springfield Arms Company (not the National Armory). The Belknap weapons, like their other hardware, were known for their combination of ruggedness, serviceability and reasonable prices. This slide-action shotgun, the Belknap Model B64, is a typical product, being simple, easy-to-use, but thoroughly effective. It is a 12 gauge gun with a 28 inch barrel.

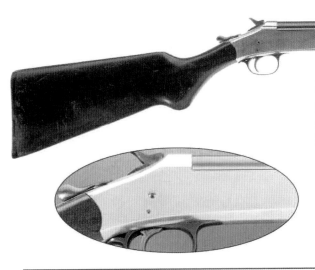

Here we show a "Volunteer" single-action shotgun with a .410 gauge, 26 inch barrel. Volunteer was one of the many brand names used by Belknap, one of their suppliers under this name being the Crescent Fire Arms Company.

## BROWNING SHOTGUNS

Browning shotguns were made in Belgium by Fabrique Nationale at Herstal when most production switched to B.C. Miroku in Japan (see above). They are sold in the United States under the Browning label and are listed here rather than under either Belgium or Japan.

## BROWNING MODEL AUTO-5

**SPECIFICATIONS**

**Type:** semi-automatic shotgun

**Origin:** Browning (Fabrique Nationale, Herstal, Belgium).

**Caliber:** 12 gauge

**Barrel Length:** see text

The Auto-5 recoil-operated, semi-automatic shotgun was designed by John Browning and has been produced in great numbers in Belgium, Japan and the United States, but always under the Browning label. It was made by Fabrique Nationale in Belgium from 1903 to 1939, then by Remington in the United States on Browning's behalf from 1940 to 1942. Production returned to Belgium again in 1952 and remained with FN until 1976, by which time FN's total production since 1903 had totalled 2,750,000. Production then switched to B.C. Miroku in Japan, where it continued until 1999, when production ended with a "final tribute" series of one thousand.

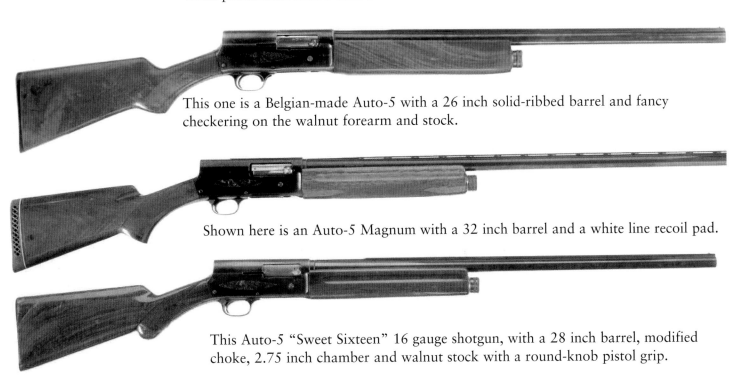

This one is a Belgian-made Auto-5 with a 26 inch solid-ribbed barrel and fancy checkering on the walnut forearm and stock.

Shown here is an Auto-5 Magnum with a 32 inch barrel and a white line recoil pad.

This Auto-5 "Sweet Sixteen" 16 gauge shotgun, with a 28 inch barrel, modified choke, 2.75 inch chamber and walnut stock with a round-knob pistol grip.

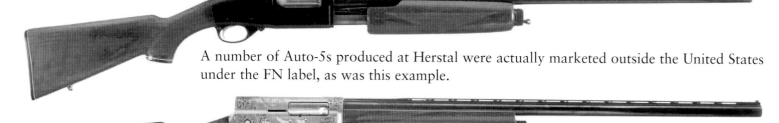

A number of Auto-5s produced at Herstal were actually marketed outside the United States under the FN label, as was this example.

Finally, we have an engraved Gold Classic, actually Number 443 out of a total of 500 produced. It has a 12 gauge, 28 inch vent-ribbed barrel and the receiver is covered in high relief engraving together with a bust of John M. Browning and the words "Browning Gold Classic."

## BROWNING SUPERPOSED DIANA GRADE 3 SHOTGUN

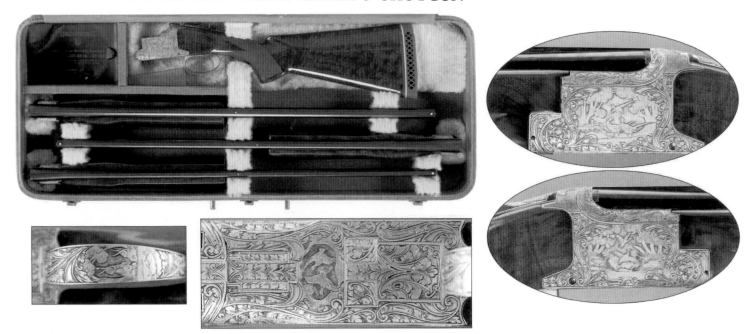

**SPECIFICATIONS**

**Type:** over-and-under shotgun

**Origin:** Browning (Fabrique Nationale, Herstal, Belgium).

**Caliber:** 12 gauge

**Barrel Length:** two 28 inch

These two Browning Superposed shotguns both have Diana Grade Three finish but, even so, they are by no means identical. The first features two superposed 30 inch, 12 gauge barrels, of which the top one is vent-ribbed. However, the gun is also supplied with an additional single-barrel unit, also vent-ribbed, which obviously has to match the fittings of the superposed unit, so the lower barrel is plugged. The deep-relief engraving has been carried out by R. Kowalski and features pheasants on the left and ducks on the right, with two quails on the bottom, and rabbits on the trigger guard. The walnut stock is fitted with a Pachmayr white line recoil pad.

This one is the same model, also in 12 gauge but with 30 inch barrels, with engravings designed by Felix Funcken. These engravings, while generally similar to those on the first weapon are demonstrably by a different hand.

## BROWNING LIEGE OVER-AND-UNDER SKEET SHOTGUN

**SPECIFICATION**
**Type:** over-and-under (superposed) skeet shotgun
**Origin:** Browning (Fabrique Nationale, Herstal, Belgium).
**Caliber:** 12 gauge
**Barrel Length:** 27.5in

The Browning Liege 12 gauge over-and-under was manufactured by FN, Herstal from 1973 to 1975, and was made in only three barrel lengths – 26.5, 28 and 30 inches – all with vented ribs and a variety of chokes. It had a boxlock action and blued finish with checkered walnut stock. Shown here is the Grand De Luxe version with a Broadway vented rib and skeet chokes. The action is engraved with scrollwork and wild life scenes, signed by R. Denil.

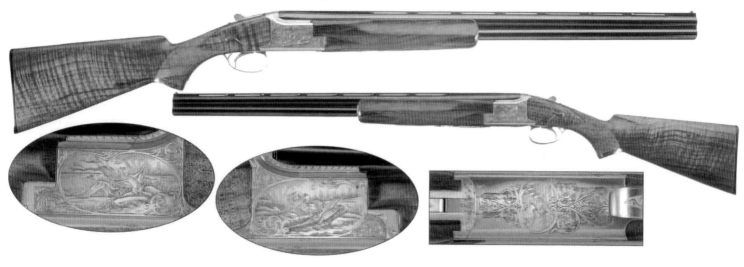

## BROWNING LIGHTNING

**SPECIFICATION**
**Type:** over-and-under shotgun
**Origin:** Browning (Fabrique Nationale, Herstal, Belgium).
**Caliber:** see text
**Barrel Length:** see text

The Browning Superposed (over-and-under) shotgun, in 12 gauge only, was introduced in 1930 and remained in production at Fabrique Nationale in Belgium, until 1940. There were four grades of finish: Grade I, Pigeon, Diana and Midas. The model returned to production in 1947 in both 12 gauge and 20 gauge, with two further gauges, 28 and .410 gauge, being added in 1959. During this period the finishes were numbered from Grade I to Grade VI. A third production period lasted from 1960–76, when there were some minor internal modifications and finish designations reverted to those used in the pre-war period, but with the addition of Pointer between Pigeon and Diana.

The gun shown here was built in 1966 and has a 26.5 inch vent-rib barrel, some engraving and a gold-washed trigger.

## BROWNING DOUBLE-AUTOMATIC SHOTGUN

The "Double Automatic" derives its name from the fact that its tubular magazine holds just two rounds, giving it no more firepower than a double-barreled or over-and-under shotgun, but perhaps with a slight saving in weight. It was marketed between 1954 and 1972. The example shown here has a 30 inch barrel, but lengths of 26 and 28 inches were also available.

**SPECIFICATIONS**
**Type:** semi-automatic shotgun
**Origin:** Browning (Fabrique Nationale, Herstal, Belgium).
**Caliber:** 12 gauge
**Barrel Length:** see text

## BROWNING WATERFOWL SERIES

**SPECIFICATIONS**
**Type:** over-and-under shotgun
**Origin:** Browning (Fabrique Nationale, Herstal, Belgium).
**Caliber:** 12 gauge
**Barrel Length:** 28in

The Browning superposed shotgun was very popular and the good response to the top grades led to a series of "Presentation Grade" models. Among these was the "Waterfowl" series, which consisted of three annual editions limited to exactly 500 each. All were in 12 gauge, with 28 inch vent-ribbed, blue/satin grey, barrels, French grey action and triple X fancy black walnut stock with round knob stock. The action, trigger and trigger guard were all engraved in deep relief and all had gold-inlaid vignettes of two birds on the left and right of the action, and a bird's head on the trigger guard. Each gun was also inscribed with its unique number; i.e., "... of 500." Each of the three series was named for and depicted a particular bird in the engraved vignettes. First was the "Mallard" issued in 1981.

The second issue, in 1982, was the "Pintail".

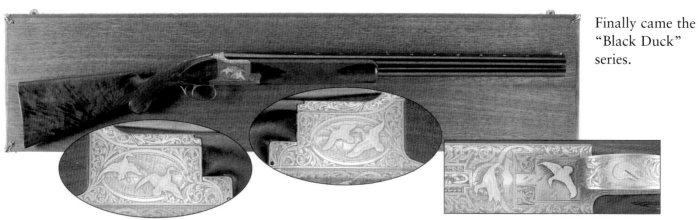

Finally came the "Black Duck" series.

## BROWNING BPS SLIDE-ACTION SHOTGUN

**SPECIFICATIONS**

**Type:** slide-action shotgun

**Origin:** Browning (B.C. Miroku, Japan)

**Caliber:** see text

**Barrel Length:** see text

The BPS series of Browning slide-action shotguns was introduced by B.C. Miroku in 1977, shortly after they had taken over much of the American company's production. The BPS features vent-ribbed barrels in various lengths, all of which are fitted for Invector screw-in chokes; calibers are 10, 12, and 20 gauge, and there is a five round tubular magazine. Barrels and action are of steel and the stock and forearm are of synthetic composition. One unusual feature is that they are fitted with bottom ejection, making them equally suitable for use by left or right-handed shooters.

## BROWNING MODEL BT-99 SINGLE-BARREL TRAP GUN

**SPECIFICATIONS**

**Type:** over-and-under shotgun

**Origin:** Browning (B.C. Miroku, Japan)

**Caliber:** 12 gauge

**Barrel Length:** 32/34in

The BT-99, manufactured in Japan by B.C. Miroku, was introduced in 1968 and versions remain in production today. It is a boxlock, single-barrel, break-open trap gun, with either 32 or 34 inch vent-ribbed barrel, with the muzzle tapped for a screw-in choke. It is fitted with automatic ejectors.

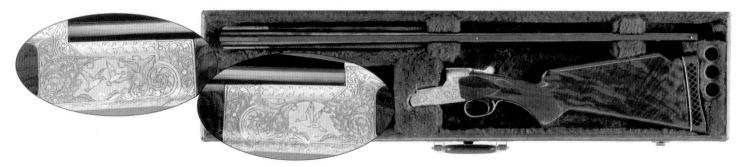

We show here a boxed BT-99 Pigeon-grade with a 32 inch barrel, deep relief engraving featuring pigeons and a triple X fancy walnut stock with a trap-style recoil pad.

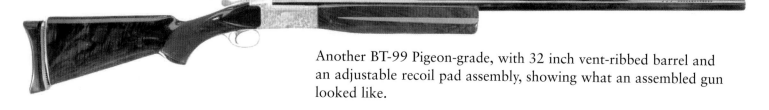

Another BT-99 Pigeon-grade, with 32 inch vent-ribbed barrel and an adjustable recoil pad assembly, showing what an assembled gun looked like.

## BROWNING MODIFIED TRAP GUN

**SPECIFICATIONS**

**Type:** trap shotgun
**Origin:** Browning (Fabrique Nationale, Herstal, Belgium)
**Caliber:** 12 gauge
**Barrel Length:** 32in

It goes without saying that owners are entitled to do what they want with their guns once they have bought them, but the results may not always be happy, as in this case. This gun started as a standard Lightning over-and-under but little of that original weapon remains. The top barrel has been cut off and plugged and an elaborate (and unsightly) vented rib installed above the remaining barrel. The stock has also been altered by the addition of a 1.7 inch extension to the comb.

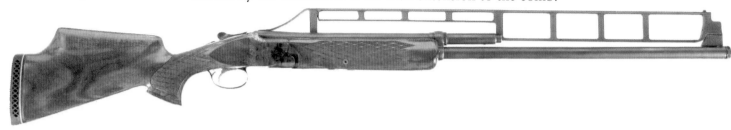

## BROWNING OVER-AND-UNDER EXHIBITION GRADE SET

This quite exceptional set consists of a Browning with three separate barrels and a carrying-case, all decorated to exhibition standard. The barrels, all vent-ribbed and

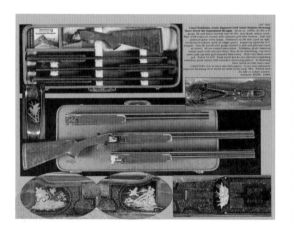

28 inches long, are in three gauges – .410, 20 and 28 – are choked skeet/skeet, and each is marked with its gauge in gold wire at the breech end. Each barrel has its own forearm of matching exhibition-grade walnut with extensive checkering. The receiver is fine scroll engraved with gold wire borders, and with gold/platinum game-scene inlays – pheasants on the left, quail on the right and woodcock on the bottom. There is also a duck on the trigger guard. The highest-grade American

**SPECIFICATIONS**

**Type:** takedown, over-and-under shotgun set
**Origin:** Browning (Fabrique Nationale, Herstal, Belgium)
**Caliber:** .410, 20, 28 gauge
**Barrel Length:** 28in

## BROWNING OVER-AND-UNDER SHOTGUN

**SPECIFICATIONS**

**Type:** semi-automatic shotgun
**Origin:** Browning (Fabrique Nationale, Herstal, Belgium).
**Caliber:** .410 gauge
**Barrel Length:** 28in

The .410 caliber over-and-under shotgun was made to a very high standard by Fabrique Nationale in Belgium and then engraved by Master-Engraver Angelo Bee of Chatsworth, California. The action is decorated with, on the left, a quartet of quail in a prairie scene and on the right a trio of doves in flight, while on the floor is a single woodcock, all inlaid in gold and surrounded by gold inlaid vines and lining. Gold wire and vines also decorate the tang, trigger guard and latch. The work is signed "A. Bee."

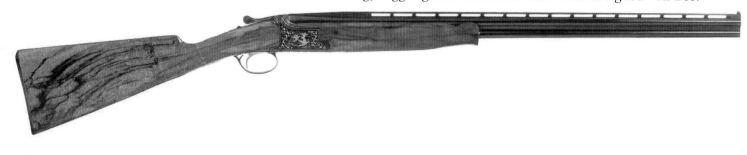

# BROWNING MODEL MAXUS

The Maxus is Browning's latest offering of semi-automatic shotgun. Manufactured at the original Browning factory at Herstal, Belgium, this shotgun boasts four varieties of finish, Maxus Hunter, Maxus Mossy Oak Duck Blind, Maxus stalker and Maxus Sporting Carbon fiber. There are two chamber lengths available, 3 or 3½ inches. The styling of this semi-auto is very up to date and compact looking, the flat ventilated rib on the barrel really adds to the purposeful appearance of the weapon. The Maxus is comparatively lighter than most other semi-autos in this class, at a mere 6lbs 14oz when fitted with a 26 inch barrel.

This 12 gauge Maxus has the matte black finish.

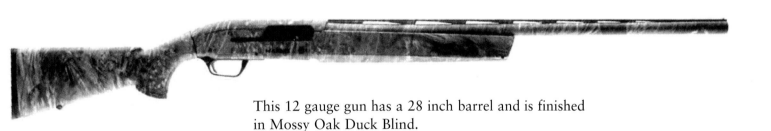

This 12 gauge gun has a 28 inch barrel and is finished in Mossy Oak Duck Blind.

The Maxus also comes with a composite carbon fiber stock and forend for extra lightness.

## SPECIFICATIONS

**Type:** semi-automatic shotgun
**Origin:** John Browning, (Fabrique Nationale, Herstal, Belgium)
**Caliber:** 12 gauge
**Barrel Length:** 26, 28 inches
**Weight:** 6lbs 14oz, 6lbs 15oz

## BURGESS TAKEDOWN SHOTGUN

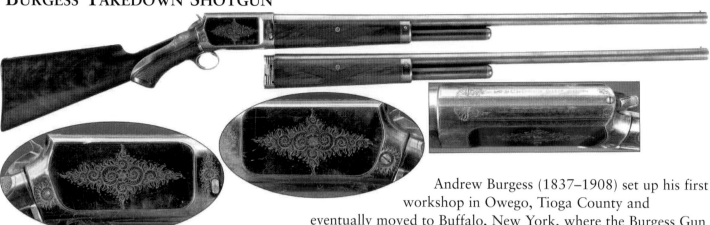

**SPECIFICATIONS**
**Type:** takedown, slide-action shotgun
**Origin:** Burgess Gun Company, Buffalo, New York
**Caliber:** 12 gauge
**Barrel Length:** 30in

Andrew Burgess (1837–1908) set up his first workshop in Owego, Tioga County and eventually moved to Buffalo, New York, where the Burgess Gun Company flourished from 1892 to 1899 when it was purchased by Winchester. Burgess was a prolific inventor and held an unusually large number of patents, many of which were incorporated into arms produced by other makers. This takedown shotgun was manufactured between 1892 and 1899, and is in 12 gauge with two 30 inch barrels, one on the gun and one spare. It is in Burgess deluxe finish with Damascus finish on the barrels and leaf and scroll engraving on the sides and bottom of the blued receiver, trigger guard and forearm cap. This particular weapon was sold at auction for $4,600 in 2003.

## CLABROUGH & BROTHERS DOUBLE-BARREL SHOTGUN

**SPECIFICATIONS**
**Type:** double-barrel shotgun
**Origin:** Clabrough & Brothers, San Francisco, California
**Caliber:** 16 gauge
**Barrel Length:** 30in

J.P. Clabrough and Brothers were a San Francisco-based gunmaking company, which was active in at least 1870–75 and probably much longer. This engraved 16 gauge double-barrel shotgun has two 30 inch barrels and is nicely decorated with engravings on the lockplates and scrolls and borders on the forearm.

## COLT MODEL 1878 DOUBLE-BARREL SHOTGUN

**SPECIFICATIONS**
**Type:** double-barrel shotgun
**Origin:** Colt's Patent Fire Arms Manufacturing Company, Hartford, Connecticut,
**Caliber:** see text
**Barrel Length:** see text

Colt's Model 1878 was made in 10 or 12 gauge, with 28, 30 or 32 inch barrels, and only 22,690 had been manufactured when production ceased in 1889. It had Damascus pattern barrels with modified chokes and 2.75 inch chambers. The stock and forearm were made of good quality walnut, with a checkered round-knob pistol grip. Among experts and collectors this is considered to be one of the finest shotguns ever made in the United States.

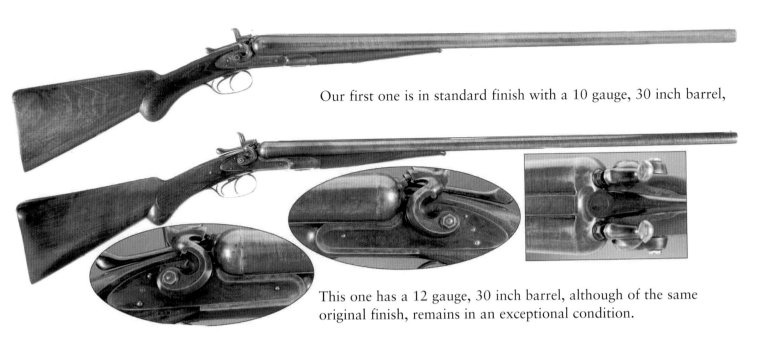

Our first one is in standard finish with a 10 gauge, 30 inch barrel,

This one has a 12 gauge, 30 inch barrel, although of the same original finish, remains in an exceptional condition.

## COLT MODEL 1883 DOUBLE-BARREL SHOTGUN

The Model 1883 was in production until 1895, during which time 7,386 were produced, and which experts join with the Colt Model 1878 as being among the best American shotguns ever made. Like the Model 1878, the Model 1883 was in either 10 or 12 gauge and had barrels of 28, 30 or 32 inches in length. The example seen here is a 10 gauge with a 30 inch barrel; it was made in 1891.

**SPECIFICATIONS**
**Type:** double-barrel shotgun
**Origin:** Colt's Patent Fire Arms Manufacturing Company, Hartford, Connecticut,
**Caliber:** see text
**Barrel Length:** see text

## CRESCENT ARMS DOUBLE-BARREL

The Crescent Fire Arms Company was established in Norwich, Connecticut in 1892 but was taken over the following years by H. & D. Folsom Arms Company of Broadway, New York City. Folsom was a large-scale arms importer and wholesaler who needed to add a U.S. manufacturing facility to their already extensive interests. The Crescent guns quickly established a good reputation and were sold under a bewildering number of brand names through a wide variety of stores and mail-order houses. The weapon seen here is a side-by-side, 16 gauge, hammerless shotgun with 28 inch barrels which bears one of the company's better known trade names, the "Peerless."

**SPECIFICATIONS**
**Type:** double-barrel shotgun
**Origin:** Crescent Fire Arms Company, Norwich, Connecticut
**Caliber:** 16 gauge
**Barrel Length:** 28in

# EASTERN ARMS SINGLE-BARREL SHOTGUN

**SPECIFICATIONS**
**Type:** single-barrel shotgun
**Origin:** Eastern Arms (Iver Johnson)
**Caliber:** 20 gauge
**Barrel Length:** 27.75in

This was another of the many shotguns produced by a major manufacturer for a hardware company, in this case by Iver Johnson for Sears & Roebuck, using the trade name "Eastern Arms." It is a 20 gauge weapon with a 27.75 inch barrel and, like all such "Hardware Guns," as they are called, it is simple, straightforward and robust.

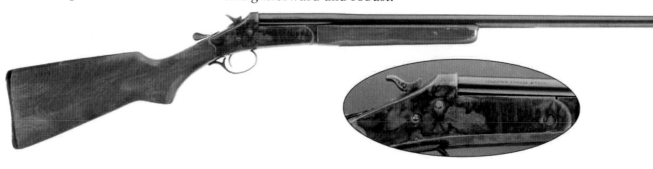

# FEDERAL GAS RIOT GUN

**SPECIFICATION**
**Type:** anti-riot shotgun
**Origin:** Federal Laboratories Incorporated of America
**Caliber:** 37mm
**Barrel Length:** 12in

This is a very basic riot gun and this example was issued at one time to the Highway department of the Illinois State Police. It was designed and made by Federal Gas Laboratories Inc, of Pittsburgh, Pennsylvania and operated on the "tip-up" principle to fire standard 37mm (1.5 inches) cartridges. The weapon was used to fire gas cartridges and there is a fixed sight on the breech marked "50 yards" and a folding sight on the receiver marked for 75 and 100 yards.

# FOX STERLINGWORTH DOUBLE-BARREL SHOTGUN

**SPECIFICATIONS**
**Type:** double-barrel shotgun
**Origin:** A.H. Fox, Philadelphia, Pennsylvania
**Caliber:** 12 gauge
**Barrel Length:** 28in

Ansley H. Fox was active as a firearms maker from 1896, first in Baltimore, Maryland and later in Philadelphia, Pennsylvania. In 1930, however, the company was taken over by the Savage Arms Company, although the latter continued to make Fox Model B shotguns until the 1970s. The Sterlingworth shotguns, made from 1911 to 1946, were double-barreled weapons with 26, 28 or 30 inch barrels and extractors; automatic ejectors were also available, and double triggers were normally fitted. The example seen here is 12 gauge, with a 28 inch barrel, a walnut stock and, unusually, a single trigger. The owner of this particular weapon has added a 2 inch extension to the stock (which is unfinished) and a recoil pad.

## FOX SINGLE-BARREL TRAP SHOTGUN

**SPECIFICATIONS**

**Type:** single-barrel shotgun
**Origin:** A.H. Fox, Philadelphia, Pennsylvania
**Caliber:** 12 gauge
**Barrel Length:** 32in

Another example of Fox's workmanship when still an independent company, this was one of some 570 single-barrel trap guns, designed in 1918–19 and made between 1919 and 1936. There were four grades – J, K, L and M – and the example seen here is grade JE, with the E-suffix indicating that it is fitted with automatic ejectors. It has a 32 inch, 12 gauge barrel and has some fine engraving on barrel and action.

## FRIGON FT-1 DOUBLE-BARREL SHOTGUN

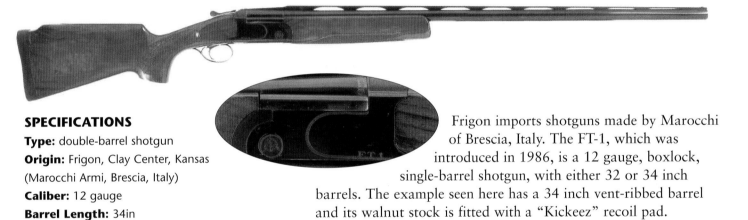

**SPECIFICATIONS**

**Type:** double-barrel shotgun
**Origin:** Frigon, Clay Center, Kansas (Marocchi Armi, Brescia, Italy)
**Caliber:** 12 gauge
**Barrel Length:** 34in

Frigon imports shotguns made by Marocchi of Brescia, Italy. The FT-1, which was introduced in 1986, is a 12 gauge, boxlock, single-barrel shotgun, with either 32 or 34 inch barrels. The example seen here has a 34 inch vent-ribbed barrel and its walnut stock is fitted with a "Kickeez" recoil pad.

## HARRINGTON & RICHARDSON SPECIAL FORCES SHOTGUN

**SPECIFICATION**

**Type:** combat shotgun
**Origin:** Harrington & Richardson Inc, Worcester, Massachusetts,
**Caliber:** 12 gauge
**Barrel Length:** 28in

These shotguns were purchased from Harrington & Richardson in the 1970s by the Special Forces – the Green Berets – for use in the Vietnam War. Their main use was to be given as gifts to the Montagnard people, who lived in the mountains, and were ultra-loyal, first to the French and subsequently to the United States in their fight against Communism. Not only was these weapons' origin clear from their general appearance, but they were actually inscribed "Special Forces Model" so that possession of one after the fall of the country made the owner's sympathies only too clear. As a result, all but a very few were destroyed and examples such as this are very difficult to find.

# ITHACA SINGLE-BARREL TRAP GUN

## SPECIFICATIONS

**Type:** single-barrel trap shotgun
**Origin:** Ithaca Gun Company, Ithaca, New York
**Caliber:** 12 gauge
**Barrel Length:** 32

The original Ithaca single-barrel trap gun used a lock designed by Emil Flues of Bay City, Michigan and was in production from 1914 to 1922; this one is a Flues model in Grade 5E finish.

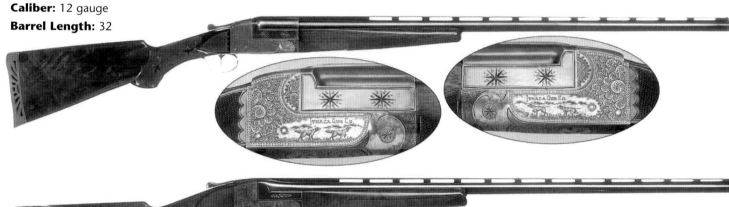

It was then replaced by a new design by one of Ithaca's own staff, Frank Knickerbocker, which was produced from 1922 to 1988; this was a very popular weapon among champion trap shooters, by whom it was known, quite simple, as "The Knick." It was marketed in a variety of grades, the example seen here being in Grade 4E, and which is engraved with scenes of an Indian archer and a trap shooter.

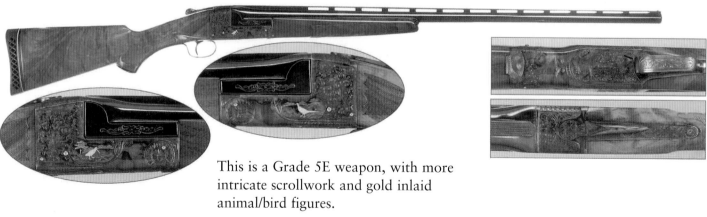

This is a Grade 5E weapon, with more intricate scrollwork and gold inlaid animal/bird figures.

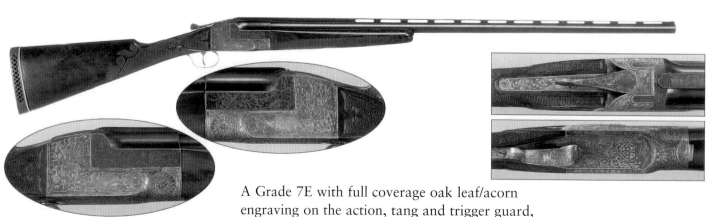

A Grade 7E with full coverage oak leaf/acorn engraving on the action, tang and trigger guard, together with bird scenes on the action.

# IVER JOHNSON CHAMPION SHOTGUN

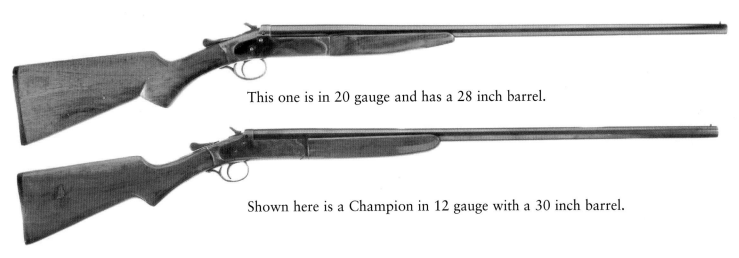

## SPECIFICATIONS
**Type:** single-barrel
shotgun
**Origin:** Iver Johnson Arms
Inc., Middlesex, New Jersey
**Caliber:** see text
**Barrel Length:** see text

The Champion was a straightforward single-barrel shotgun, which entered production at the Iver Johnson factory in 1909. It was produced in several gauges, with 26, 28, 30 or 32 inch barrels. It had external hammers and automatic ejectors. The basic model had a blued barrel, but there was also the Matted Rib grade, with a 12, 16 or 20 gauge matte rib barrel and a Trap grade with a 32 inch barrel. The Standard was made from 1909–56; the Matte Rib from 1909–48 and the Trap from 1909–42. The Champion was also produced as a "Hardware Gun" for various retail chains and mail order companies under their own trade names; e.g., Eastern Arms, Volunteer, etc. We show here a Champion in .410 gauge and with a 26 inch barrel.

This one is in 20 gauge and has a 28 inch barrel.

Shown here is a Champion in 12 gauge with a 30 inch barrel.

# KRIEGHOFF COMBINATION

## SPECIFICATIONS
**Type:** combination rifle/shotgun
**Origin:** Krieghoff International Ottsville,
Pennsylvania (Heinrich Krieghoff Gun
Co, Ulm, Germany)
**Caliber:** 7mm/16 Gauge
**Barrel Length:** 25in

Heinrich Krieghoff was one of the many German firearm manufacturers operating in Suhl in Thuringia up to 1945. When forced to close down after the war, it re-established itself in the West, in this case in Ulm. The company has set up a subsidiary in the United States, Krieghoff International, which imports the factory's products. This is a combination 7mm rifle and 16 gauge shotgun, fitted with a Carl Zeiss 4x telescopic sight on a claw sight for rapid removal. The stock has a cheek piece and is fitted with a recoil pad.

## KRIEGHOFF MODEL 32 SUPERPOSED SHOTGUN

**SPECIFICATIONS**

**Type:** superposed shotgun

**Origin:** Krieghoff International, Ottsville, Pennsylvania (Heinrich Krieghoff Gun Co, Ulm, Germany)

**Caliber:** see text

**Barrel Length:** see text

The Krieghoff Model 32 was a series of superposed shotguns in 12, 20, 28 or .410 gauge with barrels ranging from 26.5 to 32 inches in length, which was discontinued in 1988. The first example seen here is in 12 gauge with a 32 inch vented-rib barrel, and with deep engravings on the receiver (duck on the right, bird and dog on the left). The furniture is walnut and the stock has a white line recoil pad.

The case also contains a Krieghoff Model 32, but with no less than five barrels. Four are 28 inches long in .410, 12, 20 and 28 gauge, while the fifth is 30 inches long and in 12 gauge. The entire outfit is housed in a Simmons case.

## LEFEVER DAMASCUS DOUBLE-BARREL SHOTGUN

**SPECIFICATIONS**

**Type:** hammerless, double-barrel shotgun

**Origin:** Lefever Arms Company, Syracuse, New York

**Caliber:** see text

**Barrel Length:** see text

The Lefever Arms Company was founded in 1884 by Dan Lefever a noted inventor and innovator, who was widely known as "Uncle Dan." It was based in Syracuse, New York, with Dan as company president, but in 1901 he was forced out of office. He sought revenge by founding a new company, D.M. Lefever & Sons, also based in Syracuse, New York, but this continued in business only until 1906, when he died and the company folded. Meanwhile, the original Lefever Arms Company continued in business until 1916, when it was bought by Ithaca, who continued producing Lefever shotguns until 1948.

The Lefever Damascus side-plated shotgun was made by the original Lefever Arms Company from 1885 and remained in production until 1919. It was made in four barrel lengths – 26, 28, 30 and 32 inches – and four calibers – 10, 12, 16 and 20 gauge – and in no less than eighteen grades of finish. The examples shown here are all chambered for 12 gauge.

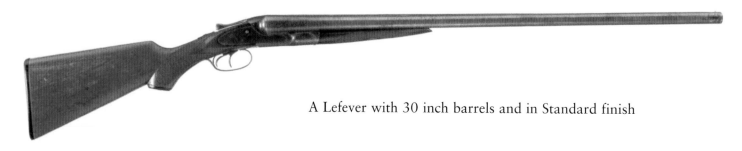

A Lefever with 30 inch barrels and in Standard finish

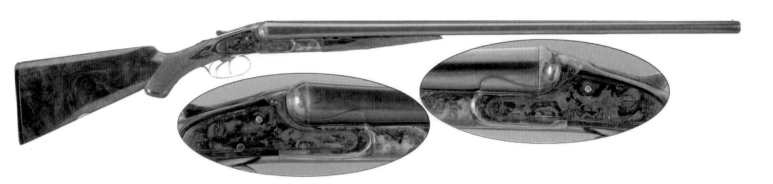

Another with 30 inch barrels, but this time in "Grade DE" finish.

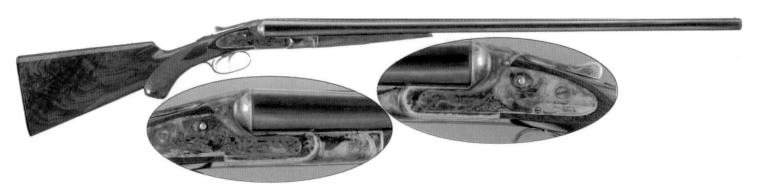

This one has a 32 inch barrel and is in "Grade EE" finish.

## LEFEVER NITRO SPECIAL DOUBLE-BARREL SHOTGUN

Having been taken over by Ithaca in 1916 (see previous entry) the company, now known as Lefever Arms Company Inc, continued production of the sidelock gun until 1919. It was the replaced in 1921 by a new gun, the Nitro Special, a boxlock design in various barrel lengths and four calibers – 12, 16, 20 and .410 gauge – which remained in production until 1948. This example is in 20 gauge, with a 28 inch barrel and single trigger.

**SPECIFICATIONS**
**Type:** double-barrel shotgun
**Origin:** Lefever Arms Company Inc, Syracuse, New York
**Caliber:** 20 gauge
**Barrel Length:** 28in

## MARLIN MODEL 44A SLIDE-ACTION SHOTGUN

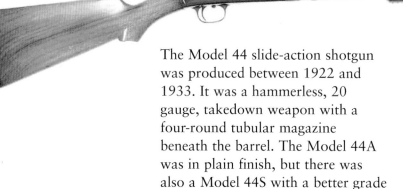

The Model 44 slide-action shotgun was produced between 1922 and 1933. It was a hammerless, 20 gauge, takedown weapon with a four-round tubular magazine beneath the barrel. The Model 44A was in plain finish, but there was also a Model 44S with a better grade walnut stock with checkering.

**SPECIFICATIONS**
**Type:** slide-action shotgun
**Origin:** Marlin Firearms Company, New Haven, Connecticut
**Caliber:** 20 gauge
**Barrel Length:** 26in

## MARLIN MODEL 90 OVER-AND-UNDER SHOTGUN

**SPECIFICATIONS**
**Type:** over-and-under (superposed) shotgun
**Origin:** Marlin Firearms Company, New Haven, Connecticut
**Caliber:** see text
**Barrel Length:** see text

The Model 90 was manufactured by Marlin between 1937 and 1963. One production run was for Sears, Roebuck and was marketed by them under the trades name "Ranger" up to 1941, and "J.C. Higgins" from 1946 onwards. The same weapon was also marketed by Marlin as the Model 90. The two shotguns shown here are both Marlin Model 90s.

The first has 28 inch, 20 gauge barrels and double set triggers and was produced after 1950 (no gap between barrels).

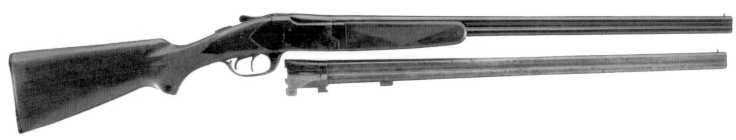

The second has .410 gauge, 28 inch barrels (plus a spare) and was also produced before 1950.

# MOSSBERG MODEL 500

## SPECIFICATIONS
**Type:** slide-action shotgun
**Origin:** O.F. Mossberg & Sons Inc, North Haven, Connecticut
**Caliber:** see text
**Barrel Length:** see text

The Mossberg Model 500 pump-action shotgun has been in production for well over 20 years, during which time many millions have been sold. There have been at least seventeen variants, ranging from standard field models, through slug (including fully rifled), bantam for young shooters, turkey, waterfowl, security and combination models, and it has also been accepted by the U.S. army. The Model 500 is marketed in a wide variety of barrel lengths, calibers and finishes, and the standard magazine holds five shells.

Shown here is a Model 500 Crown Grade with 28.25 inch vent-ribbed barrel in 20 gauge.

This one is in 12 gauge with a 28 inch vent-ribbed barrel and a Woodlands camouflage pattern finish.

Finally we have a Model 500 ATP in 12 gauge, with plastic pistol grips and no stock butt.

## MOSSBERG MODEL 835 SLIDE-ACTION SHOTGUN

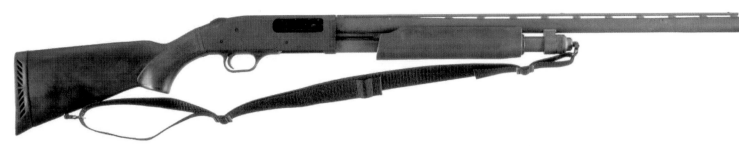

**SPECIFICATIONS**

**Type:** slide-action shotgun

**Origin:** O.F. Mossberg & Sons Inc, North Haven, Connecticut

**Caliber:** see text

**Barrel Length:** see text

The Mossberg Model 835 Ulti-Mag is a 12 gauge, pump-action shotgun, usually with a vent-ribbed barrel, and with a number of fully-camouflaged variants. We show a Model 835 with a 26 inch barrel and composition stock with a matte blue finish.

## MOSSBERG MODEL 9200 SEMI-AUTOMATIC SHOTGUN

**SPECIFICATIONS**

**Type:** semi-automatic shotgun

**Origin:** O.F. Mossberg & Sons Inc, North Haven, Connecticut

**Caliber:** see text

**Barrel Length:** see text

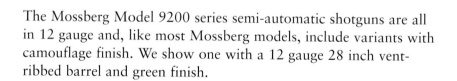

The Mossberg Model 9200 series semi-automatic shotguns are all in 12 gauge and, like most Mossberg models, include variants with camouflage finish. We show one with a 12 gauge 28 inch vent-ribbed barrel and green finish.

## NEWPORT DOUBLE-BARREL SHOTGUN

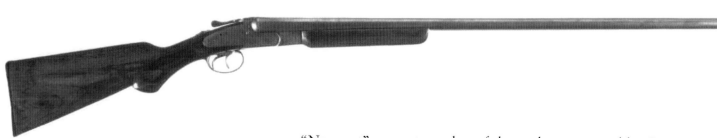

**SPECIFICATIONS**

**Type:** double-barrel shotgun

**Origin:** H & D Folsom (Crescent), New York

**Caliber:** 16 gauge

**Barrel Length:** 30 inch

"Newport" was yet another of the trade names used by Crescent, which was itself owned by H. & D. Folsom. The Newport weapons were made for the Chicago-based Hibbard, Spencer and Bartlett company. This particular example has two 16 gauge, 30 inches long barrels, side lock action with double triggers, and a tang safety.

## PARKER GH/GHE GRADE DOUBLE-BARREL SHOTGUNS

### SPECIFICATIONS

**Type:** semi-automatic shotgun
**Origin:** Parker Brothers, Meriden, Connecticut
**Caliber:** see text
**Barrel Length:** see text

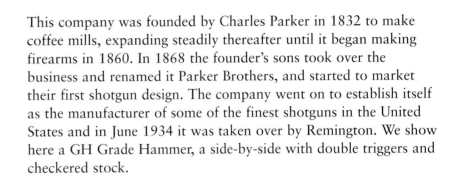

This company was founded by Charles Parker in 1832 to make coffee mills, expanding steadily thereafter until it began making firearms in 1860. In 1868 the founder's sons took over the business and renamed it Parker Brothers, and started to market their first shotgun design. The company went on to establish itself as the manufacturer of some of the finest shotguns in the United States and in June 1934 it was taken over by Remington. We show here a GH Grade Hammer, a side-by-side with double triggers and checkered stock.

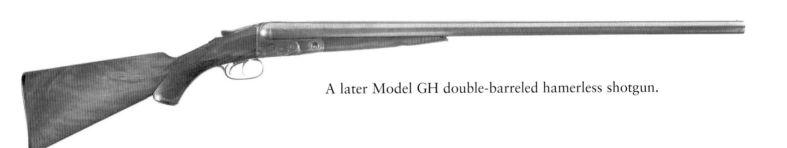

A later Model GH double-barreled hamerless shotgun.

## PARKER TROJAN DOUBLE-BARREL SHOTGUNS

### SPECIFICATIONS

**Type:** double-barrel shotgun
**Origin:** Parker Brothers, Meriden, Connecticut
**Caliber:** see text
**Barrel Length:** see text

The Trojan was a boxlock, double-barreled (side-by-side) shotgun. It was made in 12, 16, or 20 gauge and in the usual variety of barrel lengths. The example shown has a 12 gauge, 30 inch barrel with 2.6 inch chambers, and extractors. The recoil pad is a post-factory addition by one of the owners.

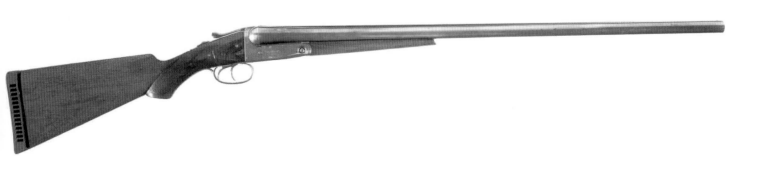

## REMINGTON-WHITMORE MODEL 1873

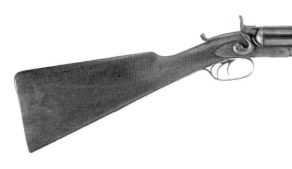

### SPECIFICATIONS

**Type:** double-barrel shotgun
**Origin:** Remington Arms Co., Ilion, New York
**Caliber:** 10, 12 gauge
**Barrel Length:** 28in and 30in

One of the attitudes that kept Remington successful was their willingness to search for the best designs and ideas no matter the source. Andrew E. Whitmore was a designer who sold the rights to his shotgun to the company, giving them in 1873 the first double-barreled weapon in their product line, and one of the first to be mass-produced at an affordable price in the United States. Versions were later (1875) offered with various rifle/shotgun barrel combinations, stronger hammer shoulders and Hepburn's patented rebounding lock.

## REMINGTON MODEL 1889

### SPECIFICATIONS

**Type:** double-barrel shotgun
**Origin:** Remington Arms Co., Ilion, New York
**Caliber:** 10, 12 gauge
**Barrel Length:** various

Remington's Model 1885 and 1887 shotguns were reasonably successful weapons, using a rotating top lever to open the action, first pioneered in the Model 1882. The Model 1889 was a redesign of the Model 1887, still with exposed hammers, and available in 10 and 12 gauge. It turned out to be remarkable successful, and over 134,000 were made before production stopped in 1908. During this time various grades and options were available, while the hammer shape was redesigned more than once. We show two Model 1889s, one with significantly shorter barrels than the other.

The documentation with this Model 1899 certifies that it was supplied to the Wells Fargo company to enable their stagecoach drivers and wayposts to defend themselves from robbery or attack.

## REMINGTON MODEL 1894 HAMMERLESS

This first Remington double-barreled shotgun to have no external hammer, the Model 1894 came in a range of quality grades, rising from A to E. Early models used "Damascus twist" construction, but steel barrels were available from 1896. A remarkably expensive special edition ($750) was offered in 1902, but only a few were made. By the time production of the Model 1894 ceased in 1910, nearly 42,000 had been sold.

### SPECIFICATIONS

**Type:** double-barrel shotgun
**Origin:** Remington Arms Co., Ilion, New York
**Caliber:** 10, 12 and 16 gauge
**Barrel Length:** various

## REMINGTON MODEL 1900

The Model 1900 was intended to offer a more economical hammerless side-by-side that the Model 1894, and was a plain, simple but reliable weapon. Barrels were available in both "Damascus twist" and gunmetal steel. Production stopped in 1910, with 98,508 made.

### SPECIFICATIONS

**Type:** double-barrel shotgun
**Origin:** Remington Arms Co., Ilion, New York
**Caliber:** 12 and 16 gauge
**Barrel Length:** various

## REMINGTON MODEL 10 PUMP-ACTION

John D. Pedersen helped Remington to develop their first slide-action shotgun which went on sale in 1908, and it became the Model 10 in 1911. A 12 gauge weapon, it had a short tubular magazine under the barrel loaded from underneath the breech. Empty shell cases were also ejected downward.

The Model 10 was originally sold in 8 grades, but more were added as time went on. There were sporting versions, hunters and riot guns, and in 1931 a Target Grade Model 10 was introduced with a ventilated top rib. Some 275,000 were made by 1928, when production stopped. We show a riot gun version.

### SPECIFICATIONS

**Type:** slide-action shotgun
**Origin:** Remington Arms Co., Ilion, New York
**Caliber:** 12 gauge
**Barrel Length:** various

## REMINGTON MODEL 10 TRENCH GUN

### SPECIFICATION

**Type:** trench gun
**Origin:** Remington Arms Co., Ilion, New York
**Caliber:** 12 gauge
**Barrel Length:** 23 and 20 in

The main order for combat shotguns placed by the U.S. army in 1917 was with Winchester (see below) but they also ordered a trench gun version of the Model 10 shotgun from Remington. It was an army requirement that trench guns should be capable of mounting a bayonet, so Remington designed a metal adaptor that clamped over the muzzle, with a bayonet boss underneath. In addition, it was necessary to protect the firer's left hand from the hot barrel when the bayonet was fixed so a wooden handguard was installed. Remington delivered approximately 3,500 of these 23 inch Model 10 trench guns to the army during World War One. Another 1,500 were delivered with 20 inch barrels.

## REMINGTON MODEL 11 AUTOLOADING SHOTGUN

A John Browning design, this recoil-operated autoloader was first offered in 1906 as the Remington Autoloading Gun, but was renamed the Model 11 Autoloading Shotgun in 1911. For most of its life it was a 12 gauge weapon, but 20 and 16 gauge were introduced in 1931–32. It turned out to be a spectacular success for the company, with over 850,000 being made; and production only finally stopped in 1948.

### SPECIFICATIONS

**Type:** semi-automatic shotgun
**Origin:** Remington Arms Co., Ilion, New York
**Caliber:** 12, 16 and 20 gauge
**Barrel Length:** 26 in

# REMINGTON ARMY MODEL 11

## SPECIFICATION

**Type:** semi-automatic shotgun
**Origin:** Remington Arms Co., Ilion, New York
**Caliber:** 12 gauge
**Barrel Length:** 26 and 20in

The U.S. government purchased a number of Model 11s, particularly during World War Two, while others were bought by police departments for anti-riot duties.

This one is a World War Two U.S. army Model 11, with a 26 inch, 12 gauge barrel.

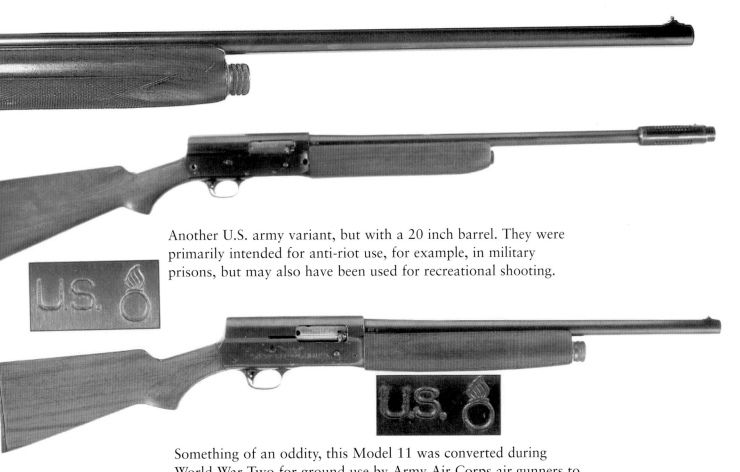

Another U.S. army variant, but with a 20 inch barrel. They were primarily intended for anti-riot use, for example, in military prisons, but may also have been used for recreational shooting.

Something of an oddity, this Model 11 was converted during World War Two for ground use by Army Air Corps air gunners to practice "leading. against aerial targets. The weapon had threaded holes in the receiver, which enabled it to be attached to the simulated aircraft fuselage, and a Cutts compensator on the muzzle.

## REMINGTON MODEL 17 PUMP-ACTION

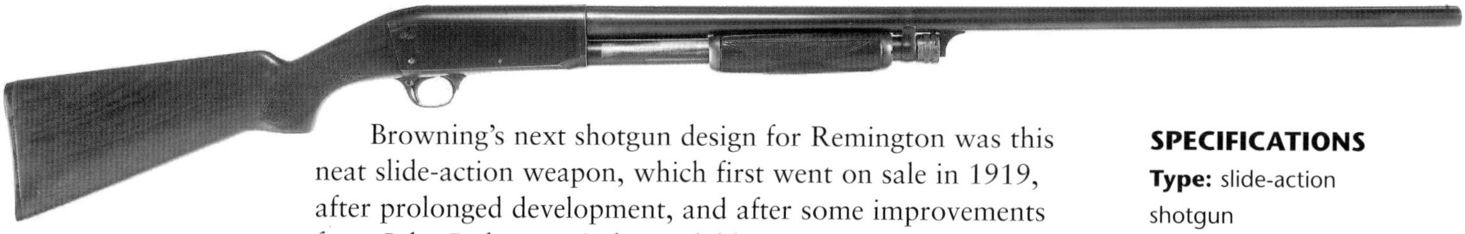

Browning's next shotgun design for Remington was this neat slide-action weapon, which first went on sale in 1919, after prolonged development, and after some improvements from John Pederson. Only available in 20-gauge, it was light, at 5lbs 12 oz, and came with a takedown frame. The under-barrel tubular magazine was loaded from under the receiver, and shell cases were ejected the same way. The Model 17 came in 5 sporting grades plus a riot grade, and 72,644 were made before production stopped in 1941.

**SPECIFICATIONS**

**Type:** slide-action shotgun
**Origin:** Remington Arms Co., Ilion, New York
**Caliber:** 20 gauge
**Barrel Length:** various

## REMINGTON MODEL 31 PUMP-ACTION

The Model 31 was developed to replace the Model 17 and Model 29, and was Remington's first side-ejecting, repeating shotgun. The Model 31 held 5 shots in the tubular magazine, although a lightweight 3-shot version was also issued in 1931, as "The Sportsman." Another success for the company, the Model 31 remained in production from 1931 to 1949, during which time some 189,000 were made, in a multitude of grades and variations. Another 179,000 or so Sportsman shotguns were also sold during this time.

**SPECIFICATIONS**

**Type:** slide-action shotgun
**Origin:** Remington Arms Co., Ilion, New York
**Caliber:** 12, 16, 20 gauge
**Barrel Length:** various

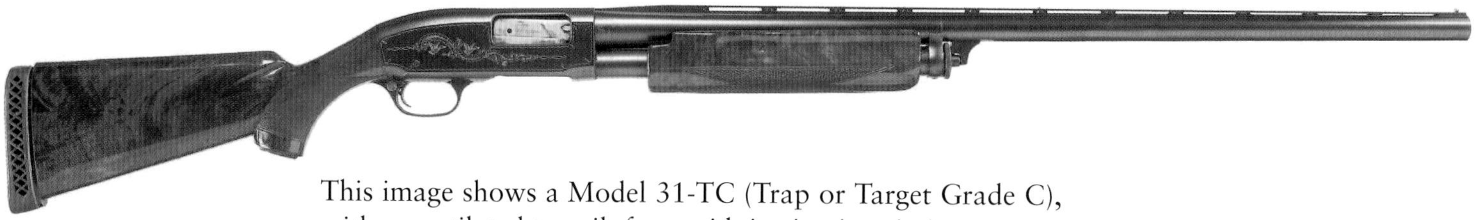

This image shows a Model 31-TC (Trap or Target Grade C), with a ventilated top rib for rapid, instinctive aiming.

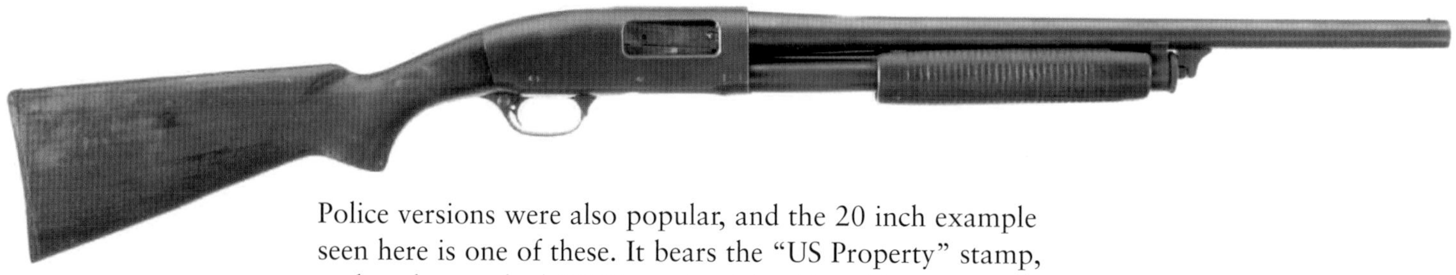

Police versions were also popular, and the 20 inch example seen here is one of these. It bears the "US Property" stamp, and is also marked "ISP" on the right side of the receiver, which suggests that it may once have belonged to a police department, possibly "Illinois State Police."

## REMINGTON MODEL 32 OVER AND UNDER

**SPECIFICATIONS**
**Type:** double-barrel over-and-under shotgun
**Origin:** Remington Arms Co., Ilion, New York
**Caliber:** 12 gauge
**Barrel Length:** various

A simple break-open shotgun, the Model 32 was Remington's first attempt at an over-and-under configuration. Launched in March 1932 it was well-made, with machine engraving on the receiver and high-grade wood with checkered fore-end and wrist. Initially it came with two triggers but from 1934 had a single selective trigger. Variations included different levels of finish and recoil pad. We show the Model 32 TC Target Grade, which has a raised, ventilated top rib and recoil pad. The Model 32 was an expensive weapon, and sales were limited to only some 5,000 during the depression years, and finally stopped when war broke out.

## REMINGTON MODEL 870

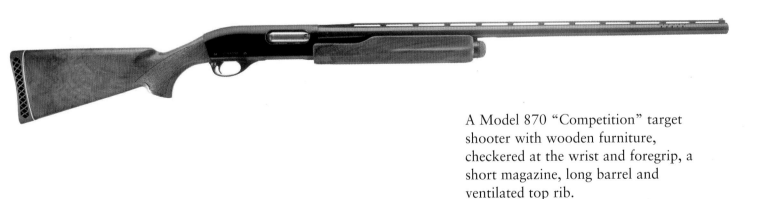

A Model 870 "Competition" target shooter with wooden furniture, checkered at the wrist and foregrip, a short magazine, long barrel and ventilated top rib.

The Remington Model 870 slide action shotgun was introduced in 1950 as a replacement for then Model 31. Originally known as the "Wingmaster", it has sprouted a whole range of variations, mainly in 12, 16 or 20 gauge, and with 20, 26, 28 or 30 inch barrels. With this weapon Remington hit on a combination of simplicity, robustness, balance and effectiveness that is still world-beating. Over fifty-five years since first going on sale, it is still one of Remington's main product lines; and as over six million have been made, it is the most popular shotgun of any type in history.

Variants include straightforward hunting shotguns, skeet, target-shooting and competition models, economical "Express" models, heavy duty "Magnum" versions for heavier loads, rifled "slug" guns for large game targets, folding stock versions and specialist military and police models.

## SPECIFICATIONS
**Type:** slide-action shotgun
**Origin:** Remington Arms Co., Ilion, New York
**Caliber:** 10, 12, 16 or 20 gauge
**Barrel Length:** 20, 26, 28, and 30in

This Model 870 Express has a short magazine and ventilated top rib

A Model 870 with dulled green finish on the metalwork but a standard wooden stock and grip. This one comes with a shorter and choked second barrel.

One of the many special edition Model 870s, this "Wildlife for Tomorrow" piece has finely finished and polished wood, and finely engraved scenes of gamebirds, picked out in gold wire.

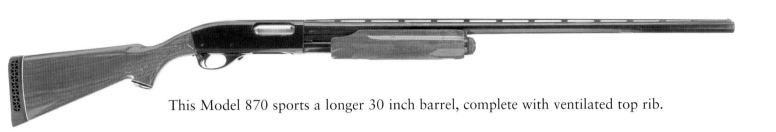

This Model 870 sports a longer 30 inch barrel, complete with ventilated top rib.

Remington Model 870 Express Turkey, with non-reflective black finish (also on the bolt) and ventilated top rib.

## REMINGTON 870 MAGNUM AND SLUG GUNS

**SPECIFICATIONS**

**Type:** slide-action shotgun

**Origin:** Remington Arms Co., Ilion, New York

**Caliber:** 10, 12, 16 or 20 gauge

**Barrel Length:** 20, 26, 28, and 30in

When larger game is hunted, users normally want a more powerful cartridge than the normal "buckshot" type. Magnum cartridges are longer than standard, with a more powerful charge and heavier load. Magnum variants of the M870 have longer chambers and often quite short barrels (20 or 26 inch).

For some targets such as deer etc, a heavy single slug is often used rather than the multiple projectiles in normal shotgun ammunition. Slug barrels are usually rifled, and many shotguns have sets of interchangeable barrels to allow the owner to set the gun up with the right kind of ammunition for a particular job.

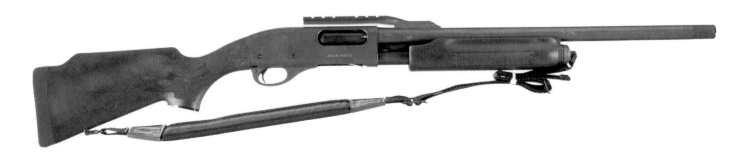

A Model 870 Magnum Special Purpose, with dull green finish to metalwork and green synthetic stock and foregrip. The stock has an integral cheek pad, while on the receiver is a mounting rail for fitting various optical and night vision sights.

Another Magnum Special Purpose, with non-reflective black finish on the receiver and bolt. It has a short magazine and barrel-mounted fore- and rearsights.

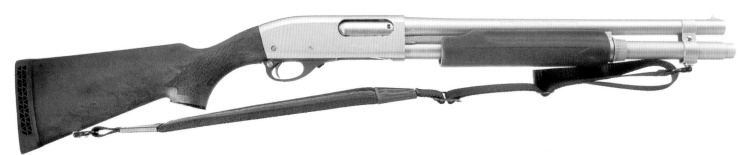

This Model 870 Magnum is the "Marine" type, where the bright satin finish on the metalwork helps prevent corrosion in salt environment. It also has a green synthetic stock and foregrip, and rubber recoil pad.

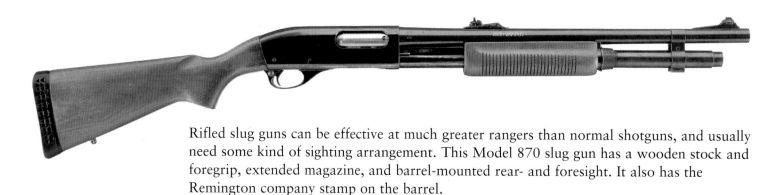

Rifled slug guns can be effective at much greater rangers than normal shotguns, and usually need some kind of sighting arrangement. This Model 870 slug gun has a wooden stock and foregrip, extended magazine, and barrel-mounted rear- and foresight. It also has the Remington company stamp on the barrel.

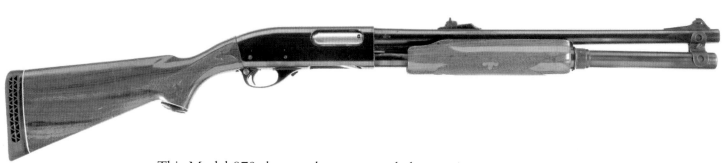

This Model 870 slug gun has an extended magazine.

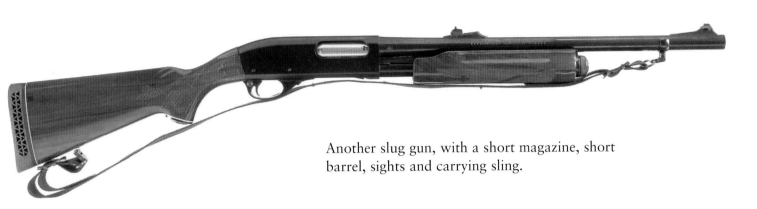

Another slug gun, with a short magazine, short barrel, sights and carrying sling.

# REMINGTON 870 MILITARY/POLICE

## SPECIFICATIONS

**Type:** slide-action shotgun
**Origin:** Remington Arms Co., Ilion, New York
**Caliber:** 12 gauge
**Barrel Length:** 14in, 18in, 20in

Model 870s used for military and police work usually have shorter barrels, making them handier for rapid aiming and easier to get in and out of vehicles. The versatile shotgun can be used for a range of ammunition types, including buckshot, solid slugs (for forcing doors open), non-lethal baton rounds and irritant gas projectiles.

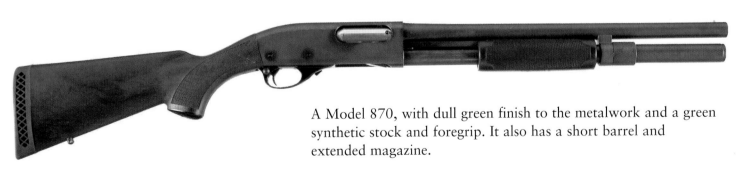

A Model 870 modified for police and military use, with synthetic pistol grip, short barrel, camouflaged detachable skeleton stock and dull green metalwork. Note that the foregrip remains checkered wood.

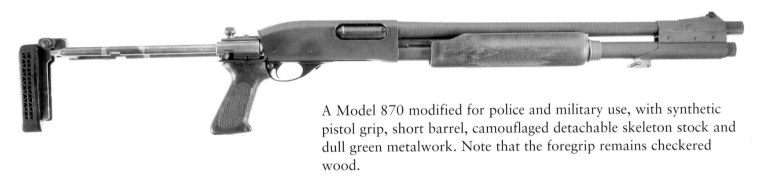

A Model 870, with dull green finish to the metalwork and a green synthetic stock and foregrip. It also has a short barrel and extended magazine.

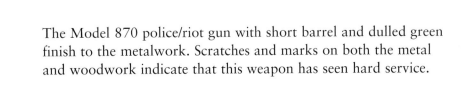

The Model 870 police/riot gun with short barrel and dulled green finish to the metalwork. Scratches and marks on both the metal and woodwork indicate that this weapon has seen hard service.

# REMINGTON MODEL 1100 AUTOLOADING SHOTGUN

## SPECIFICATIONS

**Type:** autoloading shotgun

**Origin:** Remington Arms Co., Ilion, New York

**Caliber:** see text

**Barrel Length:** 28in and 30in

Introduced in 1963, the Model 1100 was Remington revisiting the autoloading shotgun and producing a weapon to fill the gap left by the now out-of-production Model 11. Using Remington's signature smooth outline and styling, it was another success for the company. Since introduction, over 3 million have been made, and solid and reliable, it comes in a range of gauges, including 12, 12 Magnum, 16 and 20 gauges. A lightweight version is also available in 28 and .410m gauges. The two shown here have similar levels of finish, with fine scrollwork on the receiver and bolt. One shows the signs of hard usage – exactly what these fine, practical guns were intended for.

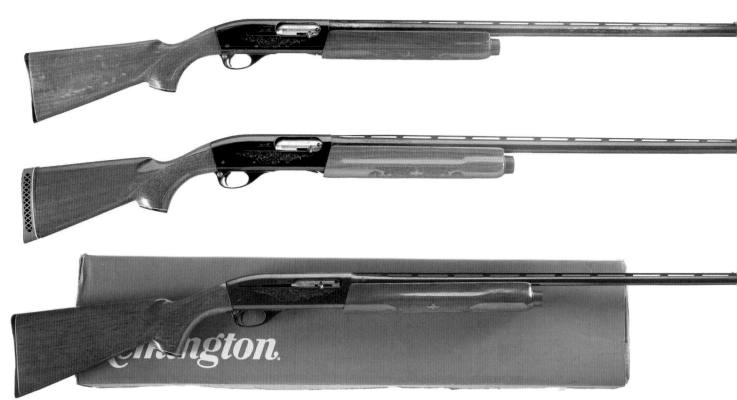

While it looks similar, this one is actually a Model 1100 LW, or Lightweight. The narrower barrel is chambered for either 28 or .410 gauge.

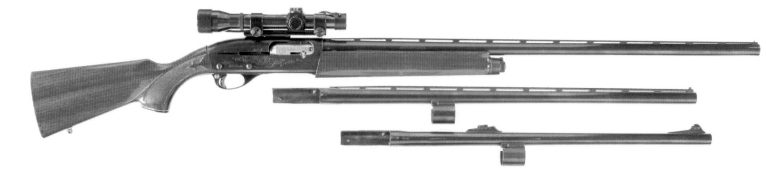

A complete shotgun "set," this Model 1100 comes with two extra barrels, on choked, and one a heavy slug or deer barrel with fore- and rearsights. The weapon also has a mounting rail above the receiver which is carrying an optical sight.

# REMINGTON MODEL 3200

## SPECIFICATIONS

**Type:** autoloading shotgun
**Origin:** Remington Arms Co., Ilion, New York
**Caliber:** see text
**Barrel Length:** 28in and 30in

The Model 3200 was introduced in 1973, the first Remington over-and-under shotgun since the Model 32, which ended production in 1941. It bears a close visual and engineering resemblance to the earlier weapon although modern production methods allow it to made quicker, more efficiently and comparatively cheaper. It was available in a range of gauges and grades.

# REMINGTON PARKER AHE

## SPECIFICATIONS

**Type:** double-barrel shotgun
**Origin:** Remington Arms Co., Ilion, New York
**Caliber:** 20 gauge
**Barrel Length:** 28in

Remington introduced this in 1988, and it is handcrafted in the Parker Gun Works division of Remington. It represents a double-barreled Parker shotgun of yesteryear, and is made to the same exacting standards as before. It has ribbed side-by-side barrels, a smooth, fast-acting single selective trigger, and fine engravings on the receiver. Only a few of these very expensive collectors' items were made.

# RICHLAND ARMS MODEL 711 MAGNUM DOUBLE-BARREL SHOTGUN

## SPECIFICATIONS

**Type:** double-barrel shotgun
**Origin:** Richland Arms Company, Blissfield, Michigan
**Caliber:** 19 gauge
**Barrel Length:** 32in

The Richland Arms Company imported Spanish-made shotguns, but ceased trading in 1986. This Model 711 Magnum is a double-barreled gun with two 10 gauge, 32 inch, solid rib barrels and 3.5 inch chambers. It has double triggers and automatic ejectors and the action is decorated with fine English scrollwork.

## RIVERSIDE SLIDE-ACTION SHOTGUN

**SPECIFICATIONS**

**Type:** slide-action shotgun
**Origin:** Riverside Arms Company (J. Stevens Arms Company, Chicopee Falls, Massachusetts)
**Caliber:** 12 gauge
**Barrel Length:** 20in

Riverside Arms Company was a trade name used by the J. Stevens Arms Company for certain types of firearm. This 12 gauge, 20 inch barrel shotgun was intended for law enforcement use and was made in about 1938.

## ROPER REVOLVING SHOTGUN

**SPECIFICATIONS**

**Type:** revolver shotgun
**Origin:** Roper Sporting Arms Co., Hartford, Connecticut
**Caliber:** 12 gauge
**Barrel Length:** 28in

Sylvester H. Roper set up the Roper Repeating Rifle company in Amerhurst, Massachusetts and began producing a range of revolver rifles and shotguns from 1867 onwards. He soon moved to Hartford and from 1869–76 manufactured weapons under the name of the Roper Sporting Arms Co. All used variations of the same theme, where a metal cartridge was rotated into place by using the rear cocking trigger, then forced up against the barrel when hit by the hammer to form a tight seal. The cartridges were unusual in that they were made from steel, were reloadable with shot and powder, and had either a percussion nipple or primer hole built-in. This shotgun had four such cartridges inside the cylindrical housing, which were accessed by a loading gate on top.

## RUGER RED LABEL OVER-AND-UNDER SHOTGUN (EARLY PRODUCTION)

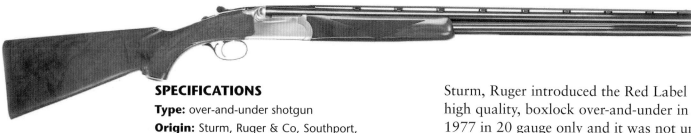

**SPECIFICATIONS**

**Type:** over-and-under shotgun
**Origin:** Sturm, Ruger & Co, Southport, Connecticut
**Caliber:** see text
**Barrel Length:** see text

Sturm, Ruger introduced the Red Label high quality, boxlock over-and-under in 1977 in 20 gauge only and it was not until 1982 that the 12 gauge version appeared. This is one of those early examples, with 28 inch vent-ribbed barrels in 20 gauge.

# RUGER RED LABEL SHOTGUNS (LATER PRODUCTION)

For over 30 years, Sturm, Ruger has been producingh high-quality, American-made over-and-under shotguns that offer a unique combination of traditional styling and Ruger reliability. The Ruger Red Label comes in 12, 20 and 28 gauges, has Briley adjustable chokes, and in a variety of finishes including stainless steel, engraved, blued and satin gray all-weather.

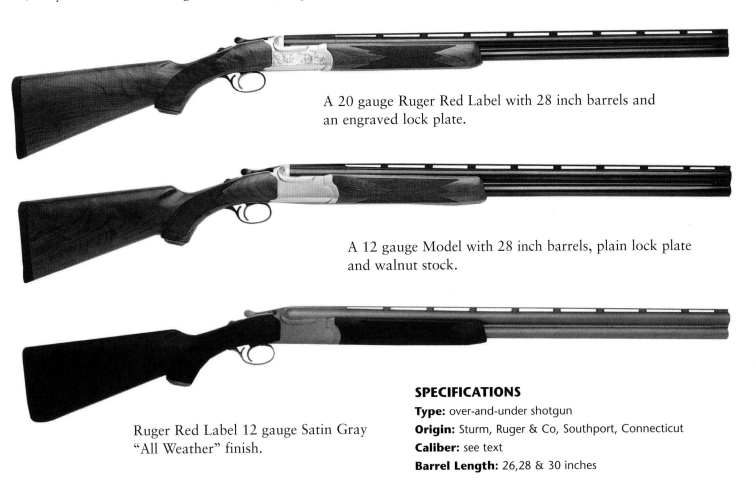

A 20 gauge Ruger Red Label with 28 inch barrels and an engraved lock plate.

A 12 gauge Model with 28 inch barrels, plain lock plate and walnut stock.

Ruger Red Label 12 gauge Satin Gray "All Weather" finish.

**SPECIFICATIONS**
**Type:** over-and-under shotgun
**Origin:** Sturm, Ruger & Co, Southport, Connecticut
**Caliber:** see text
**Barrel Length:** 26,28 & 30 inches

# RUGER GOLD LABEL SIDE-BY SIDE SHOTGUNS

Typical of the Sturm, Ruger approach is the traditional side –by –side range of shotguns to compete with the finest European and British guns. The Ruger Gold Label comes with Blued Barrels, a stainless steel brushed receiver and an American walnut stock with either straight or pistol grip. It has Briley adjustable chokes.

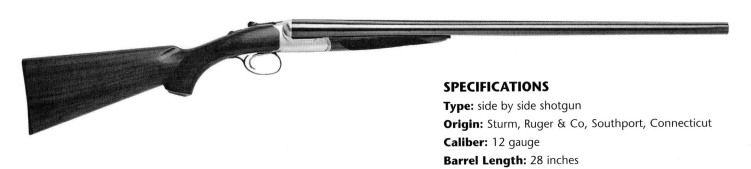

**SPECIFICATIONS**
**Type:** side by side shotgun
**Origin:** Sturm, Ruger & Co, Southport, Connecticut
**Caliber:** 12 gauge
**Barrel Length:** 28 inches

## SAVAGE MODEL 430 SUPERPOSED SHOTGUN

**SPECIFICATIONS**

**Type:** superposed shotgun

**Origin:** Savage Arms Corporation, Chicopee Falls, Massachusetts

**Caliber:** 12 gauge

**Barrel Length**: 28in

The Savage Model 420 and 430 superposed shotguns were produced between 1937 and 1943 in 12, 16 or 20 gauge and 26, 28, or 30 inch barrels. The 430 differed from the 420 only in having a checkered stock and a solid ribbed barrel. Both models were available in single- or double-trigger versions. The example shown here is a Model 430 with a 28 inch barrel with double triggers.

## SAVAGE MODEL 440T SUPERPOSED SHOTGUN

**SPECIFICATIONS**

**Type:** superposed shotgun

**Origin:** Savage Arms Corporation, Chicopee Falls, Massachusetts

**Caliber:** 12 gauge

**Barrel Length:** 30in

The Model 440T was made in Italy between 1968 and 1972 and marketed in the United States under the Savage label. It has two 12 gauge 30 inch barrels and a walnut, trap-style stock.

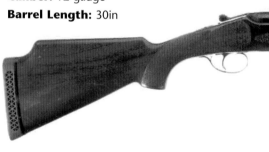

## SAVAGE MODEL 720 SEMI-AUTOMATIC SHOTGUN

**SPECIFICATIONS**

**Type:** semi-automatic shotgun

**Origin:** Savage Arms Corporation, Chicopee Falls, Massachusetts

**Caliber:** 16 gauge

**Barrel Length:** 28in

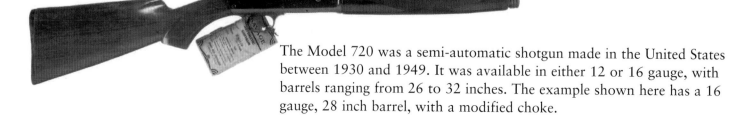

The Model 720 was a semi-automatic shotgun made in the United States between 1930 and 1949. It was available in either 12 or 16 gauge, with barrels ranging from 26 to 32 inches. The example shown here has a 16 gauge, 28 inch barrel, with a modified choke.

## SHATTUCK TWO-TRIGGER SHOTGUN

**SPECIFICATIONS**
**Type:** double-barrel shotgun
**Origin:** C.S. Shattuck, Hatfield, Massachusetts
**Caliber:** 10 gauge
**Barrel Length:** 43in

Charles S. Shattuck was a firearms manufacturer, who was in business from 1880 to 1908. His best known products were revolvers, but he also made single- and double-barrel shotguns.

## SKB SHOTGUNS

SKB is a Japanese company, formed in the Ibaraki province of Japan in 1855, its title being derived from the family's Japanese name of Sakaba, with the vowels removed. In the past, SKB's shotguns have been imported into the United States by several well-known companies, including Ithaca, but are now imported under their own name, by SKB Shotguns of Omaha, Nebraska. The produce a wide range of shotguns, some of which are shown here.

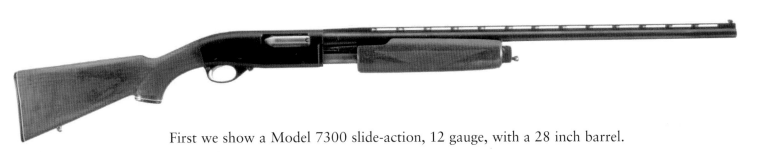

First we show a Model 7300 slide-action, 12 gauge, with a 28 inch barrel.

This is the XL 900MR semi-automatic, again in 12 gauge and with a 28 inch barrels.

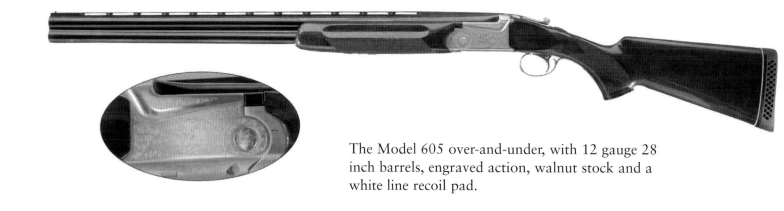

The Model 605 over-and-under, with 12 gauge 28 inch barrels, engraved action, walnut stock and a white line recoil pad.

# L.C. SMITH, EARLY HAMMERLESS DOUBLE-BARREL SHOTGUN

## SPECIFICATIONS
**Type:** double-barrel shotgun
**Origin:** Hunter Arms Company, Fulton, New York
**Caliber:** 16 gauge
**Barrel Length:** 26in

The L.C. Smith label has undergone several changes over the years. The company was formed for the manufacture of shotguns by Lyman Cornelius Smith at Syracuse, New York in 1877. He sold out in 1890 when the company was purchased by the Hunter Arms Company and moved to Fulton, New York. The Hunter company was, in its turn, purchased by the Marlin Firearms Company in 1945, who retained the L.C. Smith label until 1951 and then resurrected it for a further five years from 1968 to 1973, but it then disappeared for good.

The L.C. Smith hammerless shotguns are divided into two eras: early – made by Hunter Arms between 1890 and 1913; and late – made by Hunter Arms between 1914 and 1945 and by Marlin from 1945 to 1951. The early models were all to a standard design which featured sidelock actions, and were made in 10, 12, 16 and 20 gauge and in a variety of barrel lengths. The main variation was in the standard of materials and the quality and expense of embellishment, which rose from No.1 Grade, through No.2, No.3, Pigeon, No.4, A-1, No.5, Monogram and A-2 to the highest of them all, A-3, of which just twenty were ever made. The example seen here is No.2 Grade with 16 gauge, 26 inch barrels and a vignette of a duck and quail on the action. The wood is good quality walnut, but without any checkering.

# L.C. SMITH, LATER HAMMERLESS DOUBLE-BARREL SHOTGUN

## SPECIFICATIONS

**Type:** double-barrel shotgun

**Origin:** Hunter Arms Company, Fulton, New York/Marlin Firearms Company, Fulton, New York

**Caliber:** see text

**Barrel Length:** see text

The later variants of the hammerless side-by-side shotgun, made between 1914 and 1951, were chambered for 12, 16, 20 and .410 gauge, and appeared in the usual variety of barrel lengths. The degree of embellishment again varied, but with different names, starting with Field Grade and then working up through Teal, Trap, Specialty, Skeet Special, Premier Skeet to Eagle Grade. Above these were four more, which differed from the earlier models in that they had automatic ejection as standard: Crown, Monogram, Premier and De Luxe. In these highest grades, .410 gauge was available only in Crown Grade.

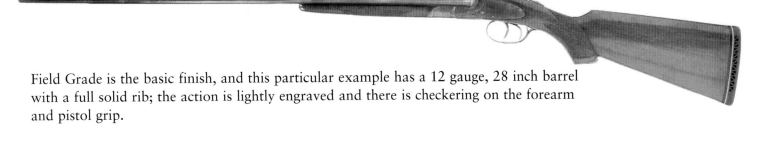

Field Grade is the basic finish, and this particular example has a 12 gauge, 28 inch barrel with a full solid rib; the action is lightly engraved and there is checkering on the forearm and pistol grip.

This one has a 12 gauge, 30 inch barrel and is in Ideal Grade finish, with slightly better quality engraving and checkering, and a trap-style, high-comb stock butt.

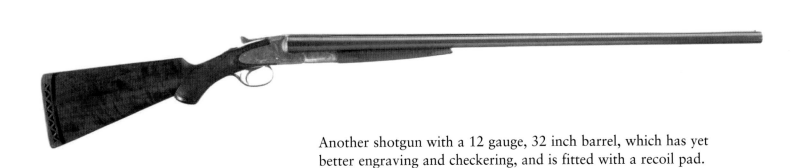

Another shotgun with a 12 gauge, 32 inch barrel, which has yet better engraving and checkering, and is fitted with a recoil pad.

## L.C. SMITH DAMASCUS HAMMER DRILLING

The majority of drillings were made in Europe, making this L.C. Smith version very rare. It has two 10 gauge shotgun barrels and a single .40 rifle barrel in a triangular configuration. There is a folding, tang-mounted rear leaf sight and a bead foresight. The stock is made of good quality walnut, as is the forearm, which also has a steel end-cap.

**SPECIFICATIONS**
**Type:** drilling (three-barrel) shotgun
**Origin:** L.C. Smith, Syracuse, New York
**Caliber:** two 10 caliber; one .40
**Barrel Length:** 23.5in

## SPRINGFIELD M1842 SHOTGUN CONVERSION

**SPECIFICATIONS**
**Type:** single-shot shotgun
**Origin:** National Armory, Springfield, Illinois
**Caliber:** .69
**Barrel Length:** 35.25in

When the Civil War ended, and men returned to their homesteads, the need was for shotguns rather than military rifles. Many war surplus rifles were converted to such civilian use by retaining the percussion lock and trigger, replacing the barrel with s smoothbore one and cutting down the stock to suit. The one shown here is typical of the type, being based on Model 1842 Rifle musket.

## STEVENS MODEL 94B SINGLE-SHOT SHOTGUN

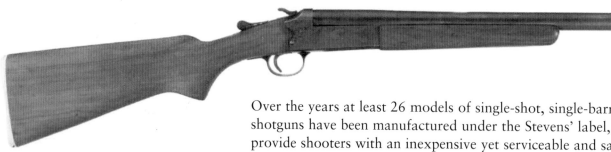

**SPECIFICATIONS**
**Type:** single-shot shotgun
**Origin:** J. Stevens Arms Company, Chicopee Falls, Massachusetts
**Caliber:** see text
**Barrel Length:** see text

Over the years at least 26 models of single-shot, single-barrel, break-open shotguns have been manufactured under the Stevens' label, intended to provide shooters with an inexpensive yet serviceable and safe weapon. They have been in the usual variety of gauges and barrel lengths, and have been generally similar in appearance. This Model 94B is typical in most respects, with a 12 gauge, 21 inch barrel and a plain walnut stock. It differs only in having had a bayonet lug welded to the underside of the barrel, about 4 inches from the muzzle, which suggests a possible military link in its past, although, since it does not bear the "US" mark and Ordnance grenade, this is unlikely to have been any of the U.S. armed forces.

## STEVENS MODEL 311-A DOUBLE-BARREL SHOTGUN

**SPECIFICATIONS**
**Type:** double-shot shotgun
**Origin:** J. Stevens Arms Company, Chicopee Falls, Massachusetts
**Caliber:** see text
**Barrel Length:** see text

The Model 311 is one of the long line of double-barrel designs produced by Stevens and there were at least thirteen different variants within the 311 series. This is a Model 311-A hammerless boxlock in 12 gauge, with a 28 inch barrel.

## STEVENS UTILITY GRADE PUMP-ACTION SHOTGUNS

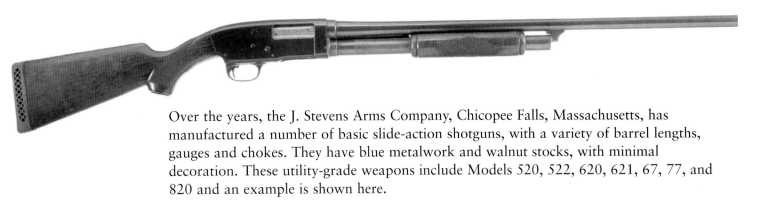

Over the years, the J. Stevens Arms Company, Chicopee Falls, Massachusetts, has manufactured a number of basic slide-action shotguns, with a variety of barrel lengths, gauges and chokes. They have blue metalwork and walnut stocks, with minimal decoration. These utility-grade weapons include Models 520, 522, 620, 621, 67, 77, and 820 and an example is shown here.

## STEVENS MODEL 520-30 TRENCH GUN

During World War One a number of trench gun conversions were ordered from Stevens, in addition to those already on order from Remington (see above) and Winchester (see below).

**SPECIFICATION**
**Type:** trench gun
**Origin:** J. Stevens Arms Company, Chicopee Falls, Massachusetts
**Caliber:** 12 gauge
**Barrel Length:** 20in

The Stevens Model 520 combat shotgun was already in service, so to meet this new requirement, Stevens modified his existing design.

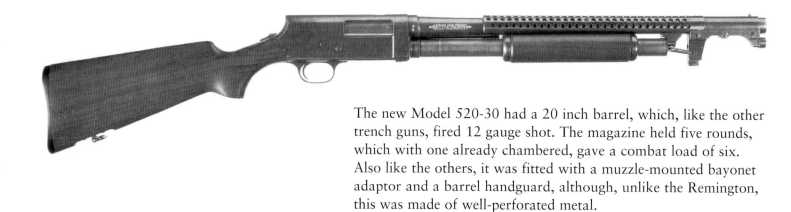

The new Model 520-30 had a 20 inch barrel, which, like the other trench guns, fired 12 gauge shot. The magazine held five rounds, which with one already chambered, gave a combat load of six. Also like the others, it was fitted with a muzzle-mounted bayonet adaptor and a barrel handguard, although, unlike the Remington, this was made of well-perforated metal.

## STEVENS MODEL 620 TRENCH GUN

### SPECIFICATION

**Type:** trench gun
**Origin:** J. Stevens Arms Company, Chicopee Falls, Massachusetts
**Caliber:** 12 gauge
**Barrel Length:** 20in

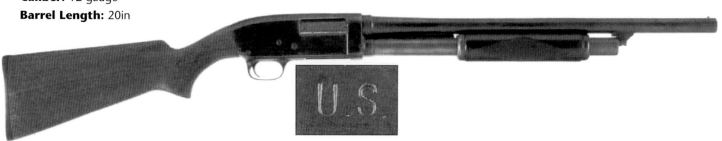

Production of World War One trench guns ceased almost as soon as the war ended; of those already completed, some were retained in store and others sold off on the civilian market. On the outbreak of World War Two, however, a new need for shotguns was foreseen and what remained of the military stocks were reissued. This still left a shortfall and among the new weapons ordered were the Stevens Model 620 riot gun seen here.

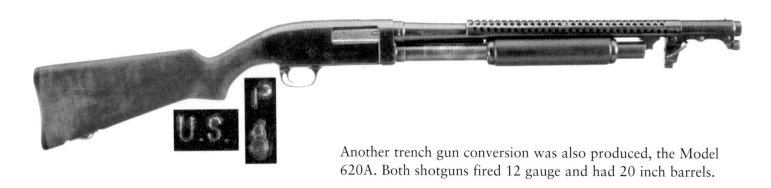

Another trench gun conversion was also produced, the Model 620A. Both shotguns fired 12 gauge and had 20 inch barrels.

## STEVENS MODEL 77E COMBAT SHOTGUN

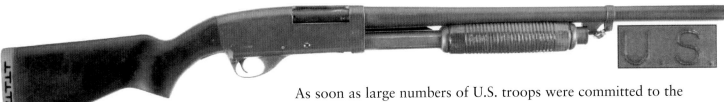

### SPECIFICATION

**Type:** combat shotgun
**Origin:** J. Stevens Arms Company, Chicopee Falls, Massachusetts
**Caliber:** 12 gauge
**Barrel Length:** 20in

As soon as large numbers of U.S. troops were committed to the land war in Vietnam, requests began to filter back to Washington for combat shotguns.

Having failed to learn the lesson from the aftermath of World War One, most of the stock of World War II weapons was no longer available, having been sold off to civilians in the 1950s, so the Government turned towards two companies for new models. As a result some 70,000 Stevens Model 77Es were procured and supplied to the troops in South-East Asia, both U.S. and allies such as the Australians and South Vietnamese. The Model 77E had a 20 inch barrel, fired 12 gauge and could be loaded with seven rounds (six in the magazine and one already chambered).

## MONTGOMERY WARD SHOTGUNS

Montgomery Ward, founded in 1872, was a Chicago-based retail and mail-order giant which went bankrupt in 2000 after 128 years in business. Like similar businesses it included firearms among its wares, which were made to Ward's specification by established manufacturers, such as Stevens, and then sold under a variety of trade-names. Sears used "Craftsman" and "J.C. Higgins", while Montgomery Ward used "Western Field" and "Hercules."

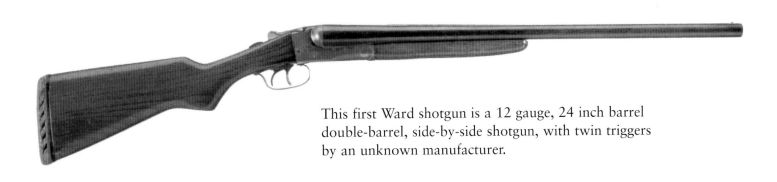

This first Ward shotgun is a 12 gauge, 24 inch barrel double-barrel, side-by-side shotgun, with twin triggers by an unknown manufacturer.

This however, is a 30 inch, 16 gauge single-barrel shotgun, which was made for Ward by Iver Johnson, based on their Champion model.

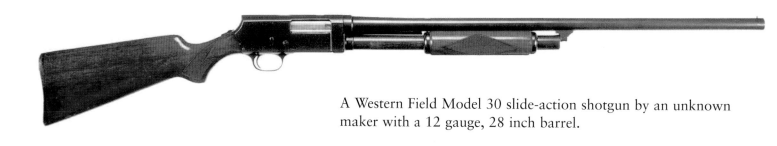

A Western Field Model 30 slide-action shotgun by an unknown maker with a 12 gauge, 28 inch barrel.

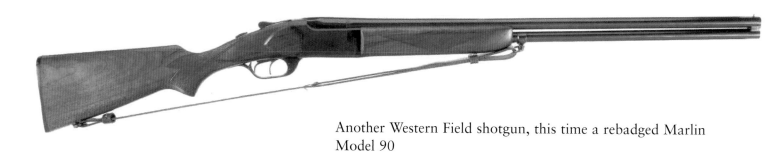

Another Western Field shotgun, this time a rebadged Marlin Model 90

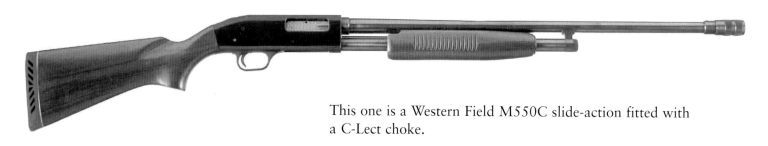

This one is a Western Field M550C slide-action fitted with a C-Lect choke.

# WEATHERBY CENTURION SEMI-AUTOMATIC SHOTGUN

## SPECIFICATIONS
**Type:** semi-automatic shotgun
**Origin:** Weatherby Corporation, Atascadero, California
**Caliber:** 12 gauge
**Barrel Length:** 30in

Weatherby was founded in 1945 and much of their earlier production effort was concentrated on high-power rifles. The Centurion, introduced in 1972, was the first shotgun, and was a gas-operated, semi-automatic, but various barrel lengths and chokes were offered. There was also a Centurion deluxe which had a vent-ribbed barrel, better quality walnut and a limited amount of engraving. The weapon seen here is a standard Centurion, with a vent-ribbed, 30 inch barrel. Production of the Centurion ended in 1981.

# WEATHERBY ATHENA OVER-AND-UNDER SHOTGUN

## SPECIFICATIONS

**Type:** over-and-under shotgun
**Origin:** Weatherby Corporation, Atascadero, California
**Caliber:** 12 gauge
**Barrel Length:** 28in

Many weapons have a story to tell and this one's is better recorded than most, having belonged to a famous modern singer. Conway Twitty (1933–93) had fifty-five singles reach Number 1 in the United States during the 20th century, more than any other singer, including such greats as Elvis, Frank Sinatra, the Beatles and Garth Brooks. Twitty died very suddenly in 1993 and unfortunately it quickly transpired that he had failed to update his will to take account of his most recent (third) marriage. This resulted in his widow and four children by earlier marriages becoming involved in a major – and very public – dispute, and since they proved incapable of agreeing on the dispersal of Twitty's assets, most had to be auctioned off, including this shotgun.

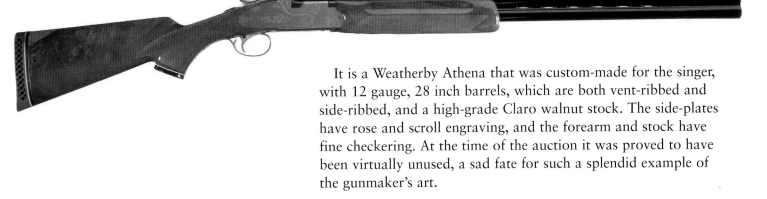

It is a Weatherby Athena that was custom-made for the singer, with 12 gauge, 28 inch barrels, which are both vent-ribbed and side-ribbed, and a high-grade Claro walnut stock. The side-plates have rose and scroll engraving, and the forearm and stock have fine checkering. At the time of the auction it was proved to have been virtually unused, a sad fate for such a splendid example of the gunmaker's art.

# WINCHESTER BREECH-LOADING DOUBLE-BARREL SHOTGUN

## SPECIFICATIONS

**Type:** double-barrel shotgun
**Origin:** Winchester Repeating Arms Company, New Haven, Connecticut
**Caliber:** 10 gauge
**Barrel Length:** 32in

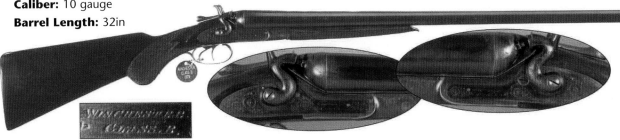

In 1879 Winchester started to import a shotgun from England which they marketed under their own name; some 10,000 had been sold when the program ended in 1884. The English maker has never been identified, but the guns all bear Birmingham proofmarks. These shotguns were not given an identifying number or name, but were known, instead, by the different grades of finish – Class D (the lowest) thru A (highest) and Match Gun – which were marked on the sideplates. The gun was sold in either 10 or 12 gauge and with either 30 or 32 inch barrels, both of which had Damascus finish. Shown here is a Winchester Breechloading Shotgun Class B, with a 10 gauge, 32 inch barrel.

## WINCHESTER MODEL 1887 LEVER-ACTION SHOTGUN

**SPECIFICATIONS**
**Type:** lever-action shotgun
**Origin:** Winchester Repeating Arms Company, New Haven, Connecticut
**Caliber:** 10 gauge
**Barrel Length:** 30.25in

Encouraged by the success of the imported shotguns (see above), Winchester bought the patent for a lever-action design from John Browning and put it into production as the Model 1887 shotgun, of which some 65,000 had been sold by the time production ended in 1901. The Model 1887 was made in 10 and 12 gauges with either 30 or 32 inch barrels, with a Riot Gun variant with a 20 inch barrel. The Model 1887 was subsequently redesigned to cope with smokeless cartridges and, as the Model 1901, was in production until 1920.

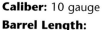

This Model 1887 is in 12 gauge with a 30 inch barrel and was made in 1891.

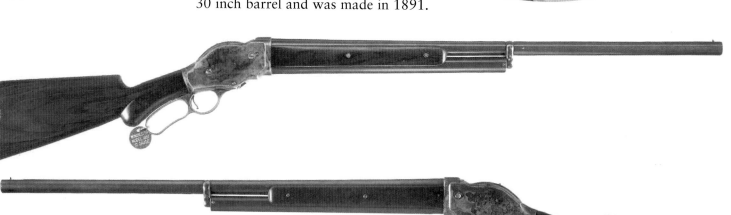

This 1892-built one has a 30 inch, 10 gauge barrel.

## WINCHESTER MODEL 1893 SLIDE-ACTION SHOTGUN

**SPECIFICATION**
**Type:** slide-action shotgun
**Origin:** Winchester Repeating Arms Company, New Haven, Connecticut
**Caliber:** 12 gauge
**Barrel Length:** 30in

Like the Model 1887 lever-action, the Model 1893 slide-action, Winchester's first, was based on a John M. Browning design. Although some 35,000 were sold between 1893 and 1897, it was only a qualified success, mainly because the action could not cope with the new smokeless loads, even though it had been designed to do so. The Model 1893 was produced in 12 gauge only, with either 30 or 32 inch barrel.

The example seen here is a special order Model 1893 with a Damascus barrel, deluxe flamegrain walnut and checkered pistol grip. As only a few deluxe models were made and the entire production run only amounted to 35,000 this is a rare weapon.

# WINCHESTER MODEL 1897 PUMP-ACTION SHOTGUN

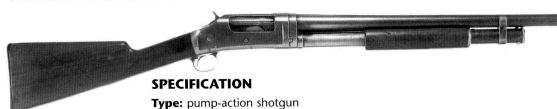

**SPECIFICATION**

**Type:** pump-action shotgun

**Origin:** Winchester Repeating Arms Company, New Haven, Connecticut

| GRADE | GAUGE | BARREL (IN) | REMARKS |
|---|---|---|---|
| STANDARD | 12, 16 | 28in (16 gauge) 30in (12 gauge) | Plain walnut stock with steel buttplate |
| TRAP | 12, 16 | 28in (16 gauge) 30in (12 gauge) | Fancy walnut with checkering |
| PIGEON | 12, 16 | 28 | As Trap, but hand- engraved receiver |
| TOURNAMENT | 12 | 30 | Select walnut; receiver top matte to reduce glare |
| BRUSH | 12, 16 | 26 | Shorter magazine, plain walnut without checkering, solid frame |
| BRUSH TAKEDOWN | 12, 16 | 26 | As above, but takedown frame |
| RIOT | 12 | 20 | Shoots buckshot, plain walnut, solid or takedown frame |
| TRENCH | 12 | 20 | As riot gun but with hand guard and bayonet fitting |

The Model 1893 was Winchester's first slide-action shotgun and was soon followed by the much improved Model 1897, which had a stronger frame and longer, better-angled stock. It was produced in a variety of models – see table. The riot and trench-gun versions are described separately. We show a Standard version with 30 inch barrel in 12 gauge.

# WINCHESTER MODEL 1897 TRENCH GUN

**SPECIFICATION**

**Type:** trench shotgun

**Origin:** Winchester Repeating Arms Company, New Haven, Connecticut

**Caliber:** 12 gauge

**Barrel Length:** 20in

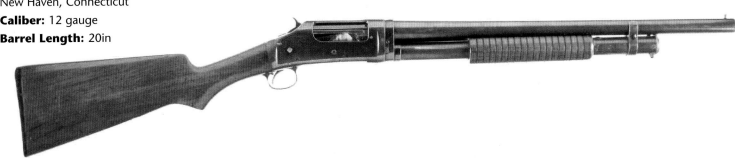

When, in 1917, the commanders in France demanded a trench gun, the first to be selected by the Ordnance Department was the Model 1897 which was readily available. With a 20 inch barrel and solid frame, it had a useful capacity of five rounds in the magazine plus one in the chamber.

However, the Ordnance Department stipulated that the weapon must have a bayonet, which caused a difficulty, since the normal bayonet had a guard ring which fitted over the muzzle of .30-30 barrel, but would not fit over the greater diameter 12 gauge barrel. This was resolved by the use of an attachment, designed at the Springfield Armory, which went over the muzzle. The image shows the Model 1897 trench gun with its associated Model 1917 bayonet and scabbard. The bayonet attachment is clearly shown with the lug protruding below the muzzle. To "fix" the bayonet, the hole in the upper part of the bayonet's crossguard was aligned with the lug, and the bayonet was then pulled towards the rifle so that the recess in the top of the handle slid over and locked onto the square lug (immediately to the right of the forward sling swivel).

The Model 1897 trench gun was reinstated in production during World War Two.

## WINCHESTER MODEL 12 PUMP-ACTION SHOTGUN

The Winchester Model 12 pump-action shotgun was designed by the legendary T.C. Johnson and having been introduced in 1912 it remained in production until 1963, by which time just under two million had been sold. It was produced in eight basic models, most of them being available in various gauges and barrel lengths, as shown in the table.

| GRADE | GAUGE | BARREL (IN) | PRODUCED | REMARKS |
|---|---|---|---|---|
| Standard | 12, 16, 20, 28 | 26, 28, 30, 32 | 1912–63 | |
| Feather-weight | 12, 16, 20, 28 | 26, 28, 30, 32 | 1959–62 | Standard, plus alloy trigger guard |
| Riot gun | 12 | 20 | 1918–63 | Military/police only |
| Trench gun | 12 | 20 | 1918–? | U.S. army only |
| Skeet | 12, 16, 20, 28 | 26 | 1933–63 | |
| Trap | 12 | 30 | 1914–63 | |
| Heavy Duck | 12 | 30, 32 | 1935–63 | |
| Pigeon | 12, 16, 20, 28 | 26, 28, 30, 32 | 1914–63 | |

There were also variations in ribs and stocks, as well as special finishes in the Custom Shop. Many variations were possible on the Standard model.

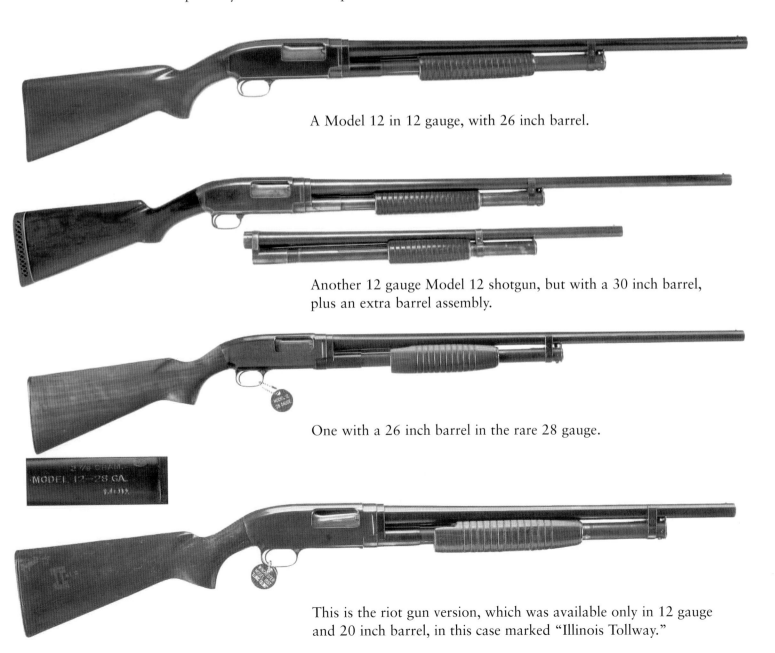

A Model 12 in 12 gauge, with 26 inch barrel.

Another 12 gauge Model 12 shotgun, but with a 30 inch barrel, plus an extra barrel assembly.

One with a 26 inch barrel in the rare 28 gauge.

This is the riot gun version, which was available only in 12 gauge and 20 inch barrel, in this case marked "Illinois Tollway."

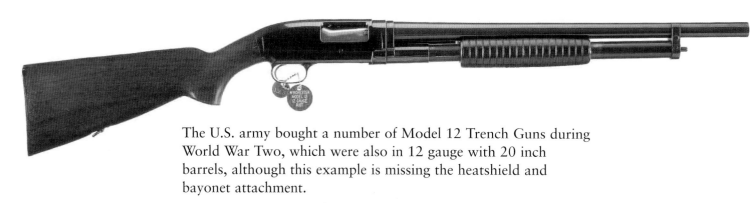

The U.S. army bought a number of Model 12 Trench Guns during World War Two, which were also in 12 gauge with 20 inch barrels, although this example is missing the heatshield and bayonet attachment.

Next came the Skeet Grade, shown here with a 26 inch barrel which is vent-ribbed with round posts; it is in the relatively unusual 28 gauge and was made in 1955.

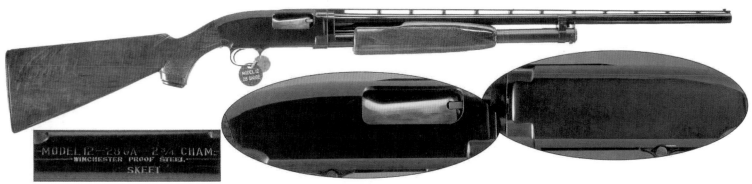

The Trap version was in production for 49 years and was available only in 12 gauge with a 30 inch barrel, but this example has been customized in the factory with the addition of a Simmons vent rib and extra fancy black walnut butt stock with adjustable cheek-piece and recoil pad.

The Heavy Duck version, here with a 30 inch barrel,

## WINCHESTER MODEL 12 SPECIAL FINISHES

We show a range of special finishes that the Model 12 has appeared in, from a spectacular hand-crafted museum-quality one-off to simpler weapons with a little engraving. All the weapons shown are in 12 gauge, with 30 inch barrels.

There could be nothing finer than a set made for the Company President's personal collection by Winchester's own engraving shop. This one-of-a-kind "Presidential Model 12 Pigeon Grade" set has three barrels, all 12 gauge and 30 inches long, one each for skeet, trap and field shooting. The whole set is housed in a custom-made black Winchester hardwood case. The barrels are scroll engraved with gold-filled Winchester address and there is an engraved pigeon above the serial number to indicate pigeon grade. Both sides of the receiver are engraved and gold inlaid, with, on the left, two dogs on point and a water-grouse in flight, and, on the right, four ducks in flight.

Another customized Model 12, this time to Black Diamond grade. It also has a 12 gauge, 30 inch barrel – in this case just one – but this time fitted with a ventilated poly-choke. The receiver is engraved with scroll and flying duck on the left, dogs and grouse on the right, with extra fancy checkering on both sides of the wrist and the forearm. There is a red rubber recoil pad. This weapon, too, is a fine piece of work, but in a more modest style.

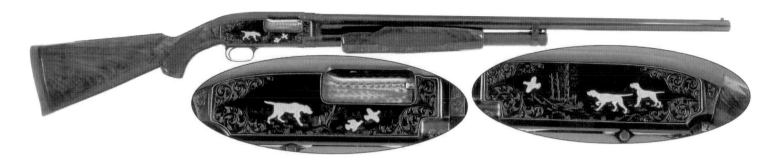

Made in 1951, a Pigeon grade with gold inlaid scenes, showing one dog and two birds on the left, two dogs and one bird on the right.

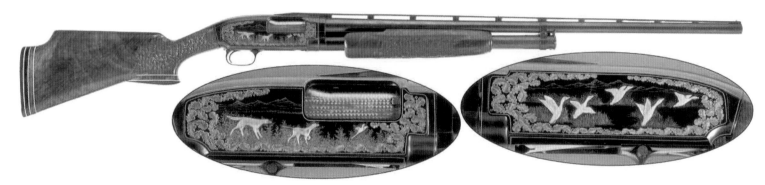

A vent-ribbed barrel Model 12, made in 1959, where the engraved scenes are more elaborate, while the stock and forearm are both carved with very elaborate oak leaves and flower motifs. The butt and pistol grip have also been customized by the addition of layers of different colored woods.

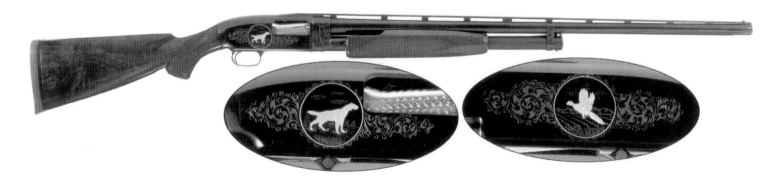

Still decorated to a high standard, this one is in a much simpler style,

And for comparison, this Model 12 is the basic model, nothing fancy or special but still perfectly capable of doing the job.

## WINCHESTER MODEL 12 MISCELLANY

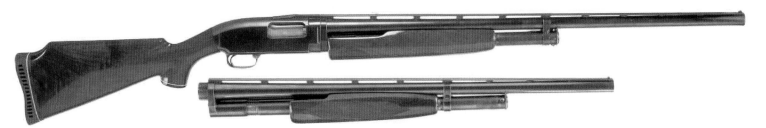

We showed earlier the Company President's very special set with three barrels, but many owners bought more than one barrel. This one is a 12 gauge with two barrels, both serial numbered to the gun, one 30 inches long (on the gun) the other 26 inches.

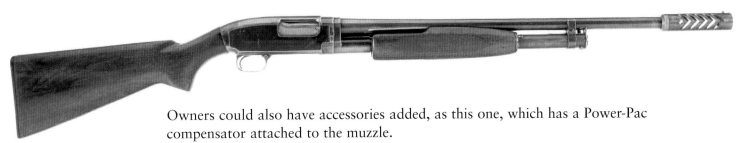

Owners could also have accessories added, as this one, which has a Power-Pac compensator attached to the muzzle.

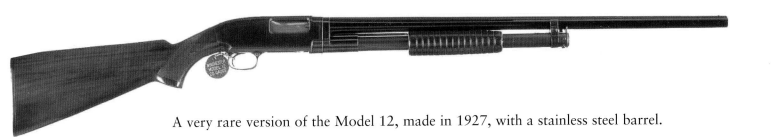

A very rare version of the Model 12, made in 1927, with a stainless steel barrel.

These two were among the very last Model 12s to be made and featured the hydro-coil recoil- absorbing stock, which was engineered out of aluminum. The system seemed to hold some promise and was strongly advocated by John Olin, who happened to be president of Winchester at the time and was a personal friend of the inventor, Eddie Wilmering, a NASA engineer. However, it proved less than popular with potential buyers and was not pursued.

# WINCHESTER MODEL 12 COMBAT

## SPECIFICATION
**Type:** combat shotgun
**Origin:** Winchester Repeating Arms Company,
New Haven, Connecticut
**Caliber:** 12 gauge
**Barrel Length:** 20in

A riot gun version of the Model 12 was introduced in 1918 and was periodically put into production to meet specific orders, until finally withdrawn in 1963.

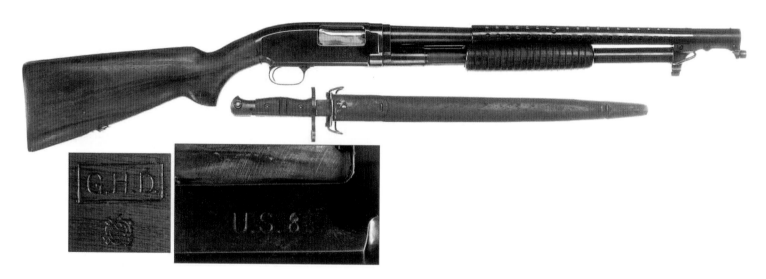

The trench gun, developed from the riot gun, was introduced in 1918, and went out of production in the early 1920s, but remained available against potential future orders from the U.S. army. We show a World War One version.

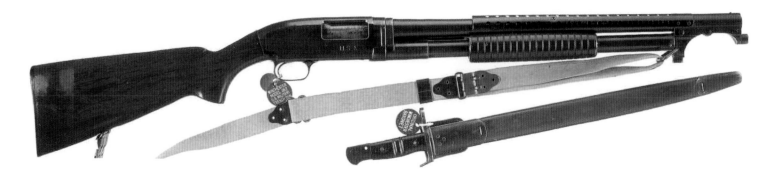

It was put back into production during World War Two and then remained in service through the Korean War until Vietnam.

# WINCHESTER MODEL 20 SINGLE-BARREL SHOTGUN

## SPECIFICATION
**Type:** single-barrel shotgun
**Origin:** Winchester Repeating Arms Company,
New Haven, Connecticut
**Caliber:** .410 gauge
**Barrel Length:** 26in

As with all other armaments firms, the end of World War One found Winchester with a huge manufacturing capability and precious few orders or models to keep it occupied. One of the company's earliest responses was the rapid development and marketing of a single-barrel shotgun – the Model 20. Production started in 1920, but ended in 1924 after some 24,000 had been made. There were severe limits to the range, in order to simplify production and keep the price down, it being made only in .410 gauge with a 26 inch barrel, while the walnut stock was of the simplest shape and had a hard rubber butt plate. Perhaps the only element of even very limited extravagance was a small lip on the fore-end. The example shown here is absolutely standard in every respect.

# WINCHESTER MODEL 21 DOUBLE-BARREL SHOTGUN

## SPECIFICATION
**Type:** double-barrel shotgun
**Origin:** Winchester Repeating Arms
Company, New Haven, Connecticut
**Caliber:** .410 gauge
**Barrel Length:** 28in

Work on the Model 21 started in the mid-1920s but financial problems affecting both the company and their potential market meant that the first guns did not leave the factory until 1931, but between then and the end of production in 1959 no less than 30,000 had been sold. The Model 21was advertised as a production-line product but, in reality, it was hand-made in order to meet customers' requests concerning barrel lengths, chokes, finish and embellishments. The Winchester Custom Shop opened in 1960 and a further 1,000-odd Model 21s were assembled there.

Rarest of all Model 21s was that in .410 gauge; no more than 50 were built between 1931 and 1959 and a further five were made in the Custom Shop era between 1960 and 1991.This is one of those five. The special feature of this gun is the exceptional standard of finish of aspects of its appearance. The engraving consists of the most intricate scrollwork on the action and the breech end of the barrels, but the only pictorial element is the figure of the Winchester rider inlaid in gold on the bottom of the frame. The furniture, made of the very highest quality walnut, is decorated in Grand American checkering with special borders and panels. There is also a high-grade leather recoil pad and the selective trigger is made of gold. There is a maroon-lined walnut case for the owner to display the shotgun and a leather takedown case for travel.

# WINCHESTER MODEL 22 DOUBLE-BARREL SHOTGUN

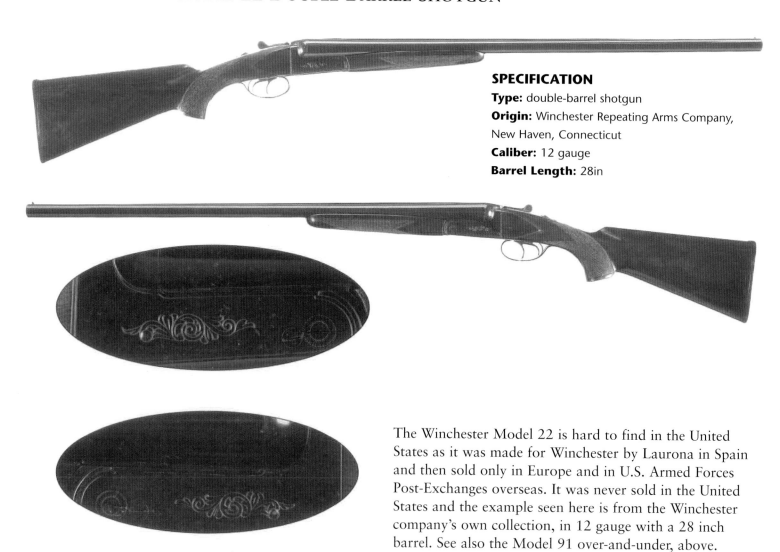

## SPECIFICATION
**Type:** double-barrel shotgun
**Origin:** Winchester Repeating Arms Company, New Haven, Connecticut
**Caliber:** 12 gauge
**Barrel Length:** 28in

The Winchester Model 22 is hard to find in the United States as it was made for Winchester by Laurona in Spain and then sold only in Europe and in U.S. Armed Forces Post-Exchanges overseas. It was never sold in the United States and the example seen here is from the Winchester company's own collection, in 12 gauge with a 28 inch barrel. See also the Model 91 over-and-under, above.

# WINCHESTER MODEL 23 DOUBLE-BARREL SHOTGUN

## SPECIFICATION
**Type:** double-barrel shotgun
**Origin:** Winchester Repeating Arms Company, New Haven, Connecticut
**Caliber:** see text
**Barrel Length:** see text

The Model 23 was a double-barrel, side-by-side, box-lock shotgun in either 12 or 20 gauge, with barrels of 25.5, 26, 28 or 30 inch lengths and was produced in seven main grades. The first is a very special Grand Canadian boxed set of two guns, the twenty-fourth in a series of fifty. The receivers are coin-finished with oak-leaf engraving and goldleaf inlay on the bottom. The forearms are beavertail design and the butt-stocks of English pattern, all being made of the finest quality walnut. One barrel is 25.5 inches in 20 gauge, the other 25.5 inches in 12 gauge.

This one is a Pigeon grade model, still of very high quality, but in a much more workmanlike canvas case.

# WINCHESTER MODEL 24 DOUBLE-BARREL SHOTGUN

The Model 24 double-barrel, side-by-side shotgun was intended to meet a gap in the medium-priced market and achieved a fair measure of success, with approximately 116,000 sold between its introduction in 1939 and its withdrawal in 1957. It was made in 12, 16 and 20 gauge, with 26, 28 and 30 inch barrels, but was available in only one grade

**SPECIFICATION**

**Type:** double-barrel shotgun

**Origin:** Winchester Repeating Arms Company, New Haven, Connecticut

**Caliber:** see text

**Barrel Length:** see text

of finish – Standard. Two examples are shown here. One is in 16 gauge with a 28 inch barrel and the other in 20 gauge with a 26 inch barrel, the only very minor difference between the two being that the latter has a white line recoil pad.

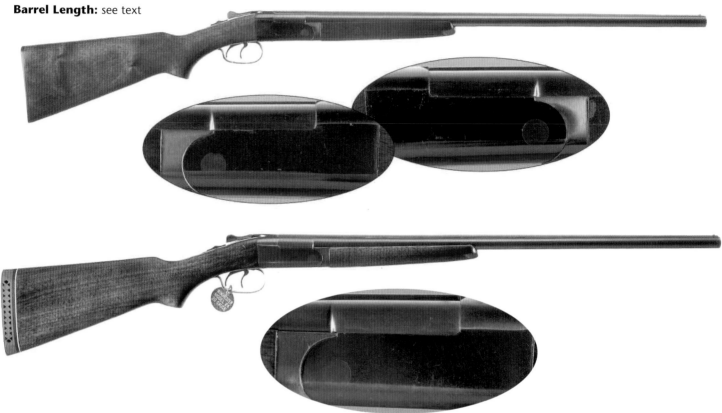

# WINCHESTER MODEL 25 SLIDE-ACTION SHOTGUN

**SPECIFICATION**

**Type:** slide-action shotgun

**Origin:** Winchester Repeating Arms Company, New Haven, Connecticut

**Caliber:** 12 gauge

**Barrel Length:** 26 or 28in

The Model 25 entered the product line in 1949. It was an attempt to produce a cheaper version of the very successful Model 12, to which it bore many similarities, but it was a solid-frame weapon, which could not be taken down. It was not a great success and production ceased after only five years, with some 88,000 sold – not a major success by Winchester standards. The example shown here, which has a 28 inch barrel, shows the simplicity of design and the plain, but perfectly adequate, finish.

# WINCHESTER MODEL 36 SINGLE-BARREL SHOTGUN

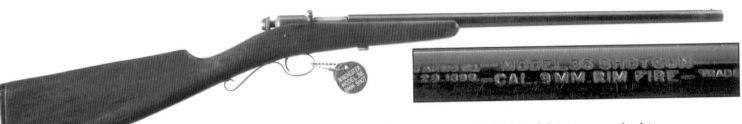

## SPECIFICATION

**Type:** single-barrel "Garden" shotgun
**Origin:** Winchester Repeating Arms
Company, New Haven, Connecticut
**Caliber:** 9mm RF
**Barrel Length:** 17.5in

Like the Model 20 (see above) the Model 36 was rushed into production in 1920 to help occupy the machinery that had fallen silent with the ending of the wartime contracts. Production started in 1920 and ended in 1927 after some 20,000 had been sold. It was a bolt-action breech loader and was cocked by a rearward pull on the firing-pin head. The company referred to it as the "Garden gun" to promote its use around the house and barn to control pests. It could fire either 9mm Long shot, 9mm Short shot or 9mm Ball.

# WINCHESTER MODEL 37 SINGLE-BARREL SHOTGUN

## SPECIFICATION

**Type:** single-barrel shotgun
**Origin:** Winchester Repeating Arms Company,
New Haven, Connecticut
**Caliber:** see text
**Barrel Length:** see text

The Model 37 entered production in 1936 and remained in the company catalog until 1963, by which time over one million had been sold. It was designed to be a simple weapon at a low price which would give it mass appeal. It was produced in various popular gauges and with barrels from 26 to 30 inches in length, but there were no variations in finish.

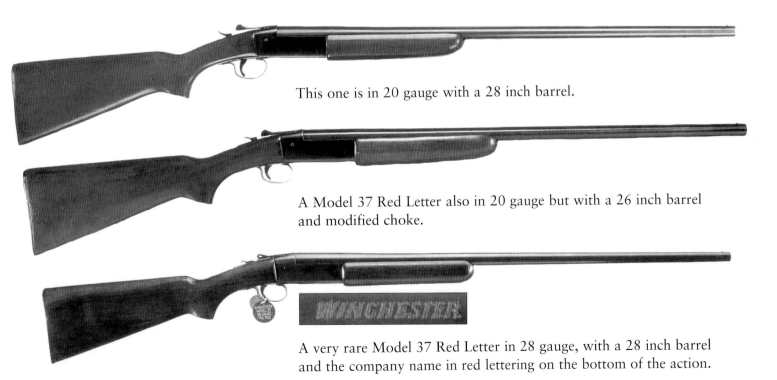

This one is in 20 gauge with a 28 inch barrel.

A Model 37 Red Letter also in 20 gauge but with a 26 inch barrel and modified choke.

A very rare Model 37 Red Letter in 28 gauge, with a 28 inch barrel and the company name in red lettering on the bottom of the action.

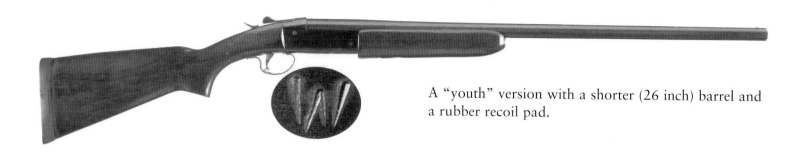

A "youth" version with a shorter (26 inch) barrel and a rubber recoil pad.

# WINCHESTER MODEL 42 SLIDE-ACTION SHOTGUN

## SPECIFICATION

**Type:** slide-action shotgun
**Origin:** Winchester Repeating Arms Company, New Haven, Connecticut
**Caliber:** .410 gauge
**Barrel Length:** 26 or 28in

The Model 42 was designed by William Roehmer around the .410 bore, and was, in many respects, a slightly scaled-down Model 12. It was produced in five basic models, with some 164,000 made in a production run lasting from 1933 to 1963. The Model 42 was made in only one caliber – .410 gauge – and with only two barrel lengths – 26 inch and 28 inch – although most versions gave a choice between plain, solid ribbed, or vent-ribbed. The grades followed the usual Winchester system of Standard (1933---63); Skeet (1933–63); Trap (1934–9); De Luxe (1940–63); and Pigeon (1945–9). Unusually, there were very few engraved Model 42s made, and fewer than 50 of the Pigeon Grade.

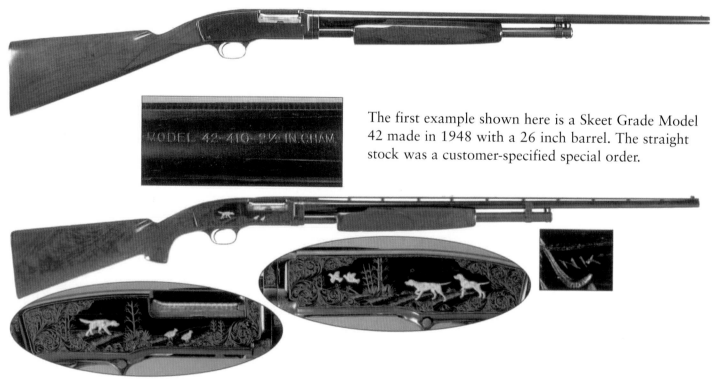

The first example shown here is a Skeet Grade Model 42 made in 1948 with a 26 inch barrel. The straight stock was a customer-specified special order.

A Pigeon grade Model 42 in .410 gauge, with a 28 inch barrel. It was made in 1933, the first year of production of the Model 42, but was returned to the Winchester factory sometime after 1950 and refurbished and upgraded, which included the engraving by Nick Kusmit.

# WINCHESTER MODEL 50 SEMI-AUTOMATIC SHOTGUN

**SPECIFICATION**
**Type:** semi-automatic shotgun
**Origin:** Winchester Repeating
Arms Company, New Haven,
Connecticut
**Caliber:** 12 or 20 gauge
**Barrel Length:** see text

Winchester had several attempts with self-loading shotguns, starting with the Model 1911 and then the Model 40, but neither of them was really satisfactory, so they tried again in 1954 with the Model 50. This used a short recoil system with a floating chamber and this time they were much more successful with some 200,000 sold by the time production ended in 1961. The Model 50 was produced in either 12 or 20 gauge and in a variety of barrel lengths. It was made in four grades – Standard, Skeet, Trap and Pigeon – and a lighter "Featherweight" version was available in all except the Trap grade.

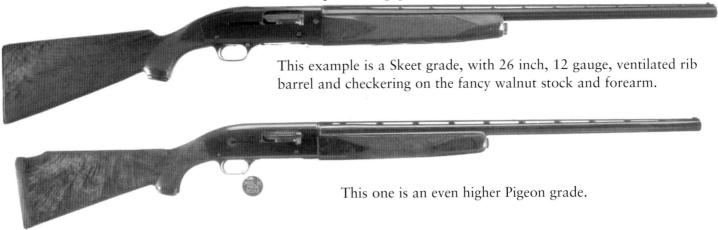

This example is a Skeet grade, with 26 inch, 12 gauge, ventilated rib barrel and checkering on the fancy walnut stock and forearm.

This one is an even higher Pigeon grade.

# WINCHESTER MODEL 59 SEMI-AUTOMATIC SHOTGUN

The Model 59 was marketed between 1960 and 1965 and had a barrel made of steel-lined fiberglass which was available in lengths between 26 and 30 inches, but only in 12 gauge. A variety of chokes could be fitted and there were two grades, Standard, in plain walnut, and Pigeon in high grade walnut, both with checkering. The example shown here is a post-1961 model fitted with a Winchester VersaLite choke tube on a 28 inch barrel.

**SPECIFICATION**
**Type:** semi-automatic shotgun
**Origin:** Winchester Repeating
Arms Company, New Haven,
Connecticut
**Caliber:** 12 gauge (but see
text)
**Barrel Length:** see text

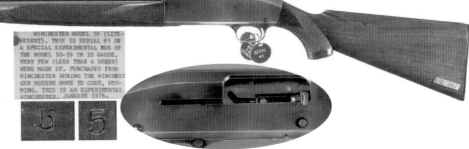

This one is the fifth and last of a very short experimental run of "ultra-lightweight" Model 59s in 20 gauge and with aluminum frames. They were all made in the highest or "Pigeon" grade, probably because the owner of the company, John Olin, took a personal interest in the project.

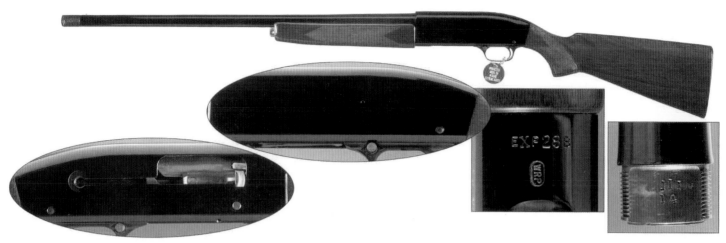

Another experimental model is shown here. This was one of four or five 14 gauge versions which were made to test aluminum shotgun shells being tested at the Winchester-Western ammunition plant at Alton, Illinois, which was also owned by John Olin.

## WINCHESTER MODEL 91 OVER-AND-UNDER SHOTGUN

### SPECIFICATION
**Type:** over-and-under shotgun
**Origin:** Winchester Repeating Arms Company, New Haven, Connecticut
**Caliber:** 12 gauge
**Barrel Length:** 28in

Like the Model 22 double-barrel, the Model 91 was made for Winchester by Spanish gunmaker, Laurona, and then sold only in Europe and in U.S. Armed Forces Post-Exchanges overseas. It was never sold in the United States and the example seen here is from the Winchester company's own collection. Like the Model 22, it is rarely found in the United States.

## WINCHESTER MODEL 101 OVER-AND-UNDER SHOTGUN

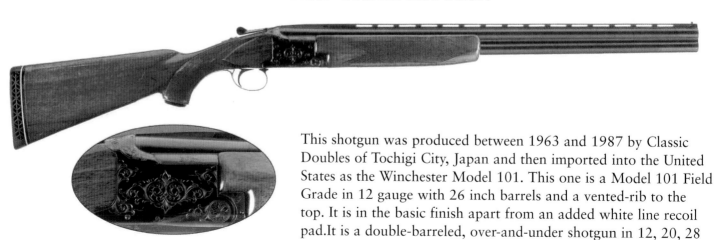

This shotgun was produced between 1963 and 1987 by Classic Doubles of Tochigi City, Japan and then imported into the United States as the Winchester Model 101. This one is a Model 101 Field Grade in 12 gauge with 26 inch barrels and a vented-rib to the top. It is in the basic finish apart from an added white line recoil pad.It is a double-barreled, over-and-under shotgun in 12, 20, 28 and .410 gauge, with vent-ribbed barrels either 26, 28 or 30 inches in length. It was a boxlock shotgun with automatic ejectors, selective trigger and an engraved receiver; it was offered in eight grades ranging from Field to Diamond.

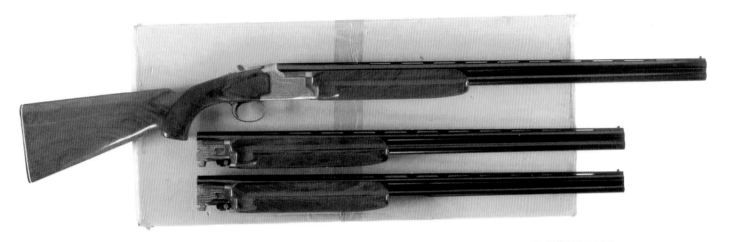

A Model 101 three-gauge Skeet set in Pigeon grade, with three 28 inch barrels for 20, 28 and .410 gauge, respectively. All three barrels have vent-ribs and individual forearms, and the whole set comes in a custom-made box.

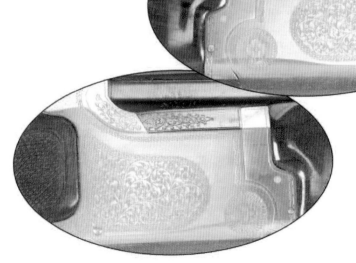

**SPECIFICATION**
**Type:** over-and-under shotgun
**Origin:** Winchester Repeating Arms Company, New Haven, Connecticut
**Caliber:** see text
**Barrel Length:** see text

This one is a "one-off" having been made to special order from the director of Winchester Canada, and is in 20 gauge with uniquely short, 24 inch barrels.

## WINCHESTER MODEL 1200 SLIDE-ACTION SHOTGUN

### SPECIFICATION
**Type:** slide-action shotgun
**Origin:** Winchester Repeating Arms Company, New Haven, Connecticut
**Caliber:** see text
**Barrel Length:** see text

The Model 1200 slide-action shotgun was made between 1964 and 1981 in 12, 16 or 20 gauges, with 26, 28 or 30 inch vent-ribbed barrels, and an alloy receiver.

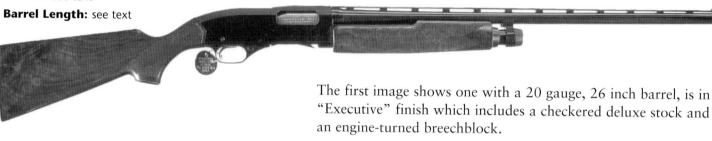

The first image shows one with a 20 gauge, 26 inch barrel, is in "Executive" finish which includes a checkered deluxe stock and an engine-turned breechblock.

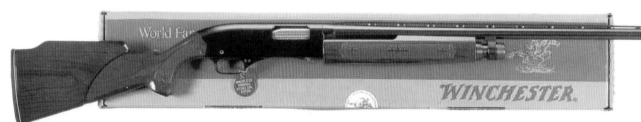

This is in 12 gauge with a 29 inch vent-ribbed barrel, but of most significance is the Hydro-coil stock, an option on the Model 1200 and, as described in the Model 12 entry, an item in which the company owner, John Olin, took a personal interest.

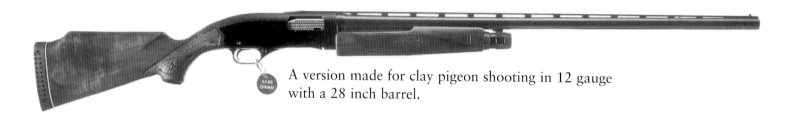

A version made for clay pigeon shooting in 12 gauge with a 28 inch barrel.

## WINCHESTER MODEL 1200 TRENCH GUN

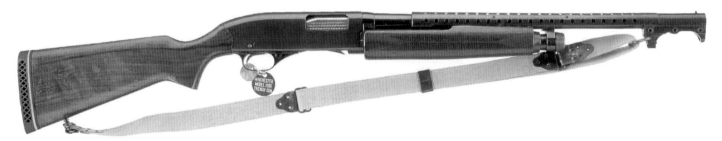

In the early 1960s Winchester developed the Model 1200 slide-action riot gun in order to meet any orders from civilian law enforcement agencies. This weapon was based almost entirely on civilian sporting shotgun components, with a 12 gauge, 18 inch barrel, an overall length of 39 inches and a capacity of five rounds (four in the magazine, one in the chamber). The Model 1200 underwent tests by the army, air force and marines but these

**SPECIFICATION**

**Type:** combat shotgun
**Origin:** Winchester
Repeating Arms
Company, New Haven,
Connecticut
**Caliber:** 12 gauge
**Barrel Length:**
20.1in

did not result in an order until 1968 when the army suddenly ordered a large quantity as the Model 1200 Trench Gun. This weapon had a 20.1 inch barrel with a vented metal handguard and a plain finish, but for reasons never made clear the army insisted on a bayonet. However, they did not specify the M7 bayonet, which was then in wide-scale use with the M16 rifle, but the long and unwieldy, 50-years-old, M1917 pattern. Fortunately, this was achieved by using the old World War One Springfield bayonet adapter which had been used on the Model 1897 Trench Gun, but the Model 1200 could equally easily have been fitted with an adapter for the M7 bayonet. It is also curious that the weapon should have been referred to as a "trench gun," a term with World War One connotations, when "combat shotgun" would have been much more appropriate. We show two Model 1200 Trench Guns, showing many differences from the Model 12, but with exactly the same bayonet adapter.

## WINCHESTER MODEL 1300 SLIDE-ACTION SHOTGUN

The Model 1300 was introduced in 1978 and remains Winchester's current production slide-action shotgun. It has been made in some 37 different grades/configurations, not all of them concurrently available. It is a takedown weapon, in either 12 or 20 gauge, but with a wide variety of barrels and chokes.

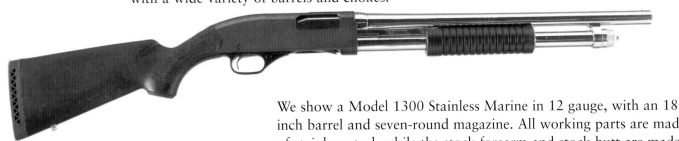

We show a Model 1300 Stainless Marine in 12 gauge, with an 18 inch barrel and seven-round magazine. All working parts are made of stainless steel, while the stock forearm and stock butt are made of a black synthetic material, with the latter having an added recoil pad. This version is designed for use in a maritime environment and to resists the corrosive effects of salt-water.

**SPECIFICATION**

**Type:** over-and-under shotgun
**Origin:** Winchester Repeating Arms Company,
New Haven, Connecticut
**Caliber:** see text
**Barrel Length:** see text

A Model 1300 Defender Pistol Grip in 12 gauge with an 18 inch barrel and an eight-round magazine.

The Model 1300 Slug Hunter with a full rifled barrel for 3 inch/12 gauge shells; the camouflage-pattern canvas sling is part of the outfit.

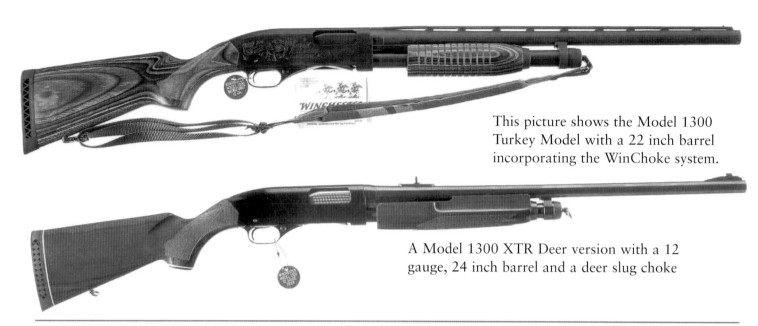

This picture shows the Model 1300 Turkey Model with a 22 inch barrel incorporating the WinChoke system.

A Model 1300 XTR Deer version with a 12 gauge, 24 inch barrel and a deer slug choke

## WINCHESTER MODEL 1370 KILN GUN

**SPECIFICATION**

**Type:** single-shot kiln gun
**Origin:** Winchester Repeating Arms Company, New Haven, Connecticut
**Caliber:** 12 gauge.
**Barrel Length:** 26in

Guns are sometimes put to strange uses which never meet the public eye. This Winchester Model 1370 is a prime example being a "kiln gun" which was designed to be used in factories with rotary kilns processing metallic and non-metallic products such as manganese, zinc, cement, lime and phosphate. The shotgun was used to blast the slag off the inner walls without having to halt the machinery. A single shot weapon, it had an unusually thick 26 inch barrel with a 2.75–3 inch chamber to fire Winchester Super X 12 shells.

## WINCHESTER SUPER X MODEL 1 SEMI-AUTOMATIC SHOTGUN

**SPECIFICATION**

**Type:** semi-automatic shotgun
**Origin:** Winchester Repeating Arms Company, New Haven, Connecticut
**Caliber:** 12 gauge.
**Barrel Length:** 26in

The Super X Model 1, produced in 1974–81, was a gas-operated semi-automatic shotgun in 12 gauge only, but with 6, 28 or 30 inch barrels. It was of all-steel construction with a vented barrel and walnut stock. The example shown here has a 26 inch skeet choked barrel and a white line recoil pad.

## WINCHESTER SUPER X MODEL 2 SEMI-AUTOMATIC SHOTGUN

Launched in 1999 this gun is the successor to the SX1 and manufactured at the Belgian factory of the Browning /Winchester group. Finished in black, walnut or Mossy Oak(shown here), with optional chambering of both 3 inch and 31/2 inch (magnum) shells.

**SPECIFICATIONS**
**Type:** semi-automatic shotgun
**Origin:** Fabrique Nationale, Herstal, Belgium
**Caliber:** 12 gauge
**Barrel Length:** 24-28 inches
**Weight:** 7¼ -7¾ lbs

## WINCHESTER SUPER X MODEL 3 SEMI-AUTOMATIC SHOTGUN

As a follow up to the X2 this model has established a reputation for speed as it is the gun used by Patrick Flanigan in setting the World Record for hand throw clays of 12 successful shots in 1.442 seconds. It is also available in 20 gauge.

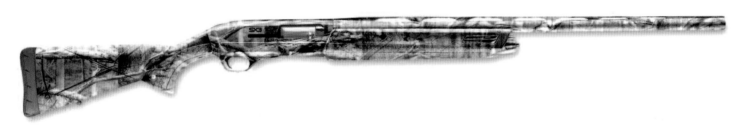

## WINCHESTER SXP PUMP-ACTION SHOTGUN

The successor to the Model 1300 series this gun is revamped to cope with sales pressure from European makes like Benelli. This gun is made in the Herstal factory like the SX3.

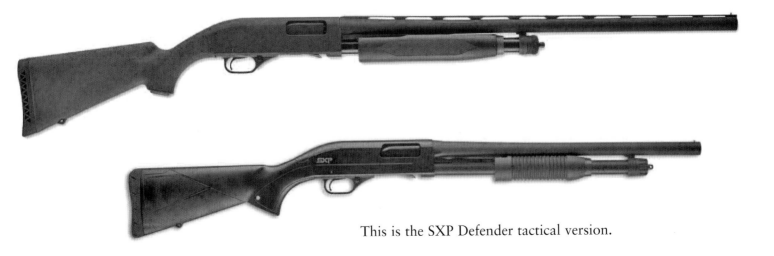

This is the SXP Defender tactical version.

## WINCHESTER COMBINATION (OVER-AND-UNDER) RIFLE/SHOTGUN

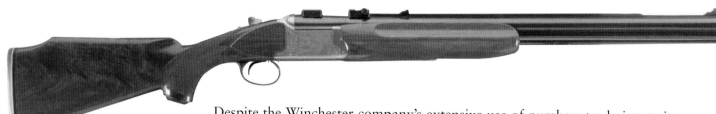

### SPECIFICATION
**Type:** over-and-under combination rifle/shotgun
**Origin:** Winchester Repeating Arms Company, New Haven, Connecticut
**Caliber:** two 12 gauge, plus one rifle (see text)
**Barrel Length:** 25in

Despite the Winchester company's extensive use of numbers to designate its models, every now and then one emerges with a simple descriptive title, such as this case which is simply known as the "Combination Gun." This was made in small numbers between 1983 and 1985, with a 12 gauge shotgun with screw-in choke, atop a rifle in .222, .223, .30-06, or 9.3mm caliber, both with 25 inch barrels.

This has the 12 gauge shotgun with 3 inch chamber and Winchester screw-in choke, combined with a .222 Remington rifle. There is a bead sight on the shotgun muzzle and a folding-leaf rear sight. Finish is to "Super Grade" standard; the action is decorated with tight scrollwork and the high quality walnut stock is fitted with a rifle-style buttpad.

## WINCHESTER CUT-AWAYS

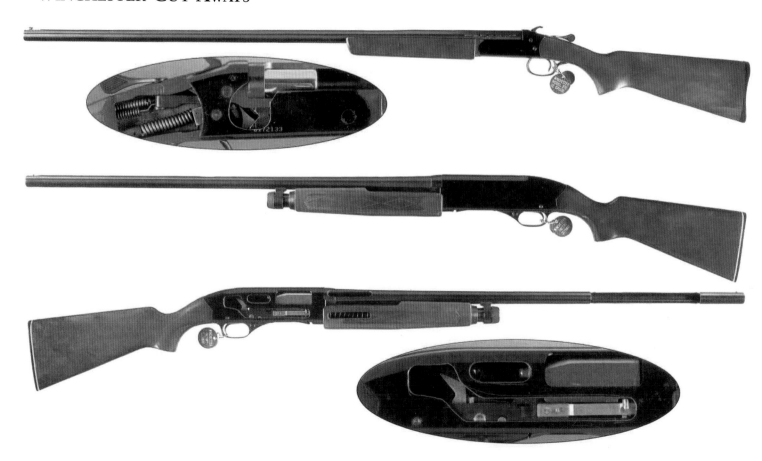

Interesting curios maybe, but cut-aways could be used for demonstration purposes by company representatives and for training purposes with technicians or owners. The Winchester convention was to cut away the action, as shown on these guns shown, but sometimes sections of the barrel were also exposed.

## BLUNDERBUSSES

Although slightly outside the normal description of a shotgun, a blunderbuss is, in essence, a very large caliber shotgun recognisable by the distinctive flared bell-mouth muzzle. They were probably originally devised for close-range defense at sea, as these large caliber weapons firing buckshot or a spray of pistol balls would be devastating to men trying to board a vessel. Interestingly, later tests have shown that contrary to general opinion, the flared muzzle actually has very little effect on the spread of shot. The large muzzle aperture would, however, make the arm much easier to reload, especially on the deck of a moving ship, and would also have a distinctly intimidating effect on any would-be attacker.

From the 17th century blunderbuss pistols were also produced for military use by cavalrymen, and for civil use by coachmen and riders. Again, the wide mouth made for easier reloading on horse or coach, and the spread of shot gave more chance of a hit in a fast-moving melee. It may not even need to be fired – as a footpad attempting to rob a coach would probably have second thoughts when the muzzle of one of these gets stuck in his face. We show here just a few sample blunderbusses.

An Ottoman blunderbuss, probably made in the late 18th/early 19th century, this one has the lock stamped with the badge of the British Honourable East India Company, suggesting that it was made in India and exported to Turkey. It has a 20 inch barrel with a 4.5 inch bell.

Another Ottoman weapon, this one has a 14 inch barrel and 4 inches bell.

This 18th century full-stocked flintlock blunderbuss was made in London by gunmaker known as Richards. It has a brass barrel, at this time often a sign of a weapon intended for naval service, as brass doesn't corrode so much in salt air. Once the user had fired the weapon, he could resort to the use of the 9.25in spring-loaded folding bayonet attached to the top of the barrel.

This .50 caliber blunderbuss has a 17 inch barrel, and is marked "DUNDERDALE/ MABSON & LABRON", who were gunmakers in Birmingham, England from 1813–1852. Unusually it has been converted to the percussion system. Again it has a brass barrel, complete with a 15 inch triangular folding bayonet on top of the muzzle.

# BEGINNINGS

## GATLING 1862

### SPECIFICATIONS

**Type:** machine gun
**Origin:** Colt Armory, Hartford, Conecticut
**Caliber:** 0.45in
**Barrel Length:** 10in

Doctor Richard J. Gatling invented the first working version of the machine gun in 1862, during the second year of the American Civil War. The war had stimulated a great deal of weapon development, and Gatling believed that a high rate of automatic gunfire would reduce the number of soldiers needed to man the battlefield, thus reducing their exposure to disease and the hazards of war. Gatling demonstrated his first weapon in 1862 in Indianapolis, Indiana, at the age of 44 and patented the gun in the November of that year. The key elements of the gun were a lock cylinder containing six strikers that revolved with six rotating gun barrels, all powered by a hand crank. (Hence Abraham Lincoln's nickname for the Gatling, the "Coffee-Mill gun.") In this sense, the weapon was not yet a true machine gun, as an external power source was required. Gatlings were fed ammunition by means of a hopper, which loaded powder and ball into the steel chambers. This resulted in gas leakage (a fairly common difficulty in revolving arms). Self-contained rim-fire cartridges were then introduced. For the time, the gun attained an extremely high rate of fire of 200 shots per minute. The Colt Armory in Hartford, Connecticut manufactured the production model of the gun. Gatling offered the gun to the Government, and was subsequently turned down by the rather reactionary General Ripley, the Chief of Ordnance. A lighter version of the gun was then introduced, which weighed 135lbs, which was mounted on a robust wooden tripod, rather like a light cannon. The illustrated gun is a 10-barrel British-made Gatling, mounted on a British carriage.

## MAXIM M1885

### SPECIFICATIONS

**Type:** machine gun
**Origin:** Vickers, Son and Maxim Ltd., Sheffield, England
**Caliber:** 0.45in
**Barrel Length:** 24.0in

Originally from Maine, Hiram Maxim moved to England in the 1880s and proceeded to design, build (largely with his own hands), test, and patent the first true automatic gun in which the recoil from the first manually loaded round was used to fire the next. He worked on the gun in partnership with the English company, Vickers. The principle of the design was that the barrel recoiled a short distance before unlocking the breechblock from it and allowing that to continue backwards under the momentum given to it, a strong fuzee spring was extended as it did so, and a cartridge was simultaneously drawn from the belt. When the bolt had reached its most rearward position the extended fuzee spring drew it forward again, so that it chambered and fired the cartridge, after which the process was repeated as long as the trigger was pressed and there were cartridges in the belt. The actual cyclic rate of fire was about 600 rounds per minute, the cartridges being of 0.45in Boxer type loaded with black powder, and the barrel got so hot that it was necessary to surround it with a brass water-jacket. The gun itself was mounted on a long tubular metal tripod with a canvas seat for the firer. It was fitted with elevating and traversing gear and was sighted to 1,000 yards (914m).

The British Army used the rifle-caliber gun, but had it mounted on a light two-wheel artillery type carriage instead of the tripod. It saw service in various colonial wars where it proved remarkably effective in breaking up mass attacks of Dervishes and the like. It was best sited on a flank, and because an enormous cloud of grey smoke resulted from its high rate of black powder fire, it was very desirable to position the weapon to take advantage of a good breeze to disperse it.

# MACHINE GUNS

## AUSTRIA

### SCHWARZLOSE MASCHINEGEWEHR MODELL 05

**SPECIFICATIONS**
**Type:** heavy machine gun
**Origin:** Osterreichische Waffenfabrik, Steyr, Austria
**Caliber:** 8mm
**Barrel Length:** 20.7in

The Schwarzlose machine gun had a characteristically slow cyclic rate of fire of about 400 rounds per minute. In many ways, the system of lubricating the cartridge case in order to assist its extraction was undesirable, although it was widely used at the time. The system often led to difficulties in service, particularly in very dry or dusty countries. Schwarzlose finally succeeded in eliminating this undesirable tendency in the gun by increasing the weight of the breechblock and the strength of the spring, and by increasing the various mechanical disadvantages working against the bolt during the initial stages of its rearward action. These improvements resulted in a second model of the gun, which first appeared in 1912. This new Schwarzlose proved to be a reliable weapon from its inception, when two of the early models fired 35,000 rounds each with minimal stoppages and no apparent loss of accuracy. It was also simple to fire and maintain and was soon in service with the Austro-Hungarian Army where it was used with considerable success. The Austrians calculated the fire of a single well-handled gun as being equivalent to that of 80 riflemen. The weapon saw service in Italy during World War II, but is now obsolete.

### STEYR AUG HBAR

**SPECIFICATIONS**
**Type:** light machine gun
**Origin:** Steyr-Mannlicher, Steyr, Austria
**Caliber:** 5.56mm
**Barrel Length:** 24.46in

The Steyr is the light machine gun version of the AUG family. It had a heavier barrel than the rifle, a large 30-shot magazine, and a folding bipod. AUG also manufactured many rifled in a modular family of armaments. The barrels and components were all interchangeable, and the even the 1970s design looked extremely futuristic. The gun had a smooth plastic body, a semi-transparent plastic magazine meant that the firer could see how much ammunition was left at a glance.

# BELGIUM

## FN 5.56MM MINIMI

**SPECIFICATIONS**

**Type:** light machine gun
**Origin:** Fabrique Nationale (FN), Herstal, Belgium
**Caliber:** 5.56mm
**Barrel Length:** 18.4in

Fabrique Nationale (FN) made a long line of successful weapons, and the 5.56mm Minimi joined this veritable coterie. Development of the weapon started in the early 1960s and it was originally designed around the 5.56 x 45mm M913 round, but this was changed to the 5.56 x 45mm SS109. Prototypes appeared in the early 1970s but the long development work did not translate into production until the early 1980s. The Minimi uses gas operation and a rotating bolt, which is locked into place by a patented FN system. The weapon is belt-fed, with the belt normally housed in a large, lightweight, 200-round plastic box, which is secured underneath, immediately in front of the trigger. The Minimi Para was designed for use by paratroops and features a shorter

barrel (13.7in long) and a telescopic butt. A Minimi Mark 2 has now been developed, which incorporates a number of minor improvements (such as a folding cocking handle). This is intended to make the gun easier to handle without changing its major features or any loss in component interchangeability. The weapon has been adopted by many armed forces, including those of Australia, Belgium, Canada, France, Indonesia, Italy, New Zealand, Sri Lanka, Sweden, and the United Arab Emirates. Production of this highly successful weapon also takes place in Australia (as the Type 89 Minimi) and in the USA (as the M249 SAW). The Minimi is normally fired from its integral bipod, but tripod is also available for use in the sustained fire role.

# CZECHOSLOVAKIA

## ZB 33

**SPECIFICATIONS**

**Type:** light machine gun
**Origin:** Ceska Zbrojovka, Brno, Czechoslovakia
**Caliber:** 0.303in
**Barrel Length:** 25.0in

The British Army held a series of trials in 1932 to select a new light machine gun to replace the venerable Lewis. The ZB 26 from Czechoslovakia was a late entry and a surprise winner. The gun classification was

derived from the fact that the Brno factory adopted the initials ZB for its international dealings. The factory had been established in 1923 and had begun experiments with a prototype automatic within a year. Vaclac Holek, a genius in the field, designed the gun. Holek had started as an ordinary workman in the factory, but he had risen rapidly. The Czechoslovakian Army's request for a new light automatic gave him his chance. Holek's design team included his brother Emmanuel and two expatriate Poles, Marek and Podrabsky. The gun the team produced was gas operated, with a piston working to a tilting breechblock, an easily removed barrel, and a vertical box magazine. It was chambered for the rimless 7.92mm German ammunition round. After exhaustive tests, it was very clear to the British that they had found a potential winner. Some modifications were necessary, principally to enable the gun to fire the British 0.303in rimmed round. The modified gun was classified as the ZGB vz30 series (which also included the vz33 with a reduced rate of fire). The barrel finning was also dispensed with, but otherwise there were no fundamental changes. Once the gun was finally accepted, the British Government decided that it should be made at Enfield. The body of the new gun, which was cut from solid metal, required 270 operations to complete it, involving 550 gauges accurate to one two-thousandth of an inch. This gives some idea of the complexity of the undertaking. The new gun entered British service in 1938 and was one of the finest infantry weapons used in World War II.

# DENMARK

## MADSEN 1902

**SPECIFICATIONS**
**Type:** light machine gun
**Origin:** Dansk Rekylriffel Syndicat A/S., Denmark
**Caliber:** 8mm
**Barrel Length:** 19.0in

The Madsen was named for the Danish Minister of War, but the British also knew the gun as the Rexer. Many weapon historians consider the weapon to be the first true light machine gun, and it was certainly very advanced for its time. The gun itself had an unusual mechanism in which the basic breech consisted of a rectangular steel frame sliding on ribs in the main body of the gun. Inside this steel frame, there was a breechblock, pivoted at the rear so that it worked in the vertical plane with three positions, locked, dropped, or raised. A curved feed arm attached to the left hand side of the box controlled the vertical movement itself. The gun was of the long recoil type in which barrel and breech both recoiled sufficiently far for the next cartridge to be stripped from the magazine and fed into the chamber. When the first round, which had to be located manually using a lever, was fired, the barrel and breech mechanism recoiled together. In the course of this movement the feed arm caused the front of the breechblock to rise, allowing the empty case to be extracted and ejected underneath it. When the rearward action was complete, a return spring took over, forcing the mechanism forward; during this stage the next round was stripped from the magazine and carried forward on top of the breechblock, which acted as a feed tray. At the proper time, the feed arm then depressed the front of the block so that the chamber was exposed and forced the cartridge in. The block then rose to the locked position and the round was fired. The Madsen was tested by many armies between 1903 and 1917 but was not adopted by any of them in substantial numbers.

# FRANCE

## HOTCHKISS M1914

In the early years of the twentieth century, machine guns were fitted with bulky waterjackets. As the water had to be replaced constantly, the jackets posed a problem in areas where water was in short supply. The Hotchkiss answer was to encircle the breech end of the barrel with five solid metal discs that increased the radiating surface area by more than ten times the original. The general shape of these discs, which were about 3.15in in diameter, can be seen at the end of the barrel. The discs made the gun an extremely serviceable

weapon, and in 1900, a United States Army board decided to test its performance against that of a water-cooled gun. Despite the rigors of the trial, the Hotchkiss performed extremely well. During the Russo-Japanese War of 1904 to 1905, the Russian Army used a water-cooled belt-fed Maxim while the Japanese used a Hotchkiss. The Japanese forces were so impressed that Japan went on to manufacture its own version of the gun. Both proved themselves to be capable of standing up to the demands of modern warfare. In 1914, the French Army found itself seriously short of automatic weapons, which trench warfare had shown to be essential in vast numbers. Fortunately, the reliable Hotchkiss was readily available and manufacture began immediately in huge quantities. The earliest models were sent to reserve units, as the regular Army was generally equipped with the Saint-Etienne 07. But once the Hotchkiss guns began to appear in large numbers, they quickly established their superiority and the French Army demanded the weapon in greater and greater numbers. In 1916, two Hotchkiss guns remained in almost continuous action for a full ten days, during

## SPECIFICATIONS

**Type:** heavy machine gun
**Origin:** Hotchkiss Company, St-Denis, France
**Caliber:** 8mm
**Barrel Length:** 31.0in

which they fired an extraordinary total of over 150,000 rounds of ammunition without suffering any greater problem than brief and easily cleared stoppages. When the U.S. Army arrived in France in 1918, twelve of its divisions were therefore equipped with the Hotchkiss Model of 1914.

# HOTCHKISS LMG

## SPECIFICATIONS

**Type:** light machine gun
**Origin:** Hotchkiss Company, St-Denis, France
**Caliber:** 8mm
**Barrel Length:** 23.5in

The Hotchkiss light machine gun was manufactured in France, but during World War I, the British cavalry was the main user of this highly portable weapon that weighed just 12kg. Like its heavy machine gun counterparts, the gun was air-cooled. It was manufactured to take the British 0.303in cartridge (fed from a metallic strip), and operated in the usual way by the action of gas tapped off from the bore and striking a piston to which the breechblock was attached. The forward action of the mechanism under the impulse of the return spring caused the bolt to turn and lock into a fitting, forming part of the barrel extension and known by the French term of fermeture nut. The cocking handle was a long rod, and its rear end was basically similar in appearance to a rifle bolt.

The British Army had found to their cost the futility of massed infantry attacks against well-entrenched defensive positions; 60,000 soldiers were lost of the first day of the Somme to withering machine gun fire, and were anxious to equip their troops with more modern weapons. The Hotchkiss was a reasonably effective light machine gun, and remained in service for many years even until World War II. During World War I, its main use was in trench warfare, where its role was to exploit any gap, and its firepower was very useful in these circumstances. It was also found to be most effective mounted in aircraft and tanks (both French and British) where short bursts of fire were required. The U.S. version of the gun was the Benet-Mercie M1909.

# CHATELLERAULT

## SPECIFICATIONS

**Type:** light machine gun
**Origin:** Manufacture d'Armes de
Chatellerault, France
**Caliber:** 7.5mm
**Barrel Length:** 19.7in

The Chatellerault Model 1924-9 light machine gun was of a conventional appearance and action, as it was a gas- and piston-operated arm with a mechanism very similar to that of the Browning Automatic Rifle. It had two triggers, the forward one for automatic fire, together with a selector that had to be previously set for the type of fire required. The gun was also fitted with a gas regulator, which could be used in conjunction with an adjustable buffer to allow the firer to vary their cyclic rate. Perhaps most important of all, the gun was designed to fire the new 7.5mm rimless round, similar in type and general performance to the German 7.92mm cartridge. There was a further modification in 1928 when the round was shortened slightly, after which the fun functioned with great efficiency. The Chatellerault was also simple to use and teach, an important matter for a country which relied

on fairly short-term conscription for the great bulk of its armed forces. In order to increase the firepower of the infantry garrisons in the Maginot Line, the French made modifications to their Model 1924-9 and this resulted in the Model 31. This was fundamentally the same weapon, but instead of the usual box magazine it was fitted with a huge side-mounted drum, similar to that of the Lewis gun in general principle but designed to hold no fewer than 150 cartridges. This gun only had a pistol grip and was designed to fire from a loophole on a swivel mounting. In order to allow a long burst without overheating the French devised a system under which a small jet of cost water was squirted into the barrel between the extraction of the empty case and the loading of the next round into the chamber.

# SAINT-ETIENNE MODEL 1907

## SPECIFICATIONS

**Type:** heavy machine gun
**Origin:** St. Etienne Arsenal, St. Etienne,
France
**Caliber:** 8mm
**Barrel Length:** 28.0in

Baron von Odkolek, a captain in the Austrian Army invented a completely new type of automatic weapon in 1893. Odkolek's gun utilized part of the gasses from one round to load and fire the next. Having no manufacturing facilities of his own, Odkolek contacted the French manufacturing company of Hotchkiss, who showed great interest in his concept. They were not only fascinated by the fantastic design of the completed weapon itself, but were greatly interested in Odkolek's system of trapping gasses from the barrel to activate the piston. After many years' work, the Saint-Etienne Model 1907 was produced. Basically, it was a Hotchkiss-type

weapon, but the piston was blown forward instead of backward to activate a mechanism of astonishing complexity. An example of this complexity was that the reversed piston operation necessitated the introduction of a rack and pinion mechanism to reverse the motion again. The mainspring, which was coiled on a steel rod, was largely exposed below the massive brass receiver, to keep it cool. 30-round strips of standard Lebel rifle cartridges fed the gun. The Saint-Etienne could also be mounted on a tripod, two models of which were produced, one in 1907 and another in 1914. The earlier version had a large brass wheel that was used for clamping the elevating gear. This superior gun became the standard French heavy machine gun during World War I.

## CHAUCHAT MODEL 1915

**SPECIFICATIONS**
**Type:** light machine gun
**Origin:** French state arsenals
**Caliber:** 8mm
**Barrel Length:** 18.5in

As war loomed in 1914, the Chauchat was rushed into production. A large part of the gun was manufactured from ordinary commercial tubing that had not been designed to withstand the strains inherent in automatic weapons firing full-scale rifle cartridges. Even the locking lugs and similarly essential parts were stamped, pressed, screwed, and generally botched together. As the photograph shows, the pistol grip was made from rough wood and the forehand grip was no more than a crudely shaped tool handle. When the gun was fired (and even this basic function proved to be unreliable and sporadic), the barrel and bolt recoiled together, the bolt being locked to the barrel by locking lugs. This action continued for the whole of the backward phase when the bolt was turned and unlocked allowing the barrel to go forward. The bolt then followed it, taking a round with

it, chambering it, and firing. The long recoil necessarily caused a great deal of vibration making it virtually impossible to hold the weapon steadyily on target when firing on automatic. A recognizable feature of the Chauchat was its semi-circular magazine, made necessary by the fact that the standard 8mm Lebel cartridge had a very wide base. The front end of the magazine was engaged first and then the rear end pulled upwards until it was engaged and the rear end then pulled upwards until it was engaged and held by the magazine catch. The first round then had to be loaded manually by means of the cocking handle. When U.S. forces arrived in France in 1918 they were equipped with the Chauchat (which they called the "Shoshos") and they found the weapon to be completely unsatisfactory, unreliable, and poorly made.

# GERMANY

## MACHINENGEWEHR MG42

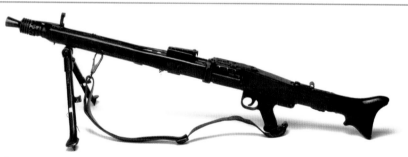

**SPECIFICATIONS**
**Type:** heavy machine gun
**Origin:** Mauser, Oberndorf, Germany
**Caliber:** 7.92mm
**Barrel Length:** 21.0in

German resources were already dwindling by the early years of World War II, and they required an effective gun that could be mass-produced as economically as possible. Once the basic design of the weapon had been established, the project was placed in the hands of Dr. Grunow, a well-known German industrialist whose forte was mass-production by metal stampings, riveting, spot-welding, brazing, and any other method that did not require complicated equipment or specialized techniques needing skilled manpower. The result of this combination of long experience, highly developed industrial skills, and a great deal of service experience, was the MG42 machine gun. It proved to

be one of the finest weapons to come out of World War II. In fact, the gun effectively set the standard for all post-war machine guns. It was an exceptionally flexible weapon that could also be produced as a light machine gun and/or tripod mounted. The gun resembled the MG34, and made use of the same principles of short recoil assisted by gas pressure from a muzzle booster, perhaps its main difference being the way in which the bolt locked. The MG34 had made use of a rotating bolt with an interrupted thread which locked into the barrel extension, but the new gun used a system originally patented by Edward Stecke, a Polish citizen, in which the bolt head carried two small rollers which were held close to the bolt until it was ready to lock when they were forced outwards into grooves in the barrel extension. The firing pin could not move forward between them until they were fully into their grooves, which ensured that the bolt was locked at the moment of firing. Once recoil started, the rollers hit a cam path that forced them inwards out of their recesses, thus unlocking the bolt and allowing the cycle to continue. The gun fired 50-round belts of the standard 7.92mm cartridge using a new and effective feed system that was widely copied. The lightness of the MG42, combined with its successful operating system resulted in a very high rate of fire of around 1,200 rounds per minute. This was described as being "like tearing calico." However, this high rate of fire resulted in vibration that had an effect on the accuracy of the gun. The muzzle break was ingeniously designed to help stabilize the weapon but the problem was never fully overcome. Some rare examples were produced with special periscope optics, stock, and trigger grip, allowing the gunner to operate the weapon from a concealed position. The MG42, which British troops nicknamed the "Spandau," was brought back into post-war German service as the MG3.

## Maxim MG08

**SPECIFICATIONS**

**Type:** heavy machine gun
**Origin:** Spandau Arsenal, Spandau, Germany
**Caliber:** 7.92mm
**Barrel Length:** 28.3in

Both the Germans and British had used early machine guns in their colonial wars, but neither army had regarded the weapons seriously. But after the Kaiser watched a demonstration of Hiram Maxim's new gun, he asserted (according to the inventor, at least), "That is the gun – there is no other." In 1899, a number of Maxim batteries (each of which consisted of four guns) were tried out at the Imperial maneuvers. Following the success of the gun in the Russo-Japanese War, a heavy Maxim gun was developed at the great Spandau factory. It came into active service in 1908. The gun was of the normal Maxim pattern, but its mount was distinctly new. Instead of either a wheeled artillery-type carriage or a tripod, the gun had a solid heavy mount based on a sledge. The gun only needed to be elevated and the forward legs swung over it so that it would be ready to drag along. When the legs were down, they could easily be adjusted so that the firers could sit, kneel, or lie down according to the type of cover available to them. By the end of 1908, every German regiment of three battalions had its own six-gun battery. The guns were carried on light horse drawn carts and the detachments, usually of four men each, marched along with extra ammunition vehicles. The German battery was under the direct command of the Regimental Commander and similar batteries were provided for the cavalry. These were more mobile, the wagons having four horses instead of two, and the detachments were mounted on horses. A modified sledge mount was also introduced at this time, which reduced the total weight significantly and allowed the individual guns to be manhandled if necessary, either by carrying or dragging. By the outbreak of war in 1914, the German Army probably had 12 or 13,000 of these guns in service, and it is thought that the MG08 may have been responsible for more deaths than any other single weapon. Our photograph shows a bipod mounted "light" version of the gun, which was not entirely successful, as it remained too heavy to be considered a true light machine gun.

# ITALY

## BREDA 37

### SPECIFICATIONS

**Type:** heavy machine gun
**Origin:** Breda Meccanica Bresciana, Brescia, Italy
**Caliber:** 8mm
**Barrel Length:** 25.0in

Breda produced a 13.2mm caliber gun in 1932 that proved to be a sound and reliable weapon. The company then scaled it down to fire the 8mm Modello 35 cartridge. The mechanism of the gun was simple. It used a piston worked by gases tapped off the bore. The piston also activated the breechblock that was locked in the firing position by the action of a ramp on the piston, which lifted the end of the block into a recess on the top of the body. The gun fired automatic only and it was possible to control its cyclic rate by the use of a gas regulator through which the gasses passed on their way to the piston head, which was interchangeable. The need to keep the gas port in its proper place in relation to the gas regulator made it impossible to increase or decrease the headspace, which was therefore somewhat larger than necessary. This naturally gave rise to the risk of ruptured cases, due to the direct lack of support by the breechblock, but Breda overcame this by the familiar method of oiling each case as it entered the chamber by means of a pump. This allowed the case to "float" in the chamber and set back firmly against the block before the pressure got too high. This system of lubricating cartridges was widely used and it is possible that Breda got the original idea from the Schwarzlose, which they had acquired from the Austrians in large numbers after World War I. But this case lubrication was not altogether satisfactory and it could sometimes cause trouble in hot and dusty climates. Surprisingly, the Italian forces did not seem overly troubled by this problem in their African campaigns. The Breda was air-cooled, and its heavy barrel (that weighed 9.7lb) allowed a satisfactory degree of sustained fire without overheating.

# JAPAN

## TYPE 96

### SPECIFICATIONS

**Type:** light machine gun
**Origin:** Japanese state arsenals
**Caliber:** 6.5mm
**Barrel Length:** 21.7in

In 1936, the Japanese were engaged in more or less continuous warfare with their ancient enemies the Chinese at this time, and practical experience led to various improvements being incorporated into the new gun. The Type 96 was still the basic Hotchkiss design, which was the mainstay of Japanese gun design. One of the principal differences from its predecessor was the abolition of the inefficient system of charger loading by hopper and the substitution of a more orthodox top-mounted box magazine. It still fired the rather unsatisfactory 6.5mm cartridge but the oil pump was situated in the magazine loader and thus completely divorced from the gun itself, which was a considerable improvement. The gun also had a quick system for changing barrels, which did something to help its capacity for sustained fire without overheating. It had a carrying handle and a distinctive one-piece butt and pistol grip combined, and would take the standard infantry bayonet, although this was largely to demonstrate the offensive spirit, since a 20lb gun makes a poor basis for a thrusting weapon. Perhaps its oddest feature was the frequent incorporation of a low-powered telescopic sight, which is not usually considered to be of great value on an automatic weapon. The cartridge used was still the reduced charge pattern employed in the previous gun, which must have continued to cause complications over the resupply of ammunition.

# RUSSIA

## DEGTYARYEV PAKHONTNYI (DP)

### SPECIFICATIONS

**Type:** light machine gun
**Origin:** Soviet state arsenals
**Caliber:** 7.62mm
**Barrel Length:** 23.8in

The gun was put into limited production in 1926, and then subjected to two years of exhaustive trials. Its full title was Ruchnoi Pulemyot Degtyaryeva Pakhotnyi, which literally translated means "Automatic Weapon, Degtyaryev, Infantry," which was abbreviated to DP. The original gun was of simple construction and contained only 65 parts, having been designed for manufacture and assembly by semi-skilled labor. The gun had some defects, principally in its very large bearing surfaces, which caused undue friction in action, its susceptibility to dirt, and overheating. The earliest modes had finned barrels to help dissipate the heat, but this problem was never fully overcome except by restricting the rate of fire. The gun was used extensively in the Spanish Civil War (1936-39) as a result of which various improvements eliminated its worst faults. The gun worked by tapped-off gas impinging on a piston and driving it to the rear, taking the bolt with it, which was then forced forward again by the action of the compressed return spring. The feed system was reasonably efficient, with a large flat single-deck drum, although its very size and thinness naturally made it susceptible to damage. Unlike the drum on the British Lewis gun, the Degtyaryev magazine was not driven by the action of the gun, but by an integral clockwork mechanism in the magazine itself. The magazine capacity was originally 49, but this was found to be excessive, and it was necessary to reduce it by two. The modified guns had removable barrels, and the mainspring was placed on its own sleeve below the receiver, which suffered from the effects of heat. The gun worked on the open bolt system and fired automatic only. The weapon gave good service during World War II and was also used in Korea and Vietnam.

## RUCHNOI PULEMYOT DEGTYARYEV (RPD)

### SPECIFICATIONS

**Type:** light machine gun
**Origin:** Soviet state arsenals
**Caliber:** 7.62mm
**Barrel Length:** 20.5in

The RPD's chief merits were its lightness and simplicity of operation. Like its predecessor from Degtyaryev, it was gas-operated, with the bolt locked by means of hinged lugs, which were normally retained flush with the body of the bolt, but which were forced outwards into recesses in the receiver so as to lock the breech at the instant of firing. The gun was belt fed, each belt holding 50 rounds. Belts could easily be connected to each other or could be coiled tightly and fitted into a sheet metal drum. The gun was fitted with a rotatable gas regulator, had a fixed barrel, and would fire only automatic, overheating being avoided by the gunner ensuring that he did not exceed 100 rounds a minute. The first model had a reciprocating cocking handle, which worked backwards and forwards with the piston, the latter having a hollow head that fitted over the gas spigot. The second model revised the piston head arrangements and added protectors for the backsights, while the third model finally incorporated a folding, non-reciprocating handle and a much-needed dust cover over the ejector opening. It was not, however, until the fourth model that any significant change was made to the gun. Its power had always been marginal as regards its capacity to move a fairly heavy belt, so the size of the piston was significantly increased in an effort to improve this. The RPD was produced in vast numbers throughout the Cold War and is still used in many similar countries and by guerrillas. It was also produced in China as the Type 56. The gun compared favourably to the M60, being lighter, more accurate, and reliable.

# PKM

## SPECIFICATIONS

**Type:** light machine gun
**Origin:** Soviet state arsenal
**Caliber:** 7.62mm
**Barrel Length:** 31.2in

The original PK, or "Machinegun Kalashnikov" was a fully automatic weapon derived from the design of the Kalashnikov rifle. The current, modernized version, or PKM remains in production. The gun fires 54mm standard Eastern Block ammunition, but this is not common to the AK47 or other weapons carried by Russian infantry units. Ammunition is belt-fed from an ammunition box clipped under the receiver. The PKM is equipped with a simple bipod. The gun was designed as a squad-level support weapon, which is also suitable for installation and vehicle mounting. It compares favorably to the American M60, some even considering it to be more accurate and reliable. The gun has a cyclic rate of fire of 650 rounds per minute, and a sustained rate of fire of 250 rounds per minute. A

heavier version of the gun, the PKMS model (PKM Stepanova, which is named after its tripod) features heavier and more stable mounting equipment. Another special version of the gun, the PKMSN2 is equipped to fit modern NSPU night sights for use in low visibility operations. PKT (PK Tank) is another development of the basic weapon, designed as a direct replacement for the SGMT Gorunov tank machine gun. Modifications for this variant include the removal of the stock, a longer and heavier barrel, an added gas regulator, and an electric solenoid trigger. The PKM and its variants have been widely exported to many different countries, and are also now manufactured in several locations outside Russia. The weapon and its many variants will doubtless be in service for many years to come.

# RUCHNOI PULEMOT KALASHNIKOVA (RPK)

## SPECIFICATIONS

**Type:** light machine gun
**Origin:** Soviet state arsenals
**Caliber:** 7.62mm
**Barrel Length:** 23.3in

In its general appearance, the RPK was essentially similar to the AK47 assault rifle, from which the original inventor, the prolific and highly successful designer Kalashnikov, developed the gun. The main external differences in this gun are its very characteristic club butt and appreciably longer and heavier barrel. It is equipped with a bipod, fitted well forward, and designed to be folded back and held by a clip when not required as a support. The weapon is gas-operated; when the first manually loaded round is

fired part of the gases pass through a vent in the barrel and thence into the cylinder visible above it, where they strike and force back the piston. The initial rearward action of the piston causes the bolt locking lugs to rotate anti-clockwise, thus allowing the breech to open, after which the bolt continues to the rear with the piston compressing the return spring as it does so. The power of the gas having been exhausted, the return spring takes over and drives the mechanism forward, and during this phase the bolt strips a round from the magazine and forces it into the chamber. It then stops, but the piston continues sufficiently to cause the locking lugs to engage with the locking shoulders after which the striker is free to fire the round and the cycle continues. There is a change lever on the right hand side of the receiver above the trigger. The RPK takes the same 30-round magazine as the rifle or a drum holding 75 rounds.

# UK

## VICKERS MK I

### SPECIFICATIONS
**Type:** heavy machine gun
**Origin:** Vickers-Armstrong Ltd., Tyneside, England
**Caliber:** 0.303in
**Barrel Length:** 28.4in

Mechanically, the Vickers was similar to the earlier Maxim, the rear impulse being produced by recoil supplemented by the action of a muzzle attachment, which deflected some of the gas. This thrust the lock backwards taking with it a round from the belt and extending the fuzee spring which was situated in an elongated box on the left-hand side of the gun. The fuzee spring then took over and forced the bolt forward and so the cycle was repeated. The gun had a remarkable capacity for sustained fire but this led to obvious problems of wear. A barrel would last for about 100,000 rounds at 200 rounds a minute, after which the rifling would have been worn away to the stage where the bullet ceased to be spun effectively by it and so lost accuracy very quickly. The barrel could be changed very quickly and as spares were carried this was not a serious problem. The gun was, of course, water-cooled with a jacket capacity of about 7 pints. This began to boil after around 3,000 rounds of steady fire at about 200 rounds per minute, which led to it steady evaporation. This happened at the rate of about one or two pints for each thousand rounds fired depending on the rate of fire and the prevailing climactic conditions. The gun was fitted with a condenser tube leading into an old-fashioned one-gallon petrol can. If some water was put into the can first, and the steam passed through it, a considerable amount of the water lost could be used again. This was an important factor in desert conditions where water was scarce. Various models of Vickers guns were produced, all of which were quite similar to one another. Some water jackets were fluted, others were plain, but this does not necessarily indicate a different mark of gun. Although the gun was heavy, it had a reputation for being superbly reliable. It gave good service in World War I, War World II, and Korea.

## LEWIS MACHINE GUN

### SPECIFICATIONS
**Type:** light machine gun
**Origin:** Birmingham Small Arms Ltd., Birmingham, England
**Caliber:** 0.303in
**Barrel Length:** 26.0in

The originator of the gun, Colonel Isaac Newton Lewis, first offered it to the U.S. Army, but it was rejected in 1912. He decided to go ahead and set up his own factory in Belgium. The Germans overran this site in 1914, and the business was handed over to the British Birmingham Small Arms Company. The principle on which the gun worked was simple. Gases were tapped off from the barrel to drive back a piston that took the bolt with it, extracting and ejecting the empty case. A stud on top of the bolt also activated a feed arm, which took the next round from the double-layer, circular magazine on top of the gun, the mechanism being equipped with two stop pawls that ensured that the magazine rotated only by the correct amount. During this backward movement a rack on the underside of the piston engaged a pinion, which wound a clock-type spring, which took over, driving the working parts forward and chambering and firing the round. The bolt was of the turning variety with lugs, which locked into

recesses in the barrel extension. In order to keep the barrel cool radial fins surrounded it, and a light outer-casing designed to keep the whole thing clean surrounded these. The gun was designed to fire automatic only, but a good gunner with a sensitive trigger finger could often fire single rounds, while "double tapping" (firing two rounds at a time) was very simple. The Lewis was also used as an aircraft weapon, being flexibly mounted and with a different sight system clamped onto it. It was fired by the observer.

## BREN

### SPECIFICATIONS

**Type:** light machine gun
**Origin:** Royal Small Arms Factory, Enfield, England
**Caliber:** 0.303in
**Barrel Length:** 25.0in

The mid-1930s saw the development of the Bren gun, based on the Czechoslovakian ZB 26. The Bren's basic mechanism was similar to that of the ZB 26, being designed for either single rounds or bursts, this being controlled by a change lever, the trigger pull being noticeably longer for single rounds than for automatic fire. There was a rather elaborate backsight with a drum and a pivoted lever carrying the aperture, and because the magazine was top-mounted, the sights were offset to the left. Each gun had a spare-parts wallet containing a combination tool and small replacement parts, and a holdall containing a cleaning kit and the second barrel. The latter could be put onto the gun in a matter of two or three seconds. Although the magazine capacity was nominally 30 it was soon found that this was too many, and the total was reduced to 28, but

even that meant that rimmed cartridge magazines had to be loaded carefully. Careless loading caused the commonest stoppage problems, but fortunately, this difficulty was easy to clear. The Bren could also be mounted onto a tripod for firing on a fixed line. The gun proved to be a most reliable and efficient gun and instilled confidence in all who used it. When Great Britain adopted the standard 7.62mm NATO round a number of the later marks of Bren were converted to fire this ammunition (in the 1950s). Designated L4A1 to L4A6, these guns are readily recognizable by the absence of the cone-shaped flash hider and the straight magazine, the latter being made necessary by the rimless NATO round. The Bren served throughout World War II and its reliability and accuracy were highly regarded.

## BESA

### SPECIFICATIONS

**Type:** heavy machine gun
**Origin:** Birmingham Small Arms Ltd., Birmingham, England
**Caliber:** 7.92mm
**Barrel Length:** 26.7in

The Czech ZB 53 gun was gas-operated but the barrel

also moved back under the force of the recoil, the timing being so arranged that the cartridge was fed into the chamber and fired as the barrel went forward. This, of course, meant that the backward force of the recoil had first to arrest and then reverse the forward movement. This had the effect of substantially diminishing the next recoil and considerably reduced various stresses and strains on the weapon. The guns

had very heavy barrels, some finned, which allowed for sustained fire, and the earlier models also had the means to vary their cyclic rate of fire from 450 to 850 rounds per minute. All reports indicated that the gun was a success; indeed, it was so reliable that in 1937 there was a possibility that it would replace the role of the Vickers gun. The reason it did not do so was due to the fact that the gun fired the 7.92mm rimless round and could not be modified to handle the rimmed 0.303in British cartridge. Some of the early prototypes sent from Czechoslovakia to England for testing were mounted on the standard Czech Model 45 tripod, which offered a rigid platform for the weapon. It could have been used to supplement the Bren, but the British

Army didn't really need another gun of this type. In 1936, the Birmingham Small Arms Company came to an arrangement with ZB under which the company was allowed to manufacture the No 53 gun, under the name Besa. The name was derived from the initial letters of Brno and Enfield and the last two letters of BSA. A larger version of the gun was produced for tanks, with a caliber of 0.59in.

# L7 GPMG

## SPECIFICATIONS

**Type:** light machine gun
**Origin:** Royal Small Arms Factory, Enfield, England
**Caliber:** 7.62mm
**Barrel Length:** 24.8in

Back in the 1950s, the British Army carried out a series of trials to find a new machine gun that could fire the newly adopted NATO standard 7.62mm round. The winner of the competition was the Belgian FN MAG (Mitrailleur a Gaz). The first guns of this type used by the British Army were manufactured in Belgium, but later examples came from the Royal Small Arms Factory at Enfield, England. This involved certain modifications to conform with British manufacturing standards. But no fundamental changes were made to the gun, which remained true to its original self. The British-made gun is designated the L7A1, but it is generally referred to as the GPMG. The new gun, like many original FN products, owes a great deal to the patents of the American John M.

Browning, one of the most successful designers in the field of firearms that the world has ever seen. It is gas-operated with a bolt locking system similar to the original Browning Automatic Rifle of 1917, its feed mechanism being virtually identical to that of the German MG42, as is its trigger. The original idea was to have two different barrels for the gun, a plain steel one for the light role and a heavy barrel with a special liner for the sustained fire role, but the latter was abandoned. Other versions included the L8A1 (co-axial gun in tanks); the L37A1 (for use in vehicles or on the ground); and the L20A1 (for use in helicopters). The L7A2 model has modified trigger and feed mechanisms, a belt box is fitted to the left side, and other minor changes have been made.

# L86 LSW

## SPECIFICATIONS

**Type:** light machine gun
**Origin:** Royal Small Arms Factory, Enfield, England
**Caliber:** 5.56mm
**Barrel Length:** 35.36in

The L86 LSW (Light Support Weapon) is part of the SA80 family of weapons. The others are the L85 IW (Individual Weapon), the SA80A2 Carbine and the L98 CGP (Cadet General Purpose). All the guns were similar in most respects, all firing the 5.56mm NATO round from a 30-box magazine, and can mount the SUSAT (Sight Unit; Small Arms; Trilux), a 4x optical sight with a tritium-powered glowing pointer for limited night sighting as well as the CWS (Common Weapon Sight) which was actually an ultraviolet night sight. The weapons were designed in the bull-pup configuration with pistol grip forward of the magazine and the mechanism in the butt. This allows the use of a long, accurate barrel in a weapon with compact dimensions. The LSW was a section-level magazine-fed light machine gun, complete with bipod, buttstrap, and rear pistol grip. It also had a longer barrel to improve muzzle velocity at its longer effective range. Otherwise,

the gun was identical to the basic L85 and the magazines and some internal parts are interchangeable. Its reputation for unreliability and fragility was also shared with the other members of the SA80 family, but work has been carried out to try and minimize its various problems.

# UNITED STATES

## COLT-BROWNING MODEL 1895

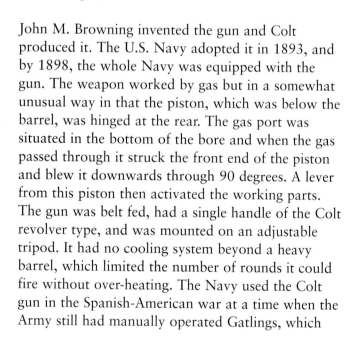

**SPECIFICATIONS**

**Type:** heavy machine gun
**Origin:** Colt Patent Firearms Co.,
Hartford, Connecticut
**Caliber:** 0.30in
**Barrel Length:** 28.0in

John M. Browning invented the gun and Colt produced it. The U.S. Navy adopted it in 1893, and by 1898, the whole Navy was equipped with the gun. The weapon worked by gas but in a somewhat unusual way in that the piston, which was below the barrel, was hinged at the rear. The gas port was situated in the bottom of the bore and when the gas passed through it struck the front end of the piston and blew it downwards through 90 degrees. A lever from this piston then activated the working parts. The gun was belt fed, had a single handle of the Colt revolver type, and was mounted on an adjustable tripod. It had no cooling system beyond a heavy barrel, which limited the number of rounds it could fire without over-heating. The Navy used the Colt gun in the Spanish-American war at a time when the Army still had manually operated Gatlings, which

led the Army to investigate the possibility of adopting it, but it was finally decided that the gun was too complex for land service. In the meantime, some modifications were made, and the eventual result, the Model 1904, was bought by a number of other countries. It so happened that when the United States entered World War I in 1917 its Army had no modern machine guns. A new model, the 1917 (Army), was ordered in considerable quantities, and about 1,500 were supplied before the end of the war. One serious defect was that it could not be used in the prone position because the 10-inch piston used to hit the ground if the gun was too low. This tendency inevitably led the United States infantrymen to nickname it the "potato digger," a name by which it is often recognized by people otherwise quite ignorant of its official designation.

## BROWNING MODEL 1917

**SPECIFICATIONS**

**Type:** heavy machine gun
**Origin:** various U.S. arsenals
**Caliber:** 0.30in
**Barrel Length:** 24.0in

Mechanical simplicity was the salient feature of the Browning M1917. This simplicity facilitated both mass production and teaching the workings of the gun to the hastily raised American troops. The first round had to be manually loaded by means of a cocking handle, which

this time, the empty case was extracted from the breech and ejected from the gun, and a fresh cartridge drawn from the belt. When this backward phase was complete, the return spring drove the working parts forward again, chambering the cartridge, locking the block to the barrel, and firing the round. This cycle could continue as long as the trigger was pressed and there were rounds left in the belt. The Browning gun was made in considerable variety, including air-cooled models for use in tanks and aircraft for which water-cooled weapons were clearly unsuitable. But no fundamental mechanical changes were made. The final modification before the outbreak of World War II resulted in the Model 1917A1 which was introduced in 1936. World War II was the first real combat test of the Browning gun since its introduction and it turned out to be an excellent weapon. It also saw a good deal of service in Korea, and was not replaced until the early 1960s when the new M60 entered service.

duplicated the action of the recoil. When the trigger was pressed, the barrel and breechlock recoiled together, for just over half an inch until pressure had dropped to a safe level and the barrel and breechlock unlocked, the barrel stopping, while the block continued backwards under its initial impetus. During

## BROWNING AUTOMATIC RIFLE

**SPECIFICATIONS**
**Type:** light machine gun
**Origin:** various U.S. arsenals
**Caliber:** 0.30in
**Barrel Length:** 24.0in

John M. Browning first demonstrated his "Automatic Rifle" in February 1917. The new weapon weighed just under 16lb and it was perfectly correct to describe it as a rifle as its general appearance and handling qualities were of this type. The first models had no bipod. In modern terminology, the gun would be described as a squad automatic weapon, as the gun was too light to be a true machine gun and too heavy to be a rifle. Browning did a lot of the initial work on the gas and piston operation of the gun at the Colt factory, but Winchester were also involved in the later development of the weapon. Manufacture began in 1918, and production totalled 50,000 units. The Allies received the BAR with great enthusiasm, as the weapon was quite unique. They ordered the gun in large quantities, with France ordering 15,000 units. But it was developed too late for extensive service in World

War I. The gun was able to fire in bursts or single rounds as required, and later models were equipped with a bipod. Another variation was introduced in 1940, the Model 1918A2, which had a light bipod attached to the tubular flash hider. Although this model only fired in bursts, it also incorporated a selector that allowed two cyclic rates; the higher one was 600, the lower 350 rounds per minute. The BAR came to be used in many countries, and was also manufactured at Belgium's Herstal factory. A number were sold to Britain in 1940 and were used to arm the Home Guard, where they gave good service but caused some problems over caliber. The BAR Model 1922 was used by the U.S. Cavalry and had a heavier, finned barrel, a bipod, and butt rest. It fired automatic only. The gun was also made in special versions for the civilian market and the FBI.

## BROWNING M1919

**SPECIFICATIONS**

**Type:** light machine gun
**Origin:** various U.S. arsenals
**Caliber:** 0.30in
**Barrel Length:** 24.0in

The Browning M1919 was originally developed for the U.S. Cavalry. The 1919A4 was derived from this model, a general-purpose light machine gun. It became the main machine gun used by the American forces in World War II. With light modifications, and changes in mounts, the gun could also be used in tanks and armored cars, as a multiple anti-aircraft gun, and in a ground role. This gun was mechanically similar to the water-cooled Browning Model 1917, but was air-cooled. Like the 1917, the 1919 also worked by the recoil power of the barrel that unlocked the breechblock in a brief rearward thrust and sent it to the rear, extracting the case as it did so. The force of the compressed return spring provided the motive power for the forward action in which a new round was stripped from the belt, chambered, and fired. The gun also had a heavy barrel enclosed in a light perforated outer casing. Feed was by means of a woven fabric belt holding 150 rounds with brass tags at each end to facilitate loading. At normal operating temperatures, the gun maintained an actual rate of fire of 60 rounds per minute for up to 30 minutes without any serious overheating problems. The weapon had a single pistol-type grip, very similar in shape and appearance to that of the Colt revolver, as was its trigger, which had no guard. This protruded almost horizontally from the rear of the receiver. When used in the ground role, the gun was mounted on the standard M2 tripod. The Browning was simple to handle and reliable in use. Stoppages were few and were easy to resolve. The M1919A6 was an improved version of the gun, and was fitted with a rifle-type butt and pistol grip, and a flash hider. The 1919 gave good service, but was ultimately replaced by the M60.

## BROWNING 0.50IN CALIBER M2

**SPECIFICATIONS**

**Type:** heavy machine gun
**Origin:** various U.S. arsenals
**Caliber:** 0.50in
**Barrel Length:** 45.0in

The M2 was first introduced in 1933 and was originally intended for use on multiple anti-aircraft mounts. A version was also developed as a tank turret gun, and another for use with a ground mount. The gun worked on the usual Browning system of short recoil. When the cartridge was fired, the barrel and breechlock (which were securely locked together) recoiled for just under half an inch when the barrel was stopped by means of an oil buffer. At this stage, the pressure had dropped sufficiently for the breechblock to unlock and continue to the rear under the initial impetus given to it by the barrel, extracting and ejecting the empty case and extracting the next live round from the belt. Once the rearward action had stopped the compressed return spring then took over and drove the working parts sharply forward, chambering the round, locking the breechblock, and firing the cartridge, after which the cycle continued as long as the trigger was pressed and there were rounds in the belt. The gun would fire automatic only, although some were equipped with bolt latches to allow single rounds to be fired if necessary. Although this gun functioned well enough mechanically, it showed an unfortunate tendency to overheat, so that 70 or 80 rounds was about the maximum that could be fired continuously without a considerable pause to allow the barrel to cool. In practice, this was completely unacceptable, so

a heavy barrelled version (the M2HB) was adopted. The extra metal in the barrel made a considerable difference and this new gun was most effective. Although both the gun and its cartridge were both heavy, it was hugely successful as an extremely powerful automatic assault weapon, especially against aircraft, helicopters, and light vehicles. The gun was used extensively during World War II, both by the United States and many other countries. It was also used in Korea, Vietnam, Somalia, the First Gulf War, the Second Gulf War, and continues to be in active service to this day.

# M60

## SPECIFICATIONS

**Type:** light machine gun
**Origin:** Saco Defence Inc., Saco, Maine
**Caliber:** 7.62mm
**Barrel Length:** 25.5in

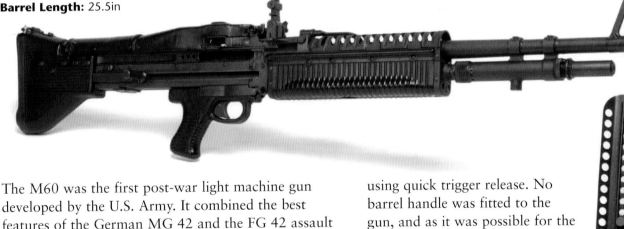

The M60 was the first post-war light machine gun developed by the U.S. Army. It combined the best features of the German MG 42 and the FG 42 assault rifle. The gun was largely manufactured from stampings, rubber, and plastics. It had a somewhat fussy, cluttered appearance and was afflicted by several basic problems. In the first place, there was no gas regulator: the supply of gas was fixed, and could not be controlled by the firer. Under certain conditions the gun either stopped, or less usually "ran away." This means that the working parts of the gun go back far enough to feed, chamber, and fire another round, but not far enough to be engaged by the sear. This means that the gun may continue to fire even after the firer's finger has been lifted from the trigger. Although this is very disconcerting, the problem is by no means limited to the M60. The difficulty could be overcome by holding onto the belt, and preventing its feeding. The gun had no system to fire single shots, but with its slow rate of fire, a good gunner could achieve single shots

using quick trigger release. No barrel handle was fitted to the gun, and as it was possible for the barrel to reach temperatures of up to 500 degrees centigrade, great care had to be taken when changing it. An asbestos mitten was issued with each gun to address this problem, but these were frequently lost in action. In this case, the gunner could use a piece of rag. One of the best features of the gun was its chromium-plated barrels, which had stellite liners for the first 6 inches from the chamber. The gun sights were adequate but the zeroing system was not. A belt or box was supplied when the gun was being used on the move, and a simple, robust tripod was available for the sustained fire role. The M60 was used extensively in Vietnam. This combat experience led to a considerably improved version of the gun that was issued as the M60E1, but many of its roles have now been assumed by the M249 (Minimi).

# AUSTRALIA

## OWEN

Australia found herself in a vulnerable position when Japan entered World War II. Most of her small army was already engaged in the Middle East theater and her vast and sparsely populated country presented an extremely attractive target to a warlike race seeking greater living room. Although there was a well-established arms factory already active at Lithgow, Australia was not a particularly industrialized nation at this time, but was forced to step up her production of arms as a matter of urgent necessity. One of the country's first efforts was the Australian Sten, which (rather inevitably) became known as the Austen. But although this was by no means a bad weapon, it never won popularity with the Australian army. The first locally designed submachine gun was the brainchild of Lieutenant E. Owen of the Australia Army. It was adopted in November 1941 and put into production immediately. This was a well-made weapon, if a little on the heavy side, and was an immediate success with the Australian troops. It was of a fairly orthodox

design and its point-of-balance was immediately above the pistol grip, which meant that it could be fired single-handed if necessary. The magazine was vertically above the gun and although this involved offset sights the idea was popular because it helped when moving through thick cover. Some early versions of the weapon had cooling fins on the barrel but this was found to be unnecessary and was discontinued. All Owens were camouflaged after 1943. A later, prototype version (Mark 2) was fitted with a different method of attaching the butt, and a bayonet lug above the muzzle compensator to receive a special tubular-haft bayonet. Overall, weight was also reduced to 7.6lb.

**SPECIFICATIONS**
**Type:** submachine gun
**Origin:** Lithgow, Australia
**Caliber:** 9mm
**Barrel Length:** 9.8in

# CHINA

## TYPE 50

As was typical of the weapons used by Communist China, their submachine gun Type 50 had its origins in a weapon first produced by the Soviet Union, in this particular case the PPSh 41. As with most other aggressive nations, the Russians soon saw the necessity for mass-produced weapons, and the new gun was made largely from heavy gauge stampings that were welded, pinned, and brazed as necessary. The gun had a normal blowback mechanism and the interior of the barrel was chromed; this was a fairly common Soviet device. One of the most distinctive features of the gun was that the front end of the perforated

**SPECIFICATIONS**
**Type:** submachine gun
**Origin:** Chinese state arsenal
**Caliber:** 7.62mm
**Barrel Length:** 10.8in

barrel casing sloped steeply backward from top to bottom, thus acting as a compensator to keep the muzzle down. In spite of its high cyclic rate of fire, the gun was reasonably accurate and could be fired in single rounds if required. The earliest versions had a tangent backsight but a simpler flip sight soon replaced this. The Chinese Communists received many of these guns in and after 1949 and started their own large-scale manufacture of them in either 1949 or 1950. Their version was essentially similar to its Russian counterpart, but had a somewhat lighter stock. It was

also designed to take a curved box magazine though it could also fire the 71-round drum, which was the standard magazine on the original Russian model. All Chinese versions had the two-range flip sight. The first locally made weapons were crude in the extreme and gave the impression of having been made by apprentice blacksmiths (as they most probably were). But they worked well which was the first and only requirement of the Chinese. The Type 50 was extensively used by the Chinese in the Korean War, and by the Viet Minh against the French in Indo-China in the 1950s.

## TYPE 54

**SPECIFICATIONS**
**Type:** submachine gun
**Origin:** Chinese state arsenal
**Caliber:** 7.62mm
**Barrel Length:** 10.0in

Like the Type 50, the Type 54 also had its origins in an original Russian gun. In this case, it was a copy of the PPD, which had been designed by A. Sudarev in 1942, who was working even as the city was under siege by the Germans. The new gun, originally known as the PPS 42, was designed and made in the city itself, so that weapons coming off the production line were in action within just a couple of hours. The gun was made of stampings from any suitable grade of metal, and was held together by rivetings, welding, and pinning. Nevertheless, it was not only cheap but also turned out to be highly effective. It worked on the simple blowback system and would only fire automatic; perhaps its oddest feature was its semi-circular compensator, which helped to keep the muzzle down but increased the blast considerably. This was followed by the PPS 43, which was also modified and

improved by Sudarev. Its most unusual feature was that it had no separate ejector in the normal sense of the word. Instead, the bolt moved backwards and forwards along a guide rod, which was of such a length that, as the bolt came back with the empty case, the end of the rod caught it a sharp blow, and knocked it clear. After the Chinese Revolution of 1949, the Soviet Union naturally supplied its new ally with a considerable quantity of arms including large numbers of the PPS 43, and by 1953, the Chinese had begun large-scale manufacture of these weapons, virtually unchanged in appearance from the Russian prototypes. The only way in which it could be distinguished was by the fact that the plastic pistol grips often bore a large letter K, although other designs, including a diamond, have also been found.

# CZECHOSLOVAKIA

## SKORPION (VZ61)

The Skorpion is a good example of the rather limited number of true machine pistols, its general dimensions being comparable to those of the Mauser pistol model 1896. Its diminutive size meant that it was of relatively limited use as a military weapon, except possibly for

tank crews, motorcyclists, and soldiers in similar conditions, for whom a compact secondary weapon was more important than pure performance. Its small calibre also served to reduce its stopping power, although this was considerably improved by the use of

**SPECIFICATIONS**
**Type:** submachine gun
**Origin:** Czech state arsenal
**Caliber:** 7.65mm
**Barrel Length:** 4.5in

automatic fire. Limited quantities of a larger version of the gun were also manufactured, which fired a 9mm round. Although this was a good deal heavier than the original weapon, it was a very similar gun. The Skorpion worked on the usual blowback system. Very light automatic weapons of this kind often have the disadvantage that their cyclic rate of fire is unacceptable high, but in the Skorpion, this problem was largely overcome by the use of a type of buffer device in the butt. The gun had a light wire butt for use from the shoulder; this could be folded forward when not required without affecting the working of the weapon. Although the size and capacity of the Skorpion reduced its military efficiency, it was an excellent weapon for police use or other forms of internal security work since it was inconspicuous and easily concealed. Its low muzzle velocity also made it relatively easy to silence. The VZ61 was sold to many African countries. Other versions fired the 9mm short round (VZ63), 9mm Mokarov (VZ65); or 9mm Parabellum (VZ68).

# FINLAND

## SUOMI MODEL 1931

**SPECIFICATIONS:**
**Type:** submachine gun
**Origin:** Tikkakoski Factory, Finland
**Caliber:** 9mm
**Barrel Length:** 34.3in

The first gun in the Suomi (the native word for Finland) series was developed in 1922 making it one of the first ever submachine guns. The famous Finnish designer Johannes Lahti devised the gun, and the first completed model appeared in 1926. These guns were effective but extremely complex, designed to fire the 7.62mm Parabellum cartridge from a magazine with such a pronounced curve that three of them placed end to end formed a complete circle. Only small numbers of this first Suomi were ever produced and its chief interest is that it became the first weapon in a series. The illustrated model, the 1931, was also designed by Lahti, but although it retained some features of the Model 26, so many adaptations were made to the gun that it was virtually a new weapon. The patent was finally granted in 1932, but the gun was already in use by the Finnish Army in 1931, hence its model designation. At the end of 1939, the Russians, having failed to persuade the Finns to make some territorial adjustments to enhance Soviet security, invaded Finland. The Finns fought back bravely and made good use of the Suomi. It worked on the normal blowback system and had no fewer than four different magazines, a single 20-round box, a double 50-round box, and two drums, one of 40-round capacity and one of 71. It was very well made of good steel, heavily machined and milled and unusually well finished. This attention to detail meant that the end product was an exceptionally reliable and robust weapon and, although it was very heavy by modern standards, (with the bigger drum magazine, it weighed over 15lbs) this at least had the merit of reducing recoil and vibration and thus increasing its accuracy, for which the gun was very well known. It was made under license in Sweden, Denmark, and Switzerland, and was used in Finland, Sweden, Switzerland, Norway, and Poland. As late as the 1980s, the Suomi was still in use by many units of the Finnish Army, although, by this time, these surviving weapons had been modified to take a modern 36-round box magazine of an improved pattern.

# GERMANY

## BERGMANN MP 18

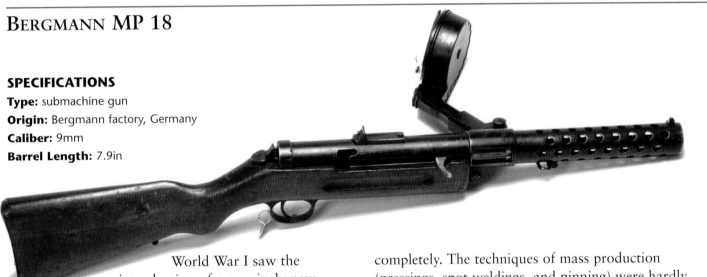

**SPECIFICATIONS**

**Type:** submachine gun

**Origin:** Bergmann factory, Germany

**Caliber:** 9mm

**Barrel Length:** 7.9in

World War I saw the introduction of a genuinely new weapon, the submachine gun. Once trench warfare had become the norm, the German Army began to arm a proportion of their infantry with stocked pistols of the Mauser and Luger types. From there, it was a short step to introduce a larger and heavier version of these weapons, with the capacity to fire in bursts. The Bergmann factory began work on a prototype weapon of this kind in 1916. The designer was Hugo Schmeisser, the famous son of an almost equally famous father. By the early months of 1918, the gun was in limited production. Always realistic, the Germans realized that at this late stage in the war, when their manufacturing capacity was already fully extended, any new weapon would have to be simple to make. The MP 18.I fulfilled this requirement completely. The techniques of mass production (pressings, spot weldings, and pinning) were hardly developed by this time, so "simple" is a relative term, compared with, say, the Sten gun of twenty-five years later. The Bergmann was machined, and although complicated milling was abandoned, the general finish of the gun was good. The Bergmann's weakest component was its magazine, which was of a type originally developed for the Luger pistol, and was too complex and too liable to stoppage to be fully reliable. The Germans proposed to have six guns per company; each was to have a number two to carry ammunition, and there were to be three hand carts in addition, which presupposed a type of barrage fire, but the weapon came too late. Its main interest is therefore in its influence on future designs, which was very significant.

## BERGMANN MP 28

An updated version of the MP 18.I, the MP 28.II appeared in 1928. The II denoted two minor modifications to the original prototype. The new Bergmann had some interesting features, including the ability to fire in both bursts and single shots using a circular stud above the trigger. For automatic fire, this had to be pushed to the right, and to the left for single shots. The gun was also equipped with an elaborate tangent backsight graduated by hundreds up to 1,094 yards, which must have been far outside any practical service range. The weapon was equipped with straight box magazines, but the magazine housing was so designed that, if necessary, it would accept the old snaildrum type. These various improvements did not

**SPECIFICATIONS**
**Type:** submachine gun
**Origin:** Haenel-Weapon Factory, Suhl, Germany
**Caliber:** 9mm
**Barrel Length:** 7.8in

change its general appearance very materially so that it still resembled the old MP 18. The Bergmann MP 28.II was manufactured in Germany at the Haenel-Weapon factory at Suhl, but there were still some restrictions placed on the domestic production of German military firearms, so the bulk of production was based at a Belgium company in Herstal, under license from Schmeisser. The Belgium Army introduced a small number of the guns to its troops in 1934. The Bergmann soon established a reputation for reliability, and was purchased in South America and by the Portuguese who used the gun as a police weapon. Although it was mainly manufactured in 9mm Parabellum, it also appeared in 9mm Bergmann, 7.65mm Parabellum, 7.63mm, and even for the American 0.45in cartridge. It seems probable that its main use was in the Spanish Civil War of 1936-39, where its robustness made it an ideal weapon for the militias.

## MP 40 (SCHMEISSER)

**SPECIFICATIONS**
**Type:** submachine gun
**Origin:** Erma factory, Germany
**Caliber:** 9mm
**Barrel Length:** 9.9in

The German Army ordered the Erma factory to design and produce an easily manufactured submachine gun for use mainly by armored and airborne troops in 1938. The new weapon was prepared very quickly, and the new gun was issued as the MP 38. It was the first weapon of its type to be adopted by the German Army since 1918. The MP 38 was also the first firearm of its type ever to be made entirely from metal and plastic, with no woodwork of any kind, and thus became the first truly modern looking submachine gun. Gone were the heavy butt and the carefully machined body, and in their place was a folding tubular metal stock and a receiver of steel tube, slotted to reduce weight. Although the MP 38 was an excellent weapon, it was relatively slow and expensive to produce. This led to the introduction of the featured weapon, the MP 40, which used the techniques of mass production, including pressing, spot-welding, and brazing, far more extensively. Perhaps its most important change was the introduction of a safety device, it having been found (as with the Sten) that a moderately severe jolt could be enough to bounce the bolt back and fire a round. Most of the later MP 40s were made with horizontal ribs on the magazine housing. Only a few were made without them. A later model was fitted with a double side-by-side magazine in a sliding housing. Known as the "Schmeisser," (although Louis Schmeisser had had nothing to do with its creation), the gun became one of the most famous weapons of World War II, some even being used by Allied soldiers in preference to their own submachine guns. Over 1,000,000 had been produced by 1945.

# HECKLER AND KOCH MP5

**SPECIFICATIONS**
**Type:** submachine gun
**Origin:** Heckler and Koch, Germany
**Caliber:** 9mm
**Barrel Length:** 8.9in

Most of the world's elite forces, including such prestigious units as the German GSG 9, the British SAS, and the London Metropolitan Police use the Heckler and Koch MP5. This famous submachine gun uses the same roller-delayed blowback operating principle as the G3 rifle and features good handling qualities as well as the interchangeability of most of its parts with other weapons in the Heckler and Koch range. The MP can fire semi-automatic, fully automatic, or three, four or five round bursts. In the latter mode, a small ratchet counting mechanism, which interacts with the sear, achieves the effect. Each time the bolt cycles to the rear of the ratchet advances one notch until the third, fourth or fifth cycle allows re-engagement of the sear. Firing also ceases the instant trigger is released, regardless of how many rounds have been fired in the current burst. The actual number of rounds in each burst is pre-set in the factory, and cannot be altered by the firer. Heckler and Koch use metal stampings and welded sub-group parts. The receiver is constructed of stamped sheet steel in nineteen operations (several combined) and is attached to the polygonal rifled barrel by a trunnion, which is spot-welded to the receiver and inned to the barrel.

The trigger-housing, butt-stock and fore-end are fabricated from high-impact plastic. The specifications above refer to the MP5A3. There is a variety of specialized versions. MP5K has a shorter barrel with a vertical foregrip underneath, and a simple cap replaces the butt. MP5SD is a series of silenced weapons, which can also be fitted with a special laser sight that allows the used to lay a laser beam on the target. There are also several stock variants. The MP5SD1 has no stock; MP5SD2 has a fixed stock; and MP5SD3 has a retractable stock.

Heckler and Koch MP5K

# ISRAEL
## UZI

The British mandate over Palestine ceased at midnight on May 14, 1948, and the Jewish state of Israel was declared. On the very next day, its Arab neighbors invaded the brand new state. Eight months of war followed, by the end of which, Israel had not only successfully defended her own territory but had also occupied some of that belonging to her attackers. Despite her success, it was clear that Israel needed a reliable new weapon, which could be made using her own resources in sufficient numbers to arm the bulk of her population. By 1950, Major Uziel Gal of the Israeli Army had designed the illustrated weapon. Production started almost immediately and continues to this day. The Uzi works on the normal blowback system and is made from heavy pressings in conjunction with certain heat-resistant plastics. The rear end of the barrel extends backward into the body and the front of the bolt is hollowed out so as to wrap round this rear projection. The magazine fits into the pistol grip, which affords it firm support and also keeps the point-of-balance above it, so that the gun can be fired one-handed, like a pistol, if necessary. The Uzi fires both

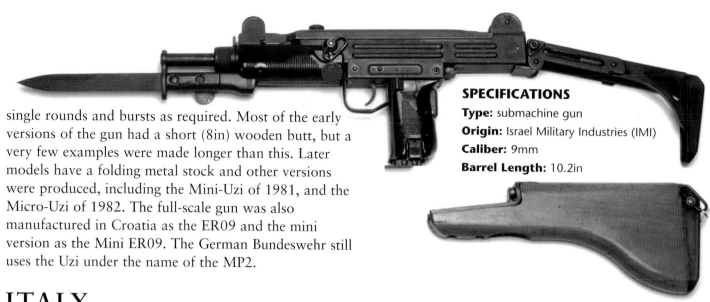

**SPECIFICATIONS**
**Type:** submachine gun
**Origin:** Israel Military Industries (IMI)
**Caliber:** 9mm
**Barrel Length:** 10.2in

single rounds and bursts as required. Most of the early versions of the gun had a short (8in) wooden butt, but a very few examples were made longer than this. Later models have a folding metal stock and other versions were produced, including the Mini-Uzi of 1981, and the Micro-Uzi of 1982. The full-scale gun was also manufactured in Croatia as the ER09 and the mini version as the Mini ER09. The German Bundeswehr still uses the Uzi under the name of the MP2.

# ITALY

## BERETTA MODELLO 38A

**SPECIFICATIONS**
**Type:** submachine gun
**Origin:** Beretta, Northern Italy
**Caliber:** 9mm
**Barrel Length:** 37.3in

Tullio Marengoni designed most of Beretta's guns, and the submachine guns produced by the Northern Italian company had a deservedly high reputation. The Modella 38A has a good claim to be regarded as Marengoni's successful submachine gun. The gun had it origins in a self-loading carbine first produced in small numbers for police use in 1935, but by 1938, it had been discharged into a true submachine gun. It was well machined and finished, which made it expensive to produce, but resulted in a very reliable and accurate aim. It functioned by normal blowback and had a separate firing pin, which was a rather unusual refinement. Its forward trigger was for single shots, the other for bursts of fire. The first model in the series can

be distinguished by elongated slots in its jacket, by its compensator, which consisted of a single large hole in the top of the muzzle with a bar across it and a folding, knife-type bayonet. Not many of these were actually produced before the elongated cooling slots were replaced by round holes, which became standard from that point. The third version had a new compensator consisting of four separate cuts across the muzzle, but no bayonet. This version remained in production for the remainder of the war, being used by both the Italian and the German armies; captured specimens were popular with Allied soldiers. The Beretta Modello 38A was also used by a number of other countries, notably Romania and Argentina.

# RUSSIA/USSR

## PPSH 41

Vast scale sproduction of the PPSh 41 did not actually begin until 1942, after extensive testing of the gun by the Russian Army in the previous year. Georgii Shpagin, a well-known Russian expert in the field, designed the gun and his contribution was honored by the use of his initial in the official designation of the

gun. The PPSh was an early and successful example of the application of mass-production techniques to the manufacture of firearms, as the gun was greatly needed for wartime fighting. As far as possible, the gun was made from sheet metal stampings, and welding and riveting were used wherever this was considered

**SPECIFICATIONS**
**Type:** submachine gun
**Origin:** Russian state arsenal
**Caliber:** 7.62mm
**Barrel Length:** 10.6in

feasible. It retained its wooden butt, but was a sturdy and reliable weapon. The gun worked on the usual blowback system with a buffer at the rear end of the receiver to reduce vibrations and had a selector lever in front of the trigger to give single rounds or bursts of fire as required. As its cyclic rate of fire was high and would have tended to make the muzzle rise when firing bursts, the front of the barrel jacket was sloped backwards to act as a compensator. Feed was either by a 71-round drum, basically similar to that of the earlier PPD series but not interchangeable with them, or by a 35-round box. To reduce wear and help cleaning, the bore and chamber of these guns were all chromed. There were two models of this gun; the first had a complicated tangent backsight, while the second had a two aperture flip sight. The Soviet armies greatly favored the submachine gun and whole battalions were sometimes armed with these weapons. It is therefore not very surprising that total production of the gun exceeded five million units. The gun was widely copied by other Communist countries, and the Chinese based their hugely successful Type 50 gun on the PPSh, a gun also mass-produced in huge numbers.

# AK-74-SU

**SPECIFICATIONS**
**Type:** submachine gun
**Origin:** Russian state arsenal
**Caliber:** 5.45mm
**Barrel Length:** 8.1in

The Soviet Army used the 7.62mm PPSh 41 and PPS 43 throughout World War II and for many years afterwards. The submachine gun, as a separate type, was then allowed to fade out of use by the Russian Army in favor of the AK-47 and AK-74 assault rifles. Despite this, other armies continued to use submachine guns. But this policy seems to have been reversed in the 1970s, and a completely new Soviet submachine gun made its appearance. The gun was based on the Kalashnikov AKS-74 assault rifle, but it was considerably smaller and lighter. The barrel was only 8.1in long and was fitted with a screw-on, cylindrical attachment at the front of which was a cone-shaped flash suppressor. Unlike the majority of submachine guns, the AK-74-SU fired standard, full-charge rifle ammunition, in this case the Russian 5.45 x 39.5mm, in addition, due to the shortness of the barrel, the gas was tapped off very close to the chamber which resulted in a very high pressure for such a small weapon, and the muzzle attachment was an expansion chamber, designed to reduce the pressure acting on the gas piston; it also served as a flame damper. The weapon was fitted with basic iron sights, the rear sight being a basic flip-over device, which was marked for 220 and 440 yards, although the latter range seemed somewhat optimistic for such a weapon. The internal mechanism was identical to that of the AK-74 except that the gas piston, return spring, and spring guide rod were shorted. The gun also had a very simple skeleton stock, which folded forwards along the left side of the weapon. It is often compared with the Colt Commando.

# SWEDEN

## CARL GUSTAV MODEL 45

**SPECIFICATIONS**
**Type:** submachine gun
**Origin:** Carl Gustav factory,
Sweden
**Caliber:** 9mm
**Barrel Length:** 8.0in

Sweden first began to manufacture a submachine gun in 1937. This was actually a slightly modified version of the Finnish Suomi and was made under license at the Carl Gustav factory. A second version of the gun, manufactured by Husqvarna, soon replaced the original. It had a shorter barrel, a very large trigger guard (to accommodate gloved fingers in the bitter Scandinavian winters) and had a much straighter stock than the original Finnish version. Although Sweden was neutral during World War II, she enlarged her army considerably to defend herself if the need should arise. It was realized that Sweden had no submachine gun suitable for mass-production, and started to develop such a gun. This process resulted in the Model 1945, but production didn't actually start until the war had ended. The gun was made of heavy gauge steel stampings, which were riveted or welded as necessary. Although these manufacturing methods were somewhat

limiting, the gun proved to be sound and reliable.

Mechanically, the Model 1945 bore a strong resemblance to the British Sten gun, but it had a rectangular stock of tubular metal which could be folded forward on the right of the gun without interfering with its working in any way. Although the gun was designed for firing on automatic only, single rounds could also be fired by anyone with a reasonably sensitive trigger finger. The gun fired a special high velocity cartridge, and the original model used the old Suomi 50-round magazine. Later versions were designed to fire a new 36-round type but as large stocks of the older magazines, which were not interchangeable, remained, the new gun was built with an easily detachable magazine housing, which could be replaced by one of the older type if required.

# UNITED KINGDOM

## STEN MARK 1

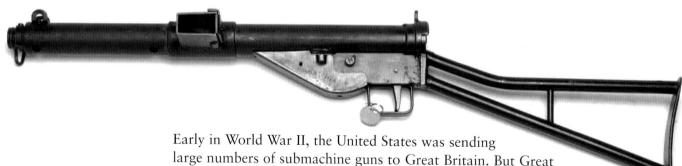

**SPECIFICATIONS**
**Type:** submachine gun
**Origin:** Royal Small Arms
factory, Enfield, England
**Caliber:** 9mm
**Barrel Length:** 7.8in

Early in World War II, the United States was sending large numbers of submachine guns to Great Britain. But Great Britain itself, and the countries of the Commonwealth, were driven by the need to raise and equip new armies, and were also engaged in supplying and replacing defunct supplies for their forces in North and East Africa, where British and Colonial troops were fighting the Italian Army. Following Britain's devastating losses at Dunkirk, it was realized that there was an urgent requirement for a simple, home-produced submachine gun. By the middle of 1941, such a gun had been designed and was in limited production, undergoing stringent user trials. This was the famous Sten. Its name was an amalgamation of the initial letters of the surnames of the two people most closely connected with its development, Major Shepherd and Mr. Turpin, added to the first two letters of Enfield, the location of the Royal Small Arms factory where the gun was first produced. As soon as the few inevitable weaknesses highlighted by the user trials were rectified, the Sten was put into large-scale production. In its various forms, it was to provide a truly invaluable source of additional automatic firepower to the British and Commonwealth forces. The gun worked on a simple blowback system with a heavy bolt controlled by a coiled spring return. But the simple concept behind the gun was belied by the original, rather elaborate, examples. These had a cone-shaped flash hider and a rather crude forward pistol grip, which could be folded up underneath the barrel when not in use. The gun could fire either single shots or bursts of fire, the change lever being a circular stud positioned just above the trigger. The Sten had some woodwork at the fore-end and as a bracer at the small of the butt. In fact, the Sten proved to be so simple to manufacture that various resistance groups even produced their own versions of the gun.

---

## STEN MARK 2 AND STEN MARK 2, SILENCED VERSION

### SPECIFICATIONS
**Type:** submachine gun
**Origin:** Royal Small Arms Factory, Enfield, England
**Caliber:** 9mm
**Barrel Length:** 7.8in

The Sten gun was in production for many years, and the first revision of the original model was the Mark 2. This was the first in a long series of changes in the general design of the gun. Effectively, it was a stripped-down version of the Mark I, designed with the intention of simplifying and speeding the manufacturing process itself. At the time of its introduction, Great Britain was fighting for her very existence, and had reached the conclusion that appearance was a very secondary consideration to efficacy. This practical thinking directly led to the Sten Mark 2, the ugliest, nastiest weapon every used by the British Army. It looked cheap because it was cheap, with its great unfiled blobs of welding metal, its general appearance of having been constructed from scrap-iron, and its depressing tendency of falling to pieces if dropped onto a hard surface. Even so, the gun did manage to incorporate one or two improvements over the Mark I. The magazine housing was now attached to a rotatable sleeve, held by a spring, so that it could be turned upwards through 90 degrees. This acted as a dust cover for the ejection opening in bad conditions. The British Army was accustomed to its high quality Short Magazine Lee Enfield rifles and handsomely finished Bren light machineguns and joked about their tin Tommy-gun but they still got good value out of it. One of the most persistent weaknesses of the wartime Sten gun was the poor quality of its magazine. In the circumstances, of hasty construction from inferior metal, this is hardly surprising. The lips were particularly susceptible to damage. This had a serious effect on the feed and led to endless stoppages. Dirt also tended to clog the magazine, and although conscientious cleaning resolved the problem to some extent, it tended to recur. Despite these many drawbacks, historically, the Mark 2 was an extremely important weapon.

Sten Mark 2, Silenced Version

## STEN MARK 6 (SILENCED)

The Sten Mark 2 marked the low point of production of this venerable weapon series. Thereafter, quality began to improve. Practically all the components for the gun were manufactured in small factories and workshops that had had no previous connection with the munitions industry, but increased experience led to a great improvement in the general finish. The Mark 3 was similar in appearance to the Mark 2, and was produced in huge numbers. This version was followed by the Sten Mark 4, which never saw full-scale production. The best Sten of all was probably the Mark 5. This gun saw active service from 1944 to the mid-1950s. Although it had many similarities to its predecessors, the Mark 5 was of a more robust construction, and was fitted with a wooden butt (some of which also had brass buttplates) and pistol grip. It was also designed to accept the standard issue bayonet.

Experiments were conducted with a silenced Mark 6, and in 1944, it was decided that there was a pressing need for a gun of this type. The standard Mark 2 silencer was fitted to Mark 5, which was then designated the Mark 6 (Silenced). The muzzle velocity of the Mark 5 bullet was in excess of the speed of sound, and this posed a number of problems from the "sonic boom" effect. These were countered by drilling gas escape holes in the barrel to bring the velocity down to the required figure. The silencer tended to heat very rapidly, so a canvas hand guard was laced over it. In fact, it wasn't considered advisable to fire bursts through the silencer except in emergencies. The gun tended to be mainly used by airborne forces and Resistance fighters in World War II and remained in use until around 1953.

## STERLING

The Sterling was originally known as the Patchett submachine gun, as it was designed by George Patchett. The gun was patented in 1942. The Sterling Engineering Company had been involved in the production of the Lanchester, but had manufactured a small number of Sterlings by the end of the war. A few of these early guns were used by British airborne troops towards the end of the war and their feedback was encouraging. The armed forces were looking for a replacement for the Sten, and the Sterling was tested alongside several other candidates. But all were deemed to be in need of further modification. Another trial was launched in 1951, and the Patchett, as the gun was still called, came out ahead of its rival weapons. It was subsequently accepted for service with the British Army

in September 1951. The gun was officially known as the SMG L2A1, but it became known as the Sterling from this time onwards. The weapon, which was well made and finished, was of the normal blowback mechanism, but it was unusual in having a ribbed bolt that cut away dirt and fouling as it accumulated and forced it out of the receiver. This allowed the gun to function well, even under the most adverse conditions. The Sterling underwent a good many modifications after its initial introduction, notably in the addition of foresight protectors, varying shapes of muzzle and butt, and on one light version of the gun, a spring-loaded bayonet. Some of the earlier models also took a straight magazine. The final production version was the L2A3, which was also produced (in a slightly modified form) in Canada as the C1 9mm submachine gun.

# UNITED STATES

## COLT COMMANDO

**SPECIFICATIONS**
**Type:** submachine gun
**Origin:** Colt Manufacturing Company
**Caliber:** 5.56mm
**Barrel Length:** 10.2in

The Colt Commando does not neatly fit into a particular category of gun. It is variously described as an assault rifle or carbine and submachine gun. But we are including it in the latter section. The weapon was a shorter and handier version of the M16 rifle and was intended for use in the Vietnam War as a close-quarter survival weapon. Mechanically, it was identical to the M16 but with a much shorter barrel, this slightly reduced the muzzle velocity and also reduced the accuracy of the gun at longer ranges. The short barrel also caused considerable muzzle flash, which had to be overcome by a 4-inch flash suppressor, if necessary, this could be unscrewed. The Colt Commando had a telescopic butt, which could be extended when the user needed to fire the weapon from the shoulder. It also featured selective fire and a holding-open device, and was actuated by the same direct gas action as the M16. In spite of the limitations of its range, the weapon nevertheless proved useful in Indochina and although it had been designed as a survival weapon it fitted the submachine gun role so well that it was later issued to the U.S. Special Operations Forces and was also used in small numbers by the British SAS.

## INGRAM MODEL 10/MAC 10

**SPECIFICATIONS**
**Type:** submachine gun
**Origin:** Military Armament Company
**Caliber:** 0.45in
**Barrel Length:** 5.75in

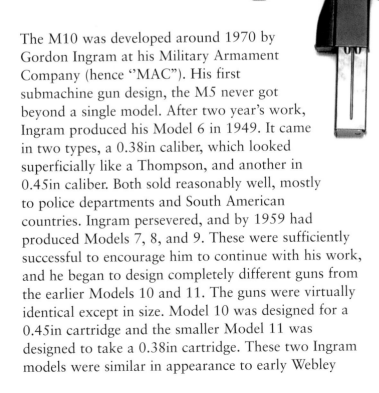

The M10 was developed around 1970 by Gordon Ingram at his Military Armament Company (hence "MAC"). His first submachine gun design, the M5 never got beyond a single model. After two year's work, Ingram produced his Model 6 in 1949. It came in two types, a 0.38in caliber, which looked superficially like a Thompson, and another in 0.45in caliber. Both sold reasonably well, mostly to police departments and South American countries. Ingram persevered, and by 1959 had produced Models 7, 8, and 9. These were sufficiently successful to encourage him to continue with his work, and he began to design completely different guns from the earlier Models 10 and 11. The guns were virtually identical except in size. Model 10 was designed for a 0.45in cartridge and the smaller Model 11 was designed to take a 0.38in cartridge. These two Ingram models were similar in appearance to early Webley automatic pistols, and worked on a blowback system but had wrap-around bolts that made it possible to keep the weapon short. This improved control at fully automatic fire. The cocking handle was on the top and was equally convenient for both right- and left-handed users; it had a slot cut into its center so as not to interfere with the line of sight. The magazine fitted into the pistol grip and the gun had a retractable butt. The whole gun was made of stampings with the exception of the barrel. Even the bolt was made of sheet metal and filled with lead. Models 10 and 11 were both fitted with suppressors, which reduced the sound considerably. Both guns were compact and reliable, capable of delivering a good amount of firepower due to their high rate of fire. Approximately 16,000 M10s were produced between 1964 and the mid-1980s, but only a few M11s were ever sold.

## M3A1 "Grease Gun"

**SPECIFICATIONS**
**Type:** submachine gun
**Origin:** Small Arms
Development Branch
**Caliber:** 0.45in
**Barrel Length:** 8.0in

Early in World War II (1941), the Small Arms Development Branch of the United States Army Ordnance Corps set out to produce an inexpensive weapon which could be mass produced using modern methods. Once the basic design had been developed, a very detailed study of the methods that were used to manufacture the British Sten gun was undertaken. Development work was so speedy that prototypes had already been tested by the end of 1942. The new weapon was designated M3, and was a highly utilitarian arm. It was almost exclusively made from stampings, and only the barrel and bolt were machined. The gun worked on the blowback method, and had no provision to fire single rounds. Its low cyclic rate made this acceptable. Its stock was of retractable wire, and it had a caliber of 0.45in, although it was easy to convert to 9mm. Its famous nickname came from its remarkable resemblance to a garage mechanic's grease gun. Large-scale use exposed some defects in the design of the gun, and several model simplifications were introduced. The revised version of the weapon was designated the M3A1. This gun also worked by blowback, but had no handle.

Instead, the firer inserted a finger into a slot in the receiver, by which method the bolt cold be withdrawn. The bolt had an integral firing pin. This was worked on guide rods, which made complicated finishing of the inside of the receiver unnecessary as they facilitated smooth functioning with very little interruption from dirt. An oil container was built into the pistol grip and a small bracket was also added to the rear of the retractable butt. This acted as a magazine filler. The gun had a box magazine that was not completely reliable in dirty or dusty conditions until the later addition of an easily removed plastic cover that eliminated this defect. By the end of 1944, the new gun had officially replaced the Thompson as the standard submachine gun of the United States Army, a more powerful weapon than the Sten that had inspired its inception. A simple flash hider was added in 1945, which was held in place by a wing nut. Some examples of the gun were also fitted with silencers.

## Thompson M1928

Colonel J. T. Thompson developed his Thompson, or "Tommy" gun during the course of World War I, but it arrived too late to be used in action. The Auto-Ordnance Corporation found that submachine guns were difficult to sell during peacetime, especially during the Great Depression. They somewhat surmounted this difficulty by advertising the gun quite heavily. This resulted in small but steady sales to law enforcement agencies, and some of the guns also found their way into the hands of various criminal types. A surprising variety of Thompson models were made. Almost all of these were 0.45in caliber and one or two were made as automatic rifles rather than submachine guns. Some examples were also produced in England by the

Birmingham Small Arms Company. The M1928A1 version was produced with several minor design changes, and was the final peacetime version of the weapon, and was more complex than the M1A1. The gun worked on the usual blowback system. Unusually, the gun also has a delay device to prevent the bolt from opening until the barrel pressure had dropped. Two squared grooves were cut into the sides of the bolt at an angle of 45 degrees, the lower ends being nearer to the face of the bolt, and an H-shaped bridge was fitted into these. When the bolt was fully home, the lower ends of the H-piece engaged in recess in the receiver. When the cartridge fired, the pressure was enough to cause it to rise, thus allowing the bolt to go back after

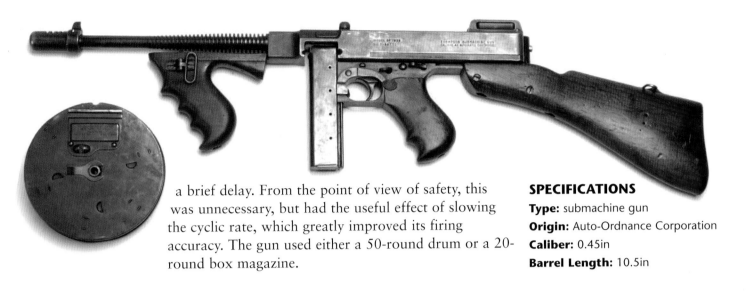

a brief delay. From the point of view of safety, this was unnecessary, but had the useful effect of slowing the cyclic rate, which greatly improved its firing accuracy. The gun used either a 50-round drum or a 20-round box magazine.

## SPECIFICATIONS
**Type:** submachine gun
**Origin:** Auto-Ordnance Corporation
**Caliber:** 0.45in
**Barrel Length:** 10.5in

# THOMPSON M1A1

## SPECIFICATIONS
**Type:** submachine gun
**Origin:** Auto-Ordnance Corporation
**Caliber:** 0.45in
**Barrel Length:** 10.5in

The real breakthrough for the Thompson submachine gun came in 1938, when the United States Army adopted the weapon. Other contemporary guns were more modern, and some were better weapons, but the Thompson had the supreme advantage of being available. Demand for the gun rose greatly at the outbreak of war. Apart from the domestic needs of the United States, Great Britain also bought as many Thompsons as it was offered from 1940 onwards. Like many other pre-war models, the Thompson had been produced with great attention to detail, but simplification was imperative to accelerate production. The result of this work was the M1, whose main mechanical difference was the abolition of the H-piece and the substitution of a heavier bolt to compensate for this. Externally, the main differences were the absence of the compensator on the muzzle, the substitution of a straight forehand for the forward pistol grip (although this had been optional on the Model 28), the removal of the rather complex backsight, and its replacement by a simple flip. The new gun could not take the 50-round drum. But this had never been entirely reliable in dirty conditions, so it was no great loss. A new 30-round box magazine was introduced and the earlier 20-round magazine also fit the new gun. Yet another simplification, the incorporation of a fixed firing pin on the face of the bolt, resulted in the M1A1 version of the gun. By then, the basic design of the weapon was almost a quarter of a century old, but the Thompson gave excellent service in the critical years between 1939 and 1945. Although it was heavy to carry, the gun was also reliable, and had excellent stopping power.

# ACKNOWLEDGEMENTS

The Publisher and Author would like to thank the following for their help in publishing this book.

Gun images by special arrangement with Patrick F. Hogan of the Rock Island Auction Company.

Machine Guns and Assault Rifles by arrangement with Major Conway at the S.A.S.C. Weapons Room and Archive.

Patrick Reardon for access to his collection of Civil War firearms.

Roy Marcot for his Civil War and hunting images.

Jean Huon for the M60 machine gun image.